WORD
BIBLICAL
COMMENTARY

WORD
BIBLICAL
COMMENTARY

VOLUME 15

2 Chronicles

RAYMOND B. DILLARD

WORD BOOKS, PUBLISHER • WACO, TEXAS

Word Biblical Commentary
2 CHRONICLES
Copyright © 1987 by Word, Incorporated

Library of Congress Cataloging-in-Publication Data
Main entry under title:

Word biblical commentary.

Includes bibliographies.
1. Bible—Commentaries   Collected Works.
BS491.2.W67   220.7'7   81–71768
ISBN 0–8499–0214–2 (vol. 15)   AACR2

Printed in the United States of America

The author's own translation of the Scripture text appears in italic type under the heading *Translation*.

5 6 7 8 9 9   AGF   9 8 7 6

To our parents:

Ray and Ruth Dillard
Ralph and Margaret Albrecht

"Parents are the pride of their children."—Proverbs 17:6

Contents

Author's Preface

Paralipomenon liber est, id est, Instrumenti veteris ἐπιτομή tantus ac talis est, ut absque illo si quis scientiam Scripturarum sibi voluerit arrogare, seipsum irrideat.
Jerome, Ad Paulinum, Epistle 53.8

Jerome wrote, "The book of Chronicles, the epitome of the old dispensation, is of such importance that without it anyone who claims to have a knowledge of the Scriptures makes himself a fool." In many ways I assent to Jerome's insight; the Chronicles are extraordinarily rich and repay manyfold the effort invested to understand them. It is to be regretted that the Chronicles remain a neglected book in the church. Yet as this volume now comes to publication, I find I also assent to A. Saltman's caveat in his introduction to Langton's commentary on Chronicles (p. 11), that "anyone who claims to know Chronicles without having a thorough knowledge of Scripture would be making an even bigger fool of himself, for least of all books of the Bible can it be studied in isolation." From its position at the end of the Hebrew canon and among the latest writings of the Old Testament, the Chronicles reflect on the history of the universe, from Adam to the Chronicler's own day; there are few issues in the history of exegesis which are not in some way touched by these books, so that along with their richness, they involve the interpreter in a labyrinth of related questions.

This commentary is the product of a number of years of study and reflection on these books. By its very nature a commentary cannot be definitive; readers of such volumes all come to the text of Scripture with different needs and questions that the writer has not anticipated or addressed. Nevertheless, it is my fervent hope that I have learned enough of Chronicles and of the Bible so as to offer useful help to those who turn to these pages.

I owe a great debt of thanks to many who have made this work possible. Westminster Theological Seminary in Philadelphia has a generous policy regarding sabbatical leaves, and I am grateful to the Board of Trustees of that institution for the portions of three leaves that were devoted to this work. The staff of the Montgomery Library at Westminster has been of immense help; in particular I appreciate the unfailingly cheerful and professional assistance of Ms. Grace Mullen and Mrs. Jane Patete. Faculty colleagues at Westminster—Profs. George Fuller, Al Groves, Tim Keller, Tremper Longman, Moises Silva—have read portions of the manuscript and have offered valued advice. My students have taught me a great deal, both from their own insightfulness and the steady stimulus of their questions. I have profited from teaching several doctoral seminars in Chronicles at Westminster and from lectureships in these books at the Trinity Episcopal School for Ministry, Myerstown Evangelical Congregational School of Theology, Gordon-Conwell Theological Seminary, and Winnipeg Theological Seminary. I have profited also from the shared research, friendship, and encouragement of other scholars who are ploughing these same fields; the consultation on the Chronicler

at the annual meeting of the Society of Biblical Literature has proved fertile
ground for interaction with others whose labors have been at least in part
devoted to this literature. I feel a particular debt of gratitude to Profs. Ralph
Klein and Hugh Williamson for their encouragement along the way. I would
also like to express my thanks to the editorial team, especially Prof. John
Watts, for the invitation to participate in the series and the assistance along
the way. I am grateful too for the assistance of Ms. Pamela Williams and
Mrs. Gail O'Neil in the preparation of indices. Many others could be added
to this list—I have been helped by a much greater number than I have mentioned, and I am grateful to all. Obviously the deficiencies of this work are
solely my own and should not be laid at the door of anyone else.

It would border on travesty to fail to mention my thankfulness both to
and for my wife Ann and our sons, Joel, Jonathan, and Joshua. Only those
who have written similar volumes know the price that is paid by an author's
family. Each has encouraged the work and endured a physically absent or
mentally preoccupied husband and father. I suspect that they have come to
think of the Chronicler as the sixth member of the household, and that
they look forward with some anticipation to his receiving a bit less attention
from me for the foreseeable future. Ann and I wanted this book to be dedicated to our parents, a very small evidence of the love we have for them.

Zionsville, Pennsylvania   RAYMOND B. DILLARD
June 1987

Editorial Preface

The launching of the *Word Biblical Commentary* brings to fulfillment an enterprise of several years' planning. The publishers and the members of the editorial board met in 1977 to explore the possibility of a new commentary on the books of the Bible that would incorporate several distinctive features. Prospective readers of these volumes are entitled to know what such features were intended to be; whether the aims of the commentary have been fully achieved time alone will tell.

First, we have tried to cast a wide net to include as contributors a number of scholars from around the world who not only share our aims, but are in the main engaged in the ministry of teaching in university, college, and seminary. They represent a rich diversity of denominational allegiance. The broad stance of our contributors can rightly be called evangelical, and this term is to be understood in its positive, historic sense of a commitment to Scripture as divine revelation, and to the truth and power of the Christian gospel.

Then, the commentaries in our series are all commissioned and written for the purpose of inclusion in the *Word Biblical Commentary*. Unlike several of our distinguished counterparts in the field of commentary writing, there are no translated works, originally written in a non-English language. Also, our commentators were asked to prepare their own rendering of the original biblical text and to use those languages as the basis of their own comments and exegesis. What may be claimed as distinctive with this series is that it is based on the biblical languages, yet it seeks to make the technical and scholarly approach to a theological understanding of Scripture understandable by— and useful to—the fledgling student, the working minister, and colleagues in the guild of professional scholars and teachers as well.

Finally, a word must be said about the format of the series. The layout, in clearly defined sections, has been consciously devised to assist readers at different levels. Those wishing to learn about the textual witnesses on which the translation is offered are invited to consult the section headed *Notes*. If the readers' concern is with the state of modern scholarship on any given portion of Scripture, they should turn to the sections on *Bibliography* and *Form/Structure/Setting*. For a clear exposition of the passage's meaning and its relevance to the ongoing biblical revelation, the *Comment* and concluding *Explanation* are designed expressly to meet that need. There is therefore something for everyone who may pick up and use these volumes.

If these aims come anywhere near realization, the intention of the editors will have been met, and the labor of our team of contributors rewarded.

General Editors: *David A. Hubbard*
Glenn Barker †
Old Testament: *John D. W. Watts*
New Testament: *Ralph P. Martin*

Abbreviations

PERIODICALS, SERIALS, AND REFERENCE WORKS

AB	Anchor Bible
AcAnt	*Acta Antiqua*
AfO	*Archiv für Orientforschung*
Ag.Ap.	Josephus, *Against Apion*
AJSL	*American Journal of Semitic Languages and Literature*
AnBib	Analecta biblica
ANEP	*Ancient Near East in Pictures*, ed. J. B. Pritchard
ANET	*Ancient Near Eastern Texts*, ed. J. B. Pritchard
Ant	Josephus, *Antiquities*
AOAT	Alter Orient und Altes Testament
ArOr	*Archiv orientální*
ASORDS	American Schools of Oriental Research Dissertation Series
ATD	Das Alte Testament Deutsch
AusBR	*Australian Biblical Review*
AUSS	*Andrews University Seminary Studies*
BA	*Biblical Archaeologist*
BARev	*Biblical Archaeology Review*
BASOR	*Bulletin of the American Schools of Oriental Research*
BBET	Beiträge zur biblischen Exegese und Theologie
BDB	F. Brown, S. R. Driver, and C. A. Briggs, *Hebrew and English Lexicon of the Old Testament*
BETS	*Bulletin of the Evangelical Theological Society*
BHS	*Biblia hebraica stuttgartensia*
Bib	*Biblica*
BibNot	*Biblische Notizen*
BJPES	*Bulletin of the Jewish Palestine Exploration Society*
BJRL	*Bulletin of the John Rylands University Library of Manchester*
BKAT	Biblische Kommentar Altes Testament
BMik	*Beth Mikra*
BOT	De Boeken van het Oude Testament
BR	*Biblical Research*
BSac	*Bibliotheca Sacra*
BT	*The Bible Translator*
BTB	*Biblical Theology Bulletin*
BWANT	Beiträge zur Wissenschaft vom Alten und Neuen Testament
BZ	*Biblische Zeitschrift*
BZAW	Beihefte zur *ZAW*
CAT	Commentaire de l'Ancien Testament
CBC	Cambridge Bible Commentary

CBQ	*Catholic Biblical Quarterly*
CBSC	Cambridge Bible for Schools and Colleges
C-M	E. L. Curtis and A. A. Madsen, *A Critical and Exegetical Commentary on the Books of Chronicles,* ICC (Edinburgh: T. & T. Clark, 1910)
CTM	*Concordia Theological Monthly*
DTT	*Dansk teologisk tidsskrift*
EI	*Eretz Israel*
EncJud	*Encyclopaedia judaica* (1971)
EvQ	*Evangelical Quarterly*
EvT	*Evangelische Theologie*
ExpTim	*Expository Times*
FRLANT	Forschungen zur Religion und Literatur des Alten und Neuen Testaments
GC	L. Allen, *The Greek Chronicles,* 2 vols., VTSup 25, 27 (Leiden: E. J. Brill, 1974)
GKC	*Gesenius' Hebrew Grammar,* ed. E. Kautzsch, tr. A. E. Cowley
HAT	Handbuch zum Alten Testament
HKAT	Handkommentar zum Alten Testament
HSM	Harvard Semitic Monographs
HTR	*Harvard Theological Review*
HUCA	*Hebrew Union College Annual*
IBC	H. G. M. Williamson, *Israel in the Books of Chronicles* (London: Cambridge UP, 1977)
ICC	International Critical Commentary
IDB	*Interpreter's Dictionary of the Bible,* ed. G. A. Buttrick, 4 vols. (Nashville: Abingdon, 1962)
IDBSup	Supplementary volume to *IDB*
IEJ	*Israel Exploration Journal*
Int	*Interpretation*
JANESCU	*Journal of the Ancient Near Eastern Society of Columbia University*
JAOS	*Journal of the American Oriental Society*
JBL	*Journal of Biblical Literature*
JBR	*Journal of Bible and Religion*
JCS	*Journal of Cuneiform Studies*
JETS	*Journal of the Evangelical Theological Society*
JNES	*Journal of Near Eastern Studies*
JPOS	*Journal of the Palestine Oriental Society*
JQR	*Jewish Quarterly Review*
JSOT	*Journal for the Study of the OT*
JSOTSup	Journal for the Study of the OT—Supplement Series
JSS	*Journal of Semitic Studies*
JTS	*Journal of Theological Studies*
J.W.	Josephus, *Jewish Wars*
KAT	Kommentar zum Alten Testament, ed. E. Sellin
KB	L. Koehler and W. Baumgartner, *Lexicon in Veteris Testamenti Libros,* 3d ed.

KHAT	Kurzer Handcommentar zum Alten Testament
KVHS	Korte Verklaring der Heilige Schrift
Leš	*Lešonénu*
LTQ	*Lexington Theological Quarterly*
NCB	New Century Bible Commentary
OTS	*Oudtestamentische Studiën*
PCB	M. Black and H. H. Rowley, eds., *Peake's Commentary on the Bible*
PEQ	*Palestinian Exploration Quarterly*
PJ	*Palästina-Jahrbuch*
PredikOT	De Prediking van het Oude Testament
RA	*Revue d'assyriologie et d'archéologie orientale*
RB	*Revue biblique*
RivB	*Rivista biblica*
RTP	*Revue de Theologie et de Philosophie*
SBLMS	SBL Monograph Series
SBT	*Studia biblica et theologica*
SBT	Studies in Biblical Theology
SEÅ	*Svensk exegetisk årsbok*
Sem	*Semitica*
SJT	*Scottish Journal of Theology*
TAPS	*Transactions of the American Philosophical Society*
TBC	Torch Bible Commentary
TIPE	K. Kitchen, *The Third Intermediate Period in Egypt* (Warminster: Aris and Phillips, 1973)
TLZ	*Theologische Literaturzeitung*
TQ	*Theologische Quartalschrift*
TRu	*Theologische Rundschau*
TynBul	*Tyndale Bulletin*
TZ	*Theologische Zeitschrift*
US	*Überlieferungsgeschichtliche Studien*, 2d ed. (Darmstadt: Wissenschaftliche Buchgesellschaft, 1967)
VT	*Vetus Testamentum*
VTSup	Vetus Testamentum, Supplements
WBC	Word Biblical Commentary
WMANT	Wissenschaftliche Monographien zum Alten und Neuen Testament
WTJ	*Westminster Theological Journal*
ZAW	*Zeitschrift für die alttestamentliche Wissenschaft*
ZDMG	*Zeitschrift der deutschen morgenländischen Gesellschaft*
ZDPV	*Zeitschrift des deutschen Palästina-Vereins*

MODERN TRANSLATIONS

ASV	American Standard Version	NAB	New American Bible
		NASB	New American Standard Bible
AV	Authorized Version		
JB	Jerusalem Bible	NEB	New English Bible

| NIV | New International Version | RV | Revised Version |
| RSV | Revised Standard Version | TEV | Today's English Version (Good News Bible) |

TEXTS, VERSIONS, AND ANCIENT WORKS

Arab	Arabic	MT	Masoretic Text
Bas	Basileion: Septuagint of Samuel and Kings	NT	New Testament
G, LXX	Septuagint	OG	Old Greek
A	Codex Alexandrinus	OL	Old Latin
B	Codex Vaticanus	OT	Old Testament
L	Lucianic recension (boc₂e₂)	Par	Paraleipomenon: Septuagint of Chronicles
V	Codex Venetus	Syr	Syriac text
L	Codex Leningradensis, B19a	Tg	Targum
		Vg	Vulgate

This commentary is based on the printed Hebrew text of the *Biblia Hebraica Stuttgartensia* (Stuttgart: Deutsche Bibelstiftung, 1967–77). Chapter and verse enumeration throughout are those of the Hebrew Bible. Where these differ from the standard English versions, references to the latter have been given in brackets following the Hebrew number. The LXX text cited is that of H. B. Swete, *The Old Testament in Greek*, 4 vols. (Cambridge: University Press, 1905–9).

BIBLICAL AND APOCRYPHAL BOOKS

Old Testament

Gen	Genesis	Isa	Isaiah
Exod	Exodus	Jer	Jeremiah
Lev	Leviticus	Lam	Lamentations
Num	Numbers	Ezek	Ezekiel
Deut	Deuteronomy	Dan	Daniel
Josh	Joshua	Hos	Hosea
Judg	Judges	Joel	Joel
Ruth	Ruth	Amos	Amos
1–2 Sam	1–2 Samuel	Obad	Obadiah
1–2 Kgs	1– Kings	Jon	Jonah
1–2 Chr	1–2 Chronicles	Mic	Micah
Ezra	Ezra	Nah	Nahum
Neh	Nehemiah	Hab	Habakkuk
Esth	Esther	Zeph	Zephaniah
Job	Job	Hag	Haggai
Ps(s)	Psalm(s)	Zech	Zechariah
Prov	Proverbs	Mal	Malachi
Eccl	Ecclesiastes		
Cant	Canticles, Song of Solomon		

New Testament

Matt	Matthew	1–2 Thess	1–2 Thessalonians
Mark	Mark	1–2 Tim	1–2 Timothy
Luke	Luke	Titus	Titus
John	John	Phlm	Philemon
Acts	Acts	Heb	Hebrews
Rom	Romans	Jas	James
1–2 Cor	1–2 Corinthians	1–2 Pet	1–2 Peter
Gal	Galatians	1–2–3 John	1–2–3 John
Eph	Ephesians	Jude	Jude
Phil	Philippians	Rev	Revelation
Col	Colossians		

Apocrypha

Add Esth	Additions to Esther	1–2–3–4 Macc	1–2–3–4 Maccabees
Bar	Baruch		
Bel	Bel and the Dragon	Pr Azar	Prayer of Azariah
1–2 Esdr	1–2 Esdras	Pr Man	Prayer of Manasseh
4 Ezra	4 Ezra	Sir	Ecclesiasticus or The Wisdom of Jesus Son of Sirach
Jud	Judith		
Ep Jer	Epistle of Jeremy		
1 Esdr	1 Esdras	Sus	Susanna
1–2–3–4 Kgdms	1–2–3–4 Kingdoms	Tob	Tobit
		Wis	Wisdom of Solomon

HEBREW GRAMMAR

abs	absolute	impf	imperfect
acc	accusative	impv	imperative
act	active	ind	indicative
adv acc	adverbial accusative	inf	infinitive
aor	aorist	juss	jussive
c	common	masc, m	masculine
coh	cohortative	niph	niphal
conj	conjunction	obj	object
consec	consecutive	pass	passive
constr	construct	pf	perfect
dittogr	dittography	pl	plural
fem, f	feminine	prep	preposition
fut	future	pron	pronoun
gen	genitive	pronom	pronominal
haplogr	haplography	ptcp	participle
hiph	hiphil	sg	singular
hithp	hithpael	subj	subject
hoph	hophal		

MISCELLANEOUS

chap(s).	chapter(s)	MS(S)	manuscript(s)
ed(s).	editor(s), edited by	Q	Qere, to be "read"
ET	English translation	tr.	translator, translated by
Gr.	Greek	v(v)	verse(s)
Heb.	Hebrew	vol(s).	volume(s)
K	Kethib, "written"		

Introduction

No interpreter of Scripture ever transcends the hermeneutical circle. There is a set of mutually informing and reinforcing relationships that exist between one's (1) hermeneutics, (2) theology, and (3) exegesis. Rather than deny such reciprocal interplay or claim to attain some vantage of neutrality or objectivity, it is more helpful for the individual interpreter to be self-conscious regarding the influence of the hermeneutical circle on his own work; the reader is helped when a writer reflects on these relationships and directly addresses how he sees the lay of the land.

I write from the perspective of an evangelical Christian. The hallmark of evangelicalism, apart from its Christology, is its high regard for the Bible as the Word of God. Evangelical theologians often describe the Bible in terms of an incarnational analogy: the Bible is described as both fully divine and fully human. It is divine in that it is the Word of God; as God's Word, it shares in the attributes of God. Just as God does not lie, so also the Bible does not lie; it does not deceive or mislead us. It is without error in all that it teaches. It is fully human in that it was revelation that did not set aside the human personalities that produced it; it was not dictated from above. The Bible is not in some sense supratemporal or supracultural; rather, it was produced by particular persons at particular historical moments, people who were influenced by their own cultures to the same depths as all other human beings. The human authors of Scripture addressed the needs of particular communities and used the literary genres and historiographical practices of their own day.

When reading Chronicles one cannot but be impressed by the theological motivation that characterizes these writings. Chronicles is through and through a theological essay; the Chronicler describes the past to demonstrate the validity of particular premises that addressed the needs of Israel in his own day. Chronicles is not only a writing of history; it is a tract.

The Chronicler was a person interacting with texts. He clearly had access to a wide variety of canonical texts; he cites passages in canonical prophets, the pentateuch, the psalms, Joshua, and preeminently Samuel-Kings. There is no compelling reason to doubt that he had access also to the wide variety of extrabiblical sources to which he so frequently refers his reader. Throughout this volume I have described the Chronicler's interaction with texts, particularly with Kings, using a variety of verbs; I have said that the Chronicler "recasts, shapes, models, enhances, modifies, transforms, edits, rewrites" the material he had before him in order to present his view of Israel's history. In describing the Chronicler's actions in this way, I do not intend to prejudge historical questions. It is my own conviction that the Chronicler is a reliable and trustworthy historian; where we are able to check his record against extrabiblical data, the picture is that of a careful author. I do not believe that the Chronicler was simply fabricating the data he needed to make his points. In most instances, however, we do not have the extrabiblical data by which to evaluate his historical information.

Yet in making these assertions regarding the reliability of Chronicles, there is also another danger to be avoided. The doctrine of Scripture should not be used in such a way as to make the Chronicler a modern historian operating under the influence of historical positivism. The Chronicler was not a newspaper journalist. He was a teacher and theologian, a painter rather than a photographer. There are no uninterpreted facts, a fact patently clear in his writings. The Chronicler wrote within the framework of culturally acceptable historiographic practices and genres. To impose on him canons for historiography that are derived from historical positivism would not only be an anachronism, but it would also strike in a fundamental way at the incarnational analogy by abstracting the Chronicler from his own time. We cannot deny to the Chronicler the liberties in the presentation of his data that his culture allowed. The Chronicler does use hyperbole on occasion; events are not always narrated in strict chronological sequence.

Just as we do not have the data by which to evaluate much of the Chronicler's historical information, so also we do not have sufficient data by which to settle in a definitive way the range of historiographical practices and genres that characterized ancient Israel. The data create two very strong impressions: that of a writer working carefully with a wide variety of reliable sources, and that of an able theologian ministering to his own people. In studying Chronicles we cannot fail to do justice to both.

The usual concerns of a commentary introduction with questions of authorship, date, text, sources, etc., have been treated in some detail in the companion volume in this series by Roddy Braun (*1 Chronicles*, WBC 14 [Waco: Word Books, 1986]). My own research agrees in the main with the conclusions presented by Braun in that introduction. We join a growing list of commentators who have written from the vantage that Chronicles and Ezra-Nehemiah are not the product of the same author.

With reference to the particular introductory concerns of 2 Chronicles, two separate essays have been included that serve as introduction to larger units of text: "The Chronicler's Solomon" introduces chaps. 1–9; "Reward and Punishment in Chronicles: The Theology of Immediate Retribution" introduces chaps. 10–36. These essays describe the Chronicler's theology, purpose, and compositional techniques; they will assist the reader to fit a particular narrative into the larger scope of the Chronicler's work.

The Chronicler has treated the reigns of several of the Judean kings at comparatively greater length. Again to provide a look at the bigger picture, shorter separate chapters have been included introducing "The Chronicler's Jehoshaphat" and "The Chronicler's Hezekiah."

Main Bibliography

A few of the items in this bibliography have not been accessible to me; they are included for the sake of other researchers working on Chronicles.

Abramsky, S. "The Chronicler's View of King Solomon." *EI* 16 (1982) 3–14. **Ackroyd, P. R.** *The Age of the Chronicler.* Supplement to *Colloquim.* Auckland: SPCK, 1970. ———. "The Chronicler as Exegete." *JSOT* 2 (1977) 2–32. ———. *Exile and Restoration: A Study of Hebrew Thought of the Sixth Century B.C.* Philadelphia: Westminster Press, 1968. ———. *I and II Chronicles, Ezra, Nehemiah.* TBC. London: SCM Press, 1973. ———. "History and Theology in the Writings of the Chronicler." *CTM* 38 (1967) 501–15. ———. *Israel under Babylon and Persia.* New Clarendon Bible. Oxford: Oxford UP, 1970. ———. "The Theology of the Chronicler." *LTQ* 8 (1973) 101–16. **Albright, W. F.** *Archaeology and the Religion of Israel.* Baltimore: Johns Hopkins Press, 1946. ———. "The Date and Personality of the Chronicler." *JBL* 40 (1921) 104–24. ———. "The Judicial Reform of Jehoshaphat." *Alexander Marx Jubilee Volume.* New York: Jewish Publication Society, 1950. **Allen, L. C.** "Further Thoughts on an Old Recension of Reigns in Paralipomena." *HTR* 61 (1968) 483–91. ———. *The Greek Chronicles.* 2 vols. VTSup 25, 27. Leiden: E. J. Brill, 1974. **Amit, Y.** "A New Outlook on the Book of Chronicles." *Immanuel* 13 (1981) 20–29. ———. "The Role of Prophecy and the Prophets in the Teaching of Chronicles." *BMik* 28/93 (1982/83) 113–33. **Barnes, W. E.** "The David of the Book of Samuel and the David of the Book of Chronicles." *The Expositor.* 7th ser. 37 (1909) 49–59. ———. "The Midrashic Element in Chronicles." *The Expositor.* 5th ser. 4 (1896) 426–39. ———. "The Religious Standpoint of the Chronicler." *AJSL* 13 (1896–97) 14–20. **Bea, A.** "Neuere Arbeiten zum Problem der biblischen Chronikbucher." *Bib* 22 (1941) 46–58. **Begg, C.** "'Seeking Yahweh' and the Purpose of Chronicles." *Louvain Studies* 9 (1982) 128–42. **Ben David, A.** *Parallels in the Bible.* Jerusalem: Carta, 1972. **Benzinger, I.** *Die Bucher der Chronik.* KHAT 20. Tubingen: Mohr, 1901. **Bertheau, E.** *Die Bücher der Chronik.* Kurzgefasstes exegetisches Handbuch zum Alten Testament 15. Leipzig: Hirzel, 1854. **Born, A. van den.** *Kronieken.* BOT. Roermond: Romen, 1954. **Botterweck, G. J.** "Zur Eigenart der chronistischen Davidgeschichte." *TQ* 136 (1956) 402–35. **Braun, R. L.** "Chronicles, Ezra and Nehemiah: Theology and Literary History." In *Studies in the Historical Books of the Old Testament,* ed. J. A. Emerton. VTSup 30. Leiden: E. J. Brill, 1979. ———. *First Chronicles.* WBC 14. Waco: Word Books, 1986. ———. "The Message of Chronicles: Rally 'Round the Temple." *CTM* 42 (1971) 502–14. ———. "A Reconsideration of the Chronicler's Attitude toward the North." *JBL* 96 (1977) 59–62. ———. *The Significance of 1 Chronicles 22, 28, and 29 for the Structure and Theology of the Work of the Chronicler.* Th.D. thesis, Concordia Seminary, St. Louis, 1971. ———. "Solomon, the Chosen Temple Builder: The Significance of 1 Chr 22, 28, and 29 for the Theology of Chronicles." *JBL* 95 (1976) 581–90. ———. "Solomonic Apologetic in Chronicles." *JBL* 92 (1973) 503–16. **Bright, J.** *A History of Israel.* 2d ed. Philadelphia: Westminster Press, 1972. **Brunet, A. M.** "Le Chroniste et ses sources." *RB* 60 (1953) 481–508; 61 (1954) 349–86. ———. "La théologie du Chroniste: théocratie et messianisme." *Sacra Pagina* 1 (1959) 384–97. **Bückers, H.** *Die Bücher der Chronik.* Freiburg: Herder, 1952. **Cancik, H.** "Das jüdische Fest: Ein Versuch zu Form und Religion des chronistischen Geschichtswerkes." *TQ* 150 (1970) 335–48. **Caquot, A.** "Peut-on parler de messianisme dans l'oeuvre du Chroniste?" *RTP,* 3d ser. 16 (1966) 110–20. **Carr, G. L.** *The Claims of the Chronicler for the Origin of the Israelite Priesthood.* Diss. Boston University, 1973.

Cazelles, H. *Les livres des Chroniques.* La Sainte Bible. Paris: Éditions du Cerf, 1954. **Cogan, M.** *Imperialism and Religion: Assyria, Judah, and Israel in the Eighth and Seventh Centuries B.C.* SBLMS 19. Missoula, MT: Scholars Press, 1974. ———. "Tendentious Chronology in the Book of Chronicles." *Zion* 45 (1980) 165–72. [Heb.] Also publ. as "The Chronicler's Use of Chronology as Illuminated by Neo-Assyrian Royal Inscriptions." In *Empirical Models for Biblical Criticism,* ed. J. Tigay. Philadelphia: University of Pennsylvania, 1985. 197–210. **Coggins, R. J.** *The First and Second Books of the Chronicles.* The Cambridge Bible Commentary on the New English Bible. London: Cambridge UP, 1976. **Cross, F. M.** "A Reconstruction of the Judean Restoration." *JBL* 94 (1975) 4–18. **Curtis, E. L.,** and **A. A. Madsen.** *A Critical and Exegetical Commentary on the Books of Chronicles.* ICC. Edinburgh: T. & T. Clark, 1910. **Déaut, R. le,** and **J. Robert.** *Targum des Chroniques.* 2 vols. AnBib 51. Rome: Biblical Institute Press, 1971. **Dillard, R. B.** "David's Census: Perspectives on 2 Samuel 24 and 1 Chronicles 21." In *Through Christ's Word,* ed. R. Godfrey and J. Boyd. Phillipsburg, NJ: Presbyterian and Reformed, 1985. 94–107. ———. "The Chronicler's Jehoshaphat." *Trinity Journal* 7 (1986) 17–22. ———. "The Chronicler's Solomon." *WTJ* 43 (1980) 289–300. ———. "The Literary Structure of the Chronicler's Solomon Narrative." *JSOT* 30 (1984) 85–93. ———. "Reward and Punishment in Chronicles: The Theology of Immediate Retribution." *WTJ* 46 (1984) 164–72. ———. "The Reign of Asa (2 Chr 14–16): An Example of the Chronicler's Theological Method." *JETS* 23 (1980) 207–18. **Dion, P. E.** "Did Cultic Prostitution Fall into Oblivion in the Postexilic Era? Some Evidence from Chronicles and the Septuagint." *CBQ* 43 (1981) 41–48. **Driver, S. R.** "The Speeches in Chronicles." *The Expositor,* 5th ser. 1 (1895) 241–56. **Dumbrell, W.** "The Purpose of the Books of Chronicles." *JETS* 27 (1984) 257–66. **Ellison, H. L.** "1 and 2 Chronicles." *The New Bible Commentary: Revised,* ed. D. Guthrie et al. London: Inter-Varsity Press, 1970. **Elmslie, W. A. L.** *The Books of Chronicles.* CBSC. London: Cambridge UP, 1916. **Engler, H.** *The Attitude of the Chronicler Toward the Davidic Monarchy.* Diss. Concordia Seminary, 1971. **Eshkenazi, T.** "The Chronicler and the Composition of 1 Esdras." *CBQ* 48 (1986) 39–61. **Fishbane, M.** *Biblical Interpretation in Ancient Israel.* Oxford: Clarendon, 1985. **Freedman, D. N.** "The Chronicler's Purpose." *CBQ* 23 (1961) 436–42. **Galling, K.** *Die Bucher der Chronik, Esra, Nehemiah.* ATD 12. Göttingen: Vandenhoeck und Ruprecht, 1954. **Gerleman, G.** *Studies in the Septuagint, II.* Lunds Universitets Årsskrift, N.F., avd. 1, vol. 43, no. 3. Lund: C. W. K. Gleerup, 1946. **Gese, H.** "Zur Geschichte der Kultsanger am zweiten Tempel." *Von Sinai zum Zion: alttestamentliche Beitrage zur biblische Theologie.* Munich: Chr. Kaiser, 1974. **Gill, M.** "Israel in the Book of Chronicles." *BMik* 13 (1968) 105–15. **Goettsberger, J.** *Die Bücher der Chronik oder Paralipomenon.* Die heilige Schrift des Alten Testaments. Bonn: Hanstein, 1939. **Goldingay, J.** "The Chronicler as Theologian." *BTB* 5 (1975) 99–126. **Graham, M.** *The Utilization of 1 and 2 Chronicles in the Reconstruction of Israelite History in the Nineteenth Century.* Diss. Emory University, 1983. **Gray, J.** *I and II Kings.* 2d ed. OTL. Philadelphia: Westminster Press, 1970. **Hanks, T. D.** "The Chronicler: Theologian of Grace." *EvQ* 53 (1981) 16–28. **Haran, M.** *Temples and Temple Service in Ancient Israel.* Oxford: Clarendon, 1977. **Herbert, A. S.** "I and II Chronicles." *PCB.* New York: Thos. Nelson, 1962. **Hobbs, T.** *Second Kings.* WBC 13. Waco: Word Books, 1985. **Im, T.-S.** *Das Davidbild in der Chronikbüchern: David als Idealbild des theokratischen Messianismus für den Chronisten.* Frankfurt am Main: Peter Lang, 1985. **Japhet, S.** "Chronicles, Book of." *EncJud* 5 (1971) 517–34. ———. "Conquest and Settlement in Chronicles." *JBL* 98 (1979) 205–18. ———. "The Historical Reliability of Chronicles." *JSOT* 33 (1985) 83–107. ———. "Interchanges of Verbal Roots in Parallel Texts in Chronicles." *Leš* 31 (1967) 165–79. ———. *The Ideology of the Book of Chronicles and Its Place in Biblical Thought.* Jerusalem: Bialik, 1977. ———. "The Supposed Common Authorship of Chronicles and Ezra-Nehemiah Investigated Anew." *VT* 18 (1968) 330–71. **Jenni, E.**

"Aus der Literatur zur chronistischen Geschichtschreibung." *TRu* 45 (1980) 97–108. **Johnstone, W.** "Guilt and Atonement: The Theme of 1 and 2 Chronicles." In *A Word in Season*, ed. J. Martin and P. Davies. JSOTSup 42. Sheffield: JSOT Press, 1986. 113–38. **Katzenstein, H. J.** *The History of Tyre.* Jerusalem: Schocken Institute for Jewish Research, 1973. **Kegler, J.,** and **M. Augustin.** *Synopse zum chronistischen Geschichtswerk.* Frankfurt am Main: Peter Lang, 1984. **Keil, C. F.** *The Books of the Chronicles.* Tr. A. Harper. Grand Rapids: Wm. B. Eerdmans, 1966. **Kitchen, K. A.** *The Third Intermediate Period in Egypt.* Warminster: Aris and Phillips, 1973. **Kittel, R.** *Die Bücher der Chronik.* HKAT I/6. Göttingen: Vandenhoeck & Ruprecht, 1902. **Kropat, A.** *Die Syntax des Autors der Chronik verglichen mit der seiner Quellen.* BZAW 16. Giessen: Alfred Töpelmann, 1909. **Langton, S.** *Commentary on the Book of Chronicles.* Ed. A. Saltman. Ramat-gan: Bar-Ilan UP, 1978. **Lemke, W. F.** "The Synoptic Problem in the Chronicler's History." *HTR* 58 (1965) 349–63. ―――. *Synoptic Studies in the Chronicler's History.* Diss. Harvard Divinity School, 1963. **Longacre, R.** *Anatomy of Speech Notions.* Lisse: Peter de Ridder, 1976. **Mathias, D.** *Die Geschichte der Chronikforschung in 19. Jahrhundert unter besonderer Berucksichtigung der exegetischen Behandlung der Prophetennachrichten des chronistischen Geschichtswerkes.* 3 vols. Leipzig: Karl-Marx Universität, 1977. **McConville, J.** *I and II Chronicles.* Daily Study Bible. Philadelphia: Westminster Press, 1984. **McKay, J.** *Religion in Judah under the Assyrians.* SBT 2d ser. 26. Naperville, IL: Alec R. Allenson, 1973. **McKenzie, S.** *The Chronicler's Use of the Deuteronomistic History.* HSM 33. Atlanta: Scholars Press, 1985. **Mendenhall, G. E.** "The Census Lists of Numbers 1 and 26." *JBL* 77 (1958) 52–66. **Michaeli, F.** *Les livres des Chroniques, d'Esdras et de Néhémie.* CAT 16. Neuchâtel: Delachaux et Niestlé, 1967. **Micheel, R.** *Die Seher- und Prophetenüberlieferungen in der Chronik.* BBET 18. Frankfurt am Main: Peter Lang, 1983. **Montgomery, J.** *A Critical and Exegetical Commentary on the Books of Kings.* ICC. New York: Scribners, 1951. **Mosis, R.** *Untersuchungen zur Theologie des chronistischen Geschichtswerkes.* Freiburger theologische Studien. Freiburg: Herder, 1973. **Mowinckel, S.** "Erwagungen zum chronistischen Geschichtswerk." *TLZ* 85 (1960) 1–8. **Myers, J. M.** *I and II Chronicles.* AB 12, 13. Garden City, NY: Doubleday, 1965. ―――. "The Kerygma of the Chronicler: History and Theology in the Service of Religion." *Int* 20 (1966) 259–73. **Newsome, J. D., Jr.** *The Chronicler's View of Prophecy.* Diss. Vanderbilt University, 1973. ―――. "Toward a New Understanding of the Chronicler and His Purposes." *JBL* 94 (1975) 204–17. **Noordtzij, A.** *De Boeken der Kronieken.* 2 vols. KVHS. Kampen: J. H. Kok, 1957. ―――. "Les intentions du Chroniste." *RB* 49 (1940) 161–68. **North, R.** "The Chronicler: 1–2 Chronicles, Ezra, Nehemiah." In *Jerome Bible Commentary*, ed. R. E. Brown et al. Englewood Cliffs, NJ: Prentice-Hall, 1968. ―――. "Does Archaeology Prove Chronicles Sources?" In *Old Testament Studies in Honor of Jacob M. Myers*, ed. H. N. Bream et al. Philadelphia: Temple UP, 1974. ―――. "The Theology of the Chronicler." *JBL* 82 (1963) 369–81. **Noth, M.** *Überlieferungsgeschichtliche Studien.* 2d ed. Darmstadt: Wissenschaftliche Buchgesellschaft, 1967. **Osborne, W.** *The Genealogies of 1 Chronicles 1–9.* Diss. Dropsie University, 1979. **Payne, J. B.** "I and II Chronicles." *Wycliffe Bible Commentary*, ed. C. Pfeiffer and E. Harrison. Chicago: Moody Press, 1962. ―――. "The Validity of Numbers in Chronicles." *BSac* 136 (1979) 109–28, 206–20. **Petersen, D. L.** *Late Israelite Prophecy.* SBLMS 23. Missoula, MT: Scholars Press, 1977. **Plöger, O.** "Reden und Gebete im deuteronomistischen und chronistischen Geschichtswerk." *Aus der Spätzeit des Alten Testaments. Göttingen: Vandenhoeck und Ruprecht, 1971.* **Polzin, R.** *Late Biblical Hebrew: Toward an Historical Typology of Biblical Hebrew Prose.* HSM 12. Missoula, MT: Scholars Press, 1976. **Rad, G. von.** *Das Geschichtsbild des chronistischen Werkes.* BWANT 4/3. Stuttgart: Kohlhammer, 1930. ―――. "The Levitical Sermon in I and II Chronicles." *The Problem of the Hexateuch and Other Essays.* Tr. E. Dicken. New York: McGraw-Hill, 1966. **Randellini, L.** "Il Libro delle Cronache nel decennio 1950–60." *RivB* 10 (1962) 136–56. **Rehm, M.** *Textkritische Untersuchungen zu den Parallel-*

stellen der Samuel-Königsbücher und der Chronik. Münster: Aschendorff, 1937. **Richardson, H. N.** "The Historical Reliability of Chronicles." *JBR* 26 (1958) 9–12. **Rigsby, R.** *The Historiography of Speeches and Prayers in the Books of Chronicles.* Diss. Southern Baptist Theological Seminary, 1973. **Romerowski, S.** "Les règnes de David et Salomon dans les Chroniques." *Hokhma* 31 (1986) 1–23. **Rothstein, J. W.,** and **Hänel, J.** *Das erste Buch der Chronik.* KAT 18/2. Leipzig: A. Deichert, 1927. **Roubos, K.** *I Kronieken.* PredikOT. Nijkerk: Callenbach, 1969. ———. *II Kronieken.* PredikOT. Nijkerk: Callenbach, 1972. **Rudolph, W.** *Chronikbücher.* HAT 1/21. Tübingen: J. C. B. Mohr, 1955. ———. "Problems of the Books of Chronicles." *VT* 4 (1954) 401–9. **Saebœ, M.** "Messianism in Chronicles? Some Remarks to the Old Testament Background of the New Testament Christology." *Horizons in Biblical Theology* 2 (1980) 85–109. **Schaefer, G. E.** *The Significance of Seeking God in the Purpose of the Chronicler.* Diss. Southern Baptist Theological Seminary, 1972. **Schumacher, J. H.** "The Chronicler's Theology of History." *The Theologian* 13 (1957) 11–21. **Seeligman, I. L.** "Die Auffassung von der Prophetie in der deuteronomistischen und chronistischen Geschichtsschreibung (mit einem Exkurs über das Buch Jeremiah)." *Congress Volume, Göttingen, 1977.* VTSup 29. Leiden: E. J. Brill, 1978. ———. "The Beginnings of Midrash in the Book of Chronicles." *Tarbiz* 49 (1979–80) 14–32. **Shaver, J.** *Torah and the Chronicler's History Work: An Inquiry into the Chronicler's References to Laws, Festivals, and Cultic Institutions in Relation to Pentateuchal Legislation.* Diss. University of Notre Dame, 1984. **Slotki, I. W.** *Chronicles.* London: Soncino Books, 1952. **Smit, E. J.** "Death and Burial Formulas in Kings and Chronicles Relating to the Kings of Judah." *Biblical Essays.* Ninth Meeting of Die Outestamentiese Werkgemeenskap in Suid-Afrika, University of Stellenbosch, July, 1966. Potchefstroom: 1966. **Soggin, J. A.** *A History of Ancient Israel.* Tr. J. Bowden. Philadelphia: Westminster Press, 1985. **Spieckermann, H.** *Juda unter Assur in der Sargonidenzeit.* Göttingen: Vandenhoeck und Ruprecht, 1982. **Stinespring, W. F.** "Eschatology in Chronicles." *JBL* 80 (1961) 209–19. **Swart, J.** *De Theologie von Kronieken.* Groningen: Gebroeders Hoitsema, 1911. **Thiele, E. R.** *The Mysterious Numbers of the Hebrew Kings.* Rev. ed. Grand Rapids: Zondervan, 1983. **Throntveit, M.** *The Significance of the Royal Speeches and Prayers for the Structure and Theology of the Chronicler.* Diss. Union Theological Seminary in Virginia, 1982. **Torrey, C. C.** "The Chronicler as Editor and Independent Narrator." *AJSL* 25 (1908–9) 157–73, 188–217. ———. *The Chronicler's History of Israel.* New Haven: Yale UP, 1954. **Vannutelli, P.** *Libri Synoptici Veteris Testamenti.* Rome: Pontifical Biblical Institute, 1931. **Watson, W. G. E.** "Archaic Elements in the Language of Chronicles." *Bib* 53 (1972) 191–207. **Weinberg, J. P.** "Die Natur im Weltbild des Chronisten." *VT* 31 (1981) 324–45. **Welch, A. C.** *The Work of the Chronicler: Its Purpose and Date.* London: British Academy, 1939. **Wellhausen, J.** *Prolegomena to the History of Ancient Israel.* Tr. Menzies and Black. New York: Meridian Books, 1957. **Welten, P.** *Geschichte und Geschichtsdarstellung in den Chronikbüchern.* WMANT 42. Neukirchen: Neukirchener Verlag, 1973. **Wenham, J. W.** "Large Numbers in the Old Testament." *TynBul* 18 (1967) 19–53. **Westermann, C.** *Basic Forms of Prophetic Speech.* Tr. H. C. White. Philadelphia: Westminster Press, 1967. **Wilda, G.** *Das Königsbild des chronistischen Geschichtswerkes.* Bonn: Rheinische Friedrich-Wilhelms-Universität, 1959. **Willi, T.** *Die Chronik als Auslegung.* FRLANT 106. Göttingen: Vandenhoeck und Ruprecht, 1972. ———. "Thora in den biblischen Chronikbüchern." *Judaica* 36 (1980) 102–5, 148–51. **Williamson, H. G. M.** "The Accession of Solomon in the Books of Chronicles." *VT* 26 (1976) 351–61. ———. "Eschatology in Chronicles." *TynBul* 28 (1977) 115–54. ———. *Israel in the Books of Chronicles.* London: Cambridge UP, 1977. ———. *1 and 2 Chronicles.* NCB. London: Marshall, Morgan, and Scott, 1982. ———. "The Origins of the Twenty-four Priestly Courses: A Study of 1 Chronicles 23–27." In *Studies in the Historical Books of the Old Testament,* ed. J. A. Emerton. VTSup 30. Leiden: E. J. Brill, 1979. **Wilson, R. R.** *Prophecy and Society in Ancient Israel.* Philadelphia: Fortress Press, 1980.

The Chronicler's Solomon   (2 Chr 1–9)

Bibliography

Any effort to elucidate the purpose and theology of the Chronicler must take account of the author's distinctive handling of David and Solomon; an extensive literature has surveyed the subject. The bibliography here is a selective list, but will lead to the wider literature.

Abramsky, S. "The Chronicler's View of King Solomon." *EI* 16 (1982) 3–14. **Ackroyd, P.** "History and Theology in the Writings of the Chronicler." *CTM* 38 (1967) 501–15. **Braun, R.** "The Message of Chronicles: Rally 'Round the Temple." *CTM* 42 (1971) 502–14. ———. "Solomon, the Chosen Temple Builder: The Significance of 1 Chronicles 22, 28, and 29 for the Theology of Chronicles." *JBL* 95 (1976) 581–90. ———. "Solomonic Apologetic in Chronicles." *JBL* 92 (1973) 503–16. **Brunet, A.** "La théologie du Chroniste: Théocratie et messianisme." *Sacra Pagina* 1 (1959) 384–97. **Caquot, A.** "Peut-on parler de messianisme dans l'oeuvre du Chroniste?" *RTP* 16 (1966) 110–20. **Dillard, R.** "The Chronicler's Solomon." *WTJ* 43 (1980) 289–300. ———. "The Literary Structure of the Chronicler's Solomon Narrative." *JSOT* 30 (1984) 85–93. **Freedman, D.** "The Chronicler's Purpose." *CBQ* 23 (1961) 436–42. **Mosis, R.** *Untersuchungen.* 130–38. **Porten, B.** "The Structure and Theme of the Solomon Narrative (1 Kgs 3–11)." *HUCA* 38 (1967) 93–128. **Romerowski, S.** "Les règnes de David et Salomon dan les Chroniques." *Hokhma* 31 (1986) 1–23. **Stinespring, W.** "Eschatology in Chronicles." *JBL* 80 (1961) 209–19. **Williamson, H.** "The Accession of Solomon in the Books of Chronicles." *VT* 26 (1976) 351–61. ———. "Eschatology in Chronicles." *TynBul* 28 (1977) 115–54.

The reigns of David and Solomon as recorded in Chronicles are markedly different when compared with the earlier accounts in Samuel-Kings; though the central events of their lives are found in both records, they are set in different theological frameworks largely motivated by the needs of their respective audiences. The outlines of the Chronicler's distinctive treatment of Solomon appear in high relief by examining both (1) his deletion of material from the Sam/Kgs account and (2) his use of models around which to shape his version of Solomon.

1. *The Chronicler's omissions.* The deuteronomic historian had divided the reign of Solomon into two distinct periods, a time of blessing and obedience (1 Kgs 1–10) followed by apostasy and judgment in the form of the schism (1 Kgs 11–12). The concern with centralization of worship, particularly with frequenting the high places in Judah (1 Kgs 3:2–4; 12:31–33; 13:2, 32–33; 14:22–23; 22:43; 2 Kgs 12:3; 14:4; 15:4,35; 16:4; 17:11, 29–41; 18:4, 22; 21:3; 23:5–20), became the canon also for condemning the actions of Solomon (1 Kgs 11:1–13). The era of blessing ended with attacks from adversaries (11:14–25) and rebellion from within (11:26–40); the schism itself was attributed to judgment for the sins of Solomon (11:1–6, 31–33). Solomon's corvée labor and his numerous wives made him the negation of the ideal king (Deut 17:17; 1 Sam 8:11–18; 1 Kgs 11:1–6; 4:6–7, 22–28; 5:13–18; 9:15–23; 12:3–19). For the deuteronomic historian the record of the sins of Solomon, as well as those of David, was one more ingredient in the answer for his exilic

audience to the "why" for the destruction of Jerusalem; though David and Solomon were Israel's glorious kings, they too had their part in the failure to live according to God's covenant with his people, a failure that ultimately issued in judgment.

In contrast the Solomon portrayed in Chronicles differs considerably. Any fault or transgression which might tarnish the image of David and Solomon has been removed (that is, with the exception of the account of David's census [1 Chr 21] and perhaps somewhat regarding the first attempt to move the ark [1 Chr 13]). Instead the Chronicler portrays glorious, obedient, all-conquering figures who enjoy not only divine blessing but the total support of the people as well; he presents us not only the David and Solomon of history, but also the David and Solomon of his messianic expectation.

Parenthetically, it should be stated that the nature of the Chronicler's eschatological expectation is highly debated. Scholarly opinion is divided between two extremes and a host of mediating positions: on the one hand, many find the author's messianic/eschatological expectations central to the book, while others view the Chronicler as espousing the view that the purposes of God were so realized in the restoration community as to leave little if any place for eschatological expectation. For a survey of positions and bibliography, see Braun, "Apologetic," 506–7; a recent summary of the issue is also found in Williamson, "Eschatology." See also Brunet, Caquot, and Stinespring.

With reference to Solomon in particular, the account of the accession is striking. Instead of the bedridden, aging David who only saves the kingdom for his son Solomon at the last moment due to the promptings of Bathsheba and Nathan (1 Kgs 1), the Chronicler shows a smooth transition of power without a ripple of dissent: David himself publicly announces Solomon's appointment and is present for his anointing; Solomon's designation as successor is greeted with enthusiastic and total support on the part of the people, including the other sons of David, the officers and mighty men in the army (1 Chr 28:1–29:25), the very groups that had participated in Adonijah's attempted coup (1 Chr 29:24; 1 Kgs 1:7–10). The Chronicler also deletes the record of Solomon's compliance with David's request that he take vengeance on David's enemies after his death (1 Kgs 2). Gone too are the sins for which the deuteronomic historian had condemned Solomon (1 Kgs 11); the blame for the schism is shifted from Solomon to Jeroboam (2 Chr 13:6–7).

While the Chronicler's ennobling of Solomon is effected by his deletion of any blemish found the the Kings account, these are not the only omissions he makes in line with his own central concerns; not just Solomon's sins are missing, but also some accounts which would have enhanced a favorable portrayal of the king. Since the Chronicler's account of Solomon's reign is given almost exclusively to his concern with the temple (2 Chr 2–7), narratives not showing any involvement with the cult are omitted. Even the enduement with wisdom is not wisdom in the abstract (1 Kgs 3:16–4:34) but is specifically wisdom to build the temple (see below, 2.c.).

2. *The Chronicler's models.* It is not sufficient to look at what the Chronicler omits alone; it is also necessary to assess his positive contributions. In the case of his account of Solomon the author appears to have used three distinct models to shape the record.

a. *Solomon as a second David.* Braun ("Apologetic," 506–14) has developed these parallels at some length. Solomon, like David, is king by divine choice; in ways not paralleled in Samuel-Kings, the Chronicler has twice recorded Solomon's name in divine pronouncements regarding David's successor (1 Chr 22:7–10; 28:6). The only occurrences in the OT of the term בחר "choose" in reference to the divine choice of any king after David are found in 1 Chr 28:5–6, 10; 29:1 in reference to Solomon (Braun, "Solomon the Chosen," 588–90). As king by divine election Solomon, like David, enjoys the complete and immediate support of all the people; the Chronicler had elaborated at length on the support of "all Israel" for David at his accession (1 Chr 11–12), and now does so also for Solomon (1 Chr 28–29; cf. 29:22–25). Both kings are shown as having extensive concerns with the cult and the temple and its personnel. In some respects Solomon is even more idealized than David in Chronicles: no blame whatsoever attaches to Solomon as it had to David (1 Chr 21, and perhaps to a lesser extent, 1 Chr 13); Solomon enjoys the privilege of building the temple that had been forbidden to his father. While the earlier history could say that "Solomon did evil . . . and did not follow the Lord completely, as David his father had done" (1 Kgs 11:6), the Chronicler can praise Rehoboam's early years as a time when the nation walked "in the ways of David and Solomon" (2 Chr 11:17).

b. *The succession of Moses and Joshua as a paradigm for that of David and Solomon.* Williamson ("Accession," 351–56) develops the argument that the transition of leadership from Moses to Joshua provided the model used by the Chronicler to portray the transfer of leadership from David to Solomon. He notes the following ingredients in the Chronicler's account:

(1) The disqualification of Moses and David from achieving their chief goals—the one to enter the land, the other to build the temple—is intimately related to the appointment of their respective successors (Deut 1:37–38; 31:2–8; 1 Chr 22:5–13; 28:2–8) under whom these goals are realized.

(2) The installation of Joshua had been the object of earlier form critical studies; Williamson ("Accession") and Braun ("Solomon the Chosen," 586–88) both note the presence of the same elements for this *Gattung* in the appointment of Solomon. Not only are the various elements of the genre present, but there are also numerous phrases directly parallel in the two accounts (Williamson, "Accession," 353–54):

"Be strong and take courage" (חזק ואמץ): Deut 31:7, 23; Josh 1:6, 7, 9; 1 Chr 22:13; 28:20 (cf. Deut 31:6 and 1 Chr 28:10)

"Do not be frightened or dismayed" (אל תירא ואל תחת or equivalents): Deut 31:8; Josh 1:9; 1 Chr 22:13; 28:20 (cf. Deut 31:6)

"The Lord your God is with you" (עמך יהוה אלהיך or equivalents): Deut 31:6, 8, 23; Josh 1:5, 9; 1 Chr 22:11, 16; 28:20; 2 Chr 1:1

"He will never leave you nor forsake you" (לא ירפך ולא יעזבך or equivalents): Deut 31:6, 8, Josh 1:5; 1 Chr 28:20

Stress on prospering through observance of the law: Deut 31:5; Josh 1:7–8; 1 Chr 22:12–13; 28:7–9

(3) Both Moses and David make double announcements regarding the appointment of their successors, once in a private meeting (Deut 1:23; 1 Chr 22:6) and also publicly (Deut 31:2; 1 Chr 28:8).

(4) Both Joshua and Solomon enjoy the immediate and wholehearted support of the people (Deut 34:9; Josh 1:16–20; 1 Chr 29:23–24).

(5) It is twice reported of both Joshua and Solomon that God "magnified" each (Josh 3:7; 4:14; 1 Chr 29:25; 2 Chr 1:1); the piel of גדל is used in all four instances.

A sixth point could be added to Williamson's five: both Joshua and Solomon lead the Israelites into "rest" (Josh 11:23; 21:44; 1 Chr 22:8–9); Braun ("Solomon the Chosen," 582–86) describes the Chronicler's distinctive handling of the "rest" concept in reference to David and Solomon.

Other parallels between Joshua and Solomon are not unique to Chronicles, but do enter the overall picture: (i) The conscription of alien labor for construction and further service in the tabernacle and temple: Joshua impresses the Gibeonites into service at the place of worship (Josh 9:26–27), just as Solomon would also conscript alien labor (2 Chr 2:2, 17–18; 8:7–10). (ii) Both men received divine enduement with wisdom (Deut 34:9; 2 Chr 1).

c. *Solomon and Huram-abi as the new Bezalel and Oholiab.* The third model which the Chronicler borrows to fashion his account of Solomon derives from the building of the tabernacle. The Chronicler draws numerous parallels between the building of the tabernacle and the building of the temple; particularly he casts his Solomon and Huram-abi as the new Bezalel and Oholiab.

(1) *Solomon as the new Bezalel.* Of the thousands who labored in the building of both the tabernacle and the temple, Bezalel and Oholiab and Solomon and Huram-abi are the only ones to be named for their roles. More particularly Bezalel is singled out as the one chosen by God by name (Exod 31:1–11; 35:30–36:2; 38:22–23); Oholiab is in the secondary role as helper (31:6). Solomon too is singled out for the building task (1 Chr 22:9–10; 28:6–29:2). Solomon and Bezalel are both of the tribe of Judah (Exod 31:2; 35:30; 38:22). Both receive wisdom from God for the building task (Exod 31:1–3; 35:30–35; 2 Chr 1). It is striking to note that the only two references to Bezalel outside the accounts of the building of the tabernacle in Exodus are found in Chronicles (1 Chr 2:20; 2 Chr 1:5). It is only after his seeking God at the altar built by Bezalel (2 Chr 1:5) that Solomon is endued with wisdom. For the author of Kings this was wisdom in general, wisdom shown in judicious decisions (1 Kgs 3:16–28), effective administration (4:1–28), and international reputation (4:29–34). But for the Chronicler it was specifically wisdom for building: he omits 1 Kgs 3–4 and proceeds directly to the building of the temple. In Chronicles Hiram does not praise God for giving David "a wise son over this great people" (1 Kgs 5:21 [7]), but for "a wise son who will build" (2 Chr 2:11 [12]).

(2) *Huram-abi as the new Oholiab.* The Chronicler's presentation of Solomon as the second Bezalel is enforced by his handling of Huram-abi as the second Oholiab. This is seen by modifications the Chronicler introduces in three areas: arrival time, skill inventory, and ancestry. The deuteronomic historian records the labor of Huram-abi only after he has reported the completion of the temple and palace (1 Kgs 6:38–7:1); Huram appears only to cast the bronzes needed for the temple construction (1 Kgs 7:13–47). In contrast the Chronicler makes it clear that Huram-abi was involved with the building activities from the very beginning, just as was Oholiab; Huram-abi's services are sought and offered in the first exchange of correspondence between Solomon and Hiram of Tyre (2 Chr 2). Nor are his labors confined to bronze

alone as was the case in Kings (1 Kgs 7:14); the Chronicler records a more extensive skills inventory (2 Chr 2:13 [14]) so that it is the same as the skills of Bezalel and Oholiab (Exod 31:1–6; 35:30–36:2; 38:22–23). While the author of Kings reports that Huram's mother was a widow from the tribe of Naphtali (1 Kgs 7:14), the Chronicler describes her as a widow from Dan (2 Chr 2:13 [14]), thus giving Huram-abi the same tribal ancestry as Oholiab (Exod 31:6; 35:34; 38:23; see *Comment* at 2:14).

LITERARY STRUCTURE

The Chronicler has presented his account of Solomon in a chiastic or palistrophic arrangement. A chiasm is a symmetrical literary device in which items in the first half of the piece are recapitulated in a balanced fashion in the inverse order in the second half; ordinarily the items in the center represent the focal moment of the narrative, either the moment of greatest dramatic tension or the features of central interest to the author.

The following outline approximates the literary structure the Chronicler used in presenting his Solomon; each of the headings will be described below:

A. Solomon's wealth and wisdom   (1:1–17)
   (Trade in horses, 1:14–17)
  B. Recognition by Gentiles / dealings with Hiram   (2:1–16)
    (Yahweh's love for Israel, 2:11)
    C. Temple construction / gentile labor   (2:17–5:1)
      (Gentile labor, 2:17–18)
      (Completion of temple, 5:1)
      D. Dedication of temple   (5:2–7:10)
        1. a.   Summons
            b.   Sacrifice
            c.   Music
            d.   Glory cloud
               2. Solomon speaks to the people (6:1–11)
                  a. Exodus   (6:5)
                  b. Choice of Jerusalem (6:6–11)
               2'. Solomon speaks to God   (6:12–42)
                  a. Promises to David   (6:16–17)
                  b. Eyes open; hear and
                     forgive   (6:18–42)
        1'. d'. Glory cloud
            c'.   Music
            b'.   Sacrifice
            a'.   Dismissal
      D'. Divine response   (7:11–22)
               2". God speaks to Solomon   (7:12–18)
                  b. Eyes open; hear and
                     forgive   (7:13–16)
                    a. Promises to David   (7:17–18)
               2'". God speaks to the people   (7:19–22)
                  b. Choice of Jerusalem   (7:19–21)
                  a. Exodus   (7:22)

   C'. Other construction / gentile labor   (8:1–16)
       (Gentile labor, 8:7–10)
       (Completion of temple, 8:16)
 B'. Recognition by Gentiles / dealings with Hiram   (8:17–9:12)
     (Yahweh's love for Israel, 9:8)
A'. Solomon's wealth and wisdom   (9:13–28)
    (Trade in horses, 9:25–28)

A/A': Solomon's wealth and wisdom. Thematically 1:1–14 and 9:13–24 both
deal with the broad subject of Solomon's kingdom: his consolidation of rule
within (1:1, 13) and the recognition of his rule without (9:13–14, 22–24).
More narrowly both are concerned with his wealth and wisdom.

The strongest connection between these two sections is the nearly verbatim
repetition of the information about Solomon's trade in horses and the repetition of the aphorism comparing cedar with sycamore and silver with stone
(1:14–17; 9:25–28). This passage occurs in its full form only once in the
deuteronomic history of Solomon (1 Kgs 10:26–29; cf. 5:1, 6 [4:20, 26]). The
Chronicler's repeating the passage early in his history is a clue to his structural
intent. Since the Chronicler omitted the material used in Kings to show the
fulfillment of God's promises to Solomon (1 Kgs 3:16–4:34), the repetition
of this material at this point constitutes that fulfillment.

B/B': Recognition by Gentiles / dealings with Hiram. The Chronicler has rather
extensively edited the correspondence with Hiram of Tyre. At first glance
this material may not appear intrinsically paired with the visit of the queen
of Sheba, but the Chronicler has given a clear indication of his intention to
parallel the two accounts by inserting a separate small utterance into Hiram's
letter to Solomon in which Hiram attributes Solomon's rule to Yahweh's love
for Israel (2:11). The identical wording is found in the queen's praise (9:8),
though it occurs only once in the parallel history (1 Kgs 10:9). The parallel
between the two sections is reinforced by the fact that references to Solomon's
maritime ventures with Hiram bracket the account of the queen's visit (also
in 1 Kgs 8:17–9:12), so that Hiram, who is a focal character in 2:1–16, is
also kept to the fore in 8:17–9:12.

C/C': Temple and other construction / gentile labor. These sections are united
around concerns with Solomon's building activities; both emphasize his use
of gentile labor (2:17–18; 8:7–10). Though 8:1–10 is concerned with noncultic
construction, the section is linked to 3:1–5:1 by a description of the ceremonial
provisions Solomon had made for the temple (8:12–15). The earlier section
ended with a note regarding the treasuries and the statement that the work
was finished (5:1), and the counterpart ends with a similar note (8:15–16).
Unless the Chronicler intends to associate 8:16 and 5:1, 8:16 appears thor-
oughly out of place; it reintroduces the subject of actual construction and
completion of the temple well after that narration was already completed.

D/D': Dedication and divine response. This section is the most convoluted in
its general structure. One immediately notes the doubled report of the appearance of the glory cloud and its effect on the ministering priests (5:2–14;
7:1–10); both sections speak of sacrifices and musical accompaniment. It is
tempting to explain these two accounts genetically, i.e., by appeal to redaction

criticism: since 7:1–3 is unique to Chronicles, this would be designated the Chronicler's account; since 5:11, 14 parallel 1 Kgs 8:10–11, this could be judged the insertion of a later redactor influenced by the order in Kings (Rudolph, 211). If one allows that the Chronicler has staged the material in a chiastic fashion, a redaction critical explanation would not be necessary: the two appearances of the glory cloud are one and the same, repeated for structural necessity.

The two theophanies frame two speeches by Solomon, one to the assembled people (6:4–11) and one in the dedicatory prayer (6:14–42). Though many years have elapsed in the interval (see *Comment* at 7:11), the Chronicler's version of the divine response to Solomon's prayer is also twofold: part to Solomon ("you" is singular, 7:12–18) and part to the people ("you" and other personal referents are plural, 7:19–22). As can be noted from the outline, the themes in each part of the divine response correspond to themes in Solomon's speeches, but in reverse order as would be expected in a chiastic outline: D2 corresponds to D2''' while D2' corresponds to D2''.

The center of a chiasm is ordinarily the peak moment of dramatic tension or the central interest of the writer. Scholars have long recognized the centrality of cult in Chronicles, and that the Chronicler has written his accounts of David and Solomon largely in terms of their involvement with the temple. However, though the Chronicler is so concerned with the temple, his actual account of its construction is considerably shorter than that found in the parallel account. His account does not focus on the building itself, but rather on the dedicatory addresses of Solomon and the divine response. In Chronicles particularly these speech materials constitute the "charter" for the remainder of the Chronicler's historiography; the author will seek again and again to demonstrate the realization in Israel's history of the principles announced in Solomon's prayer and in God's response. This is especially clear in that most famous passage in Chronicles, 2 Chr 7:14, a passage unique to Chronicles and overtly articulating the "theology of immediate retribution" which will guide his subsequent assessment of Israel's history after the schism. These speech materials in the center of his account of Solomon constitute the "spectacles" through which the Chronicler would assess the past; see the essay introducing 2 Chr 10–36, "Reward and Punishment in Chronicles: The Theology of Immediate Retribution."

The argument for viewing the Chronicler's Solomon narrative as a chiasm would be enhanced if it could be shown that the author in all probability also used the same device as the scaffolding for other narratives. H. Williamson has demonstrated that two passages which appeared to be in disjointed disarray are in fact examples of studied symmetry constructed in chiasms; see his discussions of 1 Chr 2 (*JBL* 98 [1979] 351–59) and 1 Chr 11–12 (*OTS* 21 [1981] 164–76).

Whatever speculation scholars may indulge in regarding the history of redaction of the individual literary units and sources the Chronicler had at his disposal, in several extended pericopes there remain the traces of a unitary purpose and of a contrivance in structure that most naturally comport with a single author of considerable skill and genius.

Solomon's Request for Wisdom (1:1–17)

Bibliography

Ehrlich, E. *Der Traum im Alten Testament.* BZAW 73. Göttingen: de Gruyter, 1953. **Gilbert, M.** "La structure de la prière de Salomon (Sg 9)." *Bib* 51 (1970) 301–31. **Holladay, J.** "The Stables of Ancient Israel: Functional Determinates of Stable Construction and the Interpretation of Pillared Building Remains of the Palestinian Iron Age." *The Archaeology of Jordan and Other Studies.* Berrien Springs: Andrews UP, 1987. **Kapelrud, A.** "Temple Building, A Task for Gods and Kings." *Or* 32 (1963) 56–62. **Oppenheim, A. L.** *The Interpretation of Dreams in the Ancient Near East.* TAPS n.s. 46/3. Philadelphia: American Philosophical Society, 1956. **Pritchard, J.** "The Megiddo Stables: A Reassessment." In *Near Eastern Archaeology in the Twentieth Century,* ed. J. Sanders. Garden City, NY: Doubleday, 1970. **Richter, W.** "Der Traum und Traumdeutung in AT." *BT* (1963) 202–30. **Seow, C.** "The Syro-Palestinian Content of Solomon's Dream." *HTR* 77 (1984) 141–52. **Zalevsky, S.** "The Revelation of God to Solomon in Gibeon." *Tarbiz* 42 (1973) 214–58.

Translation

[1] Solomon son of David strengthened his hold on the kingdom, for Yahweh his God was with him and greatly[a] exalted him. [2] Solomon spoke to all Israel—to the commanders of thousands and hundreds, to the judges and all the leaders of all Israel (the heads of the families). [3] And Solomon, together with the entire assembly, went to the high place at Gibeon, for there was the tent for meeting God,[a] which Moses the servant of Yahweh had made in the wilderness.

[4] Now David had already brought the ark up from Kiriath-jearim to the place he had prepared for it, for he had pitched a tent for it in Jerusalem. [5] But the bronze altar that Bezalel son of Uri son of Hur had made was there[a] before the tabernacle of Yahweh, so Solomon and the assembly sought it[b] there. [6] Solomon went up to the bronze altar before Yahweh at the Tent of Meeting and offered a thousand burnt offerings upon it.

[7] That night God appeared to Solomon and said to him, "Ask whatever you wish, and I will give it to you."

[8] Solomon said to God, "You have shown great faithfulness to my father David and have made me king in his place. [9] Now, Yahweh God, let your promise to David my father be confirmed, for you have made me king over a people as numerous as the dust of the earth. [10] Now give me wisdom and knowledge that I might lead this people, for who can govern this great people of yours?"

[11] And God said to Solomon, "Since this is what you desire and you have not asked for wealth, riches, and honor, or the life of your enemies, nor have you asked for a long life—but you have asked for wisdom and knowledge that you may govern my people over whom I have made you king—[12] wisdom and knowledge are granted to you. And I will also give you wealth, riches, and honor such as no king before you has ever had, nor will any after you."

[13] So Solomon went from before the Tent of Meeting at the high place in Gibeon to Jerusalem,[a] and he reigned over Israel.

[14] Solomon acquired chariots and horses; he had fourteen hundred chariots and

twelve thousand horses, which he kept in chariot cities and near at hand in Jerusalem.[a]
¹⁵ *The king made silver and gold in Jerusalem as common as stones, and cedar plentiful as the sycamore fig in the hill country.*
¹⁶ *Solomon's horses were imported from Egypt and Que;*[a] *the king's merchants acquired them from Que for a price.* ¹⁷ *They imported a chariot from Egypt for six hundred sheqels of silver and a horse for a hundred and fifty. Thus all the kings of the Hittites and Arameans imported them through their hands.*

Notes

1.a. The Chronicler frequently uses the adv למעלה in the sense "greatly, exceedingly, highly" (1 Chr 14:2; 22:5; 23:17; 29:3, 25; 2 Chr 1:1; 16:12; 17:12; 20:19; 26:8), a sense broader than the usual "upward, above." This use is not found in Ezra/Neh and appears to be a stylistic trait unique to the Chronicler; as such it is one more ingredient in the argument against regarding Chr/Ezra/Neh as a unity. See Japhet, "Common Authorship," 357–58; and Polzin, *Late Hebrew*, 140–41.

3.a. The phrase אהל מועד האלהים occurs only here and is ambiguous; האלהים could modify either "tent" ("God's Tent of Meeting" NIV, JB, NAS) or "meeting" ("tent for meeting God" NEB, TEV). The gen in G and Vg makes these versions likewise ambiguous at this point. The function of the tent as a place to receive revelation (Num 12:1–16) and the immediate purpose of Solomon's visit ("to seek him," 1:5) favor the latter translation; however, the concept that it is God's tent is also present in the phrases אהל יהוה (1 Kgs 2:28–30), אהליך (Ps 15:1; cf. 61:5 [4]), and אהלו (Ps 27:5–6).

5.a. Reading שם with G, Vg, and some Heb. MSS; MT שם is supported by Tg and Syr.

5.b. The referent of the pronom object in וידרשהו is ambiguous: "him" (= God; NAB, RSV, NIV) or "it" (= the altar; G, Vg, NAS, AV, NEB, JB). The former is favored by the sustained emphasis in Chronicles on "seeking God." However, the Chronicler is drawing parallels with his earlier narrative in 1 Chr 13, and 1 Chr 13:3 speaks specifically of resorting to/seeking the ark; see *Comment* at 1:1–3.

13.a. G and Vg both read that Solomon came "from" the high place at Gibeon; however, the translators have given the sense required by the context and this cannot, therefore, be viewed as evidence for an alternate text using the prep מן. The translation here "gerrymanders" the phrases a bit but attempts to leave the text untouched. Any appeal to uses of preps in cognate languages would seem improbable for this late a stage of biblical Heb.; cf. Watson, *Bib* 53 (1972) 200.

14.a. Lit., "with the king in Jerusalem," presumably a reference to the royal precincts and palace complex.

16.a. Traditionally מקוא was viewed as a noun meaning "collection, mass"; hence the translation "in droves, each drove for a price" (ASV). Modern scholarship has identified it as a place name and translates "from Que." See *Comment* below.

Form/Structure/Setting

The Chronicler's account of Solomon is given almost entirely to his building of the temple (2 Chr 2–7); in light of the author's modeling his Solomon as a new Bezalel (see the introductory essay, "The Chronicler's Solomon"), chap. 1 also becomes part of the temple building account which properly includes all of 1 Chr 21–2 Chr 7. Unlike the parallel narrative, in Chronicles the wisdom Solomon receives is specifically wisdom to build. Beyond his concern with Solomon as temple builder, the Chronicler speaks also of the "riches, wealth, and honor" (1:12) that God had promised and had given to Solomon. To demonstrate the fulfillment of these promises other than wisdom, before he takes up the building account, the author introduces 1:14–17, repeating at an earlier point the material in 9:25, 27–28 // 1 Kgs 10:26–28. This repetition is part of his overall chiastic structuring for the Solomon narrative. After his report of Solomon's dream at Gibeon, the deuteronomic historian proceeded to demonstrate the practical sagacity of Solomon (1 Kgs 3:15–4:34), but this material is omitted by the Chronicler for whom Solomon's wisdom, like Bezalel's, is shown in building the house of God. See *Comment* at 2:12.

Though the Chronicler's primary source for the accounts in this chapter appears to be the book of Kings, the narrative is extensively rewritten. However, it still shows much in common with other ancient Near Eastern dream narratives, particularly the Ugaritic report of Keret's dream; the two texts have in common sacrifice before and after the dream, a dialogue with deity, the deity's asking the king what he wishes, and the king's answering with what he does not want before specifying his request.

The dream narrative is a subunit within the larger temple building narrative. Kapelrud (*Or* 32 [1963] 56–62) noted ten items commonly present in ancient Near Eastern literature depicting a temple built by a king; these items and the corresponding passages in Chronicles and the tabernacle account are as follows:

(1) A temple to be built—Exod 25:1–8; 1 Chr 28:11–21
(2) The king visits a temple overnight—Exod 24:12–18; 2 Chr 1:2–7
(3) A god reveals what to do and gives plans—Exod 25:8–30:38; 1 Chr 28:2–3, 11–19; 2 Chr 1:7–12
(4) The king announces intentions to build—Exod 35:4–10; 36:2–35; 2 Chr 2:1–10
(5) Master builder and materials (cedar, gold, silver) secured—Exod 31:1–6; 35:4–29; 36:3–7; 1 Chr 22:14–15; 29:1–9; 2 Chr 2:7–14
(6) Temple finished according to plan—Exod 39:42–43; 2 Chr 5:1; 6:10
(7) Offerings and dedication—Exod 40:9–11; 2 Chr 6:12–42; 7:4–7
(8) Assembly of people—Exod 39:32–33, 42–43; 2 Chr 5:2–13
(9) God enters the temple—Exod 40:34–35; 2 Chr 5:13–14; 7:1–3
(10) King is blessed and promised dominion—2 Chr 7:12–18

The account of the building of the temple in Chronicles shows its dependence on the tabernacle pericope and follows the outline observed by Kapelrud more closely than does the account in Kings: the securing of the wise master builder comes at the outset of construction instead of at the end (1 Kgs 7), and there is a greater stress on the divine origin of the plans (1 Chr 28:11–19). Chap. 1 fills the second and third slots of Kapelrud's outline. The outline embraces the work of both Solomon and David, establishing their unity in the one great work of building the temple. Kapelrud is troubled with why the narrator in Kings does not go immediately from Solomon's vision to the building account without the digression of 1 Kgs 3:16–4:34; he suggests that "Solomon's visit to Gibeon and his announcement of his intention were originally connected and have been divided by an author who wanted to bring in the wisdom theme" (p. 60). Kapelrud does not notice that the sequence in Chronicles fits his expectation.

Chap. 1 is divided by the use of the following paragraphing devices available to the Hebrew narrator: v 1, explicit change of subject; v 4, the contrastive

אבל followed by a circumstantial clause; v 7, the suspension of the use of the *waw*-consecutive and beginning the sentence with a temporal phrase, "that night." Vv 7–13 are repartee paragraphs; the last clause of v 13 וימלך על ישראל might form an inclusio with the ויתחזק שלמה על מלכותו of v 1, an inclusio setting off the entire dream episode.

Comment

1–3 "Strengthened his hold." The hithpael of חזק is common in Chronicles, particularly in connection with royal accession. It embraces any steps taken to consolidate the king's power and to secure the throne from dangers within and without (12:13; 13:21; 27:6; cf. 1 Chr 11:10). It covers the construction of fortifications (17:1–2; 27:6; 32:5), gathering an army (17:1–2; 23:1; 25:11), and instituting reforms (15:8). "Solomon strengthened his hold over the kingdom" is synonymous with the parallel text (1 Kgs 2:46b) "the kingdom was firmly established in Solomon's hands," a passage that summarizes Solomon's taking vengeance for his father and eliminating any threats to the throne (1 Kgs 2:5–46). The Chronicler eliminates these unpleasantries as out of accord with his portrait of Solomon, summarizing them in the oblique allusion to Solomon's strengthening his hold on the kingdom. Cf. the similar use of the hithpael of חזק in 21:4.

"Exalted him." The Chronicler twice uses the piel of גדל in reference to Solomon (1:1; 1 Chr 29:25). The same verb is also used twice in reference to Joshua (Josh 3:7; 4:14), suggesting that the Chronicler has used the succession of Moses and Joshua as a paradigm for his account of the succession of David and Solomon. See the introductory essay, "The Chronicler's Solomon" and Williamson, *VT* 26 (1976) 355–56.

V 2 provides a brief but important glimpse into the military and tribal organization of early monarchic Israel. The military units were composed of "hundreds" and "thousands" raised by a levy along ancient tribal and clan lines and led by the "heads of the families"; beyond this force raised by clan conscription, David and Solomon also had a standing army of professional soldiers. The units "hundreds" and "thousands" presumably represented divisions along clan and phratry or subphratry lines; the number of men at arms in each unit would be a function of the size of the clan and need not correspond in a literal way to the number one hundred or one thousand.

Though in Kings the visit of Solomon to Gibeon is presented essentially as an act of private devotion, the Chronicler has described the pilgrimage as a national assembly. The king no doubt never went anywhere outside Jerusalem without a fairly large retinue, and an even greater number may have accompanied him on this occasion; the Chronicler is concerned to portray "all Israel" acting in concert. Williamson (193–94) notes the parallels the Chronicler is effecting with the first acts of David: just as David immediately after his accession in Chronicles made a pilgrimage with all Israel to seek the ark (1 Chr 13:1–6), the Chronicler shows Solomon as immediately leading a national pilgrimage concerned with cultic matters. David went to seek the ark (1 Chr 13:3); Solomon, to seek the altar of Bezalel (1:5—see *Notes*). The reference to the fact that the ark had already been moved (1:4) further shows the Chronicler's awareness in this context of the report in 1 Chr 13.

4–6 For the account of the movement of the ark from Kiriath-jearim, see 1 Chr 15:1–16:6 and 2 Sam 6:12–23; for the manufacture of the altar, see Exod 38:1–8. Bezalel is only mentioned in two books of the Bible: Exodus and Chronicles. His mention in connection with Solomon's visit to Gibeon associates Solomon's gift of wisdom for building the temple with the earlier gift of wisdom to Bezalel for building the tabernacle. There are numerous parallels; see "Solomon and Huram-abi as the New Bezalel and Oholiab" in the introductory chapter, "The Chronicler's Solomon."

7 The Chronicler has omitted both statements in the parallel passage (1 Kgs 3:5,15) that the appearance of God to Solomon was in a dream. In spite of the difficulties of trying to read the author's mind many commentators have taken this as a theologically motived change, either (1) to enhance the status of Solomon by making the revelation more immediate and direct (C-M, Myers; cf. Num 12:6–8) or (2) because dreams had fallen into disrepute by the time of the Chronicler (Ackroyd, Coggins, Michaeli; cf. Jer 23:25–32). Cf. Brunet, *RB* 61 (1954) 353. It may also be the case that the difference represents nothing more than the Chronicler's effort to abridge the passage: even the Chronicler's audience would not likely have differentiated between a revelation "to Solomon in a dream of the night" and simply "at night." See the discussion in Lemke's dissertation, *Synoptic Studies,* 83–85. One change the author makes in his *Vorlage* tends to associate Solomon's revelation deliberately with another dream (see 1:9 below), so it is improbable that there is conscious evasion of dream in this instance.

8 This verse abridges 1 Kgs 3:6–7. Though the statement that Solomon is but a "small boy" (1 Kgs 3:7) may appear depreciating to Solomon, the Chronicler does not object to calling him "young and inexperienced" (1 Chr 22:5; 29:1; cf. 2 Chr 13:7). At the time of his accession Solomon was likely to have been about twenty years old.

9 For the "great people too numerous to count or number" of 1 Kgs 3:8 (an expression found first in the Bible in reference to Ishmael—Gen 16:10), the Chronicler has substituted "a people as numerous as the dust of the earth," a description used in God's promise to Jacob, another situation where a dream was involved (Gen 28:14; cf. Gen 13:16). Williamson (*IBC,* 62–64) has discussed the emphasis in Chronicles on Jacob/Israel; interest in the father of the twelve tribes reflects the author's concern with "all Israel."

10 "Lead." "Go out and come in" is ordinarily used in a military sense of leading an army (1 Chr 11:2; 1 Sam 18:13,16), but as applied to the "man of peace" refers to adequate civil government.

11 There may be a touch of irony here: Solomon had already taken the lives of prominent enemies (1 Kgs 2:5–46—see *Comment* at 1:1 above), though no doubt others were left.

The phrase "my people over whom I have made you king" is not found in the parallel text at 1 Kgs 3:11. The Chronicler frequently introduces the theocratic ideal into his account: throne and kingdom belong to Yahweh; the king is vice-regent (1 Chr 17:14; 28:5–6; 29:23; 2 Chr 9:8; 13:4–8). For the significance of this theme to the post-exilic audience, see *Comment* at 9:8.

12 "Length of days" is omitted from the list, presumably reflecting that Solomon's reign was not longer than that of any king before or after him.

14   The chariot became a part of Israel's military equipage under Solomon. The term translated "horses" could also represent "charioteers, horsemen." The MT shows considerable variation on the number of horses in Solomon's possession; see *Comment* at 9:25 for a discussion.

Pillared buildings uncovered in the excavations of Megiddo were identified by the original excavators as stables and were immediately associated with the notes regarding Solomonic chariot cities (1 Kgs 9:17; 10:26–29; 2 Chr 8:6). Yadin's studies led to a reassessment of the stratigraphy and showed that the structures at Megiddo belonged to a century or more later, perhaps at the time of Ahab (*BA* 33 [1970] 66–96). Pritchard ("The Megiddo Stables: A Reassessment") questioned whether the buildings were stables at all; the discovery of a large number of pottery vessels *in situ* in a similar building excavated at Beersheba led many to conclude that the buildings were storehouses. Other buildings of similar design have been unearthed in the excavations of Hazor, Tel-el-Hesi, Tell Abu Hawam, Tell Qasile, and outside Palestine at Bastam near Lake Urmia and possibly Tell el-Amarna in Egypt. The whole issue has been reexamined at length by Holladay ("Stables"); his research in stable design led him to conclude that the buildings were indeed stables.

15   The terrain of Israel is very stony. The sycamore fig was quite common and not highly valued (Isa 9:10); it grew in great numbers in the Shephelah (1 Chr 27:28). Cedar, on the other hand, was highly prized. This verse is repeated in 9:27 as a part of the overall chiastic structuring of the reign of Solomon.

16   Cf. 2 Chr 9:25–28. Solomon's kingdom straddled the sole land bridge between three continents: Europe, Asia, and Africa. His control of the trade routes through this vital area, most particularly between Syria and Egypt, made him the middleman in the contemporary arms race. The Chronicler is dependent on 1 Kgs 10:28–29 as his source, and some difficulties have been felt with this passage.

(1) For Solomon to be serving as a middleman between the suppliers of horses and the suppliers of chariots, Albright ("Review of J. Montgomery, *A Critical and Exegetical Commentary on the Books of Kings,* ICC (New York: Scribner's, 1951)" *JBL* 71 [1952] 249; cf. Bright, *History,* 2d ed., 212) proposed that ממצרים be dropped from 1:16 // 1 Kgs 10:28 as "vertical dittography" from 1:17 // 10:29, and that the clause regarding price be moved to 1:16 // 10:27 with the following result: "The source of Solomon's horses was from Cilicia. The king's traders bought them from Cilicia at the price of 150 silver sheqels for each horse. And a chariot was imported and delivered from Egypt at the price of 600 silver sheqels."

(2) Others (see Gray, *I and II Kings,* 268–69; and Katzenstein, *History of Tyre,* 113–14) read ממצרים as "from Musri." Que and Musri are mentioned together in Assyrian texts suggesting they are located in Cilicia and Cappadocia, though the identification has been disputed (Tadmor, "Que and Muṣri," *IEJ* 11 [1961] 143–50; Albright, "Silicia and Babylonia under the Chaldean Kings," *BASOR* 120 [1950] 22–25). If this approach is followed, the horses are from Que and Musri, and Solomon is in the middle with chariots from Egypt.

(3) Gray (*I and II Kings,* 269) sees little basis for the notion of Solomon's "alleged traffic in horses and chariots" on such a grand scale; he regards the text as saying no more than that the Hittites and Arameans got their

chariots and horses from the same sources and for the same price as Solomon; Solomon's imports were for his own use. This approach does not commend itself: the Hittites and Arameans could not import chariots by any overland routes that did not confront Solomon's monopoly over these routes and his "mark-up" on price. The passage in both histories seeks to account for Solomon's enormous wealth. However, the G of 1 Kgs 10:29 does read בים "by sea" for ביד "through their agency."

(4) It is not necessary to separate the horses in Cilicia from the chariots in Egypt as done in (1) and (2) above in order to effect a situation whereby Solomon could profit from the arms trade. Though the data come from a couple of centuries later, numerous Assyrian texts show that "Nubian horses" were one of the most prized goals of Assyrian trade with Egypt. This larger breed of horse was distinguished from the smaller cavalry breeds acquired in part through Urartu to the north in the eighth century (S. Dalley, "Foreign Chariotry and Cavalry in the Armies of Tiglath-pileser III and Sargon II," *Iraq* 47 [1985] 31–48). Assyrian officials imported both the horses and the foreign experts to serve their chariot corps. In addition to the differences in the breeds used for cavalry and chariotry, the animals would have been trained differently and broken to different bits and harnesses. It is probably safe to infer that Egyptian horses and chariots were similarly prized commodities in the Solomonic period. Clearly Deuteronomy had Egypt in mind as a source for the horses and not for chariots alone; see Deut 17:16 and its prohibition against "going back that way again." The large scale rearrangement of the text proposed by Albright appears unwise in the absence of any clear textual evidence that some place other than Egypt is intended.

Explanation

In addition to modeling Solomon after Bezalel and associating him with the latter's altar at the time of his own enduement with wisdom, other theological concerns of the Chronicler are apparent in the chapter.

In Kings Solomon's visit to the high place at Gibeon is presented essentially as an act of private devotion; the Chronicler has recorded instead a national cultic assembly in which representatives of "all Israel" assemble in Jerusalem and journey to the high place. The Chronicler had earlier shown the same concern to introduce "all Israel" into the record of David's reign (1 Chr 11:4 // 2 Sam 5:6; 1 Chr 11–12); the unity and fullness of the people continue through the reign of Solomon.

In Kings the major yardstick for judging the kings of the Southern Kingdom was their attitude toward the high places; the deuteronomic historian felt it necessary to be somewhat apologetic about Solomon's visit to the high place at Gibeon, in spite of God's self-revelation there (1 Kgs 3:3–4). In contrast the Chronicler is not at all apologetic, but has legitimized this visit by his reference to the tabernacle and Bezalel's altar there, data not provided in Kings. Since the tabernacle was there, the high place is the legitimate goal of Solomon's short pilgrimage; rather than apologize for Solomon's appearance there, the Chronicler feels obligated to explain why David did not worship there (1 Chr 21:29–30). Unlike the author of Kings (1 Kgs 11:4–13, 33), the Chronicler does not mention any of Solomon's other visits to high places. There is no direct evidence for the tabernacle's having been moved to Gibeon, although the move may have been made after the slaughter of the priests at Nob (1 Sam 21:1–9; 22:6–23).

As part of his idealization of David and Solomon the Chronicler uses the language of the patriarchal promises with reference to their reigns (Gen 15:5; 22:17; 26:4 // 1 Chr 27:23; Gen 13:16; 28:14 // 2 Chr 1:9—see *Comment* at 1:9). The Chronicler appears to attribute the sinfulness of David's census to an implied distrust of Yahweh's fulfilling his promises (1 Chr 27:23; 21:3). Not only the promises of posterity, but also of land have their realizations under these two messianic figures (1 Chr 13:5; 2 Chr 9:26; Num 34:3–9; Gen 15:18–21). See Japhet's further discussion, "Conquest and Settlement," *JBL* 98 (1979) 205–18.

Several features of the passage are developed in the NT. Paul borrows the Bezalel/Oholiab model for a description of the relationship of himself and Apollos to the church at Corinth; in describing himself as a σοφὸς ἀρχιτέκτων, "a wise master builder," Paul is borrowing terminology from the Septuagint that was used in reference to Bezalel (1 Cor 3:10; Exod 35:32, 35; see the introductory essay, "The Chronicler's Solomon"). James may also be reflecting on this supreme example of the gift of wisdom (James 1:5; cf. Eph 1:17). As a king who receives revelation and officiates at an altar, Solomon incorporates aspects of prophet/priest/king.

Solomon Arranges for Materials and Workmen (1:18–2:17 [2:1–18])

Bibliography

Avigad, N. "The Chief of the Corvée." *IEJ* 30 (1980) 170–73. **Fensham, F. C.** "The Treaty between the Israelites and the Tyrians." *Congress Volume, Rome, 1968.* VTSup 17. Leiden: E. J. Brill, 1968. **Greenfield, J.,** and **M. Mayrhofer.** "The ʾalgummim/ ʾalmuggim Problem Reexamined." *Hebräische Wortforschung.* VTSup 16. Leiden: E. J. Brill, 1967. **Katzenstein, J.** *History of Tyre.* 77–115. **Mendelsohn, I.** "On Corvée Labor in Ancient Canaan and Israel." *BASOR* 167 (1962) 31–35. ———. *Slavery in the Ancient Near East.* London: Oxford UP, 1949. ———. "State Slavery in Ancient Palestine." *BASOR* 85 (1942) 14–17. **Pardee, D.** "An Overview of Ancient Hebrew Epistolography." *JBL* 97 (1978) 321–46. **Rainey, A.** "Compulsory Labor Gangs in Ancient Israel." *IEJ* 20 (1970) 191–202.

Translation

1:18 [2:1] *Solomon proposed*[a] *to build a temple in honor of the name of Yahweh and a royal palace for himself.*

1 [2] *Solomon conscripted seventy thousand carriers and eighty thousand quarrymen to work in the hills and three thousand six hundred overseers to supervise them.*

2 [3] *Solomon sent this message to Hiram king of Tyre:*

"You sent cedar to my father David when he built his royal residence. 3 [4] *Now I his son*[a] *am about to build a temple for the honor of the name of Yahweh my God, to consecrate it to him for burning incense before him, for regularly setting out the consecrated bread, and for making burnt offerings every morning and evening, on sabbaths, new moons, and the appointed feasts of Yahweh our God, for this is a perpetual duty for Israel.*

4 [5] *"The temple that I am going to build will be great, for our God is greater than all gods.*[a] 5 [6] *But*, *who can build a temple for him when heaven itself, even the highest heaven, cannot contain him? And who am I that I should build a temple for him, except as a place to burn offerings before him?*

6 [7] *"Now send me a skilled man who can do the work in gold, silver, bronze, iron, and in purple, crimson, and violet yarn, someone who is also skilled as an engraver; he will work with my craftsmen in Judah and Jerusalem who were provided by my father David.* 7 [8] *Also send me cedar, pine, and algum wood from Lebanon, for I know that your servants are skilled in cutting the timber of Lebanon.* 9 [8] *My servants will work with your servants to prepare an ample supply of timber for me, for the temple I am building will be great and wondrous.* 9 [10] *I will pay your servants who fell the trees twenty thousand cors of ground*[a] *wheat, twenty-thousand cors of barley, twenty thousand baths of wine, and twenty thousand baths of oil."*[b]

10 [11] *Hiram replied and sent this letter to Solomon: "It is because Yahweh loves his people that he has made you king over them."* 11 [12] *Hiram said further:*

"Blessed be Yahweh, God of Israel, who has made heaven and earth and has given King David a wise son who has the intelligence and discernment to build a temple for Yahweh and a palace for himself.

12 [13] *"Now I am going to send you a skillful and experienced craftsman, Huram-abi.* 13 [14] *He is the son of a woman from Dan; his father was a Tyrian. He is skilled in working with gold, silver, bronze, iron, stone, and wood, as well as purple, violet and crimson yarn and fine linen; he knows engraving and can execute any design given him. He will work with your craftsmen and the craftsmen of my lord David your father.*

14 [15] *"Now let my lord send to his servants the wheat and barley, wine and oil of which he spoke.* 15 [16] *We will cut all the timber you need from Lebanon and will bring it to you at Joppa by raft on the sea; you can then transport it to Jerusalem."*

16 [17] *Solomon took a census of all the aliens in the land of Israel like the census David his father had made, and there were found to be one hundred fifty-three thousand and six hundred.* 17 [18] *Of these he made seventy thousand carriers, eighty thousand quarrymen, and three thousand six hundred supervisors to keep the people working.*

Notes

1:18 [2:1]a. For this use of אמר see 2 Chr 28:10, 13; 1 Kgs 5:19; Josh 22:33; alternatively it could be taken as "command, give orders" to build.

3 [4].a. "His son" (בנו) is inserted with G; its omission in MT appears to be a haplogr with בונה.

4 [5].a. See the same or equivalent formula in 1 Chr 22:5; 29:1; Exod 18:11; Ps 86:8; Deut 10:17.

9 [10].a. MT מכות "crushed, beaten" is taken by extension to mean "ground" wheat, though this use is otherwise unattested. Vg appears to have been influenced by the difficulty of the term and the use of מכלת in 1 Kgs 5:25 [11] (= מאכלת), "provisions." For G developments, see Allen, *GC*, 1:198.

9 [10].b. The twenty thousand baths of oil are missing in G^B, certainly due to a homoiotel of εἴκοσι χιλιάδας.

Form/Structure/Setting

The first sentence in this narrative (1:18 [2:1]) serves as the aperture or stage for the narrative of the temple building as a whole; the closure of the narrative is marked by the similar phraseology of 7:11. The remainder of the chapter constitutes one episode in the larger narrative and is itself a narrative discourse on the preparations for the building work.

The chapter is structured around a chiastic outline as follows:

A   Conscription of laborers (2:2)
  B   Solomon's letter (2:3–10)
  B'   Hiram's letter (2:11–16)
A'   Conscription of laborers (2:17–18)

Chiasm is the basic device used by the author in his presentation of Solomon's reign; see "Literary Structure" in the introductory essay, "The Chronicler's Solomon." The conscription account in this chapter also has its counterpart in the larger narrative at 8:7–10. Repetition of vocabulary and themes is the hallmark of literature using chiastic structure; the Chronicler's fondness for the device should caution against labeling the repetition a product of a lapse in memory on the Chronicler's part (C-M, 320) or the result of later redactional activity (Ackroyd, 103).

The two letters, like all examples of this genre in the OT, have been adapted to their narrative context and do not show many of the characteristic introductory and concluding formulae found in extrabiblical Hebrew letters (Pardee, *JBL* 97 [1978] 322–23, 330–31). Not only have they been adjusted to their narrative frame, they appear also to have been reshaped by the Chronicler from their presumably more original form in Kings (1 Kgs 5:15–26 [1–12]; 7:13–14) to give expression to his own concerns. The Chronicler's hand is discernible particularly in the skill list he assigns to Solomon's request and to Huram-abi, as a part of his effort to parallel these two men with their earlier counterparts Bezalel and Oholiab; his hand is also discernible in the long list of cultic functions incorporated in the correspondence (2:4), so similar to other lists inserted in his history (1 Chr 6:34 [49]; 23:13, 28–32; 2 Chr 13:11; 29:11).

Josephus twice claims that the Tyrian archives contained in his day copies of correspondence between Hiram and Solomon, "so that if anyone wished to learn the exact truth, he would, by inquiring of the public officials in charge of the Tyrian archives find that their records are in agreement with what we have said" (*Ant.* 8.55; *Ag.Ap.* 1:111). This statement is probably rhetorical embellishment on the part of Josephus; copies of the correspondence are likely to have disappeared before the time of the Chronicler.

The following paragraphing devices are used in the introductions and texts of the two letters: (1) repetition of explicit subject without change of subject in the intervening material (2:2 [3]; 2:11 [12]); (2) similar phraseology in the first sentence of one paragraph to the first sentence of the succeeding paragraph (2:2 [3]; 2:10 [11]), often called "head-head linkage" by discourse analysts (R. Longacre, *Anatomy of Speech Notions* [Lisse: Peter de Ridder, 1976] 204); (3) the use of ועתה to introduce requests or conclusions (2:6 [7], 12 [13], 14 [15]); cf. 1:9, 10; (4) a circumstantial clause (2:4 [5]).

Comment

1:18 [2:1] The Chronicler only infrequently mentions the royal palace (2:12; 7:11; 8:1; 9:11) and gives no details on its construction such as found in Kings (1 Kgs 7:1–12). He may be presuming the reader's familiarity with the other account (Rudolph, 199); the absence of detail on the palace comports well with the Chronicler's interest in Solomon primarily as the builder of the temple.

1 [2]   See *Comment* at 2:17–18.

2 [3]   According to Josephus (*Ag.Ap.* 1.117) Hiram ascended the throne after the death of his father Abibaal ca. 970 B.C.; he was nineteen years old at his accession and reigned for thiry-four years. Josephus is the main source of chronological information on the Phoenician kings, though estimates of the worth of his data vary; see the discussion in Katzenstein, *Tyre,* 80–84. The Chronicler consistently writes the name "Huram," a variant of the form used in Kings, "Hiram." Both are shortened forms of the name *'Aḥîrām*

(Harris, *Grammar of the Phoenician Language* [New Haven: American Oriental Society, 1936] 75).

The Chronicler had earlier reported David's preparations for building the temple and his construction of his own palace using materials from the Phoenicians (1 Chr 14:1 // 2 Sam 5:11; 1 Chr 22:4).

3 [4]   Such lists of cultic duties are common insertions betraying the Chronicler's own hand; see *Form/Structure/Setting.* With reference to incense, see Exod 30:1–10; 37:25–29; 40:27; Lev 16:13; 1 Chr 28:18; 2 Chr 26:16–20; Haran (*Temples and Temple Service in Ancient Israel,* 230–45) provides an extensive discussion of incense rites known from the OT. For provisions regarding the Bread of the Presence, see Exod 25:23–30; 40:22–24; Lev 24:5–9; 1 Sam 21:1–6; 1 Chr 28:16; 9:31–32; 23:29; 2 Chr 13:11; 29:18. A summary of Israel's feasts is found in Num 28:1–29:39.

5 [6]   The Chronicler borrows from the dedicatory speech of Solomon to include in this correspondence a statement on the transcendence of God (1 Kgs 8:27 // 2 Chr 6:18).

"Who am I" is a common protestation of humility (Exod 3:11; 1 Sam 18:18; 2 Sam 7:18; 1 Chr 29:14).

6 [7]   The Chronicler makes some of his most significant modifications to the record in Kings at this point by reporting the request for a craftsman in the initial exchange of letters, rather than after the building report, and by modifiying the skill list so that it is the same as that of Bezalel and Oholiab, rather than simply skill in bronze (1 Kgs 7:13–14). The significance of these changes is explored in the section "Solomon and Huram-abi as the New Bezalel and Oholiab" in the introductory essay, "The Chronicler's Solomon."

This is the only occurrence of the phrase "Judah and Jerusalem" in the history of the united monarchy, though it is common after the schism (20:17; 24:6, 9, 18, 23; 29:8; 32:12, 25; 34:3, 5; 35:24; 36:4, 10, 23). Ackroyd (104) regards this as a slip on the part of the Chronicler into thinking of the restricted southern community of his own time; it also stands to reason, however, that should David have assembled craftsmen for the work, they would have been near the site where the work was to be done, i.e., in "Judah and Jerusalem." For David's assembling the work force, see 1 Chr 22:14–16; 28:21; 29:5, all passages unique to the Chronicler.

7 [8]   The identity of algum wood (or almug wood, 1 Kgs 10:11–12) is not known with certainty (see Greenfield and Mayrhofer, VTSup 16, 83–89). Apparently Hiram not only traded in prized domestic woods like cedar and pine, but also imported other exotic woods for trade. 1 Kgs 10:11–12 // 2 Chr 9:10–11 identify it as an import from Ophir, in which case it would not be "cut in Lebanon" unless this reference is to further drying and fashioning. However, Assyriological sources report the import of *elammakku*-wood from northern Syria; if this Akkadian term is a cognate to *almug*-wood, then it would have been grown in Lebanon as well. The parallel text at 1 Kgs 5:20 [6] mentions only a request for cedar, though Hiram's response promises both cedar and pine (5:22 [8]).

9 [10]   The Bible elsewhere speaks of Tyrian dependence on foodstuffs shipped from Israel (Ezek 27:17; Acts 12:20); Tyre may have been rich in trade but apparently needed substantial imports to feed her population. The *cor* is a unit of dry measure, slightly above six bushels, for a total of 125,000 bushels each of wheat and barley. The *bath* is a unit of liquid measure, approximately six gallons, though the precise standard for these measures at a given time and locality is not known with confidence.

These figures should be compared with those in 1 Kgs 5:25 [11]. The following differences emerge: (1) Kings makes no mention of barley and wine. (2) The oil in Kings appears to be a better quality (שׁמן כתית) than that mentioned in Chronicles. Although the MT of Kings mentions only twenty baths, this should be emended to read twenty thousand with Bas. (3) Kings appears to speak of an annual payment to the Phoenician court, whereas Chronicles speaks of a one-time payment to the workmen provided by Hiram. The differences are sufficiently great to suggest that the two histories are dealing with two different sources concerned with different aspects of Solomon's bargain with Hiram. No effort should be made to derive the Chronicles figures from Kings through textual corruption or theological aggrandizement. One can only speculate about the Chronicler's source. The important thing for the Chronicler is that just as Solomon initiated the correspondence instead of Hiram, so also Solomon sets the terms of payment rather than Hiram.

10 [11]   In a similar diplomatic context, the queen of Sheba also recognizes Solomon's rule as a token of Yahweh's love for his people (2 Chr 9:8 // 1 Kgs 10:9); cf. Deut 7:7–8; Isa 43:4; 63:9; Jer 31:3; Zeph 3:17; Mal 1:2–3; Ps 47:5 [4]. The repetition of this statement in speeches by gentile monarchs shows the Chronicler's effort to present his account of Solomon's reign in a palistrophic or chiastic arrangement; see further "Literary Structure" in the introductory essay, "The Chronicler's Solomon."

11 [12]   The only other occurrence of the phrase שׂכל ובינה "intelligence and discernment" is in 1 Chr 22:12; here the gentile king Hiram extols Solomon for those qualities David had prayed he would show.

A comparison with the parallel text vividly reinforces the Chronicler's view that Solomon's wisdom was particularly wisdom for building. In 1 Kgs 5:21 [7] Hiram extols God's gift of a wise ruler, "a wise son over this great people"; the Chronicler inserts instead "a wise son who has the intelligence and discernment to build the temple of Yahweh and a royal palace for himself."

12 [13]   In the other references this Tyrian craftsman is named simply "Hiram" (1 Kgs 7:13, 40, 45) or the variant "Huram" (2 Chr 4:11). The use of אבי and אביו here and in 2 Chr 4:16 may be part of his name or a title to be translated as "my/his master (craftsman)." For this use of אב, see Gen 45:8; Judg 17:10. Mosis (*Untersuchungen*, 167) considers this use of the fuller name with the ending *-ab* as one more part of the effort to parallel Huram-abi and Oholiab by giving the names the same ending.

13 [14]   The parallel text traces Huram-abi's descent from a widow of Naphtali instead of Dan (1 Kgs 7:14). J. Liver (*Encyclopedia Biblica* 3 [1958] col. 123) suggested that the tribal territory of Dan lay in the district of Naphtali; others have accounted for the discrepancy by suggesting that (1) Naphtali may be used geographically as the location of her residence, and Dan as her actual genealogical relationship, or (2) her lineage may have been through parents of two different tribes. However one accounts for the discrepancy, it is clear that the Chronicler has assigned Huram-abi a Danite ancestry to further perfect the parallel with Oholiab; rabbinic exegesis recognized this connection and viewed Huram-abi as a descendant of Oholiab (Katzenstein, *Tyre*, 100). For the full scope of the Chronicler's patterning, see "Solomon and Huram-abi as the New Bezalel and Oholiab" in the introductory essay, "The Chronicler's Solomon." Historically the Danites had longstanding connections with Tyre and Sidon (Judg 18:7, 27–30); see the discussions in Katzenstein, *Tyre*, 65–67; Talmon, "Gezer Calendar," *JAOS* 83 (1963) 181; Mazar, "The Cities of Dan," *IEJ* 10 (1960) 65–77, esp. 71.

The verse is structured by the three infinitives: לעשות, לפתח, and לחשב. The parallel text at 1 Kgs 7:14 mentions only his skill in bronze and lists his castings in that medium alone (1 Kgs 7:15–47). The Chronicler, however, reports that his skills were coextensive with those of Bezalel and Oholiab.

Hiram's use of אדני "my lord" in reference to both David and Solomon (v 15) has been taken to imply vassalage on Hiram's part. Although the Chronicler may have enhanced the status of David and Solomon by the use of this designation in Hiram's mouth, it could equally be viewed as the language of a shrewd merchant to a client. Though the census account embraced territory in the vicinity of the Phoenician cities (2 Sam 24:6–7), there is no evidence of military subjugation. The actual relationship between Israel and Tyre was one of parity, not vassalage: (1) note the use of "brother" in 1 Kgs 9:13; cf. also 1 Kgs 20:33; (2) Hiram's services required full recompense, hardly a sign of vassalage (1 Kgs 5:23 [9]); (3) the treaty between the powers gives no hint of subordination (1 Kgs 5:23 [9]). The relationship between Hiram and Solomon may have been cemented by diplomatic marriage (1 Kgs 11:1, 5).

15 [16]   The Chronicler adds the note that the logs from Hiram would come by sea to Joppa; cf. 1 Kgs 5:23 [9]) and Ezra 3:7. The materials would then be transferred overland on the road past Gezer; this implies that Solomon was already in control of the area of Gezer which must have been given him very early in his reign at the time of his marriage to Pharaoh's daughter (1 Kgs 9:16–17; see Kitchen, *TIPE*, 280, par. 235, n. 221; and Malamat, "Aspects of the Foreign Policies of David and Solomon," *JNES* 22 [1963] 10–17). Reliefs from Sargonic Khorsabad portray typical Phoenician ships with their horse-head prows and horse-tail sterns transporting logs by sea; the logs were both loaded on the decks and towed in rafts behind the ships (Katzenstein, *Tyre*, 243).

16 [17]   The phrase ארץ ישראל "land of Israel" occurs ten times in the OT, four of them in Chronicles: once each in the reigns of David (1 Chr 22:2, also in connection with a census of aliens), Solomon (2:17), Hezekiah (30:25), and Josiah (34:7), all occasions when the geographical extent of the land was great. See Japhet, *Ideology*, 365–66; and Williamson, *IBC*, 123.

The reference to David's census is presumably to the account in 1 Chr 21, but more specifically to the enrollment of aliens mentioned in 1 Chr 22:2. Solomon, like Joshua before him, pressed alien labor into service of the cult; see "The Succession of Moses and Joshua as a Paradigm for That of David and Solomon" in the introductory essay, "The Chronicler's Solomon." For 2:17–18, see the parallel at 1 Kgs 5:27–32 [13–18]; cf. 2 Chr 8:7–10 // 1 Kgs 9:20–23.

The question of whether Solomon imposed corvée labor on Israelites has provoked considerable discussion. Both the Chronicler and the deuteronomic historian insist that such labor was exacted from resident aliens alone (2 Chr 2:17–18; 8:7–10; 1 Kgs 9:15, 20–22). Israel imposed compulsory labor on subservient peoples, just as it had been imposed on them (Gen 49:15; Exod 1:11; Deut 20:10–11; Josh 9:21–27; 16:10; Judg 1:28, 33). Rainey (*IEJ* 20 [1970] 199) notes that part of the purpose of the census under both David and Solomon would be to register those liable for compulsory labor in the previously unconquered territory and Canaanite enclaves.

In spite of the evidence that compulsory labor was confined to aliens, several lines of argument indicate it was also imposed on native Israelites. (1) In the parallel text at 1 Kgs 5:27–32 [13–18], the deuteronomic historian names yet another group of thirty thousand workers sent to Lebanon in shifts of ten thousand, so that each man spent one month per quarter in the logging operations. This group is omitted entirely by the Chronicler and may have been native Israelites; the levy had been raised "from all Israel" (1 Kgs 5:27 [13]). (2) Jeroboam had served as the corvée officer over the house of Joseph, implying Israelite servitude in the corvée (1 Kgs 11:28). (3) The plea of the northern tribes for easing the yoke and their subsequent stoning of Adoniram, the officer in charge of the corvée, portray the degree to which the forced labor was despised by the Israelites (1 Kgs 12:3–4, 18–19). (4) The warning of 1 Sam 8:10–17 is best understood on the background of the existence of the practices it condemns.

Many efforts have been made to resolve this conflict; a summary of prior research and yet another suggestion are found in Dillard, "The Chronicler's Solomon," *WTJ* 43 (1980) 294–96. The Israelites were apparently not subject to the full range of compulsory labor to which aliens could be impressed.

Avigad's recent publication (*IEJ* 30 [1980] 170–73) of a seal "belonging to Pela'yahu (son of) Mattityahu, who is over the corvée" provides the first extrabiblical confirmation of this officer; the title is the same as that borne by Adoram/Adoniram (2 Sam 20:24; 1 Kgs 4:6; 5:28 [14]; 12:18). Though the Bible makes no further mention of this office, the practice of using forced labor doubtless continued (1 Kgs 15:22 // 2 Chr 16:6; Jer 22:13).

17 [18]   1 Kgs 5:30 [16] mentions only 3,300 supervisors instead of 3,600. There is, however, considerable variation in the G of 1 Kgs 5:16: some MSS agree with Chronicles, while G^L has 700 and G^O has 500; it is quite possible that the variation simply reflects a transmission problem. Others explain the difficulty by noting that the 250 Israelite foremen (8:10) should be added to the 3,600 supervisors of 2:18, for a total of 3,850. The text of Kings reports 550 foremen (1 Kgs 9:23), which when added to the 3,300 supervisors of 1 Kgs 5:30 [16] gives the same total of 3,850. On this basis a group of 300 was once counted as supervisors and once as foremen.

Explanation

2 Chr 2 is parallel to 1 Kgs 5:15–26 [1–12]; 7:13–14; several of the Chronicler's omissions from the parallel material may reflect his concerns. In the Kings account Hiram initiates the correspondence with Solomon (1 Kgs 5:15 [1]), whereas the Chronicler reports the initial exchange as originating

with Solomon. Rudolph (199) finds this to be evidence that the Chronicler wanted to emphasize the initiative of Solomon so that he postponed the good wishes from Hiram to Solomon to the reply of Hiram (2:11–12). On the other hand, this omission may reflect a simple abridgment of the parallel account (Lemke, *Synoptic Studies,* 87–88).

The Chronicler also omits reference to the reason David was disqualified from building the temple (1 Kgs 5:17 [3]). The Chronicler's omission in this regard should be assigned to the fact that he has given an alternative explanation for this disqualification: not that David was always so busy with wars, but because of the amount of blood he had shed (1 Chr 22:8; 28:2–3). The omission of reference to the rest given to Solomon and to the promises to David (1 Kgs 5:18–19 [4–5]) is probably due to abridgment in light of the fact that this material is used by the Chronicler earlier at 1 Chr 22:9–10; 28:5–7 (see Braun, *JBL* 95 [1976] 582–86). The Chronicler has forged a contrast between David the "man of war" (1 Chr 28:3) and Solomon the "man of rest" (1 Chr 22:9).

While the Chronicler's omissions often reflect his interests, these interests are most clearly seen by examining his positive reshaping of the earlier record. In addition to assigning initiative in the correspondence with Hiram to Solomon, the Chronicler has also used this correspondence as a vehicle for his modeling of Solomon and Huram-abi as a new Bezalel and Oholiab; see the introductory essay, "The Chronicler's Solomon." In the Kings account the request for a skilled workman is not reported until after the narrative of the building of the temple and palace (1 Kgs 6:38–7:1, 13–14); the Chronicler associates Huram-abi with Solomon from the outset of the building enterprise, in the same way that Oholiab accompanied Bezalel from the beginning. While the request in Kings was for a worker skilled in bronze and reports only Huram-abi's castings in this metal (1 Kgs 7:13–47), the Chronicler assigns Huram-abi an expanded skill list the same as that of Bezalel and Oholiab (2:7, 13–14), underscoring once again the continuity between the building of the temple and the tabernacle, between the Mosaic and Davidic covenants. He also modifies the ancestry of Huram-abi to assign him to the Danites, the tribe of Oholiab.

The Chronicler has expanded the letters of Solomon and Hiram with sections extolling the glory of God and the temple (2:4–6, 11–12). Hiram's praise of God should be compared with that of the queen of Sheba (9:7–9) and Cyrus (36:23); the praise of God by the Gentiles is a common theme of prophetic expectation (Isa 11:10–15; 14:1–2; 45:14–15; 49:22–23; 56:3–8; 66:18–23; Mic 7:16–17; Zeph 3:10; Hag 2:7; Zech 8:18–23; 14:16–21; Mal 1:11).

The Chronicler also introduces into Solomon's letter reflection on the tension between the transcendence and immanence of God; he imports phraseology drawn from the prayer at the dedication of the temple (6:18 // 1 Kgs 8:27): even the highest heaven cannot encompass God, much less a building contain him; though he may reveal himself in his name and in his glory in a place, prayers addressed there are answered from heaven (6:20–21 // 1 Kgs 8:29–30). The building is not strictly a residence for God, but a place to make sacrifices to him; cf. Isa 66:1–3.

NT authors develop several themes exhibited in these passages. Paul, the wise master builder (1 Cor 3:10), and Apollos are the Bezalel and Oholiab of the church at Corinth (1 Cor 3:5–17). Hiram's praise of Israel's God shows an element of prophetic hope also developed in the NT where the Gentiles are also declared to be "my people" and sing the praises of God (Rom 15:7–12; 11:11–32; 9:25–26; 1 Pet 2:10). Even the Chronicler's emphasis on the use of alien labor for the building of the temple (cf. Isa 60:10–14) may be viewed as an adumbration of the NT church/temple built by Jew and Gentile alike (1 Cor 3:5–10; 1 Pet 2:4–10; Gal 3:26–29). For the NT the ultimate resolution of the problem of the transcendence and immanence of God is the God/man, "the radiance of glory and the exact representation of his being" (Heb 1:3), who "tabernacled" in our midst (John 1:14). The visible glory of God would ultimately come to the second temple in the person of Jesus Christ.

The Temple Building   (3:1–17)

Bibliography

Aharoni, Y. "The Israelite Sanctuary at Arad." In *New Directions in Biblical Archaeology,* ed. Freedman and Greenfield. Garden City, NY: Doubleday, 1969. **Albright, W. F.** *Archaeology and the Religion of Israel.* 142–55. **Busink, T. A.** *Der Tempel von Jerusalem.* 2 vols. Leiden: E. J. Brill, 1970, 1980. **Davey, C.** "Temples of the Levant and the Buildings of Solomon." *TynBul* 31 (1980) 107–46. **Garber, P. L.** "Reconstructing Solomon's Temple." *BA* 14 (1951) 2–24. **Gooding, D.** "Temple Specifications in MT and LXX." *VT* 17 (1967) 143–72. **Gutmann, J., ed.** *The Temple of Solomon.* Missoula, MT: Scholars Press, 1976. **Mohlenbrink, K.** *Der Tempel Salomos.* Stuttgart: Kohlhammer, 1932. **Ouelette, J.** "Le vestibule du Temple de Salomon, était-il un bit ḥilâni?" *RB* 76 (1969) 365–78. ———. "The Solomonic Debir According to the Hebrew Text of 1 Kings 6." *JBL* 89 (1970) 338–43. ———. "The Yāṣiaʿ and the Selāʿôt: Two Mysterious Structures in Solomon's Temple." *JNES* 31 (1972) 187–91. **Parrot, A.** *The Temple of Jerusalem.* New York: Philosophical Library, 1955. **Rupprecht, K.** *Der Tempel von Jerusalem: Grundung Salomos oder jebusitisches Erbe?* Berlin: de Gruyter, 1977. **Shaffer, S.** *Israel's Temple Mount.* Jerusalem: Achiva Press, 1975. **Watzinger, C.** *Denkmäler Palästinas.* 2 vols. 1933–35. **Wright, G. E.** "Solomon's Temple Resurrected." *BA* 4 (1941) 17–31. ———. "The Stevens' Reconstruction of the Solomonic Temple." *BA* 18 (1955) 41–44.

Translation

[1] *Solomon began to build the temple of Yahweh in Jerusalem on Mount Moriah where the Lord had appeared[a] to David his father, on the site which David had prepared at the threshing floor of Ornan the Jebusite.* [2] *He began to build in the second month[a] of the fourth year of his reign.*

[3] *Now these are the foundations which Solomon laid for the building of the temple of God: the length (using the old standard for the cubit) was sixty cubits, and the width, twenty.* [4] *The portico, which was in front of the temple[a] was as long as the temple was wide, twenty cubits, and the height was twenty cubits;[b] he overlaid the interior with pure gold.*

[5] *As for the large chamber, he paneled it with pine, covered it with fine gold, and decorated it with palm tree and chain designs.* [6] *He embellished the chamber with the beauty of precious stones; the gold was the gold of Parvaim.* [7] *He covered the chamber with gold—the beams, doorframes, walls, and doors—and he carved cherubim on the walls.*

[8] *He also built the Most Holy Place. Its length was also the same as the width of the temple, twenty cubits, and it was twenty cubits wide. He covered it with six hundred talents of fine gold.* [9] *The weight of the gold for the nails was fifty shekels; he also covered the upper chambers with gold.*

[10] *He made two sculpted[a] cherubim for the Most Holy Place and overlaid them with gold.* [11] *The total wingspan of the cherubim was twenty cubits. One wing of the first cherub was five cubits long and touched the wall of the temple, while the other wing was five cubits long and touched the wing of the other cherub.* [12] *One wing of the other cherub was five cubits long and touched the wall of the temple, while the other wing was five cubits long and touched the other cherub.[a]* [13] *The*

wings of these cherubim spread twenty cubits; they stood on their feet facing the outer chamber.

¹⁴ *He also made the veil of violet, purple, and crimson yarn and fine linen and embroidered cherubim on it.*

¹⁵ *He also made two pillars in front of the temple, thirty-five cubits long; the capital on top of each was five cubits.* ¹⁶ *He had made chain designs in the inner chamber;*ᵃ *he also put them on top of the pillars. He also made a hundred pomegranates*ᵇ *and attached them to the chains.* ¹⁷ *He erected the pillars in front of the temple, one on the south and one on the north; he named the one on the south Jachin and the one on the north Boaz.*

Notes

1.a. Contrast NAB, "which he pointed out to David his father." However, the niph of ראה ordinarily has the meaning "be seen, appear" and is not used in a causative sense,"show, designate."

2.a. בשני has been omitted as dittogr with השני. Some take it as a reference to "the second day," but it is not found in the parallel text at 1 Kgs 6:1, nor in the text of Chr in G, Vg, or Syr. The day of the month is ordinarily expressed with the cardinal number with לחדש or יום.

4.a. The insertion of the words "of the temple" is an effort to cope with the difficulty of the Heb. text; it is not intended to suggest a transmission error resulting in the loss of הבית. Both 1 Kgs 6:3 (על פני היכל) and Par (κατὰ πρόσωπον τοῦ οἴκου) do supply the additional noun, but in the case of Par this is probably due to assimilation to the parallel text (Allen, GC, 1:198–99). Rudolph (202) suggests reading עלפניו "in front of it," and cites Syr and A, though this reading in these two translations probably reflects the difficulty felt by the translators rather than actually attesting to an alternative text.

4.b. Reading "twenty cubits" with one G MS, Syr, and A for the MT "one hundred and twenty." The addition of a portico four to six times higher than the remainder of the building is unlikely. Although the textual evidence for reading "twenty cubits" is not strong, the MT may have arisen from a confusion of אמות "cubits" and מאות "hundred": note the use of אמות before the number in the other measurements in the context (3:3, 4, 8, 11, 12, 13, 15); cf. the K/Q at Ezek 42:16.

10.a. צצעים occurs only here. RSV follows G (ἔργον ἐκ ξύλων = מעשה עצים); however, G should probably be viewed as coping with a difficult word rather than as a valid attestation to an alternative text. The cherubim were carved from wood and overlaid with gold (1 Kgs 6:23, 28). The lexicons take the word as cognate with an Arabic root meaning "fashion" (BDB, 858), "fashion by melting" (KB, 810).

12.a. 3:12 is missing in GᴮB, raising the possibility that the verse is a dittogr of 3:11 in the MT, or a haplogr in Gᴮ. (1) If 3:12 is viewed as a dittogr in the MT, the translation of v 11b would be as follows: "One wing of each was five cubits long and touched the wall of the temple, while the other wing was five cubits long and touched the wing of the other cherub." Throughout this account the Chronicler has abridged the materials in 1 Kgs 6; such an abridgment here is at least possible. (2) If 3:12 is viewed as part of the original text, most commentators suggest emending to reverse in effect the easily confused words האחד and האחר at the beginning and end of the verse to secure a better sense: "The wing of the other cherub . . . touched the wing of the first cherub." Rudolph (204) notes that the MT can have this meaning without textual reconstruction; cf. the use of האחד . . . האחד in the sense "the one . . . the other" at Exod 18:3–4.

16.a. In a context concerning the two pillars, it is improbable that the Chronicler would suddenly take up the subject of the decoration of the *debîr*. Most commentators suggest emending to כרביד "like a necklace" in place of בדביר; there is no extant textual support for this alteration. 1 Kgs 6:21 does speak of chain designs in reference to the Most Holy Place, though a different term is used (cf. 1 Kgs 7:17; 2 Chr 3:5).

16.b. 1 Kgs 7:20 speaks of two hundred pomegranates, but as the total amount for both pillars.

Form/Structure/Setting

In light of the dominant role the temple plays in the Chronicler's history the most striking feature of his account of the building of the temple is its brevity: forty-six verses in Kings (1 Kgs 6:1–38; 7:15–22) compared to seventeen in Chronicles. Much of the extensive detail regarding the architecture of the temple is omitted (6:4–19, 22, 26, 29–38; 7:15, 17b–20, 22), along with the description of Solomon's palace (7:1–12; see *Comment* at 2:1). The Chronicler adds only a few details not found in the parallel text (3:1, 6, 8b–9, 14). At the very least the author is depending on the reader's knowledge of the account in Kings, for without that information his description of the temple is relatively opaque; additional factors are also operative in his abbreviation of the account (see *Explanation*).

From the standpoint of discourse analysis, the account of the building of the temple in Chronicles is an expository discourse; the focus is on the subject matter rather than the performers, and a chronological sequence should not be assumed (Longacre, *Anatomy*, 197–202, 210). The use of paragraphing devices other than those most commonly encountered in narrative discourse is symptomatic of the expository character of the account. The repetition of ויחל לבנות (3:1–2) gives the temporal setting for the entire account; the next paragraph is begun with a topical sentence (. . . ואלה הוסד, 3:3). Use of an initial direct object is a topicalization device also marking a new paragraph (3:5). The remainder of the paragraphs in this chapter and into the next are marked by the repetition of ויעש (3:8, 10, 14, 15); Williamson (208) sees in this use of ויעש a further effort on the part of the Chronicler to draw parallels with the account of the tabernacle construction, where this verb form occurs almost forty times (Exod 36:8–39:32).

Comment

1–2 This is the only biblical reference identifying the temple mount with Moriah, the place of Abraham's sacrifice, "the mount of the Lord" (Gen 22:2, 14). At the same place that Abraham held a knife above his son, David saw the destroying angel with sword drawn to plunge into Jerusalem (1 Chr 21:1–22:1; see R. Dillard, "David's Census: Perspectives on 2 Samuel 24 and 1 Chronicles 21," in *Through Christ's Word*, ed. R. Godfrey and J. Boyd [Phillipsburg: Presbyterian and Reformed, 1985] 94–107). The legitimacy of the temple site is shown not only from the census account (1 Chr 22:1), but also from the life of Abraham (Gen 22). The use of the niphal of the verb ראה may entail a further allusion to Gen 22:8, 14 ("יהוה יראה").

A strict translation of the text would appear to require "which he [Solomon] established on David's site at the threshing floor of Ornan. . . ." Several difficulties arise with taking the text in this sense: (1) The more immediate possible subject is David. (2) The verb הכין is frequently used of David's preparations for building the temple or the place of the ark (1 Chr 15:3, 12; 22:3, 5, 14; 28:2; 29:3, 16–19; 2 Chr 1:4; 2:6 [7]). (3) The phrase מקום דויד would be unique to this passage as a designation for the temple site. The

versions (G, Vg, NEB, NIV, RSV, NASB, JB) read the phrase as if it were the
more common word order במקום אשר הכין דויד "in the place which David
prepared." Cf. Exod 23:20; 1 Chr 15:3.

The parallel text (1 Kgs 6:1) dated the building of the temple from the
Exodus. The Exodus is not given the same degree of theological importance
by the Chronicler, who frequently omits references to it in the parallel passages (1 Chr 17:5 // 2 Sam 7:6; 2 Chr 6:11 // 1 Kgs 8:21; 2 Chr 6:39–40 //
1 Kgs 8:50–53) in favor of a greater emphasis on the patriarchs. See the discussions in Japhet, *JBL* 98 (1979) 217–18, and *Ideology,* 322–27; Brunet, *RB* 61
(1954) 361–62; Williamson, *IBC,* 64–66; North, *JBL* 82 (1963) 377–78; Ackroyd, *CTM* 38 (1967) 510–12.

Following the chronology proposed by Albright, the work on the temple
was begun in 959 B.C. (Rowton, "Date of the Founding of Solomon's Temple,"
BASOR 119 [1950] 20–22). Following the chronology of Thiele (*Mysterious
Numbers,* rev. ed., 28–29), the temple was begun in 966 B.C.

3–4 As the text implies, Israel knew at least two standards for the cubit:
a short cubit (17.4 inches) and a long cubit (20.4 inches; see Ezek 40:5;
43:13), both apparently based on an Egyptian dual standard of six and seven
palms. There is some debate about which the Chronicler intends as the "old
standard." In the excavations of the temple at Arad, Aharoni ("Israelite Sanctuary," 35–36) noted that the north-south measurement of the main hall was
nine meters (or twenty short cubits) in stratum XI (tenth century), while in
stratum X (ninth century) it had been enlarged to 10.5 meters (or twenty
long cubits). He concluded that the standard for the cubit changed in the
period between these two levels. The explanation is appealing, but one cannot
rule out the possibility of the coexistence of both standards over a long period
of time. Depending on which standard is thought to have been in use, the
Solomonic temple would have been either ninety by thirty feet, or one hundred
five by thirty-five feet. See also A. Kaufman, "Determining the Length of
the Medium Cubit," *PEQ* 116 (1984) 120–32.

The terms צפה (3:4, 6, 10) and חפה (3:5, 7, 8, 9) may require some adjustment to differing contexts. Here an overlay to give the appearance of solid
gold may be appropriate for the entrance to the temple, but in other cases
"inlay" appears more appropriate. The carefully carved figures in fine woods
were probably not covered completely by the gold sheeting, or the reverse,
the carved figures were overlaid with gold leaf contrasting with the surrounding flat wood surfaces. See Wright, *BA* 4 (1941) 21; and Garber, *BA* 14
(1951) 16.

Several grades of gold are mentioned in this and the parallel contexts
(זהב טהור, 3:4; זהב טוב, 3:8; זהב פרוים, 3:6; זהב סגור, 1 Kgs 6:20–21).
Our knowledge of ancient metallurgy is yet insufficient to specify the characteristics of these refined products. The gradations of holiness in approaching the Most Holy Place were matched by the increasing value of the materials used in closer proximity to the ark and Most Holy Place. Foundries
and assayers were often attached to ancient temples; see the discussion at 2
Chr 24.

6 *Parvaim* is ordinarily taken as a geographical term designating the provenance of this gold; it may refer to Sak el-Farwein in Yemama. The precise

reference of the term has long been forgotten; the translators of Syr and Vg omit it, while G simply transliterates it. Postbiblical literature gave the place mythical connotations; see Fitzmeyer, *The Genesis Apocryphon of Qumran Cave One*, 2d rev. ed. (Rome: Pontifical Biblical Institute, 1971) 94–95; P. Grelot, "Parwaïm des Chroniques a l'Apocryphe de la Genèse," *VT* 11 (1961) 30–38; H. Del Medico, "*Zahab Parwayim*," *VT* 13 (1963) 158–86; Grelot, "Retour au Parwaïm," *VT* 14 (1964) 155–63; North, "Ophir/Parvaim and Petra/ Joktheel," *Fourth World Congress of Jewish Studies* (Jerusalem, 1967) 1:197– 202. *Cant. Rab.* on Cant. 3:10 describes the gold of Parvaim as having "a red hue like the blood of a bullock," though this is probably a popular etymology associating Parvaim with פר, "bull."

8–9 Six hundred talents would be approximately twenty-three tons (twenty-one metric tons) of gold, an amount not mentioned in the parallel text in 1 Kgs 6. The amount is enormous, but only a small fraction of the amount the Chronicler records David as having amassed for the building work (1 Chr 22:14). Rudolph (203) suggests the number is symbolic, either of a fifty-talent contribution from each of the twelve tribes, or of one year's revenue for Solomon (9:13). See also Mosis, *Untersuchungen*, 142–43.

The fifty-shekel amount is quite small compared to what precedes; it is the equivalent of about twenty ounces. Gold may be too soft to function well as a nail. Most have viewed this amount as the quantity of gold leaf used to cover the heads of nails or tacks that held the sheets of gold in place on the walls; cf. the tabernacle account, Exod 26:32, 37. The RSV has followed G, taking it as a ratio of the weight of gold to the weight of the nails: for each shekel of nails, there were fifty shekels of gold; however, this appears to have developed in G to simplify a difficult text. Syr omits it altogether, either as a difficult text or due to homoioteleuton with זהב.

The context describes the Most Holy Place (3:8–14), but no "upper chambers" are mentioned elsewhere specifically in connection with this room; cf. 1 Chr 28:11. 1 Kgs 6:2, 20 specify that the ceiling height of the building was thirty cubits, while that of the Most Holy Place was twenty cubits. The inner chamber of several excavated temples was built on an elevated platform; if the Most Holy Place were built on a similar platform five cubits high, a space of five cubits would remain above the Most Holy Place and below the ceiling of the remainder of the building. Perhaps this area above the Most Holy Place was gilded with the gold leaf.

14 The veil is not mentioned in the parallel text in 1 Kgs 6. Since the parallel text does speak of doors separating the Most Holy Place from the outer chamber (1 Kgs 6:31–32), many have taken the veil as a projection onto the first temple from the temple of the Chronicler's day under the influence of the tabernacle account (Exod 26:31–33; see C-M, 327). The veil is also not mentioned in connection with Ezekiel's temple. Others regard the absence of the veil in 1 Kgs 6 as due to a textual error: פרכת is said to have been confused with ברתיקות (1 Kgs 6:21) due to similarity of consonants; in the absence of supporting textual evidence, this is purely conjectural (see Rudolph, 204–5). Since the veil was present in the tabernacle and in the Herodian temple (Matt 27:51; Josephus, *J.W.* 5.5) it would seem probable that it was also found in the first temple and should be regarded as an accurate addition by the Chronicler. See Vattioni, "Il velo del tempio dei cherubini," *RevBIt* 7 (1959) 67–68.

15–17 No feature of temple architecture has generated as much interest as the pillars Jachin and Boaz. These pillars were not unique to the temple of Solomon, but were a common feature in ancient temples. Similar pillars are found in the excavated remains of numerous first- and second-millennium temples; they are portrayed in wall paintings, on coins, and in a clay model of a temple from Cyprus and are often mentioned by ancient historians referring to a number of different temples. Though there is no doubt that the pillars were a common architectural feature in ancient temples, little unanimity exists beyond this assertion. Difficulties attend their size, placement, names, and function.

Various scholars have described them as fire cressets, cosmic pillars, maṣṣe-bôth, Egyptian obelisks, mythological mountains between which the sun (-god) appeared (cf. Zech 6:1), trees of paradise, means of determining the equinox, gateposts, etc. As much as they have kindled the interest of the modern reader, the Bible itself does not clearly articulate their function. See the following literature: Albright, "Two Cressets from Marisa and the Pillars of Jachin and Boaz," *BASOR* 85 (1942) 18–26; Albright, *ARI*, 144–48; A. Audin, "Les piliers jumeaux dans le monde sémitique," *ArOr* 21 (1953) 430–39; T. Busink, *Der Tempel*, 1:299–321; W. Kornfeld, "Der Symbolismus der Tempelsäulen," *ZAW* 74 (1962) 50–57; H. May, "The Two Pillars Before the Temple of Solomon," *BASOR* 88 (1942) 19–27; C. Meyers, "Jachin and Boaz in Religious and Political Perspectives," *CBQ* 45 (1983) 167–78; Ouelette, "Le vestibule du Temple de Salomon," *RB* 76 (1969) 365–78, esp. 375–78; R. Scott, "The Pillars Jachin and Boaz," *JBL* 58 (1939) 143–49; Yeivin, "Jachin and Boaz," *EI* 5 (1958) 97–104. The Chronicler has considerably shortened his description of the pillars; this should be attributed to his general reduction of the entire description of the temple architecture. Since there is no evidence that the second temple had similar structures (they were also not found in Herod's temple), the reduced attention given them may reflect their irrelevancy to the post-exilic community. There is no direct support for the common assertion that the pillars evoked pagan associations for the Chronicler who for this reason shortened his account of them (Rudolph, 205; Michaeli, 152).

There has been some debate over whether the pillars were freestanding in front of the temple or built into the portico structure to support the architrave (as shown in the remains of the chapel at Tell Tainat). On the basis of the evidence from most temples, the consensus among archeologists is that the pillars were freestanding; their function was symbolic and decorative rather than structural. For the arguments in favor of their supporting the architrave, see Ouelette, *RB* 76 (1969) 375–78.

The names of the pillars have also produced a wide variety of opinion, some transparently less probable than others; they have been viewed (1) as the names of donors or builders; (2) as a reference to other gods; (3) as the names of maṣṣebôth that stood on the site prior to the time of David; (4) as predicates of deity: "He is the one who establishes; in him is strength"; (5) together as a verbal sentence, "he establishes in strength"; (6) as opening words of two longer inscriptions in some way associated with dynastic oracles; (7) as ancestral names of King Solomon.

This passage and G of Jer 52:21 give the height as thirty-five cubits, while 1 Kgs 7:15, 2 Kgs 25:17, and Jer 52:21 all give eighteen cubits. A number of explanations have been offered. The Chronicler is thought to have added the height, circumference, and capitals (18 + 12 + 5; cf. 1 Kgs 7:15) through some misreading of the text (C-M, 328–29; Rudolph, 204). Others harmonize by suggesting that the total height of both pillars is intended (note the addition of the word "together" in the NIV). Others suggest a misreading of numeral or alphanumeric writing systems (לה read for י״ח; Payne, *BSac* 136 [1979] 121–22). All these explanations are ingenious, but none appears very probable.

Explanation

The Chronicler's surprising curtailment of the deuteronomic account of the building of the temple should be traced not only to the author's relying on the reader's knowledge of the parallel account, but also to the elimination of much detail which was likely irrelevant to the community of the second temple period. Much of the architectural detail of Solomon's temple would have been insignificant for the much more modest structure of the Chronicler's day (Hag 2:3–9; Zech 4:10; Ezra 3:12–13, Josephus, *Ant.* 15:11). For the Chronicler, continuity with the past in the temple was less a matter of architecture than of location: the additions he makes to his narrative show this concern with the legitimate site of the sanctuary (1 Chr 21:27–22:1; 2 Chr 3:1); the temple site is given double warrant, both from the incident at Ornan's threshing floor and from the life of Abraham (Gen 22).

If the theocracy stood on the twin pillars of the cult and the Davidic dynasty, then during the Persian rule over the restoration community, the theocracy revolved around the cult as the available "means of grace." Hopes may have flourished for the reinstitution of Davidic rule, but the temple was the present reality for post-exilic generations.

The NT makes extensive use of temple imagery. The gospels report Jesus' teaching that his body was the temple of God (Matt 12:6; 26:61; 27:40; Mark 14:58; 15:29; John 2:19–21); Peter and Paul extend this teaching to individual Christians (1 Cor 3:16–17; 6:19; 2 Cor 6:16; Eph 2:21–22; 1 Pet 2:4–5). The veil of the temple was torn at the death of Christ (Matt 27:51; Mark 15:38; Luke 23:45); his death opened a way into the Most Holy Place (Heb 9). The writer of Hebrews treats the earthly temple/tabernacle as a pattern of the heavenly one (8:5; 9:23). In the letter to the church at Philadelphia, the overcomer is made an inscribed pillar in the temple (Rev 3:12). The New Jerusalem is a perfect cube, like the Most Holy Place; there is no temple there since the entire city has been made the dwelling of God (Rev 21:15–23). Abraham, who was seeking a heavenly city (Heb 11:8–10), had once visited the earthly Zion (Gen 22:2; 2 Chr 3:1). The site at which Abraham held a knife above his own son was the place where the destroying angel held a sword above Jerusalem (Gen 22; 1 Chr 21; 2 Chr 3:1); it was there that through the centuries hundreds of thousands of animals would die beneath a blade as sacrifices, until ultimately the blade of divine justice would find its mark in God's own Son.

The Temple Furnishings   (4:1–5:1)

Bibliography

In addition to those works listed at the beginning of the previous chapter, consult the following:

Bagnani, G. "The Molten Sea of Solomon's Temple." In *The Seed of Wisdom: Essays in Honor of T. J. Meek,* ed. W. McCullough. Toronto: University of Toronto Press, 1964. 114–17. **Groot, J. de.** *Die Altäre des Salomonischen Tempelhofes.* Stuttgart: Kohlhammer, 1924. **Haran, M.** *Temples and Temple Service in Ancient Israel.* Oxford: Clarendon Press, 1977. **Langhe, R. de.** "L'autel d'ar du temple de Jérusalem." *Bib* 40 (1959) 476–94. **Meyers, C.** *The Tabernacle Menorah: A Synthetic Study of a Symbol from the Biblical Cult.* ASORDS 2. Missoula, MT: Scholars Press, 1976. **North, R.** "Zechariah's Seven-Spout Lampstand." *Bib* 51 (1970) 183–206. **Scott, R.** "The Hebrew Cubit." *JBL* 77 (1958) 205–14. ———. "Weights and Measures of the Bible." *BA* 22 (1959) 22–40. **Shiloh, Y.** "Iron Age Sanctuaries and Cult Elements in Palestine." In *Symposia Celebrating the Seventy-fifth Anniversary of the Founding of the American Schools of Oriental Research,* ed. F. Cross. Cambridge: American Schools of Oriental Research, 1979. **Wiener, H.** *The Altars of the Old Testament.* Leipzig: Hinrichs, 1927. **Wylie, C.** "On King Solomon's Molten Sea." *BA* 12 (1949) 86–90. **Zuidhof, A.** "King Solomon's Molten Sea and (π)." *BA* 45 (1982) 179–84.

Translation

[1] *He also made the bronze altar, twenty cubits long, twenty cubits wide, and ten cubits high.*
[2] *He made the cast Sea, circular in shape, ten cubits from brim to brim and five cubits high; a line thirty cubits long would encircle it.* [3] *Figures resembling oxen[a] were beneath the rim around the entire circumference, ten to a cubit;[b] they completely encircled it in two rows cast with the Sea.* [4] *It stood on twelve oxen, three facing north, three facing west, three facing south, and three facing east. The Sea was above them, and their hindquarters pointed inward.* [5] *It was a handbreadth thick; its brim was fashioned like the brim of a cup in the shape of a lily blossom. Its capacity was three thousand baths.[a]*
[6] *He also made ten basins for washing and put five on the south and five on the north. The implements for the burnt offerings were rinsed in these, while the Sea was for the priests to wash in.*
[7] *He made ten golden lampstands according to their specifications and put them in the outer chamber, five on the south and five on the north.*
[8] *He also made ten tables and placed them in the outer chamber, five on the south and five on the north. And he made a hundred golden bowls.*
[9] *He made the court of the priests, and the great court, and the doors for the court; he overlaid the doors with bronze.* [10] *He put the Sea south of the temple[a] toward the southeast.*
[11] *Huram made the pots,[a] the shovels, and the bowls.*
Huram completed all the work he had done for King Solomon on the temple of God:

[12] *the two pillars,*
the bowl-shaped[a] *capitals on top of the two pillars,*
the two networks to decorate the two bowl-shaped capitals on top of the pillars,
[13] *the four hundred pomegranates for the two networks (two rows of pomegranates*
for each network) to decorate the two bowl-shaped capitals on top of the pillars.
[14] *He made the stands and also the basins atop the stands;*[a] [15] *the one Sea, and*
the twelve oxen beneath it, [16] *the pots, and shovels, and forks,*[a] *and all related*
implements Huram-abi[b] *made for King Solomon for the temple of Yahweh from*
polished bronze. [17] *The king cast them in clay beds in the Plain of the Jordan*
between Succoth and Zarethan.[a] [18] *Solomon made all these things—an exceeding*
great number, so much that the weight of the bronze could not be determined.

[19] *Solomon also made the furnishings for the temple of God: the golden altar,*
the tables[a] *on which was the Bread of the Presence,* [20] *the lampstands of pure*
gold and their lamps,[a] *to burn as prescribed before the inner chamber,* [21] *the floral*
work, the lamps, and the tongs of gold (they were of solid gold), [22] *the wick trimmers,*
the bowls, ladles, and censers of pure gold, and the entrance[a] *to the temple and*
the doors (the inner doors to the Most Holy Place and the doors of the temple
entering the outer chamber)—all of gold.

[5:1] *When all the work Solomon had done for the temple of Yahweh was completed,*
he brought the things his father David had dedicated—the silver, and gold, and
all the furnishings—and put them in the treasuries of the temple of God.

Notes

3.a. In 1 Kgs 7:24 these protuberances are called פקעים "gourds"; see *Comment*.
3.b. Context requires understanding עשר באמה differently than in v 2 // 1 Kgs 7:23.
5.a. There is some variation regarding the capacity. The MT of 1 Kgs 7:26 reports two thousand baths; however, the capacity is not given in the OG and is found only in some Lucianic MSS of Bas. Josephus (*Ant.* 8.79) records three thousand baths. Wylie (*BA* 12 [1949]) suggests that the capacity in Kings was calculated on the volume of a hemisphere, while that in Chronicles assumed a cylindrical shape. The diversity in the textual evidence, however, makes scribal error the more likely occasion for the differences.
10.a. הבית has been inserted with G and the parallel at 1 Kgs 7:39. Allen (*GC* 2:138) regards this as an example of parablepsis in the MT. The word omitted is redundant, however, and its inclusion in Par may reflect the dependence of that translation on Bas.
11.a. Cf. 1 Kgs 7:40 סירות "basins"; the same series of items recurs in 1 Kgs 7:45.
12.a. MT והגלות והכתרות translated as גלות הכתרות (4:12, 13; 1 Kgs 7:41, 42).
14.a. For the two occurrences of the verb עשה the parallel text at 1 Kgs 7:43 has עשר and עשרה "ten." G specifies ten stands, but does not repeat the number for the basins. Par may be an assimilation toward Bas.
16.a. Cf. 1 Kgs 7:45 מזרקות "pots"; see 14:11.
16.b. See *Comment* at 2:13. Rudolph (208) regards אביו as indicating that in Solomon's service Huram had become "his master craftsman" as he had earlier been "my master craftsman" for Hiram of Tyre. G (ἀνήνεγκεν) may have read ויבא. Allen (*GC* 2:127) suggests G read אביל, a form derived from יבל.
17.a. With the parallel at 1 Kgs 7:46 instead of the MT *Zeredah*. The two may be alternative names for the same site. Zarethan is clearly located east of the Jordan (Josh 3:1, 14–17; 1 Kgs 4:12) in the valley. A town Zeredah is known as the birthplace of Jeroboam I (1 Kgs 11:26), though this town was likely in the hill country of Ephraim.
19.a. The parallel at 1 Kgs 7:48 has the sg, "table." See *Comment*.
20.a. "And their lamps" is an addition not found in the parallel text; the result is that the lamps are mentioned twice, here and in v 21. Cf. 1 Kgs 7:49. The stand and lamps are also mentioned together in 1 Chr 28:15 (3 times) and 2 Chr 13:11.
22.a. Cf. 1 Kgs 7:50 פתות "door sockets."

Form/Structure/Setting

See the parallel passage at 1 Kgs 7:23–51. Chronicles adds material in 4:1, 6b–9; an extensive section of the parallel text has also been omitted (1 Kgs 7:27–38 [see *Comment* at 4:14]).

Rudolph (207, 209) considers only vv 2a, 3a, 6–9 as original and regards the remainder as an insertion from Kings at a later point in transmission. Several features in the chapter may betray the outlines of its compositional history. (1) The sudden extensive dependence on the parallel text in the chapter is in marked contrast to the abridgment of the parallel material in chap. 3. (2) At the grammatical level there is some difficulty in determining the subject in this section. Solomon performs the actions from 3:1, 3; however, the subject in the text parallel to 3:15–4:16 (1 Kgs 7:13–45) is the Tyrian craftsman Huram-abi who is abruptly introduced from the parallel at 4:11 (= 1 Kgs 7:40). (3) The introduction of the lamps at 4:20 (see *Comment*) makes for a somewhat uneven repetition. These items may assist in distinguishing stages of composition and are in themselves plausibly understood as evidence for redactional activity, though one cannot be dogmatic. See the discussion in Williamson, 211–12.

The paragraph structure of chap. 4 is determined by the continuing use of ויעש (4:1, 2, 6, 7, 8, 9, 11, 19) to introduce new paragraphs; see *Form/Structure/Setting* in the preceding chapter. Other paragraph level devices are the use of the explicit subject (4:11), the repetition of the subject without an intervening change of subject (4:11), and the repetition of the final clause of one paragraph at the beginning of the next ("tail-head linkage," 4:18–19).

Comment

1 *The bronze altar.* The MT of Kings does not report the construction of the bronze altar in the temple court, though it is subsequently mentioned (1 Kgs 8:64; 9:25; 2 Kgs 16:14). Its omission in Kings should probably be attributed to a homoioarchon with ויעש at 1 Kgs 7:22–23. Suggestions that the Deuteronomist thought of Solomon as having used David's earlier provisional altar (2 Sam 24 // 1 Chr 21) or using bare rock for the sacrifices would fail to account for the subsequent references to the altar. Rudolph (207) argues that the text of Chronicles betrays dependence on a no longer extant text of Kings for its description of this altar: (1) the occurrence in 2 Chr 4:1 of the word קומה for "height" reflects the customary usage of Kings (1 Kgs 6:2, 10, 20, 23, 26; 7:2, 15, 16, 23, et passim) rather than גבה as found in 2 Chr 3:4; (2) in Chronicles the numbers ordinarily follow the dimension rather than precede it (2 Chr 3:4 vs. 1 Kgs 6:3). The dimensions favor a step-altar similar to that described by Ezekiel (Ezek 43:13–17); the base would then be a square twenty cubits on each side, topped by several smaller platforms or terraces attaining a height of ten cubits above the base.

2–6 *The Sea and the basins.* The Chronicler assigns to the Sea and the basins a function in ritual cleansing of the priests and the sacrificial implements. This addition by the Chronicler gives these vessels the same function as that of the laver in the tabernacle (Exod 30:18–21); the inclusion of this information is one more example of the Chronicler's efforts to parallel the building of the temple and the tabernacle. Most interpreters have viewed the Sea as symbolic of the primeval sea or chaos ocean over which Yahweh rules in triumph (Ps 29:10; 74:12–17; 89:9–10; 93:3–4; 98:7–9; 104:1–9; Isa 51:9–10; Hab 3:8–10); it is Yahweh who rules over the Sea, not the Babylonian Marduk or the Canaanite Baal whose victories are recorded in mythological literature. If the function of the Sea in the temple courtyard is primarily that of cosmological symbolism, then the Chronicler could be viewed as demythologizing the Sea of the pagan associations it may have evoked by giving it instead a utilitarian function (C-M, Rudolph, Albright, Michaeli, Coggins). There is, however, insufficient evidence to determine which was the original use intended for the Sea or to associate either view of it with a different time period or sociological group. Biblical imagery pertaining to water is multifaceted: it not only represents the threatening waters which must be subjected to God, but also water for cleansing and purification (Exod 30:18–21; Lev 15:5–11; Ezek 36:25; Zech 13:1; Ps 51:7, 10; Isa 1:16). In Ezekiel's temple vision the brazen Sea has been replaced by a life-giving river (Ezek 47:1–12; cf. Rev 22:1–2). If the Sea was to be used by the priests for ablution, some stairs or other means of ascent must also have been provided, but are not mentioned. The twelve bulls forming the base were likely symbolic of the tribes of Israel; three tribes at each of the four compass points is reminiscent of the arrangement of camp in the wilderness (Num 2) and of Ezekiel's vision of the city gates (Ezek 48:30–35).

Many commentators have noted that the circumference of the Sea (thirty cubits) divided by its diameter (ten cubits) does not yield the value of π (3.14159). Most likely the number thirty represents a round figure for the circumference. Some suggest that thirty cubits was the circumference of the inside rim, while if a handbreadth were added (ca. three inches; cf. v 5), the circumference of the outside rim would approach the figure for π quite closely. Zuidhof (*BA* 45 [1982]) suggests that the diameter was measured from rim to rim, but that the circumference was measured at the narrower waist beneath the flared, lily-like rim (v 5), the point at which it would be easiest to draw a line around the vessel.

The Chronicler describes the protuberances on the side of the Sea as "figures resembling oxen," a departure from their being called "gourds" in 1 Kgs 7:24. The description in Kings could be attributed to the Deuteronomist's effort to avoid a reference to oxen because of his hatred for the idols of the Northern Kingdom; he may have regarded them as symbols incongruous with the true worship of Yahweh (Myers, Francisco). It must be asked, however, why the Deuteronomist would be troubled by these small images when the Sea itself was standing atop twelve large bulls. An alternative approach sees the text of Kings as correct and views the Chronicler's בקרים as a copyist's error, perhaps under the influence of the following reference (v 4) to twelve bulls (C-M, Keil). This approach, however, does not account for the additional term in Chronicles (דמות); nor is the alternative attested in extant textual data.

While the tabernacle had a single lampstand, a single table for the consecrated bread, and a single laver, Solomon's temple had ten of each. The description of these mobile basins is much more elaborate in 1 Kgs 7:27–40.

For a discussion of the Sea and the basins and archeological parallels, see Busink, *Der Tempel* 1:326–52. The decoration on the panels of these wheeled stands (lions, bulls, cherubim) and their being likened to chariots (1 Kgs 7:32–33) evokes imagery of the divine chariot (Ezek 1:4–28) with its wheels, creatures, and the sound of rushing water; cf. 1 Chr 28:18.

7 *The lampstands.* The lamps were made and burned "according to specification" (4:7, 20). The specifications for construction and use may be those of the tabernacle account (Exod 25:31–40; 37:17–24); this would comport well with the Chronicler's effort to parallel the construction of the temple with that of the earlier shrine. However, the specifications for the construction could also be those of 1 Chr 28:11–19, particularly 28:15. Though the lamps are not described in detail, Zechariah's vision (4:1–3) may reflect a memory of the lamps of the first temple. Each lampstand would have been topped by a bowl with seven lamps on its perimeter; there is ample archeological attestation for lamps of this type (North, *Bib* 51 [1970] 183–206). If the lamps in Solomon's temple were of a different shape than the lampstand of the tabernacle, there is probably also an attendant shift in its primary symbolic function from that of a "tree of life" (appropriate to the seven-branched menorah of the tabernacle) to a light motif, perhaps representative of the presence of God (Meyers, 185–88). Only one menorah was found in the second temple (1 Macc 1:21; 4:49), presumably in the seven-branched shape represented on the arch of Titus. The Talmud harmonizes by placing both the tabernacle menorah and the ten lampstands in Solomon's temple: "You must therefore say that the menorah stood in the middle with five menorahs to the right of it and five to the left of it" (*Menaḥ.* 98b). The data in Chronicles appear to equivocate on the number of lampstands: either ten lampstands along with the ten tables (4:7–8), or only one lampstand (13:11). 2 Chr 4:6–9 is unique to Chronicles, though the lamps are mentioned in the summary of 1 Kgs 7:49 // 4:20.

8 *The tables.* The fact that there were ten tables is only mentioned here and in v 19; their function is uncertain. (1) Since the ten lampstands are similarly distributed five on the north and five on the south (4:7), the lampstands may have stood on these tables which should be distinguished from the table used for the Bread of the Presence. (2) The tables may have been used for the Bread of the Presence. Although the tabernacle accounts (Exod 25:23–40; Lev 24:5–9) and Ezekiel's temple vision (Ezek 41:22) mention only one table for this purpose, the temple design may have multiplied the number of tables as it had the number of lamps. Cf. the plural in 1 Chr 28:16 and 2 Chr 4:19, but contrast the singular in the parallel passage in 1 Kgs 7:48. Other passages suggest that the Chronicler knew of only one table for the Bread of the Presence (2 Chr 13:11; 29:18; cf. 1 Chr 9:32; 23:29). Josephus (*Ant.* 8.88–90) does speak of more than one table, but also distinguishes the one table for the Bread of the Presence from the rest. See Busink, *Der Tempel* 1:288–92.

9–10 *The courts.* The term עזרה is unique to 2 Chronicles (4:9; 6:13) and Ezekiel (43: 14, 17, 20; 45:19) as a designation for the temple courts, doubtless reflecting the terminology of the second temple period. The court of the priests corresponds to the inner court of 1 Kgs 6:36; 7:12; both histories report that the temple had two courts (1 Kgs 7:12; 2 Kgs 23:12), though Kings does not mention the doors.

11–22 *The work in bronze and gold.* The shovels were used to remove the coals and ashes from the altar hearth and to dump them into pots; the sprinkling bowls received the blood of the sacrificial victims (Exod 27:3; 38:3; Num 4:14). For a discussion of the pillars, see *Comment* at 3:15–17. Solomon's source for the immeasurable quantities of bronze (4:16–18) is not known; current interpretations of the archeological data indicate that the copper deposits at Timna and in the valley of Elath were not mined during the Solomonic period (F. Singer, "From These Hills . . . ," *BARev* 4 [1978] 11–25). The casting was done in the Jordan Valley about halfway between the Dead Sea and the Sea of Galilee, far from the traditional site for the mines.

The golden altar is the altar of incense (1 Chr 28:18; Exod 30:1–10; 2 Chr 26:16–20). According to 1 Kgs 6:31–35, the doors to the Most Holy Place and the temple itself were made of wood covered with hammered gold sheeting.

14 This is the first reference in Chronicles to these stands; it is incorporated from the parallel text at 1 Kgs 7:43. If the passage is original with the Chronicler, it is another instance of his assuming the audience's familiarity with the other narrative (1 Kgs 7:27–37).

17 The parallel at 1 Kgs 7:46 (מעבה האדמה "thickness of the ground") is often emended to מעברת האדמה "the ford at Adamah." Adamah was a city in the Jordan Plain (Josh 3:9–17), identified with Tell ed-Damiyeh on the delta of the Jabbok. Rudolph (209) suggests that the Chronicler had the disturbed text before him and understood it as a place name as required by context; he finds the suggestion "clay beds" hard to accept. However, since מעבה and עבי are etymologically related, a better explanation may be to view the Chronicler as adjusting to the current linguistic usage of his audience. The context suggests the meaning "clay beds" as the location where molds for the bronze castings could be made.

5:1 *The things dedicated by David.* See 1 Chr 18:1–13; 26:25–27; 29:1–5. Just as the spoil taken from Egypt had gone into the building of the tabernacle, so also the spoil of Israel's enemies built the temple. The prophets often portray the wealth of the nations at the disposal of Israel (Isa 60:10–14; Mic 4:13; Zech 14:14). David's generosity stimulated the giving of the people (1 Chr 29:6–9); their giving is another parallel chosen by the Chronicler with events at the building of the tabernacle (Exod 35:4–36:7). The dedicated things were stored in the treasuries of the temple (1 Chr 26:26; 28:12), though these rooms are not described in the Chronicler's account of the construction (1 Kgs 6:5–10).

McConville (125) suggests the statement that the temple was completed (ותשלם) is a play on Solomon's name; Solomon, the chosen temple builder, brings his task to fulfillment.

Explanation

If the Chronicler was the source for all the material in this section (see the discussion under *Form/Structure/Setting*), it is striking that so much more attention is given to the temple accouterments than to the building itself (2 Chr 3). Interest in the furnishing and implements of temple service is of a piece with the author's pervasive concern with the cult and presumably had immediate relevance to the needs of his readers. The temple vessels represent an important continuity theme into the restoration period; see *Comment* at 29:18–19.

NT authors frequently draw imagery from the tabernacle or the temple; see the *Explanation* in the preceding chapter. The author of Hebrews views the old covenant shrines as a copy of the heavenly one (Heb 9), and he reflects on the paraphernalia and furnishings; the work of Christ is the reality which the service there anticipated (Heb 10). John saw the Christ standing among seven lampstands (Rev 4:12–20); in the holy city the Lamb of God is the lamp (Rev 21:23–24; 22:5). There is no cosmic Sea in the heavenly Jerusalem (Rev 21:1); the great basin in the temple court has been replaced by the life-giving river (Rev 22:1–2; cf. Ezek 47:1–12). Instead of the twelve loaves on the table (Lev 24:5–9) in the presence of God, the church partakes of one loaf (1 Cor 10:17).

The Installation of the Ark (5:2–14)

Bibliography

Cody, A. *A History of the Old Testament Priesthood.* Rome: Pontifical Biblical Institute, 1969. **McConville, J.** "Priests and Levites in Ezekiel: A Crux in the Interpretation of Israel's History." *TynBul* 34 (1983) 3–31. **Rad, G. von.** "The Tent and the Ark." In *The Problem of the Hexateuch and Other Essays.* New York: McGraw-Hill, 1966. **Welch, A.** "The Chronicler and the Levites." In *The Work of the Chronicler.* London: British Academy, 1939.

Translation

[2]*Then Solomon summoned to Jerusalem the elders of Israel and all the heads of the tribes, the leaders of the families*[a] *of the children of Israel, to bring up the ark of the covenant of Yahweh from the City of David (that is, Zion).* [3]*Everyone in Israel gathered to the king for the festival in the seventh month.*

[4]*When all the elders of Israel had come, the Levites*[a] *took up the ark.* [5]*They carried the ark and the Tent of Meeting and all the sacred furnishings that were in the Tent; the priests and Levites*[a] *carried them,* [6]*while King Solomon and all the congregation of Israel who had gathered around him before the ark were sacrificing so many sheep and cattle that they could not be recorded or counted.* [7]*The priests brought the ark of the covenant of Yahweh to its place beneath the wings of the cherubim in the inner chamber of the temple, the Most Holy Place.*

[8]*The cherubim spread their wings over the place of the ark and covered*[a] *the ark and its poles from above.* [9]*The poles were so long, however, that the ends of the poles could be seen from the Holy Place*[a] *in front of the inner chamber, though they could not be seen outside. They*[b] *are there to this very day.* [10]*There was nothing in the ark except the two tablets that Moses had put there at Horeb when*[a] *Yahweh made a covenant with the children of Israel after they had come out of Egypt.*

[11]*And it came about that when the priests came out of the Holy Place (for all the priests who were present had sanctified themselves, regardless of their divisions;* [12]*all the Levites who were musicians—Asaph, Heman, Jeduthun, their families and relatives—were dressed in fine linen and were standing east of the altar with cymbals, harps, and zithers; a hundred and twenty priests were with them blowing trumpets),* [13]*the trumpeters and musicians were in unison, as with one voice to give praise and thanks to Yahweh. Accompanied by trumpets, cymbals, and other musical instruments, they began to sing, praising Yahweh,*

> *"for he is good,*
> *his faithfulness is everlasting,"*

and the temple was filled with a cloud.[a] [14]*The priests were unable to remain to perform their service because of the cloud, for the glory of Yahweh had filled the temple of God.*

Notes

2.a. Cf. 1:2. These statements give a glimpse into the social structure of early and premonarchic Israel. The national assembly included representation from all the tribes down to the level of a subphratry (בית אב, "extended family").

4.a. The parallel at 1 Kgs 8:3 reads "priests" instead of Levites; see *Comment.*

5.a. With G, Vg, many Hebrew MSS and 1 Kgs 8:4, והלוים; MT, הלוים "the levitical priests." A similar textual problem occurs at 23:18; 30:27; Ezra 10:5. See *Comment.*

8.a. ויסכו may be a metathesis of ויסכו (1 Kgs 8:7), though they are partially synonymous.

9.a. With a few Hebrew MSS, G, and 1 Kgs 8:8, הקדש מן; MT, הארון מן. Most regard the substitution of ארון in Chr MT as the work of a careless scribe; L. Allen (*JTS* 22 [1971] 150) sees "the ark" as a marginal gloss to explain the singular of ויהי in the final clause of the verse; a later scribe would have understood the gloss as a correction for הקדש. Leaving the MT unaltered would produce a translation as follows: "the ends of the poles extending from the ark could be seen in front of the inner chamber."

9.b. Some Hebrew MSS, G, Syr, Tg, and 1 Kgs 8:8 have the plural ויהיו; the plural in the versional evidence, however, should be understood as required by the target languages rather than as attesting to an alternative text. Vg retains the singular by providing the subject "the ark."

10.a. The relative אשר may conceivably be understood as "by which," i.e., "the two tablets Moses had put there at Horeb, by which Yahweh made a covenant with the children of Israel. . . ." See *Preliminary and Interim Report on the Hebrew Old Testament Text Project* (Stuttgart: United Bible Societies, 1976) 2:307.

13.a. The redundant בית יהוה has been omitted from the translation as a gloss. Several possibilities exist other than omitting the phrase as a gloss: (1) The phrase could be taken as a construct, "the temple was filled with the cloud of the temple of Yahweh." This would be contrary to the accentuation and would also be a unique designation for the cloud. (2) It could be treated as an appositional expansion on the initial occurrence of הבית, "the temple, the temple of Yahweh, was filled with a cloud." (3) G appears to be influenced by v 14, "the temple was filled with the cloud of the glory of Yahweh." (4) Perhaps the least probable possibility is to view the text as a nominal sentence with a deleted subject (*Preliminary and Interim Report on the Hebrew Old Testament Text Project*, 2:450–51), "the temple was filled with a cloud; *it was/became* the temple of Yahweh."

Form/Structure/Setting

2 Chr 5:2–14 is taken largely verbatim from 1 Kgs 8:1–11; the Chronicler's distinctive interests are reflected in the addition of 5:11b–13a and a small change in 5:4.

The paragraphs of this section are marked out by the following devices: (1) the particle אז introducing a proposal/response paragraph (5:2–3); (2) an explicit change of subject (5:4); (3) the use of ויהיו (5:8) and ויהי (5:11).

Rudolph suggests that 5:11–14 was not a part of the Chronicler's original work for the following reasons: (1) Since he regards the twenty-four priestly divisions (1 Chr 24) as a later insertion, any subsequent references to them must also represent later additions (5:11b–12a; see Williamson, "The Origins of the Twenty-Four Priestly Courses," VTSup 30 [1979] 251–68). (2) Both instances in which the temple singers wear בוץ are attributed to a later glossator (5:12; 1 Chr 15:27). (3) Since 5:11a, 13b–14 report the appearance of the glory cloud before Solomon's solicitation of the divine appearance (6:41) and the actual appearance itself (7:1–2), the Chronicler himself would not have written 5:11b, 13b–14 which were subsequently mechanically introduced from 1 Kgs 8:10–11.

The validity of Rudolph's first two arguments for the secondary character of 5:11b–13a depends on the validity of his argument for regarding the related passages as secondary; both arguments are rebutted by Williamson (215–16). The third argument, however, is (1) at the expense of the rhetorical structure of the Chronicler's presentation of the reign of Solomon (2 Chr

1–9). If the narrative of his reign is structured as a chiasm, the repetition of the appearance of the glory cloud in 5:11a, 13b–14 and 7:1–2 is a feature of chiastic ordering and would represent original material; see "Literary Structure" in the introductory essay "The Chronicler's Solomon." In a chiastic structure the double reference to the appearance of the glory cloud would not suggest two separate instances, but only one, as demonstrable in other narratives showing a similar structure (see G. Wenham, "Coherence of the Flood Narrative," *VT* 28 [1978] 336–48). Williamson (216) distinguishes between the two appearances of the cloud, the one in the holy place visible to the priests only (5:13–14) and the other, the fire at the altar outside visible to all Israel (7:1–3). (2) Similarly, the introduction of the musicians into this account effects a parallel with the earlier account of the movement of the ark (1 Chr 13:8; 15:16–28) and can only be excised at the expense of that parallel. (3) The appearance of the cloud in 5:14 is also reported in the parallel at 1 Kgs 8:11; the response of Solomon (6:1–2) appears to presume the cloud's appearance. Mosis (*Untersuchungen*, 148, n. 71) summarizes other opinion in favor of regarding 5:11–14 as secondary.

Comment

2–3 One of the most characteristic features of the Chronicles is the author's concern with "all Israel," a theme he frequently introduces where it would be unparalleled in his Samuel/Kings *Vorlage*. Here, however, this theme so congenial to the author's interests is already present in the parallel text at 1 Kgs 8:1–2.

The festival of the seventh month was the Feast of Tabernacles (7:8–10). According to 1 Kgs 6:38 the temple was completed in the eighth month of Solomon's eleventh year; the dedication must have taken place during the month before the actual completion of the work. The month is designated by its Canaanite name Ethanim in the parallel passage (1 Kgs 8:1); the Hebrew designation for the month was Tishri. Note the Chronicler's omission of the month name at 3:2 // 1 Kgs 6:1.

4–7 One of the central tenets of the Wellhausen school was that the distinction between priests and Levites was unknown before the exile. Since the earlier history reported that the ark was moved by the priests (1 Kgs 8:3), the Chronicler's assigning the task to the Levites instead (5:4) has long been viewed by biblical scholars as indicative of a post-exilic concern to keep the two offices distinct. More recent biblical scholarship has tended to soften the dictum of Wellhausen by recognizing the distinction between priest and Levite in the pre-exilic literature as well; nevertheless, it is a clear concern of the Chronicler to accentuate the differences between the two offices (1 Chr 23:24–32). The Levites were charged with the transfer of the ark (5:4; 1 Chr 15:2, 11–15; Num 4:24–28), but only the priests could enter the Most Holy Place and handle the sacred furnishings (5:7; Num 4:5–20).

There is no record of the transfer of the tabernacle from Gibeon (1:3) to Jerusalem. However, the phrase "Tent of Meeting" is used exclusively of that structure and should not be transferred to the temporary structure erected by David for the ark (1 Chr 16:1; 2 Chr 1:4) without clear warrant. The movement of the tabernacle to Jerusalem implies that it was stored in the temple precincts once dismantled.

9 The phrase "to this day" or its equivalent is common in Chronicles (1 Chr 4:41, 43; 5:26; 13:11; 17:5; 2 Chr 8:8; 10:19; 20:25; 21:10; 35:25); here it is taken from the parallel text (1 Kgs 8:8), though this is not always the case. For both Kings and Chronicles the ark had long disappeared by the time of their composition. C-M (338) regard this as an example of the Chronicler's lack of concern to harmonize his account with actual conditions. However, in light of the usage here and in other passages, one is prompted to ask whether the literal "to this day" should be understood as idiomatic for "from then on" or "in perpetuity"; if this suggestion of idiomatic usage is correct, the phrase cannot be used to unravel the redactional history of the individual pericopes. See B. Childs, "A Study of the Formula 'Unto This Day,'" *JBL* 82 (1963) 279–92.

10 The statement that nothing was in the ark except the tablets of the law (5:10 // 1 Kgs 8:9) implies familiarity with a tradition that the ark had at one time contained more than the tablets alone. The NT is familiar with this tradition and speaks of a jar of manna and Aaron's rod as having been in the ark (Heb 9:4) with the tablets. The OT itself, however, only speaks of the rod and the jar of manna as having been placed in front of the ark (Exod 16:32–34; Num 17:10–11).

11–14 Most of the material in these verses is not paralleled in Kings; it consists of a variety of themes that occur frequently in Chronicles. The Chronicler's interest in the levitical musicians is widely recognized and pervasive (1 Chr 6:31–47; 15:16–16:6; 23:5; 25:1–31; 2 Chr 20:19; 29:25–29; 35:15). The same refrain (5:13) is heard in other ceremonies (1 Chr 16:34, 41; 2 Chr 7:3, 6; 20:21); throughout there is the author's general delight in cultic pageantry.

The 120 priests probably represented an ad hoc group of musicians, in keeping with the fact that the priests were not serving in their usual divisional rotations (5:11), though it is possible also that they consisted of five representatives from each of the twenty-four courses.

Explanation

This section of Chronicles owes its form largely to 1 Kgs 8, though while accepting the earlier tradition, the Chronicler has recast it with small modifications that reflect his own interests. One characteristic of the Chronicler's writing is his effort to parallel earlier records; see the introductory essay, "The Chronicler's Solomon," for examples of this. Here he parallels Solomon's movement of the ark to the temple with the earlier effort by David to transfer the ark to Jerusalem; the following features are in common:

(1) A national assembly: 1 Chr 13:1–5; 15:3; 2 Chr 5:2–3
(2) Sacrifices during the procession and installation: 1 Chr 15:26; 16:1; 2 Chr 5:6
(3) Musical accompaniment: 1 Chr 13:8; 15:16–28; 2 Chr 5:12–13
(4) A royal blessing for the people: 1 Chr 16:1–3; 2 Chr 6:3

Several of these elements were borrowed from the earlier narrative: sacrifices and the royal blessing are mentioned in the parallel passages of Samuel; musical accompaniment is also noted for the initial abortive effort to move the ark (1 Chr 13:8; 2 Sam 6:5); the dedication of the temple is attended by all Israel in both narratives (5:2–3; 1 Kgs 8:2–3). It is the Chronicler's contribution, however, to draw out the full-blown parallels between these incidents, particularly reflecting his interest in the cultic musicians and in "all Israel."

In general the Chronicler has modeled his account of the building of the temple on the earlier manufacture of the tabernacle; at completion both structures receive divine approval through the appearance of the cloud/pillar. The inability of the priests to perform their functions because of the presence of the cloud (5:14; 7:1–2) repeats the experience at the dedication of the tabernacle (Exod 40:34–35); the disciples would find their contact with the transfigured and glorified Christ similarly overwhelming (Matt 17:6–7).

The Dedicatory Speeches   (6:1–42)

Bibliography

Adinolfi, M. "Le 'opere di pietà liturgica' di David in 2 Chron. 6.42." *Bibbia e Oriente* 8 (1966) 31–36. **Beuken, W.** "Isa. 55.3–5: The Reinterpretation of David." *Bijdragen* 35 (1974) 49–64. **Bordeuil, P.** "Les 'grâces de David' et 1 Maccabees 2:57." *VT* 31 (1981) 73–76. **Caquot, A.** "Les 'grâces de David': à propos d'Isaïe 55/3b." *Sem* 15 (1965) 45–59. **Williamson, H.** "Eschatology in Chronicles." *TynBul* 28 (1977) 115–54. ———. "'The Sure Mercies of David': Subjective or Objective Genitive?" *JSS* 23 (1978) 31–49.

Translation

[1] [a]*Then Solomon said, "Yahweh has said that he would dwell in a dark cloud;* [2]*I have built this magnificent temple for you as a place for you to dwell forever."* [3]*The king turned, and while the whole assembly of Israel was standing there, he blessed the entire assembly of Israel.* [4]*And he said,*

"Blessed be Yahweh, the God of Israel, who by his hands has fulfilled what he promised with his own mouth to David my father. [5]*For he said, 'Since the day that I brought my people out of Egypt, I have not chosen any city among all the tribes of Israel to have a temple built there for my name,* [a]*nor have I chosen any man to be leader over my people Israel.* [6]*But I have chosen Jerusalem that my name should be there,*[a] *and I have chosen David to be over my people Israel.'*

[7]*"It had been the intention of David my father to build a temple for the name of Yahweh, the God of Israel.* [8]*But Yahweh said to David my father, 'As for your intention to build a temple for my name, you have done well to intend this.* [9]*But you will not build the temple; rather,*[a] *your son, one who comes from your loins, will build the temple for my name.'* [10]*Yahweh has kept the promise he made; I have succeeded David my father, and I sit on the throne of Israel just as Yahweh promised, and I have built the temple for the name of Yahweh, the God of Israel.* [11]*I have placed there the ark which contains the covenant that Yahweh made with the children of Israel."*[a]

[12]*He*[a] *stood before the altar of Yahweh in front of all the congregation of Israel and spread out his hands.*[b] [13]*Now Solomon had made a bronze platform, five cubits long, five cubits wide, and three cubits high, and had placed it in the middle of the court; he stood upon it, knelt down on his knees before the entire assembly of Israel, and spread out his hands toward heaven,*[a] [14]*and said,*

"O Yahweh, God of Israel, there is no god like you in heaven or on earth, one who shows covenant faithfulness[a] *with your servants who walk wholeheartedly before you,* [15]*and which you have shown to your servant my father David in keeping what you promised to him, what you spoke with your own mouth and fulfilled with your own hand, even this day.*

[16]*"And now Yahweh, God of Israel, keep for your servant David my father what you promised him, when you said, 'You will never lack a man to sit before me on the throne of Israel, if only your sons will watch their conduct and walk in my law*[a] *just as you have walked before me.'*

[17] "Now Yahweh, God of Israel, let the promise you made to your servant David be confirmed.

[18] "But will God really dwell with man[a] on earth? Indeed, heaven itself, even the highest heaven, cannot contain you, and certainly not this house that I have built. [19] Yet take heed to your servant's prayer and his plea, O Yahweh, my God; hear the cry and the prayer your servant makes before you,[a] [20] that your eyes be open toward this temple day and night, this place where you said you would put your name, and that you might hear the prayer your servant makes toward this place. [21] Hear the pleas of your servant and of your people Israel when they pray toward this place; hear from your dwelling place, from heaven, and when you hear, forgive.

[22] "When a man wrongs his neighbor and is required[a] to take an oath, and he enters an oath[b] before your altar in this temple, [23] then hear from heaven and act; decide between your servants, requiting the guilty by bringing his conduct on his own head, and acquitting the innocent and rewarding him as his innocence deserves.

[24] "When your people Israel are defeated before an enemy because they have sinned against you, and they return, and confess your name and pray, and plead for mercy before you in this temple, [25] then hear from heaven and forgive the sin of your people Israel; restore them to the land you gave to them and to their fathers.

[26] "When the heavens are shut up and there is no rain because they have sinned against you, and they pray toward this place, and confess your name, and turn from their sin for which you afflicted them,[a] [27] then hear from heaven and forgive the sin of your servants and your people Israel, that you might teach them the right way to live; provide rain for your land that you gave to your people as an inheritance.

[28] "When there is famine in the land, or pestilence, or blight, or mildew, or locust or grasshopper, or when enemies besiege them in the land of their cities,[a] whatever sickness or disease might come, [29] when a prayer or plea is made by any person or by anyone among your people Israel—each aware of his sickness and pain and spreading out his hands toward this temple—[30] then hear from heaven where you dwell and forgive; since you know the heart of each person, reward each as his conduct deserves, for you alone know the heart of the children of men, [31] so that they might fear you and walk in your ways all the days that they live in the land you gave to our fathers.

[32] "And also for the foreigner who is not from your people Israel, but comes from a distant land because of your great name, your strong hand, and your outstretched arm, when he comes and prays toward this temple, [33] then hear from heaven where you dwell, and do according to all that the foreigner asks of you, so that all the peoples of the earth may know your name, and fear you the way your people Israel does, and know that this house that I have built bears your name.

[34] "When your people go to war against their enemies, wherever you send them, and they pray to you toward this city you have chosen and this temple that I have built for your name, [35] then hear from heaven their prayer and their plea, and uphold their cause.

[36] "When they sin against you—for there is no one who does not sin—and

you deliver them over to an enemy who takes them captive to another land, whether distant or near, ³⁷and they have a change of heart in the land where they are captive, and they repent and plead with you in the land of their captivity, and say, 'We have sinned, done evil, and been wicked,' ³⁸and they turn to you with all their heart and soul in the land of their captivity where they are being held, and pray toward their land which you gave to their fathers and the city you have chosen and this temple I have built for your name, ³⁹then hear from heaven where you dwell their prayer and plea; uphold their cause and forgive your people who have sinned against you.

⁴⁰*"Now, O my God, let your eyes be open and your ears attentive to prayer offered in this place.* ⁴¹*And now, arise, Yahweh God, to your resting place, you and the ark of your might. O Yahweh God, let your priests be clothed with salvation; let your saints rejoice in good.* ⁴²*O Yahweh God, do not reject your anointed ones;* ᵃ *remember the faithful deeds of David your servant."*

Notes

1.a. The parallel to 6:1–2 at 1 Kgs 8:12–13 has been relocated in Bas to the end of Solomon's prayer (1 Kgs 8:53) and supplemented with an additional line to read "Then Solomon spoke concerning the temple he had finished building, and said, 'Though he put the sun in the heavens, the Lord has said that he would dwell in darkness. . . .'" Agreement in the Hebrew texts suggests editorial reworking by the G translator at this point.

5–6.a-a. This section is not found in the parallel text at 1 Kgs 8:16 from which it appears to have been omitted by homoiotel with לֹהְיוֹת שְׁמִי שָׁם. Nor is the section preserved in its entirety in either of the Greek versions: the first half is missing in Bas and the second half in Par. Here we have the unusual instance where the text of Chronicles may be superior to the text of Kings and the two Greek versions. All the lines were preserved in the Latin column of the Complutensian Polyglot, in which 2 Chr is based on the OL rather than Vg (Lemke, *Synoptic Studies*, 97–98).

9.a. Many Hebrew MSS read כִּי־אָם, but these are corrections. There is no reason to suggest a transmission error omitting אָם; the Chronicler has also used כִּי alone in this sense where the earlier text has כִּי־אָם in 2 Chr 18:7 // 1 Kgs 22:8 and 25:4 // 2 Kgs 14:6. It may reflect a diachronic development between the time of the two authors or a stylistic preference of the Chronicler.

11.a. Instead of "the children of Israel," 1 Kgs 8:21 reads "our fathers when he brought them out of the land of Egypt." See *Comment* at 6:4–6.

12.a. 1 Kgs 8:22 specifies the subj "Solomon."

12.b. 1 Kgs 8:22 adds "toward heaven"; cf. v 13.

13.a. V 13 is missing in the parallel account at 1 Kgs 8:22, and the additional material in Chr has often been related to the author's *Tendenz* (see *Comment*). A homoiotel between the last words of vv 12 and 13 (וַיִּפְרֹשׂ כַּפָּיו) is the more probable explanation, although no extant text attests to the fuller text for Kings.

14.a. הַבְּרִית וְהַחֶסֶד as hendiadys.

16.a. "In my law" in place of "before me" (1 Kgs 8:25).

18.a. "With man" is missing in 1 Kgs 8:27, but is found in both Bas and Par.

19.a. 1 Kgs 8:28, Bas, and Par add "today." No particular reason suggests the omission of הַיּוֹם as a textual error; its presence in Par may reflect assimilation toward Bas. See Allen, *GC* 1:201. Michaeli's suggestion (158) that the omission of "today" represents an effort to give the prayer "permanent value," so that it could be used in the future as well as in the present, is improbable; omission of the word does not render the prayer more suitable for ongoing liturgical use—its usefulness for further recitation would seem quite unaffected by the presence or absence of that word.

22.a. Lit., "he [the plaintiff] imposes an oath on him [the defendant], requiring him to swear. . . ."

22.b. Taken as the syntactic equivalent of בָּא בְאָלָה (Ezek 17:13; Neh 10:30 [29]). Bas and Par appear to have understood as בָּא וְאָלָה "comes and swears."

26.a. Reading תַעֲנֵם with G and Vg for MT תַעֲנֶם "you answer them."

28.a. Lit., "in the land of their gates." "Gates" is often used as a reference to the city as a whole (Isa 14:31; Ps 87:2; Deut 12:12). Bas in the parallel text (1 Kgs 8:37 = ἐν μιᾷτῶν πόλεων) could attest to an alternative text (באהד שעריו), or represent an effort to cope with the unusual Heb.; cf. Par (κατέναντι τῶν πόλεων αὐτῶν).

42.a. "Your anointed one" (sg) in the parallel at Ps 132:10; Par τό πρόσωπον σοῦ appears to be an error on the copyist's part (Allen, *GC* 2:55).

Form/Structure/Setting

2 Chr 6 is a nearly verbatim reproduction of 1 Kgs 8:12–50. The Chronicler has omitted 1 Kgs 8:51–53; in place of this passage he has introduced 6:40–42, a free citation of Ps 132:1, 8–10.

In spite of its tight correspondence to the parallel passage, the Chronicler has used the pericope, particularly Solomon's dedicatory prayer (6:12–42), as a central focus of his own account of Solomon's reign. See the discussion under "Literary Structure" in the introductory essay "The Chronicler's Solomon."

The chapter is structured by the three different addresses by Solomon (6:1–2, 3–11, 12–42), each increasing in length; the individual petitions of the dedicatory prayer form separate paragraphs.

Comment

1–2 These verses are Solomon's response to the appearance of the glory cloud indicating divine acceptance of the temple. The cloud that had appeared at Sinai (Exod 20:21; Deut 4:11; 5:22) and in which God revealed his presence would now have a permanent dwelling place ("a place for you to dwell forever") in contrast to the portable shrine/tabernacle. The darkness of the Most Holy Place was a dwelling suited to the dark cloud (Exod 20:21).

3 Turning from facing the temple toward the congregation, Solomon blesses the people. David had similarly blessed a national cultic assembly (1 Chr 16:2; cf. 1 Chr 16:43; 2 Chr 31:8; 1 Kgs 8:55).

4–6 The divine promise to David is not cited in any of its canonical forms, but appears rather to be a free composition integrating the choice of Judah and Jerusalem (1 Chr 28:4; 2 Chr 12:13; 33:7) and of David (1 Chr 17; 28:2–10). From the time of the Exodus to the building of the temple, God had not chosen a permanent dwelling (1 Chr 17:4–6).

It is widely recognized (Japhet, *Ideology*, 382–88; North, *JBL* 82 [1963] 376–78; Ackroyd, *CTM* 38 [1967] 510–12; Williamson, *IBC*, 64–66) that the Chronicler attenuates the emphasis in the earlier history on the Exodus. Three times in this chapter allusions to the Exodus are abridged or eliminated (6:11 // 1 Kgs 8:21; 1 Kgs 8:51, 53) from the form in which they occur in the parallel account. However these alterations are related to the overall theology of the Chronicler (see 6:40–42 below), it is necessary to strike a balance and recall the other references to the Exodus event which dot the Chronicler's history (1 Chr 17:21; 2 Chr 5:10; 6:5; 7:22; 20:10); the deliverance from Egypt was not unimportant to the Chronicler.

7–11 As above (6:4–6) the report of the divine revelation to David is a digest of several utterances (1 Chr 17:4–14; 22:7–10; 28:2–7), rather than a precise quotation of any one. The earlier history gave the reason for David's inability to build the temple as the warfare on all sides that had consumed his time (1 Kgs 5:2–3); the Chronicler shifts the emphasis slightly, giving as the reason the amount of bloodshed associated with David in contrast to Solomon, a man of peace (1 Chr 22:8–9; 28:3).

The accession of Solomon and the completion of the temple were for the Chronicler stages in the inauguration of the Davidic covenant. Instead of exhausting God's promises so that the Chronicler would show no eschatological expectations or royalist hopes in the post-exilic period, these realizations of God's promises were but the beginning of an unending dynasty (6:14–17; 13:5; 21:7; 23:3; 1 Chr 17:12–17, 23–27; 22:10; 28:7–8).

12–13 Since v 13 is unique to the Chronicler, scholars have often viewed it as a tendentious insertion on the part of the author in order to prevent the appearance that Solomon was usurping priestly functions before the altar (Michaeli, C-M, Wellhausen; cf. 26:16–21) or have viewed the raised platform as a cultic practice of the Chronicler's own day read back into the Solomonic period (Coggins). A text critical solution is far more probable. In addition to the probable homoioteleuton (see *Notes* at 6:13), (1) the syntax of the measurements favors the conclusion that the passage was originally also found in Kings: the Chronicler ordinarily uses גבה for "height" instead of קומה, which is more characteristic of Kings, and in Chronicles the numbers ordinarily follow the dimension rather than precede it. See *Comment* at 4:1 for a similar example; Mosis (*Untersuchungen,* 144–46) provides a full discussion. (2) Kings does report that the king stood after kneeling during his prayer (1 Kgs 8:54), but does not report that he knelt at the beginning of the prayer unless the passage in 2 Chr 6:13 was also original in Kings. (3) Iconographic remains from the ancient Near East often portray dignitaries standing or kneeling on platforms while performing cultic duties. Examples can be found in Pritchard, *ANEP,* fig. 576, p. 490; and C. Jones, *Old Testament Illustrations* (London: Cambridge UP, 1971), fig. 173. The Chronicler also speaks of a special place for the king to stand in the temple precincts (2 Chr 23:13), though its relationship to this platform is uncertain.

For spreading the hands as a gesture of prayer, cf. Exod 9:29, 33; 1 Kgs 8:54; Ezra 9:5; Job 11:13; Ps 44:21 [20]; 2 Macc 3:20. See O. Keel, *The Symbolism of the Biblical World,* tr. T. Hallett (New York: Seabury Press, 1978) 308–23.

14–17 For the Chronicler completion of the temple does not exhaust the promises of God, but represents an incipient stage; Solomon praises God for fulfilling what he had spoken to David (6:14–15), and yet prays that God would keep his promise for the future (6:16–17). Cf. 6:7–11. A passage of this type makes it difficult to eliminate royalist/messianic hopes from the Chronicler's theology.

The prayer has a stately majesty, as marked by the threefold invocation "Yahweh, God of Israel" (6:14, 16, 17).

The "walk before me" of 1 Kgs 8:25 is "concretized" (Willi, *Die Chronik,* 125) by the Chronicler as "walk in my law." The author shows a "concept of authoritative writings through which the will of God is revealed to every generation of Israel" (Childs, *Introduction,* 648), i.e., the concept of canon is well developed in his time. Willi (*Judaica* 36 [1980] 102–5, 148–151) is of the opposite opinion, arguing that the Chronicler's references to torah are to living praxis and not to a religion of the book.

18–21 The Chronicler had earlier reflected on the tension between the transcendence and immanence of God by recording a similar, partially verbatim, allusion to the matter into Solomon's correspondence with Hiram of Tyre (2:4–5). While the emphasis in this prayer is on viewing the temple as a house of prayer, the earlier reflection on transcendence emphasized the temple as a place for sacrifice (2:5). Both passages were effectively combined in Isa 56:7.

22–23 Solomon's prayer transfers to the temple the oath procedure which had ordinarily been administered at the tabernacle or other holy sites (Num 5:13; Lev 6:3–6; Judg 11:11; Amos 8:14). Similar procedures are elaborated for cases of default (Exod 22:7–15), adultery (Num 5:11–31) and theft (Lev 6:3–5). Taking an oath was a solemn act (Lev 19:12; 15:1, 4; Ezek 17:13–19; Ps 15:4), ordinarily accompanied by a self-maledictory curse; the terror of the accompanying curse was apparently designed to elicit a confession (Judg 17:1–4). Lifting the hand toward heaven was the common gesture while making the oath (Gen 14:22; Exod 6:8; Deut 32:40; Ps 144:8; Isa 62:8; Dan 12:7; Ezek 20:5; Rev 10:5–6).

24–25 Though the major motifs of the prayer are the Davidic dynasty, the temple, and prayer itself, two recurring themes are war (6:24–25, 34–37) and the land (6:25, 27, 28, 31, 38); twice the author chooses the ordinarily more concrete and specific term אדמה (6:25, 31) instead of the more common ארץ.

26–27 Ancient Israel was an agrarian society with sufficient rainfall in most of the land that irrigation was not necessary. Agriculture was dependent on the regularity of the seasonal rains, particularly both the early rains to soften the ground for plowing in the fall, and the latter rains to swell the crop before harvest in the spring; adequate rainfall was a sign of divine blessing, and low rainfall of divine anger (Lev 26:3–4; Deut 11:13–14; 28:23–24; Prov 16:15; Jer 3:3; 5:24; Hos 6:3; 10:1; Joel 2:23; Cant 2:11; Acts 14:17; Heb 6:7; Jas 5:17; Amos 4:6–8). The divine response to Solomon's prayer about drought is a promise of healing the land (7:13–14).

28–31 W. Shea ("Famines in the Early History of Egypt and Syro-Palestine," Diss. University of Michigan, 1976) describes famines in the ancient Near East as deriving from natural causes such as drought, disease, or insects (Gen 12:10; 26:1; 41:1–57; Ruth 1:1; 2 Sam 21:1; 24:13 // 1 Chr 21:12; 1 Kgs 18:1–2) or from warfare through the confiscation and burning of crops (Judg 6:3–6; 15:3–5) and siege (Lev 26:25–26; 2 Kgs 6:24–25; 25:1–3; 2 Chr 32:11; Isa 51:19; Jer 14:11–18; 16:4; 21:7–90; 52:6). The fear of famine and hope of escaping it are common themes (Ps 30:18–19; Job 5:20–22; Jer 5:12; 42:13–22).

"Pestilence" refers to diseases affecting animals (Exod 9:3; Ps 78:48–50) or men (Lev 26:25–26; Num 14:12; 2 Sam 24:13 // 1 Chr 21:12; Ezek 5:12; 7:15), and possibly, in this context, crops. Israel's unique geographical location on the sole land bridge between the continents of Europe, Asia, and Africa and the large amount of commerce through the area would have made the land subject to the easy spread of outbreaks and epidemics from the surrounding regions.

The technical vocabulary of ancient culture—its scientific terminology, the jargon of a trade, its pharmacopoeia and medical terminology—is often difficult to translate. Here ירקון and שדפון appear to designate plant diseases caused by extremes of moisture: ירקון derives from a root meaning "green" and suggests mildew that forms where there is too much moisture for the plants, while שדפון derives from a root meaning "scorch" and may refer to the rust fungi which form in overly dry conditions or to the premature arrival of the hot sirocco winds from the deserts south and east which shrivel crops before harvest (Gen 41:6; see O. Boronski, *Agriculture in Iron Age Israel* [Winona Lake: Eisenbrauns, 1987] 158–60).

The richness of Hebrew vocabulary (at least ten terms and possibly others) designating the locust in its various species and molting stages betrays the indelible impression their threat made in the biblical world; the devastation they were capable of bringing made them an apt image for invading armies destroying all in their path (Judg 6:5; Isa 33:4; Jer 46:22–23; 51:27; Joel 2:1–27; Nah 3:15). Only three of the hundreds of species in the area are characterized by the gregarious phase; combinations of moisture conditions favorable to reproduction and temperature-induced behavior appear to be responsible for the dreaded swarming that defoliates most natural and cultivated vegetation. ארבה is the general term for the locust in its adult flying stages; חסיל designates one of the successive molting stages (instars) during development. See J. Thompson, "Joel's Locusts in the Light of Near Eastern Parallels," *JNES* 14 (1955) 52–55.

While reciting this list of public calamities—warfare, famine, crop failures, locust invasions—the prayer turns to private concerns. The prayer of the nation (6:21, 25, 27) is in the final analysis the prayer of needy individuals; God alone knows the needs of each heart (Ps 139:4; Matt 6:8; Luke 16:15; John 2:24–25).

32–33 Although the author of Chronicles is often held to be the same as for Ezra-Nehemiah, these two collections breathe a different spirit in their attitudes toward foreigners and outsiders (Ezra 4:1–4; 9:1–3; Neh 9:2; 10:28–31; 13:1–3, 23–27). The prophets envisage the Gentiles coming to Jerusalem to worship the Lord (Isa 56:6–8; Ps 87; Zech 8:20–23; 14:16–21).

34–35 Although this plea for assistance in battle is not mentioned in the divine response to Solomon's prayer (7:12–22), the Chronicler is tireless in his effort to show that God did indeed answer this particular petition; the prayers of his people in time of battle issued in victory over the Egyptians (12:1–8), the Northern Kingdom (13:13–16), Zerah the Cushite (14:11–12), Arameans (18:31–32), Moabites and Ammonites (20:5–17), Edomites (25:7–11), and Assyrians (32:20–22). The frequency with which the Chronicler reiterates God's responsiveness in time of battle attests to the centrality of this prayer in the author's Solomon narrative. The message that God responds to prayer in times of military tension may have had in the Chronicler's mind an immediate homiletic value to the national aspirations of the restoration community.

36–39 The prayer turns again to the matter of captivity after defeat in battle (6:24–25); the attention given this disaster suggests that the report of Solomon's prayer in both Kings and Chronicles has been influenced by the exile to Babylon. Nevertheless, the reference to the exile does not exhaust the significance of this petition for the Chronicler; just as he had repeatedly illustrated the divine response to prayer in time of battle (see 6:34–35 above), so also he exhibits the operation of this petition both *distant and near* (6:36) in passages unique to the Chronicler: temporary captivity is reported for part of the population of Judah in nearby Samaria (28:6–15) and for Manasseh in distant Babylon (33:10–13).

For the practice of directing prayer toward Jerusalem, see Dan 6:11 [10] and Jonah 2:5 [4].

40–42 What ground can be offered that God should grant Solomon's requests? In the Kings account of the prayer, the ground for God's answer is his unique relationship to Israel deriving from the Exodus (1 Kgs 8:50–53). The Chronicler, however, omits these verses from his *Vorlage,* as he does with other material pertaining to the Exodus (see 6:4–6 above); instead he grounds the expectation of God's favorable response to Solomon's prayer in the divine promises to David. In place of the theme of election and redemption in the Exodus, the Chronicler introduces a free citation of Ps 132:1, 8–10. Ps 132 is itself a psalm of ascents recalling the righteous deeds of David in seeking a place for God to dwell, the movement of the ark to Jerusalem, and the divine choice of the city and David's dynasty; the entire psalm is a fitting citation in the context of the temple dedication.

"Your anointed ones" is potentially a reference to the priests mentioned immediately before. However, it would appear better to refer it to David and Solomon: the singular of Ps 132:10 which clearly referred to a king has been made plural in Chronicles to embrace both kings. Cf. the similar expansion from a singular referent (David, 1 Kgs 8:66) to both David and Solomon (2 Chr 7:10).

Scholars have long debated the correct understanding of the phrase חַסְדֵי דָוִיד; it occurs only here (6:42) and in Isa 55:3 (cited in Acts 13:34). H. Williamson (*JSS* 23 [1978] 31–49) has summarized the arguments most recently. The point at issue is whether to take the genitive as subjective ("the faithful deeds of David") or objective ("faithfulness to David"). The ancient versions are for the most part ambiguous on this question, and in any case would represent only the interpretation of the translators; although the preponderant use of the governed noun with חֶסֶד is a subjective genitive, this does admit of exceptions and cannot settle the issue. The strongest arguments in favor of taking the phrase with an objective genitive are that (1) this is the apparent usage in the only other occurrence in Isa 55:3 (though it has been debated there as well), and (2) the overall context of Solomon's prayer which recalls God's faithfulness to David (6:4–11, 15–17). This writer inclines, however, toward the subjective usage: (1) Even if one grants that the objective is correct for Isa 55:3, that would not settle the case for 2 Chronicles; some direct literary dependence on Isa 55 would have to be demonstrated. (2) Although the context does celebrate God's fidelity to David and does echo Nathan's oracle (1 Chr 17), there is another context that must be kept in mind. 2 Chr 6:42 may be a paraphrastic allusion to Ps 132:1; there is little question in that context that the faithful actions of David are in view (Ps 132:1–5). Rather than seek to explain 2 Chr 6:42 by Isa 55:3, the context from which it is drawn (though not a précise verbal parallel) should have a controlling influence. (3) The only other occurrences in Chronicles where the plural חסדי governs a genitive (a pronominal suffix, 2 Chr 32:32; 35:26) are both unquestionably subjective genitives; both refer to the faithful deeds of kings.

Explanation

Although the dedicatory prayer of Solomon is taken almost verbatim from the parallel passage (1 Kgs 8), the Chronicler has given the prayer a centrality and importance that it does not have in the earlier history. The importance the Chronicler attached to the prayer can be seen in several ways. (1) The prayer and the divine response to it are at the center of a large chiastic narrative embracing the entire account of Solomon's reign; see the discussion under "Literary Structure" in the introductory essay "The Chronicler's Solomon." Ordinarily in a chiastically structured narrative the items in the center of the chiasm represent the focal point of the narrative. (2) The prayer at the dedication is longer than the actual account of the building of the temple itself (2 Chr 3), unlike the parallel in 1 Kgs 6. Though length of treatment is not necessarily an index of importance, it seems safe to infer that the prayer of Solomon was of greater interest to the Chronicler and his audience than the details of the temple architecture. (3) It is widely recognized that the Chronicler's treatment of the divided kingdom is structured around the theme of immediate retribution, the coherence of deed and effect which produces blessing for obedience and judgment for disobedience. This basic conviction is articulated as a "charter" for the subsequent history in the divine response to Solomon's prayer (7:11–22), most particularly in 7:13–16, a passage unique to the Chronicler. For the Chronicler then, the theology of immediate retribution grows out of Solomon's own prayer. The author has grounded the leitmotif of the remainder of his history in this prayer, giving the prayer a centrality not found in Kings. This also comports well with the tendency of the Chronicler to use speech materials to give prominence to his theological viewpoints.

Solomon's prayer in both histories appears to be influenced by an exilic or post-exilic setting: the prayer presumes the possibility of exile and return (6:24–25, 36–39) and emphasizes the temple as a place toward which one prays (6:20, 21, 26, 29, 32, 34, 38) rather than as a place of sacrifice. The petitions are sufficiently general that one might suggest the prayer had liturgical use through a large part of Israel's history, a fact which would also explain its importance to post-exilic generations.

In 2 Chr 6 Solomon is performing the duties of a king toward the cult and takes on almost a priestly role through his officiation. It is interesting to compare this prayer with John 17, a passage popularly called the "high priestly prayer of Jesus." Both prayers are concerned with the glory of God, manifest in the cloud at the temple and in the presence of the Son of God

(John 17:1, 5, 10, 22, 24); both prayers constitute somewhat of a "charter" for the subsequent history of the people of God and are basically oriented to generations to follow (John 17:6, 9, 20). Both prayers occur at the completion of work undertaken by divine appointment (5:1; 6:10–11; John 17:4); both are concerned to solicit divine protection for those who follow (John 17:11–12, 15). But for all of their similarities, two prayers could hardly contrast more as representatives of the old and the new covenant.

The dedicatory prayer of Solomon developed the theme of the temple as a place for prayer, the prayer of Jew and Gentile alike; the same theme is developed in the accounts of the cleansing of the temple in the NT (Matt 21:13; Mark 11:17; Luke 19:46; John 2:16–17; see Isa 56:7).

Dedicatory Festival and Divine Response (7:1–22)

Bibliography

Braun, R. "Chronicles, Ezra, and Nehemiah: Theology and Literary History." In *Studies in the Historical Books of the Old Testament*, ed. J. A. Emerton. VTSup 30. Leiden: E. J. Brill, 1979. **Japhet, S.** "Conquest and Settlement in Chronicles." *JBL* 98 (1979) 205–18. **Williamson, H.** "Eschatology in Chronicles." *TynBul* 28 (1977) 115–54.

Translation

[1]When Solomon finished praying, fire descended from heaven and consumed the burnt offering and the sacrifices, and the glory of Yahweh filled the temple. [2]The priests were not able to enter the temple of Yahweh because the glory of Yahweh had filled the temple of Yahweh. [3]All the children of Israel were watching while the fire descended and the glory of Yahweh was above the temple; they bowed down on the pavement with their faces on the ground; they worshiped and praised Yahweh, "for he is good, his faithfulness is everlasting."

[4]The king and all the people were offering sacrifices before Yahweh. [5]King Solomon offered a sacrifice of twenty-two thousand oxen and a hundred and twenty thousand sheep. The king and all the people dedicated the temple of God. [6]The priests stood at their posts, as did the Levites who had Yahweh's musical instruments[a] which King David had made[b] for giving thanks to Yahweh—"for his faithfulness is everlasting"—and which David had used when he offered praise. Opposite them, the priests were blowing trumpets, while all Israel was standing.

[7]Solomon consecrated the middle of the courtyard in front of the temple of Yahweh; he offered the burnt offerings[a] and the fat of the fellowship offerings there since the bronze altar that Solomon had made[b] could not accommodate the burnt offering, grain offering, and fat portions.

[8]Solomon also observed the festival at that time for seven days, and all Israel with him—an exceeding great assembly—from Lebo-hamath to the brook of Egypt. [9]On the eighth day they held an assembly—for they had observed the dedication of the altar for seven days and the festival for seven days; [10]so on the twenty-third day of the seventh month he sent the people to their tents, happy and with merry hearts because of the good Yahweh had done for David and Solomon and Israel his people.

[11]Solomon completed the temple of Yahweh and the royal palace; he succeeded in all that he intended to do in Yahweh's temple and in his palace. [12]Then Yahweh appeared to Solomon at night, and he said to him,

"I have heard your prayer and have chosen this place as mine for a temple for sacrifices.

[13]"If I shut up the heavens so there is no rain, or command the locust to devour the land, or send a pestilence against my people, [14]if my people who are called by my name will humble themselves, and pray, and seek my face, and turn from their wicked ways, then will I hear from heaven; I will forgive their sin and heal their land.

¹⁵ *"Now my eyes will be open and my ears attentive to prayer in this place.*
¹⁶*Now I have chosen and consecrated this temple that my name should be there
forever, my eyes and my heart there for all time.*

¹⁷ *"As for you, if you will walk before me just as your father David did,
doing all I command you, if you observe all my statutes and precepts,* ¹⁸*then I
will establish the throne of your kingdom*^a *just as I covenanted*^b *with David
your father, saying, 'You will never fail to have a man ruling*^c *in Israel.'*

¹⁹ *"But if you*^a *turn away and forsake my statutes and commandments which
I have set before you, and you go and serve other gods and worship them,*
²⁰*then I will uproot them*^a *from my land that I gave them and this temple that
I consecrated for my name; I will cast*^b *them from my presence and make them*^c
an object of ridicule and a taunt among all peoples.

²¹ *"And as for this temple which is*^a *so imposing,*^b *it will be appalling to all
who pass by. They will say, 'Why has Yahweh done such a thing to this land
and this temple?'* ²²*People will answer, 'It is because they forsook Yahweh the
God of their fathers who brought them from the land of Egypt. They laid hold
of other gods and worshiped and served them; therefore, he brought against
them all this disaster.'"*

Notes

6.a. The construction is ambiguous; the sense could be either "Yahweh's instruments of
music" (cf. NIV) or "instruments of music to the LORD" (cf. NEB, RSV). Cf. the constructions in 1
Chr 16:42; Neh 12:36.

6.b. See 1 Chr 23:5, 2 Chr 29:26–30; Amos 6:5.

7.a. The parallel text at 1 Kgs 8:64 adds ואת המנחה, also mentioned in 7b // 1 Kgs 8:64b.
Failure to mention the grain offerings in the first half of the verse may reflect a haplogr or
homoioarchon, but no extant textual evidence includes the words at this point.

7.b. See 2 Chr 4:1.

18.a. 1 Kgs 9:5 adds "over Israel forever."

18.b. Instead of כרתי, 1 Kgs 9:5 has דברתי "I spoke."

18.c. Instead of "a man ruling in Israel," 1 Kgs 9:5 has "a man on the throne of Israel."
Cf. Mic 5:2.

19.a. Note the shift to 2d person pl; see the discussion under *Form/Structure/Setting*.

20.a. Note shift to 3d person pl. G, Syr, and Vg contain 2d pl for the 3d pl suffs in this
verse; though the evidence from the versions is fairly uniform and may suggest an alternative
Heb. text, it is equally probable that they reflect the influence of the MT context. See Allen,
GC 2:97.

20.b. 1 Kgs 9:7, אשלח.

20.c. Cf. 1 Kgs 9:7, "And Israel will become. . . ." Though the suff is sg, it appears in the
context to refer to the people, not to the temple, the fate of which is taken up in the next
verse. Contrast Rudolph, 217.

21.a. Contrast 1 Kgs 9:8, יהיה.

21.b. G^L adds ἐρημωθήσεται, and Tg יהא חרוב, both additions which suggest an original
text that contained יהיה לעיין, "[this temple] shall be ruins," lost through haplogr due to
the similar appearance of עליון; alternatively these additions could be assimilations toward
Mic 3:12.

Form/Structure/Setting

2 Chr 7 corresponds closely to the parallel text at 1 Kgs 8:54–9:9. The
Chronicler has modified the material in his source through additions and

deletions to achieve the chiastic structure he used to present the reign of Solomon (see "Literary Structure" in the introductory essay, "The Chronicler's Solomon") or to otherwise reflect his particular concerns.

The fire/cloud theophany of 7:1b–3 appears to duplicate the account in 5:13–14. A duplication of this sort often prompts biblical scholars to assign the accounts to different editorial hands—either the first account (Rudolph) or the second account (Galling) will be assigned to a later redactor while the other is derived from the Chronicler himself. However, this sort of speculation is unnecessary if the author's architecture for the entire narrative is appreciated; in a chiastic narrative repetition would be expected.

The divine response to Solomon's prayer contains an address to Solomon (7:12–18) and an address to the people (7:19–22); both of these sections parallel Solomon's earlier address to God (6:12–42) and to the people (6:1–11). The same themes occur in both sets of addresses, once again showing the contours of a chiastic narrative.

The addition at 7:6 is amenable to similar treatment. The Chronicler's concern with the Levitical musicians is well known and is reflected in the inclusion of the material in 7:6, but that is only part of the story; the note about the Levitical musicians is the necessary parallel to 5:12–13.

Other modifications of the parallel text (additions at 7:9b–10a, 12b–15 and the omission of 1 Kgs 8:54b–61) seem better understood in other ways; see *Comment*.

The paragraphs in the chapter are all marked by the use of the explicit subject "Solomon" (7:1, 4–5, 7, 8, 11). There is some ambiguity in this regard with reference to 7:4–5; the circumstantial clause (7:4) could be viewed as closing the previous paragraph, and the repetition of 7:5 would begin the next paragraph (often called by discourse analysts "tail-head linkage," when similar wording ends one paragraph and begins the next), or the repetition could be viewed as a major device marking the onset of a new section. The latter approach is contextually more appropriate—both the people and Solomon offered sacrifices, but detail is given regarding Solomon's offerings.

Comment

1–3 This second report of the appearance of the fire and glory of Yahweh parallels the earlier account (5:13–14) and probably refers to the same incident, narrated twice to achieve the literary balance of a chiasm. It should be compared with other appearances of fire from Yahweh showing approval of a sanctuary or sacrifice (1 Chr 21 // 2 Sam 24; Exod 40:34–38; 1 Kgs 18; Judg 6:20–22).

A second approach to the two passages construes them in chronological sequence rather than as a duplicate account for purposes of literary balance; in this case the initial appearance was confined to the priests inside (5:13–14), while the latter incident was visible to all the people (7:3).

As previously indicated a third treatment of the two accounts excises one or the other as nonoriginal; see *Form/Structure/Setting* in chaps. 5 and 7. The abrupt introduction of previously unmentioned sacrifices in 7:1, when the offerings of the king and people are not mentioned until 7:4, has been viewed as an argument that 7:1–3 represents a later intrusion into the text (Galling, 90; see Lemke, *Synoptic Studies,* 104). However, if the two narratives of the descent of the fire and glory are regarded as two accounts of a single incident, the sacrifices consumed in 7:1 would be associated with those accompanying the movement and placement of the ark (5:4–6); these initial sacrifices were followed by others (7:4).

4–7 The Chronicler has omitted Solomon's blessing the people as reported in the parallel at 1 Kgs 8:54b–61. Gray (*I and II Kings,* 230) and C-M (347) suggest this omission reflects the Chronicler's efforts to protect the monopoly of the cultic personnel over the function of blessing the people (Num 6:23); this explanation is scarcely compelling since the author did not show a similar aversion in 6:3–4, 13. The context itself offers a more satisfying explanation: the appeal of 6:40–42 is answered with an immediate divine response, an immediacy calling for omission of the blessing in the parallel account (Ackroyd, 114).

The large number of sacrifices (also 1 Kgs 8:63) presumably provided food for the people during the fifteen days of celebration to follow (7:8–10). The fat of the fellowship offerings was burned before the people could partake (Lev 3). Wenham ("Large Numbers," *TynBul* 18 [1967] 49) notes that 22,000 oxen and 120,000 sheep would require twenty sacrifices a minute for ten hours a day for twelve days; the Chronicler probably intends these figures as hyperbole. Cf. the figures at the time of Hezekiah (29:32–36) and Josiah (35:7–9).

As part of his overall chiastic structuring of the Solomon narrative the Chronicler has introduced a note regarding the Levitical musicians. The same refrain is frequently heard in Chronicles (1 Chr 16:34, 41; 2 Chr 5:13; 7:3, 6; 20:21).

8–10 The Feast of Tabernacles was a pilgrimage festival (Lev 23:33–43) and would have brought many celebrants to Jerusalem; perhaps the scheduling of the dedication of the temple in the preceding week sought to take advantage of the large congregation that would come. The assembly provided another occasion for one of the Chronicler's favorite themes, that "all Israel" united in the observance (1 Chr 9:1; 11:1–4; 12:38–40; 13:1–8; 14:8; 15:3, 28; 16:1–3; 18:14; 19:17; 21:1–5; 22:17; 23:1–2; 28:1–8; 29:21–26; 2 Chr 1:1–3; 5:2–6; 6:3–13; 7:8–10; 9:30; 10:1–3, 16; 11:3, 13–17; 12:1; 13:4, 15; 18:16; 24:5; 28:23; 29:24; 30:1–13, 23–27; 31:6; 34:6–9, 33).

Another of the Chronicler's distinctive emphases is also present: his desire to parallel David and Solomon as much as possible; see "Solomon as a Second David" in the introductory essay, "The Chronicler's Solomon." He modifies his *Vorlage* at 1 Kgs 8:66 ("David his servant") by speaking instead of "David and Solomon" (cf. 2 Chr 11:17). Although he follows 1 Kgs 8:66 in mentioning that the congregation had come from the maximum extent of the kingdom, at 1 Chr 13:5 he had already modified the parallel text (2 Sam 6:1) to show David presiding over an assembly from the same extent ("from the Shihor of Egypt to Lebo-hamath"), thereby further perfecting the parallel of David and Solomon.

Lebo-hamath and the Wadi of Egypt are the ideal boundaries of Israel, the possession promised to the patriarchs (Gen 15:18; Num 34:5, 8; Josh

15:4, 47; 2 Kgs 14:25; 24:7; Isa 27:12; Ezek 47:15, 19; 48:1—there is some variation in these references). Lebo-hamath has comnmonly been understood to mean "the entrance to Hamath," i.e., the southern boundary of the territory controlled by Hamath, perhaps near Riblah; however, it is probably more correctly understood as the name of a city identified with Libweh on the Orontes River below Riblah. The southern boundary is here given as the Wadi of Egypt, identified with the Wadi-el-Arish emptying from the middle of the Sinai into the Mediterranean. The relation of this "Wadi of Egypt" to the term "Shihor" (1 Chr 13:5; Isa 23:3; Jer 2:18; Josh 13:3) is debated. It was clearly a waterway thought to mark the boundary of Egypt and could refer to one of the eastern branches in the Nile Delta; others regard the designation "Shihor" as synonymous with "Wadi of Egypt." See the discussion by S. Japhet, *JBL* 98 (1979) 208–10.

The Chronicler appears to be elaborating on 1 Kgs 8:65 to clarify the precise sequence of events. The dedication festival lasted seven days, from the eighth to the fourteenth of the month, and was followed by the regular observance of the Feast of Tabernacles from the fifteenth to the twenty-second day of the month. The eighth day (7:9; cf. Lev 23:39) would be the final convocation on the twenty-second, followed by dismissal on the twenty-third day of the month (7:10). Again a parallel has been achieved with David who similarly dismissed a national assembly (1 Chr 16:1–3, 43). The celebration would have included the Day of Atonement (Lev 23:26–32; Lev 16) on the tenth day, but the author is silent about it. A similar two-week observance of the temple dedications occurred under Hezekiah (30:23). See the discussions in J. Shaver, *Torah*, 143–44; A. Welch, *Work*, 37; M. Fishbane, *Interpretation*, 153.

11–22 This second appearance (1 Kgs 9:2) of God to Solomon provides the divine response to his prayer (6:14–42). In spite of its proximate juxtaposition to the prayer in both Kings and Chronicles, this second appearance came about thirteen years later, after Solomon had completed the work on his palace as well (7:11; 1 Kgs 7:1; 9:10).

The response as presented in Chronicles follows the parallel text (1 Kgs 9:1–9) fairly closely with one pivotal exception. The material in 7:12b–15 is unique to Chronicles and is programmatic for the author's presentation of the divided kingdoms (2 Chr 10–36). In 7:14, a passage more familiar than any other from his work, the Chronicler specifically enunciates the literary program for his "theology of immediate retribution." In the remainder of his record the author virtually without fail recasts the accounts in his *Vorlage* to demonstrate his conviction that both obedience and transgression have immediate consequences of blessing or punishment. See the essay introducing 2 Chr 10–36, "Reward and Punishment in Chronicles: The Theology of Immediate Retribution."

18 The Chronicler has introduced two modifications to the parallel text at 1 Kgs 9:5. For the more general "spoke to" or "promised" (דברתי) of Kings the Chronicler has substituted the specific language of covenant making (כרתי). Though the possibility exists of a textual confusion due to the similarity of the two terms, no extant evidence attests to alternative texts, and the modification should be viewed as deliberate.

But how was the post-exilic community to view the eternality of the Davidic covenant when they were without a king and subject to foreign domination? The second modification the Chronicler has made at this point may address the needs of the post-exilic community: for the "you shall never fail to have a man on the throne of Israel" in 1 Kgs 9:5, the Chronicler has substituted "you shall never fail to have a man to rule over Israel," language parallel to Mic 5:1 [2]. The author gives expression to his messianic or royalist hopes: though the throne of Israel is vacant, the continuity of the Davidic dynasty remains. The dynastic promise has not lost its validity even with the loss of the throne.

19–22 Having spoken to Solomon, God now speaks to the people; note the shift to 2d person plural in 7:19. At the dedication of the temple in all its magnificence, there is the reminder of what it could and did become: an object of ridicule, the butt of a joke, the point of a proverb (Deut 28:37; Jer 24:9).

Explanation

Solomon's prayer and God's response form the center of the author's Solomon narrative; the Chronicler will remain through the rest of his history concerned to show that God did indeed keep his promise to Solomon to answer with favor the prayers and repentance of his people. It is particularly in his addition of 7:13–15 to God's response that the Chronicler articulates most clearly the theological perspective supporting his historiographical goals. In his accounts of the reigns of the kings of Judah the Chronicler tirelessly exhibits the validity of his retributive convictions; he proceeds by taking details from the accounts as he found them in Kings, but by adding supporting and inciting incidents to provide the rationale for reward or punishment.

The basic theological questions of the restoration community revolved around its relationship to the Israel of the past—what validity did the promises of God regarding the temple and the house of David have for a community that had no king, was under foreign domination, and had only in recent history rebuilt the former temple that had been destroyed? Solomon's prayer presumably had liturgical use through much of the first temple period and was probably recited regularly in the liturgy of the post-exilic temple. The Chronicler was seeking to demonstrate the validity of those petitions and God's response through history, and by implication for his own generation as well. Though the temple had once been destroyed, God's choice of Jerusalem was still valid; though no descendant of David sat on a throne, the Davidic line had not failed (7:18). One would yet come whose origins are of old, from ancient times, to be ruler over Israel (Mic 5:2).

Solomonic Miscellany: More Dealings with Hiram, Building Projects, Cultic Observances (8:1–18)

Bibliography

Fensham, F. "The Treaty between Solomon and Hiram and the Alalakh Tablets." *JBL* 79 (1960) 59–60. ———. "The Treaty between the Israelites and Tyrians." *Congress Volume, Rome, 1968.* VTSup 17 Leiden: E. J. Brill, 1968. 71–87. **Horn, S.** "Who Was Solomon's Egyptian Father-in-Law?" *BR* 12 (1967) 3–7. **Katzenstein, H.** *The History of Tyre.* **Kitchen, K.** *The Third Intermediate Period in Egypt.* **Mazar, B.** "The Aramean Empire and Its Relations with Israel." *BA* 25 (1962) 97–120. **Redford, D.** "Studies in the Relations between Palestine and Egypt during the First Millennium B.C.: II. The Twenty-second Dynasty." *JAOS* 93 (1973) 3–17.

Translation

[1] *And it came about at the end of the twenty years during which Solomon built the temple of Yahweh and his own palace* [2] *that Solomon rebuilt the cities that Hiram had given to Solomon, and he settled Israelites there.*

[3] [a] *Solomon went to Hamath-zobah and conquered it.* [4] *He also rebuilt Tadmor* [a] *in the desert as well as all the store cities he built in Hamath.* [5] *He rebuilt Upper Beth Horon and Lower Beth Horon as fortress cities with walls, gates, and bars,* [6] *as well as Baalath and all the store cities that belonged to Solomon, all the cities for chariots and horses—anything Solomon desired, whatever he wanted to build in Jerusalem, Lebanon, and all the territory under his rule.*

[7] *As for all the people who were left from the Hittites, Amorites, Perizzites, Hivvites, and Jebusites (these peoples were not of Israel),* [8] *from their descendants who remained after them in the land—those whom the Israelites had not destroyed* [a]*—Solomon conscripted them to forced labor* [b] *to this very day.* [9] *But from among the Israelites* [a] *Solomon did not make slaves for his work;* [b] *they were soldiers, commanders of his officers* [c] *and commanders of his chariots and horsemen,* [10] *and they were his chief officers, two hundred* [a] *fifty who supervised the people.* [b]

[11] *Solomon brought the daughter of Pharaoh up from the City of David to the place he had built for her, for he said, "No wife of mine will dwell in the house of David* [a] *king of Israel, for the places where the ark of Yahweh has been are holy."*

[12] *Then Solomon sacrificed burnt offerings to Yahweh on the altar of Yahweh which he had built in front of the portico;* [13] *in accordance with the command of Moses he made offerings each day, on sabbaths, at the new moon, and at the three annual appointed feasts (the Feast of Unleavened Bread, the Feast of Weeks, and the Feast of Tabernacles).* [14] *Following the practice of his father David he appointed the divisions of priests for their service, the Levites for their duties to offer praise and to attend the priests as required day in and day out, and the gatekeepers in their divisions for each gate—for such was the instruction of David the man of God.* [15] *They did not neglect any commandment of the king concerning the priests and Levites in any respect, including the matter of the treasuries.*

[16] *All the work of Solomon was carried out, from* [a] *the day the foundation of the temple of Yahweh was laid until its completion; the temple of Yahweh was finished.* [b]
[17] *Then Solomon went to Ezion-geber and Elath on the seacoast in the land of Edom;* [18] *Hiram sent him ships under the command of his own officers, along with crews who knew the sea, and they went with Solomon's servants to Ophir and took from there four hundred and fifty* [a] *talents of gold and brought it to King Solomon.*

Notes

3.a. Chr omits 1 Kgs 9:14–17a.

4.a. 1 Kgs 9:18, K = Tamar; some MSS, G[L], Syr, Tg, and Vg with Q and 2 Chr 8:4, = Tadmor. See *Comment.*

8.a. 1 Kgs 9:21, אשר לא יכלו בני ישראל להחרימם "whom the Israelites had not been able to exterminate."

8.b. One MS, Syr, and 1 Kgs 9:21 = מס עבד; see *Comment* at 2:17.

9.a. The אשר is missing in a few MSS and in 1 Kgs 9:22; it was either missing in the *Vorlage* or ignored by the translators of G, Syr, and Vg. Its inclusion would clearly represent a more difficult text: it is unclear where the long dependent clause would join a main clause.

9.b. G τῆς βασιλεία αὐτοῦ = למלכותו.

9.c. 1 Kgs 9:22, שריו ושלשיו.

10.a. Par, 520; 1 Kgs 9:23, 550; Bas (2:35), 3,600.

10.b. 1 Kgs 9:23 adds "who were doing the work."

11.a. G ἐν πόλει Δαυίδ = בעיר דויד.

16.a. The common idiom is . . . עד . . . מן (Gen 10:19; 19:4; 46:34; et al.). The versions translate "from" of necessity, and their evidence should not be though to attest to a text with מן.

16.b. G ἕως οὗ ἐτελείωσεν Σαλωμὼν τὸν οἶκον κυρίου = עד כלות שלמה בית יהוה. The MT is correct: the last clause of 8:16 is properly parallel to the last clause of 1 Kgs 9:25; the material unique to Chr (8:13–16a) has been inserted before the statement that the temple was completed.

18.a. 1 Kgs 9:28, 420; Syr and Josephus (*Ant.* 8:164), 400.

Form/Structure/Setting

See the parallel text at 1 Kgs 9:10–28. Although the Chronicler has characteristically made some omissions (1 Kgs 9:15–16) and additions (8:11b, 13–16), the sequence of materials remains essentially the same in both histories and attests to direct dependence on the Kings account, whatever other sources the author may have had.

In the overall chiastic structure that shapes the Chronicler's account of Solomon, 8:1–16 forms the parallel to 2:17–5:1; these sections have in common their emphasis on construction projects (3:1–4:22; 8:1–6), the use of gentile labor (2:17–18; 8:7–10), and the completion of the temple (5:1; 8:16). Though 8:1–6 is concerned with noncultic construction, the section is linked to 3:1–5:1 by a description of the ceremonial provisions Solomon had made for the temple (8:12–15). Both sections end with a reference to the treasuries and the statement that the work was finished (5:1; 8:15–16); unless the Chronicler intends to associate 8:16 and 5:1, 8:16 is quite out of place—it reopens the subject of the temple construction and completion well after that narration has already been completed. See "Literary Structure" in the introductory essay, "The Chronicler's Solomon."

The maritime arrangements Solomon made with Hiram (8:17–18) rhetorically belong with chap. 9 where they are mentioned twice again (9:10, 21). The paragraphing devices used in this section are quite diverse:

(1) The introductory ויהי with a temporal phrase (8:1).
(2) Repeated explicit subject (8:3).
(3) Casus pendens (8:7).
(4) Initial direct object (8:11).
(5) Temporal marker with an explicit subject (8:12, 17). Gray (*I and II Kings,* 28, 252) regards the use of asyndetic אז as betraying the presence of an annalistic source in Kings, though this would not follow for Chronicles.

Of these devices, items (3) and (4) are aptly called "topicalization" devices; they redirect the reader's attention to the new subject by virtue of their clause initial position. Both devices have other grammatical functions in different contexts.

Comment

1–2 The Chronicler's record presents a sharp contrast to the earlier account (1 Kgs 9:1–13). In Kings, Solomon cedes the cities to Hiram either to satisfy an outstanding debt (1 Kgs 9:11) or as payment for additional gold needed to complete the work (1 Kgs 9:14). The terms of the arrangement must have been above and beyond the previously contracted annual payment (1 Kgs 5:10–11; 2 Chr 2:10). Hiram finds the cities worthless; he applied the name of a town in the territory of Asher ("Cabul," Josh 19:27) contiguous with his own borders to the entire twenty cities (1 Kgs 9:13). Hiram's designation preserves an etiological element; the town is generally identified with modern Kabul, nine miles southeast of Acre.

In Chronicles, the picture is quite different: it is Hiram who gives the cities to Solomon. Scholars have generally followed one of three different approaches to this issue: either (1) the Chronicler has fabricated the account for theological reasons, or (2) the text of Kings he had before him was corrupt, or (3) the two accounts can be historically harmonized.

Perhaps the most common reaction to the Chronicler's rewriting of this incident is to regard it as a blatant falsification undertaken with theological motivation (Wellhausen, *Prolegomena,* 187; Kittel, 119; Galling, 97; C-M, 352; Coggins, 174; Throntveit, 100–102; et al.). The Chronicler is thought to have such a high regard for Solomon that it would be inconceivable (1) for him to part with any Israelite territory or (2) for him to be in financial straits (9:13–28). There can be no real question that the Chronicler's theology and positive evaluation of Solomon have played a major role in shaping his Solomon narrative; a modification at this point would certainly be in line with his general idealization of the king. However, one must also ask whether this explanation is alone adequate. The Chronicler frequently assumes the audience's knowledge of the parallel account; in this context he relies on the reader's prior familiarity with the earlier history in connection with Solomon's otherwise unmentioned marriage to Pharaoh's daughter (8:11; 1 Kgs 3:1; 7:8; 9:16, 24; 11:1). It does not seem likely that such a blatant reversal of the earlier record would be acceptable to his audience or escape notice without undermining the author's own credibility.

Willi (*Die Chronik*, 75–78) argues that the Chronicler's *Vorlage* for 8:1–6 was corrupt and that the divergencies in his record represent his best efforts to salvage the text before him. While some of Willi's suggestions are ingenious and at least plausible, the variations between 8:1–6 and 1 Kgs 9:10–19 are much wider than textual difficulties could account for. Williamson (228–29), who is sympathetic to Willi's suggestions, rejected explaining the changes as motivated by theological concerns alone because of the presumed familiarity on the part of the audience; the same concerns would be valid in this case. If the audience were familiar with the exchange of cities as described in Kings, the Chronicler himself should have that same knowledge; the only other conclusion is the reverse, that the Chronicler did not presume familiarity with the narrative on the part of the audience.

Efforts to harmonize the two accounts have taken two forms: either (1) there was a swap of territory for mutual strategic advantage, in which Solomon ceded Israelite cities in exhange for some Phoenician cities mentioned only by the Chronicler, or (2) the Chronicler presents the sequel to Hiram's displeasure with the cities, i.e, he returned them to Solomon. The suggestion of a mutual exchange of territory is not very convincing; its sole warrant is the need to explain both accounts, and the direct dependence of 8:1 on 1 Kgs 9:10 would indicate that they refer to the same incident. If Hiram had found the cities unacceptable payment, it is probable that the cities would be returned with demand for other payment, or that they would be held as "mortgage" or "collateral" until Solomon's debt was liquidated. 1 Kgs 9:13 may imply that since the cities were worthless to Hiram, they would have been returned; Josephus (*Ant.* 8:142) reaches the same conclusion by adding the note that Hiram "sent word to Solomon that he had no use for the cities." The Chronicler's account is best understood as both preserving the image of Solomon and providing a less onerous sequel to Kings.

The Chronicler also does not mention that Pharaoh captured and depopulated Gezer before giving it to Solomon as part of his daughter's dowry (1 Kgs 9:16); see *Comment* on 2:16. Such an Egyptian incursion through Philistine territory would have been of considerable mutual advantage for Israel and Egypt. This omission was no doubt deliberate: the Chronicler may have considered it depreciating to Solomon to have a foreigner conquer a city for him (Rudolph, 219); the Chronicler is uniformly opposed to foreign alliances in the remainder of his history. The giving of a Pharaoh's daughter in marriage to a foreigner was all but unthinkable in the earlier centuries of Egyptian history—the traffic was always the other way, that of Pharaoh's taking the daughters and sisters of foreigners as wives in diplomatic marriages. Though it is not without parallel (contra Malamat, *BAR* [1979] 59; cf. Kitchen, *TIPE*, 280–82), this marriage and the attendant dowry were at least remarkable, as attested by the frequency with which Pharaoh's daughter is mentioned in 1 Kings (3:1; 7:8; 9:16, 24; 11:1). Lemke (*Synoptic Studies*, 113) feels that the opposite point could be made about the Chronicler's omission: such an event so illustrative of the power and prestige of Solomon would hardly have been dropped from the narrative! Again the precariousness and subjectivity of trying to read the author's mind are apparent. Lemke also questions whether 1 Kgs 9:16 was even in the Chronicler's *Vorlage*—the verse is not found in the major MSS of Bas or G^L, but is found only in hexaplaric MSS, where it is marked with an asterisk as an addition from the Hebrew; however, its omission in Bas could easily be the result of a haplography with the word *Gezer* in 1 Kgs 9:17a. See D. Gooding, "Text-Sequence and Translation-Revision in 3 Reigns IX, 10–X, 33," *VT* 19 (1969) 448–63.

3–6   This is the only reference in Chronicles to the military prowess of Solomon the man of peace (1 Chr 22:9). The parallel account (1 Kgs 9:17–19) on the surface appears to confine itself to building projects within the territorial control of Solomon and does not speak of the conquest of Hamath far to the north. Willi (*Die Chronik*, 76–77) regards the reference to Hamath as having developed from the Chronicler's effort to reconstruct a damaged *Vorlage*; the Chronicler read חֹמַת from the word חֹמָה, "wall" (1 Kgs 9:15); cf. Williamson, 229.

The identity of one city in particular has occasioned considerable discussion. Where the *kethib* of 1 Kgs 9:18 speaks of the fortification of Tamar, a small city near the southern end of the Dead Sea (Ezek 47:18–19; 48:28), the *qere* of that verse and 2 Chr 8:4 speak instead of Tadmor, the great caravan city in the Syrian desert 120 miles northeast of Damascus, known in the later Greek sources as Palmyra. Commentators have been quick to see here another effort on the part of the Chronicler to enhance the glory of Solomon: for the little Tamar, possibly insignificant to the author in the post-exilic period, the Chronicler substitutes the flourishing and prominent Tadmor, a more worthy object of Solomon's efforts. This explanation, however, is tenuous due to uncertainty about the text of Kings. The reading Tadmor is not only found in the *qere* of Kings, but is also attested in a number of Hebrew MSS, in the Lucianic texts of Bas, the Syro-hexapla, Vulgate, and Josephus (*Ant.* 8:153–154). Even the spellings ιεθερμάθ or θέρμαθ in G MSS may readily be understood as reflecting an underlying Tadmor rather than Tamar (Lemke, *Synoptic Studies*, 115; Gerleman, *Synoptic Studies*, 25). It is not at all clear that the Chronicler's *Vorlage* contained Tamar.

Whatever the condition of his *Vorlage*, it is clearly a part of the Chronicler's record that the kingdom under David and Solomon had reached its ideal borders (7:8; 1 Chr 13:5; 18:3). If David had extended control as far as Hamath, what could be more natural than that Solomon would campaign against Hamath? The mention of Tadmor in northern Syria may have prompted his speaking also of the conquest of Hamath. The Chronicler had already mentioned that Solomon's borders almost reached that far (7:8), and this passage reports Solomon's extension of his borders to include that great city (cf. 9:26). The designation Hamath-zobah may reflect the Assyrian-Babylonian-Persian system of provincial administration (Williamson, *IBC*, 84). Solomon did not succeed in maintaining these far northern boundaries (1 Kgs 11:23–25).

By pairing Hamath and Tadmor the Chronicler shows Solomon's sovereignty over all major arteries for trade with Mesopotamia: the main overland route (Hamath) and the desert shortcut (Tadmor) are in his control. Domination of these cities on the trade routes to the north was fundamental to Solomon's commercial endeavors and wealth.

Upper and *Lower Beth Horon* sit astride a ridge rising from the Valley of Aijalon to the plateau just north of Jerusalem. The road traversing this route provided Jerusalem's major link with the international coastal highway, the so-called Via Maris; conversely it also represented the approach from which Jerusalem was most vulnerable. The frequency with which it is mentioned in battle reports attests to its strategic importance (Josh 10:10–11; 1 Sam 13:15–18; 14:31, 46; 1 Chron 14:8–17 // 2 Sam 5:17–25). According to Egyptian records Shishak's attack came up this road; in 1917 British troops fought along the ridge in stormy weather. The most graphic account reports the defeat of Seron by the armies of Judas Maccabeus in 166 B.C. (1 Macc 3:13–24); after his abortive effort to intervene following the outbreak of the first Jewish revolt, Cestius Gallus and the Roman Twelfth Legion suffered disastrous losses along the Beth Horon ridge during their retreat (Josephus, *J.W.* 2:278–486).

There are two possible candidates for the location of Baalath. Since the immediate context in Chronicles concerns the Gezer–Beth Horon–Jerusalem road, Josephus is likely correct in his assertion that it was near Gezer (*Ant.* 8:152); it was probably the site named in the territory originally allocated to Dan (Josh 19:44). The other possible identification is not as probable: the mention of Tamar south of the Dead Sea in the parallel text (1 Kgs 9:18) might warrant identification with the Baalath in the territory of Simeon (Josh 19:8). If a small textual error were allowed, Baalath could refer instead to Baalah, a name for Kiriath-jearim (1 Chr 13:6). Kiriath-jearim was along the second route into the central Benjamin plateau; the mention of Kiriath-jearim alongside the Beth Horons would then refer to fortification of both routes up from the Valley of Aijalon. Cf. G^B βαλάα with G^A βαλάαθ.

11 The Chronicler presumes that his audience is already familiar with the diplomatic marriage of Solomon and Pharaoh's daughter; see *Comment* at 8:1–2. Both accounts (here and 1 Kgs 9:24; cf. 1 Kgs 3:1) report that Solomon moved the daughter of Pharaoh from the City of David to the quarters he had built for her; only the Chronicler adds the reason for the transfer—the sanctifying presence of the ark required her removal.

The Chronicler may be using Solomon's action to provide sanction for a practice known more clearly in later Judaism. During the second temple period women could not enter the sanctuary or proceed beyond the special "court of the women" in the temple precincts except for sacrificial purposes; similarly women were segregated from men in synagogue worship, and men alone had access to the room where the Torah shrine ("the ark") was housed. The wording "no wife of mine" does imply that gender was the issue rather than the fact that Pharaoh's daughter was a Gentile (1 Kgs 11:1–8; Ezek 44:9).

12–15 The author expands his source (1 Kgs 9:25) with emphasis on the detailed observance of the Mosaic commands (Lev 23:1–37; Num 28–29) and Davidic prescriptions (1 Chr 23–26); he specifies the three annual feasts mentioned in Kings and adds the observance of weekly sabbaths and the new moon. The text is ambiguous regarding the extent of the king's participation; it could cover any degree of involvement from simply decreeing the observances to personal officiation in the worship.

16 This is the second occasion that the Chronicler reports the completion of the temple; the verse in unique to Chronicles and forms the rhetorical counterpart to 5:1 as part of the author's overall chiastic structuring of his Solomon narrative. See the discussion in *Form/Structure/Setting*.

17–18 The unique position of Israel as the sole land bridge between Europe-Asia and Africa is itself sufficient explanation for the vast wealth accruing to Solomon from his virtual monopoly over all commerce through the region. Not only did he have mastery of the routes to the north (8:4), he also controlled the overland access south and undertook maritime trade in the commodities of Africa and beyond (9:21; 1 Kgs 10:22). The Phoenician expertise in craft technologies and monumental architecture that Solomon had hired once before extended beyond these areas to shipbuilding and sea-manship as well; Phoenician renown for seamanship was celebrated by the prophets (Isa 23:1, 14; Ezek 27). Solomon undertook a joint venture to mutual benefit with Hiram to exploit the maritime trade to the south; a similar oppor-tunity would later also bring Jehoshaphat into alliance with Ahaziah, king of Israel (20:36–37 // 1 Kgs 22:49–50).

The location of Ophir has long been a subject of debate. Ophir has been identified with India (Josephus, *Ant.* 8:164), Punt (Somaliland) on the coast of Africa (Albright), and west or south Arabia (Montgomery, 38–39, 177; Gray, *I and II Kings*, 256). The three year duration of the voyages (9:21 // 1 Kgs 10:22) suggests a remote location, unless seaborne commerce was re-stricted to seasons when the prevailing winds were favorable; the identity and source of the commodities procured is also a factor, but this is complicated by the fact that Ophir itself could be a transfer point in the trade with more distant regions and not the native environment of the goods. All in all the identification of the location of Ophir remains an open question.

The divergence in the MT of the two histories on the quantity of gold Solomon received (1 Kgs 9:28 = 420 talents; 8:18 = 450 talents) is a minor question of text transmission. Considerable variation is found in both Bas and Par as well as in Syr and Josephus; see *Note*.

Explanation

Modern historians setting out to record the reign of Solomon would proba-bly place great emphasis on the geopolitical aspects of his empire; they would emphasize his conquests and military prowess. If they described at all Solomon's building projects, they would devote as much time to Solomon's other monu-mental architecture, his palace and public buildings, and not simply the temple alone. The Chronicler clearly has other foci. He devotes the largest part of his narrative to presenting Solomon as a temple builder; even in this context largely devoted to "secular" concerns, the Chronicler reiterates Solomon's central involvement in cult (8:11–16).

The Chronicler downplayed Solomon's military prowess in part because of the contrast he had drawn between Solomon the man of peace and David the man of war (1 Chr 22:8–9; 28:3). However, in this one passage in which he does record Solomon's conquests and fortifications, he presents Israel at its maximum borders in the north (8:3–4) and in the south (8:17–18). For his post-exilic audience in the tiny province of Judah, this probably reflected more than simply the idealization of the "good old days," but rather the glowing embers of unextinguished national hopes embodied in God's promises to the fathers (see *Comment* at 8:3–6; 7:8–10).

Similarly, for his post-exilic audience in subservience to the Persians, reminders of gentile servitude (8:7–10) to Israel's God, cult, and king were probably not simply fond memories of the past, but expressed hopes for the future also embodied in the prophets (Isa 60; 55:5; 56:6–8; Mic 4:1–5; Zeph 3:9–11; Zech 8:20–23; 9:9–10; 14:10–19; cf. Ps 72:8–11).

More on Solomon's Wealth and Wisdom; His Death (9:1–31)

Bibliography

Abbott, N. "Pre-Islamic Arab Queens." *AJSL* 58 (1941) 1–22. **Albright, W. F.** "The Ivory and Apes of Ophir." *AJSL* 37 (1921) 144–45. **Beek, G. Van.** "Frankincense and Myrrh." *BA* 23 (1960) 69–95. **Bulliet, R.** *The Camel and the Wheel.* Cambridge, MA: Harvard UP, 1975. **Clark, W. E.** "The Sandalwood and Peacocks of Ophir." *AJSL* 36 (1920) 103–19. **Greenfield, J.,** and **M. Mayrhofer.** "The *ʾalgummîm/ʾalmuggîm* Problem Reexamined." *Hebräische Wortforschung.* VTSup 16. Leiden: E. J. Brill, 1967. **Groom, N.** *Frankincense and Myrrh: A Study of the Arabian Incense Trade.* London: Longman, 1981. **Liptzin, S.** "Solomon and the Queen of Sheba." *Dor leDor* 7 (1979) 172–86. **Nielsen, K.** *Incense in Ancient Israel.* VTSup 38. Leiden: E. J. Brill, 1986. **Philips, W.** *Qataban and Sheba.* New York: Harcourt, Brace and Co., 1955. **Pritchard, J.,** ed. *Solomon and Sheba.* London: Phaidon Press, 1974. **Scott, R.** "Solomon and the Beginnings of Wisdom in Israel." In *Wisdom in Israel and in the Ancient Near East,* ed. M. Noth. VTSup 3 (1955) 262–79. **Steglitz, R.** "Long Distance Seafaring in the Ancient Near East." *BA* 47 (1984) 134–42. **Ullendorf, E.** *Ethiopia and the Bible.* London: Oxford UP, 1968. ———. "The Queen of Sheba." *BJRL* 45 (1963) 486–504. **Wapnish, P.** "Camel Caravans and Camel Pastoralists at Tell Jemmeh." *JANESCU* 13 (1981) 101–21.

Translation

[1]*The queen of Sheba heard of Solomon's fame,*[a] *and she came to Jerusalem with a very large retinue, with camels carrying spices, gold in abundance, and precious stones, in order to test Solomon with hard questions. She came to Solomon and spoke with him about everything she had in mind,* [2]*and Solomon answered all her questions; nothing was too difficult for Solomon to explain to her.*

[3]*When the queen of Sheba had seen the wisdom of Solomon and the house*[a] *that he had built,* [4]*the food on his table, the seating of his officials, the servants attending him in their livery, his cup bearers in their livery,*[a] *and the sacrifices*[b] *that he offered in the temple of Yahweh, she was breathless.* [5]*She said to the king, "The rumor I heard in my own land about your achievements and your wisdom was true,* [6]*but I did not believe what they told me until I came and saw with my own eyes. Indeed, not even half the magnitude of your wisdom*[a]*was reported to me; you surpass the reports I had heard.* [7]*Happy are your men*[a]—*happy these your servants who attend you continually and hear your wisdom!* [8]*Blessed be Yahweh your God who delights in you and has set you on his throne*[a]*as king for Yahweh your God.*[b] *Because your God loves Israel and upholds*[c] *it forever, he has appointed you over them as king to maintain justice and righteousness."* [9]*Then she gave the king a hundred and twenty talents of gold, spices in great quantity, and precious stones; there had never been spices like those the queen of Sheba gave Solomon.* [10]*(The servants*[a] *of Hiram and the servants of Solomon*[b] *who brought gold from Ophir also brought algum wood and precious stones;* [11]*with algum wood the king made gateways*[a] *for the temple of Yahweh and the royal palace, as well as harps and lyres for the musicians; there had never been anything like them in the land of Judah.*[b]*)*

¹²*Then King Solomon gave the queen of Sheba all she desired and asked for, above and beyond what she brought to the king; then she departed and returned with her retinue to her own land.*

¹³*Now the weight of the gold that came to Solomon each year was six hundred sixty-six talents,* ¹⁴*besides what the merchants and traders*ᵃ *brought; all the kings of Arabia*ᵇ *and the governors of the land were bringing gold and silver to Solomon.*

¹⁵*King Solomon made two hundred large shields of hammered gold; six hundred shekels of hammered gold went into each shield.* ¹⁶*He also made three hundred small shields of hammered gold; three hundred shekels of hammered gold went into each shield. The king put them in the Palace of the Forest of Lebanon.*

¹⁷*The king also made a great throne of ivory and inlaid it with pure gold.* ¹⁸*The throne had six steps, and a footstool*ᵃ *of gold was attached to it; there were armrests on each side of the seat, and a lion stood beside each armrest.* ¹⁹*Twelve lions stood on the six steps, one at both sides of each step. Nothing like it had been made for any other kingdom.*

²⁰*All of King Solomon's vessels were of gold, and all the utensils of the Palace of the Forest of Lebanon were of pure gold; silver was reckoned as of no value in the days of Solomon.* ²¹*The king had ships sailing to Tarshish*ᵃ *with Hiram's servants;*ᵇ *once every three years these ships would bring gold and silver, ivory, apes, and monkeys.*

²²*King Solomon outdid all the kings of the earth in wealth and wisdom.* ²³*All the kings of the earth were seeking audience with Solomon to hear the wisdom that God had put in his heart;* ²⁴*year after year they brought their gifts—articles of silver and gold, garments, weapons,*ᵃ *spices, horses and mules.*

²⁵*Solomon had four thousand*ᵃ *stalls for horses and chariots and twelve thousand horses; he stationed them in the chariot cities and with the king in Jerusalem.*

²⁶*He ruled over all kings from the Euphrates to the land of the Philistines and the border of Egypt.* ²⁷*The king made silver*ᵃ *in Jerusalem as common as stones, and cedar as plentiful as the sycamore fig in the hill country.* ²⁸*Horses were imported from Egypt and from all other lands for Solomon.*

²⁹*As for the rest of Solomon's acts, from first to last, are they not written in the records of Nathan the prophet, the prophecy of Ahijah the Shilonite, and the visions of Iddo the seer concerning Jeroboam son of Nebat?* ³⁰*Solomon ruled in Jerusalem over all Israel for forty years.* ³¹*Then he rested with his fathers, and they buried him in the city of David his father, and Rehoboam his son ruled in his stead.*

Notes

1.a. 1 Kgs 10:1 adds לשם יהוה "for the name of Yahweh."

3.a. "House" is ambiguous; it could refer to the temple or the palace or the entire royal/sacral precinct.

4.a. Not in 1 Kgs 10:5.

4.b. With 1 Kgs 10:5 (עלתו); Par and Bas, ὁλοκαυτώματα. Chr MT, "his upper chamber by which he entered the temple," suggests a processional stairway or some other structure linking the palace and the temple complex (cf. 9:15, 12:9–11; Jer 22:13–15), but probably derives from a transmission error.

6.a. 1 Kgs 10:7 adds וטוב; see *Comment.*

7.a. Bas (1 Kgs 10:8) αἱ γυναῖκες σοῦ = נשיך, "your wives." The Chronicler's studied avoidance of reference to Solomon's many wives would make *wives* improbable as original text for Chronicles, contra NEB.

8.a. 1 Kgs 10:9, "on the throne of Israel"; see *Comment*.

8.b. "As king for Yahweh your God" is not in 1 Kgs 10:9.

8.c. להעמידו "upholds it" is not in 1 Kgs 10:9; both Par and Bas include στῆσαι·

10.a. 1 Kgs 10:11 אני חירם "ships of Hiram."

10.b. "Servants of Solomon" is not in 1 Kgs 10:11.

11.a. The term מסלה occurs 27 times in the OT, ordinarily with the meaning "public road, highway." However, this meaning does not fit the 3 occurrences in Chronicles (1 Chr 26:16, 18; 2 Chr 9:11). Roads were ordinarily unpaved in the ancient Near East; for the rare road or processional way stone might have been used, but a costly exotic wood is an improbable paving material. Numerous alternatives have been offered: Syr "bench"; NEB "stands"; JB "floorboards"; RSV "steps." Par (ἀναβάσεις) need not imply that the Chronicler's *Vorlage* contained מעלות; cf. MT and G of Ps 84:6. The parallel passage contains the *hapax legomenon* מסעד (= G ὑποστηρίγματα "supports"), and many commentators correct Chr MT by 1 Kgs 10:12. The translation offered here follows the suggestion of D. Dorsey ("Another Peculiar Term in the Book of Chronicles: מסלה, Highway?" *JQR* 75 [1984–85] 385–91) based on an Akkadian cognate designating the gateway or entranceway to temples and palaces; these structures may have been constructed from or decorated with this exotic wood and would be a probable place for gatekeepers (1 Chr 26:16, 18).

11.b. 1 Kgs 10:12, "So much algum wood has not been imported or seen to this day."

14.a. 1 Kgs 10:15, מסחר הרכלים "the wares of the merchants."

14.b. 1 Kgs 10:15, מלכי הערב "kings of the west." α′, σ′, and Vg on 1 Kgs 10:15 read with Chr MT, "Arabia."

18.a. 1 Kgs 10:19, וראש עגל לכסא מאחריו "its back had a rounded top." The difference in Chronicles at this point is commonly assigned to theological motivation: hostility to the golden calves (1 Kgs 13, Exod 32) is thought to have prompted the Chronicler to change the image to that of a lamb (כבש) or footstool (כבש), just as the Masoretes were motivated to read in Kings ראש עגל "round top" rather than ראש עֵגֶל "the head of a calf," a reading found in some Heb. MSS. However, for an example to the contrary, where the Chronicler does not show an aversion to calf/bull imagery, see 4:3. There is a possibility of textual corruption. The entire reference is omitted in Par, though the MT is supported by a group of Lucianic texts. At best this passage can be adduced only as a quite tenuous example of *Tendenz* (Lemke, *Synoptic Studies*, 120–21).

21.a. 1 Kgs 10:22 אני תרשיש "ships of Tarshish"; see *Comment*.

21.b. 1 Kgs 10:22 אני חירם "Hiram's ships."

24.a. Par and Bas στακτήν "oil, perfume."

25.a. 1 Kgs 10:26 "1,400 chariots"; Par and Bas "4,000."

27.a. Cf. 1:15. The MT of Kgs and Chr agrees, while Bas and Par add "gold."

Form/Structure/Setting

Chap. 9 closely follows the parallel account in 1 Kgs 10:1–28, 11:41–43 apart from some minor modifications. The major change from the parallel material is the omission of 1 Kgs 11:1–40, a passage which reports Solomon's straying due to his foreign wives, the LORD's subsequent anger and determination to wrest most of the kingdom from him, the raising of adversaries who freed Edom and Aram from Israelite sovereignty, and the rebellion of Jeroboam. All of these matters are out of accord with the Chronicler's portrayal of Solomon's glorious, peaceful, and righteous reign; the Chronicler prefers to conclude his account of Solomon by introducing the note, not paralleled at this point in Kings (cf. 1 Kgs 5:1), that Solomon ruled from the Euphrates to the border of Egypt (9:26).

Though most of his material is borrowed from the parallel account, it is necessary to appreciate the uniqueness of the Chronicler's own structuring of his material; see "Literary Structure" in the introductory essay, "The Chronicler's Solomon." The author has used his account of the queen's visit as a counterpart to his earlier narrative of Solomon's relations with another gentile ruler, Hiram king of Tyre (2:1–16). His intention to parallel these two narratives is indicated by his bracketing the queen's visit with references to Solomon's dealings with Hiram (8:17–18; 9:10–11), and by his placing once again in the mouth of a gentile ruler the recognition that Solomon's reign over Israel is because of Yahweh's love for the nation (9:8; 2:11). The other material elaborates on the earlier theme of Solomon's wealth and wisdom with which the author began his narrative, repeating the account of the trade in horses (1:14–17; 9:28) and the comparative evaluation of silver and cedar (1:15; 9:27). These repetitions should not be thought of as clumsy compositional technique or lapse of memory on the part of the author, but rather as deliberate signposts of the overall structure he has contrived.

The incident with the queen of Sheba (9:1–12) is a self-contained narrative with its own internal structure. The onset of two paragraphs is marked by the use of the explicit subject and the perfect tense of the verb (9:1, 12). A second paragraph begins with a repetition of the explicit subject (9:3). The remainder of the chapter is subdivided by other devices commonly found on paragraph boundaries: ויהי clauses (9:13, 25, 26) and ויעש with an explicit subject (9:15, 17—cf. 4:1, 2, 6, 7, 8, 9, 11, 19).

Comment

1–12   The visit of the queen of Sheba is described as a wisdom encounter and emphasizes the admiration of a gentile ruler for the wealth and wisdom of Solomon. While a firsthand observation of Solomon's wisdom might have been worth the arduous and hazardous journey across 1,400 miles of desert from ancient Saba (roughly modern Yemen), commercial interests were probably the more basic motivation. The economy of ancient Saba was built on trade in frankincense and myrrh. Access to sea trade through Tyre (Ezek 27:22–23) to the Mediterranean world required passage through Solomon's monopoly on the overland routes; negotiations with him concerning the trade in these aromatic resins would have been worthy of the queen's attention. Solomon's own naval operations to the south, references to which bracket the narrative of the queen's visit (8:17–18; 9:10–11), may have prompted her trip; the joint maritime ventures of Solomon and Hiram may have been cutting into the queen's overland routes. See the discussions of the overland routes in Wapnish, Groom, and Nielsen (*Bibliography* above).

Several features of the passage comport well with its historical basis. Female rulers played important roles in pre-Islamic Arabia (Abbott, *AJSL* 58 [1941] 1–22), and classical historians mention the fabulous wealth of the area. Diodorus Siculus, who traveled in Arabia in the first century B.C., says of the Sabaeans that "this tribe surpasses not only the neighboring Arabs but also all other men in wealth and in their several extravagancies. For in the exchange and sale of their wares they, of all men who carry on trade for the sake of the silver they receive in exchange, obtain the highest price in return for things of the smallest weight" (3:47:5). Frankincense and myrrh were in high demand for use in pharmacopoeia and cosmetics, embalming, and primarily as a part of religious offerings (Isa 60:6; Jer 6:20). The demand and the repeated taxation along the route contributed to the extraordinary cost; it was indeed the case that frankincense and myrrh could rank alongside gold as gifts fit for a king (Matt 2:11).

The Chronicler's version of the queen's visit follows 1 Kgs 10:1–13 fairly closely. Several minor modifications could be tendentious, but cannot be adduced with much confidence. In Chronicles the queen speaks "with him" (9:2) rather than "to him" (1 Kgs 10:2); she sees the "wisdom of Solomon" (9:3), but not "all the wisdom" (1 Kgs 10:4). Both these changes may be in the interest of assuring Solomon's superior position and the inexhaustibility of his wisdom, but one cannot be dogmatic. Pritchard (*Solomon and Sheba*, 10–11) suggests that the omission of the word "and prosperity" (וטוב, 1 Kgs 10:7) is due to the fact that by the Chronicler's time it was the wisdom rather than the wealth of Solomon which was the predominant interest; the queen expresses wonder only at the "greatness of your wisdom" (9:6). However, in light of the extended attention given to Solomon's wealth in the immediate context (9:10–28), more caution is needed before suggesting *Tendenz* behind such a small departure from the parallel text.

One modification introduced by the Chronicler is clearly related to his larger interests. Solomon sits not "on the throne of Israel" (1 Kgs 10:9), but on the throne of God (9:8). The author has similarly modified other texts or has introduced his own material to make the same point, that the throne and kingdom belong to God (1 Chr 17:14; 28:5; 29:23; 2 Chr 13:8). The relevance for the post-exilic community could not be lost: Israel may be under foreign domination (Persia), but the kingdom remains secure; God always was and remains the real king of Israel, even when no descendant of David sits on a throne, and he promises that the kingdom will endure forever (9:8).

10–11 The joint maritime venture of Solomon and Hiram is mentioned within the larger narrative of the queen's visit in Kings, and therefore also in Chronicles; it may have been prompted by the fact that their trade initiative was oriented to the same region from which the queen had come. The Chronicler may be seeking to enhance Solomon's role; he refers not to the ships of Hiram alone (1 Kgs 10:11), but to the joint efforts of both kings (9:10).

13–28 These concluding notes on the united monarchy must not be isolated from the scope of the author's overall presentation. The Chronicler has set before his readers two righteous kings ruling virtually without fault or blame over a united people. He has kept the entire nation to the fore, providing genealogies for twelve tribes (1 Chr 1–9), by referring repeatedly to the action of "all Israel" (1 Chr 9:1; 11:1–4; 12:38–40; 13:1–8; 14:8; 15:3, 28; 16:1–3; 18:14; 19:17; 21:1–5; 22:17; 23:1–2; 28:1–8; 29:21–26; 2 Chr 1:1–3; 5:2–6; 6:3–13; 7:8–10; 9:30), and by showing the land occupied at its ideal extent (7:8; 9:26; 1 Chr 18:1–13; cf. 2 Chr 1:9; 1 Chr 27:23–24; Gen 15:5, 18–19). It is to this glorious kingdom with its temple that the Gentiles come bringing their labor, their wealth, and seeking wisdom (1 Chr 18:1–13; 20:2–3; 22:3–4, 14; 26:27–28; 2 Chr 2:2–18; 8:7–9; 9:1–28). These features cumulatively are scarcely a simple recalling of fond memories from an idealized past, a mere recitation about the "good old days"—rather they represent an eschatological program and give expression to the fondest hopes

of many in the restoration community for the day that a David/Solomon redivivus would again in righteousness lead Israel to glory among the nations, a
day when the Gentiles would once again make their pilgrimage to Jerusalem.

13–14 Solomon's control of the trade routes generated enormous revenues. The 666 talents was beyond the revenue generated by trade imposts
and taxation from the governors of the various districts (1 Kgs 4:7–28); the
amount presumably represented a sum produced by Solomon's own mercantile
ventures and tribute paid him. Gray (*I and II Kings*, 264) follows van den
Born in suggesting that the total was derived by adding the sums in 1 Kgs
9:28 (420), 9:14 (120), and 10:10 (120), but not only does the total not precisely
agree, these incidental payments should not be regarded as annual sums.

15–16 The fate of these shields is described in 12:9–11 // 1 Kgs 14:26–
28. The Chronicler does not provide a description of the Palace of the Forest
of Lebanon like that found in 1 Kgs 7:1–12.

In biblical Hebrew, when the unit of weight is not specified with the amount,
as in these two verses, the *shekel* is ordinarily assumed. The NIV has specified
instead the *beka* (half-shekel), apparently to harmonize with the figure of
three minas for the small shields in 1 Kgs 10:17. Using a mina of fifty shekels,
the three minas (150 shekels) would correspond to three hundred half-shekels.
The solution is ingenious but not commended by common Hebrew usage.
An alternative approach assumes that the unit of measure in 1 Kgs 10:17 is
the heavy mina (= 100 shekels), so that the three minas would equal three
hundred shekels. G^B does omit the entire line specifying the weight of the
small shields, but this omission is most naturally viewed as a pre-G error
associated with other line omissions of similar length (Allen, *GC* 2:136).

21 Commodities of trade often represent alien lexical items in any given
language. This is the case with the terms translated here as "ivory, apes,
and monkeys." These terms were already difficult for Josephus and the translators of G; see Gray (*I and II Kings*, 263), Albright (*AJSL* 37 [1921] 144–45),
and Clark (*AJSL* 36 [1920] 103–19).

Tarshish has ordinarily been identified with a port in the western Mediterranean; Jonah (1:3) set sail for there to escape God's bidding to go to Nineveh.
Many suggestions have been made regarding the original site of Tarshish,
most commonly identified with Tartessus in Spain. Steglitz (*BA* 47 [1984]
134–42) considers the circumnavigation of Africa a possibility. However, it
is improbable that ships bound for the western Mediterranean would operate
out of Ezion-geber; the length and hazard of the journey would make it
unlikely, and the fact that it would probably be commercially unfeasible also
rules against it. Scholars have often suggested that though the term Tarshish
was originally a geographical name, it came to be applied to a type of ship
used on long journeys; Albright (*BASOR* 83 [1941] 22) referred the designation
to refinery ships. However, it is difficult to avoid the conclusion that the
Chronicler considered these ships as traveling (הלך—9:21; 20:37) to Tarshish.
It is not necessary to conclude that the author was ignorant either of the
type of vessel or of the geography; whatever the original meaning of the
term, by the author's time it appears to have become a popular designation
of a fabled distant place, roughly the equivalent of "going to the ends of
the earth" (cf. Ps 72:10; Isa 2:16; see Gordon, *IDB* 4:517).

25 The number of Solomon's chariot horses is surrounded by a thicket of textual difficulties; a somewhat oversimplified chart of the data from the relevant passages is presented below:

	2 Chr 9:25	2 Chr 1:14	1 Kgs 5:6	1 Kgs 10:26
MT:	4,000 stalls for chariot horses	1,400 chariots	40,000 stalls for chariot horses	1,400 chariots
G:	"	"	"	4,000 stalls for chariot horses

Assuming one horse to a stall and teams of two, the ratio of four thousand stalls to fourteen hundred chariots would allow for spare animals and would be a plausible figure; however, the diversity and interrelatedness of the variants suggests a basic difficulty in the history of transmission, such that it is not possible to speak with confidence regarding the original text.

By repeating the reference to Solomon's horses (here and in 1:14) and his wealth in silver and gold (9:27; 1:15) the Chronicler further perfects the rhetorical symmetry of his entire account of Solomon's reign.

28 See *Comment* at 1:16.

29–31 At first glance here and in general (1 Chr 29:29; 2 Chr 13:22; 26:22; 33:19) the Chronicler appears to have used among his sources independent collections of prophetic materials—perhaps homiletical histories, or "hagiographa," or records resembling the canonical prophetical books. While such independent collections may have been at the disposal of the author, both 2 Chr 20:34 and 32:32 suggest that by the Chronicler's own day these independent collections were already incorporated into anthologies or other annalistic sources, and that the sources named after individual prophets may be portions of the larger collection. Some scholars have concluded that the Chronicler's citations of writing attributed to a prophet refer to material the author has taken from Samuel/Kings and not from any other independent source; the prophets named are contemporaries of the king whose reign is described.

The involvement of Nathan (2 Sam 7 // 1 Chr 17; 2 Sam 12; 1 Kgs 1) and Ahijah (1 Kgs 11:29–30; 12:15; 14:2–6, 18; 15:29) in the affairs of the kingdom is well attested; works by or concerning both are elsewhere appealed to by the Chronicler as his sources (1 Chr 29:29; 2 Chr 10:15). Though Iddo is cited as an authority for the Chronicler's account of the reigns of Solomon, Rehoboam (12:15), and Abijah (13:22), nothing is known of his personal activities. Since he is said to have had visions concerning Jeroboam son of Nebat, it is tempting to equate him with the unknown prophet who speaks against the altar in Bethel (1 Kgs 13). Josephus's identification of that prophet as Ἰάδων shows that this identification had already been made in tradition (*Ant.* 8:231; cf. Lemke, *Synoptic Studies,* 126–27).

Explanation

The concluding portions of the Solomon narrative in Kings and Chronicles are a study in contrasts. Where the one reports Solomon's lack of wisdom shown in his apostasy with his gentile wives, the other ends with Solomon's wisdom displayed before a gentile woman (9:1–12) and admired by the nations (9:22–26). Where the one reports the tokens of divine displeasure seen in the announcement of the division of the kingdom and in the disintegration of the empire through successful rebellions (1 Kgs 11:9–40), the other brings Solomon to his death in tranquility, enjoying the submission of his vassals, the honor of other nations, and ruling over his empire at its maximal extent (9:22–26). The compiler of Kings wrote a tract for exiles, answering to the "why" for the great exile and captivity, judgment to which even David and Solomon contributed; the Chronicler provided a desciption of the past in terms of his aspirations for the future. See *Comment* at 9:13–28.

The visit of the anonymous queen of Sheba to Solomon is among the most enduringly popular narratives of the OT; it is the stimulus for nearly endless elaboration in the literature of Judaism, Christianity, and Islam, and in the graphic arts as well. Storytellers have put this narrative in the service of many traditions and have specified her name, listed the hard questions she put to Solomon, reported her conversion to monotheism, turned the encounter into a sexual seduction and elaborated on the lineage of their progeny, or offered a variety of often fantastic legendary accretions.

Christian interpretation has developed the passage along the two prominent themes, Solomon's wealth and wisdom. The magi from the East with their gifts of frankincense, gold, and myrrh repeat the journey of the queen of Sheba; the wealth and admiration of the Gentiles flow to Israel's king as a realization of prophetic hopes (Isa 60:6; Ps 72:10, 15). Jesus himself appeals to the passage (Matt 12:42; Luke 11:31) in commenting that the queen "came from the ends of the earth to listen to Solomon's wisdom, and now one greater than Solomon is here."

Reward and Punishment in Chronicles: The Theology of Immediate Retribution (2 Chron 10–36)

Bibliography

Braun, R. "Chronicles, Ezra, and Nehemiah: Theology and Literary History." In *Studies in the Historical Books of the Old Testament*, ed. J. A. Emerton. VTSup 30. Leiden: E. J. Brill, 1979. ———. "The Message of Chronicles: Rally 'Round the Temple." *CTM* 42 (1971) 510–11. **Dillard, R.** "The Reign of Asa (2 Chr 14–16): An Example of the Chronicler's Theological Method." *JETS* 23 (1980) 207–18. **Japhet, S.** *The Ideology of the Book of Chronicles and Its Place in Biblical Thought.* 159–208. **Johnstone, W.** "Guilt and Atonement: The Theme of 1 and 2 Chronicles." In *A Word in Season*, ed. J. Martin and P. Davies. JSOTSup 42. Sheffield: JSOT Press, 1986. 113–38. **North, R.** "The Theology of the Chronicler." *JBL* 82 (1963) 369–81. **Rad, G von.** *Old Testament Theology.* Tr. D. Stalker. 2 vols. New York: Harper Row, 1962. 1:347–50. **Rudolph, W.** "Problems of the Books of Chronicles." *VT* 4 (1954) 401–9. **Schaefer, G.** *The Significance of Seeking God in the Purpose of the Chronicler.* **Wellhausen, J.** *Prolegomena to the History of Ancient Israel.* 203–10. **Welten, P.** *Geschichte und Geschichtsdarstellung in den Chronikbüchern.* 9–186. **Williamson, H.** "Eschatology in Chronicles." *TynBul* 28 (1977) 149–54. ———. *1 and 2 Chronicles.* 31–33. ———. *Israel in the Books of Chronicles.* 67–68.

SURVEY OF RETRIBUTION THEOLOGY

General description

Though the history of research in Chronicles has been characterized by vigorous debate surrounding the author's theology, date, and purpose, on one theme of his historiography there is a near consensus. The Chronicler's adherence to a "theology of immediate retribution" provides his dominant compositional technique, particularly formative in his approach to the history of Judah after the schism. "Retribution theology" refers to the author's apparent conviction that reward and punishment are not deferred, but rather follow immediately on the heels of the precipitating events. For the Chronicler sin always brings judgment and disaster, while obedience and righteousness yield the fruit of peace and prosperity. Even a cursory reading of the text reveals the contours of the writer's convictions; they are both (1) specifically articulated and (2) demonstrated in his reshaping of narratives.

Specifically articulated. In a number of passages unique to the Chronicler, i.e., not found in the parallel text in Samuel/Kings, the author gives the reader a glimpse of his literary program by directly articulating the theme of retribution theology. Consider the following passages:

> Be careful to follow all the commands of the LORD your God, that you may possess this good land and pass it on as an inheritance to your descendants forever. And you, my son Solomon, acknowledge the God of your father, and serve him with

wholehearted devotion and with a willing mind, for the LORD searches every heart and understands every motive behind the thoughts. If you seek him, he will be found by you; but if you forsake him, he will reject you forever (1 Chr 28:8b–9).

If my people who are called by my name will humble themselves and pray and seek my face and turn from their wicked ways, then will I hear from heaven and will forgive their sin and will heal their land (2 Chr 7:14).

This is what the LORD says: "You have abandoned me; therefore, I now abandon you" (2 Chr 12:5).

The LORD is with you when you are with him. If you seek him, he will be found by you, but if you forsake him, he will forsake you (2 Chr 15:2).
Listen to me, Judah and people of Jerusalem! Have faith in the LORD your God and you will be upheld; have faith in his prophets and you will be successful (2 Chr 20:20).

Though it is not the first such notice, of these passages 2 Chr 7:14 constitutes a programmatic statement of great importance; it is probably the most widely known passage in Chronicles, though references to it in popular and homiletical literature commonly apply it in contexts quite foreign to the author's original use. Solomon's prayer at the dedication of the temple is a "charter" for the subsequent history of Israel; the prayer in both histories presumes the possibility of exile and return (6:24–25, 36–39 // 1 Kgs 8:33–34, 46–50). Both histories also report God's second appearance to Solomon in answer to the dedicatory prayer (7:11–22 // 1 Kgs 9:1–9); God tells Solomon that he will deal with Israel in accordance with the terms of Solomon's requests. The Chronicler, however, has introduced 7:13–15 into God's speech to Solomon; this insertion spells out the key concepts and vocabulary of retribution theology. In times of distress or calamity, if the people will humble themselves, pray, seek God, and turn from wickedness, then God will respond. Each of these terms and their synonymns recur again and again in the Chronicler's history demonstrating that God has indeed kept his promise to Solomon. "Seeking God" (דרשׁ, בקשׁ) or the failure to do so becomes the touchstone for weal or woe (1 Chr 10:13–14; 22:19; 28:9; 2 Chr 11:16; 12:14; 14:4, 7; 15:2, 4, 12, 13, 15; 16:12; 17:4; 18:4; 19:3; 20:4; 22:9; 25:20; 26:5; 30:19; 31:21; 33:12; 34:3); similarly "humbling oneself" (כנע) or the failure to do so determines the divine response (2 Chr 12:6, 7, 12; 28:19; 30:11; 33:12, 19, 23; 34:27; 36:12). Prayer (1 Chr 4:10; 5:20; 21:26; 2 Chr 13:12–15; 14:11; 18:31; 20:9; 30:18, 27; 32:20, 24; 33:13, 18–19), "turning" (2 Chr 15: 4; 30:6, 9; 36:13), and "healing" (2 Chr 30:20; 36:16) occur at critical moments.

It is not sufficient, however, to speak only of these terms without also taking account of their antonyms which likewise carry much of the burden of the Chronicler's convictions. The opposite responses to humbling oneself and seeking God are introduced through the use of "abandon, forsake" (עזב, 1 Chr 28:9, 20; 2 Chr 7:19, 22; 12:1, 5; 13:10–11; 15:2; 21:10; 24:18, 20, 24; 28:6; 29:6; 34:25) and "be unfaithful, rebellious" (מעל, 1 Chr 2:7; 5:25;

10:13; 2 Chr 12:2; 26:16, 18; 28:19, 22; 29:6; 30:7; 36:14; for this term see particularly W. Johnstone, "Guilt and Atonement").

Shaping narratives. Beyond the specific announcement of retribution theology as his approach, the Chronicler is untiring in his efforts to demonstrate the validity of this principle as it operated in the history of Israel. Since 2 Chr 7:14 announced a program for Israel's future, the Chronicler concentrates on the period after the schism. Of the twenty-six chapters devoted to this period, about half of the material is unique to the Chronicler, without parallel in Kings; the vast majority of this nonsynoptic material is directly in the service of retribution theology as the Chronicler seeks to provide the theological rationale for the events he narrates.

The repertoire of motifs used by the author for showing divine favor or displeasure is fairly stable. Acts of piety and obedience are rewarded with success and prosperity (1 Chr 22:11, 13; 29:23; 2 Chr 14:7; 26:5; 31:21; 32:27–30—contrast 13:12), building programs (2 Chr 11:5; 14:6–7; 16:6; 17:12; 24:13; 26:2, 6, 9–10; 27:3–4; 32 29–30; 33:14; 34:10–13—contrast 16:5), victory in warfare (13:13–18; 14:8–15; 20:2–30; 25:14; 26:11–15; 27:5–7; 32:20–22), progeny (1 Chr 3:1–9; 14:2–7; 25:5; 26:4–5; 2 Chr 11:18–22; 13:21; 21:1–3), popular support (2 Chr 11:13–17; 15:10–15; 17:5; 19:4–11; 20:27–30; 23:1–17; 30:1–26; 34:29–32; 35:24–25), and large armies (2 Chr 11:1; 14:8; 17:12–19; 25:5; 26:10). Conversely disobedience and infidelity bring military defeat (2 Chr 12:1–9; 16:1–9; 21:8–11, 16–17; 24:23–24; 25:15–24; 28:4–8, 16–25; 33:10; 35:20–24; 36:15–20), the disaffection of the population (2 Chr 16:10; 21:19; 24:25–26; 25:27–28; 28:27; 33:24–25), and illness (16:12; 21:16–20; 26:16–23—contrast 32:24). Alongside cultic offenses and the failure to seek God and to humble oneself, foreign alliances represented failure to trust God and always resulted in judgment (16:2–9; 19:1–3; 20:35–37; 22:3–9; 25:7–13; 28:16–21; 32:31; contrast 8:17–18; 9:21).

We will content ourselves with only a few examples of how the Chronicler has recast the narratives in Kings to demonstrate his convictions about immediate retribution. The reign of almost any king from the period of the divided kingdoms would serve equally well (with the possible exception of 2 Chr 35–36 where the accounts covering the last monarchs are so brief), but we will compare the narratives concerning Rehoboam and Uzziah.

In Kings the account of an individual reign ordinarily proceeds along the following pattern (the references are to the reigns of Rehoboam and Uzziah): (1) accession notice and synchronism (1 Kgs 14:21; 2 Kgs 15:1–2); (2) basic theological judgment (1 Kgs 14:22–24; 2 Kgs 15:3–4); (3) incident(s) that occurred during the reign, ordinarily reported without any theological rationale expressed (1 Kgs 14:25–28; 2 Kgs 15:5); (4) reference to other sources, the death and succession notice (1 Kgs 14:29–31; 2 Kgs 15:6–7).

In contrast the Chronicler is rarely willing simply to report an incident without providing the inciting rationale. For the Chronicler, reporting Rehoboam's obedience to the message of Shemaiah results in demonstrable blessing in the form of building programs (11:5–12), popular support (11:13–17), and progeny (11:18–23). Similarly he would not simply recount the invasion of Shishak and the military humiliation of Judah without first noting that Rehoboam had forsaken the law of God and been unfaithful (12:1–2).

The account of Uzziah in Kings would have presented some difficulty for the Chronicler. From his vantage it is somewhat a non sequitur to report that Uzziah did what was right in God's eyes, but nevertheless died of leprosy (2 Kgs 15:3–5). The account in Chronicles is distinguished immediately by its much greater length, for where Kings was willing simply to say Uzziah had done what was right, the Chronicler shows how this issued in the blessings of military victory (26:4–8), building programs (26:9–10), and a large army (26:11–15). How then did Uzziah contract leprosy? His pride led to his downfall (26:16)—while he was defying courageous priests who had confronted him for usurping their divinely appointed functions, leprosy broke out on his forehead and he was hastened out of the temple (26:17–20). That is *immediate* retribution.

Wellhausen's comment (*Prolegomena*, 209) is a fitting summary:

> Joram, Joash, and Ahaz, who are all depicted as reprobates, build no fortresses, command no great armies, have no wealth of wives and children; it is only in the case of pious kings (to the number of whom even Rehoboam and Abijah also belong) that the blessing of God also manifests itself by such tokens. Power is the index of piety, with which it accordingly rises and falls.

In any case where a particular theological theme is prominent, one runs the risk of reductionism in overdrawing its influence. Yet it needs to be specified that the theology of immediate retribution in Chronicles is certainly not confined to his account of the postschism kings; it is found also in the account of the united kingdom and in the genealogies.

There is a sense in which retribution theology could be extended to cover the entire account of the united monarchy. The major difference between the account of the united kingdom and the narratives following the schism has to do with the absence of reported transgression during the reigns of David and Solomon. Chronicles presents Solomon without any record of blame, and in the case of David, only two incidents report wrongdoing: the sin of Uzzah in the movement of the ark (1 Chr 13:7–10) and the sinful census (1 Chr 21). Both of these incidents are taken almost verbatim from Samuel, though they are put to different use in Chronicles; in both cases the immediacy of judgment for wrongdoing is a prominent feature congenial to the Chronicler's approach. Since there is so little record of wrongdoing in his account of the united monarchy, one would expect the tokens of divine blessing to be widely illustrated in the Chronicler's account of that period, and they are. Divine favor is shown in military victories (1 Chr 11:2–9; 14:8–17; 18:1–20:8), large armies (1 Chr 11:10–12:40; 27:1–24), prosperity (1 Chr 18:9–11; 20:2; 26:20–32; 27:25–31; 29:1–9; 2 Chr 1:12–17; 9:9–28), popular support (1 Chr 11:10–12:40; 28:1; 29:21–25), progeny (1 Chr 14:3–4), and the most important building project of all—the temple itself.

Not only do the genealogies contain some of the characteristic vocabulary of the author's approach, some of the short narratives within the genealogies betray his hand. God answers the battle prayer of those who trust him (1 Chr 5:18–22), but he abandons those are are unfaithful (1 Chr 5:23–26).

The pervasiveness of the themes of retribution theology betrays the essential unity of the Chronicles. It is concentrated mainly in his account of the divided kingdoms, and that is what one would expect in light of the pivotal importance of 2 Chr 7:14; it is less prominent in the record of the united kingdoms, largely due to the author's idealizing of that period; it is least prominent in the genealogical materials, as one would expect by virtue of the genre itself.

Also in order to avoid reductionism, the cautions of Rudoloph (VT 4 [1954] 405–6) should be remembered. The Chronicler has not reduced the principle of retribution to its logical extreme, such that it is a barren and unalterable law in his writings. Punishment does not always follow hard on the heels of transgression, not until the prophets come with their warnings and offers of mercy from God. Not every attack of an enemy army is due to transgression (2 Chr 32:1; 16:1; 25:13).

Source

Examples of immediate reward or punishment are found in all layers of biblical tradition. The uniqueness of the Chronicler in this regard is not simply the presence of these themes, but rather the frequency with which they have been reiterated. It must be asked what stimulus produced this rewriting of Israel's history making such extensive and consistent use of principles of retribution.

The writer of Chronicles had the version of Israel's history in Samuel/Kings before him. These books do portray instances of immediate retribution (1 Sam 3:30–34; 5:9; 25:36–39; 28:16–19; 2 Sam 12:13–14; 21:1; 24:11–12; 1 Kgs 13:4; 2 Kgs 1:16–17; 2:23–24; et al.), but for the most part, particularly in the history of the divided kingdoms, the approach to sin and guilt is that of delayed judgment culminating in the exile of the Northern and Southern kingdoms. Punishment erupts as the cumulative weight of guilt and sin from the Exodus onward provokes the divine response (2 Kgs 17:7–22; 21:10–15). This approach to sin and guilt in Kings was dictated in part by the needs of the original audience—for a generation in exile, the basic question "How could it have happened? Did God fail?" had to be answered; the destruction of Jerusalem did not represent the failure of God to keep his word to David and Jerusalem, but rather he had responded finally to the sin of the people and kings (Ezra 5:12).

While this approach to guilt may account well for the exile and the destruction of Jerusalem, it is easy to see that the exiles themselves might question the justice of God; in their eyes they were suffering not for sins that they had committed, but rather for the sins of their ancestors (Ezek 18:25; Lam 5:7). Ezekiel's fellow exiles were fond of the well-used proverb, "The fathers eat sour grapes, and the children's teeth are set on edge" (Ezek 18:2; cf. Jer 31:29). To that generation Ezekiel delivered the command of God to no longer use that proverb (18:3). Ezekiel goes on to deliver the lengthiest and most direct articulation of retribution theology found in the Scriptures. His basic thesis is that the righteous will live, while the soul that sins will die (18:4, 13, 17–32); the point is driven home with three examples, that of a righteous man who does right, that of the wicked son of a righteous father, and that of the righteous son of a wicked father (18:5–18). The thesis is that each individual or generation will stand or fall in terms of its own obedience and that a gracious God does not take delight in punishing the wicked.

Surely it is not possible to demonstrate a direct dependence of Chronicles on Ezekiel for these themes; too many issues surrounding the composition and date of both books would preclude any certainty. If it was not the book of Ezekiel itself or the influence of his disciples, at least a similar line of development may have stimulated a review of Israel's history to emphasize that deferred judgment was not always the case, but rather that God had dealt with each generation as its deeds deserved, though always with the offer of mercy. The Chronicler's approach was not offered as a contradiction to Kings, but as a counterpoise.

In this regard the Chronicler may have been warning the restoration community against any complacency or presumption that punishment might be deferred for their wrongdoing as it had been in the past. For a nation once again "serving the kingdoms of other lands" (2 Chr 12:8), survival and blessing were found through seeking God and humbling oneself before him.

Approaching the New Testament

Examples of both immediate and deferred judgment are found in the NT. In addition to the deferred judgment of the eschatological day of reward and punishment (e.g., 2 Thess 1:7–10), some incidents portray individuals bearing the consequences of their actions in the present age. Disregard for the Lord's table brought illness and death to some (1 Cor 11:30); misrepresenting themselves cost Ananias and Sapphira their lives (Acts 5:1–10). Paul sums it up by reminding Timothy that "the sins of some men are obvious, reaching the place of judgment ahead of them; the sins of others trail behind them" (1 Tim 5:24).

At least one other passage requires mention. In John 9 we see both of these strains for understanding guilt. The disciples asked Jesus about the blindness of a man nearby. "Who sinned?" they said, "this man [the approach of Chronicles] or his parents [the approach of Kings]?" Jesus surprised the disciples with a third alternative they had not considered; he answered, "Neither this man nor his parents sinned, but this happened so that the work of God might be displayed in his life."

The Schism   (10:1–19)

Bibliography

Aberbach, M., and **L. Smolar.** "Jeroboam's Rise to Power." *JBL* 88 (1969) 69–72. **Braun, R.** "A Reconsideration of the Chronicler's Attitude toward the North." *JBL* 96 (1977) 59–62. **Buccellati, G.** *Cities and Nations of Ancient Syria.* Rome: Istituto di Studi del Vicino Oriente, University of Rome, 1967. **Cohn, R.** "Literary Techniques in the Jeroboam Narrative." *ZAW* 97 (1985) 33–35. **Evans, C. D.** "Naram Sin and Jeroboam: The Archetypical *Unheilsherrscher* in Mesopotamian and Biblical Historiography." In *Scripture in Context, II,* ed. W. Hallo, J. Moyer, and L. Perdue. Winona Lake: Eisenbrauns, 1983. 97–125. **Evans, D.** "Rehoboam's Advisers at Shechem, and Political Institutions in Israel and Sumer." *JNES* 25 (1966) 273–79. **Finkelstein, J.** "Ammiṣaduqa's Edict and the Babylonian 'Law Codes.'" *JCS* 15 (1961) 91–104. **Fox, M.** "Ṭôb as Covenant Terminology." *BASOR* 209 (1973) 41–42. **Gooding, D.** "Jeroboam's Rise to Power: A Rejoinder." *JBL* 91 (1972) 529–33. ———. "Problems of Text and Midrash in the Third Book of Reigns." *Textus* 7 (1969) 1–29. ———. "The Septuagint's Rival Versions of Jeroboam's Rise to Power." *VT* 17 (1967) 173–89. **Gordon, R.** "The Second Septuagint Account of Jeroboam: History or Midrash?" *VT* 25 (1975) 368–93. **Halpern, B.** "Sectionalism and the Schism." *JBL* 93 (1974) 519–32. **Klein, R.** "Jeroboam's Rise to Power." *JBL* 89 (1970) 217–18. ———. "Once More: Jeroboam's Rise to Power." *JBL* 92 (1973) 582–84. **Lemche, N.** "Andurārum and Mišarum: Comments on the Problem of Social Edicts and Their Application in the ANE." *JNES* 38 (1979) 11–22. **Levy, J.** "The Biblical Institution of *Deror* in the Light of Akkadian Documents." *EI* 5 (1958) 27–31. **Malamat, A.** "Kingship and Council in Israel and Sumer: A Parallel." *JNES* 22 (1963) 247–53. ———. "Organs of Statecraft in the Israelite Monarchy." *BA* 28 (1965) 34–65. **Moran, W.** "A Note on the Treaty Terminology of the Sefire Stelas." *JNES* 22 (1963) 173–76. **Seebass, H.** "Zur Königserhebung Jerobeams I." *VT* 17 (1967) 325–33. **Weinfeld, M.** "The Counsel of the 'Elders' to Rehoboam and Its Implications." *Maarav* 3 (1982) 27–53. **Williamson, H.** *Israel in the Books of Chronicles.* ———. "'We Are Yours, O David': The Setting and Purpose of 1 Chronicles 12:1–23." *OTS* 21 (1981) 164–76.

Translation

¹ *Rehoboam went to Shechem, for all Israel had come to Shechem to make him king.* ² *And so it was* ᵃ *that when Jeroboam son of Nebat heard (he was still in Egypt where he had fled from King Solomon), he returned from Egypt.* ᵇ ³ *They sent and called him; so Jeroboam and all Israel* ᵃ *came and spoke to Rehoboam, saying,* ⁴ *"Your father made our yoke burdensome. Now* ᵃ *lighten the burdensome service and the heavy yoke your father imposed on us, and we will serve you."* ⁵ *And he said to them, "Wait* ᵃ *three days, and then come back to me." So the people left.*

⁶ *King Rehoboam sought the advice of the elders who had attended Solomon his father when he was alive; he said, "How do you advise me to answer these people?"* ⁷ *They said to him, "If you will be kind to these people and satisfy them* ᵃ *and grant favorable terms to them, they will be your servants ever after."* ⁸ *But he rejected the advice the elders had given him and sought the advice of the young men who had grown up with him and had attended him.* ⁹ *He said, "What do you advise? How shall we* ᵃ *answer these people who say, 'Lighten the yoke your father imposed on us'?"* ¹⁰ *The young men who had grown up with him said, "Here is how you should speak to these people who say to you, 'Your father made our yoke*

heavy, but you must make it easier for us.' You should say to them, 'My little finger is thicker than my father's waist. [11]*Now my father made you carry a heavy yoke, but I will add to it. My father flailed you with whips, but I will scourge you with scorpions.'"*

[12]*Jeroboam*[a] *and all the people*[b] *came to Rehoboam on the third day, just as the king had ordered when he said, "Come back to me on the third day."* [13]*The king spoke to them harshly; King Rehoboam rejected the advice of the elders* [14]*and spoke to them according to the advice of the young men. He said, "My father made your yoke heavy,*[a] *and I will add more to it. My father flailed you with whips, but I will scourge you with scorpions."* [15]*The king did not listen to the people, for this turn of events was from God in order that Yahweh might confirm the word he spoke through Ahijah the Shilonite to Jeroboam son of Nebat* [16]*and all Israel because the king had not listened to them.*[a] *The people replied to the king,*

> *"What portion have we in David,*
> *What part in Jesse's son?*
> *Each of you to your tents, O Israel!*
> *Now see*[b] *to your own house, David!"*

So all Israel went to their tents, [17]*and Rehoboam ruled over the children of Israel who inhabited the cities of Judah.*

[18]*Then King Rehoboam sent out Hadoram,*[a] *who was in charge of forced labor, but the children of Israel stoned him to death; so Rehoboam hastened to mount his chariot and flee to Jerusalem.* [19]*From that day to this Israel has been in rebellion against the house of David.*

Notes

2.a. G repositions the parallel material in 1 Kgs 12:2–3a to a point after 1 Kgs 11:43; see *Form/Structure/Setting.*

2.b. 1 Kgs 12:2, וַיֵּשֶׁב ירבעם במצרים "Jeroboam dwelt in Egypt." Par appears to have assimilated the Kgs MT, possibly through incorporating a marginal gloss, and contains both lines: καὶ κατῴκησεν Ἱεροβοὰμ ἐν Ἀιγύπτῳ καὶ ἀπέστρεψεν Ἱεροβοὰμ ἐξ Ἀιγύπτῳ. Chr MT may have followed a different text of Kings.

3.a. 1 Kgs 12:3 וכל קהל ישראל; Par πᾶσα ἡ ἐκκλησία. This set of data has been explained by a variety of scenarios; see particularly the exchange between Gooding (*VT* 17 [1967], *JBL* 91 [1972]) and Klein (*JBL* 89 [1970], *JBL* 92 [1973]); see also Allen, *GC* 1:203–4. The discussion is sufficiently complex and inconclusive as to warrant omission here.

4.a. A few Heb. MSS and Vg ואתה; see 1 Kgs 12:4 ואתה עתה.

5.a. Par and 1 Kgs 12:5 add לכו. Par (πορεύεσθε) does not appear to have assimilated to Bas (ἀπέλθετε), but rather to be improving the Greek by specifying a term unnecessary in the Hebrew.

7.a. 1 Kgs 12:7, "if you will be a servant to these people and serve them. . . ." Though the Chronicler does tone down the note of servitude, the concept of king as servant of the people was widespread throughout the ancient Near East (Weinfeld, *Maarav* 3 [1982] 28–32).

9.a. So also 1 Kgs 12:9; Vg, Bas and Par as singular, "I."

12.a. Jeroboam is not mentioned in G of 1 Kgs 12:12. See *Form/Structure/Setting.*

12.b. So 1 Kgs 12:12 and Par; Bas, "all Israel."

14.a. With many Hebrew MSS, G, and 1 Kgs 12:14, אבי הכביד; MT, אכביד "I will make your yoke heavy." The parallel in v 11 with the second half of the verse and the fact that the Chronicler is following Kings so closely favor the former reading. It is easy to see how the text could have been garbled to produce the latter text, though one could possibly argue that it was a deliberate change to enhance the culpability of Rehoboam.

16.a. Many Hebrew MSS, Syr, OL, and Tg add ראו (cf. 1 Kgs 12:16): ". . . to Jeroboam son of Nebat. When all Israel saw that the king had not listened. . . ." An alternative treatment views the "all Israel" as *casus pendens*: "As for all Israel, since the king would not listen. . . ." The translation adopted here follows G and treats the MT verse division as misguided; the Chronicler's modification of his *Vorlage* would have the effect of enhancing somewhat the culpability of Rehoboam for the schism (Williamson, 239).

16.b. Vg *pasce* = רעה "shepherd."

18.a. The name is known in several other spellings: 1 Kgs 12:18 אדרם. Par reflects a longer spelling, Ἀδωνειράμ, harmonizing with 1 Kgs 4:6; 5:28 [14].

Form/Structure/Setting

The Chronicler has borrowed this material directly from his *Vorlage* at 1 Kgs 12:1–19 with only minor modifications (see *Notes* at 10:3, 7, 14, 16). Though the situation in Chronicles appears simple enough, it is complicated by a textual question in Kings pertaining to Jeroboam's precise role in the events of the schism.

3 Bas contains two rival accounts of Jeroboam's place in the schism; they differ on the time of his arrival from exile in Egypt and on the level of his participation in the revolt. In the one (3 Bas 11:26–12:24) Jeroboam does not rebel while Solomon is alive, takes no active role in the negotiations with Rehoboam, and is only invited to take the throne of the North after the rebellion. In the other account (3 Bas 12:24a–z) Jeroboam takes several overt steps in rebellion against Solomon, including besieging Jerusalem, and at the time of Solomon's death, he returns to instigate and lead in the rebellion. The MT of 1 Kgs 12 is commonly regarded as a contradictory conflation of these two accounts of the schism (Montgomery, Gray, et al.): 1 Kgs 12:2–3a appears to bring him on the scene early, while 1 Kgs 12:20 suggests he arrived only at the end of the chain of events which brought him to the throne. The most common solution to this difficulty is to regard 1 Kgs 12:2–3a as a later intrusion into Kgs MT from 2 Chr 10, since it has also been placed in a different position in Bas (at 1 Kgs 11:43). Since Jeroboam is also not mentioned in G of 1 Kgs 12:12, and since 1 Kgs 12:20 has no counterpart in 2 Chr 10, the MT of Kings is reconstructed to view Jeroboam as arriving late and having a low profile in the events of the schism.

Gooding (*VT* 17 [1967] 180–81) has argued plausibly, however, that the MT of 1 Kgs 12 can be read in an unforced way which would not imply a contradiction between 12:2–3a and 12:20, and further that the rival G versions represent midrashic editorializing. The assembly in 12:20 may well have been a subsequent meeting on another occasion than the initial stage of the revolt (12:2–3a).

It is also possible that the narrative in 1 Kgs 12 reflects a chiastic structure on the following lines:

A Rehoboam to be king (12:1)
  B Jeroboam's arrival (12:2)
    C Israel speaks to Rehoboam: issue of forced labor (12:3–4)
      D 1. Three day break (12:5)
         2. Advice of elders (12:6–7)
         3. Advice of young men (12:8–11)

D' 1. Three day break (12:12)
    2. Advice of elders (12:13)
    3. Advice of young men (12:14–15)
  C' Israel speaks to Rehoboam: issue of forced labor (12:16–19)
  B' Jeroboam's arrival (12:20)
A' Jeroboam to be king; Rehoboam king of house of David (12:20)

If this structure was consciously followed by the compiler of Kings, it is possible that the second reference to Jeroboam's arrival (B/B') should be attributed to a structural necessity involved in the use of a chiasm.

However the issue is handled in Kings, it is clear that for the Chronicler Jeroboam was present early and active in the events leading to the schism.

While the advice of the young men and the elders may reflect a kind of bicameral authority in ancient Israel (Malamat, *JNES* 22 [1963] and *BA* 28 [1965]), one should not overlook the presence of themes from the wisdom literature that (1) the counsel of the wise and experienced is preferable to that of the young and immature, and that (2) tyranny is folly.

The paragraphs of the entire narrative are marked primarily by the repetition of an explicit subject ("King Rehoboam," 10:1, 6, 18). The repetition of phrases from the end of a preceding paragraph often marks the onset of a new paragraph; the repetition of the three-day time period from 10:5 marks a new paragraph at 10:12.

2 Chr 10 itself is set off as a distinct episode both by its occurrence after the death formula for Solomon (9:29–31) and by the summary statement that Israel has been in rebellion against the house of David "to this day" (10:19).

Comment

1 Strategically located at the eastern mouth of the pass between Mount Gerizim and Mount Ebal, with an ample water supply and fertile plain, Shechem was a military, political, and religious center for ancient Israel from the time of the patriarchs. Abraham and Jacob both worshiped there (Gen 12:6–7; 33:18–20). Jacob's sons Simeon and Levi attacked the city after the rape of their sister Dinah (Gen 34). Joseph searched there for his brothers (Gen 37:12–14), and his bones were eventually interred there (Josh 24:26; Acts 7:16). Shechem was a site of covenant renewal under Joshua (Josh 24), and it was one of the designated cities of refuge (Josh 21:21). The abortive kingdom of Abimelech failed there (Judg 9). The fate of the city during the invasions of the Assyrians and Babylonians is not mentioned; during the intertestamental period it became the religious center of the Samaritans (John 4). Rehoboam journeys to this ancient site of politics, worship, and covenanting; though no covenant is specifically mentioned, the procedure appears quite analogous to that followed with David (2 Sam 3:6–21; 5:1–3; cf. 2 Chr 23:3).

2 The author presumes his reader's familiarity with the parallel history at 1 Kgs 11:26–40; as a part of his idealizing the reign of Solomon, the

writer does not mention any details regarding Jeroboam, apart from his name in a source he acknowledges (9:29).

Presumably what Jeroboam "heard" was the news of Solomon's death and the succession of Rehoboam. Bas places this verse immediately after 1 Kgs 11:43. This would allow sufficient time for his return from Egypt to be present at the beginning of negotiations with Rehoboam.

4 The issues were heavy taxation and forced labor, and the delegates from the Northern tribes were negotiating reductions as a condition of recognizing Rehoboam's sovereignty. Assyriological literature provides numerous examples of royal decrees exempting individuals and cities or districts from taxes, forced labor, or military conscription; these exemptions could be directed toward the entire nation in a *mešārum* edict. In some periods of Mesopotamian history, at sometime during the first few years of their reigns kings were expected to publish a *mešārum* edict providing for manumission from certain types of slavery and the cancellation of a variety of taxes (Finkelstein, *JCS* 15 [1961] 91–104; Levy, *EI* 5 [1958] 27–31; Lemche, *JNES* 38 [1979] 11–22). While this practice is demonstrable for Mesopotamian rulers, the evidence for such decrees in ancient Israel is indirect, as in this instance where the Northern delegates seem to expect such remissions. In biblical tradition release from servitude and debt was tied to the cycles of sabbatical and jubilee years (Lev 25:8–55) rather than the onset of a king's reign. This provision for a periodic regularity in granting relief from debt and slavery need not preclude the possibility of such decrees at royal initiative, possibly to quell a rebellion or provide economic stimulus.

Both Kings and Chronicles avow that forced labor was not imposed on the Israelites by Solomon (2:17–18; 8:7–10; 1 Kgs 9:15, 20–22), yet both record what appear to be instances of the practice. The hatred of the corvée (10:4) and the dispatch of Hadoram (10:18) both presume its application to Israelites. The practice continued under subsequent kings and was denounced (1 Kgs 15:22 // 2 Chr 16:6; Jer 22:13–14). See the longer discussion of this issue in *Comment* at 2:17–18.

6–11 Malamat (*JNES* 22 [1963] and *BA* 28 [1965]) finds in the consultation with two groups of advisers evidence for the existence of a bicameral authority in ancient Israel on whose prerogatives the authority of the king may have depended, particularly when the monarchy was weak. It is not difficult to demonstrate the importance of the elders in Israel's patriarchal/tribal society (2 Sam 3:17; 5:3; 17:4, 15; 1 Kgs 20:7–8; 1 Chr 11:3). It is more difficult to establish the identity of the "young men" as a governing authority. This second body could be civil servants or ministers, often distinguished from the elders (Judg 8:14; 1 Kgs 21:8; 2 Kgs 10:5). Malamat suggested that the "young men" were royal princes, half-brothers of Rehoboam from the numerous wives and consorts of Solomon. Ahab's seventy sons constituted one such group (2 Kgs 10:1–6). Rehoboam would later single out Abijah from among the royal sons as their leader (2 Chr 11:18–23); Abijah may have organized his court similarly (13:21). Jehoshaphat provided for his progeny and the royal succession, singling Jehoram out from among his sons; royal sons also participated as a group in Adonijah's attempted coup (1 Kgs 1:9). Not only in Israel, but also in Babylon young men of royal birth were chosen to "stand in the king's palace" (Dan 1:3–4). The fact that these royal sons are as a group called "youngsters" probably represents a touch of irony or even contempt for the notion that wisdom was to be found with the young (Job 12:12; contrast Eccl 4:13). Rehoboam was forty-one at the time of his accession (12:13; 1 Kgs 14:21); neither he nor those who had grown up with him were "striplings," though they were short of the status and wisdom of the elders.

7 Context argues strongly that דברים טובים, "good words," be more than mere verbal placation; the Northern tribes are looking for a modification in royal prescriptions as a condition of fealty. Cognates of the term טוב and its translation equivalents appear in a large number of extrabiblical texts as synonymous with "condition, treaty, pact, concord" (Moran, *JNES* 22 [1963]; Fox, *BASOR* 209 [1973]). Similar significance probably attaches to the term in 2 Kgs 25:28–29; 2 Sam 7:28; 1 Sam 25:30. Weinfeld (*Maarav* 3 [1982] 45–51) has demonstrated that the idiom דָּבֶר דָּבָר often occurs in biblical (1 Sam 20:23; Isa 8:10; Zech 1:13) and extrabiblical texts in the sense "make an agreement." In this context then we should think not solely of "pleasing words," but of a more formal diplomatic treaty or covenant similar to that attending the accession of David (2 Sam 5:3) or Joash (23:1, 16).

10 It is at least possible that קְטָנִי, "my little thing," is euphemistic for the penis, a sense which would add rash vulgarity to the charge of foolishness against the young men.

11, 14 Various ancient authorities identify the "scorpion" as a whip tipped with weights and barbs. There is no direct evidence as yet for the existence of such an instrument in ancient Israel or the contemporary ancient Near East; the device described by ancient writers may have been a Roman innovation, though it is fairly probable that it antedates the Romans. A more basic difficulty is that any identification with a type of lash is at the expense of the metaphor: just as Rehoboam's little finger was thicker than his father's waist, so also the punishment he would inflict is similarly exaggerated.

15 See 10:2. The Chronicler again presumes the reader's familiarity with the parallel history (1 Kgs 11:29–33). Since he has presented Solomon as blameless, the Chronicler would hardly include the information that the schism itself was attributable to Solomon's sins.

16 The rejection formula is a poetic antithesis to the earlier affirmations of support directed toward David (1 Chr 12:19; Williamson, *OTS* 21 [1981] 172–76). Printing the two utterances side-by-side highlights the contrast:

We are yours, O David,	What portion have we in David?
And with you, O son of Jesse!	What part in Jesse's son?
Peace, peace to you and peace	Each of you to your tents,
to your helpers,	O Israel!
For your God helps you.	See to your own house, David!

Earlier versions of this rejection formula were heard from Nabal (1 Sam 25:10) and Sheba (2 Sam 20:1). The slogan here uttered by the Northern tribes may already have been used as a byword of the popular resistance to the Davidic dynasty, finally flaming into open revolt.

17–18 The Chronicler has modified the parallel at 1 Kgs 12:18 by one small change: instead of "all Israel stoned him," our author chose to say "the children of Israel stoned him." The Chronicler does not show an aversion to using the phrase "all Israel" with reference to the Northern Kingdom— that is done in 10:16. The effect of this slight modification is that the identical phrase "the children of Israel" is used of both Southern (10:17) and Northern (10:18) tribes—both are equally the children of Israel (Williamson, *IBC*, 109). The Chronicler may have regarded the Southern Kingdom, and particularly the restoration community, as the spiritual successor of earlier Israel, but he does not do so by excluding the North.

Among the various issues about wisdom in this chapter, one can only wonder about the choice of the chief corvée officer as Rehoboam's envoy to the North. It was a choice which confirmed the king's announced intention not to relent in his exactions. The recent publication of a seal "belonging to Pela‘yahu (son of) Mattityahu, who is over the corvée" is the first extrabiblical confirmation of the office held by Hadoram; the identical phrase אשר על המס is used in the seal and 10:18 (Avigad, *IEJ* 30 [1980] 170–73). The seal is of unknown provenance and probably dates to the seventh century on palaeographic grounds.

19 For the Chronicler's use of the phrase "to this day," see *Comment* at 5:9.

Explanation

Any historical event is ordinarily the product of a complex of factors such that a single explanation is not sufficient; the schism was such an event. The biblical text alludes to the sociopolitical ills that attended the splendor of the Solomonic empire; the hated corvée and heavy taxation are undoubted factors that fanned the dissatisfaction in the North. Not so apparent as a factor is the kingdom typology itself: the united monarchy was a personal union around the persons of Saul, David, and Solomon of two distinct entities. The Northern ten tribes and the Southern two were heirs of a long history of independent action and self-perception reaching back to the conquest period. Israel and Judah remained identifiable entities under Saul (1 Sam 11:8), David (2 Sam 2:4–8; 3:10; 5:5; 24:9), and Solomon (1 Kgs 1:35). It should not come as a surprise then that these two entities should separate after a period of social/political turmoil and during a time of dynastic crisis; Ahijah's prophecy of a division into ten and two was quite probable (1 Kgs 11:29–33).

The Bible does not come to us as socioeconomic or geopolitical history, however. The biblical authors were concerned to record a divine, moral judgment about the kingdom of Yahweh. But even here no simple answer is given; rather, answers are offered that show an awareness of the multiplicity of factors. For the author of Kings, the schism is above all the product of the sinfulness of Solomon, particularly his involvement with the idol worship of his numerous wives who led him astray (1 Kgs 11:1–13); judgment for wrongdoing was the cause par excellence. A subsidiary theme in Kings is the fulfillment of prophecy: the compiler's concern with the efficacy of the prophetic word is shown in his recounting the realization of Ahijah's utterances (1 Kgs 11:19–39; 12:15). Rehoboam's folly is an attendant factor.

For the Chronicler, however, things must be a bit different. He had presented the reign of Solomon as blameless, a rule enjoying the undivided support and allegiance of the people. Certainly the chapter shows an awareness of the social and political ills left from Solomon's reign, but where does the blame go for the schism if the Chronicler will not tarnish Solomon? His answer was twofold: (1) Jeroboam's lust for power, and (2) Rehoboam's folly. While 13:7 is pivotal in deciding the relative weight of these two factors, neither can be excised. In Kings Jeroboam appears more the beneficiary of divine prophecy; but in Chronicles the omission of the prophecy of Ahijah puts Jeroboam's actions more to the fore as leader and instigator. The note of prophetic fulfillment is present, but in a more subdued fashion (10:15). In the absence of direct accusation toward Solomon's conduct, the folly of Rehoboam ("young and indecisive," 13:7) is the more prominent.

Isaiah had bemoaned the day when, as judgment on Judah and Jerusalem, Yahweh would make "boys their officials, mere children to govern them," when "the young would rise against the old, the base against the honorable" (Isa 3:4–5). Israel had already experienced this at least once by Isaiah's day. But Isaiah was also the one who spoke of Israel's hope as "a child born to us . . . and the government shall be upon his shoulders." For that child there would be none of the folly of Rehoboam, but he "will be called Wonderful Counselor, Mighty God, Everlasting Father, Prince of Peace. Of the increase of his government and peace there will be no end. He will reign on David's throne and over his kingdom, establishing and upholding it with justice and righteousness from that time on and forever" (Isa 9:6–7). The yoke of Solomon had been burdensome, and in haughty arrogance Rehoboam would make it yet heavier; what a contrast to another son of David, one who was gentle and humble, and invited the weary and burdened to "take my yoke upon you and learn of me . . . for my yoke is easy and my burden is light" (Matt 11:28–29).

The Reign of Rehoboam, 931–913 B.C. (11:1–12:16)

Bibliography

Aharoni, Y. *The Land of the Bible.* Tr. and ed. A. Rainey. 2d ed. Philadelphia: Westminster Press, 1979. 323–33. **Alt, A.** "Festungen und Levitenorte im Lande Juda." *Kleine Schriften zur Geschichte des Volkes Israels.* Vol 2. Munich: C. H. Beck, 1953. **Beyer, G.** "Beiträge zur Territorialgeschichte von Südwestpalästina im Altertum. I. Das Festungssystem Rehabeams." *ZDPV* 54 (1931) 113–70. **Dorsey, D.** *The Roads and Highways of Israel during the Iron Age.* Diss. Dropsie University, 1981. **Fritz, V.** "The 'List of Rehoboam's Fortresses' in 2 Chr 11:5–12—A Document from the Time of Josiah." *EI* 15 (1981) 46–53. **Goldingay, J.** "The Chronicler as Theologian." *BTB* 5 (1975) 99–126. **Green, A.** "Israelite Influence at Shishak's Court?" *BASOR* 233 (1979) 59–62. **Herrmann, S.** "Operationen Pharao Schoschenks I in östlichen Ephraim." *ZDPV* 80 (1964) 55–79. **Junge, E.** *Der Wiederaufbau des Heerwesens des Reiches Juda unter Josia.* BWANT 75. Stuttgart: Kohlhammer, 1937. **Kallai, Z.** "The Kingdom of Rehoboam." *EI* 10 (1971) 245–54 (Heb.). **Kitchen, K.** *The Third Intermediate Period in Egypt.* **Mazar, B.** "The Campaign of Pharaoh Shishak to Palestine." *Congress Volume, Strasbourg, 1956.* VTSup 4. Leiden: E. J. Brill, 1957. **Na'aman, N.** "Hezekiah's Fortified Cities and the LMLK Stamps." *BASOR* 261 (1986) 5–21. **Noth, M.** "Die Schoschenkliste." *ZDPV* 80 (1964) 55–79. **Redford, D.** "Studies in Relations between Palestine and Egypt during the First Millennium B.C.: II. The Twenty-second Dynasty." *JAOS* 93 (1973) 3–17.

Translation

[1] *Rehoboam went to Jerusalem and he mustered the house of Judah and Benjamin, a hundred and eighty thousand select troops who could wage war, to fight with Israel to restore the kingdom to Rehoboam.*
[2] *Then the word of Yahweh came to Shemaiah the man of God, saying,* [3] *"Speak to Rehoboam son of Solomon, king of Judah, and to all Israel[a] in Judah and Benjamin[b] saying,* [4] *'Thus says Yahweh: You must not go up to fight your brothers;[a] each return to his own house, for this thing is from me.'" And they heeded the words of Yahweh and turned back from going against Jeroboam.[b]*
[5] *Rehoboam returned to Jerusalem and he rebuilt cities as fortresses in Judah.* [6] *He rebuilt Bethlehem, Etam, Tekoa,* [7] *Beth-zur, Soco, Adullam,* [8] *Gath, Mareshah, Ziph,* [9] *Adoraim, Lachish, Azekah,* [10] *Zorah, Aijalon, and Hebron to be fortified cities in Judah and Benjamin.* [11] *He strengthened the fortresses and put commanders in them with supplies of food, oil, and wine;* [12] *he stored shields and spears in every one of the cities and made them very strong. And so Judah and Benjamin were his.*
[13] *Now the priests and Levites through all Israel resorted to him from all their territories;* [14] *the Levites left all their common lands and their own property and came to Jerusalem, because Jeroboam and his sons had rejected them from serving as priests of Yahweh* [15] *and had appointed for himself priests for the high places and the goat and calf idols[a] he had made.* [16] *After them those from all the tribes of*

Israel who set their hearts on seeking Yahweh the God of Israel came to Jerusalem to sacrifice to Yahweh the God of their fathers. [17] They strengthened the kingdom of Judah and supported Rehoboam son of Solomon for three years, walking[a] in the way of David and Solomon for three years.

[18] Rehoboam married Mahalath, the daughter[a] of David's son Jerimoth and of Abihail, the daughter of Jesse's son Eliab. [19] The sons she bore him were Jeush, Shemariah, and Zaham. [20] After her he married Maacah daughter of Absalom, who bore him Abijah, Attai, Ziza, and Shelomith; [21] Rehoboam loved Maacah daughter of Absalom more than all his wives and concubines. In all, he had eighteen wives and sixty[a] concubines, twenty-eight sons and sixty daughters.

[22] Rehoboam appointed Abijah son of Maacah crown prince, leader among his brothers, in order to make him king. [23] He showed discretion by dispersing some of his sons throughout the districts of Judah and Benjamin to all the fortified cities; he gave them abundant provisions and sought many wives[a] for them.

[12:1] And it came about when Rehoboam had established his rule and consolidated his power[a] that he and all Israel with him forsook the law of Yahweh. [2] So it was that, because they had been unfaithful to Yahweh, Shishak king of Egypt came up against Jerusalem in the fifth year of Rehoboam [3] with twelve hundred chariots, sixty thousand horsemen, and innumerable troops from the Libyans, Sukkites, and Cushites that came from Egypt. [4] He captured the fortified cities of Judah and came to Jerusalem.

[5] Shemaiah the prophet came to Rehoboam and the leaders of Judah who had gathered in Jerusalem because of Shishak, and he said to them, "Thus says Yahweh, 'You have abandoned me, so I have abandoned you to Shishak.'" [6] The leaders of Israel and the king humbled themselves and said, "Yahweh is righteous."

[7] When Yahweh saw that they had humbled themselves, the word of Yahweh came to Shemaiah, saying, "Since they have humbled themselves, I will not destroy them, but will allow them barely[a] to escape; my wrath will not pour out on Jerusalem through Shishak, [8] but they will be his servants. They will know the difference between serving me and serving the kingdoms[a] of other lands."

[9] Shishak king of Egypt went up against Jerusalem and seized the treasures of the temple of Yahweh and the treasures of the royal palace. He took it all, including the gold shields that Solomon had made. [10] So King Rehoboam made bronze shields to replace them and entrusted them to the commanders of the escort who guarded the entrance of the royal palace. [11] Whenever the king went to the temple of Yahweh, the escorts came and carried them and then returned them to the guard room. [12] Since Rehoboam had humbled himself, the anger of Yahweh turned from him and did not destroy him completely; also in Judah there was some good.

[13] King Rehoboam consolidated his power in Jerusalem and ruled. Rehoboam was forty-one years old when he became king, and he ruled seventeen years in Jerusalem, the city which Yahweh had chosen from among all the tribes of Israel to put his name there. His mother's name was Naamah; she was an Ammonite. [14] He did evil, for he did not set his heart on seeking Yahweh.

[15] The events of Rehoboam's reign, from beginning to end, are they not[a] written in the accounts of Shemaiah the prophet and Iddo the seer for genealogical enrollment.[b] There was war between Rehoboam and Jeroboam all their days. [16] Rehoboam rested with his fathers and was buried in the city of David. Abijah[a] his son ruled in his place.

Notes

3.a. 1 Kgs 12:23, "to all the house of Judah and Benjamin."

3.b. 1 Kgs 12:23 adds "and the rest of the people."

4.a. 1 Kgs 12:24 adds "the children of Israel."

4.b. 1 Kgs 12:24 has "they turned to go according to the word of Yahweh" instead of "turned back from going against Jeroboam."

15.a. 1 Kgs 12:32 does not contain the words "and the goat and calf idols."

17.a. MT verb is pl; NEB and JB have followed G with sg, "he walked."

18.a. K בן‎, "son"; some MSS, G, T, and Vg agree with Q.

21.a. G^B and OL, "thirty"; Josephus also gives the number as "thirty" (*Ant.* 8:250), suggesting he used Par or a Heb. text having that number. See Allen, *GC* 1:16, 106. Driver ("Abbreviations in the Massoretic Text," *Textus* 1 [1960] 125–28; and "Once Again Abbreviations," *Textus* 4 [1964] 82–86) explained this and several other examples as instances of confusion deriving from a system of numerical abbreviations based on the use of initial letters (שׁשׁים‎, שׁלשׁים‎).

23.a. The MT as it stands may be interpreted as "he sought many wives (for them)," though it is also possible that a haplogr has occurred from a more original text וישׁאל להם המון‎. RSV, NEB, and JB ("he procured wives for them") appear to regard המון‎ as a confusion arising from להם‎. The inclusion of "for them" may be a requirement for target languages like English, i.e., should be attributed to translational dynamics rather than to an alternative text.

12:1a. For the Chronicler's use of the hithp of חזק‎, see *Comment* at 1:1.

7.a. There is some ambiguity around the significance of כמעט‎: it is used in a temporal sense (NIV: "soon give them deliverance") or a quantitative sense (ASV: "some deliverance"; NEB: "barely escape"); both appear to satisfy the context equally well.

8.a. NEB "rulers" is presumably based on the Phoenician cognate *mmlkt*, "kings, rulers"; cf. Myers, 73. Contrasting serving Yahweh to serving other kings may be contextually more fitting, but invoking a cognate to establish a variant meaning for the same term used in the context in its ordinary sense "kingdom" (9:19; 11:1; 13:5, 8) is probably unwise.

15.a. הלא‎ (cf. 9:29; 25:26) may be related to Ugaritic *hl*, "behold." Cf. BDB 520a; Watson, *Bib* 53 (1972) 193–94.

15.b. The hithp of יחשׂ‎ is unique to Chr, Ezra, and Neh; it occurs 20 times with the meaning "to enroll in a genealogy." Its occurrence in this context has long troubled translators; G translates καὶ πράξεις αὐτοῦ, ordinarily the equivalent of ודרכיו‎, while RSV and NEB confine it to a marginal reading. The obvious way of understanding the text as it stands is that the Chronicler used a genealogical source attributed to Iddo, presumably the source from which he drew the genealogical material he cites for Rehoboam's family (11:18–23).

16.a. Kings gives his name as אבים‎ "Abijam"; see *Comment*.

Form/Structure/Setting

1 Chr 11–12 parallels 1 Kgs 12:21–14:31, but with extensive modifications reflecting the Chronicler's interests. As a member of the post-exilic community, the author's interests center in Judah and Jerusalem; he does not ordinarily report on the events in the North unless they impinge on the Southern Kingdom. The Chronicler omits details of the construction of the high places at Dan and Bethel, as well as the appearance and subsequent death of an unnamed prophet who denounced Jeroboam's cult; he deletes as well the journey of Jeroboam's wife to seek an oracle from Ahijah regarding the death of a son (1 Kgs 12:23–14:20).

Although the tendency to delete most details pertaining to the Northern Kingdom is itself a sufficient factor to account for these omissions, another factor may be operative. The deuteronomic historian showed considerable interest in prophetic "hagiographa" and incorporated many narratives in which the prophet is himself the central figure in the story; his accounts of Ahijah, Elijah, Elisha, and others commonly included a miraculous element and were concerned with the efficacy of the prophetic pronouncements. In Chronicles, however, there is only one narrative resembling the prophetic biographies of Kings: the consultation with Micaiah ben Imla, drawn almost verbatim from Kings (2 Chr 18 // 1 Kgs 22). In Chronicles the ministry of the prophets is not described in terms of miracles or the interaction of prophets with one another or even in narratives in which the prophet is himself focal. Rather the writer presents the prophets primarily as guardians of the theocracy; almost every king in the Davidic succession has his prophetic counterpart. The prophets make pronouncements of weal and woe depending on the responses of the monarchs. While omission of materials dealing with the North explains the deletion of much of the parallel material in the Chronicler's account of the kingdoms after the schism, and would include omission of prophetic hagiographa set in the North, the author's distinctive handling of the prophets is a probable secondary factor. It would also account for the omission of the material concerning the unnamed prophet, the old prophet from Bethel, and Ahijah (1 Kgs 13:1–14:20) and would influence his inclusion of the second and third appearances of Shemaiah in his account of the reign of Rehoboam (12:5–7).

Goldingay (*BTB* 5 [1975] 102–4) suggests that the Chronicler's account of Rehoboam was structured around the narratives concerning Jeroboam in 1 Kgs 12:25–14:20 such that each section in the deuteronomic account has an equivalent in Chronicles:

1. Jeroboam fortifies cities (12:25); so does Rehoboam (11:5–12).
2. Jeroboam seeks strength through religious policies (12:26–33); Rehoboam finds strength through Jeroboam's religious policies (11:13–17).
   a. Jeroboam fears loss of people (12:26–27); Rehoboam gains people (11:16–17a).
   b. Jeroboam founds sinful cult (12:28–30); Rehoboam practices correct cult (11:17b).
   c. Jeroboam ignores priests and Levites (12:31–33); Rehoboam gains priests and Levites (11:13–15).
3. The consequences of Jeroboam's actions are trouble for him (13:1–32), whereas Rehoboam's actions produce blessing (11:18–21).
4. Jeroboam's son Abijah is prevented from succeeding him (13:33–14:20), but Rehoboam's son Abijah is prepared for succession (11:22–23).

Not all of the parallels Goldingay suggests are that obvious (e.g., 1 Kgs 12:28–30 // 11:17b), nor are the passages in the same sequence. However, at a rhetorical level Rehoboam's early reign is in sharp contrast to the events in the North.

The material unique to Chronicles in these chapters is incorporated in the service of the author's theology of immediate retribution (11:6–13; 12:3–9a, 12–14); see the sections of *Comment* and *Explanation*. One can only speculate regarding the sources for the additional material. The closing formula (12:15–16) refers to genealogical records which may have served as a basis for the information about Rehoboam's family (11:18–23). The "accounts of Shemaiah"(12:15) would be the logical source for the additional materials on his appearances in connection with the invasion of Shishak, though his speeches do strongly show the Chronicler's own theological concerns. Redaction critical speculation yields few confident results at this point. Shemaiah's second and third appearances (12:5–8) may have existed in the past as a part of a prophetic lawsuit narrative; there are vestiges of an indictment and announcement of judgment (12:5), the subsequent acknowledgment of the suzerain's justice (12:6), and the restoration of the penitent vassal (12:7–8).

The list of cities fortified by Rehoboam (11:5–10) has been variously attributed to a source from the time of Josiah (Junge, Alt, Fritz) or Hezekiah (Na'aman). Current interpretations of the archeological evidence suggest that Lachish at the time of Rehoboam was a city without walls and had only a small fortified palatial building (Na'aman, *BASOR* 261 [1986] 6; D. Ussishkin, "Excavations at Tel Lachish—1973–1977," *Tel Aviv* 5 [1978] 27–31). Beth-zur appears to have been settled in the eleventh century but subsequently abandoned and without a major settlement in the tenth to ninth centuries. If these readings of the archeological data are correct, Beth-zur was desolate at the time of Rehoboam, and Lachish was not yet a fortified city. The list attributed by the Chronicler to the time of Rehoboam would then have to be dated to a later time. Aijalon and Gath present similar problems (Na'aman, 6–7). While skill in archeological method continues to grow, this data is often subject to reinterpretation; today's results from archeological investigation become tomorrow's footnotes about earlier errors. At a methodological level one has to question the relative weight of the epigraphic and archeological evidence: written evidence from the Chronicler who was so much closer to the events and sources is set against the interpretation of data from partial excavations. The list of cities fits very well the political and military concerns of Rehoboam; see *Comment* below.

Most striking in the Chronicler's account is his attenuation of the negative judgment on Rehoboam's reign found in Kings. The general indictment for deuteronomic conerns (1 Kgs 14:22–24) is missing and has been replaced by a less specific statement (12:14) somewhat qualified by his obedience (11:4; 12:6) and the recognition of "some good" in Judah (12:12).

The structure of the passages is fairly obvious from the subjects introduced. The main device appearing on paragraph boundaries is the use of the explicit subject (11:1, 5, 13, 18, 22; 12:5, 9, 13), though not every occurrence of an explicit subject marks the onset of a new paragraph (11:21; 12:10). A major break in the narrative is marked by two וַיְהִי-clauses (12:1–2). Similar wording regarding the humbling of Rehoboam may form an inclusio between 12:7 and 12:12.

Comment

1:11 The internecine warfare that would characterize the first fifty years of the divided kingdoms is momentarily averted by the intervention of Shemaiah; warfare would become the status quo for Jeroboam and Rehoboam (12:15 // 1 Kgs 14:30). The "truce" between them may have been influenced by the danger from Egypt and the need to prepare (11:5–12), just as danger from Assyria would later effect a temporary peace between Israel and Aram over disputed territory (1 Kgs 20, 22).

The number of troops is quite large, though already found in the parallel at 1 Kgs 12:21, and not nearly as large as the muster of 580,000 under Asa

(14:8), or the 470,000 of military age in Judah as determined by David's census (1 Chr 21:5), or the 307,500 troops of Uzziah (26:10), or the 300,000 of Amaziah (25:5). There is no indication that the Chronicler understood these as anything other than plain numbers; efforts to reduce the figures by appeal to the use of אֶלֶף, "thousand," as a military unit or the name of a military officer are unconvincing.

3–4 The Chronicler has modified 1 Kgs 12:23 ("all the house of Judah and Benjamin and the rest of the people") to read "all Israel in Judah and Benjamin," a change commonly interpreted as expressing the Chronicler's view that after the schism Judah and Benjamin were alone "true Israel" (von Rad, *Geschichtsbild,* 31; Rudolph, 227); cf. 10:17 and 12:1. More recent studies (Williamson, *IBC;* Braun, *JBL* 96 (1977) 59–62; Japhet, *Ideology*) have sought to moderate the perception that the Chronicler made claims of exclusivity for the South. Certainly the Chronicler wished to make the point that Judah was in unbroken continuity with Israel of the past. Though the North was in a state of political rebellion and cultic apostasy, and had virtually disappeared by his own day, our post-exilic author never lost the vision of the twelve tribes as necessary to a whole Israel. The Northern tribes are part of "all Israel" (1 Chr 1–9), are brethren (11:4), and just as capable of repentance (28:6–15) as the South was of apostasy (28:1–5, 16–25). While "to your tents, O Israel" (10:16) may have been a call to arms for rebellion, "return each to his house" (11:4) signals no war.

5–12 The Chronicler departs from his *Vorlage* at this point, though there is some parallelism: Kings goes on to report building activities on the part of Jeroboam in Shechem and Penuel (1 Kgs 12:25), possibly a stimulus for the Chronicler to report fortification construction under Rehoboam.

Scholars disagree on the date of the list the Chronicler used as a source for his list of cities; see above, *Form/Structure/Setting.* Those who accept a date from the time of Rehoboam disagree on whether the fortification of the fifteen sites was undertaken before or after the invasion of Shishak. The absence of a northern border of fortified cities in the list may reflect early hopes for military reunification with the North. Though the list is given before the invasion account, it is possible that the Chronicler has dischronologized the record in order to use the building motif as part of his showing divine blessing during the years that Rehoboam "walked in the ways of David and Solomon" (11:17). Cf. the dischronologization of the family records in 11:18–23.

The potential for invasion from Egypt was always present, but Jeroboam's return from shelter with Shishak would be ample stimulus for a fortification program. The fealty Jeroboam would likely owe to Egypt made Rehoboam the target in the middle—whether for attacks with the collusion of Jeroboam or attacks against a recalcitrant Jeroboam seeking to ignore the allegiance pledged the Pharaoh. Rehoboam's military situation was fairly clear; preparations for an Egyptian attack should have begun immediately, even if the work could not have been completed in the five years before Shishak arrived.

At first glance it is striking how small a territory was embraced by Rehoboam's defensive perimeter. The line of cities suggests that Rehoboam was confident of holding only the Shephelah and the Judean hills, and that he virtually conceded his inability to maintain sovereignty in the Negev and gulf regions as well as over the coastal plain and its important highway. Shishak's own account of his invasion shows that he did move up along the coastal highway while protecting his flanks with raids through the Negev. Vassals commonly rebelled at times of dynastic crisis; Edom had already sought to escape Solomon's yoke with the collusion of the Pharaoh (1 Kgs 11:14–22, 25) and may have been able to make incursions into Israel's contiguous territory with the encouragement of Egypt in the crisis following Solomon's death.

Though the line of fortresses represents a de facto concession of territory and the demise of the Solomonic empire, it is nevertheless strategically well considered. Each fortress defends important roads into the heart of Judah. Hebron, Beth-zur, and Bethlehem are either on or immediately adjacent to the north-south ridge road which was the major artery into Jerusalem. Etam, Tekoa, and Ziph protected approaches to this road from the east; later Moab, Ammon, and Edom would cross the Dead Sea to attack from this side and be repulsed near Tekoa (20:1–28). On the south Adoraim and Ziph protected access on roads connecting with Beersheba, Aroer, and Arad.

On the west a chain of fortresses dotted the low-lying hills rising from the coastal plain; the fortresses were located in the chalk valleys that had formed natural roadways through the soft limestone of the Shephelah. Beginning in the north, Aijalon was at the base of the all-important road going up the Beth Horon ridge into the central Benjamin plateau north of Jerusalem. Its strategic importance is known from the period of the conquest (Josh 10:10–11) and the contest with the Philistines (1 Sam 13:15–18; 14:31, 46; 1 Chr 14:8–17 // 2 Sam 5:17–25). Solomon had also fortified this highway (8:5 // 1 Kgs 9:17; cf. *Comment* at 8:3–6). Shishak's own account of his invasion itinerary shows that this was the road he took into the hill country. Hellenistic forces under Seron were routed along this ridge (1 Macc 3:13–24) in the mid-second century B.C., as was the Roman Twelfth Legion during the first revolt (Josephus, *J.W.* 2:278–486). The British fought along the same road during stormy weather in 1917; Turkish forts still dot the ridge. Aijalon was also connected to another route through Chephirah into the area north of Jerusalem and was along the north-south route through the chalk valley separating the Shephelah from the hill country through Adullam, Keilah, T. Beit Mirsim, and Beersheba.

Further south Zorah was fortified at the mouth of the Soreq Valley to guard the east-west route passing between it and Beth-shemesh; this route connected with the coastal highway at Jabneh and reached into the hill country at Jerusalem. A connecting branch passed through Ashdod, Ekron, and Timnah and appears to be the road assumed in the return of the ark from Philistine territory (1 Sam 6); the road also formed a portion of the boundary of Judah (Josh 15:10–11; Dorsey, 315).

South of the Aijalon and Soreq valleys the next ascent into the hill country is through the Elah Valley; the road here connected Philistine Gath with Bethlehem and, by another spur through Adullam and Keilah, with Bethzur. Rehoboam fortified Azekah and Soco at the entrance to this valley where David had earlier confronted Goliath (1 Sam 17).

The only site about which there is some question in the list of Rehoboam's fortresses is Gath. Philistine Gath would be to the west of Rehoboam's line of fortifications; it was a Philistine city at the time of Solomon (1 Kgs 2:39) and in the eighth century (Amos 6:2), and there is no indication of Israelite conquest (Aharoni, *Land,* 330). The site referred to is more probably Moresheth-gath (T. Judeideh), a site north of Mareshah; it could have been referred to simply as "Gath," or a haplography due to the similarity with the word "Mareshah" could have produced the present text. Both sites protect the entrance to the Guvrin Valley and roads to Hebron. It was along this road that Asa turned back the army of Zerah (14:9–10).

Lachish formed the pivotal southwestern corner of Rehoboam's fortifications. It was a junction for a road north to the rest of the fortresses, south to Egypt, and connected with the coastal highway on the west and through Adoraim to Hebron on the east.

The strategic considerations reflect the realities of Rehoboam's position. Apart from the uncertainties deriving from the archeological evidence, no compelling reasons demand redating the list to the time of Josiah or Hezekiah.

13–17 As an additional sign of divine blessing, the faithful priests and Levites of the Northern tribes abandon their common lands and private property (1 Chr 6:54–60; Num 35:1–5; Lev 25:32–34), prompting a similar defection following their example on the part of citizenry whose loyalty to Yahweh and his temple transcended their identification with tribal homelands. Jeroboam's fear that loyalty to the temple would reunite the kingdom (1 Kgs 12:26–27) apparently had some basis in fact; allegiance to Jerusalem for many, according to the Chronicler, was at great personal expense.

The Chronicler's own hand in shaping this pericope is seen in the use of the theme of "seeking God," a theme basic to retribution theology, and in his concern with the Levites.

Jeroboam's sons (11:14) could be "successors" (NEB), but this sort of telescoped blanket statement about the Northern Kingdom would not characterize the Chronicler. More probably the actual sons of Jeroboam held positions of authority like that of other royal sons (2 Sam 15:1–6; 1 Kgs 1:9), including those of his contemporary Rehoboam (11:22–23).

The Chronicler has enhanced the apostasy of Jeroboam in two ways. (1) He has added a reference to the goat idols, not known from Kgs, and has thereby indicated a transgression of Lev 17:7. (2) He has also made explicit Jeroboam's rejection of the levitical priests, rather than simply reporting his indiscriminate hiring practices as done in 1 Kgs 12:32; 13:33. The שעירים, "goats, hairy ones," are commonly treated in the ancient and modern versions as demons or satyrs: G here uses a doublet, εἰδώλοι, "idols," and ματαίοι, "profane things"; at Isa 13:21 and 34:14 the chosen equivalent is δαιμόνια, "demons." Vg gives *daemonum* and Tg שׁדיא. Snaith ("The Meaning of שעירים," *VT* 25 [1975] 115–18) argued that the satyr imagery is an unwarranted intrusion of Greco-Roman models into a Palestinian environment and proposed an identification with Canaanite rain gods or fertility deities.

Since Syria-Palestine does not yield evidence of any theriomorphic deities, and since deities in the region are commonly portrayed standing on the back of an associated animal, it is a widely held opinion that Jeroboam's calves were not originally intended to be idols per se, but rather simply the pedestals above which the invisible Yahweh stood; only later biblical writers/editors would have missed the distinction and viewed them as idols. However, it should be kept in mind that while the Levant does not show evidence of theriomorphic deities, this stricture does not apply to the iconography of Egypt, where deities are routinely portrayed in animal form. The two instances of calf idol production in the Bible occur on the heels of experience in Egypt, at the Exodus (Exod 33) and at Jeroboam's return from exile there. See further J. Oswalt, "The Golden Calves and the Egyptian Concept of Deity," *EvQ* 45 (1973) 13–20.

17 "Three years." One way the Chronicler demonstrates the cycles of obedience and blessing or sin and punishment that are the basis of retribution theology is by introducing chronological notes into his record. Here the author informs his reader that the period of blessing and obedience lasted three years, followed by abandoning the law of God (12:1) presumably in the fourth year, and the subsequent attack of Shishak in the fifth (12:2). Kings does not follow this schema and mentions only the fifth year (1 Kgs 14:25).

"Ways of David and Solomon." This phrase is symptomatic of the Chronicler's idealization of Solomon; considering the portrait of Solomon in Kings, one would not expect that author to make such a statement. Contrast his evaluation that Solomon's "heart was not fully devoted to Yahweh his God as the heart of David his father had been" (1 Kgs 11:4) with the Chronicler's favorable assessment of Rehoboam's "walking in the ways of David and Solomon."

18–22 For the Chronicler large families are a sign of divine blessing (1 Chr 3:1–9; 14:2–7; 25:5; 26:4–5; 2 Chr 13:21; 21:1–3). It is not impossible that Rehoboam had eighteen wives and sixty concubines, twenty-eight sons and sixty daughters before the fifth year of his reign, i.e., by age forty-six (12:13), though it does seem improbable that his harem could have been this large before his accession. It is far more natural to see this as a total for his family through the duration of his reign of seventeen years. If this latter is the case, the Chronicler has chronologically relocated these genealogical notes to include them with the blessings of building programs (11:5–12) and a loyal populace (11:13–17), prior to narrating Rehoboam's disobedience and subsequent punishment.

While the Chronicler does consider large families the product of divine blessing, it is striking that the potentially largest family—that of Solomon due to his many wives—goes unmentioned; presumably his silence on this point reflects the condemnation of Solomon for transgressions due to the many wives as reported in Kings (1 Kgs 11:1–13; Deut 17:17). The Chronicler not only does not mention the large number of Solomon's wives, but he alludes to Pharaoh's daughter only in passing (8:11).

The genealogical section may also have the intent of explaining why the eldest son did not receive the kingdom. Though there are several examples in the Bible where the rights of primogeniture have been set aside by a father (Gen 17:19–21; 48:13–20; 1 Kgs 1:32–37; 2 Sam 3:3–4; 1 Chr 26:10), the law sought to protect the rights of the firstborn (Deut 21:15–17) and specifically rejects greater love for one wife as grounds for transferring the privilege to another son. For the firstborn son of a king primogeniture included appointment as crown prince (2 Chr 21:3). The appointment of Ahijah may also have begun a kind of coregency.

18 "Jerimoth" is not named among the sons of David in any other passage; he may have been the son of a lesser wife or concubine (1 Chr 3:9).

20 "Maacah daughter of Absalom." She was probably the granddaughter of David's son Absalom. Absalom had a beautiful daughter named Tamar and three sons (2 Sam 14:27). Since the sons do not appear to have survived childhood (2 Sam 18:18), Maacah must have been born to Tamar through a marriage to Uriel of Gibeah (2 Chr 13:2, LXX).

23 Extant records from some ancient Near Eastern rulers testify to their concern to secure the succession and an orderly transition of power. Rehoboam's dispersal of the royal princes not only extended control of the royal family into the outlying districts but also may have made planning any coup d'état more difficult. Awareness of difficulties in David's own household (2 Sam 15; 1 Kgs 1) was probably a contributing factor, though these incidents are not mentioned by the Chronicler.

12:1–4 The Chronicler's hand in reshaping the account in Kings is transparent here. Kings makes no judgment regarding the reasons for Shishak's attack, but for the Chronicler defeat and humiliation in warfare are the consequence of divine judgment. "Abandon, forsake" (עזב) and "be rebellious" (מעל) are key vehicles for the Chronicler's theology of retribution; see below on 12:5–8. The author does not spell out the precise nature of this abandoning and infidelity; presumably the transgressions are those described in 1 Kgs 14:22–24; cf. 12:14. The Chronicler will later suggest an additional reason for Rehoboam's political failures, his youth and immaturity (13:7).

Here (12:1) "all Israel" refers to the Southern Kingdom, but also as including citizenry from the other tribes (11:13–17). The "law of Yahweh" implies a canonical corpus, at least equivalent to the Pentateuch by the Chronicler's own time; cf. 17:9; 6:16.

Shishak (945–924 B.C.) was the founder of the twenty-second dynasty and achieved the reunification of a divided Egypt, a goal that had eluded his predecessors. As long as Israel remained militarily powerful under Solomon in its position along Egypt's northern and eastern borders, Shishak could do little more than harbor rebels (1 Kgs 11:26–40) and foster rebellion among Solomon's vassals (1 Kgs 11:14–22). After Solomon's death and the disintegration of his empire, and with a client of Egypt on the throne of the Northern Kingdom, Shishak's forces could sweep through and around Israel and Judah at will. So great is the concern of the biblical authors with Jerusalem that were the Bible our only source regarding this campaign, it would seem that Shishak attacked Judah alone, primarily for the prize of Solomon's golden shields in Jerusalem. However, in Shishak's own record of the campaign written on the walls of a temple at Karnak, more than 150 towns are named, but Jerusalem is not mentioned. From Shishak's topographical list it emerges that the kingdom of Israel and the Negev of Judah were in fact the main objectives of the expedition. Several features of the text make it difficult to reconstruct the precise line of march. Various scholars have evaluated the text (Aharoni, Herrmann, Mazar, Noth); a survey of previous research and a fresh synthesis of the data are given in Kitchen, *TIPE*, 432–47. Shishak advanced along the coastal highway to Gaza and then to Gezer or Makkedah, depending on how a damaged portion in the text is reconstructed; detachments were dispatched to raid in the Negev and protect the Pharaoh's rear flank. The main body of the army may have proceeded to Megiddo, or alternatively, the main troop or at least a "flying column" advanced through Aijalon and up the Beth Horon ridge to Gibeon. At Gibeon Shishak or his representatives probably received the submission and tribute of Rehoboam, thus averting catastrophe for Jerusalem and accounting also for the fact that the city is not mentioned in Shishak's list. The remainder of Shishak's campaign was conducted in Ephraim and Manasseh, through the Jezreel Valley and down the Harod Valley toward Beth-shean and the Transjordan regions, though the order of march remains debatable.

Of the cities that Rehoboam fortified, only Aijalon is mentioned in Shishak's list, though Shishak is said to have conquered the fortresses of Judah (12:4). It may be mute testimony to the success of Rehoboam's fortifications and to the fact that they were undertaken before the Pharaoh's campaign; Shishak attacks sites west and south of Rehoboam's defensive perimeter. Alternatively the other fortified cities may have submitted to Shishak and paid tribute, possibly on Rehoboam's orders, just as did Jerusalem. The mention of Aijalon also establishes the line of attack up the Beth Horon ridge. The major thrust of the campaign was against the Northern Kingdom, suggesting a punitive expedition against a recalcitrant Jeroboam.

3 "Sukkites." The reference to the Sukkites confirms the antiquity of the Chronicler's sources for his account of Shishak's campaign. Though they are not mentioned in the parallel in Kings, the Chronicler has included a reference to this group of Libyan forces from the oases of the western desert; the Sukkites (Egyptian *Tjukten*) are known from Egyptian records primarily from the thirteenth and twelfth centuries B.C. See further Kitchen, *TIPE*, 295. The significance of the term was lost to the G translators; see A. Brawer, "'Sukkites' in 2 Chr 12:3," *BMik* 13 (1967) 127, and Allen, *GC* 1:23.

5–8 According to G. Schaefer (*Seeking*, 28–29), of the 165 speeches in Chronicles, 95 have parallels in Samuel/Kings; many of the nonparallel speeches tend to be longer. Of these the speeches of prophets and kings are particularly important as vehicles for the Chronicler's own theological assessments. The formula "you have abandoned me; I have abandoned you" or an approximate equivalent appears in similar speech materials in 1 Chr 28:9; 2 Chr 15:2; 24:20 and demonstrates the hand of the author in the presentation of speeches. The outworking of the programmatic statement that "if my people . . . will humble themselves . . ."(7:14) is vividly portrayed in this narrative; Yahweh does take account of the humility and penitence of king and people and lessens the consequences of Shishak's attack.

9 The G translators made explicit in the parallel text (1 Kgs 14:26) the deduction that the gold for Solomon's shields came from David's plunder; cf. 1 Chr 18:7–11; 26:26–28.

12 The Chronicler reiterates his conclusion that it was by humbling himself before the LORD that Rehoboam escaped (12:7), but he also adds the note that there was "some good" in Judah. The good is left undefined—it may have been the very acts of contrition themselves, the many faithful in the kingdom, the residual benefit of God's promises to David, or simply the favor shown to his people Israel.

13–14 This information occurs at the beginning of the Kings account (1 Kgs 14:21–22); Rudolph (235) regards its insertion here as the work of a later editor.

With reference to the overall verdict on Rehoboam's reign, see *Form/Structure/Setting*. The *evil* Rehoboam did no doubt refers to those things mentioned at this point in the parallel text (1 Kgs 14:22–24). *Seeking God* echoes 7:14 once again and is one of the most characteristic terms of the Chronicler's theology.

16 "Abijah" is "Abijam" in Kings. There are a variety of ways to account for the varying forms of his name: these may be no more than orthographic variants or the difference between his given name and a throne name. One other possibility has intrigued scholars: if Abijam ("my father is Yam") contains a reference to the Canaanite god Yam, the Chronicler (whose opinion about that king is much more positive than that found in Kings) or a later editor could have corrected the name to Abijah ("My father is Yah"); this way of construing the data is a possibility, but no more probable than the others.

Explanation

The reign of Rehoboam is the author's first opportunity to demonstrate how he will treat the reigns of kings after the schism; it provides a virtual paradigm for the program announced in the divine response to Solomon's prayer at the dedication of the temple (7:14). Almost all the changes the Chronicler has made in his *Vorlage* have served the purpose of highlighting the fact that God responds with blessings for obedience and with punishment for transgression. Though Kings reports the obedience of Rehoboam to Shemaiah's first speech (1 Kgs 12:21–24), the Chronicler goes on to show how this obedience issued in prosperity and power (11:5–12), popular support (11:13–17), and progeny (11:18–23). Though Kings reports the invasion of Shishak and the loss of Solomon's shields (1 Kgs 14:25–28), that author makes no theological judgment regarding those events; contrast the Chronicler, however, who provides the theological rationale for both the attack and the narrow escape of Judah. All the key terms ("seek, humble, abandon/forsake, rebel") the Chronicler uses to convey his theology of immediate retribution occur in these chapters.

Rehoboam's reign marks the first time Jerusalem suffers military humiliation since it became the City of David; it had never experienced in Israelite hands "servitude to the kingdoms of other lands" (12:8, a passage unique to Chronicles). Penitence and fidelity in Rehoboam's day had opened a way to escape disaster, just as a penitent community had enjoyed restoration to their land and temple in the days preceding the Chronicler's own times. The author's message to the post-exilic community, now living in servitude under the Persian empire, could not be missed: the path to freedom and to the amelioration of Judah's difficulties lay in seeking God and in humbling oneself before him, while turning from that path could bring only disaster. The passage is a warning against presumptuous transgression, for "the soul who sins is the one who will die" (Ezek 18:4, 20, 24). Perhaps the closest analog to these chapters in the NT is Paul's setting before the church the issues of servitude, righteousness, and freedom (Rom 6:16–18).

The Reign of Abijah,
913–911/10 B.C.　(13:1–23 [14:1])

Bibliography

Klein, R. "Abijah's Campaign against the North (II Chr 13)—What Were the Chronicler's Sources?" *ZAW* 95 (1983) 210–17. **Koch, K.** "Zur Lage von Ṣemarajim." *ZDPV* 78 (1962) 19–29. **Mendenhall, G.** "The Census Lists of Numbers 1 and 26." *JBL* 77 (1958) 52–66. **Payne, J. B.** "The Validity of Numbers in Chronicles." *BSac* 136 (1979) 109–28, 206–20; also in *Near East Archaeological Society Bulletin*, n.s. 11 (1978) 5–58. **Rad, G. von.** "The Levitical Sermon in I and II Chronicles." *The Problem of the Hexateuch and Other Essays.* Tr. E. Dicken. New York: McGraw-Hill, 1966. **Wenham, J.** "Large Numbers in the Old Testament." *TynBul* 18 (1967) 19–53.

Translation

[1] *In the eighteenth year of King Jeroboam, Abijah*[a] *began to rule over Judah;* [2] *he ruled three years in Jerusalem. His mother's name was Maacah,*[a] *daughter of Uriel of Gibeah.*[b] *There was war between Abijah and Jeroboam.*[c]

[3] *Abijah went into battle with four hundred thousand select troops, and Jeroboam deployed eight hundred thousand select troops against him.*

[4] *Abijah stood on Mount Zemarayim in the hill country of Ephraim and said,*

"Hear me, Jeroboam and all Israel! [5] *Should not you know that Yahweh has given kingship over Israel to David forever—for him and his sons it is a covenant of salt.* [6] *But Jeroboam son of Nebat, a servant of Solomon son of David, arose and rebelled against his master.*[a] [7] *Some worthless scoundrels gathered around him and opposed Rehoboam son of Solomon, when Rehoboam was young and inexperienced and not strong enough to resist them.*

[8] *Now you are planning*[a] *to resist the kingdom of Yahweh in the hands of the sons of David. You are a great horde, and you have with you the golden calves that Jeroboam made for you as gods.* [9] *Haven't you driven out the sons of Aaron and the Levites and made priests for yourselves like the peoples of other lands? Now anyone who comes for consecration with a young bull and seven rams can become a priest to what are not gods!*

[10] *But as for us, Yahweh is our God and we have not forsaken him. The priests who serve Yahweh are the sons of Aaron, and the Levites assist them.* [11] *Every morning and evening they present burnt offerings and fragrant incense to Yahweh; they set out the stacks*[a] *of bread on a table ritually clean and light the lamps on the golden lampstand every evening. Indeed we are observing the requirements of Yahweh our God, but you have forsaken him.* [12] *Behold God is with us at the lead;*[a] *his priests have trumpets to sound the battle cry against you. O children of Israel, do not fight with Yahweh, the God of your fathers, for you will not succeed!"*

[13] *Now Jeroboam had sent troops around behind them for an ambush, so that the main force was in front of Judah while the ambush was behind.* [14] *Judah turned, and to their surprise the battle raged in front and behind them. They cried out to Yahweh, and the priests blew the trumpets;* [15] *each man of Judah raised the battle cry.*

So it was, that when each man of Judah raised the battle cry, God routed Jeroboam and all Israel before Abijah and Judah. [16] *The Israelites fled before Judah, and God delivered them into their hand.* [17] *Abijah and his men inflicted heavy losses on them; there were five hundred thousand casualties among Israel's select troops.* [18] *The Israelites were subdued on that occasion, and the men of Judah were victorious, because they relied upon God.*

[19] *Abijah pursued Jeroboam and captured these cities from him: Bethel, Jeshannah, and Ephron,*[a] *together with their surrounding villages.* [20] *Jeroboam did not regain power during the days of Abijah; Yahweh struck him down and he died.*

[21] *Abijah consolidated his power; he married fourteen wives and had twenty-two sons and sixteen daughters.*

[22] *The rest of the matters concerning Abijah—both his words and deeds*[a]*—are written in the commentary of the prophet Iddo.* [23] [14:1] *Abijah rested with his fathers, and they buried him in the city of David. Asa his son ruled in his place, and the land was quiet in his*[a] *days for ten*[b] *years.*

Notes

1.a. "Abijah" is consistently named "Abijam" in Kings; see *Comment* at 12:16.

2.a. G, Syr, and the parallel text at 1 Kgs 15:2; MT and Vg, "Micaiah."

2.b. 1 Kgs 15:2 identifies her as the "daughter of Abishalom"; see *Comment*.

2.c. Note the parallel at 1 Kgs 15:6, "there was war between Rehoboam and Jeroboam." Some Hebrew MSS and Syr read "between Abijam and Jeroboam"; the verse is missing, however, in the OG of Bas.

6.a. "Master" is pl in its MT form, but uniformly translated as a sg in the versions. The word ordinarily occurs in a pl form as an "intensive pl of rank" (BDB, 10) having a sg referent.

8.a. Cf. the use of אמר in 1:18 [2:1].

11.a. מערכת ordinarily means "row, formation"; the difficulty with "rows" in reference to the Bread of the Presence is simply logistics: the twelve disc-shaped loaves would not likely fit on a table the size of that prescribed. Even though unleavened, the loaves contained about a gallon of flour each and would have to occupy a surface roughly eighteen by thirty-six inches (Lev 24:5–9; Exod 37:10–16). It may not be necessary to assume that the same size table or quantity of flour was always used, though both seem probable; the other avenue open is to suggest an arrangement other than rows, i.e., stacks.

12.a. ראש is ambiguous in this context: it could be "commander, leader" or "at the front, lead."

19.a. With the Q, many MSS, and the versions; K, "Ephrayin."

22.a. In place of "both his words and deeds," 1 Kgs 15:7 has "and all that he did."

23 [14:1].a. G has specified the antecedent, "in the days of Asa."

23 [14:1].b. Syr and Arab, "twenty."

Form/Structure/Setting

Though there can scarcely be any doubt that the Chronicler had 1 Kgs 15:1–8 before him as he undertook to write his account of the reign of Abijah, only the introductory and concluding formulae are strictly parallel in any sense. Where Kings describes a sinful king not wholly devoted to God, a king maintained only because of God's fidelity to David, the Chronicler presents instead a victorious leader and preacher of righteousness. Apart from the introductory and concluding formulae, the only contact between the two canonical accounts may have been that the remark regarding warfare between Rehoboam and Jeroboam (1 Kgs 15:6—but see *Notes* regarding a textual difficulty) stimulated the Chronicler to substitute an account of a war with Jeroboam during Abijah's short reign. The Chronicler's account is three times longer than that of his *Vorlage.*

Von Rad's analysis ("Levitical Sermon") of speech materials in Chronicles did not include a discussion of Abijah's speech, even though it is among the longest examples available; the categories of his analysis are, nevertheless, quite applicable. Von Rad described an outline for levitical sermons as consisting of doctrine, application, and exhortation, accompanied by appeal to earlier biblical texts. In the case of Abijah's speech, the doctrinal basis is the divinely established legitimacy of the dynasty of David and the Jerusalem cult (13:5, 10–12a); these doctrines are applied to the immediate situation with the verdict that Jeroboam had led the people to abandon the worship and kingdom of Yahweh (13:6–9). On this basis the king exhorts the Northerners, "do not fight against the LORD, the God of your fathers, for you will not succeed" (13:12b). The basis for both doctrines is established by allusion to earlier biblical materials (2 Sam 7 // 1 Chr 17; Exod 29:1–21; 28:1; Lev 8–9). Von Rad (278) also noted that a biblical text often "stands at the end by way of climax, as a kind of final trump card with which the speaker takes the decisive trick against his hearers"; though it is not the end of his speech, the allusion to the "no-gods" of Hos 8:6 is a climactic moment in Abijah's address (13:9). Von Rad also noted the way in which the Chronicler has presented kings as prophetic preachers (19:6–7; 20:20; 32:7–8; 14:7).

There is pervasive evidence of the Chronicler's own hand in the shaping of the speech: (1) the vocabulary of retribution theology is found in his use of עָזַב, "forsake" (13:10, 11) and צָלֵחַ, "succeed" (13:12); (2) the insertion of lists of cultic duties (13:10–11) is also characteristic of the Chronicler (1 Chr 9:28–32; 23:28–31; 2 Chr 2:4; 8:12; 29:4–7, 18–19); (3) he also frequently makes the point that the kingdom of Israel is the kingdom of Yahweh (13:8; cf. 1 Chr 17:14; 28:5; 29:11, 23; 2 Chr 9:8). While there is no good reason to question that a speech was made by Abijah, it is apparent that the author has also made it a vehicle for his own concerns.

Overlaying the entire passage are the motifs of holy war. Battles displaying the power of Israel's God are commonly fought against much larger armies (13:3; Deut 20:2; 2 Chr 14:8–9; 20:2); a pre-battle speech by a priest, prophet, or king assures that God is with Israel's army and will give victory (13:5–13; Deut 20:1–4; 2 Chr 20:5–17). An offer of peace may be tendered to the opposing forces (13:5–13; Deut 20:10). Cultic purity for the combatants is a prerequisite (13:10–11; 1 Sam 21:4–5; Josh 5:1–8; 7:13; 2 Chr 20:3–4); victory follows the blowing of the trumpets by the priests and the battle cry from the army (13:12–15; Num 10:8–9; 31:6; Josh 6; 2 Chr 20:18–22).

Klein (*ZAW* 95 [1983] 210–17) surveys the possible sources for materials in this pericope, with particular focus on the geographical details of Abijah's battle (13:4, 19). He concludes that all of the Chronicler's departures from Kings can be explained as due to a divergent text of Samuel-Kings, to his own theological viewpoints, and to his use of an old Benjamite list (Josh 18:21–24) to provide geographical concreteness for Abijah's victory; none of the material is necessarily from extrabiblical sources. Because he finds the same cities in the list in Josh 18:21–24, Klein concludes the Chronicler borrowed cities from this list for his own battle narrative. However, while it may be reasonable to use 2 Chr 13:4, 19 to assist in restoring the text of Josh 18:21–24, it is hardly surprising that two sources reporting events within the borders of Benjamin would mention some of the same cities. There is a high probability that some of the same cities would be mentioned, and this vitiates the value of these city names as evidence that the Chronicler borrowed them from Josh 18 to provide concreteness for an otherwise spurious story. While it is clear that the Chronicler frequently patterns material after earlier biblical narratives, as a methodological question one has to ask whether the ability to connect sets of biblical data (size of the armies in 13:3 and 2 Sam 24:9; the city named in 13:4, 19 with Josh 18:21–24) is always to be construed as evidence of dependence and reuse.

The major paragraph-level device the Chronicler continues to favor is the repetition of the explicit subject (13:3, 4, 13, 19, 21). In earlier Hebrew the use of ויהי with a following infinitive construct repeating part of the preceding clause was often a major episode or narrative level device (described as tail-head linkage by discourse analysts), but here (13:15b) it does not appear to function in quite the same way. Within the speech itself two paragraphs are marked primarily by the contrast of "you"(13:8) and "we"(13:10); ועתה (13:8) is also commonly found on paragraph boundaries.

Comment

1–2   This is the only instance in which the Chronicler provides a synchronism with the Northern king in an introductory formula.

"Maacah" was the wife of Rehoboam (11:20), the mother of Abijah (13:2), and the mother of Asa (15:16). In 15:16 the word "mother" must be understood as "grandmother" unless a different woman of the same name was one of Abijah's wives; since the succession was from father to son (12:16; 14:1), Abijah and Asa should not be construed as brothers. Maacah is both "daughter of Abishalom" (a variant of Absalom—1 Kgs 15:2) and "daughter of Uriel of Gibeah" (13:2); see *Comment* at 11:20.

3   The numbers appear once again quite high. The known total military casualties of the United States during World War II (1939–45) were 1,076,245, the dead numbering more than 400,000 and the wounded more than 600,000; for France during the same time period, there were 741,462 casualties, of whom 200,000 were deaths. The casualties for the Northern Kingdom for this one battle are set at 500,000 (v 17).

Scholars have generally taken one of several approaches to these large numbers. (1) It is suggested that אלף, ordinarily "thousand," was also a term designating a military unit which at full strength may have numbered considerably less than a thousand, much as a Roman centurion ordinarily commanded a unit smaller than a hundred (cf. Judg 6:15; Num 1:16; Mic 5:1; 1 Sam 10:19–21). (2) Another approach repoints אלף as *ʾalluf*, "commander, colonel" and would see the armies as having eight hundred or four hundred officers. (3) A third avenue is to understand that the Chronicler intends these numbers as hyperbolic, not literal figures of an actual headcount, but rather as indexes of the magnitude of the victory God gave to Abijah. Each of these approaches is subject to serious objections and none can claim to be satisfactory. See the discussions in Payne, Wenham, and Mendenhall. Klein (*ZAW* 95 [1983] 217) views the figures of 800,000 and 400,000 as derived from David's census; the MT of 2 Sam 24:9 gives 800,000 in Israel and 500,000 in Judah, though the Lucianic text of 2 Sam 24:9 and Josephus both give 400,000 for Judah.

4–12 The speech of Abijah has two foci: the legitimacy of the Davidic dynasty and the legitimacy of the Jerusalem cult. The kingdom of David is in reality the kingdom of Yahweh; Jeroboam is a rebel surrounded by worthless scoundrels. The cultic personnel and apparatus of the South are divinely ordained, while those of the North serve "no-gods." The speech has commonly been interpreted as an anti-Samaritan polemic, particularly so by scholars who have held to an early date for the Samaritan schism and to the unity of Chronicles, Ezra, and Nehemiah as the work of the "Chronicler"; for the arguments against this view, see Williamson, *IBC,* particularly with reference to Abijah's speech, pp. 111–14. The Chronicler's hand is evident in shaping the speech; see the discussion under *Form/Structure/Setting.*

4–5 Mount Zemarayim is probably to be identified with the town of the same name on the northern borders of Benjamin (Josh 18:22). It is usually associated with Ras ez-Zeimara about five miles northeast of Bethel in the hill country between et-Taiyibeh and Rammun. Koch (*ZDPV* 78 [1962]) places it in the Jordan valley northeast of Jericho. Williamson (252) suggests yet a third alternative in Khirbet el-Mazāriᶜa, the most imposing peak in the region and some two kilometers west of Ras ez-Zeimara. If Mount Zemarayim in the hill country of Ephraim (2 Chr 13:4) is the same as the town in the allotment of Benjamin (Josh 18:22) it is mute testimony to the position of Benjamin as the buffer and battleground between the Northern and Southern Kingdoms.

The context implies that a "covenant of salt" is an eternal and efficacious covenant, though the precise social or religious character of such a covenant is not known. The "salt of the covenant" was necessary for a sacrifice to be efficacious (Lev 2:13); W. Robertson Smith (*Lectures on the Religion of the Semites,* 2d ed. [1894] 270) related the reference to the sacredness of the bond acknowledged among Arabs between persons who have "eaten salt" together. The covenant made with David was as permanent as the covenant made with Israel in the wilderness (Num 18:19; Coggins, 195).

6–7 Two quite different understandings of Abijah's speech and of the Chronicler's assessment of the schism hinge on the identification of the antecedent of the "him" of 13:7. Did the scoundrels gather around Jeroboam or Rehoboam?

Williamson (252–53; *IBC,* 112–13) contends that Rehoboam is the correct reference. "Master" is the immediate antecedent and unquestionably does refer to Rehoboam. Williamson also notes that the Chronicler does not mention any group gathering around Jeroboam in the same way that the young men gathered about Rehoboam to persuade him not to follow the advice of the elders (10:8); he also argues that ויתאמצו על "nowhere else" has the meaning "defy," but rather "prevail over" or "persuade." Williamson is not alone in his approach to the passage; Josephus (*Ant.* 8:277) also read this verse as a reference to Rehoboam's following the advice of wicked men when he was young and inexperienced. Rehoboam is assigned a large measure of the blame for the schism; Abijah's speech does not criticize the Northerners for failing to submit to Rehoboam, but rather reiterates Rehoboam's failures already articulated in 2 Chr 10. The reference to Rehoboam's youth reinforces this interpretation: he was the same age as his advisors (10:8). Since the schism was ordained by God (10:15), why would the Chronicler criticize the failure of the Northerners to submit to Rehoboam's rule?

Most commentators, however, have understood the antecedent of "him" as Jeroboam. Condemnation of the Northern Kingdom is the overarching feature of the immediate context: Jeroboam's rebellion, resisting the kingdom of God, the illegitimate cult—all these are contrasted to the situation in the South; in this context it would seem a digression to assign blame to Rehoboam if the passage can be understood in a natural way as yet further heightening Jeroboam's culpability. The statement that "now you are planning to resist the kingdom of Yahweh" (13:8) is best understood applied to the Northern Kingdom with the implication "just the way you/your fathers did when you/they resisted Rehoboam" (13:7). The argument from the meaning of אמץ is also without much value: this is the only occurrence of the hithpael form of that verb followed by the preposition על, and it would be unwise to argue that an extended meaning for one of the other stems is the only appropriate one in this context; the uncertainty about the verb requires greater reliance on the immediate context and its concern with the wrongs in the North and resistance to the kingdom of Yahweh. 2 Chr 10:2–3 // 1 Kgs 12:2–3 does speak of those who gathered around Jeroboam and made him the leader of their rebellion. If this identification of the antecedent of "him" with Jeroboam is correct, quite different conclusions follow. The Chronicler had exonerated Solomon of all blame for the schism as part of his overall idealization of the reign of both David and Solomon; see the introductory essay, "The Chronicler's Solomon." Having eliminated the blame for the schism in connection with Solomon's sin (1 Kgs 11), where will the Chronicler assign the blame? Certainly Rehoboam bears some of the onus (2 Chr 10), but the full weight of reproof is assigned to Jeroboam and his congeners; Abijah warns the next generation not to repeat their sin. Commonly the Chronicler has been read as quite hostile to the Northern Kingdom; in his generally well-founded zeal to redress the excesses of that reading of Chronicles, Williamson may have overdrawn his evidence in this pericope.

Solomon was also called young and inexperienced at the time of his accession (1 Chr 22:5; 29:1), but David had made careful provisions for a smooth transition of power by securing the allegiance of the nation's leadership to Solomon (1 Chr 28–29), a benefit that Rehoboam did not have.

8–9 For the Chronicler the kingdom of David was the kingdom of God; that kingdom was forever to be in the hands of David's descendants. For the post-exilic audience to which he wrote, an audience living without a Davidic king, this speech must have expressed their hopes and aspirations. The speech argues from the two foci of legitimate king and legitimate cult; in the Chronicler's own day legitimate cult was a reality with the second temple, and aspirations for political freedom fired hopes for the reestablishment of the Davidic dynasty. Israel as the kingdom of Yahweh is one of the Chronicler's favorite themes (1 Chr 17:14; 28:5; 29:11, 23; 2 Chr 9:8).

For consecration to the priesthood the law specified a young bull and two rams (Exod 29:1); the increase to seven rams may reflect the current practice in Jerusalem as well at the time of the schism, or possibly "inflation" in the new kingdom of Jeroboam, enhancing for the Chronicler the idea that the office was for sale. "Come for consecration" is expressed literally in the idiom "fill the hand" (Exod 28:41; 29:9, 29, 33, 35; 32:29; Lev 8:33; et al.)

10–11 Such lists of cultic duties are common insertions by the Chronicler (see *Form/Structure/Setting*); they give voice also to the importance of the cult in the post-exilic period and probably represent something of the confidence of the restoration community in its own cultic rectitude. The duties catalogued here are all performed daily except for setting out the Bread of the Presence which was to be done on a weekly basis (Lev 24:8). With reference to the incense, see *Comment* on 9:1–12.

12–18 Abijah's speech and the following battle narrative show many of the motifs common in holy war ideology; see *Form/Structure/Setting*. שׁען ("trust," 13:18) is one of the less frequent terms in the Chronicler's vocabulary of retribution theology (14:10; 16:7–8).

19 The cities are all known from the pre-exilic period (contra Welten, *Geschichte*, 116–29); Jeshanah should possibly be inserted at 1 Sam 7:12 and Josh 18:22 for text critical reasons (Klein, *ZAW* 95 [1983] 212–16). The historical reliability of the information in this verse has been the subject of some debate; see the bibliography in Williamson, 254–55.

The calf idol from the shrine at Bethel was apparently with Jeroboam's army (13:8) as a battle palladium, much as Israel had earlier used the ark; it must have been withdrawn before Bethel was taken. Bethel passed back into Northern possession prior to Baasha's fortifying Ramah (16:1); the calf idol was eventually reinstalled in Bethel (2 Kgs 10:29).

20 One means by which Abijah may have blocked any resurgence under Jeroboam would have been a treaty with Aram to open a second front to Jeroboam's north; though the treaty is not directly mentioned in any biblical text, it is implied in Asa's speaking of his father's treaty with Aram (16:3; 1 Kgs 15:19). Asa sought to use the same ploy (16:1–6). The Chronicler ordinarily considers reliance on a foreign power a sign of distrust in Yahweh (16:7–9; 19:1–3; 25:7–10; 28:16–21).

The verse correctly implies that Jeroboam outlived Abijah (13:20a; cf. 1 Kgs 15:9). The report of his death is telescoped and should be compared with the similar immediate report of the death of a defeated enemy in the case of Sennacherib (2 Kgs 19:37), even though about twenty years would elapse between his defeat in 701 B.C. and his death. The death notice for Jeroboam in 1 Kgs 14:19–20 has no note of divine retribution.

21 The Chronicler often uses numerous progeny as a sign of divine blessing; see the *Comment* at 11:18–21. For the Chronicler's use of התחזק, "consolidated his power," see the *Comment* at 1:1.

22–23 [14:1] The concluding notices for the reign of Abijah are slightly different than the Chronicler's ordinary practice: the phrase "from first to last" (וראשנים והאחרנים) is missing, and the other sources are not introduced with the usual rhetorical question "Are they not written . . ." (9:29; 12:15).

Iddo is cited as a source under other "titles" (9:29; 12:15), but only here under the "Midrash of the Prophet Iddo." The term *midrash* occurs only here and in 24:27; its precise connotations are not known. The term may mean simply "annotations" or "commentary," or it may have already begun to develop in the direction of the sense it would have in later rabbinic exegesis. It is not implausible that a work showing features of later exegesis would have been available in the Chronicler's own day; the elaboration and commentary on Scripture which became known as "midrash" was already known by the period of the Qumran sect (Lemke, *Synoptic Studies*, 146). In the absence of fuller evidence surrounding the use of the term, one can only speculate.

The Chronicler frequently introduces chronological notes not found in Kings into his account. These notes play a particularly important role in his recounting the reign of Asa; see the discussion at 15:19. This ten-year period would have covered roughly 910-900 B.C., i.e., until the invasion of Zerah.

The Chronicler makes a distinctive use of the "rest" concept (G. von Rad, "There Remains Still a Rest for the People of God," *The Problem of the Hexateuch and Other Essays*, trans. E. Dicken [New York: McGraw-Hill, 1966] 97–98; R. Braun, *JBL* 95 [1976] 582–86); forms of שקט (1 Chr 22:9, 18; 23:25; 28:2; 2 Chr 14:4–5 [5-6]; 15:15; 20:30) and נוח (13:23 [14:1]; 14:4–7 [5–8]; 20:30; 23:21) are the primary vehicles. The concept is introduced in 1 Chr 22:9 during the tranquil and godly reign of Solomon and is applied subsequently to point to the peace attending other godly reigns.

Explanation

Numerous lines of evidence suggest that the Chronicler wrote to an audience well familiar with Israel's historical traditions; in particular he was able to presume that his audience already knew the version of Israel's history in the book of Kings. But to an audience that probably was well aware of the deuteronomic historian's judgment on the reign of Abijah, the Chronicler gave an opposite moral judgment. The writer of Kings devoted his account to Abijah's sinfulness; in quantity he said more about God's fidelity to David than he actually reported about Abijah. The Chronicler on the other hand has presented us with a prophet king, a preacher of righteousness enjoying the benefits and blessing of his fidelity. Yet Judaism, and subsequently Christianity, would both accept both versions as word of God.

The import of Abijah's sermon was not likely lost on the post-exilic community for which the Chronicler wrote. The theocracy stood on twin pillars: the Davidic covenant and the temple cult, both the foci of Abijah's condemnation of the North. The post-exilic community had enjoyed the reinstitution of the temple cult; the revitalization of Israel awaited the reestablishment of political freedom under Davidic rule. The Chronicler is so often treated as if he offered no eschatological expectation and was an advocate of the status quo; that reading of Chronicles, however, cannot grapple adequately with the forcefulness with which the Chronicler reiterates the eternality of God's promises to the house of David (1 Chr 17; 22:10; 28:6–7; 2 Chr 6:16; 7:17–18; 13:4, 8). The post-exilic community might be under foreign domination, but the kingdom remains secure: God always was the real king of Israel (13:8), even when no descendant of David sat on a throne.

The Chronicler will later draw on his account of the reign of Abijah to show that the South could sink to the same level of apostasy as had the North; see the discussion of 2 Chr 28.

One passage in the NT makes a similar argument to that in 13:8; Gamaliel warned his hearers about the irresistibility of the kingdom of God (Acts 5:38–39).

The Reign of Asa,
911/10–870/69 B.C.   (14:1 [2]–16:14)

Bibliography

Dillard, R. "The Reign of Asa (2 Chr 14–16): An Example of the Chronicler's Theological Method." *JETS* 23 (1980) 207–18. **Rudolph, W.** "Der Aufbau der Asa-Geschichte." *VT* 2 (1952) 367–71.

Translation

¹[²]*Now Asa did what was good*[a] *and right in the eyes of Yahweh his God.*[b] ²[³]*He removed the foreign altars and the high places; he smashed the sacred pillars and cut down the Asherah poles.* ³[⁴]*He ordered Judah to seek Yahweh the God of their fathers and to keep the law and the commandments;* ⁴[⁵]*he removed the high places and the incense altars from all the cities of Judah, and the kingdom was at peace under him.*

⁵[⁶]*Since the land was at peace, he built fortified cities in Judah; he had no wars to fight during those years, for Yahweh had given him rest.* ⁶[⁷]*He said to Judah, "Let us fortify these cities and construct walls around them with towers and barred gates. The land is still ours because we have sought Yahweh our God— we sought him,*[a] *and he has, given us rest on every side." And so they built and prospered.*

⁷[⁸]*Asa had an army of three hundred thousand from Judah armed with large shields and spears, and an army of two hundred eighty thousand*[a] *from Benjamin armed with small shields and bows; all these were valiant fighters.* ⁸[⁹]*Now Zerah the Cushite came out against them with an army a million strong and with three hundred*[a] *chariots, and he came as far as Mareshah.* ⁹[¹⁰]*Asa went out to meet him and deployed for battle in the valley of Zephathah*[a] *at Mareshah.* ¹⁰[¹¹]*Then Asa cried out to Yahweh his God, "O Yahweh, there is no one but you who can help the powerless against the mighty. Help us, Yahweh our God, for we trust in you, and it is in your name that we have come against this horde. You are Yahweh our God—let no man prevail against you."* ¹¹[¹²]*So Yahweh struck down the Cushites before Asa and Judah. The Cushites fled,* ¹²[¹³]*and Asa and the army with him pursued them as far as Gerar.*[a] *So many fell among the Cushites that they could not recover, for they were crushed before Yahweh and his army. They took great quantities of booty,* ¹³[¹⁴] *and destroyed all the cities around Gerar, for the dread of Yahweh had come upon them, and they plundered all those cities since there was much plunder in them.* ¹⁴[¹⁵]*They also attacked the camps*[a] *of the herdsmen and seized many sheep and camels, and then returned to Jerusalem.*

¹⁵:¹*Now the spirit of God came upon Azariah son of Oded,* ²*and he appeared before Asa and said to him, "Hear me, Asa and all Judah and Benjamin! Yahweh is with you when you are with him. If you seek him, he will be found by you, but if you forsake him, he will forsake you.* ³*For a long time Israel was without the true God and without a priest to teach*[a] *and without instruction.* ⁴*But in their distress they turned to Yahweh the God of Israel; they sought him and he was*

found by them. [5]*In those times it was not safe to travel about, for there was great turmoil for the inhabitants of all lands.* [6]*One nation was crushed by another, one city by another city, for God harassed them with every kind of adversity.* [7]*But you be strong, and do not lose courage,*[a] *for there is a reward for your labor."*

[8]*When Asa heard these words and the prophecy,*[a] *he took courage and removed the detestable idols from all the land of Judah and Benjamin and from the cities he had captured in the hill country of Ephraim, and he refurbished the altar of Yahweh which stood in front of the portico of the temple*[b] *of Yahweh.* [9]*Then he assembled all Judah and Benjamin along with those resident among them from Ephraim, Manasseh, and Simeon, for great numbers had come over to him when they saw that Yahweh his God was with him.* [10]*They gathered in Jerusalem in the third month of the fifteenth year of the reign of Asa,* [11]*and offered sacrifices to Yahweh at that time from the plunder; they presented seven hundred oxen and seven thousand sheep.* [12]*They entered into a covenant to seek Yahweh the God of their fathers with all their hearts and souls.* [13]*Any who would not seek Yahweh the God of Israel were put to death, whether small or great, man or woman.* [14]*They swore an oath to Yahweh with loud acclamation and shouting and with trumpets and horns.* [15]*All Judah rejoiced about the oath, for they had sworn it with all their hearts; they sought him with all their will,*[a] *and he was found by them, and Yahweh gave them rest round about.*

[16]*Furthermore, King Asa deposed Maacah his grandmother*[a] *from her position as queen mother, because she had made a vile*[b] *Asherah pole; Asa cut down her vile idol, pulverized it,*[c] *and burned it in the Kidron Valley.* [17]*Though he did not remove the high places from Israel,*[a] *nevertheless the heart of Asa was wholly committed all his life.* [18]*He brought to the temple of God all the votive offerings given by his father and himself*[a]*—the silver, the gold, and the cultic implements.* [19]*There was no more warfare*[a] *until the thirty-fifth year of the reign of Asa.*

[16:1]*In the thirty-sixth*[a] *year of the reign of Asa, Baasha king of Israel went up against Judah and built Ramah to cut off all access to Asa king of Judah.* [2]*So Asa brought out the silver and gold*[a] *from the treasuries of Yahweh's temple and the royal palace, and he sent it to Ben-hadad*[b] *king of Aram, whose capital was in Damascus, saying,* [3]*"Let there be an alliance between you and me as there was between my father and your father. See how I have sent you silver and gold. Now you go break your alliance with Baasha king of Israel so that he will withdraw from me."* [4]*Ben-hadad took heed of King Asa and sent the officers of his armies against the cities of Israel; they attacked Iyyon, Dan, Abel-maim,*[a] *and all the store cities*[b] *of Naphtali.*

[5]*So it was that when Baasha heard of it, he stopped fortifying Ramah and ceased any work on it.*[a] [6]*Then King Asa took all the men of Judah,*[a] *and they carried away the stones and timbers with which Baasha had fortified Ramah, and he used them to fortify Geba*[b] *and Mizpeh.*

[7]*At that time Hanani the seer came to Asa king of Judah and said to him, "You have relied upon the king of Aram and not on Yahweh your God; therefore, the army of the king of Aram*[a] *will escape from your grasp.* [8]*Were not the Cushites and Libyans a great army with a vast number of chariots and horsemen? But when you relied upon Yahweh, he delivered them into your hand,* [9]*for the eyes of Yahweh roam through all the earth to strengthen those whose hearts are fully committed to him. You have done a foolish thing, so from now on you will have war."* [10]*Asa*

was provoked with the seer; he was so angry about this that he put him in stocks. Asa also oppressed some of the people at that time.

11 Now the events of Asa's reign, from beginning to end, are written in the book of the kings of Judah and Israel. 12 In the thirty-ninth year of his reign Asa became ill with diseased feet until his illness became grave; but even while he was ill he did not seek Yahweh, but the physicians. 13 In the forty-first year of his reign Asa lay with his fathers and died. 14 They buried him in the tomb he had dug ᵃ for himself in the City of David; they lay him on a bier covered with spices and skilfully blended aromatics, and they kindled a huge fire in his honor.

Notes

14:1 [2].a. "The good" not found in 1 Kgs 15:11.

1 [2].b. 1 Kgs 15:11, "in the eyes of Yahweh, like David his father."

6 [7].a. G translators, of course, had an unvocalized text before them and read דְּרַשְׁנוּ (= ἐξεζήτησεν ἡμᾶς), "we sought the LORD our God and he sought us"(NEB, Rudolph, Myers, Williamson). MT has read "we sought [him]" a second time, as a recapitulation (for emphasis?). "Seeking God" is a pervasive vehicle for the author's retribution theology. The subj of the verb is nearly always men; God is the subj rarely and in contexts where the sense of the verb is judgmental (1 Chr 28:9; 2 Chr 24:22). The Chronicler may be protecting the sovereignty or transcendence of God: he may say "if you forsake God, he will forsake you"(15:2; 12:5; 1 Chr 28:9), but he does not say (unless here) "if you seek him, he will seek you"; rather he seems deliberately to use a circumlocution, "if you seek him, he will be found by you"(1 Chr 28:9; 2 Chr 15:2, 4, 15).

7 [8].a. G and Josephus (*Ant.* 8:291), "two hundred and fifty thousand."

8 [9].a. Syr, Arab, "thirty thousand."

9 [10].a. Zephathah is otherwise unknown; it should not be equated with Zephath of Judg 1:17. At Mareshah a valley provides a natural pass through the Shephelah, via Nezib or Idna to the ridge route at Hebron; this may have been the "Valley of Zephathah." G read "north of Mareshah." (κατὰ βορρᾶν = צפנה).

12 [13].a. Gᴸ read "Gedor." A Gedor is mentioned as the southern limit of the conquests of the Simeonites (1 Chr 4:39; cf. Gen 10:19; note the presence of Simeonites in Asa's reform, 15:9), though 1 Chr 4:39 should be emended (with G) to "Gerar." MT is almost certainly correct: Gerar would represent the northeastern range of Egyptian influence, ten miles east of the international coastal highway, and a significant military objective.

14 [15].a. Lit., "tents of cattle," an expression unique to this passage. G glosses with a proper name, presumably that of an Arabian tribe familiar to the Alexandrians of the Ptolemaic period; for a discussion of the G developments, see Allen, *GC* 1:167.

15:3.a. Gᴮ is missing "without a priest to teach," most likely due to a homoioarchon (וללא).

7.a. Lit., "may your hands not weaken," idiomatic for becoming discouraged or demoralized. Cf. 2 Sam 4:1; Isa 13:7; Jer 6:24; 50:43; Ezek 7:17; 21:12; Zeph 3:16; the same idiom is also used in Lachish ostracon VI.

8.a. Omitting MT "Oded the prophet." The MT as it stands could be correct only (1) if the "prophecy of Oded" were some heretofore unmentioned source abruptly introduced at this point, though it does seem implausible that any other than the prophecy of "Azariah son of Oded" (15:1) is intended; or (2) if the word "Oded" were revocalized as a verb meaning "prophesy." The root עדד, though used in the Zakir inscription, cannot be said with certainty to occur as a verb in biblical Heb. (See R. Wilson, *Prophecy and Society in Ancient Israel* [Philadelphia: Fortress Press, 1980] 131; and T. Willi, *Die Chronik*, 221–22). Since the word "prophecy" (והנבואה) is not in the constr state, it is most probably construed as having originally stood alone before the incorrect and partial insertion of a marginal gloss. Gᴮ and Vg, which read "prophecy of Azariah son of Oded," should be viewed as corrections of the MT.

8.b. The words "of the temple" are not in the MT and were inserted for clarity. Par regularly translates אולם using ναός (1 Chr 28:11; 2 Chr 8:12; 15:8; 29:7, 17), ordinarily the translation equivalent for היכל, "temple, sanctuary, inner chamber." See Allen, *GC* 1:59.

15.a. Alternatively, "they had sworn with all their hearts and all their will; they sought him and he. . . ."

16.a. With 1 Kgs 15:13, Bas, and Par; MT, "the king removed Maacah, the grandmother of Asa."

16.b. The noun מפלצת occurs only here and in the parallel at 1 Kgs 15:13, so that its precise significance is difficult to determine. The cognates (Job 9:6; 21:6; Isa 21:4; Ezek 7:18; Ps 55:6; Jer 49:16) connote trembling, terror, or shuddering, and hence, "vile," for this context. Vg (*simulacrum Priapi*, "image of Priapus," the god of procreation; representation of the phallus) regarded the term as referring to a phallic symbol; G (λειτουργοῦσαν, "priestess, minister,") may have read מפלחת for the first occurrence.

16.c. Not found in G, Syr, or 1 Kgs 15:13, possibly a later gloss to conform to the fate of the golden calf (Exod 32:20; Deut 9:21).

17.a. "From Israel" is not found in the parallel at 1 Kgs 15:14; see *Comment*.

18.a. G, "the dedicated things of his father David and the dedicated things of the temple." In the first instance Par is probably influenced by the frequent references to the material dedicated by David (1 Chr 18:11; 26:20–28; 28:12; 2 Chr 5:1; 7:5); for the second, cf. 1 Kgs 15:15.

19.a. Contrast 1 Kgs 15:16, "there was warfare between Asa and Baasha king of Israel all their days"; see *Comment*.

16:1.a. G, "thirty-eighth year"; see the discussion in Dillard, *JETS* 23 (1980) 213, n. 25. G may be following an alternative text that has assimilated to 16:12, so that the disobedience is placed in the year immediately before Asa's disease.

2.a. 1 Kgs 15:18, "silver and gold which were left in the treasuries," alluding to the earlier despoliation by Shishak (1 Kgs 14:25–26).

2.b. 1 Kgs 15:18 adds his patronymic, "son of Tab-rimmon and Hezion."

4.a. 1 Kgs 15:20, "Abel-beth-maacah." Since "Abel" itself appears to mean "watercourse," it is questionable whether מַיִם is the correct pointing; since most other city names using "Abel" are east of the Jordan, it is possible that the vowels read by Tg are correct (מָיִם = "in the west"). See Rudolph, 246.

4.b. 1 Kgs 15:20, כנרות, "Galilee, Kinnereth." G (περιχώρους "surrounding country") appears to have read either מסבות or סביבות.

5.a. 1 Kgs 15:21, "withdrew to Tirzah."

6.a. 1 Kgs 15:22 adds "no one was exempt."

6.b. 1 Kgs 15:22 adds "of Benjamin."

7.a. G^L, "Israel" instead of "Aram"; see *Comment*.

14.a. Or, "bought."

Form/Structure/Setting

The Chronicler has devoted far more attention to the reign of Asa than the earlier history; while Kings covered his reign in sixteen verses, the Chronicler has nearly tripled that amount, expanding his *Vorlage* to forty-seven verses. The account in Kings follows the outline the author commonly used: introductory synchronism (15:9–10), basic theological judgment (1 Kgs 15:11–15); incidents during the reign (15:16–22); death and succession formula (15:23–24). The Chronicler has, as customary for him, omitted the introductory synchronism with the Northern Kingdom (1 Kgs 15:9–10—though for reservations on this point, see W. Lemke, *Synoptic Studies*, 147). The Chronicler then proceeded to modify material taken from his *Vorlage* and to incorporate extensive nonsynoptic material (14:2 [3]–15:15; 16:7–10); his rewriting of the reign of Asa is primarily in the service of his theology of immediate retribution in order to demonstrate the blessings attending Asa's fidelity and the punishment following his failure to trust the Lord.

Since so much of the material unique to Chronicles involves incidents in which prophets (Azariah and Hanani) are central figures, it is surprising that the author does not cite as his source some collection of prophetic records as he so often does (1 Chr 29:29; 2 Chr 9:29; 12:15; 13:22; 20:34; 26:22;

32:32; 33:19). Rather we hear only of "the book of the kings of Israel and Judah" (16:11; cf. 25:26; 27:7; 28:26; 32:32; 35:27; 36:8), presumably some sort of official records, perhaps an annalistic collection; in two passages (20:34, 32:32) collections of records about prophets are already integrated into such an annalistic source. One can only speculate as to whether this single source itself provided all of the material unique to the Chronicler, or whether it is referred to simply by way of additional information, or whether it is a reference to the canonical book of Kings. The Chronicler's account of the reign of Asa is also marked by the insertion of a large number of chronological notices not found in Kings (13:23 [14:1]; 15:10; 15:19; 16:1; 16:12; 16:13), a fact which would comport well with the use of an annalistic source; chronological notices regularly provide the Chronicler with a framework for dividing a given reign into periods of obedience and disobedience, thereby showing the outworking of retribution theology. Annals would also be a probable source for information on Asa's military actions which comprise so much of the Chronicler's account. The source cited for the Kings account ("the book of the annals of the kings of Judah"—1 Kgs 15:23) contained additional information regarding "the cities he built"; this reference could have prompted the Chronicler's inclusion of 14:5–6 [6–7], though building projects are a common feature the Chronicler includes to show divine blessing.

Whatever the nature of the sources at his disposal, the author's hand in reshaping them to demonstrate the validity of retribution theology is apparent (see *Explanation*), particularly in speech materials. Key terms and concepts of retribution theology abound: seeking God (14:6 [7]; 15:2, 4, 12, 13, 15; 16:12), forsaking God (15:2); trusting God (14:10 [11]; 16:7, 8), rest and peace as divine blessing (13:23 [14:1]; 15:5, 6, 7, 15, 19—and the opposite, 15:6, 16:9), prayer in time of battle (14:10 [11]).

The Chronicler provides religious instruction frequently through the vehicle of interpolated speeches. Von Rad ("Levitical Sermon") identified the structure of many of the speeches in Chronicles as (1) doctrine—the basis on which God is prepared to help; (2) application—a look back into history showing that God's nearness should not be taken for granted; and (3) exhortation—the call to faith and promise of a reward. The sermons of Azariah and Hanani provide instructive examples. "Doctrine" for Hanani's sermon is the futility of relying on earthly might (16:7), a futility illustrated in the successful campaign against Zerah ("application," 16:8); Hanani's exhortation urges Asa to renewed trust, for God strengthens those whose hearts are wholly committed to him (16:8)—though the element of promise is present, there is also a pronouncement of judgment, that Asa would have war from then on (16:9). Azariah's sermon appeals to the necessity of seeking God ("doctrine," 15:2), illustrates the principle from Israel's past ("application," 15:3–6), and concludes with "exhortation" to renewed courage and the promise of reward (15:7). Both speeches quote other biblical texts (see *Comment*).

Rudolph (240–41) finds a number of "seams" in the Asa narrative. (1) If Asa had already initiated a reform and had removed the foreign altars and high places (14:2–4), one would not expect to hear this same sort of action reported again (15:8–15). (2) Since Azariah's speech does not betray any knowledge of a reform already under way, but rather appears to be an initial admonition to reform, Rudolph concludes that the entirety of 15:1–15 is a doublet to 14:2–4, and that the doubling of the accounts had probably already occurred in the author's extracanonical sources. The validity of both these issues is inextricably bound up with the chronological notices introduced by the Chronicler; see *Comment* at 15:19. (3) Rudolph also concludes that 15:16–18 represents an intrusion introduced by a later editor from 1 Kgs 15:13–15 since the statement that Asa did not remove the high places (15:17) is an obvious contradiction of 14:2, 5, and since the statement that Asa's heart was blameless all his days (15:17) contradicts the record of his transgression in 16:7–12. Rudolph rather quickly dismisses other explanations; see *Comment* at 15:17.

The Chronicler appears to be using his account of Asa's reign as a model for that of his son Jehoshaphat. See the introductory chapter to 2 Chr 17–20, "The Chronicler's Jehoshaphat."

A wide variety of paragraph-level syntactical devices appear in the Asa narrative:

(1) 14:1 [2]—explicit subject without intervening change in subject
(2) 14:4 [5]—an example of "tail-head" linkage: the initial sentence repeats part of the last sentence of the preceding paragraph ("the land was quiet")
(3) 14:6–7; 16:1–4—both are proposal/response paragraphs
(4) 14:8; 16:5—both introduced by ויהי clauses
(5) 15:1; 16:11—*casus pendens*
(6) 15:8—infinitive construct in a temporal phrase
(7) 15:16—וגם
(8) 16:1—another example of a "tail-head" linkage: a date formula ends one paragraph (15:19) and begins the next (16:1)
(9) 16:7–10—a paragraph-level inclusio: the paragraph begins and ends with בעת ההיא, "at that time."

Comment

14:1–4 [2–5] The Chronicler repeats the basic theological judgment on the reign of Asa that is found in 1 Kgs 15:11, that it was a reign pleasing to God. However, he omits 1 Kgs 15:12 which reports the expulsion of the cultic prostitutes and the removal of the idols made by his fathers; the Chronicler proceeds to introduce his own material from 14:2 [3]–15:15, and only resumes copying the text of Kings with 1 Kgs 15:13 // 2 Chr 15:16. The Chronicler omits all four references found in Kings to cultic prostitutes (1 Kgs 14:24; 15:12; 22:47 [46]; 2 Kgs 23:7), possibly to suppress abhorrent memories, though more likely because cultic prostitution was not practiced widely in post-exilic Judah, and references to it were somewhat irrelevant to his audience (P. Dion, *CBQ* 43 [1981] 41–48). His failure to mention the removal of the idols made by Asa's ancestors should probably be traced to the more favorable account he has given of the reigns of Solomon, Rehoboam, and Abijah.

That Asa "removed the foreign altars and high places" (14:1 [2]) is in tension with the statement that "he did not remove the high places from Israel" (15:17); many regard these two statements as flat contradictions or a measure of the author's incompetence as a historian. Rather than quickly dismiss efforts to ease the apparent contradiction as unconscionably harmonistic, it would be more plausible to assume that in the author's mind the two statements were not in tension; it is unlikely that either the author or a later editor would contradict himself in such short compass. (1) Since 15:17 occurs toward the end of Asa's reign, presumably in some proximity to his thirty-fifth year from the narrator's viewpoint (15:19), and 14:2 refers to early reforms, an intervening period of up to thirty years is possible. The two statements could be understood as no more than evidence of the resilience of the indigenous cults which plagued Judah's history and required repeated reformation. (2) It is also possible that the Chronicler's insertion of the words "from Israel" in 15:17 (not in the // at 1 Kgs 15:14) is intended to indicate that Asa did not remove the high places from the cities earlier belonging to the Northern Kingdom and then under his sway; contrast the explicit statement that he removed the high places "from all the cities of Judah" (14:4 [5]). Rudolph (241) criticizes two other solutions, that 15:17 be understood as saying that Asa did "not completely" remove the high places (Theodoret), or that the high places in 14:2 were the high places of the foreign deities also mentioned, whereas the subsequent reference was to Yahwistic worship centers (Noordtzij)—both solutions which are admittedly less plausible. This difficulty is not unique to the Chronicler's account of Asa, but recurs in his statements that Jehoshaphat did (17:6) and did not (20:33) remove the high places. The destruction of the pillars and Asherah poles, the high places and altars is in accord with the injunctions of Deut 7:5; 12:3; 16:21–22.

The theme of "seeking God" (14:3 [4]) occurs nine times in the three chapters devoted to the reign of Asa. The "law of God" probably refers to canonical writings, though for the contrary opinion, see T. Willi, *Judaica* 36 (1980) 102–5, 148–51.

The precise meaning of the term חמנים (14:4 [5]) is not known with certainty. Older lexical authorities commonly translated it as "sun pillar," though more recent interpretations of the archeological data had achieved some consensus to translate "incense altars." The term is still debated; see Williamson, 260; and Myers, 83.

5–6 [6–7]   The Chronicler commonly reports on the building projects of godly kings; he makes no mention of such projects in his account of the reigns of kings under divine censure. These two verses are a fairly direct articulation of his historiographical concepts: obedience brings peace ("no wars . . . for Yahweh had given him rest"; "we sought him and he has given us rest") and the prosperity to build ("they built and prospered"). See the essay introducing 2 Chr 10–36, "Reward and Punishment in Chronicles: The Theology of Immediate Retribution."

Asa's short speech (14:6 [7]) is one of the few speeches in Chronicles that is not a prayer or a sermon or a prophetic speech.

7–14 [8–15]   Solomon had prayed that Yahweh would hear his people's prayer in time of battle (6:34), and the Chronicler reports several incidents similar to Asa's prayer (14:10 [11]) reinforcing God's responsiveness (13:14–18; 18:31; 20:5–20; 32:20–22; 1 Chr 5:20—all passages unique to the Chronicler or modified from their form in Kings). See Throntveit, *Significance*, 79–82.

Several motifs of holy war also characterize this battle narrative: Israel's army facing a much more numerous foe (14:7–8 [8–9]; 13:3; 20:2; Deut 20:1), a pre-battle speech or prayer (14:10 [11]; 13:5–11; 20:5–17; Deut 20:2–4), Yahweh at the lead in the battle while the army is described largely as passive (14:11–12 [12–13]; 13:15–16; 20:22–24; Deut 20:4), the fear of Yahweh coming upon the foe (14:13 [14]; Exod 23:28; Deut 7:20, 23).

The invasion of Zerah would have taken place between the tenth and fourteenth year of Asa, i.e., between 900–897 B.C.; this period would correspond to the twenty-fifth to twenty-ninth years of Pharaoh Osorkon I, according to the chronology proposed by Kitchen (*TIPE*, 467). It has been demonstrated that the Hebrew and Egyptian names of Zerah and Osorkon do not correspond, so that the two individuals cannot be equated by virtue of having the same name. Osorkon was a king of Libyan origin; Zerah is not called a king and was a Nubian (Cushite). It is possible that Osorkon, already an old man, dispatched a force into Palestine under a Nubian general named Zerah, seeking to take plunder in emulation of Shishak (Kitchen, *TIPE*, par. 268, n. 372); note the linking of Nubians and Libyans in 16:8.

Others do not accept this historical reconstruction and have proffered different views. (1) Welten (*Geschichte*, 129–40) is particularly influenced by the stylistic presence of the Chronicler in the narrative, and concludes that the entire episode was the author's fabrication. (2) Albright ("Egypt and the Early History of the Negev," *JPOS* 4 [1924] 146–47) postulates the existence of an Egyptian garrison of Nubian mercenaries at Gerar, but there is no evidence that Shishak established such a garrison as a buffer state; Gerar is mentioned only as the end point of Asa's pursuit (14:11 [12]) and not as the source of the invasion. (3) Other scholars dismiss involvement with Egypt; Egypt is not mentioned in the narrative. "Cush" is understood not as a reference to Nubia, but rather as a region of Midian on the northeastern shore of the Gulf of Aqabah: in Hab 3:7 the phrase "tents of Cushan" parallels "the curtain of Midian"; Moses, whose father-in-law was a priest of Midian (Exod 2:16–21; 3:1), had married a "Cushite" woman (Num 12:1), and many scholars assume that these passages refer to the same woman. Since 14:14 [15] mentions camels and possibly bedouin herdsmen, the attack of Zerah is treated as a much smaller local flare-up in which nomadic tribes pressure Judah's southern flank for better pasturage. The objections to this approach are several. The mere mention of camels and herdsmen does not create a bedouin invasion; one could equally well see the commissary, porters and camp followers for the invading army, or even a sedentary population engaged in caravan trade. Wapnish ("Camel Caravans and Camel Pastoralists at Tell Jemmeh," *JANESCU* 13 [1981] 101–21) argues that one main branch of the spice trade itinerary intersected the coastal highway at Tell Jemmeh, ten miles west of Gerar/T. Abu Hureira (cf. Y. Aharoni, "The Land of Gerar," *IEJ* 6 [1956] 26–32). The mention of the Libyans (16:8) is most plausibly understood with an Egyptian origin for the invasion; when compared with 12:3, it is clear that the Chronicler regarded this as a major international incident. The size of the armies involved probably represents some degree of hyperbole, though this is a subjective judgment, reducing the narrative to a clash with bedouin over pasturage taxes credulity. Jehoshaphat would later receive tribute from the region of Asa's campaign; see *Comment* at 17:10–11.

7–8 [8–9] The numbers appear quite high; it is especially difficult to think that an otherwise unknown Zerah could field a million troops. Several different approaches have been taken to the large numbers in Chronicles; see the discussion at 13:3. If אלף is taken as a military unit, Zerah's army had 1,000, and the army of Asa had 580, and the actual number of troops would remain a matter of conjecture; similarly if אלף is repointed as *ʾalluf* (officer, colonel), the number of officers would be specified, but not the size of the total army. However, these ways of reducing the size of the armies are open to serious objection. In this particular context, it is difficult to escape the conclusion that the Chronicler intends these as actual numbers, though hyperbolic. Asa's army is the army of Yahweh (14:12 [13]). Cf. 1 Chr 12:22: David had an army "like the army of God," and numbering in excess of 340,000 (12:23–40); reducing the numbers in 1 Chr 12:22 using these other approaches to 2,000 officers (Wenham, *TynBul* 18 [1967] 26–27, 44–45) or even 398 (Payne, *BSac* 136 [1979] 214–15) would seriously undercut the Chronicler's intention to present the "army of God." In this context with its emphasis on the magnitude of the victory because God helped the weak against the strong (14:10 [11]), reducing the numbers to an indeterminate figure through some artifice would also undercut the point the author is seeking to make.

15:1–7 Apart from this passage Azariah is otherwise unknown. His speech rehearses a number of the prominent themes of Chronicles and shows the author's hand in its composition: Yahweh will be with the people and will reward obedience (15:2, 7); he is found by those who seek him, but forsakes those who are derelict toward him (15:2; cf. 12:5; 24:20; 1 Chr 28:9).

The post-exilic community probably saw the speech as quite applicable to its own life. The exile could have been regarded as a period without a proper cultic establishment in place and operational, a time when God had abandoned the people (15:3); the adversity and strife faced by the restoration community mirrored the unsafe commerce (cf. Zech 7:14; Ezra 8:31), turmoil, and harassment of which Azariah spoke (15:4–6). The promises of his speech, that God could be found and would reward their labor, would have immediate homiletical relevance; for the Chronicler the desired response may have been similar to that of Azariah's hearers (15:8–15). Three essentials for the faith of the restoration community are articulated: the true God, the teaching priest, and the torah (15:3).

3–4 From antiquity these verses have been variously interpreted. The Tg takes them as a description of the Northern Kingdom. Though there are no finite verbs in 15:3, the tenses of G and Vg show that they took the verses as a prophecy for the future (cf. Hos 3:4). Others see them as generalized statement applying to past or future (Keil, 361) or as a generalized comment on the history of Israel. Most commentators have understood the verses as a description of the period of the judges; 15:4 is easily understood as describing the cyclical pattern of affliction and deliverance that characterized that period. Von Rad's analysis of the levitical sermon in Chronicles requires a reference to the past as the basis for the exhortation (see *Form/Structure/Setting*).

Teaching was a duty of the priests (Lev 10:11; Deut 33:10; Jer 18:18; Hos 4:6–7; Mal 2:7). In the Chronicler's presentation, by analogy with the teaching delegation sent out by Jehoshaphat (17:7–9), teaching the law probably involved a written torah. However, one cannot preclude the possibility that "torah" in this case was no more than oral instruction in religious and legal precepts. See 6:16.

8 Asa's reform was not confined to Judah and Benjamin, but also embraced territory he had captured in the hill country of Ephraim. This is a tacit admission that there had been conflict between Judah and Israel prior to the thirty-sixth year of Asa's reign (16:1), even though no details of these conquests are given. Contrast the statement that there was war between Asa and Baasha throughout their reigns (1 Kgs 15:16) with the statement that there was no war until the thirty-fifth year (15:19). See the discussion at 15:19.

There is no record of any damage to the altar—certainly not during the reigns of the preceding godly kings. The refurbishing of the altar probably refers to needed maintenance that may have been deferred.

9 The Chronicler's concern with "all Israel" is one of his most pervasive themes; from the vantage point of the post-exilic community, he has not simply written off the Northern tribes. Here Asa enjoys the loyalty of many Northerners, as had Rehoboam before him (11:13–17). The Chronicler speaks of actions in the North on the part of several of the kings of Judah. Asa's son Jehoshaphat put garrisons in the cities of Ephraim captured by his father (17:2) and sent a teaching delegation into the North (19:4). Hezekiah invited Israelites from Beersheba to Dan to celebrate the Passover (30:5, 11); Josiah's reform reached into "Ephraim, Manasseh, Simeon, and as far as Naphtali" (34:6; cf. 34:21, 33). Though there is the steady call for reform in the North and for the recognition of the Jerusalem cult, the Chronicler's attitude to the North is not one of exclusivism (cf. Ezra 6:17).

Simeon was a Southern tribe (1 Chr 4:28–43; Josh 19:1–9) long assimilated into Judah by the Chronicler's time; it is curious that here and in 34:6 Simeon is included in a list of the Northern tribes. The attack of Simeon and Levi against Shechem (Gen 34) may recount a foothold for that tribe in the hill country ordinarily ascribed to Ephraim and Manasseh, or at least provide a basis in biblical tradition for understanding the Shechem region as a homeland of Simeon (cf. Noth, *US,* 178). Another historical reconstruction suggests that Edomite incursions following the collapse of the united kingdom displaced the Simeonites northward, though this situation must have been reversed by the time of Hezekiah (1 Chr 4:41; cf. Rudolph, 247; Myers, 89; Williamson, *IBC,* 104).

10–15 This ceremony of covenant renewal probably was concurrent with the celebration of the Feast of Weeks (Pentecost; Exod 23:16; 34:22; Lev 23:15–21; Num 28:26–31; Deut 16:9), one of the great pilgrim festivals (Deut 16:16) that would have brought crowds loyal to the Jerusalem temple from the surrounding regions; the third month of Asa's fifteenth year probably fell in May/June of 895 B.C. The plunder offered (15:11) was taken from the victory over Zerah, particularly the seized cattle (14:14 [15]). The campaign of Zerah was presumably in the preceding year, unless the Chronicler intends to present the victory over Zerah as followed immediately by the further reforms and covenant renewal; late spring and summer were ordinarily the seasons for warfare, and the third month would have come barely at the end of the harvest season, perhaps too early for Zerah's invasion to have come in the same year.

The execution of those who would "not seek Yahweh the God of Israel" (15:13) may seem harsh by modern standards, but it is in accord with Deut 17:2–7; 13:6–10.

16–18 The Chronicler resumes following Kings at this point (1 Kgs 15: 13–15).

The importance attainable by a queen mother is also attested in the accounts of Bathsheba, Jezebel, and Athaliah; see the discussion in N. Andreasen, "The Role of the Queen Mother in Israelite Society," *CBQ* 45 (1983) 179–94. With reference to Maacah, see *Comment* at 11:20. The Kidron Valley runs north-south on the eastern side of Jerusalem, between the city and the Mount of Olives; it was the site where materials cleared in cultic reforms were also burned on other occasions (2 Kgs 23:4–6; 2 Chr 29:16; 30:14). For a recent survey of the data regarding Asherah poles, see J. Day, "Asherah in the Hebrew Bible and Northwest Semitic Literature," *JBL* 105 (1986) 385–408.

Asa's failure to remove the high places from Israel should not be considered a contradiction to 14:2 [3]; see *Comment* there. Nor is the statement that he was faithful all his life necessarily contradicted by the following narrative (16:1–10)—it says no more than that he was faithful through the thirty-fifth year of his reign (15:19).

For the Chronicler the premier example of a king's giving votive offerings and cultic implements is David (1 Chr 18:11; 22:3, 14; 29:1–5); though such giving commonly came from the spoils of war, it was not an act confined to kings (1 Chr 26:27). For Abijah and Asa, if their gifts derived from the spoils of war, they must have been from their respective battles with Jeroboam and Zerah.

19 The Chronicler appears virtually to negate his *Vorlage* at 1 Kgs 15:16, which says that there was continuous warfare between Asa and Baasha; however, the Chronicler has already tacitly intimated prior military conflict between them (15:8), though of a smaller scale not requiring the full-scale mobilization and the diplomatic moves that Asa would make.

The Chronicler frequently inserts chronological data into his accounts of individual reigns; these chronological notes provide the scaffolding for dividing the accounts into periods of obedience or disobedience. While the Kings account of Asa's reign contains no chronological information beyond the accession and death notices, the Chronicler's account contains half a dozen dates dividing Asa's reign into periods that demonstrate the principle of retribution so dear to the author; see the essay introducing 2 Chr 10–36, "Reward and Punishment in Chronicles: The Theology of Immediate Retribution."

The Kings account reported that Asa was a godly king (1 Kgs 15:11–15), that he fought with Baasha throughout his reign and hired Ben-hadad at one point (15:16–22), and that in his old age he acquired some foot disease (15:23). Several aspects of the deuteronomic account confronted the Chronicler with difficulties in terms of his own convictions about retribution. (1) If

Asa were a righteous king, why would he have war throughout his reign? Rest from enemies, peace, and prosperity are the lot of the righteous (1 Chr 22:8–9; 2 Chr 14:5–6; 15:15; 20:29–30). (2) Severe illness is the result of sin and guilt in Chronicles (2 Chr 21:16–20; 26:16–23), so why would the righteous Asa die of a foot disease (Rudolph, 239)? The Chronicler reworks the account as he found it in Kings; he uses chronological notes to provide a framework that will demonstrate the validity of his retribution theology.

1. *13:23 [14:1]* The Chronicler notes that after Asa's accession, the land was quiet for ten years, a statement that contrasts with 1 Kgs 15:16 which describes warfare between Asa and Baasha throughout their reigns. The Chronicler proceeds to elaborate on Asa's reform, essentially interpolating between 1 Kgs 15:12 and 13 a large block of material unique to his account (2 Chr 14:4–15:15). This material is rich in the concepts of retribution theology: it elaborates on Asa's building programs, his trust in God and the subsequent victory over the much more numerous forces of Zerah, and his responsiveness to the word of God through Azariah.

2. *15:10* The Chronicler reports a covenant renewal in the fifteenth year of Asa's reign; he incorporates his distinctive concerns with "all Israel" and "seeking God."

3. *15:19* The statement that there was no [more] war until the thirty-fifth year is again in tension with 1 Kgs 15:19. The Chronicler has emphasized the peace and rest in the reign of Asa (13:23 [14:1]; 14:4–6 [5–7]; 15:3–7).

4. *16:1* The first recorded conflict between Baasha and Asa is set in Asa's thirty-sixth year. This time Asa fails to trust the LORD as he had in his battle with Zerah; for the Chronicler foreign alliances are always culpable (2 Chr 19:1–20:37; 28:1–36). The Chronicler incorporates a fourth speech unique to his account, the speech of Hanani announcing punishment in the form of war for Asa from then on. Asa imprisons the prophet and oppresses some of his subjects.

5. *16:12* Asa contracts a foot disease in his thirty-ninth year, and becomes gravely ill, but still will not "seek the LORD."

6. *16:13* Asa dies in the forty-first year of his reign. The author provides additional details on his death and burial.

The Chronicler has reshaped the account he found in Kings by elaborating and reinforcing the divine favor enjoyed by an obedient king and by making explicit the nature of the transgressions that led to his disease and death.

However characteristic of the Chronicler his treatment of Asa might be, a substantive problem remains. 1 Kgs 15:33 records that Baasha ruled for twenty-four years, while 1 Kgs 16:8 reports that Elah succeeded Baasha in the twenty-sixth year of Asa. It is obvious that Baasha could not have been alive in the thirty-sixth year of Asa's reign where 2 Chr 16:1 places him. Efforts to address this difficulty have followed basically one of two polar approaches (see the summary in Dillard, *JETS* 23 [1980] 207–18; and Williamson, 255–58). (1) One approach repudiates any harmonization pressure and regards the chronological notices as part and parcel with the Chronicler's imposition of his basic retributive concerns on the narrative. The chronological data is simply a vehicle by which the author demonstrates again the validity of retribution theology; see M. Cogan, "The Chronicler's Use of Chronology as Illuminated by Neo-Assyrian Royal Inscriptions," in *Empirical Models for Biblical Criticism*, ed. J. Tigay (Philadelphia: University of Pennsylvania Press, 1985) 197–210. (2) Another approach seeks to harmonize the chronological data in the various accounts. Harmonistic chronology is primarily associated with the work of E. Thiele (*The Mysterious Numbers of the Hebrew Kings* [Grand Rapids: Zondervan, 1951, 1965, 1983]), though Thiele's suggestion for the Asa chronology was already known by Keil as the approach of the "older commentators." This approach conjectures that the dates in 2 Chr 15:19 and 16:1 are references to the date of the schism (931 B.C. for Thiele). Thus Thiele is able to deduct the twenty years of prior reigns (seventeen for Rehoboam, three for Abijah) from the references to Asa's thirty-fifth and thirty-sixth years, so that they become instead the fifteenth and sixteenth years of his reign and harmonize quite nicely with the years of Baasha. The following scheme results:

> *Year 15:* Zerah invades (14:9–15; 15:19). Asa's success against Zerah encourages many Northerners to defect to the South, prompting Baasha to fortify Ramah "so that no one could go out or come in to Asa" (16:1).
> *Year 16:* Baasha's offensive; Asa's treaty with Ben-hadad (16:1–10).
> *Years 39–41:* Asa's disease and death (16:11–14).

This solution is ingenious, but probably not acceptable without serious consequences for the Chronicler as a historian. (1) Of the hundreds of bits of data for the chronology of the divided monarchy, this would be the only occasion of dating from the schism. It would be unique to this passage and, therefore, a case of "special pleading" to appeal to it. (2) It ignores the plain statement of the text that these were the thirty-fifth and thirty-sixth years of Asa's reign; Keil rejected the solution for this reason. The formulae used for the regnal years are identical to the formulae used throughout Chronicles (1 Chr 26:31; 2 Chr 3:2; 13:1; 15:10; 16:12, 13; 17:7; 34:8; 36:22) as well as in Kings and generally throughout the rest of the OT to cite regnal years of individual kings. To follow this solution one must conclude that the Chronicler misunderstood some sources dating from the schism, or that the confusion had already taken place in sources he used, for that was certainly not his intent or practice. (3) This reconstruction would also play havoc with the Chronicler's theological argument: the foot disease as retribution would come over twenty years after the offense. The cycles of obedience-reward and sin-punishment that are the major compositional technique of the Chronicler would thereby be destroyed. Another harmonistic approach achieves the same results by postulating a textual error deriving from the use of Hebrew alphabetic characters to represent numerals. On this basis, the י (10) and the ל (30) which are somewhat similar in the older Hebrew/Canaanite alphabet were confused by a copyist, and hence the numbers thirty-five and thirty-six arose from an original fifteen and sixteen. This argument is subject to the same objection mentioned above, that it would invalidate the characteristic argument of the Chronicler that punishment follows transgression immediately. Further, no extant text testifies to the postulated text.

In sum, the theological function served by the chronological notes in the Asa narrative is clear, but the important question of how to harmonize these notes with the chronology in the MT of Kings has as yet no ready solution. Variant chronological data in the OG does not ease the difficulty here, nor has that data yielded a systematic chronlology (see J. Shenkel, *Chronology and Recensional Development in the Greek Text of Kings* [Cambridge, MA: Harvard UP, 1968). Thiele's dates for the individual reigns account for most of the chronological data in the MT with minimal textual difficulty, and they correspond to the dates derived from primarily Assyriological records and the Ptolemaic canon; though some problems remain, Thiele's dates are the best provisional basis for approaching the chronology of the divided kingdoms.

16:1 According to 1 Kgs 15:33; 16:8, Baasha was dead long before Asa's thirty-sixth year; see *Comment* at 15:19. Baasha's objective in fortifying Ramah is stated: to cut off access to Asa. Ramah is ordinarily identified with er-Ram, five miles north of Jerusalem. Its location was well suited for Baasha's objective: Ramah was on the major north-south ridge route by-passing Jerusalem (Judg 19:11–13) and within sufficient proximity to threaten any east-west traffic in the central Benjamin plateau using the important Beth Horon ridge.

2–6 The Arameans were implacable foes for the Northern Kingdom through most of its history. Asa follows the time-honored practice of opening conflict on a second front to ease pressure against Judah from the North (28:16–21); he probably was following the example set by his father Abijah (16:3; see *Comment* at 13:20). Evaluated for its political savvy Asa's enlistment of Ben-hadad's aid outmaneuvered Baasha; the writer of Kings reports the event without any theological evaluation. For the Chronicler, however, such foreign alliances betray a lack of trust in Yahweh (16:8).

A basalt stela possibly from the mid-ninth century B.C. was found just north of Aleppo and contained a reference to a Ben-hadad. Albright (*BASOR* 87 [1942] 23–29; 100 [1945] 16–22) reconstructed the badly damaged second line so that the text reported that the stela had been erected by "Ben-hadad, son of Tab-rimmon, son of Hezion," the precise patronymic of Ben-hadad in 1 Kgs 15:18 // 2 Chr 16:2. Albright went on to identify this Ben-hadad with the Ben-hadad who figures prominently as the adversary of the Omrides from 1 Kgs 20 to 2 Kgs 8. Others considered these as two different Ben-hadads. Though Albright's reconstruction was widely disseminated in the popular secondary literature, reexamination of the second line by F. Cross (*BASOR* 205 [1972] 36–42), W. Shea (*Maarav* 1/2 [1978–79] 159–76), and others has led to the rejection of his historical and epigraphical conclusions.

The route taken by Ben-hadad's forces followed one branch of the main international highway past Iyyon and Abel-beth-maacah and would therefore have been a prime strategic concern for Baasha; Tiglath-pileser III, king of Assyria, would take the same route over a century later (2 Kgs 15:29).

Mizpeh is ordinarily identified with Tell en-Nasbeh; if this identification is correct, Asa had moved his defensive perimeter a couple miles north of Ramah. Excavations at Tell en-Nasbeh do reveal defensive fortifications usually associated with Asa's building program. There is some debate, however, over whether Mizpeh is to be identified with Tell en-Nasbeh or Nebi Samwil, the highest point in the region. The most compelling argument in favor of the identification with Tell en-Nasbeh is its location immediately adjacent to the major north-south highway from Jerusalem to Shechem (Jer 41:4–6), whereas Nebi Samwil is located further to the south and west. The cistern dug in Mizpeh at Asa's command to insure the city's water supply was put to unusual use three centuries later after a slaughter in the city (Jer 41:7–9). Geba has also been identified with different sites, either Jeba or Tell el-Ful.

7–10 The Chronicler commonly uses speech materials as a vehicle for theological pronouncements affirming his own convictions. For the Chronicler, regardless of whatever diplomatic skills may have been represented, such foreign alliances inevitably betray the failure to trust Yahweh (19:1–20:37; 28:1–36; cf. 1 Kgs 20:32–43). Peace and rest are the lot of the righteous king (1 Chr 22:8–9, 18; 2 Chr 14:5–6; 15:15; 20:29–30); disobedience brings warfare and defeat (21:8–10; 28:5–8, 17–18; 24:23–24; 36:17–20).

The textual variant in G^L on 16:7 at first glance appears probable: Hanani tells Asa that his reliance on the king of Aram instead of Yahweh will cost him victory over the king of Israel; victory over Baasha is the issue in the immediate context. However, to some extent, victory over Baasha was secured through Asa's alliance with Ben-hadad, even if Baasha himself did escape. It appears rather that Hanani is saying that Asa would have had victory not only over Baasha, but also over Ben-hadad if he had remained faithful. Victory over both Israel and Aram best fits the symmetry in the speech: the Chronicler mentions the earlier victory over two enemies, the Cushites and Libyans (16:8); since the Libyans are not mentioned in the earlier account (14:8–14 [9–15]), the mention of both here suggests understanding Hanani's speech as implying victory over two foes as well.

Asa responds to Hanani's speech by imprisoning him and oppressing others who may have been supporters of the prophet (16:10); this is the first incident recorded in the Bible of the royal persecution of a prophet.

11–14 Baasha's attack had come in Asa's thirty-sixth year of reign (16:1); Asa's foot disease was contracted in the thirty-ninth year. In Chronicles retribution commonly comes in the following year (12:2; 24:23); the sequence of events probably went somewhat as follows: year thirty-six, Baasha's attack; year thirty-seven, Beh-hadad opens a second front north of Baasha; year thirty-eight, dismantling Baasha's fortifications in Ramah, reusing the material in Geba and Mizpeh, the prophet's condemnation of Asa; year thirty-nine, Asa's disease.

For the Chronicler disease is one form that judgment can take (21:16–20; 26:16–23; contrast 32:24). Asa's foot disease has been variously diagnosed as gangrene developing from a vascular obstruction, gout, or dropsy; see Williamson, 276–77, for a summary. It is doubtful that the Chronicler himself had any information as to the nature of the disease more precise than the broad designation "foot disease." If the disease had become debilitating, a short coregency with Jehoshaphat was possible, but there is no explicit mention of such. A. Shinan and Y. Zakowitch ("Midrash on Scripture and Midrash within Scripture," *Scripta Hieroslymitana* 31 [1986] 272) suggest the Chronicler is providing a pun based on the king's name; אסא in Aramaic is a term for "physician." Cf. the similar play on Jehoshaphat's name in connection with his judicial reform (2 Chr 19).

The Chronicler provides substantially more information on Asa's burial than was found in Kings; 16:14 is unique to Chronicles. Noth (*US*, 143) considers the nonsynoptic information in the Chronicler's burial notices (16:14; 21:20; 24:25; 26:23; 32:33) as free compositions probably based on apocryphal post-exilic traditions current in Jerusalem, whereas Rudolph (249) attributes the information to the Chronicler's source. Such opposing conclusions are a salutary reminder of how precarious and subjective conclusions can be when reached on the basis of insufficient evidence; see W. Lemke, *Synoptic Studies*, 155.

The fire accompanying his burial was not cremation, but rather a memorial and honorific rite customarily attending the death of kings (21:19; Jer 34:5).

Explanation

The Chronicler's handling of the reign of Asa is exemplary of his usual methodology for dealing with the post-schism kings of Judah. The Chronicler ordinarily accepts the basic, broad evaluation of each reign that was made by the deuteronomic historian; the only exceptions to this practice occur in the cases of Abijah and somewhat with reference to Solomon and Manasseh. However, rather than operate at the level of the broad evaluation alone, the Chronicler commonly takes details from the Kings account and elaborates upon them; individual reigns are divided into two or more distinct periods and evaluated in light of his theology of immediate retribution. The doctrine of retribution is made applicable not to the reign of the king as a whole alone, but to details within the reign. In the case of several kings to whom the Chronicler is quite favorably disposed, religious fidelity is demonstrated early and through the largest part of a reign, so that the apostasy is relegated to the final few years (17:3; 29:3; 32:4; 34:3; see R. Braun, *Significance*, 171).

The outworking of this procedure in the case of Asa is clear. The writer accepts the basic evaluation of his reign from Kings (14:1 [2] // 1 Kgs 15:10). He takes details from the Kings account (details of the reform, the wars with Baasha, the death from a foot disease) and elaborates upon them in light of his convictions about retribution; see *Comment* at 15:19. Each detail is provided with its cause or results: reforms issue in victory, peace, prosperity, and the loyalty of the populace (chaps. 14–15); war and disease follow infidelity (chap. 16). The reign is divided into two periods, and apostasy is confined to the last few years.

The Chronicler commonly uses speech materials to announce themes important to him; the speech materials often seem to have direct homiletical relevance for the post-exilic period. Building, prosperity, and the possession of the land depend on seeking God (14:6 [7]); even though facing numerically insurmountable opposition, no one can prevail against God (14:10 [11]). In spite of the ferment and tumult of the past, there is reward for labor (15:2–7); do not rely on political alliances but on God (16:7–9).

The Chronicler reports the earliest royal persecution of a prophet (16:10). Hanani becomes the first in a long line to suffer death or imprisonment after delivering the prophetic word of God to political powers (18:25–26; 24:20–22; Jer 20:1–2; 26:11, 20–23; Matt 5:11–12; 23:29–37; Mark

6:17–18; Luke 11:47–50; John 16:2; Acts 7:51–60; 12:1–5; 16:23–26; 2 Cor 11:23–31; Rev 18:24).

Membership in the covenant community required submission to the LORD; death was the alternative (15:13). In the New Covenant, no less than the Old, those who will not give fealty to the LORD have no place in his kingdom (1 Cor 6:9–10; Eph 5:5; Rev 21:8; 22:14–15).

The Chronicler's Jehoshaphat, 872–848 B.C. (2 Chr 17–20)

When one compares the handling of Jehoshaphat in Kings and Chronicles, the disparity of length in the two accounts is immediately apparent. Though the deuteronomic historian notes his accession in 1 Kgs 15:24, the larger context in Kings is more concerned with the Northern Kingdom (1 Kgs 15:25–16:34), and particularly with the reign of Ahab as the backdrop for the ministry of Elijah (1 Kgs 17–21). The deuteronomic historian gives only the briefest account of Jehoshaphat's reign, most of which is the largely formulaic language of the introduction and conclusion (1 Kgs 22:41–50). Though the battle for Ramoth-gilead is found in both accounts (1 Kgs 22:1–40; 2 Chr 18:1–19:3), in Kings the context makes the primary function of that narrative to account for the death of Ahab, but in Chronicles the same account is put to quite different use.

The Chronicler, on the other hand, devotes considerable attention to Jehoshaphat (2 Chr 17–20), devoting nearly as much attention to his reign as to that of Hezekiah (2 Chr 29–32) and giving him an unqualified endorsement (22:9; contrast 20:33). The Chronicler had also considerably expanded his account of the preceding reign of Asa, and his Asa narrative may have served as a paradigm for his account of Jehoshaphat. The following parallels should be noted:

1. Both accounts concern pious kings whose reigns could be outlined as follows: (a) reform, building programs, and large armies (14:2–8; 17:1–19); (b) battle report (14:9–15; 18:1–19:3); (c) reform (15:1–19; 19:4–11); (d) battle report (16:1–9; 20:1–30); (e) transgression and death (16:10–14; 20:31–21:1).

2. The reform accounts in both reigns are thought by many scholars to be duplicates of the same event: Asa's suppression of heterodox worship (14:2–6) may have been one aspect of the reforms endorsed by Azariah the prophet (15:1–19; see *Comment* at 15:19); Jehoshaphat's teaching mission (17:7–9) may have been the reflex of a larger judicial reform (19:4–11).

3. Both kings are said to have suppressed the high places (14:2–5; 17:6) and not to have done so (15:17; 20:33); (see *Comment* at 14:2–5).

4. Both enjoy the rewards of their piety in building programs (14:7; 17:2, 12), peace (14:1; 17:10), large armies (14:8; 17:12–19). God was with both (15:9; 17:3), and the fear of Yahweh was on the nations (14:14; 17:10; 20:29) during their reigns.

5. Prophets indict both for their entangling foreign alliances (16:7–9; 19:1–3; cf. 20:35–37). Two prophets minister during the reigns of each: Azariah and Hanani for Asa; Jehu and Eliezer for Jehoshaphat. Like Asa and Jehoshaphat the relationship between two of the prophets is father-son; Hanani (16:7) was the father of Jehu (19:2; 20:34).

6. The Chronicler may be using a paronomasia on the name of both kings. A. Shinan and Y. Zakowitch ("Midrash on Scripture and Midrash within Scripture," *Scripta Hierosolymitana* 31 [1986] 272) suggest that the Chronicler is

using a word play on Asa's name. אסא in Aramaic is a term for physician (16:11–14). Jehoshaphat, whose name means "Yahweh judges," is the one who appoints judges for Judah (19:4–11).

The Chronicler may be indicating his intention to parallel the accounts of Asa and Jehoshaphat by his twice comparing Jehoshaphat to his father (17:3—see *Notes* regarding the textual difficulty; 20:32 // 1 Kgs 22:43); Asa and Jehoshaphat are explicitly paired together as a standard of comparison against Jehoram in 21:12.

One must not underestimate, however, the differences between the Chronicler's narrative of Asa and Jehoshaphat. Williamson (278) finds a marked contrast with the Chronicler's account of Asa in the lack of a rigid chronological framework for the reign of Jehoshaphat. Though there are two battle reports for each king, the sequence is reversed: Asa begins with a victory during a period of fidelity, but ends with an alliance that provoked prophetic rebuke. The reverse is true for Jehoshaphat: he is compromised by his alliance with Ahab (19:1–3), but his next battle (2 Chr 20) is more like Asa's first.

Though the Chronicler has devoted much more space to this king than did the deuteronomic historian, one should not overstate the contrast. Most of the account in Kings is cited nearly verbatim by the Chronicler (1 Kgs 22:1–35 // 2 Chr 18:2–34; 1 Kgs 22:41–46, 49 // 2 Chr 20:31–36). Of those portions unique to Chronicles, many contain elaborations on themes alluded to in the Kings account, suggesting a greater influence for the author's Kings *Vorlage* than might be apparent simply from noting verbatim parallels. The following issues mentioned in Kings may have precipitated the Chronicler's elaboration: the issue of the high places (1 Kgs 22:43; cf. 2 Chr 17:3–6), the comparison with Asa (1 Kgs 22:43; 2 Chr 17:3; 20:32), peace with Israel (1 Kgs 22:44; cf. 2 Chr 17:1; 18:1), his military exploits (1 Kgs 22:45), particularly with reference to Edom (1 Kgs 22:47; 2 Chr 20).

The basic compositional influence for the Chronicler's record of Jehoshaphat is the same as for his accounts of other reigns—his theology of immediate retribution. Fidelity and obedience are rewarded with building programs, wealth and honor, peace and victory, but infidelity is greeted with swift rebuke (19:1–3) and punishment (20:37).

Jehoshaphat, Faithful and Blessed (17:1–19)

Bibliography

Albright, W. F. "The Judicial Reform of Jehoshaphat." *Alexander Marx Jubilee Volume.* New York: Jewish Publication Society, 1950. **Macholz, G.** "Zur Geschichte der Justizorganisation in Juda." *ZAW* 84 (1972) 314–40. **Welch, A. C.** *The Work of the Chronicler.* 73–77. **Whitelam, K.** *The Just King: Monarchical Judicial Authority in Ancient Israel.* JSOTSup, 12. Sheffield: JSOT Press, 1979. **Wilson, R.** "Israel's Judicial System in the Preexilic Period." *JQR* 74 (1983) 229–48.

Translation

[1] *Jehoshaphat his son ruled in his place and strengthened himself against Israel.* [2] *He stationed troops in all the fortified cities of Judah and established garrisons[a] in the land of Judah and in the cities of Ephraim that Asa his father had captured.*

[3] *Yahweh was with Jehoshaphat because he walked in the earlier[a] ways of his father[b] and did not seek Baal.* [4] *Rather he sought the God of his father and followed all his commandments,[a] and not the practice of Israel.* [5] *Yahweh established the kingdom in his hand, and all Judah brought gifts to Jehoshaphat, so that he had great riches and honor.* [6] *His heart exulted in the ways of Yahweh, and further, he removed the high places and the Asherah poles from Judah.*

[7] *In the third year of his reign he sent his officials Ben-hayil,[a] Obadiah, Zechariah, Nethanel, and Micaiah to teach in the cities of Judah.* [8] *With them there were the Levites Shemaiah, Nethaniah, Zebadiah, Asahel, Shemiramoth, Jehonathan, Adonijah, Tobijah,[a] and Tob-adonijah[b]—all Levites; Elishama and Jehoram—both priests—were also with them.* [9] *They taught in the cities of Judah. They had the book of the law of Yahweh with them and went through all the cities of Judah teaching the people.*

[10] *The dread of Yahweh fell upon all the kingdoms of the lands around Judah, and they did not make war with Jehoshaphat.* [11] *Some of the Philistines were bringing gifts to him, and silver as tribute;[a] the Arabs also were bringing him flocks, 7,700 rams and 7,700 goats.*

[12] *Now Jehosphaphat became more and more powerful; he built fortresses and store cities in Judah* [13] *and had many supplies in the cities of Judah. He also had an army of seasoned troops in Jerusalem,* [14] *registered by their clans as follows:*
from Judah, the officers over units of a thousand:
Adnah, the commander, and with him 300,000 seasoned troops;
[15] *next to him, Jehohanan, the commander, with 280,000;*
[16] *next to him, Amasiah ben Zikri, who volunteered for the*
service of Yahweh with 200,000 seasoned troops;
[17] *from Benjamin, the valiant soldier Eliada with 200,000 men*
armed with bow and shield;
[18] *next to him, Jehozabad, with 180,000 armed troops.*
[19] *These were the men who served the king, apart from those whom the king had stationed in the fortified cities through all Judah.*

Notes

2.a. The term נציבים could refer either to a garrison or to an officer or official. The point in the context appears to be that larger forces were stationed in the fortified cities, as opposed to the smaller contingents in the unfortified towns.

3.a. Contrast NIV: "because in his early years he walked in the ways. . . ." The term "years" is not found in the text, nor does the Chronicler make the point that in his later years Jehoshaphat did not walk in the ways of his father. The decision on how to translate הראשנים "former, earlier" is bound up with the text-critical decision regarding the word *David*; cf. n. 3.b.

3.b. MT, "in the earlier ways of his father David"; a few Hebrew MSS and G omit דויד, "David." The Chronicler does not divide the reign of David into good vs. evil periods in the way done in the deuteronomic history; though he does often presume his reader's familiarity with the parallel history, it is improbable in light of his own idealization of David that he would here refer to the presentation of David's reign in Samuel. Omitting "David," the immediate antecedent would be Asa, for whom the Chronicler does present a chronological scheme dividing the earlier good years from the later evil ones; futhermore, the comparison to Asa is explicitly made in the parallel history and later in the Chronicler's own narrative (1 Kgs 22:43 // 2 Chr 20:32). Since David is so often the standard of comparison, it is easy to understand why a scribe might gloss the text with his name at this point; none of the typical types of scribal errors would readily account for its omission.

4.a. G (except G^L) reads "commandments of his father." The insertion τοῦ πατρὸς αὐτοῦ is an erroneous clarification similar to the insertion of *David* in the preceding verse.

7.a. G τοὺς υἱοὺς τῶν δυνατῶν = בני חיל, "valiant men" (cf. 1 Chr 5:18; 2 Chr 28:6).

8.a-b. *Tobijah* is missing from OG. Either a copyist or translator skipped over *Tobijah* due to homoioarchon, or *Tob-adonijah* is a conflation and dittogr of the two previous names.

11.a. This appears to be the only instance where משא means "tribute"; cf. the use of נשא with מנחה in the sense "tributaries" (2 Sam 8:2, 6).

Form/Structure/Setting

Apart from a snippet of the introductory formula (17:1a // 1 Kgs 15:24b), the material in 2 Chr 17 is unique to the Chronicler. The chapter is structured by further explicit elaborations on the the general statements introduced in 17:1–6 (Williamson, 280): Jehoshaphat's army and fortifications (17:2) are developed in 17:12b–19; his wealth and honor (17:5) are described in 17:10–12a; aspects of his religious devotion (17:3, 6) are elaborated in 17:7–9.

Whatever sources may have been available to the author for these materials, the chapter bears the unmistakable imprint of the Chronicler's characteristic motifs and vocabulary. Building programs and large armies (17:2, 12–19) are common items the author uses to show divine favor; the most characteristic act of the pious kings in Chronicles is their "seeking God" (17:4; see the essay introducing 2 Chr 10–36, "Reward and Punishment in Chronicles: The Theology of Immediate Retribution"). Other vocabulary is also characteristic of the Chronicler: פחד יהוה ("the dread of Yahweh," 14:13 [14]; 17:10; 19:7; cf. 20:29) and כל ממלכות הארצות ("all the kingdoms of the lands," 1 Chr 29:30; 2 Chr 12:8; 17:10; 20:29; cf. 20:6).

Rudolph (249) thought he had isolated a source for 17:1b–2; see *Comment*. Considerable discussion has also centered on whether 17:7–9 and 19:4–12 are doublets; see *Comment* at those passages.

The major paragraph-level syntactic devices in the chapter are the ויהי-clauses at 17:3, 10, 12 and the temporal phrase at 17:7.

Comment

1–2 The Chronicler ordinarily uses the word הִתְחַזֵּק in the sense "to consolidate one's power over" the kingdom (1:1; 12:13; 13:20 [21]; 21:4; 27:6; 32:5; see *Comment* at 1:1–3). If this use is intended here, Israel would refer to the Southern Kingdom and Ephraim to the Northern. In vv 4–5, however, Israel would refer to the Northern Kingdom and Judah to the Southern. These differing terms of reference in vv 1–6 prompted Rudolph (249) to identify two different sources: vv 1–2 from a source used by the Chronicler, and vv 3–6 from the Chronicler himself. However, context suggests instead the translation adopted here: "strengthened himself against Israel," i.e., against the Northern Kingdom. Apparently Jehoshaphat was fully aware of the preceeding half century of warfare over the territory between the two kingdoms and sufficiently concerned about the powerful Ahab to his north so as to take the precaution of fortifying his borders. The Ephraimite cities were captured initially by Abijah (13:19), held by Asa (15:8), and now by his son Jehoshaphat. Though the cities in question were primarily in the territory of Benjamin, some were also in the hills of Ephraim (15:8). This initial posture of hostility to the North on the part of Jehoshaphat would soon turn to one of treaty and marriage alliance (18:1); the Chronicler may be elaborating on the point already found in his *Vorlage* that Jehoshaphat was the one who "made peace" (1 Kgs 22:44) with Ahab, reflecting on the fact that their initial relationship was one of hostility.

3–4 In these verses the Chronicler twice compares Jehoshaphat with his father Asa; see the introductory section "The Chronicler's Jehoshaphat" regarding the way in which the author has used Asa's reign as a paradigm for that of Jehoshaphat.

The statements that Jehoshaphat did not follow the Baals (v 3) or the practices of Israel (v 4) are mutually explanatory. Though the author could be alluding to the calf worship in the Northern Kingdom (11:15; 13:9), it is more probable that he is assuming his reader's familiarity with the flourishing Baal cult in the North under Ahab and Jezebel as described in the deuteronomic history; he is making the point that though Jehoshaphat would eventually wrongly ally himself with the North, this alliance did not sway his devotion to Yahweh. The term *Baal* is plural in its grammatical form, either (1) as an "emphatic plural" similar to the use of *'elohim* with a singular referent, or conceivably (2) as a reference to local representations of Baal worshiped under a variety of designations.

"Yahweh was with" Jehoshaphat, as he had been with Solomon (1:1), Abijah and Judah (13:12), and Asa (15:9).

5–6 Wealth, honor, and fame are part of the repertoire of themes which show divine favor in Chronicles. Not only do David and Solomon enjoy these tokens of God's pleasure (1 Chr 29:2–5, 28; 2 Chr 9:13–27), but so do Jehoshaphat (17:5; 18:1), Uzziah (26:8, 15), and Hezekiah (32:27).

This is the only passage in Chronicles where the phrase וַיִּגְבַּהּ לִבּוֹ, "his heart was lifted up," must have a positive sense; its ordinary use in Chronicles (26:16; 32:25) and in the rest of the OT is negative, "be haughty."

The Chronicler states that Jehoshaphat removed the high places (17:6), but later following his *Vorlage* appears to reverse himself (20:33 // 1 Kgs 22:43). The same apparent contradiction occurs in the Chronicler's account of Asa's reign (14:2 [3]; 15:17). One way this contradiction has been handled is by suggesting that only the statements that the kings removed the high places were original with the Chronicler (14:2; 17:6), and that the contradictory statements were introduced only later by another editor inserting material from the parallel history (15:17 // 1 Kgs 15:14; 20:33 // 1 Kgs 22:43; cf. Elmslie, 236–37). However, the parallels between Asa and Jehoshaphat suggest that these apparent contradictions were a part of the conscious schematization of their reigns on the part of the Chronicler himself rather than the careless labors of a later redactor; see the introductory section, "The Chronicler's Jehoshaphat." Alternative explanations apply equally well for these historical difficulties in the case of both kings; see *Comment* at 14:2–5.

7–9 The third year of Jehoshaphat's reign may actually have been the first year of his sole reign, following a presumed coregency necessitated by his father's debilitating disease (16:12). Though his total reign (872–848 B.C.) was twenty-five years, Jehoshaphat would have carried on the affairs of state for his stricken father during the period from 872–869 B.C. (Thiele, *Mysterious Numbers,* rev. ed. [1983] 96–97).

Jehoshaphat's teaching mission portrays him in the light of the ideal king of Deut 17:18–20. It is an ideal of royal responsibility for law and justice which is pervasive in the ancient Near East (Whitelam, *Just King,* 17–38, 207–18). The teaching duty of the cultic personnel is well established in biblical tradition (Deut 33:10; Lev 10:11; Jer 18:18; Mal 2:7; Hos 4:6; cf. 2 Chr 15:3). Though the five officials would have served primarily as representatives of the crown, their presence assigns and legitimates a teaching role also for laity. The Chronicler's interest in the lay members may reflect the practice of the emergent synagogues in the post-exilic period.

There is no way to establish with confidence the contents of the "book of the law of Yahweh." Though by the Chronicler's own day such a designation would probably refer to the Pentateuch, one cannot insist on that significance for the time of Jehoshaphat. At the very least, however, presuming the historical worth of the material, this pericope does attest to the early existence of authoritative writings regulative of Israel's life, i.e., it speaks of the concept of canonical writings at a time far earlier than critical reconstructions have ordinarily allowed (cf. S. Leiman, *The Canonization of Hebrew Scripture* [Hamden, CT: Connecticut Academy of Arts and Sciences, 1976] 20–21).

Many scholars have viewed the teaching mission as a duplicate of the judicial reform account (19:4–11); the author may have had two sources describing the reforms from different vantages. While this is certainly a possibility, nothing precludes understanding the text as it presents itself, as essentially two different stages in Jehoshaphat's reforms.

10–11 The Chronicler notes the dread of Yahweh on the part of the nations for both Jehoshaphat (20:29) and Asa (14:14; cf. 1 Chr 14:17), and he makes the point regarding both that they enjoyed periods of peace. Peace is one of the tokens of divine favor in Chronicles (14:1; cf. 1 Chr 22:9); the statement that the nations would "not make war" (cf. 15:19) on Jehoshaphat is conceptually related to the Chronicler's distinctive use of the rest concept (20:30; 14:6–7; 1 Chr 22:9; see R. Braun, *JBL* 95 [1976] 582–86).

The "Arabs" were probably the desert tribes south and southwest of Judah in territory contiguous with the Philistines; they inhabited the region where Asa had fought his campaign against Zerah the Ethiopian (14:9–15), and their paying tribute to Jehoshaphat may derive largely from his father's earlier victories in the area. Depending on the date assigned for the work of the Chronicler, for the author's audience this region would have been associated with the growing power of the Nabateans (Elmslie, 238).

12–19 It appears from this passage that the clan levy which provided Israel's army in the early- and premonarchic periods was still the basis for conscription in the mid-ninth century B.C. אלף is used as a military synonym for the more family-oriented term משפחה, "phratry, clan" (Mic 5:1 [2]; Judg 6:15; Num 1:16; 1 Sam 10:19; 23:23; cf. F. Andersen, "Israelite Kingship Terminology and Social Structure," *BT* 20 [1969] 36–37); 2 Chr 1:2 equates the heads of the families with the military and political leadership.

If the numbers are simply totaled, Jehoshaphat is presented as having a standing army in Jerusalem composed of 1.16 million men. Scholars have pursued several avenues to cope with such large figures. (1) Since the בית אב, "clan," is a subdivision of a tribe, it is suggested that an אלף is a military unit actually composed of considerably less than 1,000 men (J. B. Payne, *BSac* 136 [1979] 109–28, 206–20; J. Wenham, *TynBul* 18 [1967] 19–53; cf. G. Mendenhall, *JBL* 77 [1958] 52–66). But even if the average "1,000" were reduced to 100 or even 50 men, Jehoshaphat would still have between 58,000 and 116,000 troops quartered in Jerusalem, a figure that still appears high in light of population estimates for Iron Age Jerusalem. Mendenhall ("The Census Lists of Numbers 1 and 26," *JBL* 77 [1958] 52–66) suggested that an *'elef* consisted of 5 to 14 men, a reduction which would reach more probable figures. (2) It is possible that the text does not intend that all were quartered in Jerusalem at the same time, but only that the respective divisions served on rotation (1 Chr 27:1–15) or that each division was represented by a smaller number of troops. Though such a scenario is possible, the Chronicler's pointed distinction between the troops just numbered and those in the outlying cities (17:19) suggests he thought of the total as a standing army.

However the problem with such large numbers is solved, it is clear that large armies are an index of royal piety for the author (13:3; 14:8; 25:5; 26:11–15). The figure assigned to Jehoshaphat is roughly triple that assigned to Abijah, Asa, Amaziah, and Uzziah, and approximately the same as the number of fighting men in the Northern tribes according to the Chronicler's account of David's census (1 Chr 21:5). The Chronicler is seeking to show the degree to which divine favor rested on Jehoshaphat. See *Comment* at 28:5–8.

Explanation

The Chronicler begins his account of Jehoshaphat by presenting him in an entirely favorable light. The chapter should be read with an eye to the author's efforts to effect a parallel between Asa and Jehoshaphat; see the introductory section, "The Chronicler's Jehoshaphat."

The Chronicler reminds his post-exilic audience once again that God never fails to reward fidelity. He calls attention to the importance of the public teaching of the law; the path to honor among the nations is found in obedience to it.

The NT also speaks of teaching missions commissioned by Israel's king. Jesus sent out the seventy (Luke 10:1–24; cf. 3 John 5–8); the resurrected Christ commissions his disciples to teach among the nations (Matt 28: 19–20).

Jehoshaphat's Involvement with Ahab (18:1–19:3)

Bibliography

Crenshaw, J. *Prophetic Conflict.* Berlin: de Gruyter, 1971. **Halevi, R.** "Micha ben Jimla, The Ideal Prophet." *BMik* 12 (1966/67) 102–6. **Haller, E.** *Charisma und Ekstasis. Der Erzählung von dem Propheten Micha ben Jimla.* Munich: Kaiser, 1960. **Seebass, H.** "Zur 1 Reg 22:35–38." *VT* 21 (1971) 380–82. **Vries, S. de.** *Prophet Against Prophet.* Grand Rapids: Wm. B. Eerdmans, 1978. **Wilson, R.** *Prophecy and Society in Ancient Israel.* Philadelphia: Fortress Press, 1980. **Würthwein, E.** "Zur Komposition von 1 Reg 22:1– 38." In *Das ferne und nahe Wort,* ed. F. Maass. BZAW 105. Berlin: Töpelmann, 1967.

Translation

[1] *Jehoshaphat had great riches and honor, and he allied himself with[a] Ahab by marriage.* [2] *After some years he went down to Ahab in Samaria; Ahab slaughtered many sheep and cattle in his honor and in honor of his entourage, and he urged him to go up against Ramoth-gilead.*

[3] *Ahab king of Israel said to Jehoshaphat king of Judah, "Will you go with me to Ramoth-gilead?" And he said to him, "I am as you are, and my people as your people;[a] we will go with you into battle."*

[4] *Then Jehoshaphat said to the king of Israel, "First seek the word[a] of Yahweh."* [5] *So the king of Israel assembled the prophets—400 men—and he said to them, "Shall we[a] go to war against Ramoth-gilead, or should I refrain?" And they said, "Go. God[b] will deliver them into the hand of the king."*

[6] *Then Jehoshaphat said, "Is there no other prophet of Yahweh here that we may inquire of him?"* [7] *"There is one other man," said the king of Israel to Jehoshaphat, "through whom we can inquire of Yahweh, but I hate him since he never prophesies good concerning me, but only evil throughout his life. He is Micaiah son of Imlah." And Jehoshaphat replied, "The king shouldn't say that."* [8] *So the king of Israel called one of his ministers and said, "Bring Micaiah son of Imlah at once."*

[9] *Now the king of Israel and Jehoshaphat king of Judah were each sitting on their thrones dressed in their robes, holding court at the threshing floor by the entrance to the gate of Samaria, while all the prophets were prophesying before them.* [10] *Now Zedekiah son of Kenaanah had made for himself some iron horns, and he said, "Thus says Yahweh, 'With these you will gore the Arameans until they are destroyed.'"* [11] *And all the prophets were prophesying similarly; they said, "Go up against Ramoth-gilead and you will be victorious, for Yahweh will deliver them into the king's hand."*

[12] *Now the messenger who had gone to call Micaiah said to him, "Look, the prophets are speaking[a] favorably for the king with one accord. Now let your own speech be like one of theirs; you also speak favorably."* [13] *But Micaiah said, "As Yahweh lives, I can only speak whatever my God[a] says to me[b]."*

[14] *So he went to the king, and the king asked him, "Should we[a] go to war against Ramoth-gilead or should I refrain?" And he answered, "Go, and be victorious![b] They will be delivered into your hands."[c]*

¹⁵Then the king said to him, "How many times must I adjure you to speak to me only the truth in the name of Yahweh!" ¹⁶And Micaiah answered, "I saw all Israel scattered over the hills like sheep without a shepherd, and Yahweh said, 'They have no masters; let each return to his house in peace.'"

¹⁷And the king of Israel said to Jehoshaphat, "Didn't I tell you that he never speaks favorably concerning me, but only evil!" ¹⁸Then Micaiah said, "ᵃHear now the word of Yahweh! I saw Yahweh sitting on his throne with all the army of heaven standing on his right and on his left, ¹⁹and Yahweh said, 'Who will entice Ahab king of Israelᵃ so that he will go to war and fall in Ramoth-gilead?' ᵇOne suggested this, and another, that. ²⁰Then a spirit came and stood before Yahweh and said, 'I will entice Ahab,' and Yahweh said to him, 'How?' ²¹And he said, 'I will go out and become a lying spirit in the mouths of all his prophets.' And Yahweh said, 'You will entice, and furthermore, you will succeed. Go and do so.' ²²Now behold, Yahweh has put a lying spirit in the mouth ofᵃ these your prophets, and Yahweh has decreed disaster for you."

²³Then Zedekiah son of Kenaanah approached and struck Micaiah on the cheek, and said, "Which way did the spirit of Yahweh leave me to speak to you?" ²⁴Micaiah replied, "You will find out on that day when you go to an inner room to hide yourself."

²⁵ Then the king of Israel said, "Take Micaiah and turn him over to Amon the city magistrate and to Joash the king's son, ²⁶and tell them, 'Thus says the king: put this man in prison and feed him a reduced ration of bread and water until I return in safety.'" ²⁷"If you ever return in safety," Micaiah said, "Yahweh has not spoken by me." He added, "Mark my words, all you people."

²⁸So the king of Israel and Jehoshaphat king of Judah went up against Ramoth-gilead. ²⁹The king of Israel said to Jehoshaphat, "I will disguise myself and goᵃ into battle, but you wear yourᵇ royal robes." And the king of Israel disguised himself, and they went into battle.

³⁰Now the king of Aram commanded the officers of his chariotry,ᵃ "Do not fight with great or small, but only with the king of Israel."

³¹And it came about that, when the chariot officers saw Jehoshaphat, they said, "It is the king of Israel!" and they wheeled about toward him to attack. Jehoshaphat cried out ᵃand Yahweh helped him; God drew them away from him.ᵃ ³²When the chariot officers saw that it was not the king of Israel, they stopped pursuing him.

³³One man drew his bow at random,ᵃ and he shot the king of Israel between the joints of his armor. The king said to his driver, "Pull about and get me out of the fighting! I've been wounded!" ³⁴The battle raged all that day, while the king of Israel was proppedᵃ up in his chariot facing the Arameans. Toward evening, at the time of sunset,ᵇ he died.

¹⁹:¹ Jehoshaphat king of Judah returned safely to his palace in Jerusalem. ²Jehu son of Hanani, the seer, appeared before him and said to King Jehoshaphat, "Is it right to help the wicked and to make alliances with those who hate Yahweh? Because of this wrath has come upon you from Yahweh. ³But some good things have been found in you, inasmuch as you removed the Asherahs from the land and set your heart on seeking God."

Notes

1.a. G ἐν οἴκῳ Αχααβ, "in the house of Ahab."

3.a. Chr omits "my horses are your horses" (1 Kgs 22:4), but adds the clause "we will go with you into battle" not found in the parallel.

4.a. Par (except for Par^L) and Bas (1 Kgs 22:5) omit "word."

5.a. 1 Kgs 22:6, Bas, and Par, "Shall I go"; cf. 18:14 and 1 Kgs 22:15.

5.b. 1 Kgs 22:6: אדני.

12.a. Reading דברו with Par and Bas (1 Kgs 22:13).

13.a. 1 Kgs 22:14, "Yahweh."

13.b. 1 Kgs 22:14, Bas and Par add אלי, "to me"; omission from MT possibly due to haplogr with אלהי.

14.a. See note at 18:5.

14.b. 1 Kgs 22:15, Par and Syr read both impvs as sgs.

14.c. 1 Kgs 22;15, "Yahweh will deliver them into the hand of the king."

18.a. Par = לא כן; Bas = לא כן לא אנכי, "not so! not I."

19.a. "King of Israel" is missing in 1 Kgs 22:20 MT, but found in Bas and Par.

19.b. Chr MT repeats אמר, probably a dittograph; it is absent from 1 Kgs 22:20, Bas and Par.

22.a. 1 Kgs 22:23, Bas, Vg, and some mss of Par add "all," i.e., "all these prophets of yours."

29.a. Both verbs are inf absolutes.

29.b. Par and Bas "my robes." This may reflect an effort on the part of the Bas translator to enhance the story by heightening Ahab's effort to evade Micaiah's prophecy and by explaining the assault against Jehoshaphat. For Par it probably reflects that translator's dependence on Bas.

30.a. 1 Kgs 22:31 specifies the number of chariot commanders as thirty-two.

31.a.-a. Not found in 1 Kgs 22:32; see *Comment.*

33.a. Par follows Bas εὐστόχως "with good aim." MT is literally "in his innocence," i.e., without deliberateness or intention, at random; cf. 2 Sam 15:11.

34.a. 1 Kgs 22:35 uses the hoph ptcp.

34.b. From this point the Chronicler omits details regarding the death of Ahab (1 Kg 22: 35b–40).

Form/Structure/Setting

The appearance of Micaiah before Ahab and Jehoshaphat is the only extended prophetic narrative in Chronicles; its inclusion in these books is all the more surprising in light of the author's comparative disinterest in the affairs of the Northern Kingdom. Commentators have commonly attributed its inclusion to the Chronicler's desire to portray a true prophet or to continue a positive portrayal of Jehoshaphat's fidelity to the LORD (18:4); neither of these reasons is compelling in light of the numerous other prophetic narratives the Chronicler omitted from his *Vorlage* and in light of the author's verdict on the entire incident (19:1–3).

Insofar as we attempt to read the author's mind, the concluding note (19:1–3) probably represents the key to the inclusion of this narrative. The Chronicler has consciously sought to model Jehoshaphat in Asa's image (see the introductory essay, "The Chronicler's Jehoshaphat"); Asa had received a prophet's condemnation for his involvement in a foreign alliance (16:1–9), and the inclusion of this incident perfects the parallel between the two kings. The notices with which both historians conclude their accounts give the moral of their narratives: the deuteronomic historian ends his account by emphasizing the fulfillment of the prophetic word in the death of Ahab (1 Kgs 22:36–39), an emphasis important throughout the deuteronomic history (Deut 18:14–22); the Chronicler omits this notice from his *Vorlage,* and replaces it with a moral equally important to him, that righteous kings must trust Yahweh and avoid entangling foreign alliances (19:1–3; cf. 16:1–9; 20:35–37; 25:6–8; 28:16–23). For the deuteronomic historian the efficacy of the prophetic word was one ingredient in the "why" for the exile; for the Chronicler, avoiding foreign alliances maintained the separate identity of the restoration community. We have in effect two sermons from the same text, each of the histories putting the same narrative to different purposes. The concluding notice of such parallel narratives is also diagnostic of the author's intent, for example, in the accounts of David's census: the Chronicler, who is so reluctant to report any wrongdoing on the part of David, includes the census narrative in order to account for the acquisition of the temple site (1 Chr 21:29–22:1; 2 Chr 3:1), information omitted in the deuteronomic account (2 Sam 24).

Scholarly discussion of the Micaiah narrative has focused on its literary history prior to attaining its canonical form in 1 Kgs 22. The major issues have concerned (1) the identification of its form critical genre (political narrative, prophetic narrative, battle report), (2) the sequence and nature of the redaction of the earlier materials, (3) the question of whether Ahab was always the "king of Israel" in the original narrative, and (4) the contribution of this account to the debate about false vs. true prophecy. Both Würthwein and DeVries isolate two separate sources combined with each other in a complex history of redaction, though the methodology and results of both are most tenuous and hyper-critical. DeVries (4–7) provides a history of research in the pericope.

In a sense, however, all the traditional critical tools are irrelevant at this point for the Chronicles: the Chronicler himself would have been ignorant of any literary history for the narrative and would have received it in roughly its present form in 1 Kgs 22; speculation about its literary history is more properly the province of a commentary or study on Kings. The Chronicler, however, does represent one more step in the redactional process and has taken a previous unit of tradition into the service of his own interests, as outlined above.

In addition to his changing the moral of the narrative by reporting a different end to the account from what was found in his *Vorlage*, most other changes introduced by the Chronicler are minor. The narrative is introduced somewhat differently (18:1) than 1 Kgs 22:1; Jehoshaphat's status is enhanced while Ahab's is attenuated (18:2 vs. 1 Kgs 22:3); the Chronicler also specifies the nature of Jehosphat's crying out (18:31 // 1 Kgs 22:32). See *Comment* below on these passages.

The narrative is structured primarily by its series of repartee paragraphs which constitute one of the longest dialogues in the OT; these paragraphs can be classified by their respective types: proposal/response (18:4–5, 12–13, 15–22, 28–29), question/answer (3, 6–7, 14, 23–24), command/execution (8, 25–27, 30–32). Other paragraphs are introduced using a ויהי-clause (18:1–2), circumstantial clause (18:9–11), or explicit change of subject and location (19:1–3).

Comment

1–2 The Chronicler has modified the introduction to the narrative from that found in his *Vorlage* at 1 Kgs 22:1. The mention of Jehoshaphat's wealth and honor resumes themes from chap. 17 and focuses attention on Jehoshaphat, with whom the Chronicler is concerned, rather than on Ahab. Jehoshaphat's role in the narrative is enhanced by the deference shown him and his entourage (18:2), information not found in the parallel account. The Chronicler also adds the note regarding the alliance effected by the marriage of Jehoshaphat's son Jehoram to Athaliah, daughter of Ahab; this additional note furthers the author's central concern in the Micaiah narrative with the evil of foreign alliances (19:1–3; see above *Form/Structure/Setting*) and sets the stage also for the disaster that would result from this marriage (22:10–12). The Chronicler may also be expressing his attitude toward Jehoshaphat's involvement with Ahab through his use of the term "entice" (סית), a verb which ordinarily connotes prompting to wrongdoing or inciting to evil (1 Chr 21:1; 2 Chr 32:11, 15); however, the verb is also used in some contexts (18:31) in a morally neutral sense.

Since the Chronicler has not reported the previous battles in the contest over Ramoth-gilead (see *Comment* at 22:5–6), particularly the treaty after the battle at Aphek (1 Kgs 20:26–43), he introduces his narrative with a more general chronological reference ("after some years") instead of the specific note that this incident was three years later (1 Kgs 22:2). Apparently Benhadad had not returned the contested territory in accordance with the earlier treaty (1 Kgs 20:34); after their cooperation in repulsing Shalmaneser III at the battle of Qarqar in 853, Ahab and Ben-hadad return to their local war for Ramoth-gilead (see C. F. Whitley, "The Deuteronomic Presentation of the House of Omri," *VT* 2 [1952] 137–52).

3 The Chronicler omits most of 1 Kgs 22:3, further diminishing Ahab's importance in his narrative.

4–5 The role of the prophets in the military ideology of ancient Israel is widely attested. Call narratives frequently emphasize their function against the nations (Exod 3:9–11; Jer 1:10; Ezek 3:4–7); the inclusion of extensive oracles against foreign nations in many of the canonical prophets attests to this role. They are often found providing war oracles as spokesmen for the Divine Warrior (1 Kgs 12:21–24 // 2 Chr 11:1–4; 1 Kgs 20:13, 28; 2 Kgs 3:11–19; 6:12–22; 7:1–7; 13:14–20; Isa 7:3–25; Jer 21; 2 Chr 20: 14–19).

6–8 One criterion by which the true prophet was recognized in the OT was that he in his preaching often stood alone, running against the tide of popular expectation; his opposition to the vox populi (Crenshaw, *Conflict*, 24–36) became a hallmark of the true prophet (36:16; 2 Kgs 17:13–15; Neh 9:26; Jer 25:4; 26:4–5; 28; 29:24–32; Matt 23:33–37). The vox populi and the vox pseudoprophetae were all but identical, so that agreement with the popular consensus made the prophetic message suspicious at the outset. Such suspicion appears to underlie Jehoshaphat's awareness that he was yet to hear the word of Yahweh.

Apart from this incident nothing is known of Micaiah son of Imlah. Some have identified him with the unnamed prophet who pronounced judgment on Ahab because of the lenient treaty he granted Ben-hadad (1 Kgs 20: 35–43).

9–11 The hithpael of נבא denotes the characteristic possession behavior of prophets (Num 11:25–27; 1 Sam 10:5–13; 19:20–24). Symbolic actions were viewed as partaking of the efficacy of the prophet's utterance. Cf. Jeremiah's interchange with Hananiah (Jer 27:2; 28:1–17). Yahweh is described as like a bull goring the nations with horns in Deut 33:17.

14 The Chronicler may have introduced one minor change in this verse in light of his theological concerns. Three different times the writer of Kings records the urging of the prophets to attack Ramoth-gilead, for "Yahweh will deliver it into the hands of the king" (1 Kgs 22:6, 12, 15); the Chronicler has copied him in the first two instances (2 Chr 18:5, 11). However, in this last case the Chronicler has made one modification: rather than "Yahweh will deliver it into the king's hands," he has written "it will be delivered into the king's hands." Even though the author is using irony, for the Chronicler Yahweh's name must be divorced from this false utterance in the mouth of a true prophet (Coggins, 215–16).

16 The imagery of sheep without a shepherd is also found Num 27:16–17; Isa 13:14; Zech 10:2; 13:7. "In peace" contrasts to the fate of Ahab; cf. 18:26–27; 19:1.

18–22 The role of the heavenly council in Israel's warfare was ordinarily the mustering of the heavenly army to fight in Israel's behalf, arousing even the forces of the cosmos to join the Divine Warrior in a joint venture with the nation against the enemies of God (Isa 13:1–13; Joel 4:9–12 [3:9–12]; 2 Kgs 6:15–19; 7:6; cf. P. Miller, "The Divine Council and the Prophetic Call to War," *VT* 18 [1968] 100–107). Here, however, that customary role is reversed: the heavenly council devises the death of Ahab and the defeat of Israel's armies.

This section of the Micaiah narrative gives graphic expression to the claim of the later canonical prophets that the false prophets were speaking lies (Jer 23:14, 25–26, 32; 27:10, 15; Ezek 13:8, 9, 19; Zech 10:2; 13:3). For delusion as a motif of divine punishment, cf. Matt 24:23–24; 2 Thess 2:9–12; Rev 13:13–14; 19:20.

24 The term ראה may be a pun—Zedekiah was a seer, but would only truly see in the day that his prophecy was unfulfilled (Elmslie, 244; Slotki, 242).

25–26 Jeremiah was similarly imprisoned in the house of the king's son because he was a possible source of demoralization for the army (Jer 38:1–6). Joash is not listed among the sons of Jehoshaphat in 21:2; the title "son of the king" probably referred to other members of the royal family, but could also be the official title of a royal appointee (Jer 36:26; 38:6; see Gray, 453–54).

Prisoners received reduced rations; cf. Isa 30:20; Jer 38:9; Matt 25:43.

27 The clause "Mark my words, all you people" is missing from the parallel text in most texts of Bas and has, therefore, been commonly regarded by commentators as a gloss on 1 Kgs 22:28 in order to associate the opening utterances of Micah of Moresheth (Mic 1:2) with Micaiah. If it is to be treated as a gloss on 1 Kgs 22:28, the same gloss must have been in the Chronicler's *Vorlage*. See E. Ball. "A Note on 1 Kgs 22:28," *JTS* 28 [1977] 90–94).

28–29 Various reasons can be offered for Ahab's desire to disguise himself. Obviously the desire to escape detection or identification is the ordinary motivation for such a ruse (Gen 38:14; 1 Sam 28:8; 1 Kgs 14:2); in one other battle report, disguise appears to be an effort to evade a "prophetic" utterance

(35:22). Ahab may have anticipated the tactic adopted by the king of Aram (18:30–31). There is some debate regarding the meaning of the verb traditionally translated "disguise;" see *Comment* at 35:22.

Ahab's sending Jehoshaphat into battle dressed in his royal regalia in effect made Jehoshaphat the target, as subsequent developments in the narrative confirm. This incident is one ingredient that has caused many scholars to speculate that the Northern Kingdom under Ahab and Omri exercised hegemony over Judah.

30–31 The chariots were to act as an independent force with the sole goal of killing Ahab; a similar tactic was used by the king of Moab in his attempt to break through to the king of Edom (2 Kgs 3:26; Elmslie, 245).

The parallel text (1 Kgs 22:32) does not contain the additonal clauses, "and Yahweh helped him; God drew them away from him." In the Kings MT Jehoshaphat cries out presumably either for help from his men or to alert the opposing chariotry that he was not Ahab. For the Chronicler, however, this becomes a cry to God in prayer; it is one more way in which the Chronicler shows God's responsiveness to Solomon's prayer at the dedication of the temple (6:34–35; 7:14) and to prayer in the midst of battle (1 Chr 5:20; 2 Chr 13:14–15; 14:11–12; 20:9; 32:20; cf. 33:13). However, Bas[L] does contain the additional phrase καὶ κύριος ἔσωσεν αὐτόν, the equivalent of ויהוה עזרו. This suggests that the Chronicler may have been following a Hebrew text for Kings which already had at least the first clause, and could have contained the second as well; alternatively the Chronicler could have glossed the first clause in his *Vorlage* by adding the second (Lemke, *Synoptic Studies,* 159). Whether the additional clauses originated with the Chronicler or were already found in his *Vorlage,* they represent material quite congenial to his own viewpoint.

33–34 DeVries (106) aptly comments, "That 'accidental' arrow was Yahweh's arrow—make no mistake about it!"

The Chronicler drops his *Vorlage* at the end of v 34. The compiler of Kings was quite interested in the death of Ahab (1 Kgs 22:35–40; cf. 20:41– 42; 21:19–29; 22:17, 28), but the Chronicler has put the narrative to a different use. The Chronicler does not record much detail about the kings of Israel; his interest in the Micaiah narrative is shown in his own postscript (19:1–3).

19:1–3 These verses represent the key to the Chronicler's use of the Micaiah narrative; the story provided him with a further parallel between Asa and Jehoshaphat and the opportunity to underscore the evil of foreign alliances and the failure to trust Yahweh. See the discussion above under *Form/Structure/Setting.*

Other marks of the author's style also characterize these verses. Williamson (*OTS* 21 [1981] 166–67) describes the Chronicler's distinctive use of the root עזר, "help." Beyond 18:31 above God's help for the king is found in 1 Chr 5:20; 12:19; 2 Chr 14:10 [11]; 25:8; 26:7, 15; 32:8, whereas seeking the help of others or helping the ungodly leads only to disaster (here and 28:16, 23 [twice]). "Seeking God" is among the most important themes in the Chronicles; see the introduction essay to 2 Chr 10–36, "Reward and Punishment in Chronicles: The Theology of Immediate Retribution." "Some good" in Judah at the time of Rehoboam also mitigated that king's guilt (12:12; cf. 24:16; 31:20).

Jehu ben Hanani is the son of the prophet who had also rebuked Asa for his involvement in a foreign alliance (16:7–10). Jehu must have been a very old man at this time: he was active during the reign of Baasha (1 Kgs 16:1), a contemporary of Asa against whom his father had prophesied. See H. Seebass, "Tradition und Interpretation bei Jehu ben Chanani und Ahia von Silo," *VT* 25 (1975) 175–90.

Jehoshaphat is said both to have removed the Asherahs and not to have removed them (19:3; 20:33), presuming that removal of the poles also entailed destruction of the high places. The same apparent contradiction is found with reference to Asa; see the introductory essay "The Chronicler's Jehoshaphat" and *Comment* at 14:2–5.

There is ample background in ancient Near Eastern and biblical materials for translating אהב as "make an alliance, be faithful to an alliance"; see W. L. Moran, "The Ancient Near Eastern Background of the Love of God in Deuteronomy," *CBQ* 25 (1963) 77–87.

Explanation

The Chronicler's central concern in the Micaiah narrative was the opportunity it afforded him to condemn foreign alliances, a theme he develops with some frequency (see above, especially *Form/Structure/Setting*); this passage begins and ends on that note (18:1; 19:1–3). Avoiding foreign alliances was for the Chronicler one aspect of the central demand of the covenant that Israel show exclusive loyalty to Yahweh her God. The Chronicler's frequent introduction of this theme into his history must have had rhetorical relevance for the post-exilic community: though facing opposition and afforded many opportunities to trust in foreign powers or alliances, Judah in the restoration period was urged to trust in her God alone.

The OT appeals to a variety of criteria for distinguishing true from false prophecy. These criteria can be gathered under three heads as criteria focusing (1) on the revelatory means, (2) on the message, and (3) on the man himself. All three come into play to a greater or lesser extent in the Micaiah narrative. (1) A variety of revelatory means are sanctioned or forbidden in the OT (e.g., Num 12:6; Deut 13:1; 18:9–13). Preeminently the prophet was to be a man possessed by the spirit (Num 11:16–30; 24:2; 1 Sam 10:5–13; 19:17–24; 2 Kgs 2:7–14; Mic 3:8; Zech 7:12; 2 Chr 20:14, et al.); his message derived from his access to the heavenly council to hear the words of God (Num 12:8; Isa 6; Ezek 1–2; Jer 1:4–10; 23:18–22; Zech 3:7). Both the possession of the spirit (18:23–24) and the heavenly council (18:18–21) figure in the debate over true prophecy in the Micaiah narrative. (2) The prophet's message was not to be in the name of other gods (Deut 13:1–5) or to contradict previous revelation (1 Kgs 13). The true prophet is recognized because his words come to pass (Deut 18:14–22; 2 Chr 18:16, 25–27); he stands against the tide and the vox populi (see *Comment* at 18:6–8). (3) The canonical prophets appeal also to a moral criterion to invalidate the claims of their opponents to have the true word of God (Jer 14:14; 23:10–14; 29:21–23; Ezek 13:21–22; Mic 2:11; cf. Matt 7:15–20; 2 Tim 3:6). Though there are a number of examples of violence on the part of prophets in the OT, the NT invokes the moral criteria for the man of God (1 Tim 3:1–13; Titus 1:6–9; James 3:13–18) in saying that he is not to be violent, "a striker" (kjv—Titus 1:7; 1 Tim 3:3). His conduct should contrast to that of Zedekiah (18:23).

While the passage abounds in criteria distinguishing true from false prophecy, it also enigmatically affirms divine responsibility for false prophecy (Deut 13:3; 2 Chr 18:18–22).

The passage speaks eloquently of the sovereignty of God. It was not Ahab who ruled over Israel, seated on his throne surrounded by his flattering prophets, but Yahweh sitting on his throne surrounded by the host of heaven.

The Micaiah narrative in part probably underlies the developing doctrine of Satan in the OT (Gen 3; 1 Chr 21:1; Job 1–2; Zech 3:1), so that by the NT, Jesus can describe the devil as "a liar and the father of lies" (John 8:42–47; cf. 2 Thess 2:9–12).

In time another shepherd/king would die and his sheep would be scattered, but he would not die for sins that he had committed (18:16; Zech 13:7; Matt 26:31).

Jehoshaphat's Judicial Reform   (19:4–11)

Bibliography

Albright, W. F. "The Judicial Reform of Jehoshaphat." *Alexander Marx Jubilee Volume.* New York: Jewish Publication Society, 1950. **Knierim, R.** "Exodus 18 and die Neuordnung der mosaischen Gerichtsbarkeit." *ZAW* 73 (1961) 146–71. **Macholz, G.** "Zur Geschichte der Justizorganisation in Juda." *ZAW* 84 (1972) 314–40. **Phillips, A.** *Ancient Israel's Criminal Law.* Oxford: Blackwell, 1970. **Rofé, A.** "The Law about the Organization of Justice in Deuteronomy (16:18–20; 17:8–13)." *BMik* 65 (1976) 199–210. **Welten, P.** *Geschichte und Geschichtsdarstellung.* 184–85. **Whitelam, K.** *The Just King.* JSOTSup 12. Sheffield: JSOT Press, 1979. **Wilson, R.** "Israel's Judicial System in the Preexilic Period." *JQR* 74 (1983) 229–48.

Translation

⁴*Though Jehoshaphat lived in Jerusalem, he went out again among the people from Beersheba to the hills of Ephraim, and he brought them back to Yahweh the God of their fathers.* ⁵*He appointed judges throughout the land in all the fortified cities of Judah, city by city,* ⁶*and he said to the judges, "Pay attention to what you are doing, for it is not for man that you judge, but for Yahweh, and he will be with you when you render a decision.* ⁷*Now may the fear of Yahweh be upon you; take care what you do, for with Yahweh there is no injustice, partiality, or bribery."*

⁸*Jehoshaphat also appointed in Jerusalem judges from among the Levites and priests and the leaders of the families of Israel to administer the law of Yahweh and to settle disputes. They lived*ᵃ *in Jerusalem,* ⁹*and he gave them these instructions:*
"*You must serve in the fear of Yahweh with faithfulness and singleness of heart.* ¹⁰*In any case*ᵃ *that comes before you from your fellow citizens who live in their cities, whether it concerns bloodshed or violations of laws, statutes, ordinances or regulations, you are to warn them not to sin against Yahweh, lest his wrath come on you and your fellow countrymen. Do this, and you will not sin.*
¹¹*"Amaraiah the chief priest*ᵃ *will be over you in any matter concerning Yahweh, and Zebadiah*ᵇ *son of Ishmael, the leader of the tribe of Judah, in any matter concerning the king. The Levites will serve you as officers of the court. Be strong and resolute, and may Yahweh be on the side of the good."*

Notes

8.a. Reading וַיֵּשְׁבוּ. MT וַיָּשֻׁבוּ, "they returned to Jerusalem." G (τοὺς κατοικοῦντας) and Vg (*habitatoribus*) appear to have read a ptcp, יוֹשְׁבֵי, "inhabitants," i.e., "disputed cases among the inhabitants of Jerusalem." See J. Heller, "Textkritisches zu 2 Chr 19:8," *VT* 24 (1974) 371–73; cf. *Comment* below.

10.a. G "*any man* who brings a case" is a secondary development; the original πᾶσαν was later adapted to πᾶς ἀνήρ, or כל was itself (and only here in Par) translated as "any man." See Allen, *GC* 2:40.

11.a. The Chronicler routinely designates the high priest as כהן הראש, rather than כהן גדול, the chosen designation in other post-exilic writings (Haggai, Zechariah, Ezra, Nehemiah); this suggests that the Chronicler was not one and the same with the compiler of Ezra-Nehemiah. See Japhet, *VT* 18 (1968)," 343–44; and J. Baily, "The Usage in the Post-Restoration Period of Terms Descriptive of the Priest and High Priest," *JBL* 70 (1951) 217–27.

11.b. A few Heb. MSS, Syr, and Arab, זכריהו, "Zechariah."

Form/Structure/Setting

For the Chronicler the account of Jehoshaphat's judicial reform fits with his overall effort to parallel the reign of Jehoshaphat with that of his father Asa; see the introductory essay, "The Chronicler's Jehoshaphat." Both kings initiate reforms in two stages; both were instrumental in effecting religious revivals during their reigns (19:4; 15:8–15).

The major questions about the pericope have concerned (1) whether the material came from the Chronicler's own hand or some other source, (2) its relation to the judicial program of Deut 16:18–17:13, and (3) the historicity of the account.

(1) Evidence for the Chronicler's own compositional technique can be seen in his describing the borders of the land from south to north, i.e., "from Beersheba to Mount Ephraim" (19:4; cf. 30:5; 1 Chr 21:2), and in his frequent use of the title "the God of their fathers" (19:4; cf. Japhet, *Ideology*, 19–23; and Williamson, 287–88). However, apart from these items in v 4, the remainder of the passage does not appear to be typical of the Chronicler's compositional style. Speech materials are most characteristically used by the Chronicler as a vehicle for his concerns; the absence from Jehoshaphat's speeches of the frequent key vocabulary for retribution theology is quite noticeable. The Chronicler appears to be using the judicial reform (19:5–11) as one aspect of what Jehoshaphat accomplished during his tour of the cities to call the people back to the God of their fathers; in the absence of evidence for his own distinct compositional style, one would expect that he is here following an earlier source rather closely. The Chronicler's ordinary practice is to mention the priests before the Levites (1 Chr 9:2, 10–16; 13:2; 15:11; 24:6, 31; 28:13, 21; et al.); the reversal of this practice in 19:8 also suggests that the Chronicler is directly incorporating a source rather than editing himself (cf. 17:7–9; Williamson, 288).

(2) That the Chronicler was using another source is corroborated by the dependence of 19:5–11 on Deut 16:18–17:13. Some differences are found in the two passages: (1) the Chronicler speaks only of the fortified cities of Judah (19:8) where Deut 16:18 speaks of appointing judges "in every town"; (2) the Chronicler has a tribal officer, "the governor of the house of Judah," serving in the appeals court, where Deut 17:9 has a "judge"; (3) the "heads of the families" (19:8) are not mentioned in Deuteronomy. Williamson (288–89) argues that these differences in Chronicles reflect an earlier stage in judicial development: the centralization took place first in those garrison cities most readily subject to the king before it could be extended into the towns; the diminishing importance of tribal officers and family heads has been understood as evidence that the present form of Deuteronomy is later than the source which the Chronicler used for his account of Jehoshaphat's reform. See also the discussions of Whitelam, Knierim, Macholz, and Rofé.

(3) Opinions have covered a wide range with reference to the historicity of the account. On the more radical side, Wellhausen (*Prolegomena*, 191) dismissed it as an etiological explanation of Jehoshaphat's name ("Yahweh judges"). Others have found the account to be a valuable source describing a major shift in Judean judicial administration, a narrative about "whose general

historicity there can hardly be any doubt" (Myers, 108). Where Wellhausen saw only the projection of judicial practices from the Chronicler's own day into the past, Albright ("Judicial Reform") instead argued from parallels to an Egyptian judicial reform during the reign of Ḥaremḥab in the fourteenth century B.C. The Egyptian king preceded Jehoshaphat by five hundred years, but both texts describe the king's tour of the country, the appointment of judges in the large towns, royal exhortations concerning bribery and extortion, and cultic officials with judicial roles. It is not necessary to suggest any direct dependence on the Ḥaremḥab decree for Jehoshaphat's reform to appreciate that the decree does show striking parallels to 2 Chr 19:5–11 and that it does establish even greater antiquity for the type of reform attributed to Jehoshaphat; see Whitelam, *Just King*, 203–5.

Some centralization of judicial authority must be presumed during Israel's transition from a tribal confederacy to a centralized monarchy. The practices described could have antedated Jehoshaphat in the ancient Near East by many centuries; there is no compelling reason to deny the historicity of the account. It should also be noted, however, that the judicial reform of Jehoshaphat may not have instituted new or heretofore unseen practices in Israel—transition to a centralized judiciary could well have preceded him—but could be understood simply as a reform to eliminate corruption in judicial practice.

The Chronicler may well have been seeking to cite a precedent or to otherwise legitimate practices in his own day, but this does not automatically undercut his use of historically reliable information.

Comment

4 The Chronicler credits several of the kings with efforts at religious revival among the people: Asa (15:8–15); Joash (24:4–11); Hezekiah (30:1–31:1); Josiah (34:3–7); and even Manasseh (33:16–17). The "again" (וישב) implies that this account is a sequel to the earlier teaching mission. Jehoshaphat retained control of the territory contested and won earlier by his father Asa and traveled into the hills of Ephraim (15:8; cf. 13:4; 1 Chr 6:52 [67]). The Chronicler describes the land from south to north, rather than the more customary north to south (30:5); on one occasion he deliberately reverses the sequence found in his *Vorlage* (1 Chr 21:2 // 2 Sam 24:2).

5 The fortified cities would represent centers of royal control and administration, and hence would be the cities of choice for a royal judiciary. The garrisons of troops in the fortified cities could repress any opposition to the judicial changes that might have come from the traditional local judiciary or powerful local families. For the comparison with the judicial program of Deuteronomy, see above *Form/Structure/Setting*.

Commentators commonly assume that this represented an innovation on the king's part, a move toward centralization and away from the local courts administered by town elders. Though a process of centralization is to be expected with the rise of the monarchy, it is worth noting that nothing in the text itself requires the understanding that this was an innovation introduced by Jehoshaphat. According to the Chronicler some royal judicial bureaucracy existed at the time of David and Solomon; cultic personnel were serving in a judiciary "away from the temple," i.e., presumably in the towns (1 Chr 26:29; cf. 1 Chr 23:4; 2 Chr 1:2). Though there has been considerable debate about the source and date for the lists of officials in 1 Chr 23–27, the Chronicles as we have them, i.e., in their present canonical shape, show elements of a centralized judiciary well before Jehoshaphat. It may be that Jehoshaphat further centralized control; it is, however, also possible that he was involved in reforming an already existing system that had become corrupt through partiality and taking bribes, forms of injustice addressed in his speech (19:7).

6–7 Judicial authority in Israel was not the prerogative of autonomous power; rather it depended upon and expressed the rule of Yahweh and was to reflect his own attributes of righteousness, justice, and fairness. Judges acted in behalf of kings or other men only in a derivative sense—in reality they were the agents of Yahweh who was present at their decisions. Yahweh loves and is known by his justice (Ps 9:16; 11:7). The frequent biblical injunctions against bribery attest to the extent and persistence of the practice; the poor who could not afford the bribe were in this way the prey of the rich (Exod 23:6–8; Deut 1:17; 16:18–20; 1 Sam 8:3; Ps 15:5; Prov 17:23; Isa 1:21–23; 5:22–23; Mic 3:11; 7:3; Zech 7:9–10).

8 See *Notes* above. The MT reads וישבו as "and they returned to Jerusalem"; the scribes apparently understood the statement as a concluding remark to Jehoshaphat's journey (19:4), but the intervening material concerning appointments in Jerusalem makes this seem unnatural. G and Vg attest to an alternative text which would have the effect of making the court in Jerusalem that heard appeals from outlying areas also the court of original jurisdiction for the inhabitants of Jerusalem. Though one must give due weight to the agreement of G and Vg, allowing direct access to the appeals court in Jerusalem for the inhabitants of that city would seem contrary to the equity and fairness that prompted the reform itself. Repointing the text to read "they lived in Jerusalem" refers the statement to the immediately preceding context: the priests and Levites ordinarily lived outside the city and served in Jerusalem on rotations; these cultic personnel and the family leaders appointed to the Jerusalem court would reside in the city on a more permanent basis.

"Israel" in this verse must refer to the Southern Kingdom.

8–11 Though it is not explicitly mentioned, there probably also existed a lower court in Jerusalem, so that the appeals court would not be the court of original jurisdiction for any inhabitant of Jerusalem.

The right of appeal to a higher judicial authority is found in Israel's most ancient traditions; Moses himself would hear cases too hard for the appointed judges (Deut 1:8–18; Exod 18:17–26).

The priests and Levites had some judicial role in the Jerusalem court, but no such role is mentioned for them in the local courts. It may be that their authority in judicial matters was confined to the higher court, but cf. 1 Chr 26:29. The judicial role for cultic personnel was not a new one; it may have originated with the use of sacral lots for divination (1 Sam 14:36–45; 2 Sam 21:1).

The need to have two different presiding justices reflects the tension which commonly existed in the ancient Near East between the interests of the crown and the temple, particularly in the control of revenues accruing to each from their great wealth; one can imagine that jurisdictional questions were common. The same tension between crown and cult is important again in 2 Chr 24; cf. 1 Chr 26:30, 32. The "officers" (שׁטרים) were probably the bureaucrats—clerks, bailiffs, etc.—that assisted the court; the earlier traditions of local courts also speak of this office in premonarchic times (Deut 29:9 [10]); Josh 8:33; 23:2; 24:1; cf. Whitelam, *Just King*, 198). "Amariah" should probably be identified as the third high priest after Solomon constructed the temple (1 Chr 5:37 [6:11]).

Williamson (279) sees the phrase "lest his wrath come upon you" as an important key to how the Chronicler is developing his material. The deuteronomic historian's account of Israel's battle with Moab had ended with great wrath against Israel (2 Kgs 3:27); the Chronicler omits this narrative and substitutes instead Jehoshaphat's victory over a Transjordan coalition (2 Chr 20), showing in the king's fidelity how wrath can be averted.

Explanation

The Chronicler's record of Jehoshaphat's judicial reform was probably included by him at least in part to give historical precedent for judicial practices in his own time; he shows a historical realization of judicial practices enjoined in Deuteronomy, and simultaneously illustrates the separation of judicial function in the political and sacral realms. For the post-exilic period this division into "matters concerning the king" and "matters concerning Yahweh" was crucial: for the Jews of succeeding centuries, "matters concerning the king" were largely those of foreign overlords such as the Persians, Greeks, and Romans, while authority within the daily life of Judaism increasingly revolved around the temple.

This division between political and sacral was sometimes ambiguous; jurisdictional questions and divided loyalties would be inevitable even within the Jewish commonwealth, though certainly even more so when Judah was dominated by a foreign power. The issue of jurisdiction would remain thorny and ultimately unresolved; centuries later some Pharisees sought to entrap Jesus on the question (Matt 22:17–22), but it received its most severe test when Jesus was shuttled from trial to trial—first before priests and teachers of the law, then before Roman officers (Luke 22:66–23:25; Matt 26:57–67; 27:11–26).

Jehoshaphat provided a judicial system for Israel; Paul does so for the fledgling church (1 Cor 6:1–11; 1 Tim 5:17–21; cf. Matt 19:28).

The speeches of Jehoshaphat as recorded in Chronicles reflect a large body of biblical teaching regarding the concern of God with justice. Justice will always be subject to perversion, until he who is the Just is also the Judge (Rev 20:11–15; 1 Pet 2:23).

Jehoshaphat's Battle near Tekoa; His Death (20:1–21:1)

Bibliography

Dorsey, D. *The Roads and Highways of Israel during the Iron Age.* Diss. Dropsie University, 1981. **Gese, H.** "Zur Geschichte der Kultsänger am zweiten Tempel." *Von Sinai zum Zion: alttestamentliche Beiträge zur biblische Theologie.* Munich: Chr. Kaiser, 1974. 147–58. **Ilan, Z.** "Jehoshaphat's Battle with Ammon and Moab." *BMik* 18/53 (1972/73) 205–11. **Kasher, R.** "The Salvation of Jehoshaphat—Its Dimensions, Parallels, and Significance (2 Chr 20:1–30)." *BMik* 31 (1985/86) 242–51. **Noth, M.** "Eine palästinische Lokalüberlieferung in 2 Chr. 20." *ZDPV* 67 (1945) 45–71. **Petersen, D.** *Late Israelite Prophecy.* 54–77. **Rad, G. von.** *Der Heilige Krieg im alten Israel.* Göttingen: Vandenhoeck & Ruprecht, 1952. **Welten, P.** *Geschichte und Geschichtsdarstellung.* 140–53.

Translation

[1] *After a time, the Moabites and Ammonites along with some of the Meunites*[a] *came to make war on Jehoshaphat.* [2] *Some men came and reported to Jehoshaphat, "A vast horde is coming against you from beyond the Sea, from Edom.*[a] *They are already in Hazazon Tamar" (that is, En-gedi).*

[3] *Jehoshaphat was afraid, and he determined to seek Yahweh; he proclaimed a fast for all Judah.* [4] *Judah gathered to seek help*[a] *from Yahweh; they came from every city in Judah to seek Yahweh.*

[5] *Jehoshaphat stood in the assembly of Judah and Jerusalem*[a] *in the temple of Yahweh in front of the new courtyard,* [6] *and said,*

"O Yahweh, God of our fathers, are you not the God of heaven?[a] *You rule over all the kingdoms of the nations; power and might are in your hand, and no one can withstand you.* [7] *O our God, did you not dispossess the inhabitants of this land before your people Israel and give it forever to the descendants of Abraham your friend?* [8] *They occupied it and built in it*[a] *a sanctuary in honor of your name, saying,* [9] *'If there should come against us calamity, sword, flood,*[a] *plague or famine, and we stand before this temple and before you, for your name is*[b] *in this house, and we cry out to you because of our enemies, then may you hear and save.'* [10] *But now, look! The people of Ammon, Moab, and Mount Seir—whom you did not allow Israel to attack when they came from the land of Egypt, so that they turned aside and did not destroy them—* [11] *they are now themselves repaying us by trying to drive us out of your*[a] *possession which you gave to us.* [12] *O our God, will you not judge them, for we have no power against this vast horde that has come against us. We do not know what we should do, but our eyes are on you."*

[13] *Now all the men of Judah, including their dependents, wives and children, were standing before Yahweh.* [14] *Then in the midst of the assembly the spirit of Yahweh came upon Jahaziel son of Zechariah son of Benaiah son of Jeiel son of Mattaniah, a Levite of the line of Asaph, and he said,*

[15] *"Pay attention, all Judah, inhabitants of Jerusalem, and King Jehoshaphat. Thus says Yahweh to you: Do not fear, do not be dismayed because of this great*

horde, for the battle is not yours, but God's. ¹⁶Tomorrow march down against them. They will be coming up the Ascent of Ziz;ᵃ you will find them at the end of the gorge, east of the Desert of Jeruel. ¹⁷It is not you who will fight this battle. Take your positions, stand and watch Yahweh's victory. He is with you, O Judah and Jerusalem. Do not fear or be dismayed. Tomorrow go out before them, for Yahweh is with you."

¹⁸The Jehoshaphat bowed with his face to the ground, and all the people of Judah and Jerusalem fell down before Yahweh to worship him. ¹⁹Levites from the lines of Kohath and Korah stood to praise Yahweh the God of Israel with a very loud voice.

²⁰ They arose in the morning and went out to the Desert of Tekoa. As they set out, Jehoshaphat stood and said, "Hear, O Judah and inhabitants of Jerusalem! Have faith in Yahweh your God, and you will be upheld; have faith in his prophets, and you will succeed." ²¹After consulting with the people, he appointed men to sing to Yahweh and to praise the splendor of his holinessᵃ as they went out in front of the army, saying, "Give thanks to Yahweh, for his faithfulness is everlasting."

²²As soon as they began to sing and praise, Yahweh sent ambushes against the men of Ammon, Moab, and Mount Seir who had come against Judah, and they were defeated. ²³The men of Ammon and Moab rose up against the men from Mount Seir to annihilate and destroy them; when they had exterminated the men from Seir, they helped to destroy one another.

²⁴When Judah came to the overlook in the desert and looked toward the enemy horde, they saw only corpses lying on the ground—no one had escaped. ²⁵Jehoshaphat and his men went to collect the plunder; they found a great number of cattle,ᵃ equipment, clothing,ᵇ and valuables, which they took until they could carry no more.ᶜ

There was so much plunder that it took three days to collect it, ²⁶and on the fourth day they assembled in the Valley of Berakah, and there they blessed Yahweh; that is why the place is known to this day as the Valley of Berakah.

²⁷All the men of Judah and Jerusalemᵃ set out with Jehoshaphat at their head to return to Jerusalem in joy, for Yahweh had given them cause to rejoice over their enemies. ²⁸They entered Jerusalem and went to the temple of Yahweh with harps, lutes, and trumpets.

²⁹The fear of God fell on all the kingdoms of other lands when they heard how Yahweh had fought against the enemies of Israel. ³⁰The kingdom of Jehoshaphat was at peace, because his God had given him rest on all sides.

³¹ᵃJehoshaphat ruled over Judah. He was thirty-five when he began to reign, and he ruled in Jerusalem for twenty-five years. His mother's name was Azubah daughter of Shilhi. ³²He walked in the way of his father Asa and did not turn from it; he did what was right in the eyes of Yahweh. ³³However, he did not remove the high places, and the people still did not set their hearts on the God of their fathers. ³⁴As for the other events of the Jehoshaphat's reign, from beginning to end, they are written in the accounts of Jehu son of Hanani which are includedᵃ in the book of the kings of Israel.

³⁵ Some time later Jehoshaphat king of Judah allied himself with Ahaziah king of Israel, who provoked him to do wrong.ᵃ ³⁶He made an alliance with him to build ships that could go to Tarshish; they built the ships in Ezion-geber. ³⁷Eliezer son of Dodavahu ᵃ from Mareshah prophesied against Jehoshaphat, and said, "Since

you have allied yourself with Ahaziah, Yahweh will destroy what you have made."
So the ships were wrecked and could not set sail for Tarshish.

21:1 *Jehoshaphat rested with his fathers and was buried with his fathers in the*
City of David, and Jehoram his son ruled in his stead.

Notes

1.a. With G Μωαίων, "Meunites"; MT, "Ammonites." Cf. *Comment.*

2.a. With 1 MS, OL; MT, "Aram." Cf. *Comment.*

4.a. Cf. מיהוה לבקש and לבקש את יהוה לבקש מן לבקש implies a dir obj (Ezek 7:26; Isa 1:12; Dan 1:8) elided here in the MT, but specified in the translation as "help."

5.a. For the MT "Judah and Jerusalem," cf. 20:15, 17, 18, 20, 27; a few MSS, G, and T, "Judah in Jerusalem." G has possibly assimilated under the influence of the preceding בקהל or the following בבית. Cf. Allen, *GC* 2:93.

6.a. The rhetorical questions could be continued through the entire verse; they function in fact as affirmations and are here translated as such.

8.a. MT adds לך, "for you"; it is missing in G, Syr., and Vg. Cf. Allen, *GC* 2:56, 145.

9.a. With Gᴸ, ἄκρις = שטף, "flood." MT, either "sword of judgment" (Vg) or "sword, judgment. . . ." The Chronicler alludes to Solomon's dedicatory prayer in which warfare, plague, and famine are specifically mentioned (6:28, 36–37). Apart from the possible pl. in Ezek 23:10, this would be the only use of שפוט as an absolute noun meaning "judgment"; a simple metathesis would yield the form translated by Gᴸ.

9.b. A few mss and Gᴸ add נקרא, "is invoked."

11.a. G and Tg, "our possession." Both G and Tg may have been influenced by the first pl. suffix on the immediately preceding word or the last word in the verse.

16.a. Many have suggested that the article on the form הציץ derives from misreading a ה, so that the name of the ascent is related to the name of the locale, i.e., Hazazon Tamar (20:2). Cf. the G transliterations: Gᴮ Ἀσάε, Gᴸ Ασιωα, others Ασσης, Ασσις, etc.

21.a. Or, "to praise him in holy array." Cf. Cross, *BASOR* 117 (1950) 19–21.

25.a. The MT is possibly acceptable as it stands: the items of plunder listed could all have been found *on them,* i.e., on the corpses; pack animals may not have made the ford or steep ascent. However, for בהם G (κτήνη) apparently read בהמה, "cattle," commonly taken as part of the spoils of battle (14:14 [15]; 1 Chr 5:20–21); the conjunction on ורכוש also favors the G text. See L. Allen, "More Cuckoos in the Textual Nest," *JTS* n.s. 24 (1973) 73.

25.b. MT "corpses" appears unlikely as an item in a list of plunder. Read with a few mss. and Vg, בגדים, "clothing," a common item of plunder (2 Kgs 7:8, 15; 1 Sam 27:9; 31:8–9). The confusion in the MT likely arose from the similarity of the consonants.

25.c. G omits "until they could carry no more." This use of לאין is an idiom peculiar to the Chronicler (14:12 [13]; 1 Chr 22:4; cf. C-M, 411).

27.a. G "to Jerusalem." Cf. the similar variant above at 20:5.a.

31.a. G preserves three different concluding notices for the reign of Jehoshaphat: (1) the parallel to this passage in 2 Par 20:31–21:1; (2) the parallel to 1 Kgs 22:41–48 in 3 Bas; and (3) an insertion following 1 Kgs 16:28 in 3 Bas 16:28a–h. All three differ from one another; though the nature of the Chronicler's *Vorlage* cannot be stated with confidence, traces of his own unique style suggest his reworking of whatever material he may have had before him. See Lemke, *Synoptic Studies,* 160–70; cf. also *Comment* below.

34.a. העלה is a hoph perf of עלה; the use of this form of the verb is rare in the OT (Judg 6:28; Nah 2:8), and in this meaning occurs only here. In later Heb. the hiph of the verb was used in the sense "record, enter in a book"; cf. Lemke, *Synoptic Studies,* 166–67.

35.a. Contrast NEB, "he [Jehoshaphat] did wrong in going with him. . . ."

37.a. G Ὠδειά, Gᴸ Δουδίου may have read דודיהו.

Form/Structure/Setting

Most of the material in 2 Chr 20 is unique to Chronicles. The account of Jehoshaphat's battle with a Transjordan coalition is not found in the deuteronomic history; though both histories describe a disaster to Jehoshaphat's trading fleet (20:35–37; 1 Kgs 22:49–50), the Chronicler's version is sharply different from that in Kings.

Efforts to evaluate the historicity of the battle account have commonly taken one of four forms (cf. the summary in Petersen, 70–71). (1) 2 Chr 20 has been viewed as a historical midrash on 2 Kgs 3 (Wellhausen, Kautzsch, Benzinger). Both histories mention the involvement of Moabites in a campaign against Jehoshaphat, a battle oracle from a prophet, and the confusion in the enemy ranks so that they slaughtered one another. These similarities led to the conclusion that the Chronicler had recast the earlier narrative as a vehicle for his own theological concerns, and that the account was of little historical worth. (2) Noth (*ZDPV* 67 [1945] 45–71) was not impressed by the scanty parallels with 2 Kgs 3, but rather with the geographical detail associated with the area between En-gedi and Tekoa; he concluded that the Chronicler had used a local tradition regarding an attack by early Nabataeans from Meun, southeast of Petra, sometime late in the fourth or early in the third century. (3) Rudolph (258–59) essentially followed Noth's argument, but modified it by rejecting Noth's identification of the Meunites with a group as late as the Nabataeans and by arguing that the Chronicler had used an earlier written source that had reliably reported an Edomite coalition against Jehoshaphat. (4) Since the Chronicler's battle reports are highly stylized and have common themes (cf. 13:3–20; 14:8–14 [9–15]), Welten (140–53) concluded that one cannot draw historical conclusions from the account in 2 Chr 20.

Unless the geographical detail is arbitrarily dismissed as literary mimesis, the most defensible course among these options appears to be acceptance of the historicity of the account. However, it is equally important to recognize as well the *Tendenz* of the Chronicler in this narrative and his other battle reports; he has concentrated on the epic dimensions of the battle, reported it along lines of his retribution theology, and has emphasized the significance of the cultic personnel to the course of the battle. The Chronicler has probably deliberately substituted this account for the battle report in 2 Kgs 3, but there is no inherent reason to reject the possibility of a Transjordan coalition against Jehoshaphat—for that matter, it would be the more surprising if enmity and conflict with eastern neighbors had not occurred during his reign. In his summary notice concerning the reign of Jehoshaphat the compiler of Kings invites the reader to consult his sources regarding other military exploits of Jehoshaphat (1 Kgs 22:46 [45]); the Chronicler has provided precisely that sort of additional information and omits this reference from his own parallel reign summary (20:34). The "sermonic" character of the Chronicler's account need not undercut its basis in historical fact.

Numerous different planes of form critical and redaction critical analysis interlock and overlay in the passage. (1) Jehoshaphat's battle has the contours of a holy war narrative: battle oracles, Israel's army in the role of spectators while Yahweh fights for them, music, self-destruction and obliteration of the enemy (cf. Deut 7; 20). (2) Within the larger holy war narrative, there is a lament ritual (20:5–12), followed by a priestly/prophetic oracle of salvation (20:14–17). Jehoshaphat's speech should be compared with psalms commonly classified as laments (Ps 44, 60, 74, 79, 83, 89; cf. Joel 1–2). The items that often appear in such laments (Petersen, 72) are the recitation of past favors (20:6–7), protestation of innocence and statement of trust (20:8–9), the complaint (20:10–11), and the plea (20:12). The lament is answered by a salvation oracle (20:15–17); a number of prophetic oracles have been identified possibly as responses to national laments (see G. Ogden, "Prophetic Oracles against Foreign Nations and Psalms of Communal Lament," *JSOT* 24 [1982] 89–97; and "Joel 4 and Prophetic Responses to National Laments," *JSOT* 26 [1983] 97–106). The main components of such oracles are all found in 20:15: the addressees are identified, instructed to "fear not," and provided assurances. (3) The battle narrative in its earliest form may have originated as an etiological account (20:26), subsequently elaborated with holy war themes, and finally incorporated by the Chronicler for his own distinctive portrait of Jehoshaphat and at least partially concerned with (4) the character of prophecy in the post-exilic period. The Chronicler here and in other passages (see *Comment* at 20:14) illustrates prophetic function for hierocratic personnel. Petersen (55–96) finds this claim to prophetic function on the part of Levites in tension with other post-exilic prophetic materials. Rather than finding the prophetic claims of the Levitical musicians a carry-over from pre-exilic cultic prophecy, Petersen (62) follows the redaction critical analysis of Gese (*Vom Sinai zum Zion*, 147–58) and relates such prophetic appellations to the latest stages of the singer traditions as an innovation on the part of the Chronicler and his compatriots.

The chapter is structured by a common repertoire of paragraphing devices, largely deictic elements (indicating changes in time or location): (1) ויהי-clauses with a temporal phrase (20:1, 25b, 29); (2) change in explicit subject (20:3, 18, 27); (3) use of explicit subject without an intervening change of subject (20:5); (4) circumstantial clauses (20:13, 14); (5) other devices reporting change in time or location (20:20, 22, 35).

Comment

1–2 Jehoshaphat fights a coalition of three peoples—known later in the chapter as the Ammonites, Moabites, and the people from Mount Seir (20:22–23). In these first two verses, however, textual difficulties cloud the exact composition of the opposing forces.

The reading of the MT in v 1 ("Moabites, Ammonites, along with some of the Ammonites") appears redundant and improbable due to its double mention of the Ammonites. Most authorities have followed G, "Meunites." The name and location of the Meunites probably survive in the Arab town Maʿan, twelve miles southeast of Petra on a pilgrim route connecting Damascus and Mecca. The Chronicler associates the Meunites with the Ammonites once again as among those bringing tribute to Hezekiah (26:7; cf. 1 Chr 4:41). This would place the Meunites in the region traditionally associated with Mount Seir, a mountain range extending the entire length of Edom. There has been some debate about this identification, however. Though numerous passages firmly associate Mount Seir and Edom as virtual synonyms (Ezek 25:8; 35:15; Num 24:18; Judg 5:4; Gen 36:8, 9), other passages suggest a location for Seir west of the Arabah and south of Beersheba and the biblical

Negev (Deut 1:44; 2:1; Josh 11:17; 12:7; see J. Bartlett, "The Land of Seir and the Brotherhood of Edom," *JTS* n.s. 20 [1969] 1–20); e.g., 1 Chr 4:41–43 reports attacks of the tribe Simeon against Meunites and inhabitants of Seir and probably speaks of campaigns and settlements to the south rather than east of the Arabah.

The solution regarding the location of Seir and the Meunites is intertwined with the textual difficulty in v 2. The messenger reports to the king that a vast army is attacking from "Aram." Aram is not otherwise mentioned as a member of the three-party coalition through the remainder of the chapter. It is at least possible that the coalition undertook its attack at the prompting of its northern neighbors the Arameans, but this explanation is not probable. The messenger appears to be reporting the direction from which the attack is coming, i.e., Jehoshaphat is being attacked from the south by way of En-gedi. One medieval Hebrew MS and the OL support reading "Edom" in place of the MT "Aram," and adopting this reading would help clarify the location of Seir and the Meunites in the Chronicler's mind, though it would still remain possible to suggest a site for Seir south of the Negev. One common scenario would be that the forces of Ammon and Moab journeyed south around the southern end of the Dead Sea and picked up the contingent of Meunites from Seir—wherever Seir is located, the force is described as coming from Edom. Alternatively, since the opposing army is said to have come "from over the sea," some have suggested a route south from En-gedi to the shallow ford across the sea to the Lisan and then ascending into Moab; on this routing Seir would most naturally be identified with Edom (see the discussion in Dorsey, 276–77). However, the textual witnesses in favor of the reading Edom are not at all compelling—the one Hebrew MS attesting to this variant most likely represents a development within the Massoretic tradition and is an example of the common confusion of the consonants ד and ר; it should not be thought of as direct attestation to a correctly copied earlier form of the text. The OL variants are more difficult, but are also not likely to be direct evidence. This is to say, then, that the decision to read Edom is not properly a text critical decision in itself, but is a conjectural one favored by geopolitical factors.

The attacking armies are described as הָמוֹן רַב, "a vast horde," a favorite way in which the Chronicler designates a numerically superior enemy in other battle narratives showing holy war themes (13:8; 14:10 [11]).

3–4 "Seeking God" is one of the main themes of the Chronicler's theology; see the essay introducing 2 Chr 11–36, "Reward and Punishment in Chronicles: The Theology of Immediate Retribution." Fasts were commonly proclaimed in times of war or other calamity (Judg 20:26; 1 Sam 7:6; 31:13; 2 Sam 12:16–22; Zech 7).

5–12 The "new court" before which Jehoshaphat stood is difficult to identify with certainty. It is potentially the large court of the temple (4:9). However, it is also possible that the Chronicler uses the term *new* from the vantage of the rebuilt temple of his own time; it is not clear that the earlier temple of Solomon distinguished between an inner court (court of the priests) and an outer court (court of the people).

Jehoshaphat's speech takes the form of a national lament; see above under

Form/Structure/Setting and the more detailed study in Petersen, 72–73; and Throntveit, *Significance*, 87–93. It has earlier been argued that Solomon's prayer at the dedication of the temple and the divine response to it constituted a charter for the subsequent history of Israel in the Chronicler's presentation (see *Explanation* in chap. 6). Here the Chronicler portrays Jehoshaphat as making a direct appeal to Solomon's prayer (20:9; cf. 6:28, 34), a prayer which God had promised to hear and answer (7:12–14).

Jehoshaphat's appeal is also based on other events of past history. Deut 2 provides a catalogue of peoples that Israel had been prevented from annihilating or attacking; now it is these same peoples who allied themselves against Israel to drive them from the land that was God's own possession (20:10–11; 6:27; cf. Lev 25:23–24; Jer 2:7; Ezek 36:5; 38:16). Jephthah's messengers recite this same history in greater detail (Judg 11:14–27).

Powerlessness before a numerically greater foe (20:12) is a characteristic theme in holy war narratives and the epic battle accounts in Chronicles (13:3; 14:9–11).

Abraham is also described as God's friend in Isa 41:8. The Chronicler also conjoins Abraham and the building of the temple (20:7–8) in 3:1, where he locates the temple at the site of Abraham's offering of Isaac.

13–14 The Chronicler has probably substituted this battle narrative for the account of war with Moab found in his *Vorlage* (2 Kgs 3); not only has he substituted one battle for another, but he has also substituted cultic personnel in the role occupied by a popular prophetic figure (Elisha) in the earlier narrative (Petersen, 77). The Chronicler shows a similar interest in the prophetic function of cultic personnel in several other passages as well (1 Chr 25:1–8; 2 Chr 34:30 // 2 Kgs 23:2; 2 Chr 29:25; 35:15). These passages have ordinarily been understood as evidence for the existence of cultic prophecy in the first temple period. Petersen rejects that explanation and argues instead that the Chronicler's interest in cultic prophecy represents the viewpoint on prophecy held by hierocratic elements during the post-exilic period and in effect presents rival claims to traditional prophetic roles on the part of Levitical groups. The data to which Petersen appeals could be interpreted differently; it need not be construed to deny precedent for a pre-exilic prophetic role for cultic personnel, nor does it necessarily betray rival claims from sociological groups (theocratic/hierocratic vs. eschatological/apocalyptic) in the restoration period. It is, however, important to realize that the Chronicler is legitimating practices and claims regarding the character of prophecy in his own day; as the traditionally known prophetic order is disappearing from Israel, those functions pass increasingly to temple personnel.

The Chronicler provides a linear genealogy for Jahaziel to a depth of at least five generations; this would bring his pedigree back to the time of David's organization of the temple personnel. Jahaziel is traced to the line of Asaph and would therefore be among the Levitical musicians (1 Chr 25:1).

15–17 Jahaziel's speech is commonly identified as a salvation oracle following the national lament given by Jehoshaphat; see above under *Form/Structure/Setting*. However, his speech also resembles quite closely the prescribed speech from a priest before battle (Deut 20:2–4). The salvation oracle and holy war forms appear melded in this speech. Holy war themes predominate, e.g., the numerical superiority of the foe, the passivity of Israel when the divine warrior fights in its behalf, the injunctions not to fear. Cf. the exhortations in 1 Sam 17:47; Exod 14:13–14; Ps 91:7–8.

The previous enumeration of Jehoshaphat's army had assigned 1.16 million troops to his forces (17:12–19). Whether the army numbered thirty or one million, it was still necessary to rely on God (Elmslie, 253).

It is not possible to identify the Desert of Jeruel with certainty. At least two candidates are possible for the Ascent of Ziz. East of Tekoa the route divides (1) to one running down the Wadi Hasasa to the Dead Sea at a point about five miles north of En-gedi; this route may preserve the name of the Ascent of Ziz and the region of Hazazon, if a proposed textual emendation is adopted (see note 16.a. above). (2) The more probable route descends from Tekoa directly to En-gedi; this road appears to have two branches, each marked by a chain of Iron Age sites (Dorsey, 334–35; cf. M. Har-El, "Israelite and Roman Roads in the Judean Desert," *IEJ* 17 [1967] 18–26; Z. Ilan, *BMik* 18/53 [1972/73] 205–11).

18–21 The injunction to "have faith in his prophets" is a remarkable indication of the conception of prophetic authority within Israel. In this context, however, it must not be overlooked that the prophets the author is speaking of are the Levitical musicians—one had just delivered a salvation oracle—and the musical praise for the battle march (20:21) and even the night before (20:19) was itself prophesying (1 Chr 25:1–8). There can be little doubt that the office of the Levitical musicians was of great importance to the Chronicler; a prophetic function among the temple singers of his own day is provided legitimation in the past. His singling out the Kohathites and a subclan within that larger group, the Korahites (1 Chr 6:22, 37–38) may indicate some ascendancy on the part of this family (Gese, Petersen).

The modern historian may be tempted "to poke fun at Jehoshaphat in Chronicles for sending out the temple choir to meet an invading army; it is still funnier when the choir puts the foe to flight and causes great slaughter with a few well-directed psalms" (W. Stinespring, *JBL* 80 [1961] 209). Though the role of the musicians may be enlarged or enhanced in the eyes of a modern historian, one must not forget the role of music in warfare ancient and modern; armies through the millennia have gone into battle to musical cadence. Particularly within Israel's tradition of holy war music has been assigned an important function (13:11–12; Josh 6:4–20; Judg 7:18–20; Job 39:24–25); music accompanies the appearance of the divine warrior to execute judgment (Ps 47; 96; 98). Yahweh marches at the head of the armies of heaven and Israel (Deut 33:2–5, 26–29; Josh 5:13–15; Judg 5; Ps 68:8–13; 2 Kgs 6:15–19; 7:6; Isa 13:1–13; Joel 3:9–12 [4:9–12]; Hab 3); his appearance on the Day of Yahweh is marked by a trumpet blast (Exod 19:16, 19; Isa 18:3; 27:13; Amos 2:2; Zeph 1:14–16; Zech 9:14; Matt 24:31; 1 Cor 15:52; Rev 8–9; 10:7; 11:15).

Jehoshaphat delivers the pre-battle speech; in this regard he fulfills a function assigned to a priest in Deut 20:2–4, though the speech prescribed there more closely resembles that given by Jahaziel (20:15–17). The speech may exhibit some dependence on Isa 7:9b (von Rad, *Problem of the Hexateuch*, 274; Petersen, 74).

22–26 The battle cry ordinarily heard is replaced by a chorale (Williamson, 300; Petersen, 75). Yahweh set ambushes, literally "those who lie in wait," against the foe. In the history of exegesis these have been identified with groups of Judean soldiers or even contingents from one or the other of the coalition armies. Most probably the Chronicler intends the appearance of the heavenly army to confound and confuse (2 Sam 5:24; 2 Kgs 7:5–7; Isa 13:4; Ezek 1:24; 2 Kgs 19:35). Other instances in Israel's traditions speak to the confusion in battle that brings armies to self-destruction (Judg 7:22; 1 Sam 14:20; 2 Kgs 3:23); the prophets also portray such destruction for the enemies of Israel (Ezek 38:21; Hag 2:22; Zech 14:13; Curtis, 410).

The account of the battle near Tekoa may have first been preserved in an etiological narrative to explain the name of the Valley of Berakah; see above *Form/Structure/Setting.*

27–28 The army returns to the temple confirming the answer to prayer offered there; see *Comment* at 20:5–12. Several psalms might be identified as divine warrior litanies sung on the return to the temple from victorious holy war; Ps 24, 68, 118, 136 might be representative of the songs sung in the festal procession after victory.

29–30 The rhetorical question of Jehoshaphat's prayer had been answered (20:6)—Yahweh does rule over the kingdoms of the nations. Two tokens of divine blessing in the Chronicler's theology are prominent in these verses. (1) The righteous king enjoys victory over the nations, is held in awe by them, and receives their tribute (1 Chr 14:17; 18:2, 6; 2 Chr 9:22–23; 17:10; 32:23). (2) Rest from enemies and times of peace are rewards for righteousness (14:4, 6 [5, 7]; 15:15; 1 Chr 22:9); for the Chronicler's distinctive use of the rest concept, see Braun, *JBL* 95 (1976) 582–86.

31–34 Chronicles reports a reign of twenty-five years for Jehoshaphat while 2 Kings reports twenty-two (eighteen in 2 Kgs 3:1 and four more in 8:16). These figures are reconciled by suggesting a coregency with his father Asa for three years, probably due to the severity of his father's illness as well as in order to arrange for a secure succession (16:10–14); Kings speaks only of his years of sole reign after his father's death.

The Chronicler has sought to model his account of Jehoshaphat on that of his father Asa; see the introductory essay, "The Chronicler's Jehoshaphat." Two aspects of that modeling are reiterated here, both dependent on 1 Kgs 22:43–44. (1) Jehoshaphat is specifically likened to his father Asa (20:32; cf. 17:3). (2) Both kings are said both to have removed the high places (14:2–5; 17:6) and not to have done so (15:17; 20:33). Similar approaches can be taken to this question as done with reference to Asa; see *Comment* at 14:2–5.

The Chronicler has omitted from his own concluding summary the references in his *Vorlage* to the removal of the shrine prostitutes (1 Kgs 22:47–48 [46–47]); the author omits all four references in Kings to this practice (see *Comment* at 14:2–5; cf. P. Dion, *CBQ* 43 [1981] 41–48). He has also omitted reference to sources regarding Jehoshaphat's other wars (1 Kgs 22:46 [45]), possibly because (1) he had already reported such in his own account of the battle of Tekoa (see above *Form/Structure/Setting*), or (2) because of his emphasis on the peace enjoyed by Jehoshaphat (20:30), or (3) because the reference was not in his *Vorlage,* as seen in its absence from G of 1 Kgs

22:46. Similarly, rather than report that the people continued to offer sacrifices and incense on the high places (1 Kgs 22:44), the Chronicler has substituted terms more characteristic of his own vocabulary, that the people "did not set their hearts on the God of their fathers" (20:33).

The Chronicler cites as his source a prophetic work, but also indicates that this work was contained in a larger collection, "the book of the kings of Israel." Cf. 32:32. The nature of this larger source can only be a matter of speculation: it could be a history of both kingdoms or of the Southern or Northern Kingdom alone; it is not likely to be a reference to the canonical books of Kings since Jehu plays so little role there. Jehu appears in 1 Kgs 16:1, 7, 12 to pronounce judgment on Baasha and Elah in the Northern Kingdom; he appears in Chronicles otherwise only in 19:2 to repudiate Jehoshaphat's involvement with Ahab. The one prophet ministers in both kingdoms. His father Hanani is probably the prophet imprisoned by Asa (16:7). If this latter identification is correct, in biblical references to them the career of the son spans that of the father.

35–37   The Chronicler's account of Jehoshaphat's maritime venture contrasts to that of 1 Kgs 22:49–50 [48–49]. In Kings, Jehoshaphat's ships never set sail, but are destroyed in port; Jehoshaphat turns down an offer from Ahaziah son of Ahab to undertake a joint venture. The Chronicler begins with an alliance between Jehoshaphat and Ahaziah, and the destruction of the ships is the result of divine displeasure with that alliance. Though G gives two different accounts of this maritime venture in 3 Bas 22:48–49 [49–50] and 3 Bas 16:28 (see above *Form/Structure/Setting*), and though there may be some question regarding the Chronicler's *Vorlage*, the textual differences are not at all sufficient to account for the differences found in Chronicles. Harmonizations are easy to provide: Jehoshaphat's first effort was also an alliance with Ahaziah, even though not mentioned by Kings; the offer from Ahaziah of a second effort to build a fleet was rejected by Jehoshaphat after the prophet's intervention reported in Chronicles. The Chronicler's own hand in the narrative is clearly seen in his opposition to any foreign alliances; for the Chronicler, foreign alliances are inherently a breach of faith in Yahweh and always result in judgment (16:2–9; 19:1–3; 22:3–9; 25:7–13; 28:16–21; 32:31). The Chronicler had already developed this theme in connection with Jehoshaphat's involvement with the dynasty of Ahab (see *Form/Structure/Setting* in the section on 18:1–19:3); contrast his handling of Solomon's maritime venture with Hiram (8:17–18; 9:21).

"Tarshish" ships are trading vessels; see *Comment* at 9:21.

Explanation

Chap. 20 is replete with themes dear to the Chronicler: his basic concern with retribution theology, the centrality of Solomon's dedicatory prayer and God's promise in 7:14 to hear the prayer of his people who seek him, the need to depend on God rather than foreign alliances. See the introductory essay to 2 Chr 10–36, "Reward and Punishment in Chronicles: The Theology of Immediate Retribution." Beyond these characteristic themes, all of which had practical relevance for the restoration community, this portion of the Chronicler's history touched his audience on a number of other planes.

Enemies from the past may have represented a present threat. The Chronicler may be reporting events from the past since the emergence of the Nabateans prompted a renewed interest. Peoples who had been spared when Israel came out of Egypt and who had attacked Israel during her wanderings had later been plundered by David (1 Chr 18) and their wealth used in the building of the temple. Under Jehoshaphat they had been defeated and their armies plundered once again. They proved to be resilient foes through the history of the kingdoms, and even into the post-exilic period. Rehearsing that history may have provided the Chronicler's audience a perspective on present foes or threats.

In the absence of an Israelite monarchy the temple would occupy an increasingly important role in the restoration and intertestamental periods. With the diminution of the prophetic order claims to prophetic function and succession arise among cultic personnel; the Chronicler legitimates a prophetic role for temple musicians in his own day by providing a precedent from the past.

The persistence of holy war themes in a work addressed to the small restoration community is striking. They were a politically subservient nation existing by the grace of their Persian overlords. The Chronicler reiterated through his appeal to holy war motifs that numbers and power do not count when Yahweh fights for Israel. These holy war motifs in Chronicles make little sense if the community was content with the status quo, ready to live as a hierocracy under foreign rule. To the contrary, the Chronicler's inclusion of holy war narratives bespeaks the presence of an eschatological hope, a longing for the Day of Yahweh, when the divine warrior would conquer in behalf of his people as he had done so often so long ago. The Chronicler, as an advocate of the temple and its personnel, could nevertheless have an eschatological program; hierocracy in the status quo is not necessarily opposed to eschatology and apocalypticism, but can exist in the same individuals without being assigned to separate sociological support groups. Ultimately the divine warrior does definitively fight for his people and frees them from alien domination (Rev 19:11–21; cf. T. Longman III, "The Divine Warrior: The New Testament Use of an Old Testament Motif," *WTJ* 44 [1982] 290–307).

The Reign of Jehoram, 853–841 B.C.
(21:2–20)

Bibliography

Hanson, J. D. "The Song of Heshbon and David's Nir." *HTR* 61 (1968) 297–320. **Katzenstein, H.** "Who Were the Parents of Athaliah?" *IEJ* 5 (1955) 194–97. **Mosis, R.** *Untersuchungen.* 178–79. **Shenkel, J.** *Chronology and Recensional Development in the Greek Text of Kings.* HSM 1. Cambridge, MA: Harvard UP, 1968. 68–82, 101–2. **Strange, J.** "Joram, King of Israel and Judah." *VT* 25 (1975) 191–201. **Willi, T.** *Die Chronik als Auslegung.* 63–64. **Williamson, H.** "Eschatology in Chronicles." *TynBul* 28 (1977) 115–54.

Translation

[2] *Jehoram had brothers,*[a] *other sons of Jehoshaphat—Azariah, Jehiel, Zechariah, Azaryahu,*[b] *Michael, and Shephatiah—all these were sons of Jehoshaphat, king of Israel.*[c] [3] *Their father gave them many gifts—silver and gold and other costly items, as well as fortified cities in Judah; but he gave the kingdom to Jehoram since he was the firstborn.*

[4] *When Jehoram was established over the kingdom of his father, he consolidated his position and put all his brothers to the sword, along with some of the leaders of Israel.* [5] *Jehoram was thirty-two years old when he became king, and he ruled in Jerusalem for eight years.* [6] *He walked in the ways of the kings of Israel as the house of Ahab had done, for his wife was a daughter of Ahab, and he did evil in the eyes of Yahweh.* [7] *But Yahweh was not willing to destroy the house of David*[a] *because of the covenant he had made*[b] *with David and because he had promised to maintain a lamp for David and his descendants forever.*

[8] *During his reign Edom revolted against Judah and installed its own king.* [9] *So Jehoram crossed over with his officers and all his chariotry. The Edomites surrounded him and his chariot officers,*[a] *but he arose by night and broke through.*[b] [10] *Edom has been independent of Judah to this day.*[a]

Libnah also revolted from Jehoram's rule at that time, because he had forsaken Yahweh the God of his fathers. [11] *He even made high places in the hills*[a] *of Judah; he seduced the inhabitants of Jerusalem and led Judah astray.*

[12] *A letter came to him from Elijah the prophet; it said:*

"*Thus says Yahweh the God of your father David: since you have not walked in the ways of your father Jehoshaphat or the ways of Asa King of Judah,* [13] *but in the ways of the kings of Israel, and you have seduced Judah and the inhabitants of Jerusalem just as the house of Ahab did, and you have even killed your own brothers from your father's house,*[a] *men who were better than you,* [14] *therefore Yahweh will strike your people, your children, your wives and all your possessions with a heavy blow.* [15] *You yourself will be gravely*[a] *ill with a chronic disease of the bowels, until your bowels come out because of the disease.*"

[16] *Yahweh aroused against Jehoram the spirit*[a] *of the Philistines and the Arabs who lived near the Cushites.* [17] *They went up against Judah, broke down her defenses,*

and carried off all the property found in the royal palace, as well as the king's children and wives.[a] *There was not a son left to him except Jehoahaz,*[b] *the youngest of his sons.*

[18] *After all this Yahweh afflicted him with an incurable disease of the bowels.* [19] *It continued for some time, until two days before his demise, his bowels prolapsed because of his illness; he died in horrible pain. His people did not make a fire in his honor as they had done for his fathers.* [20] *He was thirty-two years old when he began to reign, and he ruled for eight years in Jerusalem. He passed away to no one's sorrow; they buried him in the city of David, though not in the tombs of the kings.*

Notes

2.a. G specifies six brothers.

2.b. Since two brothers are named Azariah, commentators commonly suggest a textual corruption and may emend one or the other to a similar name, e.g., Uzziah. There is no inherent reason that these two sons, perhaps born to different wives, must have had different names; there is a minor differentiation in the spelling (Azaryah vs. Azaryahu). The fact that both names persist throughout the textual witnesses suggests that they were originally the same.

2.c. The *sebir*, many MSS, G, Syr, Vg, and Arab read Judah. Cf. v 4; see *Comment*.

7.a. 2 Kgs 8:19, "Judah."

7.b. 2 Kgs 8:19, "for the sake of David his servant." See *Comment*.

9.a. The Chronicler has faithfully copied 2 Kgs 8:21—the translation difficulty felt with the passage is already evident there. Following the ordinary sequence in the translation, the text appears to say that Jehoram "arose by night and struck the Edomites who had surrounded him and his chariot officers." But this translation would imply a victory on Jehoram's part, a notion foreign to the context which shows rather judgment on Jehoram and a successful revolt by Edom. The verb נכה in battle reports ordinarily means to "strike, hit, attack, conquer"; however, the context appears to require in this passage that it refer to Jehoram's escape from threat, i.e., that he "broke through."

9.b. 2 Kgs 8:21 adds "and the people fled to their tents."

10.a. "To this day" is taken from the Chronicler's source at 2 Kgs 8:22; see *Comment* at 5:9.

11.a. The *sebir*, many Heb. MSS, G, and Vg, ערי, "cities." Cf. 20:4; 23:2.

13.a. G υἱοὺς τοῦ πατρός σου = בני אביך, "sons of your father."

15.a. 2 Heb. MSS have רעים, "evil, wicked." G (πονηρᾷ) and Vg (pessimo) could arguably be translations of either Heb. term, or the translations may have assimilated to v 19 (Rudolph).

16.a. G does not translate "spirit."

17.a. G τὰς θυγατέρας αὐτοῦ, "and his daughters." Cf. 21:14. Allen (*GC* 1:131) does not see this as suggesting an alternative text ובנתיו, but rather as a free rendering of the word "women": the mention of sons suggested "daughters."

17.b. An alternative form of his usual name Ahaziah; cf. 22:1. There is some variation in G, Tg, and Syr.

Form/Structure/Setting

The Chronicler had greatly expanded his account of the reigns of Asa and Jehoshaphat; a similar expansion characterizes his handling of Jehoram: nine verses in the parallel account (2 Kgs 8:16–24) compared to twenty verses in Chronicles. The Chronicler omits only small snippets of the Kings account, but adds information concerning Jehoram's fratricide (21:1–4), his erection of high places (21:11), the letter from Elijah (21:12–15), loss of territory and family to the Philistines and Arabs (21:16–17), and the nature of his death (21:18–19).

The Chronicler's additions are characteristic of his editing narratives to demonstrate the validity of retribution theology; see the introductory essay to 2 Chr 10–36, "Reward and Punishment in Chronicles: The Theology of Immediate Retribution." Beyond this larger *Tendenz* that characterizes his handling of the various reigns, the Chronicler more specifically has presented the reign of Jehoram as the undoing of the accomplishments of Asa and Jehoshaphat. He is specifically contrasted to those two kings (21:12). Whereas Asa and Jehoshaphat were successful in campaigns to the east and south (chap. 20; 14:9–15), Jehoram loses control of these areas (21:8–10). Philistines and Arabs paid tribute to Jehoshaphat (17:11), but they rebel against Jehoram (21:16). Asa and Jehoshaphat had suppressed the worship at the high places (14:2–5; 17:6), but Jehoram fostered it (21:11).

One can only speculate regarding the sources available to the Chronicler for his additional material. Some of the material may have derived from official chronicles, e.g., the list of Jehoshaphat's sons (21:2), the military incidents (beyond those already in his *Vorlage*; 21:16–17), notices about his burial (21:20). The historicity of the letter from Elijah has long been disputed; see *Comment* below. A prophetic anthology similar to those cited in his sources would be a possible source (cf. 1 Chr 29:29; 2 Chr 9:29; 12:15; 13:22; 20:34; 26:22; 32:32; 33:19). This letter, along with other exemplars in the OT, lacks the characteristic epistolary features found in extrabiblical materials, e.g., identification of addressee, initial greetings, concluding formulae; letters found in the Hebrew portions of the OT include only the body of the letter or summaries of the message (D. Pardee, "Ancient Hebrew Epistolography," *JBL* 97 [1978] 322).

The author may have intended to group his narrative in a palistrophe as follows:

A Chronology (5)
  B Wrongdoing (royal sons) (4, 6–7)
    C Rebellion of Edom and Libnah (8–11)
      D Letter from Elijah (royal sons) (12–15)
    C' Rebellion of Philistines and Arabs (16–17)
  B' Punishment for wrongdoing (royal sons) (17–19)
A' Chronology (20)

Paragraph breaks in the chapter are indicated by the use of an explicit subject (21:4, 12, 16) or a change of subject with a temporal marker (21:8, 10, 18).

Comment

2–3   For the Chronicler numerous progeny was one index of divine favor (11:18–22; 13:21; 1 Chr 25:5; cf. *Comment* at 11:18–22). The Chronicler could have characteristically used such information to show God's blessing on Jehoshaphat, but instead, in this case, Jehoram's murder of his brothers serves to accent the depth of his wickedness. By dispersing his sons through the kingdom Jehoshaphat was following the wise example of Rehoboam (11:23) both to extend royal power and presence in the outlying districts and to avert a dynastic crisis by securing the succession of the chosen son.

The Chronicler's description of Jehoshaphat as the king of "Israel" (v 2) is corrected in many of the ancient versions and some manuscripts to read "king of Judah"; cf. the similar use with reference to the royal officials in v 4. The reading "Israel" is obviously favored as the more difficult reading—a scribal correction to alleviate the difficulty would readily explain the change to "Judah," particularly in light of the use of the phrase "kings of Israel" in v 13. Though the Chronicler was not unqualifiedly hostile to the Northern Kingdom, from the vantage of the post-exilic period he appears to regard Judah as the legal and moral successor of the united Israel, and he uses the term "Israel" with reference to the Southern Kingdom in numerous instances (Williamson, *IBC*, 102). Rudolph (265) regards the use in v 2 as reflecting the language of the original royal chronicle which the Chronicler may have had as a source.

4 "Consolidated his position." On the Chronicler's use of the hithpael of חזק, see *Comment* at 1:1–3. Solomon similarly eliminated potential rivals at the time of his accession, including at least one of David's sons (1 Kgs 2). There is both irony and retributive justice in that Jehoram sets in motion events that would ultimately lead to the near obliteration of his own line (22:10; 2 Kgs 11:1). Jehu (2 Kgs 10:11) and Abimelech (Judg 9:56) also sought to eliminate all potential rivals.

Though "princes of Israel" could be understood as indicating the presence of princes from the Northern Kingdom in Judah in the retinue of Athaliah (N. Andreasen, "The Role of the Queen Mother in Israelite Society," *CBQ* 45 [1983] 190), the use of the phrase "king of Israel" with reference to Judah (v 2) permits a similar understanding here.

5–6 The Chronicler copies his *Vorlage* quite closely at 2 Kgs 8:17–19. The chronological information of v 5 is repeated in v 20, forming somewhat of an inclusio. The reign of Joram of Israel is said to have begun in the eighteenth year of Jehoshaphat (2 Kgs 3:1) and the second year of Jehoram of Judah (2 Kgs 1:17); Jehoram of Judah is also reported to have begun his reign in the fifth year of Joram of Israel (2 Kgs 8:16). This data can be reconciled by positing a coregency on the part of Jehoram and Jehoshaphat (see Thiele, *Mysterious Numbers* [1983] 57–58, 99–101). Jehoram would have begun his coregency with Jehoshaphat in 853 B.C. That was the year of the battle of Qarqar, and Jehoshaphat may have accompanied the forces of Ahab in an alliance against Shalmaneser III; Jehoshaphat's absence could have stimulated the appointment of Jehoram as coregent and assignment of the brothers to outlying districts. The coregency would have continued until 849/ 848 when Jehoram would begin his sole reign of eight years. The second year of Jehoram in 2 Kgs 1:17 would refer to the second year of his coregency, whereas his accession in the fifth year of Joram (2 Kgs 8:16) would be the first year of his sole reign.

The Chronicler presumes that his readers are familiar with the account and nature of Ahab's rule; cf. 18:1 and 22:2 [3]. The lineage of Athaliah is uncertain. She is described as the "daughter" both of Ahab (21:6) and of Omri (22:2 // 2 Kgs 8:26). The Peshitta harmonizes 21:6 with 22:2 by reading "sister of Ahab"; cf. G^L of 22:2 and 2 Kgs 8:26. בת can mean "female descendant," so it is possible that she was the granddaughter of Omri. Her son Ahaziah was twenty-two when he began to reign (22:2) in 841 B.C. If he had been born in 863, his mother was likely at least fifteen years old at the time of his birth, i.e., she was born before 878, at least several years before the death of Omri, and so she could be the child of Omri. See the discussion in Katzenstein, *IEJ* 5 (1955) 194–97.

7 Though the Chronicler has followed his *Vorlage* quite closely in 21:5–10a // 2 Kgs 8:17–22, in this verse he has modified the language in ways reflective of his *Tendenz*. Where Kings says Yahweh "was not willing to destroy Judah for the sake of David his servant," the Chronicler has written that Yahweh "was not willing to destroy the house of David because of the covenant he made with David." Perhaps because of his entirely negative assessment of Jehoram as a Davidic successor, the Chronicler appears to be placing greater emphasis on the unconditionality of the promises to David and his successors. The analogies with his own historical moment are instructive: though Judah had been restored in the post-exilic period, under Persian rule there would appear no prospect of the restoration of the Davidic dynasty; it is precisely when things look at a low ebb that hope is directed to future generations (cf. Williamson, 305). David's "lamp" is best explained by 1 Kgs 11:36; see the discussion in Hanson, *HTR* 61 (1968) 297–320.

8–11 In the Chronicler's theology of immediate retribution, political power is an index of piety; disobedient kings raise no great armies and are defeated in battle. The gains consolidated for Judah during the reigns of Jehoshaphat and Asa unravel under Jehoram as a consequence of his disobedience; see above, *Form/Structure/Setting*.

Edom's subservience to Judah is seen in its participation in a coalition with Joram of Israel and Jehoshaphat of Judah (2 Kgs 3); Edom had been ruled by a royal deputy (1 Kgs 22:47) at the time of Jehoshaphat, though that deputy apparently could also be called a king (2 Kgs 3:9). David had subdued Edom (2 Sam 8:13–14; 1 Kgs 11:15–17); during the reign of Solomon the territory of Edom afforded Israel access to the rich trade from Arabia and possibly access to other natural resources. Rehoboam is unlikely to have retained control after the dynastic crisis that resulted in the schism; rebellion was under way before Solomon's death (1 Kgs 11:14–22), and the list of cities fortified by Rehoboam represents concession of all but the immediate districts of Judah (2 Chr 11:5–10). One must infer then that Judean hegemony over Edom was reestablished probably during the reign of Asa or Jehoshaphat, under whom Edom is once again in a subservient role. Though Amaziah (2 Kgs 14:7) and Uzziah (2 Kgs 14:22) would achieve partial conquests of Edomite territory, Edom never fell completely under Judean sway again. Failure of the campaign against Moab (2 Kgs 3) and the Assyrian pressures in the west may have encouraged Edom's revolt at the time of Jehoram.

If the identification of Libnah with Tell es-Safi is correct, Jehoram not only had trouble to the east in Edom, but also to the west in the Philistine plain. Tell es-Safi ("Lobana") is at the western end of the Valley of Elah, i.e., on the border between Philistia and Judah. If Libnah's revolt was roughly simultaneous with the rebellion in Edom, Jehoram would have been in the tenuous position of fighting on two fronts. The city was regained by the time of Hezekiah (2 Kgs 19:8).

The other attacks mentioned by the Chronicler (21:16) from the Philistines and Arabs appear to be in the same locales as those of Edom and Libnah, i.e., to the west and southeast. Jehoram's inability to stave off the initial rebellions would naturally foment other rebellions or attacks; the Chronicler has mentioned two other regions of hostilities perhaps for symmetry with the prior two in his chiastic presentation of Jehoram's reign (see above, *Form/Structure/Setting*).

The Chronicler has followed the text of Kings quite closely until v 10b; the remainder, through v 20a, is not paralleled in Kings. The Chronicler characteristically provides a theological evaluation of a political turn of events: the rebellion of Libnah was due to Jehoram's forsaking Yahweh. *Forsake* (עזב) is one of the terms frequently used by the Chronicler to express his evaluation; see the introductory essay to 2 Chr 10–36, "Reward and Punishment in Chronicles: The Theology of Immediate Retribution."

Refurbishing the high places reversed the policy of Asa and Jehoshaphat; see above, *Form/Structure/Setting*.

12–15 In the nonsynoptic portions of the Chronicler's history the author frequently reports prophetic speeches that pronounce weal or woe on the acts of the individual kings; here, however, it is not a speech, but a letter. Jehoram was a son-in-law of Ahab, and it is Ahab's nemesis Elijah who announces judgment on Jehoram in Judah for his following the ways of the Omrides and for the fratricide that began his reign.

The historicity of the letter has been contested. The main issue is chronological: a straightforward reading of 2 Kgs 2–3 suggests that Elijah had already been taken to heaven and that he was succeeded by Elisha during the reign of Jehoshaphat. He would not have been living during the reign of Jehoram to write a letter; it is not probable that the Chronicler intends us to think the letter was written "prophetically" before Elijah's death or that it was in some way transmitted from heaven. Other arguments against the historicity of the letter are arguments from silence and less compelling, but nevertheless have some weight: (1) the deuteronomic historian held such a high view of Elijah that had he known of such a letter, he would have mentioned it, had there been so much as a hint of its existence; (2) no literary activity on the part of Elijah or Elisha is elsewhere reported in Kings; (3) their ministries are set in the Northern Kingdom. In light of this evidence most scholars have concluded that the letter is the Chronicler's own composition, reflective of his theological concerns. C-M (415) considered it a "pure product of the imagination"; Rudolph (267) called it "legendary," and Myers (122), "apocryphal."

This approach to the data is not without problems of its own, however. 2 Kgs 1:17 reports the accession of Joram of Israel in the second year of Jehoram of Judah. Joram had succeeded Ahaziah; Ahaziah's death had been prophesied at the time by Elijah (2 Kgs 1:16). This information means that Elijah was alive during the first few years of Jehoram's reign, at least during the years of a possible coregency (see above on v 5); it suggests that he may well have lived into the reign of Jehoram long enough to have knowledge of Jehoram's murder of his brothers.

Since 2 Kgs 2–3 appears to portray Elisha's independent actions after the death of his mentor, Shenkel (*Chronology*, 101–2) regards it as evidence for

competing chronological systems and concludes that the Chronicler was following a chronological scheme preserved in the OG Kings; the tension with 2
Kgs 2–3 would reflect changes in the chronology of the MT subsequent to
the composition of Chronicles. A less drastic solution to the chronological
problem suggests that the incidents of 2 Kgs 3 are dischronologized, i.e.,
not to be read as chronologically subsequent to Elijah's assumption in 2 Kgs
2: Elisha no doubt was already functioning as a prophet prior to his receiving
Elijah's mantle and could have participated in the events of 2 Kgs 3 while
Elijah was still alive. The only conclusion to be drawn from 2 Kgs 3:11 is
that Elisha, Elijah's associate, was in the camp, not that Elijah was already
dead (Keil, 397).

Though the ministry of Elijah is set in the Northern Kingdom, at least
some involvement with the South is reported in his journey to Beersheba
and on to Sinai (1 Kgs 19:3, 8), though this incident does not show any
political interaction with Judean kings.

While there are many ways in which the Chronicler's account of Jehoram
contrasts to his handling of Asa (see above, *Form/Structure/Setting*), in one
particular there is striking similarity. Elijah's letter is a succinct statement of
the Chronicler's theology of immediate retribution. For both Asa (16:12–
14) and Jehoram (21:18–19), and subsequently for Uzziah (26:16–19), unfaithfulness to Yahweh brought immediate punishment in the form of serious
illness. In addition to his illness, Jehoram would also be bereft of his wives
and children. Large families are for the Chronicler a sign of divine blessing
(see above, vv 2–3). Jehoram, who had begun his reign by destroying the
family of his father, would know a similar fate. Those whom he killed were
men "better than you," i.e., would not have committed fratricide or have
fostered apostasy.

16–17 For the Chronicler, if progeny is a measure of divine favor, their
loss shows divine anger; see above, vv 2–3, 12–15. With reference to the
attacks of the Philistines and Arabs, see above vv 8–11 and *Form/Structure/
Setting*.

The loss of sons and wives at first glance might suggest a successful sack
of Jerusalem. The Chronicler, however, is not reporting an otherwise unmentioned incursion into the capital. The attack was apparently against outlying
fortified cities; Jehoram may have dispersed his own sons and their mothers
in a way similar to Jehoshaphat and Rehoboam (see above, vv 2–3). A call
to war may have brought all together in an encampment, where the Arab
raiders were able to kill all but Ahaziah (22:1; cf. C-M, 417; Keil, 401; Williamson, 308). "All the property found in the royal palace" would refer then,
not to the treasury in Jerusalem, but to the goods belonging to the royal
household in the camp.

18–19 As with most illnesses mentioned in the OT a technical vocabulary
is not used to name or describe the disease; conjectures about the nature of
Jehoram's illness have included ulcers, colitis, chronic diarrhea, and dysentery.
Prolapse (cf. NEB) is probably too clinically precise; see Williamson, 308.

The syntax of v 19a presents some difficulty. Jehoram is said to have
died after two days (לימים שנים); this appears to contradict the protracted
nature of the disease (לימים מימים). The most common resolution to this

contradiction has been to translate לימים שנים as "two years" (NIV, NEB, KJV, RSV). Keil's suggestion (401–2) has been followed here: after a protracted illness, at the time of the end of his life (כעת צאת חקץ), Jehoram's bowels prolapsed two days (לימים שנים) before his death. A variety of other conjectures have been offered (see C-M, 418), but none appear persuasive.

The Chronicler once again contrasts Jehoram to Asa and Jehoshaphat, "his fathers" (v 12; contrast 16:14; see *Form/Structure/Setting*). The fire was not cremation, but rather an honorary rite withheld at the death of Jehoram; see *Comment* at 16:14.

20 Not only was no fire made in his honor, but Jehoram was also not buried in the royal tombs within the City of David (24:25; 26:23). This additional bit of information was not found in the parallel text (2 Kgs 8:24) and must have come from some other source (Rudolph, 269). C-M (418) and Noth (*US,* 143) viewed the Chronicler as composing freely to enhance the wickedness of Jehoram.

Perhaps it is the measure of the Chronicler's contempt for Jehoram that for the first time he makes no mention of other sources the reader might consult for additional details regarding his reign.

With reference to the chronological notices surrounding his reign, see *Comment* at 21:5–6.

Explanation

Jehoram is the first king in the Davidic succession of whom the Chronicler's judgment is totally negative (Williamson, 303). Yet it is precisely at this nadir of religious fidelity that the Chronicler reiterates and elaborates on God's promises to David (21:7). The Chronicler's treatment of the validity of the Davidic covenant in the past no doubt spoke also to the dynastic aspirations of his post-exilic audience; it is hard to believe that the author would invoke God's fidelity to this promise to David for the past unless hope of a dynastic restoration was also a feature of his own faith.

Threats to the Davidic dynasty did not only come from religious infidelity. Jehoram's efforts to secure his own position represented the first of four occasions (21:4; 21:17; 22:1; 22:8–9; 22:10–11; cf. Williamson, 304) when the very continuance of the dynasty was in jeopardy. The God who had been gracious and faithful in those historical circumstances would be faithful to the restoration community as well.

The Chronicler presents Jehoram's reign as the unraveling of the accomplishments of Asa and Jehoshaphat (see above, *Form/Structure/Setting*). His handling of this king is a paradigm for his theology of immediate retribution. Each aspect of wrongdoing brought its inevitable consequence in loss of family, territory, and health. Though the writer of the Kings account would mention only that Jehoram died, the Chronicler elaborates at some length on the terrible death he endured as the result of his wickedness. See the introductory essay to 2 Chr 10–36, "Reward and Punishment in Chronicles: The Theology of Immediate Retribution."

Irony permeates the account of Jehoram's reign. Rather than enlarging the scope of his power through seizing his brothers' cities, he loses control over Libnah and Edom; rather than securing the succession of his own children by slaughtering his brothers, he sees them suffer a similar fate; rather than securing life and happiness for himself, he suffers an agonizing and premature death; rather than gaining the devotion of his subjects, he dies unmourned and without the customary honors attending a royal funeral (McConville, 198). So it is for those who forget that the kingdom is God's (1 Chr 10:14; 17:14; 28:5; 29:11; 2 Chr 13:8).

The Reign of Ahaziah, 841 B.C.   (22:1–9)

Bibliography

Andreasen, N. "The Role of the Queen Mother in Israelite Society." *CBQ* 45 (1983) 179–94.

Translation

[1] *The inhabitants of Jerusalem made his youngest son Ahaziah king in his place since the marauders, who had come with the Arabs into the camp,* [a] *had killed all the older sons; so Ahaziah, son of Joram king of Judah, began to reign.* [2] *Ahaziah was twenty-two* [a] *years old when he began to reign, and he ruled in Jerusalem for one year; his mother's name was Athaliah, daughter* [b] *of Omri.* [c]

[3] *He too* [a] *walked in the ways of the house of Ahab, for his mother was his counselor for wrongdoing.* [4] *He did what was evil in the eyes of Yahweh, just like the house of Ahab, for they were his counselors after the death of his father, to his undoing.*

[5] *He was also following their advice when he went with Joram son of Ahab king of Israel to fight against Hazael king of Aram in Ramoth-gilead. The Arameans* [a] *wounded Joram,* [6] *so he returned to Jezreel to recover from the* [a] *wounds he had received in Rama during the war with Hazael king of Aram. Ahaziah* [b] *son of Jehoram king of Judah went down to see Joram son of Ahab in Jezreel because he had been injured.*

[7] *The downfall of Ahaziah when he visited Joram was the result of God's will. When he arrived, he went out with Joram to Jehu son of Nimshi, whom Yahweh had anointed to terminate the house of Ahab.* [8] *When Jehu was executing judgment on the house of Ahab, he also came across the officials of Judah and Ahaziah's relatives* [a] *who attended him, and he killed them.* [9] *He sought out Ahaziah and captured him hiding in Samaria; they brought him to Jehu and he* [a] *put him to death. They buried him, for they said, "he was the son of Jehoshaphat who sought Yahweh with all his heart." There was no one left to the house of Ahaziah who could assume power over the kingdom.*

Notes

1.a. G οἱ Ἀλιμαζονεῖς is difficult to explain other than as a garbled transcription of a presumed original λιμαανε for למ חנה. Cf. the G doublet in 14:14.

2.a. With 2 Kgs 8:26 and G[L]. MT, forty-two years; Par, twenty; OL, sixteen. MT cannot be correct: Ahaziah would have been two years older than his father (21:5, 20). MT could be derived either from a conflation of G and 2 Kgs 8:26 (20 + 22 = 42) in an effort to preserve both traditions (Myers, 125), or a copyist could have been confused by ערבים at the end of a line in the preceding verse (Rudolph, 268), or a numerical notation could have been misread, perhaps a confusion of כ and מ to denote twenty and forty respectively.

2.b. Or "granddaughter."

2.c. G[L] "Ahab" is a correction; see *Comment* at 21:5–6.

3.a. גם הוא is an addition in Chr MT to 2 Kgs 8:27. It relates the account of Ahaziah to the statement made about Jehoram in 21:6 // 2 Kgs 8:18.

5.a. MT הרמים = הארמים (2 Kgs 8:28). G οἱ τοξόται, "archers," may have read הָרֹמִים or הַפֹרִים.

6.a. Vg adds *multas*, "many."

6.b. With some MSS, G, Syr, and Vg; MT "Azariah" must represent a scribe's error.

8.a. MT, "sons of the brothers of Ahaziah"; G and 2 Kgs 10:13, "brothers of Ahaziah." MT in this case probably represents a harmonistic addition: the brothers of Ahaziah had already been killed (21:17; 22:1). G and 2 Kgs 10:13 represent the shorter and more difficult text; אח can be understood in the less specific sense "relatives."

9.a. With a few MSS, G, Syr, and Vg; MT, plural.

Form/Structure/Setting

The Chronicler's account of Ahaziah consists largely of an abridgment of the much longer account in 2 Kgs 8:24b–10:14. The account in Kings is written from the vantage of the Northern Kingdom and is primarily concerned with details of Jehu's coup and the fulfillment of prophetic pronouncements against the house of Ahab; it is not surprising then that the Chronicler, writing from the vantage of post-exilic Judah, would eliminate much of that material, concentrating instead on those portions of that narrative that impinged on the Southern Kingdom. There is sufficient material that closely parallels the Kings report of these events to establish that the Chronicler had the Kings account before him (cf. 2 Kgs 8:26–29 with 22:2–6); the Chronicler also appears to depend on his reader's knowledge of the parallel narrative (22:7–8). Most of the differences in the two accounts can be ascribed to the author's interest more narrowly in the history of Judah; however, the account of the death of Ahaziah presents more formidable difficulties.

The differences between the two histories on the events surrounding Ahaziah's demise represent one of the most difficult historical questions in the OT. The differences in the two accounts are in three areas (Williamson, 311; C-M, 421). (1) Chronology: in 2 Kgs 10:12–14 the slaughter of the princes and officers of Judah is reported after the murder of Ahaziah, but in Chronicles, before. (2) Place of death: in 2 Kgs 9:27 Ahaziah is said to have fled wounded toward Ibleam and dies near Megiddo; in Chronicles he is found hiding in Samaria, brought to Jehu at an unnamed place and put to death. (3) Place of burial: in 2 Kgs 9:28 his body is taken to Jerusalem for burial in the City of David; Chronicles seems to imply that he was buried at the place of his death.

What is the Chronicler's source for his additional material? If in 22:2–6 the author had closely followed his Kings *Vorlage*, why would he depart so radically from it at this point? Are the changes clearly related to his larger *Tendenz*? Can the accounts be reconciled?

It has commonly been the judgment of commentators that the Chronicler here followed some other source that is irreconcilable with the account in Kings (e.g., C-M, 421; Myers, 126; Rudolph, 269). Since the Chronicler does use his reports of the death and burial of kings to show approval or disapproval of their reigns (16:14; 21:19–20; 24:25; 25:27–28; 26:22–23), his account of the death of Ahaziah is associated with that *Tendenz:* the Chronicler does not report his burial in the City of David; rather he suffers the consequence of his association with the dynasty of Ahab by being captured in Samaria, executed, and apparently buried in the Northern Kingdom. Williamson (311–12), however, does not argue for another source: he suggests rather that the Chronicler presupposed his readers' knowledge of the earlier account and rewrote that account to express a theological judgment of retributive justice rather than an alternative history; the readers of Chronicles could be expected to recognize the difference.

Others have sought to harmonize the two accounts by essentially overlaying them something like this: Jehu went in search of Ahaziah [Chronicles]; Ahaziah had fled south from Jezreel to hide in Samaria [Chronicles]; he was brought to Jehu [Chronicles], fatally wounded near Ibleam [Kings], fled northwest toward Megiddo where he died [Kings]; his servants carried his body back to Jerusalem where they buried him [Kings]. Generally the verdict on such efforts has been that they are implausible. Rudolph (269) cites with approval the judgment of van Selms that efforts to harmonize are "fantastic"; Williamson (311) describes such scenarios as "forced and unconvincing." However, some effort to ease the tension between the two texts should not be dismissed too quickly. (1) The Chronicler may have chronologically dislocated the death of Ahaziah's relatives and servants in order to end his account on the note of the death of Ahaziah—no chronological point may be made by the narrative. Perhaps in an effort to draw parallels with Saul, the death of the family was reported before the death of the king himself (1 Chr 10:1–7; cf. Mosis, *Untersuchungen,* 179). (2) Similarly, the specification of the place of burial may be assumed from the Kings account, in which case it would be wrong to infer that the Chronicler thought Ahaziah was buried in the North. The appeal to the righteousness of Jehoshaphat as a reason for the decent burial of Ahaziah would seem more natural if "they buried him" in Jerusalem (22:9). It is difficult, however, to provide a plausible scenario for the itinerary of Ahaziah's flight before his death. The Chronicler's handling of Ahaziah's death should be compared with the account of Jehoiakim's reign; see *Comment* at 36:4–8. Three of the last four kings of Judah died in exile, and the Chronicler may have deliberately left the impression that this was also the fate of Jehoiakim; it suited his narrative purpose to do so, though both he and his post-exilic readers would have been familiar with the death of Jehoiakim in Jerusalem (2 Kgs 24:5–6). Cf. the similar question regarding the place of death for Josiah; see *Comment* at 35:20–27.

Two of the paragraphs in this pericope are introduced using the word גַּם (22:3, 5). The paragraph boundary between vv 4 and 5 is also marked by the repetition of the fact that Ahaziah was following advice from members of the house of Ahab. The onset of the paragraph at v 7 appears to be marked only by the inversion of the usual word order.

Comment

1–2 The "inhabitants of Jerusalem" may be the same as the "people of the land" who participated in the installation of a king at times of dynastic crisis (23:20–21; 26:1; 33:25; 36:1). Though the precise identity of the "people of the land" is uncertain, they are commonly associated with the landed aristocracy or ruling class; see *Comment* at 33:21–25. Otherwise, the author may be distinguishing the "inhabitants of Jerusalem" from the "people of the land," suggesting action in Jerusalem without consultation or participation on the part of the outlying districts.

The "marauders who had come with the Arabs" would have included the Philistines (21:16–17). The Chronicler's mention of their attack reiterates his convictions regarding retributive justice: Jehoram, the king who had slain all his brothers, lived to witness the death of his own sons (21:4, 13, 16–17).

3–4   It is not surprising that Athaliah was Ahaziah's counselor; this appears to have been a normal role for the queen mother in the monarchies of Israel and the ancient Near East (N. Andreason, *CBQ* 45 [1983] 188–89; cf. 1 Kgs 1:11–31; 2:13–21; 15:13; 21:5–7; 2 Kgs 10:13; 24:12, 15; Jer 13:18). The queen mother held a defined position of great political power; Athaliah is the mirror image of her own mother Jezebel in her effective wielding of that power.

The fact that members of the dynasty of Ahab in the North held such sway over Ahaziah is one more line of evidence that the Northern Kingdom exercised hegemony over Judah under Omri and his successors. The marriage of the Omride Athaliah into the Judean royal house probably reflects that influence (18:1; 21:6). Members of the royal house of Judah paid calls on Israel's ruling family (1 Kgs 22:2; 2 Kgs 9:16; 10:13); the kings of Judah participated in Israel's wars with Aram (2 Chr 18 // 1 Kgs 22; 2 Chr 22:5 // 2 Kgs 8:28), even in a subordinate role (1 Kgs 22:29–30). Joram of Judah was perhaps named after the Omride ruling at the time of his own accession (2 Kgs 8:16). Ahaziah's seeking refuge in Samaria (22:9) also testifies to that relationship.

5–6   Ramoth-gilead was located in the eastern territory of Gad and had been designated as a levitical city of refuge (Deut 4:43; Josh 21:38). Due to its location along the King's Highway and the strategic interests involved for both Aram and Israel, the region became the site of repeated conflicts between these two nations. At some point it was annexed by Damascus, perhaps during the attacks of Ben-hadad I (1 Kgs 15:20). It would have been among the cities promised to Ahab by Ben-hadad after the battle at Aphek (1 Kgs 20:26–34), but for which Ahab was later forced to go to war (1 Kgs 22). Jehu was fighting there when he was anointed as king and proceeded to slay both Joram and Ahaziah (2 Kgs 8:28–10:17); Hazael's domination of Israel would have included that region (2 Kgs 13:4–7). Though Jeroboam II may have recovered it briefly (2 Kgs 14:25–28), the region ultimately fell to the Assyrians.

Jezreel was situated at the foot of Mount Gilboa in the Plain of Jezreel; it became the location of the summer palace of the kings of Israel (1 Kgs 18:45–46; 21:1; 2 Kgs 9:30); the heads of the Omride royal family were sent to Jezreel from Samaria after Jehu's coup (2 Kgs 10:1–7).

7–9   The details surrounding Ahaziah's death contrast with the account in 2 Kgs 9:27–28; see the discussion above under *Form/Structure/Setting.*

However the historical questions are settled, it is important to see that the Chronicler has used the death of Ahaziah as one more expression of his theology of immediate retribution (see the introductory essay to 2 Chr 10–36, "Reward and Punishment in Chronicles: The Theology of Immediate Retribution"). In Kings the death of Ahaziah appears to result more from the excessive zeal of Jehu's coup—perhaps it is precisely this excess in murdering the Judean king and members of the royal household that prompted

Hosea's oracle about God's avenging the "blood of Jezreel" (Hos 1:4). For the Chronicler, however, the death of Ahaziah was the result of divine will, the inevitable outcome of his following in the ways of the house of Ahab.

One theme of the Chronicler's theology is his consistent repudiation of foreign entanglements; such alliances inevitably represent a failure to trust Yahweh (see *Comment* at 16:7–10, 19:1–3). The Chronicler has introduced his concern about alliances with the house of Ahab into his accounts of the reigns of each of the Judean kings contemporary with Ahab and his successors (18:1; 19:1–3; 21:6, 13; 22:3–4); he uses the entire narrative about Jehoshaphat's participation with Ahab in the battle of Ramoth-gilead to drive home this point (see 2 Chr 18:1–19:3, *Form/Structure/Setting*). There is ironic justice in the death of Ahaziah: the king who lived by the counsel of the Omrides shared their fate; he who had taken advice from Samaria found no refuge there at the time of his death. Alliance with the Omrides bears fruit when Athaliah seizes the throne and tries to exterminate the Davidic line.

One characteristic of the Chronicler is his occasionally presuming his audience's familiarity with the parallel history. Here he alludes to Ahaziah's visit to Joram (22:7), confident that his readers know the rest of the details.

The righteousness of Jehoshaphat provides the rationale for the proper burial of Ahaziah (22:9). The Chronicler's portrayal of the reigns of Jehoshaphat, Jehoram, and Ahaziah is one of contrasts: Jehoshaphat provided the positive image, of which Jehoram and Ahaziah were the negative (see 2 Chr 21:2–20, *Form/Structure/Setting*). Jehoshaphat, who first became entangled with the Omrides, watched a Northern king die after a battle at Ramoth-gilead, whereas Ahaziah died with a Northern king, also due to events surrounding Ramoth-gilead.

The infidelity of Jehoram and Ahaziah had brought the Davidic succession to the same point as that of Saul—no one left who could assume power over the kingdom (22:9; 1 Chr 10; cf. Mosis, *Untersuchungen*, 179).

Explanation

The Chronicler's hand in his presentation of Ahaziah is clear from his concerns with retribution theology and foreign alliances, as already discussed above.

The Chronicler spoke of a time in the past when there was no one left of the Davidic line "who could assume power over the kingdom" (22:9). Surely the lesson was not lost on his post-exilic audience: even in adversity the royal line was preserved and would eventually regain the kingdom. Davidic hopes did not die at the time of Ahaziah, Athaliah, and Joash; they should not die in the post-exilic period. The flame from the promise of God that David would never lack a descendant to rule Israel (1 Chr 17:11–14; 2 Chr 21:7) may have become little more than a smoldering wick—but it could not be extinguished.

Another theological theme recurs in the narrative, though perhaps it was not expressly a concern of the Chronicler himself. It is that tension between the sovereignty of God and the responsibility of humans. The blood of Jezreel would require avenging (Hos 1:4), even though the situation was ordained by God (22:7).

The Reign of Athaliah, 841–835 B.C.; Jehoiada's Coup (22:10–23:21)

Bibliography

Andreason, N. "The Role of the Queen Mother in Israelite Society." *CBQ* 45 (1983) 179–94. **Rudolph, W.** "Die Einheitlichkeit der Erzählung vom Sturz der Atalja (2 Kon 11)." In *FS Alfred Bertholet*. Tübingen: Mohr, 1950. 473–78.

Translation

22:10 *When Athaliah the mother of Ahaziah saw that her son was dead, she proceeded to destroy* a *the entire royal family of the house of Judah.* 11 *But Josheba* a *the daughter of the king* b *took Joash the son of Ahaziah. She stole him away from the royal children who were being put to death, and she put him and his nurse in a bedroom; Josheba, daughter of King Joram and wife of Jehoiada the priest, because she was Ahaziah's sister, hid Joash from Athaliah so that she did not kill him.* 12 *He remained hidden with them* a *in the temple of God for six years while Athaliah was ruling the land.*

23:1 *In the seventh* a *year Jehoiada consolidated his power and made a covenant* b *with the officers over the hundreds—Azariah son of Jehoram, Ishmael son of Johanan, Azariah son of Obed—and with* c *Maaseiah son of Adaiah and Elishaphat son of Zicri.* 2 *They traveled throughout Judah and gathered the Levites and the heads of the families from all the cities of Judah, and they came to Jerusalem.* 3 *The entire assembly made a covenant with the king at the temple of God.* a

Jehoiada said to them,

"Here is the king's son! He shall be king just as Yahweh has promised concerning the sons of David. 4 *This is what you must do: a third of you priests and Levites going on Sabbath duty will keep watch at the gates,* 5 *a third in the royal palace, and a third at the Foundation* a *Gate; all the people will be in the courts of the temple of Yahweh.* 6 *Let no one enter the temple of Yahweh except the priests and the Levites attending them; they may enter since they are consecrated, but all the people must observe the commandment of Yahweh.* a 7 *The Levites must surround the king, each with his weapon in his hand. Let anyone who enters the temple be put to death. Stay* a *with the king wherever he goes."*

8 *The Levites and all Judah did what Jehoiada the priest had commanded them. Each took his men coming on duty on the Sabbath as well as those going off duty, since Jehoiada the priest had not released the divisions.* 9 *Then Jehoiada gave to the captains of hundreds the spears and large and small shields that had belonged to King David and were kept in the temple of God.* 10 *He positioned all the people, each with his weapon in hand, around the king—on the north and south sides of the temple between the altar and the temple.* 11 *Then they brought out the king's son, gave him the crown and a copy of the covenant, and made him king; Jehoiada and his sons anointed him and said, "Long live the king."*

¹²*When Athaliah heard the noise of the people running and cheering the king, she went to the temple of Yahweh where the people were* ¹³*and saw the king standing by his pillar at the entrance. The officers*ᵃ *and trumpeters were beside the king, and all the people of the land were rejoicing and blowing trumpets; there were singers accompanied by musical instruments leading the celebration. Then Athaliah tore her garments and called out, "Treason, treason!"*

¹⁴ *Then Jehoiada sent*ᵃ *for the officers of the hundreds, the leaders of the troops, and he said to them, "Take her out of the precincts,*ᵇ *and let anyone who follows her be put to death by the sword!" The priest had said, "Do not kill her in the temple of Yahweh,"* ¹⁵*so they laid hands on her when she reached the entrance of the Horse Gate at the royal palace, and they killed her there.*

¹⁶*Jehoiada made a covenant between himself,*ᵃ *all the people, and the king, that they should be the people of Yahweh.* ¹⁷*Then all the people went to the temple of Baal, and they pulled it down; they smashed its altars and images and killed Mattan the priest of Baal before the altars.*

¹⁸*Jehoiada placed the oversight of the temple of Yahweh in the hands of the priests and Levites,*ᵃ *and he appointed the divisions of the priests and Levites*ᵇ *that David had assigned to the temple of Yahweh to make the burnt offerings to Yahweh in accordance with what was written in the law of Moses with rejoicing and singing, as David had ordered.* ¹⁹*He appointed gatekeepers for the gates of the temple of Yahweh so that no one who was unclean in any way might enter.* ²⁰*Then he took the officers of the hundreds, the nobles, and the rulers of the people, and all the people of the land and went*ᵃ *down with the king from the temple of Yahweh; they went through the Upper*ᵇ *Gate of the royal palace and seated the king on the throne of the kingdom.* ²¹*All the people of the land rejoiced, and the city was quiet. They had put Athaliah to death by the sword.*

Notes

10.a. 2 Kgs 11:1, וַתְּאַבֵּד. Chr MT may derive from a root of דבר meaning "destroy, overthrow," or it may represent an error in copying the Kgs *Vorlage*. Cf. Williamson, 314; Watson, *Bib* 53 (1972) 193.

11.a. MT יְהוֹשַׁבְעַת, "Joshabath"; cf. 2 Kgs 11:2, יְהוֹשֶׁבַע. The feminine ending is also found on another theophoric name formed from the root שׁבע; cf. "Elizabeth," derived from אֱלִישֶׁבַע (Exod 6:23; Luke 1:5). Par follows Bas; cf. Allen, *GC* 1:208.

11.b. 2 Kgs 11:2 at this point introduces the fact that she was also the "sister of Ahaziah"; the Chronicler provides yet additional information not found in the Kgs parallel in the second half of the verse.

12.a. 2 Kgs 11:3, אִתָּהּ, "with her"; the translator of Gᴮ (μετʼαὐτοῦ) may have read אִתֹּה, "with him." The pl suff in the MT may refer to the priest and his wife or the wife and the nurse. Cf. Allen, *GC* 1:207.

1.a. G, "eighth." G could have developed from a misread abbreviation based on the first letters of the Heb. words for the numerals (שָׁבִיעִית or שְׁמֹנִית; cf. Driver, *Textus* 4 [1964] 82) or from a missing stroke in some system of numerical notation.

1.b. G εἰς οἶκον = בבית, "into the temple," instead of MT בברית. Both בית and ברית occur in 23:1, 3 // 2 Kgs 9:4—one or the other text has assimilated to the other occurrence of the term. Cf. the similar problem in MT and Par at 34:32.

1.c. The Chronicler introduces the first three names following the preposition ל, and the last two names using the marker את. Perhaps he distinguished the last two names as not among the captains of hundreds; alternatively, the two different ways of introducing the names may represent no more than stylistic variation.

3.a. Par assimilates to Bas (2 Kgs 11:4) and adds the phrase "he showed them the son of the king." The Chronicler has already introduced the king (23:3a) and the phrase from Kgs is inappropriate in the context. Alternatively, the phrase could be missing from Chr MT due to homoiotel from two lines ending with הַמֶּלֶךְ, "the king."

5.a. 2 Kgs 9:6, "Sur Gate." Gates bearing these names are otherwise unknown; some commentators identify both with the Horse Gate of the palace (23:15, as distinguished from the city gate [Jer 31:40; Neh 3:28]).

6.a. NIV "all the other men are to guard what the LORD has assigned to them" misses the point of the context: the text does not speak of the LORD as assigning the guard posts—this is done by Jehoiada. Rather, the first half of the verse emphasizes protecting the sanctity of the temple courts in keeping with the commandment of Yahweh. See Williamson, 316.

7.a. A few MSS, G, Tg, and Vg read וְהָיוּ, "and they were / will be," rather than the imperative with the MT.

13.a. Also in 2 Kgs 11:14; Bas (οἱ ᾠδοί) read שָׁרִים, "singers."

14.a. 2 Kgs 11:15, וַיְצַו "ordered."

14.b. שְׂדֵרוֹת is frequently read as if derived from סדר ("order, row, rank"), so that the command was to "take her out between the ranks" of assembled troops. The term also has an uncertain architectural use (1 Kgs 6:9); the translation "precincts" fits the contextual concern with keeping the laws pertaining to entry to the temple (23:6, 14b–15).

16.a. 2 Kgs 11:17, בֵּין יהוה. Chr MT (בֵּינוֹ, "between himself . . .") may reflect a misreading of an abbreviation for the tetragrammaton, the yod read as a waw; however, the absence of any corroboration in the versions makes this unlikely. Alternatively the Chronicler may have considered Jehoiada as the representative of Yahweh, certainly as the representative of the temple and cultic interests in the arrangement (cf. *Preliminary and Interim Report on the Hebrew Old Testament Text Project*, 2:470; Rudolph, 272).

18.a. Inserting the conjunction with a few Heb. MSS, G, Syr, and Vg; MT, "levitical priests." See the same problem at 5:5; 30:27; Ezra 10:5.

18.b. Inserting וַיַּעֲמֵד אֶת־מַחְלְקוֹת, "he appointed the divisions," with G; the phrase was probably lost in MT due to homoiotel. Cf. 8:14 and note the parallel wording with 23:19a (See Allen, *GC* 2:140; Rudolph, 272; C-M, 433).

20.a. 2 Kgs 11:19, G, and Vg read the pl וַיּוֹרִידוּ.

20.b. 2 Kgs 11:19, הָרָצִים "runners, messengers, heralds." Variations in the gate names between Chr and Kgs are a major difficulty in this pericope; the variation could scarcely be a textual question, but may reflect updating or modernizing the gate names to those in use in the author's period as opposed to the pre-exilic city. The gate of the "heralds" may reflect a usage unique to the monarchy, such that the gate bore a different name by the Chronicler's day when royal messengers no longer frequented that entrance.

Form/Structure/Setting

The Chronicler appears to have had 2 Kgs 11:1–20 before him as he wrote this account. Apart from some evidence for an additional source, most of the differences between the two accounts can be related to the Chronicler's *Tendenz*.

The differences between Kings and Chronicles in this case are largely related to the Chronicler's "sacralizing" the coup: instead of the royal bodyguard of Carites, the role of the priests and Levites is emphasized (23:1 // 2 Kgs 11:4; 23:8 // 11:9; 23:18–20 // 11:19). Rather than simply reporting the amassing of soldiers to stage a coup, the Chronicler reports a national קָהָל, "religious assembly" (23:3 // 2 Kgs 11:4); Joash comes to the throne with the support of the people and not simply as the result of palace intrigue. The Chronicler is also concerned to protect the sacrosanctity of the temple precincts (23:5b–6, 19) and, as is typical of him, he elaborates on the role of music (23:13) and the temple staff (23:18) in the proceedings.

There has been some scholarly debate about the unity of authorship and possible multiple sources for the Kings account; see Gray, 565–69. This debate is not relevant for Chronicles since the author appears to be following a text roughly the equivalent of the Kgs MT, though modifying it to meet the needs and interests of his audience.

Though most of the differences between the accounts can be attributed to the Chronicler's *Tendenz*, some portions suggest the use of yet an additional source. The Chronicler seems to delight in lists of names, and the names in 23:1 are presumably derived from some other source. The precise details of the disposition of the guards, priests, Levites, and the people are also difficult to harmonize between the two accounts (23:4–5 // 2 Kgs 11:5–6) and may reflect some other source available to the Chronicler.

The economic and power structures in societies in the ancient Near East revolved around three foci: the governmental, religious, and private sectors. Behind the details of Jehoiada's coup in both Kings and Chronicles, it is possible to speculate regarding the tensions between these three power centers in Israel. The installation of a monarchy owing its existence to the cult and under the regency of the high priest may reflect the consolidation of political power in the hands of the temple; in the Chronicler's account, the temple officers along with tribal leaders from outside Jerusalem appear to have cooperated not only in a religious reform but also in curtailing the power of the monarchy. The tension between temple and monarchy may also underlie some of the events recorded in 2 Chr 24.

The paragraph units in the pericope are mainly marked by the use of an explicit subject (23:9, 12, 14, 16, 18); the repetition of Jehoiada's name is often on a paragraph boundary. 23:3–8 is a command/fulfillment paragraph. The boundary between 22:12 and 23:1 is marked by the temporal notice that ends one paragraph and begins the next.

Comment

10–12 Often what the biblical historians do not say is nearly as important as what they do. Here the absence of the regnal formulae giving the monarch's age, length of reign, etc., is particularly noticeable: neither the deuteronomic historian nor the Chronicler regard Athaliah as a legitimate ruler, so neither provides the customary introductory or concluding notices (C-M, 422).

The destruction of the "entire royal family" probably concentrated on potential male successors; Josheba, and presumably others, survived the slaughter even though related to the royal family. Possibly Josheba's escape from Athaliah's slaughter should be related to her position as the wife of the high priest. Josheba would have been the half-sister of Ahaziah, a daughter of Jehoram by a wife other than Athaliah; her husband Jehoiada was apparently considerably older than she (24:15). No doubt both Josheba and Athaliah had the precedent set by Jehoram in mind (21:4); as Jehoram was left with only his youngest to succeed him (21:17; 22:1), so Ahaziah would be succeeded by one who was probably the youngest of his children.

The fact that royal infants may regularly have been put into the care of wet nurses or foster mothers becomes the key to Josheba's frustrating Athaliah's plans; the suckling child was overlooked and could have escaped detection as he grew by mingling with other priests' children or perhaps as a temple devotee like the young Samuel (Gray, 570; 1 Sam 1:21–28; 3:1).

1–2 The coup of Jehu that ended the Omride dynasty in the North and brought the destruction of much of the Judean royal house (22:3–9) was undertaken at prophetic instigation (2 Kgs 9:1–13) and is generally endorsed by the biblical historians (22:7; 2 Kgs 9:24–26, 36–37; 10:17, 28–30). However, its political consequences were great. Militarily both Israel and Judah sank to their nadir. It is not surprising that the military establishment would become disaffected and long for a return to the halcyon days of the Davidic dynasty. Nor is it surprising that the temple personnel would also be eager for a change: Athaliah had fostered in Jerusalem the Baalism of Jezebel her mother (23:17), and the priests of Yahweh would be eager to return to primacy the worship of Israel's God. Though Judah may have been subservient to Israel during the dynasty of the Omrides (see *Comments* at 18:28–29; 22:3–4), that subservience would not long continue when Athaliah no longer had the backing of her powerful family in the North.

Though in Kings the emphasis is on the role played by the military in the coup (2 Kgs 11:4, "the captains of hundreds, the Carites, and the guard"), the Chronicler has underscored instead the role of the priests and Levites. The Levites had a traditional quasi-military role (see *Comment* below at 23:3–8); in the absence of a military establishment in the post-exilic period, it is not surprising that the Chronicler should emphasize the role of cultic personnel in the coup, not to mention his own concerns with the sacrosanctity of the temple precincts. One of the difficulties in the chapter, however, is determining who did participate in the coup according to the Chronicler's account. Did he so emphasize the role of the priests and Levites as not to mention the participation of other elements in society?

Though all the names in v 1, with the exception of "Elishaphat," can be found in various lists of priests and Levites (Rudolph, 271; Williamson, 315), it does not necessarily follow that the Chronicler intends us to understand this list as Levites. (1) There is no question that the Chronicler has heightened the role of the priests and Levites; he may intend us to understand the names he introduces as cultic staff, but it is at least plausible that the name list is a further specification of the officers mentioned in Kings. The individuals are identified as שרי המאות, "captains of hundreds." In the parallel at 2 Kgs 11:4 this phrase appears to refer to military officers. Furthermore, the phrase in Chronicles ordinarily designates officers over militarily organized clan and tribal subunits and may refer to officers in the standing army (1 Chr 13:1; 27:1; 28:1; 29:6; 2 Chr 1:2; 25:5; cf. Num 31:14, 28, 48). Unless 23:7, 9 are the exception, there is no passage where the Levites are themselves described as organized in units of "hundreds"; in one passage, the officers of hundreds are distinguished from the Levites (1 Chr 26:26; cf. Num 31:51–54). The Levites and priests are ordinarily described as divided according to their courses and divisions (v 8). (2) The very emphasis in the Chronicler's account on protecting the sacrosanctity of the temple grounds (23:6, 7, 14) requires that non-Levites have been present and participating in the events in such a way that their forced or unavoidable entry to the precincts was a foreseen possibility. If the captains are military officers, the prohibition against entering the temple (v 6) would have required their remaining out of the inner courtyard where much of the action takes place (v 10). (3) The high priest would not likely need to make a covenant with his temple staff—it is far more probable that this covenant was made to secure the cooperation of the military in unseating Athaliah. (4) The strongest argument in favor of regarding the captains of hundreds as Levites comes from 23:7, 9–10: the Levites are instructed to surround the king with weapons in hand (v 7), and the king is surrounded in the inner courtyard by an armed force commanded by the captains of hundreds (vv 9–10), implying that the officers were themselves Levites.

The use of כרת ברית, "make a covenant," in this instance probably implies no more than "come to terms with, make an arrrangment with"; it would suggest that Jehoiada concluded with these officers some sort of pact that would be mutually advantageous (D. McCarthy, VTSup 23 [1972] 77–81).

Whether this initial arrangement was with Levitical or military leaders, the next step in the plan to overthrow Athaliah was to enlist further popular support (23:2). This addition by the Chronicler regarding the participation of the clan and phratry leadership is probably a reflex of his "all Israel" theme: as he had shown so carefully in his account of the reign of David and Solomon (1 Chr 11:1; 12:23–40; 28:1; 29:6–9, 21–25; 2 Chr 1:2), the righteous enjoy the support of all the people (cf. 11:13–17; 15:9; 17:5); loyalty of the populace is a token of divine favor in the Chronicler's theology of immediate retribution. The broadening circle of the conspiracy may have incorporated elements from all three sectors of society: the royal/military, cultic, and private. The leaders of the ancestral families (ראשי האבות) play a role in numerous crucial moments (1 Chr 29:6; 2 Chr 1;2; 5:2; 19:8; 35:10; cf. Ezr 8:29).

3–8 The initial agreement made among the original conspirators is broadened by concluding a covenant between the king and the entire assembly. This covenant probably included the arrangements under which Joash would rule; it likely included some concessions of royal prerogatives in relationship to the temple and would have specified the regency of Jehoiada for the young king. It was probably a copy of this arrangement that was placed in the king's hands (see *Comments* at 23:11; cf. 1 Sam 10:25). Cf. other examples of covenants between the king and people (2 Sam 3:17–21; 5:3) and the need to negotiate the right of rule (1 Kgs 12:1–17). A third covenant is mentioned in 23:16.

The Chronicler has added the note not found in the parallel at 2 Kgs 11:5 that Jehoiada appealed to God's promise to David to legitimate the coup (v 3). This appeal is important in assessing the Chronicler's overall attitude to messianic/Davidic hopes during the post-exilic period: in the Chronicler's portrayal, the temple is not the seat of a satisfied theocratic status quo, but rather is the guardian and promoter of the Davidic succession. By inserting this note at this point, the Chronicler gives evidence of his own hopes for the future of the restoration community that was also under foreign rule. See Williamson, *TynBul* 28 (1977) 148–49.

The time of the shift change for the temple personnel would be an ideal time to stage the coup; the large number of personnel in the precincts and moving about would not occasion any comment or suspicion at that hour

(Gray, 572; cf. 1 Chr 24:4, 28–32; 26:12–19). Though it is probable that military personnel supported the coup (see *Comments* above at 23:1–2), one must not forget the military images often associated with the Levites: they were the guardians of the ark, itself often a military symbol; they were armed gate keepers; they frequently participated in holy war (see J. Spencer, "The Tasks of the Levites: *šmr* and *ṣbʾ*," *ZAW* 96 [1984] 267–71); there is nothing incongruous with the role assigned them in Jehoiada's coup. Jehoiada in effect has amassed a cultic army ready for holy war (cf. Exod 32:26–29).

The greatest difficulty in the chapter is harmonizing the distribution of forces with the account found in 2 Kgs 11:5–8. The list below presents the deployments so that the enumeration in each corresponds:

2 Kgs 11:5–8:
    I. Those going on duty on the sabbath
        A. One-third at the royal palace
        B. One-third at the Sur Gate
        C. One-third at the gate behind the guard
    II. Two-thirds going off Sabbath duty in the temple

2 Chr 23:4–5:
    I. Those going on duty on the sabbath
        A. One-third in the royal palace
        B. One-third at the Foundation Gate
        C. One-third at the gates
    II. The rest of the people in the temple courts

This scheme seems best to make sense of what is written, but does present a few problems of its own. (1) The various groups going on duty on the sabbath are not introduced in the same order; in the scheme above, the order of these groups in Chronicles is adjusted to that in Kings. (2) The correspondence between the third "at the gate behind the guard" and the third "at the gates" (I-C) is not clear; it is at least possible that the Chronicler has modernized this reference to some points identifiable by his audience in the second temple period. (3) The Sur Gate (סוּר) and the Foundation Gate (יְסוֹד) are understood as the same gate, the one a textual error for the other. (4) The Chronicler appears to be using the word "people" (עַם; 23:5, 6, 10, 12, 16, 17) in the sense of "an armed force" (*BDB*, 766). Though it is conceivable that the Chronicler followed some source that preserved a genuinely variant tradition to that found in the Kings MT, the dependence of Chronicles on Kings in the chapter in general would favor an effort to explain the Chr MT from Kings. At least it is fairly clear in both accounts that the group going on sabbath duty was divided into thirds, and that the remaining two thirds were stationed in the temple area.

9–11   The copy of the covenant given to Jehoiada was probably the arrangement agreed to in 23:3; alternatively it could be a copy of the law, received from the hands of a priest, as envisioned in Deut 17:18. If it represented a document somewhat curbing royal authority in favor of the temple, it may have set the stage for the disagreement between Joash and Jehoiada in 24:4–12.

The guards appear to have formed a perimeter to the north and south between the temple building and the altar. It is the same area in which Zechariah the priest would later be murdered at the order of Joash (24:21; Matt 23:35). The irony of the situation could not be appreciated at the moment: Jehoiada, who was instrumental in saving the life and kingdom of Joash from a murderous parent, was saving the man who would kill his own son.

It was appropriate that the weapons used to restore rule to a descendant of David had belonged to David.

12–13 Another usurper had similarly been alerted to a change of rule by the noise coming from the city (1 Kgs 1:39–40, 45–46). If the king was still surrounded by the guards between the temple and the altar, then his "pillar" would probably refer to one of the two great pillars, Jakin and Boaz, that stood at the entrance; the elevation of the temple platform would have given the added height to put the new king in sight of all the gathered crowd. Alternatively this pillar must have been a place associated with the royal presence or the publication of royal decrees.

The cry of "treason" in the mouth of Athaliah is itself ironic: by her own standards, there could be no treason, for power is rightly held by those who can seize it (McConville, 206).

14–15 Once again the irony is poignant: Jehoiada, who is so concerned to protect the sanctity of the temple from any murder, cannot save his own son from precisely that sacrilege (24:21).

The "Horse Gate" of the palace should be distinguished from the gate of the same name in the city wall (Jer 31:40; Neh 3:28), though both could have been oriented in the same direction. The Horse Gate of the city wall led to the Kidron Valley, "where dead bodies are thrown" (Jer 31:40), and would have made a fitting exit for Athaliah; her mother Jezebel had been trampled by horses.

The absence of the usual summary statements at the end of a reign confirms once again the judgment of the biblical historians that Athaliah was never a rightful ruler in Jerusalem.

16–17 The destruction of the Baal temple at the time of Jehoiada's coup is a reflex in Judah of the similar purge of Baalism in Israel during Jehu's coup (2 Kgs 9; cf. Deut 13:7–12 [6–11]). It is not known when a temple to Baal was built in Jerusalem. Presumably Athaliah, granddaughter of a king of Tyre and daughter of Ahab and Jezebel, was allowed to bring religious accouterments with her to Jerusalem at the time of her marriage into the Judean royal house, much as Solomon's wives had done (1 Kgs 11:1–8). The Omrides had become so identified with Baalism that coups against that dynasty inevitably entailed religious reforms and the suppression of Baalism.

According to 2 Kgs 11:17, the covenant was made "between Yahweh and the king and the people" and "between the king and the people"; the Chronicler reports Jehoiada's instituting a covenant "between himself, all the people, and the king." This probably represents no more than paraphrase on the part of the Chronicler, so that no distinctive *Tendenz* is intended; see the note at 23:16.a. Cf. the similar covenant made during Asa's reform, when those who would not seek Yahweh were also put to death (15:12–13). The three major sectors of society (royal, cultic, private) were in league.

18–19 These verses are characteristic insertions reflecting the Chronicler's concern with the cult, and particularly his interest to trace cultic practice to arrangements instituted by David (29:25–30; 1 Chr 15–16; 23–27). Concern with Davidic praxis is a fitting accompaniment to the reinstitution of Davidic rule. The sacrosanctity of the temple area has been a major concern in the Chronicler's account (v 19; 23:6, 14).

20–21 The company going from the temple to the palace consisted of "officers of hundreds, Carites, and guards" according to 2 Kgs 11:19; this becomes "officers of hundreds, nobles, the rulers of the people, and all the people of the land" in Chronicles. This change reflects the Chronicler's concern to portray the wide popular support for Jehoiada's coup; see above *Form/Structure/Setting*.

"Quiet" (שקט) is one of the terms the Chronicler frequently uses to denote the divine blessing that belongs to the faithful (13:23; 14:1, 4–5 [13:23, 14:5–6]; 20:30; 1 Chr 4:40; 22:9).

Explanation

Athaliah represented the one break in the dynastic continuity of the descendants of David. Though the queen mother played an important role in the monarchies of the ancient Near East, Athaliah was the only queen of Judah ever to rule in her own name. The "prophetic revolution" that swept away her family in the North had its counterpart in the "priestly revolution" that swept her away in the South. Just as the promise of God to David (1 Chr 17:14, 23–27) would not falter before her, so also, the Chronicler was reminding his readers, it would not falter before other kingdoms, even in the post-exilic period. The Davidic lamp would not be snuffed out (see *Comments* at 23:3–8); it still glowed in the hopes of the restoration community.

Jehoiada was in some ways a priest-king during his regency for the young Joash; this is recognized in his unique burial in the royal tombs (24:16; cf. Zech 6:9–15). For the restoration community his relationship with Joash may have reproduced or modeled the community's earlier existence under the rule of Zerubbabel and Joshua.

This portion of Scripture shares many motifs with other events in the sacred canon. (1) Athaliah becomes a Jezebel redivivus; she leads the South in the path laid out by her infamous mother (23:17). Both women were defiant at the time of their death (2 Kgs 9:30–31; 2 Chr 23:13); Jezebel is trampled by horses, a fate presumably shared by Athaliah who is slain at the Horse Gate (23:15; 2 Kgs 9:33). (2) She becomes one more example in Scripture where evil is personified in a woman (24:7; Prov 5; 6:20–7:27; Isa 47:7–8; Zech 5:5–11); the conflict between good and evil reaches a crescendo when another evil woman is slain to preserve the kingdom of God (Rev 17:1–18:20). (3) Many innocent lives would be lost to those seeking to thwart the purposes of God; Moses (Exod 2:1–10) and Jesus (Matt 2:13–18) were both providentially saved from those seeking their lives in infancy; the child of another woman (Rev 12) was similarly threatened. The purposes of God for the sons of David would not be thwarted by Athaliah, nor by the Persians in the restoration period, nor by the Romans in the early years of our era.

The Reign of Joash, 835–796 B.C. (24:1–27)

Bibliography

Graham, P. "A Connection Proposed between 2 Chr 24, 26 and Ezra 9–10." *ZAW* 97 (1985) 256–58. **Hurowitz, V.** "A Fiscal Practice in the Ancient Near East: 2 Kgs 12:5–17 and a Letter to Esarhaddon." *JNES* 45 (1986) 289–94. **Luria, B.** "In the Days of Joash, King of Judah." *BMik* 52 (1972) 11–20. **Welch, A. C.** *The Work of the Chronicler.* 78–80. **Zalevsky, S.** "The Problem of Reward in the Story of the Sin of Jehoash and His Punishment." *BMik* 21/65 (1975/76) 278–88.

Translation

[1] *Joash was seven years old when he began to reign, and he ruled in Jerusalem for forty years. His mother's name was Zibiah; she was from Beersheba.* [2] *Joash did what was right in the eyes of Yahweh all the days of Jehoiada the priest.* [3] *Jehoiada secured two wives for him, and he had sons and daughters.*

[4] *Somewhat later Joash decided to restore the temple of Yahweh.* [5] *He assembled the priests and Levites and said to them, "Go to the cities of Judah and gather the sum annually due from all Israel in order to repair the temple of God. Do it [a] right away." But the Levites did not act at once.*

[6] *The king summoned Jehoiada the high priest [a] and said to him, "Why haven't you sought to have the Levites bring from Judah and Jerusalem the tax imposed by Moses the servant of Yahweh and the assembly of Israel for the Tent of Testimony?"* [7] *(Now that wicked Athaliah and her associates [a] had broken into the temple of God and had even used all the sacred implements of the temple of Yahweh for the Baals.)*

[8] *At the king's command they made a chest and set it up outside the gate of the temple of Yahweh.* [9] *They issued a decree throughout Judah and Jerusalem to bring to Yahweh the tax that Moses the servant of God had imposed on Israel in the wilderness.* [10] *All the leaders of the people rejoiced; [a] they brought the money and cast it into the chest, until it was full.*

[11] *Whenever the Levites would bring the chest to the royal officers, and they saw how much there was, the royal secretary and the representative of the high priest would come and empty it, return it and set it back up in its place. They did this regularly and collected a great sum.*

[12] *The king and Jehoiada would give it to those [a] responsible for the work on the temple of Yahweh; they hired masons and carpenters to restore the temple of Yahweh, along with smiths for the iron and bronze to repair the breeches in the temple.* [13] *Those responsible for the work were diligent, and the restoration progressed in their charge; they restored the temple of God to its original design and repaired it.*

[14] *When they finished they brought the remaining sum to the king and Jehoiada; it was made into utensils for the temple of Yahweh: utensils for the service and for burnt offerings, ladles, and other implements of gold and silver. As long as Jehoiada lived, burnt offerings were presented continually in the temple of Yahweh.*

[15] *Jehoiada died when he was old and full of years; he died when he was a hundred thirty years old.* [16] *They buried him with the kings in the City of David, for he had done good in Israel for God and his temple.*

[17] *After the death of Jehoiada the leaders of Judah came and paid homage to the king, and he began to heed them.* [18] *They forsook the temple*[a] *of Yahweh the God of their fathers and worshiped the Asherah poles and idols. Yahweh*[b] *was angry with Judah and Jerusalem because of their offense,*[c] [19] *so he sent prophets to them to bring them back to Yahweh—he warned them, but they would not listen.*

[20] *Then the spirit of God invested Zechariah son of Jehoiada the priest, and he stood opposite the people and said to them, "Thus says God, 'Why do you transgress the commandments of Yahweh and therefore not prosper? Since you have forsaken Yahweh, he has forsaken you.'"* [21] *But they conspired against him at the king's command and stoned him to death in the courtyard of the temple of Yahweh.* [22] *King Joash had no regard for the loyalty that Jehoiada, Zechariah's father, had shown him, and he killed his son. While he lay dying, Zechariah said, "May Yahweh see and avenge."*

[23] *At the turn of the year an army from Aram went up against him; they came to Judah and Jerusalem and killed all the leaders of the people*[a] *and took all the plunder to the king of Damascus.* [24] *Though the army of Aram had come with only a small force, Yahweh delivered a much larger army into their hands, for they had abandoned Yahweh the God of their fathers; judgment was executed on Joash.* [25] *When the Arameans withdrew, they left Joash severely wounded; his ministers conspired against him because of the murder of Jehoiada's son,*[a] *and they killed him in his bed. He died and they buried him in the City of David, though not in the tombs of the kings.* [26] *These are the names of those who conspired against him: Zabad,*[a] *son of Shimeath, an Ammonite woman, and Jehozabad,*[b] *son of Shimrith,*[c] *a Moabite woman.*

[27] *An account concerning his children, the many prophecies about him,*[a] *and his restoration of God's temple*[b] *is written in the annotations to the record of the kings; Amaziah his son ruled in his place.*

Notes

5.a. G λαλῆσαι reflects different vocalization (לְדַבֵּר).

6.a. The high priest is only here in Chronicles designated הראש. This is probably best understood as an abbreviation of the Chronicler's ordinary designation כהן הראש; see Japhet, *VT* 18 (1968) 343–44; Rudolph, 274. Williamson (320) sees it as evidence for the secondary nature of vv 5b–6; see *Comment* at 24:4–7.

7.a. Athaliah had murdered any potential pretenders to the throne (22:10); בניה must then refer to her associates and retainers. Some repoint instead to בֹּנֶיהָ "her builders," or emend to כֹּהֲנֶיהָ "her priests"; both of these suggestions would refer to the Baal cult sponsored by the queen (23:17).

10.a. G καὶ ἔδωκαν probably derived from reading וישימו instead of וישמחו. Rudolph (274) regards the change from "rejoiced" to "gave" as editorial; the translator of G found rejoicing over a temple tax improbable. See Allen, *GC* 2:156.

12.a. MT is sg, possibly a collective; a few MSS and the versions read pl, as in v 13; cf. 1 Chr 22:15; 27:26.

18.a. 2 MSS read ברית, "covenant," instead of "temple"; G omits the word and translates "forsook Yahweh." The Heb. MSS reflect a misreading by copyists; the omission in G is by analogy with the Chronicler's characteristic use of "forsake Yahweh" (cf. vv 20, 24). Cf. Allen, *GC* 2:104.

18.b. MT does not specify that "Yahweh" was angry, but specification of a divine subject is required by the clause beginning with וישל ה.

18.c. G does not mention "their offense" and reads instead τῇ ἡμέρᾳ ταύτῃ, "this day." This is best explained as an internal G corruption, ἡμέρα was read in place of ἁμαρτία. GL πλημμέλεια, "offense, mistake," preserves the correct reading.

23.a. Literally "leaders of the people among the people."

25.a. 2 Kgs 12:21 [20], "they struck him at Beth Millo that goes down to Silla"; cf. *Comment*.

26.a. 2 Kgs 12:22 [21], "Jozakar": GB, "Zabel."

26.b. GB, "Zozabed."

26.c. 2 Kgs 12:22, "Shomer."

27.a. With the K; Q appears to intend "with reference to his children, may the prophecies against him increase," i.e., an allusion to the imprecation of the dying Zechariah. המשׂא does not refer to the tribute (GL, καὶ πλεῖστα λήμματα) imposed on him by the Arameans or the tax levied for the temple construction; rather it refers to the other prophecies ("burdens") alluded to in v 19. Par οἱ πέντε reflects misreading המשׂא as חמשׁה, "five."

27.b. Par τὰ λοιπά is best explained as an assimilation to Bas (12:19). See Lemke, *Synoptic Studies*, 195–96; Allen, *GC* 1:104, 209.

Form/Structure/Setting

The accounts of the reign of Joash in 2 Kgs 12 and 2 Chr 24 are quite different. Though both narratives contain accounts of the restoration of the temple and of the Aramean offensive, there is comparatively little direct verbal dependence in 2 Chr 24 on the earlier history. Since most of the variations in his account can be traced to elements in the Chronicler's outlook, scholars are divided over the question of whether the Chronicler has used some different source altogether (e.g., the Midrash on the Book of Kings [24:27]—cf. Rudolph, 273–74) or has simply recast 2 Kgs 12 in terms of his own *Tendenz*. Among those scholars who argue that the Chronicler was following 2 Kings 12, debate has focused particularly on the question of whether vv 5b–6 represent a secondary insertion into the Chronicler's original narrative (e.g., Welch, *Work*, 78–80; Williamson, 318–20; see *Comment* below on vv 4–7).

The major differences between the accounts betray the Chronicler's interests and methods. (1) The events of 2 Kgs 12 are presented in ways characteristically reflecting the Chronicler's theology of immediate retribution (see the introductory essay to 2 Chr 10–36, "Reward and Punishment in Chronicles: The Theology of Immediate Retribution"). Joash's reign is divided into two distinct periods, one of blessing and obedience followed by another of disobedience, rebuke, and judgment. Where Kings reports the attack of the Arameans without any theological evaluation (2 Kgs 12:17–18), the Chronicler describes it as judgment for forsaking the LORD (v 24); where Kings simply reports a conspiracy against the king (2 Kgs 12:20–21), the Chronicler records the reason (v 25). The death notice is similarly recast with retributive significance (v 25 // 2 Kgs 12:21). (2) The Chronicler has included a role for the Levites in the temple restoration (vv 5, 6, 11), though they are not mentioned in 2 Kgs 12; the inclusion reflects the author's pervasive concern with the Levites. (3) The Chronicler often draws parallels between the temple and the tabernacle, particularly in his account of the reign of Solomon (Williamson, 319; see the introductory essay to 2 Chr 1–9, "The Chronicler's Solomon"). The mention of the Mosaic tabernacle tax and the joy with which the people gave (vv 9–10) are two examples in this pericope.

The two accounts of the temple restoration are hard to reconcile in some of their details. Each seems concerned with different temple revenues (24:5 // 2 Kgs 12:4). Different locations are assigned the offering chest (24:8 // 2 Kgs 12:9). One account says that some of the funds were used to make cultic implements, while the other specifically rejects this use (24:14 // 2 Kgs 12:13). Whatever suggestions are offered for these differences (see *Comment* below), the underlying sociopolitical issues seem clear enough. By the twenty-third year of his reign (2 Kgs 12:6), when Joash was no longer the ward of the priest Jehoiada, a disagreement had arisen between crown and cult over how to pay for the restoration work. Joash may have been seeking to reassert royal prerogatives over the cult, prerogatives that had been curtailed in the covenant made when he was a child at the time of his accession (23:3). The priests were probably looking to the royal treasury for the necessary funds (cf. 1 Chr 29:1–5); the king, on the other hand, attempted to reallocate temple revenues (2 Kgs 12:7) so that some of the funds which had gone to the maintenance of the priests would be restricted to use in the restoration project. The priests and Levites resisted by not collecting or expending funds for the repair work. Something of a compromise appears to have been effected: Joash prevailed by reallocating the census tax; crown and cult would look to the private sector by using revenue from the census tax and by soliciting voluntary contributions. The cultic personnel had to accept some curtailment of the funds used for their maintenance (2 Kgs 12:16). See also Luria, *BMik* 52 [1972] 11–20.

The following devices are used to mark paragraph boundaries: temporal phrases (24:4, 11, 14, 17, 23) and changes in explicit subject (24:6, 8, 12, 15, 20).

Comment

1–3 The Chronicler has divided the reign of Joash into two distinct periods: the good years while Jehoiada influenced the king, and the bad years after Jehoiada's death; this is a characteristic feature in the Chronicler's accounts of the individual kings. This division is already implicit in the wording of 2 Kgs 12:3 [2], that Joash did the right "for all his days while Jehoiada instructed him" (though for a contrary reading, see Williamson, 319; Gray, 583). The Chronicler omits the mention in Kings that Joash did not remove the high places (2 Kgs 12:4 [3]); since this would be out of character with his presentation of the early years of Joash, the matter of the high places is delayed to 24:18.

Jehoiada's securing wives for Joash addressed the dynastic threat that had brought him to the throne. Through the subsequent children the Davidic dynasty would begin to rebuild and broaden after the murders of members of the royal house during the reigns of Jehoram, Ahaziah, and Athaliah. V 3 is unique to Chronicles: beyond the concern with rebuilding the Davidic household, for the Chronicler numerous progeny were a token of divine blessing (1 Chr 14:2–7; 25:4–5; 26:4–5; 2 Chr 11:18–23; 13:21). The additional material the Chronicler inserted regarding the wives and children of Joash was apparently drawn from the source he cites (24:27).

4–7 Royal initiative was crucial to the building of the temple at the time of David and Solomon; here royal initiative leads to its restoration. However, royal initiative and precedent would also have led the priests and Levites to expect the royal treasury to bear much of the expense. The king instead seeks to finance the restoration work by reallocating some of the temple income used for the maintenance of the cultic staff to the building project. The priests respond with inaction. See the discussion above under *Form/Structure/Setting*.

In Kings Joash proposed that three different sources of income—all monetary offerings—be used for rehabilitating the temple (2 Kgs 12:4). The כסף עובר איש of 2 Kgs 12:5 reflects the language of the cultic census tax in Exod 30:12–16 (עובר, "money of the one who crosses over," is paid by כל העובר, "all who cross over," 30:13; cf. 38:25–26; Num 31:48–50; Neh 10:32; Matt 17:24); this is the same sum described by the Chronicler as "the tax imposed by Moses the servant of Yahweh . . . for the Tent of Testimony" (v 6). See also J. Liver, "The Ransom of the Half Shekel," in *Yehezkel Kaufmann Jubilee Volume*, ed. M. Haran (Jerusalem, 1960), 54–67; and E. Speiser, "Census and Ritual Expiation," *BASOR* 149 (1958) 17–25. The Chronicler focuses on this source only. Characteristic of his general interests, he adds a note regarding the participation of the Levites (vv 5–6, 11) who are otherwise unmentioned in Kings apart from 1 Kgs 8:4, 12:31.

The chronology of the events is uncertain. Neither history indicates when Joash first sought to refurbish the temple or how long the delay was. The deuteronomic historian reports that during his twenty-third year (2 Kgs 12:6) Joash summoned Jehoiada a second time on this matter, implying that the delay had been considerable. In spite of his frequent use of chronological data as a vehicle for presenting his theological judgments, the Chronicler omits this chronological notice, replacing it with the less specific comment that "the Levites did not act at once" (v 5), perhaps to somewhat mitigate a negative judgment regarding the delay by the priests and Levites.

Though the sequence of events is also somewhat difficult, it is not implausible. Joash first orders the priests and Levites to make a circuit of the cities of Judah ("Israel," 24:5; cf. 24:16) to collect the temple tax (v 5) and then later summons Jehoiada to censure him for his delay in performing the tax collection itinerary (v 6). The end product is not an itineration, but rather a decree that the money be brought to the temple and deposited in an offering box. This appears to be a substantive change—probably a compromise between crown and cult, and perhaps putting the offering on more of a voluntary basis. Both Welch (*Work*, 78–80) and Williamson (319–20), however, argue that vv 5b–6 are secondary, an insertion from a later glossator seeking to harmonize the Chronicler's account with that in Kings. If vv 5b–6 are omitted, the result is a simpler narrative: Joash begins with a speech about the wickedness of Athaliah, then issues a decree that the tax be brought to the offering box; the people rejoice and give willingly. On this scenario, there is no abortive beginning, and the priests and Levites are exonerated. Williamson provides six lines of argument. (1) V 7 explains why Joash wanted to make the repairs and is an unsuitable sequel to v 6. However, v 7 can equally well be taken as a parenthetical remark by the Chronicler, elaborating on the statement in his *Vorlage* (2 Kgs 12:6) that the temple had sustained damage; the Chronicler specifies the causes of the damage, otherwise unmentioned in Kings. (2) V 8 represents a new idea on the part of the king, and we are left with no indication of the outcome of the plan originally proposed in v 5. Of course, the narrative is not smooth, but the reader is allowed to infer that the original plan was abandoned—the narrator is not compelled to state that obvious fact. (3) The expression used to designate the tabernacle (אהל העדות, "Tent of Testimony") is used only here in Chronicles, and therefore reflects the usage of a later glossator. However, it should also be noted that the Chronicler varies his own terms of reference to the tabernacle, e.g., 2 Chr 1:3 (אהל מועד האלהים), a designation used nowhere else in the Bible, but in a passage where there is no doubt that it came from the Chronicler's hand. This line of argument would be valid only if there were some additional controls; even if a particular usage is characteristic of an author, nothing precludes his using other designations. The use of עדות in this case could have been influenced by the use in 23:11. (4) Similarly the designation of the high priest as הראש is not characteristic of the Chronicler; however, it is best thought of as an abbreviation of his usual usage (see the note at 24:6.a). (5) Though the priests and Levites are summoned in v 5a, only the Levites are reprimanded in v 6. However, rather than see different authors here, it is plausible to understand that the greater number (Levites) includes the lesser (priests)—repetition would not be essential. (6) It would be surprising to find criticism of the Levites in the Chronicler's work. The Chronicler's interest in the Levites is one of the hallmarks of his history, and they are presented in a favorable light. However, even in vv 5b–6, there is some concern to attenuate the negative judgment on the Levites by removing the chronological notice found in 2 Kgs 12:6 (see the preceding paragraph). In a sense this argument could be reversed: the concern to alleviate the guilt of the priests and Levites is a mark of the genuineness of the verses in question. The Chronicler's idealization of David did not prevent at least one incident critical of his rule (1 Chr 21), nor would interest in the Levites preclude some censure for them. (7) The expression "from year to year" (v 5b) conflicts with the Chronicler's presentation of Joash's reform as a single act of repair, one collection raised for a single purpose. However, it is equally plausible to view the king's decree as reassigning this portion of the annual temple revenues for a special purpose during the particular year, or perhaps we are even to infer that the tax had not been collected for a long period, certainly not during the reign of Athaliah. Vv 5b–6 are not smooth and do present some difficulties, but the difficulties may not be so great as to require positing a later author for the section.

8–11   Donations to the first temple were not brought in the form of coins—that would be an anachronism. Judging from the analogies with Mesopotamian temples prior to the use of coinage, offerings of precious metals would have come in the form of ingots, ores, and amalgams of various grades. Some temple personnel served primarily as goldsmiths or assayers; these would refine, hammer, and cast the offerings into the desired shapes for temple paraphernalia, make ingots for storage in the temple treasury, and make repairs to damaged implements. Foundries were commonly associated with

Mesopotamian temples, and one can infer that the temple in Jerusalem probably had a similar operation (C. Torrey, "The Foundry of the Second Temple at Jerusalem," *JBL* 55 [1936] 247–60; D. Weisberg, *Guild Structure and Political Allegiance in Early Achaemenid Mesopotamia* [New Haven: Yale UP, 1967] 60–63; A. Oppenheim, "A Fiscal Practice of the Ancient Near East," *JNES* 6 [1947] 116–20).

One characteristic feature of ancient Near Eastern temples was a box or basket (Akkadian *qīpu* or *arannu*; *arannu* = Heb. אֲרוֹן, 24:8) put in an accessible location for worshipers to deposit their offerings. In the Mesopotamian temples a royal official represented the king's interests in the temple's financial affairs (cf. 24:11).

The writer of Kings locates the offering box אֵצֶל הַמִּזְבֵּחַ בְּיָמִין, "beside the altar on the south side" (2 Kgs 12:10 [9]; cf. Lev 1:16; 6:3 [6:10]); Deut 16:21; 1 Kgs 2:29). The Chronicler places it instead "outside the gate of the temple of Yahweh" (24:8). This modification appears to bring the location of the offering box into conformity with the practices of the second temple period; by the Chronicler's times access to the inner court was restricted to cultic personnel (cf. Amos 2:8; cf. also the concern to protect the sanctity of the inner court in 2 Chr 23). Otherwise the altar in this case must refer to other than the main altar in the temple courtyard, perhaps a smaller altar at the threshold; others emend the text of 2 Kgs 12:10 to read "doorpost" (מְזוּזָה; cf. Gray, 584) instead of "altar."

The Chronicler frequently draws parallels between the tabernacle and the first temple. The joyous, unfettered giving of the wilderness community (Exod 36:4–7) was repeated in the history of the first temple (1 Chr 29:1–9; 2 Chr 24:9–10); for the Chronicler this spirit of joyous giving was of homiletical relevance to encourage a similar attitude toward the second temple in his own day.

12–14 The "original design" (v 13) was the product of divine instruction (1 Chr 28:11–19) just as the tabernacle had been (Exod 25:9, 40).

The Chronicler seems deliberately to contradict the earlier record regarding the use of the funds. Where 2 Kgs 12:13–14 says that the funds were used for wages and not for ritual paraphernalia, the Chronicler specifically reports the manufacture of ritual implements (v 14). These differences are not difficult to harmonize: none of the funds were used for equipment (Kings) until the repairs were finished, and surplus monies could be redirected (Chronicles). Though the harmonization is easy, it is perhaps more germane to the intent of the Chronicler to note again how the author has drawn a parallel with the building of the tabernacle and the use of those offerings to make ritual implements and furnishings (Exod 25; 31:1–10).

"As long as Jehoiada lived" (v 14). These words form an inclusio with 24:2. They reflect the regular practice of the Chronicler to use chronological notes to divide the accounts of individual reigns into good and bad periods; the transition to the record of Joash's apostasy begins with the similar notice at the beginning of v 15.

15–16 For the Chronicler living to an advanced age was a token of divine blessing. The figure of a hundred and thirty years has been considered by many as symbolic of blessing rather than a reliable indication of Jehoiada's age at death; it places Jehoiada's death at an age older than Aaron (123—Num 33:39), Moses (120—Deut 34:7), and Joshua (110—Josh 24:29). Such longevity would be unique among age figures during the kingdom period. Further, if Josheba, Jehoiada's wife, were twenty years old at the time of the death of her father Jehoram (22:11), who himself died at forty years old (21:5), she would have lived through the one-year reign of Ahaziah (22:2) and the six years under Athaliah (22:12), and would have been about twenty-seven at the time of Jehoiada's coup; Jehoiada lived at least until some period after the twenty-third year (2 Kgs 12:6) of Joash's forty-year reign (24:1). If Jehoiada lived until only two years before the death of Joash, his wife Josheba would have been about sixty-five, i.e., half the age of Jehoiada at the time of his death, so that he would have been near eighty if she had married at about age fifteen (cf. Rudolph, 277). Many have found that age difference sufficiently improbable as to suggest that the figure is symbolic. However, marriage of much older men to younger women is a common feature among tribal societies in the modern world and presumably also in antiquity (cf. Ruth 3:10). Even though Jehoiada's age at death would be unique, there is no way positively to preclude its being an accurate figure. See A. Malamat, "Longevity: Biblical Concepts and Some Ancient Near Eastern Parallels," *AfO* Beihefte 19 (1982) 215–24.

By virtue of his regency over his young ward Joash, Jehoiada was somewhat a priest/king, and he is given a royal burial among the graves of the kings, a sharp contrast to the burial of Joash (24:25). The role played by Jehoiada may reflect also the growing influence of the high priest in the absence of a monarchy during the post-exilic period.

17–19   Bad advice once again leads to unhappy results for a king of Judah (22:3–4; 18:4–11; 10:8–11). The leaders of Judah who advised Joash are not further described; presumably they had lost influence at the time of the coup and during the hegemony of the hierocratic party and were able to reassert themselves only after the death of Jehoiada.

The Chronicler's mention of the worship of Asherah poles and idols elaborates on the statement in the parallel history that the high places were not removed (2 Kgs 12:3).

The use of עזב ("abandon, forsake") is characteristic of the Chronicler's theology of immediate retribution; see the introductory essay to 2 Chr 10–36, "Reward and Punishment in Chronicles: The Theology of Immediate Retribution." Though the Chronicler demonstrates the coherence of action and effect by showing judgment for wrongdoing, sanctions are ordinarily imposed only after a prophet offers hope of escape through repentance and forgiveness (Williamson, 323). Many prophets confronted Joash (24:19, 27), but the writer elaborates only on the death of Zechariah (24:20–22).

20–22   Zechariah's sermon after the spirit of God clothed him (לבש, 1 Chr 12:18–19; Judg 6:34) draws upon Num 14:41 where defeat before enemies is also the result of disobedience (24:23–24; Num 14:42–43; cf. Coggins, 241). Prosper (צלח) is another term frequently used in Chronicles as a vehicle for the author's theology of immediate retribution (1 Chr 22:11, 13; 29:23; 2 Chr 13:12; 14:6; 20:20; 26:5; 31:21; 32:30).

There is great irony in the passage: Zechariah, the son of the priest who had saved the throne for Joash, is murdered in the place where Joash was protected during the coup (see *Comment* at 23:9–11, 15–16); Jehoiada, who had preserved the sanctity of the temple from bloodshed, installed the king who would murder his own son there. Joash falls to treason (קשׁר, 24:25), just as Athaliah (23:13) had before him.

Jesus mentions the murder of Zechariah (Matt 23:35; Luke 11:50–51); his appeal to the records of the first and last murders in the OT indicates that Chronicles was considered the last book of the Heb. Scriptures by the time of Christ.

23–24 Punishment for the murder of Zechariah follows right away; the Chronicler characteristically uses a chronological note ("at the turn of the year") to stress the immediacy. Though Kings reports the incident without a theological evaluation (2 Kgs 12:17–18), the Chronicler specifically describes the invasion as retribution for forsaking God. There are substantive differences between the two accounts. In Kings the object of Hazael's attack was primarily the coastal plain (Gath) and the strategic coastal highway: Hazael appears to accompany the army and is deterred from attacking Jerusalem by the payment of tribute; Kings makes no mention of the wounding of Joash or the removal of the leaders of Judah, presumably the same advisers who had gained influence after the death of Jehoiada (24:17, 23).

The "turn of the year" was in the spring, at the beginning of the dry season and a period of reduced agricultural activity after harvest; it was "the time when kings go off to war" (1 Chr 20:1; 2 Sam 11:1; 1 Kgs 20:26). The coup of Jehu had left both the Northern and Southern kingdoms in a condition of great military weakness (see *Comment* at 23:1–2); Hazael was quick to exploit the advantage, reducing the army of Jehoahaz in the North to no more than needed for a good parade (2 Kgs 13:7), and taking tribute from Joash in the South.

In the holy war ideology of Israel, Yahweh fought for his people so that a small force could overcome a larger (13:3–18; 14:8–15; 1 Kgs 20:27; 1 Sam 14:6; Judg 7; cf. 25:7–8); here the reverse happened: due to the infidelity of Joash, with Yahweh's aid a smaller enemy force overturned the army of Judah.

25–26 Not only does the Chronicler add a theological evaluation not found in Kings for the attack of Hazael, he also specifies that the conspiracy against Joash was the result of his murdering Zechariah. The death notice in Chronicles also differs from that in Kings in several other respects: the burial site, conspiracy participants, and location of death are all modified.

The Chronicler commonly uses burial notices to exhibit a theme important to him: righteous kings are buried in honor, while the ignominy of the unrighteous extends even to their interment (16:14; 21:19–20; 26:23; 28:27). In this context the refusal to bury the unrighteous Joash in the tombs of the kings contrasts sharply to the burial of the righteous priest Jehoiada there (24:16).

The conspirators are named differently in Chronicles than in Kings; see notes at v 26.a,b,c. The Chronicler, probably due to the text he had before him, has understood the names of both parents as feminine (where at least Shomer (2 Kgs 12:22 [21]) appears to be a masculine name) and has added the note that they were foreign women, one an Ammonite and the other a Moabite. Ackroyd (161) sees the Chronicler's implication as that "when king (or people) turn to alien gods, their judgment will be at the hands of alien instruments"; Elmslie (279), on the other hand, sees an emphasis on the evils of foreign marriages (cf. Neh 13:23). Neither of these suggestions can be clearly demonstrated as part of the general *Tendenz* of Chronicles. See also P. Graham, "A Connection Proposed between 2 Chr 24, 26 and Ezra 9–10," *ZAW* 97 (1985) 256–58.

2 Kgs 12:21 [20] indicates that Joash was wounded at "Beth Millo on the way down to Silla"; perhaps because he was not familiar with the location or because of information in an additional source, the Chronicler says simply that they "killed him in his bed."

27 The author mentioned that a number of prophets had confronted Joash (24:19) and refers to a source containing a further account of those prophecies; the information about the children of Joash (24:3) presumably came from the same source. On the use of *midrash,* see *Comment* at 13:22.

Explanation

As with his accounts of all the kings of Judah after the united monarchy, the major operative influence in the Chronicler's recasting of the account in Kings is his theology of immediate retribution. No weal or woe is left unexplained in the reign of Joash.

Christian readers of the chapter appreciate a number of analogies and motific parallels with later events of redemptive history. While Jesus would appeal to the death of Zechariah (Matt 23:35; Luke 11:50–51) in speaking of the last murder in the OT, there was yet another son and prophet who would die (Mark 12:1–12) as the result of a conspiracy against him (Matt 26:3–4). The dying words of these two prophets contrast, the one an imprecation (24:22) and the other a plea for forgiveness (Luke 23:34). "When they hurled their insults at him, he did not retaliate; when he suffered, he made no threats" (1 Pet 2:23). Jesus too would "renovate" the temple, in three days and with living stones.

The Reign of Amaziah, 796–767 B.C. (25:1–28)

Bibliography

Luria, B. "Amaziah, King of Judah, and the Gods of Edom." *BMik* 30/102 (1984/85) 353–60.

Translation

¹*Amaziah was twenty-five years old when he became king, and he ruled twenty-nine years in Jerusalem. His mother's name was Jehoaddan; she was from Jerusalem.* ²*He did what was right in the eyes of Yahweh, though not wholeheartedly.*[a]

³*After the kingdom was firmly in his control,*[a] *he killed his servants who had assassinated his father the king.* ⁴*However, he did not execute their sons because of what is written in the law, in the book of Moses,*[a] *which Yahweh commanded, saying, "You shall not kill fathers because of their children or children because of their fathers; rather each should die for his own sins."*[b]

⁵*Amaziah assembled Judah and arranged them by their paternal families under leaders of thousands and hundreds for all Judah and Benjamin; he mustered all who were twenty years old and above. He found that there were three hundred thousand select troops ready for war, carrying shield and spear.* ⁶*He also hired one hundred thousand warriors from Israel for a hundred talents of silver.*

⁷*A man of God came to him and said, "O King, these troops from Israel must not go with you, for Yahweh is not with Israel—not with any Ephraimites!* ⁸*But if you go [with them],*[a] *fight valiantly in the battle! God will overthrow you before the enemy, for God has the power to help or to overthrow."*

⁹*Amaziah said to the man of God, "What is to be done about the hundred talents that I paid for these Israelite troops?"*

The man of God answered, "Yahweh can give you far more than this."

¹⁰*Amaziah then separated out the troops that had come to him from Ephraim in order to send them home. Their anger burned hot against Judah, and they set out for home in a rage.*

¹¹*Amaziah took heart, led his army to the Valley of Salt, and struck down ten thousand men of Seir.* ¹²*The men of Judah took ten thousand alive and brought them to the top of a cliff;*[a] *they threw them from the cliff so that all were dashed to pieces.*

¹³*Now the troops that Amaziah had turned away from going with him to battle raided towns in Judah from Samaria to Beth Horon, massacred three thousand people, and carried off much plunder.*

¹⁴*When Amaziah returned from defeating the Edomites, he brought back the gods of the people of Seir; he set them up as his gods, worshiped before them, and burned sacrifices to them.* ¹⁵*The anger of Yahweh flared against Amaziah, and he sent a prophet to him, who said, "Why are you seeking the gods of this nation when they could not deliver their own people from your hand?"*

¹⁶*While he was speaking to him, the king said to him, "Have we made you a*

counsellor to the king? Desist! Why should they cut you down?" So the prophet
stopped, but first he said, *"I know that Yahweh has determined to destroy you
because you have done this and have not heeded my counsel."*

[17] *Amaziah king of Judah consulted his advisers and sent a message to Jehoash
son of Jehoahaz son of Jehu, king of Israel, "Come let us meet face to face."*

[18] *Then Jehoash king of Israel sent a message to Amaziah, king of Judah, and
said, "A thistle in Lebanon sent a message to a cedar in Lebanon and said, 'Give
me your daughter as a wife for my son,' but a wild animal in Lebanon was passing
by and trampled the thistle down.* [19] *You[a] have defeated Edom, you say to yourself,
and now you are proud and arrogant. But go home! Why look for trouble when
you and Judah with you will fall!"* [20] *But Amaziah would not listen, for this was
from God in order that he might hand them over because they sought the gods of
Edom.*

[21] *Then Jehoash king of Israel went up, and he and Amaziah king of Judah
faced one another at Beth Shemesh in Judah.* [22] *The men of Judah were routed
before Israel and fled to their homes.* [23] *Jehoash king of Israel captured Amaziah
king of Judah, son of Joash, son of Jehoahaz,[a] at Beth Shemesh and brought him
to Jerusalem. He broke down the wall of Jerusalem from the Ephraim Gate to the
Corner[b] Gate, a distance of four hundred cubits.* [24] *He took[a] all the gold and
silver and implements found in the temple of God in the care of Obed-Edom and
in the treasuries of the royal palace along with some hostages and returned to
Samaria.*

[25] *Amaziah son of Joash, king of Judah, ruled fifteen years after the death of
Jehoash son of Jehoahaz, king of Israel.* [26] *As for the rest of the acts of Amaziah,
from beginning to end, are they not written in the book of the kings of Judah and
Israel?[a]*

[27] *From the time that Amaziah turned from following Yahweh there was a conspiracy
against him in Jerusalem, and he fled to Lachish; they sent men after him to
Lachish and killed him there.* [28] *They brought him up on horses and buried him
with his fathers in the city of Judah.[a]*

Notes

2.a. 2 Kgs 14:3, "but not like his father David; rather he did according to all his father
Joash did." Chr also omits the reference to not removing the high places in 2 Kgs 14:4.

3.a. עליו in 2 Kgs 14:5 = בידו. Par and Bas ἐν χειρὶ αὐτοῦ. Par may be influenced by Bas, or
reflect a different text than MT.

4.a. 2 Kgs 14:6, בספר תורת משה "in the book of the law of Moses."

4.b. The Chronicler switches the passive forms of מות in Deut 24:16 and 2 Kgs 14:6 to
actives. Cf. קבר in 25:28 and 2 Kgs 14:20. See Kropat, 15.

8.a. "With them" is implied in the context; one need not conjecture a way to recover באלה
or בם in the surrounding text. The syntax of the first half of the verse is difficult. The text
reads lit. "For if you go, do it, be strong in the battle; God will overthrow you. . . ." Par, "If
you endeavor to strengthen yourself with them, God will overthrow . . ."; Vg, "If you plan to
prevail in battle in this way, God will overthrow. . . ." A number of efforts have been made to
retrovert the text underlying the versions (see Rudolph, 278; Allen, *GC* 2:85, 115–16, C-M,
443); however, one could also view the versions as seeking to cope with a difficulty already
found in the MT, and therefore, not as probable witnesses to an alternative text. Others conjecture
by inserting ולא before יכשילך, "if you go [alone], fight valiantly; God will not allow you to to
fall" (see Keil, 421–22). Even though the text is difficult, it is possible to understand the MT
without modification or conjecture as slightly ironic, somewhat analogous to Micaiah's oracle

before Ahab and Jehoshaphat (18:14), in the sense "If you go, fight valiantly—but Yahweh will overthrow. . . ."

12.a. or "Sela"; see *Comment.*

19.a. הנה in 2 Kgs 14:10 = הכה. Many versions read direct discourse, הכיתי, "I have defeated," GᴸL, Tg, Vg.

23.a. "Jehoahaz" is a variant spelling of Ahaziah (cf. 21:17; cf. 2 Kgs 14:13); there is no need to suggest that "son of Jehoahaz" was transposed from after the earlier "king of Israel" (cf. 25:17; C-M, 446). "Son of Jehoahaz" is missing in G, though found in Gᴸ. A parablepsis in Par would account for the missing phrase more readily than suggesting it was not found in the translator's Heb. text (contrast Rudolph, 280; and Allen, *GC* 2:53).

23.b. With 2 Kgs 14:13 and versions, פנה "corner."

24.a. Adding ולקח "he took," with 2 Kgs 14:14. The syntax is eased considerably with a verbal predicate, though ולקח may itself be secondary in Kings; the same need to ease the syntax could have prompted its insertion there. One would expect the less awkward ויקח instead.

26.a. 2 Kgs 14:18, ספר דברי הימים למלכי יהודה "the books of the chronicles of the kings of Judah."

28.a. 2 Kgs 14:20, Bas, Par, Vg, and a few Heb. MSS, "city of David." This sort of correction in texts of Chronicles is a harmonization, perhaps unconscious, with the ordinary designation of Jerusalem in the Bible, particularly in the burial notices in Chronicles (12:16; 16:14; 21:20; 24:25; et al.). It is far easier to account for the correction than to explain a change to "Judah"; therefore, MT is likely original in this case in spite of the preponderance of external evidence. "City of Judah" is a name for Jerusalem attested in extrabiblical records (Myers, 144; C-M, 447).

Form/Structure/Setting

The Chronicler's account of Amaziah follows fairly closely the record in 2 Kgs 14:1–20, except for 25:5–16 which is unique to Chronicles and represents the Chronicler's expansion on one verse in the earlier narrative (2 Kgs 14:7). Where the author of Kings mentions the successful war with Edom only as a prelude to Amaziah's challenge to Jehoash, the Chronicler expands the account to provide the theological rationale both for the victory over Edom and the defeat before Israel.

Though the Chronicler is clearly dependent on Kings for much of his account, there has been much speculation about his sources for the nonsynoptic portion of the chapter (25:5–16). Since the development of the account is so characteristic of the author's method, and since the prophet who denounces Amaziah is unnamed, some have felt that the entire section was "wholly a product of Midrashic fantasy" (C-M, 442). However, a number of small details suggest that the author was using some other source. There is a tension between vv 9 and 13 (Rudolph, 281; Williamson, 327–29): the promise of 25:9 seems to imply that all would go well for Amaziah if he dismissed the Ephraimite mercenaries. The Chronicler also does not report any characteristic theological rationale to explain what Amaziah had done to deserve the treatment he received in the attack on the cities of Judah. Unless the author was writing under the constraint of an additional source, it is difficult to explain why he would have incorporated or simply fabricated those portions of the narrative that do not fit with the prophetic promise (Williamson, 128). Furthermore, if the Chronicler were composing of whole cloth, one would expect that the prophet be given a name or associated in some way with some other known prophetic figure; the fact that the prophet is unnamed argues instead for the genuineness of the narrative.

The onset of paragraphs in the chapter is indicated largely by the use of explicit subjects, ordinarily the name of a king (25:5, 10, 11, 13, 17, 18, 21), and the use of ויהי-clauses with an indication of time (25:3, 14, 16, 25; cf. 25:27). Some portions are structured by repartee (25:7–9; 16).

Comment

1–2 The Chronicler routinely omits synchronisms with the Northern kings in his accession notices (2 Kgs 14:1). He also omits the reference to the high places in 2 Kgs 14:4; he makes the same omission in the case of Joash (24:2 // 2 Kgs 12:4), Uzziah (26:4 // 2 Kgs 15:4), and Jotham (27:2 // 2 Kgs 15:35). The Chronicler often structures the reign of a king into a good period followed by turning away, disobedience, and judgment; therefore, negative comments are held to the second half of the account, whereas in Kings the summary judgment about a reign is given immediately and regularly concerns the high places for Judean kings. The Chronicler also omits the statement that Amaziah did not follow the practices of David, but rather the example of Joash (2 Kgs 14:3); he inserts instead a summary statement that he did what was right, though not *wholeheartedly* (15:17; 16:9; 19:9; 1 Chr 12:38 [39]; 28:9; 29:9, 19). While the Chronicler often divides an individual reign into distinct periods of obedience and disobedience, here he depicts Amaziah as fundamentally half-hearted and mediocre from the beginning (McConville, 214).

Though Amaziah is assigned a reign of twenty-nine years (2 Kgs 14:2), he was apparently the sole monarch for a much shorter period. Amaziah's son Uzziah came to the throne in the twenty-seventh year of Jeroboam II (2 Kgs 15:1). Jeroboam had a reign of forty-one years (2 Kgs 14:23), so his death occurred fourteen years after the death of Amaziah in Jeroboam's twenty-seventh year; however, when Zechariah succeeded Jeroboam II, Uzziah was already in his thirty-eighth year of reign. If this data is to be accepted at face value, Uzziah must have been coregent with his father for twenty-four years of his fifty-two-year reign, i.e., he came to regency in the fifth year of Amaziah (Thiele, *Numbers,* rev. ed. [1983] 63–64). This long coregency may have been the result of the capture of Amaziah by Jehoash of Israel (25:23). Two additional items suggest this to be the case (Thiele, 115). (1) The statement that Amaziah lived fifteen years after the death of Jehoash (25:25; 2 Kgs 14:17) is the only one of its kind in the chronological data for the kingdoms of Israel and Judah. It suggests that Amaziah was released from imprisonment in Israel after the death of his captor and outlived him by fifteen years. (2) The statement that "all the people of Judah took Uzziah when he was sixteen years old and made him king" (26:1 // 2 Kgs 14:21) may also imply that the ordinary orderly succession from dying father to eldest son had not taken place in this case; the people were forced to intervene in some way due to a crisis, presumably the capture of Amaziah. Though Amaziah may have returned to Jerusalem after his release, Uzziah would have been ruling by then for ten years and have been twenty-six years old; the power was probably shared between them, though Amaziah was the actual king and would eventually fall to a conspiracy (25:27).

3–4 Amaziah may have been motivated to avenge the death of his father when he executed the assassins; however, his own consolidation of power and elimination of potential rivals may also have been a factor (see *Comment* at 1:1–3).

The stress on individual responsibility in 2 Kgs 14:6 and its citation of Deut 24:16 were quite congenial to the emphases of the Chronicler's theology; see the introductory essay to 2 Chr 10–36, "Reward and Punishment in Chronicles: The Theology of Immediate Retribution." The principle of not punishing children for the sins of their fathers was not always observed in Israel: Achan's family was obliterated for his sin (Josh 7:24), and the children of Naboth were also eliminated when he was killed (2 Kgs 9:26). The strains both of individual responsibility and of corporate repercussions (Deut 5:9) are alike found in the OT. Jeremiah (31:29–31) and Ezekiel (18:1, 19–24), while ministering to communities suffering for the sins of the fathers, both emphasized individual responsibility. Cf. the Middle Assyrian Law, A, no. 2 (Pritchard, *ANET*, 180) in which a woman guilty of blasphemy is punished, but her husband and children were not.

5–6 Amaziah's military enrollment is similar to that by David (1 Chr 21; 27:23–24), Solomon (2:16 [17]), Asa (14:8), and Jehoshaphat (17:14–19); a folk army was raised along the lines of ancient tribal subdivisions. Twenty years old was the traditional age of enrollment (Exod 30:14; 38:26; Lev 27:3–5; Num 1; 1 Chr 27:23; 23:24; 2 Chr 31:17). The fact that Benjamin is included suggests that Judah continued to exercise hegemony in that region; according to the Chronicler, Benjamin was not counted in David's disastrous enrollment (1 Chr 21:6), though it was included in the counts of Asa and Jehoshaphat.

Amaziah's force of 300,000 is smaller than that of Asa (580,000) or Jehoshaphat (1.16 million), and the Chronicler may have intended this to explain why Amaziah hired the additional troops from Israel. The large numbers are problematic in all of these cases; see *Comment* at 13:3 and 14:8–9.

The fee paid for the mercenaries would have been one talent per thousand; with three thousand shekels in each talent, the fee would have been three shekels for each man, a sum slightly more than an ounce.

7–8 A central theme in the Chronicler's theology is the necessity of trusting God; all foreign alliances are repudiated as an implicit failure to rely on Yahweh alone (16:2–9; 19:1–3; 20:15–17; 20:35–37; 32:7–8). Commonly associated with this rejection of alliances and reliance on Yahweh is the holy war theme of Yahweh's fighting for the few against the many (13:3–18; 14:8–15; 1 Kgs 20:27; 1 Sam 14:6; Judg 7; see *Comment* at 24:23–24); Amaziah need not fear losing a fourth of his army in sending the Ephraimite mercenaries home, for Yahweh "has the power to help."

Though the Chronicler is ever open to the repentance of the Northern Kingdom or its individual citizens and to the reunification of "all Israel" (11:13–17; 28:9–15; 30:1–12; 34:33), his attitude to the Northern tribes as a political entity is that "Yahweh is not with Israel." The short speech of the unnamed man of God is reminiscent of Abijah's sermon (13:4–12; cf. 19:1–13).

11–12 The entire narrative of 25:5–16 is an expansion on the one verse in 2 Kgs 14:7. The earlier history had reported Amaziah's victory over Edom to explain his pride and subsequent challenge to Jehoash of Israel; the Chronicler has characteristically elaborated on the incident, providing the theological rationale for Amaziah's victory, as well as later for his defeat. Where "Sela" appears to be a geographical name in 2 Kgs 14:7, renamed Joktheel, in Chronicles סֶלַע is used in its ordinary meaning "cliff, precipice" and provides the means used to execute ten thousand vanquished Edomites. The site of Sela has traditionally been associated with Petra (cf. Bas of 2 Kgs 14:7); however, since Amaziah was unable to realize the strategic goal of occupying the port of Elath (26:2), it would also seem improbable that he could successfully capture the Edomite capital east of the rift valley. Further, though an argument from silence, if the name Joktheel had been given to as important a site as Petra, one would expect its recurrence in some other context (Gray, 605). Sela is a common noun and may have been used to designate a number of sites. Es-Sela, two and a half miles northwest of Bozrah (Buseira), may preserve the correct identification; it is directly across from the Ascent of the Akrabbim with which Sela is associated in Judg 1:36. See the debate on the identification of the site in Rainey, *IDB Suppl,* 800; J. Bartlett, "The Land of Seir and the Brotherhood of Edom," *JTS* n.s. 20 (1967) 1–20; M. Haran, "Observations on the Historical Background of Amos 1:2–2:6," *IEJ* 18 (1968) 207–12; C. Bennett, "Notes and News," *PEQ* (1966) 123–26. The *Valley of Salt* is the depression of the Arabah south of the Dead Sea; it was the site of an earlier victory by David (1 Chr 18:12 [13]).

13 Cf. 25:10. No reason is offered for the anger and attack of the dismissed mercenaries. Presumably they had received at least a portion of the sum agreed upon (25:6, 9). Perhaps the fact that they would not share in any spoil from the battle is the implicit reason.

The actions of the mercenaries may have been included by the Chronicler both (1) because they were in his source (see above, *Form/Structure/Setting*) and (2) as an inciting incident for Amaziah's challenge against Jehoash after his victory over Edom.

It is also worth noting that the Chronicler does not take his theology of immediate retribution to its logical extreme by making it some barren, unalterable law that admits of no exception (Rudolph, *VT* 4 [1954] 405). Here the attack of the Ephraimites is in some tension with the promise in 25:6, which suggests that all will go well for Amaziah if he is obedient; the Chronicler does not explain this plundering as the result of some transgression on Amaziah's part.

The statement that the Ephraimites plundered "from Samaria to Beth Horon" presents a difficulty. If they set out from Samaria, this plundering must be some subsequent raid after they had been dismissed by Amaziah and did not take place on the return trip. Further, Samaria would scarcely be considered a Judean town that the Ephraimites would plunder. For this reason Rudolph (278–79) conjectures that Samaria is an error for some orthographically similar name of a Judean town, perhaps Migron, a town in Judah near Gibeah (1 Sam 14:2; Isa 10:28; cf. Myers, 143; Williamson, 330). Keil (423–24) defends the text, arguing that the troops were dismissed from Amaziah's service after they had assembled in Samaria but before they had joined with Amaziah's army in Jerusalem. When Amaziah went to battle to the south against Edom, these mercenaries seized the opportunity to raid Amaziah's undefended northern frontier.

14–15 The spoliation of a vanquished people's deities is well attested in the literatures of the ancient Near East. It may at first glance seem absurd or improbable that a conquering king would worship the deities of a defeated nation. However, in the religious apologetics of the ancient Near East, not only did the royal deity assist the king in his battles, but also the deities of the opposing nation were often described as abandoning their people and coming to the aid of the attacking force. The Neo-Assyrian royal inscriptions speak of victories through the intervention of foreign deities as well as the native Assyrian gods. By appealing to the motif of divine abandonment the Assyrians were spared portraying the deities of conquered peoples as impotent or themselves vanquished before the more powerful Assyrian gods; the gods of vanquished peoples were spared humiliating defeat by being described as coming to the aid of the conqueror. A similar motif also occurs in the OT, when Yahweh abandons his people and fights with the conquering nation that he has brought to punish them. The visible component of the motif of divine abandonment was the transfer of the images out of the conquered land into the territory of the conqueror (M. Cogan, *Imperialism*, 9–21). Though the deities of Edom were no doubt attractive plunder, their being moved to Judah was probably an effort to portray visibly that they had abandoned their people and come to the aid of Amaziah. Amaziah's homage to these deities may have represented his own gratitude that they had helped him. Contrast the actions of David (1 Chr 14:12; cf. 2 Sam 5:21).

16 Amaziah's warning to the unnamed prophet must have had an impact— it came fresh on the heels of the precedent set by his father's murder of Zechariah (24:17–22). The passage nicely employs paronomasia on the four occurrences of forms derived from יעץ, "counsel," here and in v 17.

17–20 The use of "meet one another" may be another example of paronomasia—though it could potentially refer to an ordinary encounter, it is defined by its use in v 21 as meeting in battle. Cf. 2 Kgs 23:29.

Jehoash's parable about the arrogant thistle should be compared with Jotham's parable about the thornbush (Judg 9:7–15). In the eyes of the Chronicler pride was one of the cardinal sins (26:16; Williamson, 331).

Though the Chronicler has closely followed his *Vorlage* in this portion, apart from the first three words v 20 is his own insertion into the narrative. In line with his theology of retribution the author injects the specific evaluation that Amaziah did not listen because God had determined to punish him for his idolatry. Cf. 10:15 and 22:7.

21–24 It is somewhat surprising that the battle between Amaziah and Jehoash took place at Beth Shemesh instead of along their contiguous borders in the territory of Benjamin where the two kingdoms had fought so often during the first fifty years after the schism. Perhaps Jehoash had broader military goals, such as a foothold on a portion of the international coastal highway (Via Maris) or control of the east-west roads through Jerusalem connecting the coast plain with Transjordanian routes. Control over the western approaches to the Sorek Valley and points north would have given Jehoash control over commerce to and from Jerusalem from the north and west. The specification that this Beth Shemesh was in Judah may reflect that in the original Northern source used by the compiler of Kings Beth Shemesh of Judah was being distinguished from the town of the same name in Naphtali (Gray, 607).

The Ephraim Gate (Neh 8:16; 12:39), as the name implies, would have been located in the northern wall of the city, and the Corner Gate (26:9; Jer 31:38; Zech 14:10) was probably on the western wall; the precise locations depend on archaeological reconstructions of the city's perimeter in the eighth century B.C. Jehoash removed two hundred yards of the wall between the two gates, damage not completely repaired until during the reign of Uzziah (26:9).

The Chronicler, characteristic of his interest in the Levites, adds the note not found in 2 Kgs 14:14 regarding the family of Obed-Edom that David had put in charge of the temple treasuries (1 Chr 26:4–8, 15; 13:13–14).

This is the only instance (25:24 // 2 Kgs 14:14) in the Bible in which taking hostages (בני התערבות) is mentioned specifically, though the practice was similar to the actions of Nebuchadnezzar (2 Kgs 25:11); additional members of the royal family or the aristocracy and bureaucracy were probably held with Amaziah as punishment, for indemnity, or for reparations.

25–28 The text does not state how long Amaziah was held by Jehoash. The note that he outlived his captor by fifteen years may imply that he was not released until the death of Jehoash; see *Comment* on chronology above under 25:1–2.

Chronological notices are often used by the Chronicler in his efforts to demonstrate immediate retribution for wrongdoing. Where the parallel history had simply reported that there was a conspiracy against Amaziah (2 Kgs 14:19), the Chronicler adds the note (v 27a) that the conspiracy began when Amaziah turned from following Yahweh. Perhaps the same military and cultic alliance that had dethroned Athaliah and installed Joash (2 Chr 23) was once again involved to avenge the military humiliation and the spoliation of the temple. Lachish was one of the fortified cities of Judah, a seat of district government, and the recipient of royal largess in the past (11:9); though Amaziah may have hoped for loyalty from the population or officials of the city, they did not intervene in his behalf.

Explanation

The Chronicler's treatment of Amaziah incorporates many themes quite familiar by this point in his narrative. Comments in his Kings *Vorlage* have been expanded to provide the theological rationale for weal or woe and to demonstrate once again the validity of the author's theology of immediate retribution. The author's call for exclusive loyalty to Yahweh and trust in God alone is prominent in the chapter, both in the condemnation of Amaziah's idolatry and in the rejection of dependence on mercenaries in warfare.

On the whole the record of Amaziah's reign is a negative one. Apart from the brief, but clouded, victory over Edom as a reward for his obedience to the prophetic warning, the passage does not record any of the usual repertoire of indications of divine favor; rather, it is a study in opposites. Instead of royal building programs, the walls of Jerusalem are destroyed; instead of wealth from the people and surrounding nations, the king is plundered; instead of a large family, there are hostages; instead of peace, war; instead of victory, defeat; instead of loyalty from the populace and long life, there is conspiracy and regicide. The Chronicler's message for the restoration community was clear—to those rebuilding Jerusalem and restoring its walls, the Chronicler sounded again the central demand of exclusive loyalty in Israel's covenant with its LORD.

The Reign of Uzziah, 792/91–740/39 B.C. (26:1–23)

Bibliography

Browne, S. G. *Leprosy in the Bible.* London: Christian Medical Society, 1970. **Graham, J.** "Vinedressers and Plowmen." *BA* 47 (1984) 55–58. **Haran, M.** *Temples and Temple Service in Ancient Israel.* Oxford: Clarendon Press, 1978. 230–45. ———. "The Use of Incense in Ancient Israelite Ritual." *VT* 10 (1960) 113–25. **Hulse, E. V.** "The Nature of Biblical 'Leprosy' and the Use of Alternative Medical Terms in Modern Translations of the Bible." *PEQ* 107 (1975) 87–105. **Morgenstern, J.** "Amos Studies II—The Sin of Uzziah, the Festival of Jeroboam, and the Date of Amos." *HUCA* 12–13 (1937–38) 1–54. **Nielsen, K.** *Incense in Ancient Israel.* VTSup 38. Leiden: E. J. Brill, 1986. **Petersen, D.** *Late Israelite Prophecy.* 80–81. **Rainey, A.** "Wine from the Royal Vineyards." *BASOR* 245 (1982) 57–62. **Rinaldi, G.** "Quelques remarques sur la politique d'Azarias (Ozias) de Juda en Philistie (2 Chron 26, 6ss)." *Congress Volume, Bonn, 1962.* VTSup 9. Leiden: E. J. Brill, 1963. 225–35. **Sukenik, Y.** "Engines Invented by Cunning Men." *BJPES* 13 (1946/47) 19–24. **Tadmor, H.** "Azriyau of Yaudi." *Scripta Hierosolymitana* 8 (1961) 232–271. ———. "The Meʿunites in the Book of Chronicles in the Light of an Assyrian Document." In *Bible and Jewish History: Studies in Bible and Jewish History Dedicated to the Memory of Jacob Liver,* ed. B. Oppenheimer. Tel Aviv: University of Tel Aviv, 1972. 222–30. **Thiele, E.** *Mysterious Numbers* Rev. ed. 1983. 139–62. **Welten, P.** *Geschichte und Geschichtsdarstellung.* 153–63. **Yadin, Y.** *The Art of Warfare in Biblical Lands.* London: Weidenfeld and Nicolson, n.d. 325–27. **Yeivin, S.** "The Sepulchers of the Kings of the House of David." *JNES* 7 (1948) 30–45. **Zeron, A.** "Die Anmassung des Königs Usia im Lichte von Jesajas Berufung." *TZ* 33 (March/April 1977) 65–68.

Translation

[1] *All the people of Judah*[a] *took Uzziah*[b] *when he was sixteen years old and made him king in place of his father Amaziah.* [2] *He rebuilt Elath*[a] *and restored it to Judah after the king rested with his fathers.*

[3] *Uzziah was sixteen years old when he began to rule, and he was king in Jerusalem for fifty-two years. His mother was Jecoliah;*[a] *she was from Jerusalem.* [4] *He did what was right in the eyes of Yahweh, just as Amaziah his father had done.*

[5] *He sought God during the days of Zechariah who instructed him in the fear*[a] *of God. As long as he sought Yahweh, God allowed him to prosper.* [6] *He went out and fought against the Philistines and broke through the walls of Gath, Jabneh, and Ashdod; then he rebuilt towns near Ashdod and elsewhere among the Philistines.* [7] *God helped him against the Philistines, against the Arabs who inhabited Gur,*[a] *and against the Meunites.* [8] *The Meunites*[a] *brought tribute to Uzziah; his fame spread as far as the border of Egypt because he had become exceedingly powerful.*

[9] *Uzziah built towers in Jerusalem at the Corner Gate,*[a] *at the Valley Gate,*[b] *and at the angle*[c] *in the wall, and he reinforced them.* [10] *He also built towers in the wilderness and dug many cisterns, for he had livestock in the hill country and in the plain. He also had plowmen and vinedressers in the hills and in the fertile areas, for he loved the soil.*

¹¹*Uzziah had an army trained for battle, ready for war by divisions, as enrolled in the muster administered by Jeiel the scribe and Maaseiah the clerk under the direction of Hananiah, one of the king's officials.* ¹²*The number of family leaders over the fighting men was two thousand six hundred.* ¹³*They had under their command an army of three hundred seven thousand five hundred men trained for battle in a powerful force to help the king against any enemy.*

¹⁴*Uzziah provided the entire army with shields, spears, helmets, body armor, bows, and sling stones.* ¹⁵*In Jerusalem he made inventions designed by clever men on the towers and corners of the wall for shooting arrows and hurling large stones. His fame spread far and wide, for he was wondrously helped until he became powerful.*

¹⁶*But when he became powerful, his pride led to his downfall. He was unfaithful to Yahweh his God and went into the temple of Yahweh to burn incense on the incense altar.* ¹⁷*Azariah the priest, along with eighty other courageous priests of Yahweh, went in after him.* ¹⁸*They confronted King Uzziah and said to him, "It is not for you, Uzziah, to burn incense to Yahweh—rather it is for the priests, the sons of Aaron, who have been consecrated to burn incense. Leave the sanctuary, for you have been unfaithful, and you will not receive honor from Yahweh God."*

¹⁹*Uzziah became enraged while he had in his hand a censer for burning incense. While he was enraged with the priests, leprosy broke out on his forehead in the presence of the priests before the incense altar in the temple of Yahweh.*

²⁰*When Azariah the high priest, along with all the priests, turned toward him, they saw that he had leprosy on his forehead, and they hastened to bundle him out of there; even he was in a hurry to get out because Yahweh had afflicted him.*

²¹*King Uzziah was leprous until the day of his death; he lived in a separate*[a] *house, leprous and excluded from the temple of Yahweh. Jotham his son had charge of the royal palace and governed the people of the land.* ²²*The rest of the acts of Uzziah, from beginning to end, were recorded by the prophet Isaiah ben Amoz.*

²³*Uzziah rested with his fathers and was buried with his fathers*[a] *in a burial field that belonged to the kings, for they said, "He was a leper." Jotham his son ruled in his place.*

Notes

1.a. 2 Hebrew MSS and G, "people of the land"; this variant probably represents an unconscious harmonization with the more frequent phrase rather than an earlier and more correct text.

1.b. He is known by this name in 2 Chr 26, Isa 1:1, Hos 1:1, Amos 1:1, Zech 14:5; 2 Kgs 15:13, 30, 32, 34. He is known as Azariah in 1 Chr 3:12 and 2 Kgs 15:1, 6, 7, 8, 17, 23, 27. Probably the best explanation is to regard one as a birth name and the other as a throne name taken at the time of his accession (A. Honeyman, "The Evidence for Regnal Names among the Hebrews," *JBL* 67 [1948] 13–25); cf. other possible examples in the cases of Shallum-Jehoahaz (Jer 22:11), Eliakim-Jehoiakim (2 Kgs 23:34), and Mattaniah-Zedekiah (2 Kgs 24:17). The Chronicler's consistent use of "Uzziah" in this chapter may be to facilitate distinguishing the king from the high priest Azariah (26:17, 20).

2.a. MT, *Eloth* (cf. 8:17 // 1 Kgs 9:26). *Elath* is the spelling in Deut 2:8; 2 Kgs 14:22. Both forms are used in 2 Kgs 16:6.

3.a. With Q and 2 Kgs 15:2; MT, *Jekiliah*.

5.a. With a few Heb. MSS, G, Syr, Tg, and Arab, יראת; MT, ראת, "vision." The "fear of God" is common enough in Chronicles (6:31, 33; 19:9; 1 Chr 13:12), whereas instruction in the "vision of God" seems more appropriate to medieval mysticism than to the Heb. Bible.

7.a. MT, "Gur-baal" is otherwise unknown. בעל should probably be read with G as ועל "and against," which occurs two other times in the verse before the names of enemies against whom the LORD helped Uzziah and would otherwise not occur before "the Meunites." The remaining "Gur" could refer to a town known from the Amarna letters, east of Beersheba (Rinaldi, 229–30; C-M, 451–52; Williamson, 335). Tg shows some variation; different MSS read Gerar, Gazer, or Gader.

8.a. With G; MT, "Ammonites." The preceding verse mentions the Meunites. All of Uzziah's campaigns were directed to the south and southwest. Though his "restoring Elat" (v 2) could have brought him into conflict with the Ammonites, this is less probable. The Meʿunites are ordinarily taken as a reference to a people of Edom (20:1). Tadmor ("Meunites") has presented evidence from an Assyrian text for the use of this term in reference to inhabitants near the region of Kadesh-barnea; this would fit with the southern thrust of Uzziah's campaign and the spread of his fame to the borders of Egypt (v 8; Williamson, 335). Alternatively, if the MT reading is maintained, Uzziah's receiving tribute from the Ammonites would anticipate the campaign of his son Jotham there (27:5).

9.a. 25:23; Zech 14:10.

9.b. Neh 2:13, 15; 3:23; see the discussion in H. Williamson, "Nehemiah's Walls Revisited," *PEQ* 116 (1986) 84.

9.c. Neh 3:19, 24.

21.a. חפשי in Hebrew has the meaning "free." Q בית החפשית, "house of freedom," could refer to (1) his being released from his duties and functions as king, i.e., free from responsibilities, or (2) a euphemism for confinement, "free house" being in fact "isolation." The same phrase occurs in an Ugaritic text where emissaries of Baal are sent to the netherworld; unless it is also a euphemistic use, Ugaritic *bṯḫptt* seems to mean "house of corruption, filth." See Rudolph, 284, and *ZAW* 89 (1977) 418; Gray, 619–20; Watson, *Bib* 53 (1972) 193.

23.a. A few Heb. MSS, Arab, Syr, and Vg omit the second occurrence of the phrase "with his fathers." Its inclusion in MT could be the result of an unconscious scribal harmonization with other passages using the phrase with the verb "bury" (21:1, 19; 25:28; cf. 35:24), so that it should be deleted. However, since "with his fathers" occurs twice in the parallel text at 2 Kgs 15:7, it is more probable that the phrase was originally included by the author who then substituted "in a burial field belonging to the kings" for 2 Kgs 15:7 "in the city of David." The omission would then be a scribal correction since the Chronicler's point seems to be that Uzziah was in fact not buried with his fathers in the royal tombs but in a separate field.

Form/Structure/Setting

The Chronicler provides in effect a double accession notice for Uzziah; both were drawn from the parallel text. 26:1–2 was taken from the concluding notices to the reign of Amaziah (2 Kgs 14:21–22) and the other the accession notice itself (26:3–4 // 2 Kgs 15:2–3). Through his customary practice of omitting accounts concerning the Northern kings and synchronisms with their reigns (2 Kgs 14:23–15:1), the Chronicler's introduction to Uzziah is somewhat awkward—we are twice told that he was made king and that he was sixteen years old at his accession (26:1–4).

The Chronicler has borrowed most of the short parallel account of Uzziah's reign (2 Kgs 15:2–7), which is largely devoted to the formulaic accession and succession notices. He has introduced even in this short portion several changes reflecting his own concerns; see below on 26:3–4, 7.

The bulk of the Chronicler's account is unique to Chronicles (26:5–20). Whatever sources the author had at his disposal appear to reflect with accuracy the historical and political milieu of Uzziah's reign. It should be no surprise that some additional records covering such a long reign were available to the later historian beyond what was reported in Kings (Williamson, 333). It is also clear that the author has reworked the material in line with his usual practice to account for the weal and woe of the kings of Judah in terms of his theology of immediate retribution. The earlier history had reported that Uzziah did "right" and enjoyed one of the longest reigns of the Judean kings. The Chronicler elaborates by demonstrating the tokens of divine blessing that Uzziah enjoyed; divine help, victory in warfare, a large army, wealth, fame, and building programs (26:5–15) are all items in the author's usual repertoire for portraying the blessings that accrue to fidelity. For the Chronicler, however, such a righteous king should not have suffered a debilitating and disgraceful disease. Where the earlier history had reported Uzziah's leprosy without comment (2 Kgs 15:5), the Chronicler explains the anomaly by reporting Uzziah's pride and his cultic sin as the inciting reason for his disease. See the introductory essay to 2 Chr 10–36, "Reward and Punishment in Chronicles: The Theology of Immediate Retribution."

Josephus's account (*Ant.* 9.222–27) testifies to the ongoing embellishment of traditions surrounding the reign of Uzziah. Josephus describes Uzziah as usurping the role of the high priest in a major festival, presumably the Day of Atonement in which incense rites were so important; at the moment of his sin, an earthquake split the valleys (cf. Zech 14:4–5; Amos 1:1) and breached the temple wall so that a beam of light (the glory of Yahweh[?]) fell on Uzziah's head to produce the leprosy. A similar tradition is alluded to in the Targum to Isa 28:21a. See Morgenstern, *HUCA* 12–13 (1937–38) 1–20.

The chapter is structured by the usual paragraphing devices used by the Chronicler: (1) an explicit subject, commonly a king's name (26:1, 9, 14, 19, 20); (2) ויהי-clause with some indicator of time (26:5, 11, 21). The verb חזק is used to structure some portions: (1) repetition of the statement that "Uzziah became strong" ends one paragraph and begins the next, a use often called tail-head linkage (26:15–16); (2) the same verb ends two paragraphs, one concerning the external affairs of Uzziah's rule (26:8), and the other his internal policies (26:15); this use is often called tail-tail linkage.

Comment

1–2 Uzziah shared the throne during the first twenty-four years of his fifty-two-year reign in a coregency with his father (see *Comment* at 25:1–2); though his coregency began in 792/91 B.C., he did not become sole ruler until about 767 B.C. He would similarly share power with his son Jotham during the last ten years of his reign due to his illness. Uzziah was also known by the name Azariah; see *Notes* at 26:1.b.

The rule of Uzziah in the South alongside that of Jeroboam II in the North briefly restored the Israelite kingdoms to approximately the borders of the Solomonic empire—a glorious sunset especially for the North. Though Amaziah had also campaigned to the southeast, he had not been able to subdue Elat; see *Comment* at 25:11–12. Elat was the strategic port at the head of the gulf and was critical to control of the seaborne commerce with Arabia, Africa, and India. It had been subdued by Solomon (8:17–18 // 1 Kgs 9:26–28). Edom had revolted during the reign of Jehoram (21:8–10). Though Uzziah reasserted Judean control, it would be lost again during the reign of Ahaz (28:17; 2 Kgs 16:6).

3–4 It is somewhat surprising that the Chronicler would describe Uzziah as a king who did "what was right just as Amaziah his father had done"; this ascription fits the original context of 2 Kgs 15:3 from which it was borrowed and where the historian had not elaborated on the transgressions of either Amaziah or Uzziah. In the Chronicler's treatment of Uzziah such a generous judgment would scarcely seem fitting for the latter portions of his reign (26:16–21).

The Chronicler omits from the parallel text the statement that Uzziah did not remove the high places (2 Kgs 15:4); he made the same omission from the deuteronomic history in his accounts of the reigns of Amaziah, Joash, and Jotham (see *Comment* at 25:1–2). The Chronicler commonly structures the reign of particular kings into an early good period followed by one of turning away and infidelity; negative evaluations would be inappropriate for those portions of a reign that the author was presenting in a positive light and hence were omitted.

5 Uzziah, like Joash before him (24:2), had one particular adviser who helped him to remain faithful to Yahweh. Nothing more is known of this individual, unless he is identified with the Zechariah who served as a witness for Isaiah (Isa 8:2); however, the statement that Uzziah sought Yahweh "during the days" of Zechariah is best understood as implying that he had died during the reign of Uzziah. דרשׁ "seek" and צלח "prosper" are two of the key terms in the Chronicler's theology of immediate retribution.

6–8 These verses summarize Uzziah's foreign policy. His conquests were oriented to the west, south, and southeast, a fact that fits well with the rule of a powerful Jeroboam II to the north. Uzziah's conquest of Jabneh suggests that he regained control of the area through which Jehoash of Israel had attacked his father Amaziah (25:21). Jabneh is probably to be equated with Jabneel (Josh 15:11); the site would later be called "Jamnia" and would become a leading center of Jewish learning and religious life after the destruction of Jerusalem in A.D. 70. Uzziah's campaigns against the Philistines not only represented the on-going conflict of traditional enemies; no doubt Uzziah had the important strategic purpose of reasserting some control over the international coastal highway ("Via Maris"). A similar strategic goal to control a major artery of international commerce influenced the campaign against Elat (26:1–2).

The practice of building towns in conquered territories has a striking analog in our own times in the practice of Israel in encouraging Jewish settlements in the Golan and West Bank, territories conquered in the Six-Day War.

It was after his own campaigns against the Philistines and gaining control over the international coastal highway that a similar statement was made regarding the spread of the fame of David (v 8; 1 Chr 14:17).

9–10 Vv 9–15 summarize the domestic activities of Uzziah. In Chronicles building projects by the various kings are signs of divine blessing. Some of Uzziah's construction was no doubt repair of damage done by Jehoash of Israel in his campaign against Amaziah (25:23–24), though some may reflect repairs following the famous earthquake during his reign (Amos 1:1; Zech 14:5).

An impressive array of archeological evidence has been interpreted as reflecting Uzziah's building activity (see Myers, xxix; and Williamson, 336–37 for bibliography). Towers and cisterns from excavations in Qumran, Gibeah, Beersheba, and other sites have been assigned to this period; a seal bearing Uzziah's name was found in a cistern at Tell Beit Mirsim. The towers provided defensive positions, but may also have served as storehouses and as refuge for workers tending fields or livestock (1 Chr 27:25–31).

Because of his love of the soil (v 10), Uzziah could with justice be considered the patron saint of farming. After the rise of the monarchy in Israel, in addition to the landed property of free Israelites, there developed extensive crown lands through purchase, take over, or other means (1 Sam 8:12–14; 22:7; 1 Kgs 21; 2 Kgs 8:3–6; 1 Chr 27:25–31). These crown lands would have provided a source of supplies and trade commodities for the court, employment for those without other means, and could be granted as fiefs in reward for faithful service. Ordinarily only the poorest of the land served as vinedressers and laborers on royal estates (2 Kgs 24:14; 25:12; Jer 52:16; Jer 40:9–10; see Graham, *BA* 47 [1985] 55–58; and Rainey, *BASOR* 245 [1982]) 55–58).

11–13 In the Chronicler's eyes a large army was another token of divine favor; his reports of large armies are confined to the reigns of pious kings (1 Chr 12:23–40; 21; 27; 2 Chr 12:3; 13:3–4, 17; 14:9; 17:12–19; 25:5–6; 28:6–8). Uzziah's large army of course figured in the victories already described. A text from early in the reign of Tiglath-pileser III of Assyria mentions his battle with a coalition including an Azriyau of Yaudi (742 B.C. according to Thiele); this individual is almost certainly to be identified with Uzziah/Azariah. The text demonstrates that Uzziah was able to participate in resistance to the rising might of Assyria at a distance far beyond his own borders (see the discussions in H. Tadmor, "Azriyau"; and E. Thiele, *Mysterious Numbers* [1983] 139–62).

With regard to the total size of the army, see the discussions of large troop figures in *Comment* at 13:3 and 14:8–9.

14–15 The note that Uzziah provided the army with its weapons and armor reflects both Uzziah's prosperity under divine blessing and a departure from ordinary practice in expecting conscripts to provide their own arms (Judg 20:8–17; 1 Chr 12:2, 8, 24, 33; 1 Sam 13:19–22).

The description of the inventions installed on the walls of the city by Uzziah has led many to conclude that they were torsion-operated devices such as catapults. However, to the extent of our current knowledge, such torsion-operated weapons probably did not appear in the warfare of the ancient Near East before about 400 B.C., though there is some evidence that could indicate a date as much as a century earlier (see Williamson, 337–38). Welten (*Geschichte,* 111–14) takes these devices as prima facie evidence for a late date for Chronicles, arguing that the author must have lived in the first half of the third century B.C. Even if such devices appeared as early as around 500 B.C., they would still be an anachronism in Chronicles.

Yadin (*Art of Warfare,* 325–28; Sukenik, *BJPES* 13 [1946–47] 19–24) argues instead that Uzziah's inventions were not torsion-operated offensive weapons, but rather defensive constructions on the walls and towers that offered a measure of protection for archers and throwers who were otherwise exposed when wielding their weapons. This explanation is confirmed in iconography, particularly in the murals of the siege of Lachish; in these protrayals from a time shortly after the rule of Uzziah defenders on the walls are behind a screen made of wooden frames holding shields rather than exposed to fire from below as seen in earlier Assyrian reliefs. This explanation fits both the demands of the context and what we know of military technology for the period.

Statements regarding Uzziah's becoming "powerful" are used by the writer as an important structuring device in this chapter; see above, *Form/Structure/Setting*. Uzziah's own power and fame were part of a brief renaissance also in the Northern Kingdom during the rule of Jeroboam II.

16–18 The Chronicler often divides the reign of an individual king into two halves, good and bad; a chronological note ordinarily separates the two portions. It was "when he became powerful" that Uzziah's pride led to his downfall. Pride was a cardinal sin in Chronicles; see *Comment* at 25:17–20. The term מעל, "be unfaithful, rebellious," is of high frequency in Chronicles, common in the author's expression of his theology of immediate retribution; see the introductory essay to 2 Chr 10–36, "Reward and Punishment in Chronicles: The Theology of Immediate Retribution." Uzziah's faithful counsellor Zechariah must have died or otherwise fallen from favor (26:5).

Burning incense in Israel's worship was reserved to the priests (Exod 30:1–10; Num 16:40; 18:1–7), though the action of the Levites in 29:11 appears to be an exception to this rule. According to the results of traditional biblical criticism the passages confining the offering of incense to priests are all found in the priestly (P) stratum of the pentateuch; of course, P itself is commonly viewed as a document or school of thought in part defining cultic regulations and protecting priestly interests as they existed in the post-exilic period. Since the regulations regarding the incense offerings and priestly prerogatives are felt to be late, Uzziah is commonly viewed as judged by an anachronistic standard: the rules of the post-exilic hierocracy were retrojected to provide the basis for the condemnation of Uzziah. However, apart from the question of the nature and date of P, there can be no real question that incense offerings played an important role in the temple services of the ancient Near East already in the second millennium—a fact illustrated by the many texts from Mesopotamia dealing with the procurement of incense for temples and by the importance attached to the incense trade (see *Comment* at 9:1–12). Where incense was important for cultic use, one would a priori expect regulations to have developed regarding its quality, blending, and use. The presence of such regulations in Chronicles, irrespective of the question of P, could well reflect a reliable tradition regarding an action of Uzziah.

The most extensive scholarly discussion to date of incense rites in Israel's worship has been done by M. Haran (*Temples and Temple Service*, 230–45; *VT* 10 [1960] 113–25), though regrettably Haran made little use of Chronicles (Petersen, *Prophecy*, 80–81).

19–21 Uzziah's sin was a cultic transgression and brings *immediate* retribution in the appearance of a skin disease; Uzziah's pride brought him to usurp the honor or glory of the priest's role, but he would receive no honor (v 18) from the LORD. Just as a cultic sin produced a plague in the wilderness (Num

16:46–50), so also Uzziah was punished with a disease. It was the offering of incense that formed the climax of the condemnation of Jeroboam (1 Kgs 12:33; Williamson, 339). The Chronicler has similarly shown disease as a consequence of transgression in the cases of Asa and Jehoram (16:12–13; 21:12–19).

There is little doubt that the disease designated by the root צרע and its derived forms was not the disease now known by the name leprosy (Hansen's disease). Evidence from ancient medical literature and palaeopathology concur in this conclusion; furthermore, criteria by which the priests were to make their diagnosis do not fit Hansen's disease (E. Hulse, *PEQ* 107 [1975] 87–105; cf. S. Browne, *Leprosy*). Biblical data suggests that צרע covered a variety of skin diseases, possibly including psoriasis and some fungal infections.

Infectious skin diseases rendered an individual ceremonially unclean and required isolation "outside the camp" (Lev 13:46; Num 5:1–4; 12:15; 2 Kgs 7:3). Uzziah would be unable to discharge all the duties of kingship, particularly toward the temple, and so began a coregency with his son Jotham.

22–23 The Chronicler appeals to the same source, writings by Isaiah, in his account of Hezekiah (32:32); this could not be the canonical book of Isaiah which mentions Uzziah only in the notices in 1:1, 6:1, and 7:1. Some have seen in this citation another example of the Chronicler's propensity for associating the individual kings with sources carrying the names of prophets known from the period of their reigns, and therefore regard these sources as fictitious. Yet it would be surprising that no mention of Isaiah is made in the sources cited for the reigns of Jotham or especially Ahaz, who was so fully involved with Isaiah in the canonical book (Isa 7; cf. Lemke, *Synoptic Studies*, 202–3). Either the Chronicler had access to some writings otherwise unknown from biblical tradition, or the Isaiah traditions he cites were part of a larger work on the history of the kingdoms (20:34; 24:27; 32:32; cf. Rudolph, 287).

The separate burial accorded Uzziah may have been strikingly confirmed by the discovery of a Hasmonean ossuary text with the following Aramaic inscription: "Herein are the bones of Uzziah, king of Judah. Do not open." If Uzziah had been buried with the other kings such separate handling of his bones would have been less probable. Perhaps during some demolition or other construction work in the first century B.C. the tomb of Uzziah was uncovered and his bones gathered into this ossuary (Yeivin, *JNES* 7 [1948] 31–32). However, it is also possible that this inscription is but another example of the frequency and ease with which biblical data are incorrectly associated with locales and structures; tombs in particular have frequently and wrongly been associated with biblical personages (Ackroyd, 171).

Explanation

Uzziah was a great king: during his reign Judah reclaimed in the South much of the territorial extent of the Solomonic empire; the kingdom prospered through conquest, the control of strategic trade routes, and the receipt of tribute. Yet isn't it ironic that Uzziah is now largely remembered only because of his disease and the fact that it was the year of his death in which Isaiah received his call? In spite of the wealth, success, power, and conquests of Uzziah, Isaiah could see that the day was not far off when cities would lie deserted, uninhabited, ruined, and ravaged (Isa 6:11–12).

Uzziah for the Chronicler was one more example of how even legitimate power could be corrupted; with Rehoboam, Amaziah, and Joash before him, Uzziah too would succumb to wrongdoing and suffer the immediate consequence of divine retribution.

The Reign of Jotham, 750–732/31 B.C. (27:1–9)

Bibliography

Welten, P. *Geschichte und Geschichtsdarstellung.* 27–29, 66–68, 163–66.

Translation

[1] *Jotham was twenty-five years old when he became king, and he ruled sixteen years in Jerusalem; his mother's name was Jerushah, daughter of Zadok.* [2] *He did what was right in the eyes of Yahweh, just as Uzziah his father had done, except* [a] [b] *that he did not enter the temple of Yahweh,* [b] *and the people* [c] *continued their corrupt practices.* [c]

[3] *He rebuilt the Upper Gate of the temple of Yahweh and did extensive work on the wall of the Ophel;* [4] *he also built towns in the hill country of Judah and forts and towers in forested areas.*

[5] *He fought against the king of the Ammonites and was victorious over them. The Ammonites paid him that year a hundred talents of silver,* [a] *ten thousand cor of wheat* [b] *and ten thousand cor of barley; they brought him the same amount also in the second and third years.* [6] *Jotham became powerful because he determined to walk obediently before Yahweh his God.*

[7] *As for the rest of the deeds of Jotham—all his wars and his conduct* [a] *—they are written in the book of the kings of Israel and Judah.* [b] [8] *He was twenty-five years old when he became king and ruled sixteen years in Jerusalem.* [a] [9] *Jotham rested with his fathers and was buried in the City of David; Ahaz his son ruled in his place.*

Notes

2.a. רק commonly introduces an exception to a preceding statement. It frequently occurs in statements that a king did "what was right, except . . ." (1 Kgs 3:3; 2 Kgs 12:4 [3]; 14:4; 15:4, 35; 2 Chr 25:2). Myers (155–56) appears to understand the text as saying that Jotham "did what was right, except that he did not enter the temple," so that this clause would represent a negative judgment on the part of the Chronicler. However, context demands that רק be understood as introducing an exception to the immediately preceding clause, "as his father had done, except that he did not enter the temple," so that it is a positive judgment indicating that Jotham did not violate the temple precincts as Uzziah had done.

2.b-b. 2 Kgs 15:35, "only they did not remove the high places."

2.c-c. 2 Kgs 15:35, "continued to make sacrifices and burn incense on the high places."

5.a. Depending on the weight of a talent at this time, an amount between sixty-six hundred and seventy-five hundred pounds.

5.b. The capacity of a cor was between slightly above five and slightly above six bushels; ten thousand cors would be between approximately fifty-two and sixty-two thousand bushels. See *Comment* at 2:9 [10].

7.a. 2 Kgs 15:36, "all that he did."

7.b. 2 Kgs 15:36, "chronicles of the kings of Judah."

8.a. V 8 is not found in the parallel text (2 Kgs 15:37; cf. 15:33); it is also omitted in Par and Syr. It is either a dittogr of 27:1 or a marginal gloss preserving a variant on 28:1 (C-M, 455; Rudolph, 286; Allen, *GC* 1:218).

Form/Structure/Setting

The Chronicler's account of Jotham's reign is essentially a postscript to that of Uzziah; the author broadly aligns him with his father's piety (27:2), but carefully notes that Jotham committed no sacrilege (McConville, 221). This wholly positive account of Jotham represents a break in the Chronicler's practice seen in the preceding three reigns of dividing his accounts of individual kings into alternating periods of good and bad; he will follow the practice of presenting a single consistent judgment through his account of Hezekiah (Williamson, 341).

The Chronicler's account of Jotham is largely dependent on the parallel text at 2 Kgs 15:32–38. The author omits the notice in 2 Kgs 15:37 that God had stirred up the opposition of Rezin and Pekah; this note would be out of keeping with his portrayal of Jotham and was more appropriate to the consistently negative account of Ahaz (28:5). He also introduced a few small modifications that reflect his own concerns (27:2 // 2 Kgs 15:35). As is ordinarily the case, the Chronicler's own *Tendenz* is most clearly reflected in those passages unique to Chronicles; building projects, victory, and tribute are among the inventory of items which the Chronicler often uses to portray divine blessing (27:3b–6) and further perfect the parallel drawn to Uzziah (27:2).

Paragraphs in this short account appear to be marked by suspending the use of the *waw*-consecutive in favor of a clause beginning with the subject הוא (27:3, 5).

Comment

1–2 The chronological notices surrounding the reign of Jotham are complex and apparently contradictory; though Jotham is assigned a reign of sixteen years, Hoshea's accession is synchronized with his twentieth year (2 Kgs 15:30) as well as the twelfth year of Ahaz (2 Kgs 17:1). Following the chronology proposed by Thiele (*Mysterious Numbers*, 106–7, 199–200), Jotham's sixteen years included a ten-year coregency due to the illness of his father Uzziah (750–740/39 B.C.); however, the sixteen-year figure did not include a three-to-four-year overlap of his reign with that of his own son and successor Ahaz (735–732/31 B.C.), a fact that would allow for the synchronism with Jotham's twentieth year (2 Kgs 15:30). Thiele (200) dismisses 2 Kgs 17:1 as a late editorial miscalculation that threw the reign of Ahaz back twelve years. Jotham's actual sole reign was probably confined to the period between 740/39 and 735. Cf. also the approach taken by H. Stigers, "The Interphased Chronology of Jotham, Ahaz, Hezekiah, and Hoshea," *BETS* 9 (1966) 81–90.

In the accession notices for the kings of Judah the hometown of the king's mother is commonly given (13:1 [2]; 24:1; 25:1; 26:1 [3]; contrast 22:2; 29:1). Since no city is mentioned for Jerushah, it could be that she was a member of a prominent family and was sufficiently identified by her patronymic, especially if Zadok in this instance referred to the lineage of the high priests (1 Chr 5:38 [6:12]; cf. Gray, 629).

The Chronicler modified the parallel text at 2 Kgs 15:35 by omitting the reference to Jotham's failure to remove the high places and substituting in its place the note that Jotham did not enter the temple as Uzziah had done. Uzziah's act of sacrilege was not mentioned in Kings; the concern with the sanctity of the temple reflects a major element in the Chronicler's theology. The Chronicler often omits references to the high places (24:2 // 2 Kgs 12:4 [3]; 25:2 // 2 Kgs 14:4; 26:4 // 2 Kgs 15:4); these instances, like this one, occur in passages where the Chronicler is presenting a positive portrayal of individual reigns and where negative evaluations are omitted or delayed. The reference to "corrupt practices" appears to be the Chronicler's paraphrase of "making sacrifices and burning incense on the high places" (2 Kgs 15:35); some sense of the corrupt practices of the time can be gleaned from the preaching of Isaiah (Isa 1–5) and Micah.

3–4 Kings mentions only Jotham's repair of the Upper Gate of the temple (2 Kgs 15:35). For the Chronicler royal building projects are an indication of divine blessing; the author frequently records construction work during the reigns of pious kings (11:5–12; 14:6–7; 17:12–13; 26:9–10; 33:14; see the introductory essay to 2 Chr 10–36, "Reward and Punishment in Chronicles: The Theology of Immediate Retribution").

The precise identity of the "Ophel" is not known. It is ordinarily associated today with that spur of land on which the City of David was located; the wall of the Ophel may have been on the steep eastern side of that hill.

The Chronicler has already compared Jotham with Uzziah (27:2), and he appears to be deliberately perfecting the parallel. Uzziah rebuilt Corner Gate and Valley Gate (26:9), and Jotham works on the Upper Gate of the temple. Uzziah built towers in the desert and in Jerusalem (26:10), and Jotham builds towers in forested areas.

5 Jotham's reign is again an extension of Uzziah's. Uzziah had received tribute from the Ammonites (26:8), and so does Jotham. The military domination by Judah of territory across the Jordan during the reigns of Uzziah and Jotham was no doubt one factor in the eventual Syro-Ephraimite coalition against Judah (2 Chr 28; Isa 7). The fact that the Ammonites ceased their payment of tribute after the third year may reflect the rising power of Aram in the region.

A seal was discovered at Ezion-geber containing the name Jotham (*BASOR* 79 [1940] 13–15; 163 [1961] 18–22); if the individual named is to be identified with Jotham the king, it appears to have come from a period of his authority in the region prior to his sole rule and attests to Judah's military success in the area during the reigns of Uzziah and Jotham.

6 This verse is an explicit statement of the Chronicler's theology of immediate retribution: political success is found in the path of obedience; power is an index of piety. Uzziah had also become "powerful," but his power and pride had led him astray (26:8, 13, 15, 16); Jotham's power did not corrupt him.

7–9 The Chronicler omits the reference in 2 Kgs 15:37 to the confrontation with Rezin and Pekah; their attack is viewed by the author as divine judgment on Ahaz (28:5–8) and would be inappropriate to his entirely positive portrayal of Jotham. The Chronicler does acknowledge the additional wars fought by Jotham (27:7), presumably including the initial confrontation with the Syro-Ephraimite coalition and possibly including his own involvement in Uzziah's campaign against Tiglath-pileser III (cf. *Comment* at 26:11–13; Thiele, *Mysterious Numbers*, 139–61).

See the note regarding the textual difficulties surrounding v 8.

Explanation

In his presentation of Jotham the Chronicler has broken with his regular practice of dividing an individual king's reign into periods of good and bad, blessing and judgment. This break with his ordinary approach is continued through the reign of Hezekiah: the portrayal of an irreproachable Jotham contrasts sharply with the uniformly negative assessment of Ahaz on the one hand and on the other hand compares favorably with the account of Hezekiah. These three reigns are treated differently, perhaps even highlighted by the Chronicler (Williamson, 341). The sequence of a righteous man (Jotham), who has an unrighteous son (Ahaz), who is in turn followed by a righteous son (Hezekiah) is precisely the sequence used by Ezekiel to reinforce his own theology of immediate retribution (Ezek 18:5–20).

The Reign of Ahaz, 735–716/15 B.C. (28:1–27)

Bibliography

Ackroyd, P. "Historians and Prophets." *SEA* 33 (1968) 18–54. **Alt, A.** "Tiglathpilesers III erster Feldzug nach Palästina." *Kleine Schriften zur Geschichte des Volkes Israel.* Munich: Beck'sche, 1953. 2:150–62. **Cogan, M.** *Imperialism.* 73–77. **Graham, W.** "Isaiah's Part in the Syro-Ephraimite Crisis." *AJSL* 50 (1934) 201–16. **Gray, J.** "The Period and Office of the Prophet Isaiah in the Light of a New Assyrian Tablet." *ExpTim* 63 (1951–52) 263–65. **Konkel, A.** *Hezekiah in Biblical Tradition.* Diss. Westminster Theological Seminary, 1987. **McKay, J.** *Religion in Judah.* 5–12. **Mosis, R.** *Untersuchungen.* 186–89. **Oded, B.** "The Historical Background of the Syro-Ephraimite War Reconsidered." *CBQ* 34 (1972) 153–64. **Spenser, S.** "2 Chronicles 28:5–15 and the Parable of the Good Samaritan." *WTJ* 46 (1984) 317–49. **Spieckermann, H.** *Juda unter Assur in der Sargonidenzeit.* Göttingen: Vandenhoeck & Ruprecht, 1982. **Tadmor, H.** "Philistia under Assyrian Rule." *BA* 29 (1966) 86–102. **Thompson, M.** *Situation and Theology: Old Testament Interpretations of the Syro-Ephraimite War.* Sheffield: Almond Press, 1982. **Wilkinson, F.** "Oded: Proto-type of the Good Samaritan." *ExpTim* 69 (1957) 94. **Williamson, H.** *IBC.* 114–18. **Wiseman, D.** "Two Historical Inscriptions from Nimrud." *Iraq* 13 (1951) 21–26.

Translation

[1] *Ahaz was twenty[a] years old when he began to reign, and he ruled sixteen years in Jerusalem. He did not do what was right in the eyes of the LORD as his father David had done.* [2] *He walked in the ways of the kings of Israel. He erected cast idols for worshiping the Baals,* [3a] *offered sacrifices in the Valley of Ben Hinnom,[a] and passed[b] his sons[c] through the fire in accordance with the abominable practices of the nations that Yahweh had expelled before the Israelites.* [4] *He made sacrifices and burned incense at the high places on every hill and beneath every green tree.*

[5] *So Yahweh handed him over to the king of Aram. The Arameans defeated him; they captured many prisoners and took them to Damascus.[a] He was also handed over to the king of Israel who inflicted many casualties on him.* [6] *Pekah son of Remaliah killed 120,000 in Judah in one day, all soldiers, because they had forsaken Yahweh the God of their fathers.* [7] *Zicri, a warrior from Ephraim, killed Maaseiah the king's son, Azrikam the palace officer, and Elkanah the second to the king.* [8] *The Israelites took captive from their relatives 200,000 women, sons, and daughters. They also seized great quantities of plunder and took it to Samaria.*

[9] *A prophet of Yahweh was there; his name was Oded. He went out to meet the army returning to Samaria and said to them:*

"Look, it is because of the wrath of Yahweh, the God of your fathers, that he handed them over to you, and you have killed them with a rage that reaches heaven. [10] *Now you are planning to make the people of Judah and Jerusalem, both male and female, your slaves. But aren't you also[a] guilty[b] before Yahweh your God?* [11] *Now listen to me! Send back the prisoners you took from your brethren, for the wrath of Yahweh rests upon you."*

[12] *Some men among the leaders of the Ephraimites—Azariah son of Jehohanan,*

Berekiah son of Meshillemoth, Hezekiah son of Shallum, and Amasa son of Hadlai—met those returning from the war [13] *and said to them, "You must not bring those captives here, for it would make us guilty before Yahweh. Are you planning to add to our sin and guilt? Our guilt is already great, and Yahweh's wrath rests upon Israel."*

[14] *So the warriors left the prisoners and the plunder before the officers and the assembly.* [15] *The men named for this duty took charge of the prisoners. They found clothes from the plunder for all who were naked. They gave them clothes, shoes, food and drink, and anointed them with oil. They loaded all who were weak on donkeys and took them to Jericho, the City of Palms, near their brethren. Then they returned to Samaria.*

[16] *At that time King Ahaz sent to the kings* [a] *of Assyria for help.* [17] *The Edomites had invaded Judah again and had taken prisoners.* [18] *The Philistines had divested the cities of the Shephelah and the Negev of Judah, and had captured Beth Shemesh, Ayyalon, and Gederoth, along with Soco, Timnah, and Gimzo, and had occupied them.* [19] *Yahweh had humbled Judah on account of Ahaz king of Israel* [a] *because he had encouraged wickedness in Judah and had been wholly unfaithful to Yahweh.*

[20] *Tiglath-pileser* [a] *King of Assyria came against him; he made trouble for Ahaz instead of help.* [21] *Ahaz took things from the temple of Yahweh, from the royal palace, and from the officials and he gave them to the king of Assyria, but it did not help him.*

[22] *During the time of his troubles, this king* [a] *Ahaz became even more unfaithful to Yahweh,* [23] *and he made sacrifices* [a] *to the gods of Damascus that had defeated him. He said, "The gods of the kings of Aram help them. I will make sacrifices to them so they will help me." They became the downfall of Ahaz and of all Israel.*

[24] *Then Ahaz gathered together the implements from the temple of God, and he broke them into pieces; he closed the doors of the temple of Yahweh and made altars for himself at every corner in Jerusalem.* [25] *In each city of Judah he made high places to burn sacrifices to other gods, and he provoked Yahweh the God of his fathers.*

[26] *As for the rest of his deeds and practices, from beginning to end, they are recorded in the book of the kings of Judah and Israel.* [27] *Ahaz rested with his fathers and was buried in the city in Jerusalem,* [a] *though they did not inter him in the tombs of the kings of Israel. Hezekiah his son ruled in his place.*

Notes

1.a. MT and 2 Kgs 16:2; one Heb. MS, a few G minuscules, OL, Syr, and A, "twenty-five." See *Notes* at 27:8. If not a misplaced gloss to 27:8, this variant could represent harmonistic changes to cope with the difficulty surrounding the age at which Ahaz fathered Hezekiah; see *Comment* at 28:1–4.

3.a-a. Not found in the parallel at 2 Kgs 16:3.

3.b. עבר "passed through," with 2 Kgs 16:3, Bas, Par, and Tg; cf. 33:6. MT בער "burned" probably represents a simple metathesis instead of a tendential modification designed to turn a "ritual ordeal into a specific statement of human sacrifice" (Coggins, 258; cf. Lemke, *Synoptic Studies*, 207).

3.c. With MT, Par, and Bas[L] at 2 Kgs 16:3. 2 Kgs 16:3 MT, בנו "his son." Though there is no question that the Chronicler has sought to enhance the evil of Ahaz, the difference here probably does not represent a tendential change from sg to pl, but rather a difference of *plene* or *defectiva* orthography. Cf. the same problem at 33:6 and the parallel passage in 2 Kgs 21:6.

5.a. The clause "he brought them to Damascus" was omitted by G^B.

10.a. G, οὐκ ἰδού εἰμι "Am I not (with you to witness . . .)"; see 10.b.

10.b. G μαρτυρῆσαι "to witness" probably represented an error developing within G due to confusion with ἁμαρτῆσαι; a similar confusion occurs in the NT text of John 5:39. OL *peccastis* throws light on the earlier text of Par.

16.a. MT pl; cf. 30:6, 32:4. Singular in one Heb. MS, G, and Vg. The pl is in a sense the more difficult reading and makes good sense in all three contexts if taken as a reference to the dynasty or general imperial might of Assyria.

19.a. A few Heb. MSS and G, "King of Judah." According to Williamson (*IBC*, 102), this is one of eleven cases beyond any reasonable doubt in Chronicles where the word *Israel* is used with reference to the Southern Kingdom. Cf. 28:23, 27.

20.a. MT, "Till^egat-pilneser"; cf. G, Vg, and 1 Chr 5:26.

22.a., 23.a. At end of v 22 and beginning of v 23, for MT הוא המלך אחז ויזבח,

G (καὶ εἶπεν ὁ βασιλεὺς Ἐκζητήσω) appears to have read ויאמר המלך אדרש "the king said, 'I will seek the gods of Damascus. . . .'" Confusion of אחז with אמר and זבח with דרש may be the source of either variant, though neither can be convincingly argued on paleographical grounds. G's reading would introduce characteristic vocabulary of Chronicles (דרש) for the syntactically awkward הוא המלך אחז. See Allen, *GC* 2:133; Throntveit, *Significance*, 39–41. It is clear that the G translator did not have the present MT before him.

27.a. Par, 2 Kgs 16:20, and Bas, "in the city of David." MT is the more difficult; Par may reflect the influence of Bas or unconscious assimilation to parallel passages.

Form/Structure/Setting

The Chronicler's account of the reign of Ahaz is of considerable strategic importance in his treatment of the history of Judah. It was the period during which the Northern Kingdom went into exile; though the Chronicler is silent on that subject, it paved the way for his portrayal of a reunited Israel under Hezekiah (29:8–10; 30:1–31:1).

In the Chronicler's account of Ahaz several planes or layers of his literary program intersect: (1) he has modeled the apostasy of Judah after that of Israel just after the schism; (2) he has portrayed a mini-exile in the captivity and restoration of citizens of Judah (28:6–15) and captivity to other nations (28:5, 17); (3) Ahaz is the wicked son of a righteous father (Ezek 18:10–13).

(1) H. Williamson (343–49; *IBC*, 114–18) has shown how the Chronicler has reworked his account of Ahaz from that found in 2 Kgs 16 in order to effect an almost complete reversal of the relationship of North and South as found in 2 Chr 13. (a) Like Jeroboam at the time of the schism, Ahaz too makes molten images for worship (28:2). He also worships the gods of Damascus (28:10–16, 23), reflecting the charge of Abijah that Israel was worshiping the golden calves and "them that are no gods" (13:8–9). (b) Ahaz shut the doors of the temple (28:24), put out the lamps and stopped the offerings of incense and sacrifices (29:7), and neglected the shewbread (29:18). These additions to the Chronicler's account amount to the negation of Abijah's boast of orthodoxy before Jeroboam (13:11). These changes show that apostasy in the South had reached the same depths as that in the North at the time of the schism. (c) At the time of the schism, the righteous left the North to join Judah (11:13–17), but during the reign of Ahaz, righteousness was found in the North (28:9–15). Whereas at the time of the schism, Judah was obedient to the word of a prophet regarding attacking the sister kingdom (11:1–4), here it is Israel that heeds the admonition of a prophet (28:9). (d) The military

fortunes of the two kingdoms are also reversed. Contrast the fortunes of Jeroboam ("God delivered them into their hand, and Abijah and his people slew them with a great slaughter," 13:16–17) with those of Ahaz ("he was delivered into the hand of the king of Israel who smote him with a great slaughter," 28:5). At the time of Abijah it was Israel that was subjugated (13:18), whereas at the time of Ahaz, it was Judah (28:19). Ahaz is the only king of Judah for whom the Chronicler does not mention at least some redeeming feature; Ahaz is the antithesis of Abijah and the shadow of Jeroboam.

(2) Captives were seized from Judah by Aram, Samaria, Edom, and presumably the Philistines (28:5, 8, 17, 18), effecting somewhat of an "exile" for Judah contemporaneous with the exile of the Northern Kingdom. Hezekiah's prayer at the outset of his reign shows "clear overtones of the exile" (29:6–11; Williamson, *IBC*, 117–18) and points to obedience and cultic fidelity as the condition of restoration (cf. 30:8–9). It was a lesson that could not be missed by the Chronicler's audience.

(3) We have already suggested the influence of Ezekiel on the Chronicler's presentation of the divided kingdom (see the introductory essay to 2 Chr 10–36, "Reward and Punishment in Chronicles: The Theology of Immediate Retribution"). Further, in his handling of Jotham, Ahaz, and Hezekiah, he has abandoned the cyclical alternations between good and evil that characterized his accounts of the prior kings, preferring to portray them more uniformly as good or evil (with the possible exception of 32:24–26). In his account of these three reigns the Chronicler may have been seeking to duplicate the sequence of examples used by Ezekiel (18:5–18), such that Ahaz becomes the wicked son of a righteous man (Ezek 18:10–13; see chap. 27, *Explanation*).

R. Mosis (186–89) suggested that the Chronicler used the reigns of Saul, David, and Solomon as paradigms representative of the the three situations in which Israel might find itself subsequent to their reigns, and that Ahaz was treated as a kind of "second Saul" (189). However, though Mosis provides many helpful insights, his suggestions that the Chronicler used Saul as a paradigm and that Ahaz is a kind of second Saul are unconvincing; see in part the critique by H. Williamson, *IBC*, 118–19.

The Chronicler's account differs considerably from that in 2 Kgs 16:1–20; only the introduction and conclusion (28:1–4 // 2 Kgs 16:1–4; 28:26–27 // 2 Kgs 16:19–20) are reasonably close. However, one should not underestimate the influence of the Chronicler's *Vorlage* on his account. Though the details vary considerably, the author follows that same outline found in Kings; he writes about the apostasy in the land (28:1–4; 2 Kgs 16:2–4), events surrounding the Syro-Ephraimite invasion (28:5–15; 2 Kgs 16:5–6), the overture to Tiglath-pileser III (28:16–31; 2 Kgs 16:7–9), and cultic offenses (28:22–25; 2 Kgs 16:10–18). The writer appears to have been elaborating and interpreting the events reported in the parallel history in accord with some other sources at his disposal; one can only speculate regarding the nature of these additional materials. Some of the divergencies from the earlier account may represent the Chronicler's own inferences; he does not appeal to any source other than "the book of the kings of Judah and Israel" (28:26).

The divergences from the Kings account are most striking in two sections: the Chronicler's account of the Syro-Ephraimite invasion and his elaboration on Ahaz's cultic offenses. (1) The Chronicler presents the Syro-Ephraimite war as two separate campaigns (28:5–8) rather than the coalition described in 2 Kgs 16 and Isa 7. The Kings account highlights the failure of the coalition to inflict damage on Jerusalem (2 Kgs 16:5–9), whereas Chronicles emphasizes the losses of Judah (28:5–8, 16–19). The appeal to Tiglath-pileser was incited by attacks from the Edomites and Philistines instead of the Syro-Ephraimite coalition (28:16–19; contrast 2 Kgs 16:5–7). (2) Where Kings concentrates on the construction and use of Ahaz's Aramean altar (2 Kgs 16:10–16) and his despoliation of the temple for tribute payments (2 Kgs 16:8, 17–18), the Chronicler emphasizes instead the moral evil of Ahaz, his worship of Aramean deities, his closing the doors of the temple, and destroying the implements used there (28:22–25).

Comment

1–4 These vv essentially parallel 2 Kgs 16:1–4, though the Chronicler has somewhat enhanced the wickedness of Ahaz by injecting the note that Ahaz erected cast idols for worshiping the Baals and made sacrifices in the Valley of Ben Hinnom (28:2–3; see *Notes* at v 3). The reference to the cast idols is part of the Chronicler's efforts to draw a parallel between apostasy under Ahaz and the apostasy in the North at the time of the schism (13:8); see above, *Form/Structure/Setting*. The ritual of child sacrifice was associated with the Ben Hinnom Valley (33:6; Jer 7:31–32); other passages also allude to the practice (Lev 20:1–5; 2 Kgs 3:26–27, 23:10; Mic 6:7; Ezek 16:20–21). The purpose of such offerings is not known, though the context of Deut 18:10 suggests they were used at least in part for divination.

If Ahaz was twenty years old at the time of his accession and ruled until he was thirty-six, then his son Hezekiah who came to the throne at age twenty-five (29:1) would have been born when Ahaz was about eleven years old. This is either the earliest age of paternity recorded for the kings of Israel and Judah or one more example of the difficulties with the chronological notices in the MT. The chronology surrounding the reign of Ahaz is particularly difficult; see the survey of research in Konkel, *Hezekiah*, 29–43.

5–8 The Chronicler does not treat the attacks of the Arameans and Israel as a joint effort, as done in Isa 7:1–6 and 2 Kgs 16:5–7. He presents them instead as separate campaigns. The Chronicler is unfailingly hostile to foreign alliances since they demonstrate a failure to trust the Lord (16:2–9; 19:1–2; 22:3–6; 25:6–10); his desire in this pericope to present the Northern Kingdom in a favorable light (28:9–15) may have prompted him to separate the Syro-Ephraimite coalition into two separate campaigns and thereby to disentangle the Northern Kingdom from such an alliance. Israel was successful against Judah just as Judah had earlier defeated Israel (13:7–20).

Though both of the other accounts emphasize the ineffectiveness of the Syro-Ephraimite coalition in its assault on Jerusalem (Isa 7:1; 2 Kgs 16:5), the Chronicler has chosen to focus instead on the success of both armies against Judah. This modification reflects the author's theology of immediate retribution: evil kings suffer defeat in war, and this must certainly be true for Ahaz who represented the nadir of righteousness in Judah. The statement that Judah had "forsaken" Yahweh (v 6) is also characteristic of the author's theology of immediate retribution; in this particular instance it recalls the accusation of Abijah against the Northern tribes (13:9–12) and is part of the Chronicler's effort to parallel the apostasy under Ahaz with that of the Northern Kingdom at the time of the schism.

The numbers of the dead and captive are higher than is historically probable. Though it is notoriously difficult to estimate populations of ancient cities or regions, estimates of the population of Iron Age Judah rarely exceed three hundred thousand persons (Y. Shiloh, "The Population of Iron Age Palestine in the Light of a Sample Analysis of Urban Plans, Areas, and Population Density," *BASOR* 239 [1980] 25–35). If these estimates are correct, the figures of 28:6–7 would amount to complete depopulation of Judah, clearly beyond what the Chronicler intends. Efforts to reduce such large numbers by defining אֶלֶף, "thousand," as a tribal subunit or by repointing it as אַלּוּף, "commander, warrior" have not proved convincing; it appears rather that the Chronicler intends to be using these large numbers, possibly as hyberbole to enlarge on the defeat of Ahaz. Cf. the similar report of captives and spoil in 1 Chr 5:21: one would not reduce the number of captives by redefining אֶלֶף in this case unless also willing to do the same for the number of camels, sheep, and donkeys—but these do not come in tribes or as individual commanders, and it is clear that the author is intending plain numbers. See *Comment* at 14:8–9; 17:12–19.

The title "second to the king" (v 7) is otherwise only known from Esther 10:3.

9–11 Prophetic speeches are regularly the vehicles for the Chronicler's theology of immediate retribution. Nothing more is known of the prophet Oded.

The LORD was using Israel as an instrument to punish Judah, but the Northerners had overstepped their bounds with excessive zeal for the task, zeal that now made them liable to divine anger; cf. the similar theme in Zech 1:15; Isa 10:15, 40:2 (Ackroyd, 176). Elmslie (295) suggests that the Chronicler was drawing a parallel with Elisha's treatment of a captured Aramean army (2 Kgs 6:21–23). Benign treatment of the captives from Judah was all the more necessary, for the law forbade enslaving fellow Israelites (v 10; Lev 25:39–55). The Chronicler's positive attitude to the North is seen in his linking the citizens of the two kingdoms as "brethren" (v 11); even during the schism, Yahweh was their god (v10).

12–15 Such nontendential details as the names of the individuals and specifying Jericho as the city where the captives were returned suggest that the Chronicler was following some other source containing this information (Williamson, 347). Most striking is the omission of any reference to the king of Israel. This omission should be viewed as part of the Chronicler's program in the narrative: it was during the reign of Ahaz in Judah that the Northern Kingdom went into exile (30:6); the absence of a king in the North removed one more obstacle to the reunification of Israel under Hezekiah (Williamson, 344).

The response of the Ephraimite leaders is tantamount to an admission that Israel was "guilty before Yahweh" (v 10), not for wrong treatment of their brethren, but guilty of the charges leveled in 13:4–12 (Williamson, 347). Their repentance too opens the way to reunification under Hezekiah.

This pericope was undoubtedly a source for the parable of the Good Samaritan (Luke 10:25–37); see S. Spenser (*WTJ* 46 [1984] 317–49) for a recent discussion of the sources of this parable.

16–19 The inciting incident in Ahaz's seeking the help of Tiglath-pileser III was the attack of the Syro-Ephraimite coalition according to 2 Kgs 16:7; here instead it is attacks from the Edomites and Philistines. These two nations were natural allies against Judah and could have been seeking to forge overland trading routes free of Judean influence linking the strategic gulf trade through Elath with the coastal highway to the west; Uzziah had extended Judean control into the region (26:7–8). Pressure from the North (28:5) would have encouraged opportunism on Judah's southern and western flanks. The attacks from Edom may have been incited by the Arameans to further the interests of the coalition against Judah or the *Aram* of 2 Kgs 16:6 may have derived from misreading *Edom*. The cities captured by the Philistines (with the exception of Gimzo) were all along the Ayyalon, Sorek, and Elah valleys in the buffer zone of the Shephelah between the two nations or in the Negev (Arad).

The statement that Yahweh *humbled* Judah (v 19) is a characteristic theme of the Chronicler's theology of immediate retribution (7:14; 12:6–7, 12; 30:11; 32:26; 33:12, 19, 23); in this instance it serves also to reverse the military fortunes of Judah as described during the reign of Abijah (13:18; Williamson, 348). מעל, "be unfaithful," is also characteristic vocabulary for the Chronicler (1 Chr 9:1; 2 Chr 33:19; 36:14); here the identical form may reflect an effort to parallel Ahaz and Saul (2 Chr 10:13; cf. 28:22; Mosis, 31–32).

20–21 The dynamics among the petty states of Cis- and Transjordan would come to an abrupt end with the rising power of Tiglath-pileser III. Assyriological sources confirm his campaign in 734 B.C. down the coast of the Levant as far as the Wadi el-ʿArish (J. Gray, *ExpTim* 63 [1951–52] 263–65; A. Alt, *Kleine Schriften*, 2:150–62; H. Tadmor, *BA* 29 [1966] 87–90; D. Wiseman, *Iraq* 13 [1951] 21–26) where he left an Assyrian garrison that effectively cut off any possible aid from Egypt; this campaign overran the Philistine cities. In the following year Tiglath-pileser overwhelmed Israelite territories and reorganized them as three Assyrian provinces (Gilead, Megiddo, and Dor; cf. 1 Chr 5:26). Pekah of Israel was assassinated by Hoshea who presumably forestalled an Assyrian attack with tribute (2 Kgs 15:30; cf. 17:3). In 732 B.C. Tiglath-pileser captured and destroyed Damascus, executed Rezin, and reorganized the Aramean kingdom into four Assyrian provinces.

The payments Ahaz sent to the Assyrian king were but a prelude to his vassaldom (2 Kgs 16:10, 17–18); Tiglath-pileser records tribute received from Ahaz (*ANET*, 282). Though the deuteronomic historian reports at least some respite from Ahaz's overture to the Assyrian king (2 Kgs 16:9), the Chronicler views it only as a disaster for Judah.

22–23 The deuteronomic historian reports only that Ahaz copied an Aramean altar; the offerings he made on it were presumably made to Yahweh (2 Kgs 16:10–13). The Chronicler does not mention the altar itself, but rather portrays Ahaz engaged in idolatry worshiping the gods of Damascus. This statement would be all the more curious if the Assyrians had already defeated

Aram (2 Kgs 16:9–10; Elmslie, 299). Because Ahaz was meeting Tiglath-pileser III in Damascus, scholars have commonly interpreted Ahaz's altar as reflecting Assyrian worship imposed on vassal kingdoms. Cogan (*Imperialism,* 73–77) and McKay (*Religion,* 5–12) have shown that the Assyrians did not impose worship of their deities on vassal states and that the apostasy under Ahaz reflects indigenous Canaanite cults as the text of both Kings and Chronicles suggests rather than specifically Assyrian worship (see H. Spieckermann, 366–69, for the contrary opinion).

The Chronicler is perfecting the parallel between the apostasy of Judah under Ahaz and the apostasy of Israel at the time of the schism. Just as Israel worshiped idols and those that were "not gods" (13:8–9), so too Ahaz leads Judah into idolatry.

24–25 The same effort to liken the apostasy of Ahaz and Judah with that of Jeroboam and Israel is seen in these vv. Just as the Northern Kingdom had been without the true cult, Ahaz's closing the temple would deprive Judah of true worship (13:8–12; 29:6–8). The statement that Ahaz closed the temple contrasts to the report of the offerings he made there according to 2 Kgs 16:12–14. The Chronicler's enhancements of Ahaz's apostasy (28:22–25) are regarded by many as hyperbolic embellishments deduced by the Chronicler from the Kings account; C-M (p. 461) sees the closing of the temple as an effort to protect its sanctity by moving Ahaz's idolatries outside its precincts. However, the controlling purpose in most of these changes seems rather to be the effort to show that under Ahaz Judah had sunk to the same depths as Israel at the schism; see *Form/Structure/Setting.*

26–27 The Chronicler adds the note that Ahaz was not buried in the tombs of the kings in contrast to the statement that he was "buried with his fathers" (2 Kgs 16:20). He is the third king about whom the author reports the loss of this honor at death (Jehoram, 21:20; Joash, 24:25; Uzziah, 26:23; cf. 33:20).

Explanation

The Chronicler's account of the reign of Ahaz is the last in a series of theological reflections on the events surrounding the Syro-Ephraimite coalition, each reflecting the concerns and needs of the author's audience (see Thompson, *Situation,* 115–24). If Hos 5:8–7:16 is correctly understood as a series of oracles from during and after the Syro-Ephraimite war, Hosea sees in these events an occasion to indict the people for deserting Yahweh and looking to the nations for help. Isaiah, his contemporary in the South, spoke to the rulers and leaders of his day about the need for trust and confidence in the LORD in the face of the coalition's attack (Isa 7–9). For the deuteronomic historian (2 Kgs 16) the incident provided another example of cultic infidelity in Judah and of the failure of Judah's kings to live up to the deuteronomic ideal (Deut 17:14–20); Ahaz's reign was one more chapter in the litany of disobedience that explained to the exiles the reason for exile.

For the Chronicler this incident served yet other purposes. (1) Judah had reached its nadir under Ahaz. By showing that the apostasy of Judah had reached the depths of that in the Northern Kingdom at the schism, he opens the way toward repentance and reunification of "all Israel" under Hezekiah. Both South and North could be forgiven their apostasy. (2) The adumbrations of exile in the chapter prepare for instruction about restoration (29:8–10). (3) The Chronicler's treatment of Ahaz once again demonstrates the validity of the author's theology of immediate retribution.

The story of the good Samarians (28:15–16) would be told once again in slightly different guise by a prophet holding out the opportunity of repentance and restoration (Luke 10:25–37).

The Chronicler's Hezekiah, 716/15–687/86 B.C. (2 Chr 29–32)

Bright, J. *A History of Israel*. 2d ed. Philadelphia: Westminster Press, 1972. 277–308. **Brinkman, J.** "Merodach-Baladan II." *Studies Presented to A. L. Oppenheim*. Chicago: Oriental Institute, 1964. 6–53. **Broshi, M.** "The Expansion of Jerusalem in the Reigns of Hezekiah and Manasseh." *IEJ* 24 (1974) 21–26. **Catastini, A.** "Il quattordicesimo anno del regno di Ezechia (II Re 18:13)." *Hen* 4 (1982) 257–63. **Childs, B.** *Isaiah and the Assyrian Crisis*. London: SCM Press, 1967. **Clements, R.** *Isaiah and the Deliverance of Jerusalem*. JSOTSup, 13. Sheffield: JSOT Press, 1980. **Cogan, M.** "The Chronicler's Use of Chronology as Illuminated by Neo-Assyrian Royal Inscriptions." In *Empirical Models for Biblical Criticism*, ed. J. Tigay. Philadelphia: University of Pennsylvania Press, 1985. 197–210. ———. *Imperialism*. 70–110. **Fewell, N.** "Sennacherib's Defeat: Words at War in 2 Kgs 18:13–19:37." *JSOT* 34 (1986) 79–90. **Haag, H.** "Le campagne de Sennacherib contre Jerusalem en 701." *RB* 58 (1951) 348–59. **Haag, H.** "Das Mazzenfest des Hiskia." In *Wort und Geschichte—Festschrift K. Elliger*. AOAT 18. Kevelaer, 1973. 87–94. **Hallo. W.** "From Qarqar to Carchemish." *BA* 23 (1960) 33–61. **Horn, S.** "Did Sennacherib Campaign Once or Twice against Hezekiah?" *AUSS* 4 (1966) 1–28. ———. "The Chronology of King Hezekiah's Reign." *AUSS* 2 (1964) 40–52. **Hutter, M.** *Hiskija, König von Juda*. Grazer theologisches Studien, 6. Graz: Instituts für Ökumenische Theologie und Patrologie an der Universität Graz, 1982. ———. "Überlegungen zu Sanheribs Palastinafeldzug im Jahre 701 v. Chr." *BN* 19 (1982) 24–90. **Jenkins, A.** "Hezekiah's Fourteenth Year." *VT* 26 (1976) 284–98. **Jepsen, A.** "Noch einmal zur israelitisch-judischen Chronologie." *VT* 18 (1968) 31–46. **Kitchen, K.** *TIPE*. 154–72, 382–86. **Konkel, A.** *Hezekiah in Biblical Tradition*. Diss. Westminster Theological Seminary, 1987. **Kraus, H.** "Zur Geschichte des Passah-Massot-Festes in Alten Testament." *EvT* 18 (1958) 47–67. **Leeuwen, C. van.** "Sanchérib devant Jérusalem." *OTS* 14 (1965) 245–72. **Levine, L.** "The Second Campaign of Sennacherib." *JNES* 32 (1973) 312–17. **Mazar, B.** "The Campaign of Sennacherib in Judaea." *EI* 2 (1953) 170–75. **McHugh, J.** "The Date of Hezekiah's Birth." *VT* 14 (1964) 446–53. **McKay, J.** *Religion in Judah*. 13–19. **Millard, A.** "Sennacherib's Attack on Hezekiah." *TynBul* 36 (1985) 61–77. **Moriarty, F.** "The Chronicler's Account of Hezekiah's Reform." *CBQ* 27 (1965) 399–406. **Mosis, R.** *Untersuchungen*. 186–92. **Na'aman, N.** "Sennacherib's Campaign to Judah and the Date of the LMLK Stamps." *VT* 29 (1979) 61–86. ———. "Sennacherib's Letter to God on his Campaign to Judah." *BASOR* 214 (1974) 25–39. **Payne, J. B.** "The Relationship of the Reign of Ahaz to the Accession of Hezekiah." *BSac* 126 (1969) 40–52. **Petersen, D.** *Late Israelite Prophecy*. 77–85. **Rosenbaum, J.** "Hezekiah's Reform and Deuteronomic Tradition." *HTR* 72 (1979) 23–43. **Rowley, H.** "Hezekiah's Reform and Rebellion." *BJRL* 44 (1961–62) 395–431. **Shea, W.** "Sennacherib's Second Palestinian Campaign." *JBL* 104 (1985) 401–18. **Spieckermann, H.** *Juda unter Assur in der Sargonidenzeit*. Göttingen: Vandenhoeck & Ruprecht, 1982. **Stigers, H.** "The Interphased Chronology of Jotham, Ahaz, Hezekiah, and Hoshea." *BETS* 9 (1966) 81–90. **Stohlman, S.** "The Judean Exile after 701 B.C.E." In *Scripture in Context, II*, ed. W. Hallo, J. Moyer, and L. Perdue. Winona Lake: Eisenbrauns, 1983. **Tadmor, H.,** and **M. Cogan.** "Hezekiah's Fourteenth Year: The King's Illness and the Babylonian Embassy." *EI* 16 (1982) 198–201. **Talmon, S.** "Divergencies in Calendar Reckoning in Ephraim and Judah." *VT* 8 (1958) 48–74. **Thiele, E.** *Mysterious Numbers*. 3d ed. 135–36, 174–77. **Throntveit, M.** *Significance*. 155–62. **Todd, E.** "The Reforms of Hezekiah and Josiah." *SJT* 9 (1956) 288–93. **Welch, A.** *Work*. 97–121. **Williamson, H.** *IBC*. 119–30.

THE RANGE OF QUESTIONS

The accounts describing the reign of Hezekiah provide the setting for some of the most vigorously debated historical and theological questions in OT study. An enormous amount of scholarly effort has been poured into these questions; the entries above are quite selective, concentrating on more recent materials that provide summaries of the current state of the argument and entree into the larger bibliography devoted to the subject.

Historical questions tend to dominate the discussion. (1) Foremost among these is the issue of whether Sennacherib campaigned against Hezekiah once or twice, and how to resolve the apparent tension between Hezekiah's submission to the Assyrians (2 Kgs 18:13–16) and his resistance and miraculous deliverance (2 Kgs 18:17–19:37 // Isa 36:1–37:38). See the discussions by Bright, Childs, Clements, Horn, Hutter, Kitchen, Levine, Mazar, Millard, Na'aman, Rowley, and Shea. This basic question is inextricably bound up with a series of related issues. (2) These question do not involve biblical materials alone, but also the reconstruction and interpretation of a considerable number of extrabiblical sources from Mesopotamia, Egypt, and Canaan. Primary among these are the records of Sennacherib's third campaign which report his confrontation with Judah. (3) The Rabshaqeh twice appears before Jerusalem to intimidate Hezekiah and his officials; many regard 2 Kgs 18:17–19:9 and 19:9–36 as duplicate accounts (Childs, 73–103). (4) The chronological notices surrounding Hezekiah's reign are difficult to reconcile; see the discussions by Horn, Hutter, Jenkins, McHugh, Payne, Stigers, Tadmor and Cogan, and Thiele. (5) Beyond the passages that provide narrative histories of Hezekiah's reign (2 Kgs 18–20; Isa 36–39; 2 Chr 29–32), there is the additional question of which oracles of Isaiah were spawned in the Assyrian crisis of 701 and may shed some light on historical questions (Childs, 20–68). (6) Some scholars question the historicity of aspects of Hezekiah's reform. Some regard the Chronicler's portrayal of Passover under Hezekiah (2 Chr 30) as consciously developed from the deuteronomic portrayal of that feast under Josiah (2 Kgs 23:21–23). Others see Hezekiah's reform as essentially the religious outworking of his political rebellion against Assyria. See the discussions in Haag, Rosenbaum, Spieckermann, McKay, and Cogan.

Alongside these historical questions there are issues of theology and tradition history. (1) The reign of Hezekiah was a crucible for the developing ideology of the inviolability of Zion (Clements). (2) The narratives about Hezekiah in Isaiah, Kings, and Chronicles were all shaped by the concerns of their respectives compilers, and each makes a distinctive use of the material while also presenting distinctive portraits of the king.

THE NARROWER FOCUS

Though we shall have occasion to discuss or allude to most of these historical and theological questions in the subsequent chapters, our focus in this introductory essay is on this last issue, the distinctive portrait of Hezekiah in Chronicles and the author's controlling purposes.

In the eyes of the book of Kings the zenith of the divided kingdom in

Judah was reached under Josiah. This focus on Josiah may derive in part from an earlier edition of the deuteronomic history which concentrated on Josiah as the antidote for the evils of the schism (1 Kgs 13:2; 2 Kgs 23:15–18) and which therefore somewhat understated the significance of earlier reform kings as a part of its focus on Josiah. For the Chronicler, however, it is Hezekiah who is the zenith for post-schism Judah. The account of Hezekiah in Kings mentions only briefly his religious reforms (2 Kgs 18:3–7) and concentrates instead on his confrontation with the Assyrians (2 Kgs 18:8–19:37; cf. Isa 36–37), his illness, and the envoys from Merodach–Baladan (2 Kgs 20:1–19; cf. Isa 38–39). The proportion is reversed in Chronicles: the largest part of the account is given to Hezekiah's reform (2 Chr 29–31), and much less attention is paid to the Assyrian invasion (2 Chr 32:1–23), the envoys from Babylon (32:31), and his illness (32:24–26). Very little of the Chronicler's account constitutes verbal parallels with the earlier history; only about a dozen verses are strictly parallel, and these are largely the formulaic introductory and concluding notices.

It is clear that the Chronicler has quite a different outlook on Hezekiah than that which he inherited from the deuteronomic historian. A number of the Chronicler's distinctive emphases intersect in his portrayal. (1) Hezekiah reunifies Israel, reflecting the Chronicler's concern with "all Israel." (2) Hezekiah is portrayed as a second David and Solomon. (3) Hezekiah also exemplifies the operation of the Chronicler's retribution theology.

(1) With the removal of the Northern Kingdom in the fall of Samaria, for the first time since David and Solomon there is now one king over Israel. Though the Chronicler does not directly narrate the fall of the Northern Kingdom (cf. 30:6), he is concerned to show North and South united in cultic fidelity under Hezekiah (30:1–20; 31:1), reflecting the practices of the golden era under Solomon (30:26). Israel is reunited under Hezekiah in the Chronicler's eyes, not only in having one king and temple, but also in its geographical extent, embracing the land from Beersheba to Dan (30:5; cf. 1 Chr 21:2). The Chronicler uses the phrase "land of Israel" on only four occasions, one each during the reign of David (1 Chr 22:2), Solomon, (2 Chr 2:16 [17]), Hezekiah (30:25), and Josiah (34:7), all periods when the land was defined in its traditional extent (Williamson, *IBC*, 123; Japhet, *Ideology*, 365–66).

The lesson for the Chronicler's audience could not be missed. For those living in the post-exilic period, the "remnant that had escaped from the hands of the kings of" Babylon (cf. 30:6), the path to the reunification of Israel and the fulfillment of prophetic hopes was the path of cultic fidelity. For those cherishing this dream in the restoration community, the Chronicler cites an instance of its realization in the past as impetus to hope for the future.

(2) The portrayal of Israel united under a Davidic king is only one aspect of the Chronicler's modeling Hezekiah in the image of David and Solomon; see the discussion in Throntveit, 155–62; Williamson, *IBC*, 119–25.

(a) The Chronicler effects a number of parallels in the cultic sphere. At the time of their accession, both kings were concerned immediately with the temple (2 Chr 1; 2 Chr 29). He specifically likens the observance of Passover at the time of Hezekiah to the time of Solomon (30:26). Hezekiah appointed the priests and Levites to their respective divisions and duties (31:2, 11–20; 29:11–14), recalling the arrangements made by David and Solomon (1 Chr 15:3–24; 23–26; 2 Chr 8:14–15). The celebration at the dedication of Solomon's temple lasted two weeks (7:8–9), and at the time of Hezekiah, "the whole assembly agreed to celebrate the festival seven more days, so for another seven days they celebrated joyfully" (30:23).

(b) The Chronicler emphasizes Hezekiah's great wealth (32:27–29), comparable to a similar report given of Solomon (9:13–14). Hezekiah too had made shields (32:27; cf. 9:15–16; 12:9–10).

(c) Just as Gentile kings brought gifts to Solomon (9:23–24), so too Hezekiah receives gifts and is "highly regarded by all the nations" (32:23). Both kings provide exemplars of the prophetic hope of the pilgrimage of the nations to Jerusalem; see *Comment* at 9:23–24.

(d) Hezekiah is said to have done "what was right in the eyes of Yahweh, according to all that David his father had done" (29:2). Though this formula is drawn from the parallel history (2 Kgs 18:3), it nevertheless likens Hezekiah to David.

(e) Hezekiah's intercessory prayer at the passover observance (30:18–20) recalls the similar prayer of Solomon at the temple dedication (2 Chr 6). The LORD promised "healing" in response to Solomon's prayer (7:14), and granted healing in response to Hezekiah (30:20).

Mosis argued that the Chronicler had made Hezekiah a "second David" (*Untersuchungen*, 189). This was a corollary of his contention that the Chronicler had made the reigns of Saul, David, and Solomon paradigmatic for the three historical situations in which Israel might find itself: a time of apostasy (Saul), a time of good rule and blessing (David), and a period of ultimate blessing for which Israel could only hope in faith (Solomon). Since this eschatological hope must be future, the kings of Judah on Mosis's schema could only be likened to Saul or David. Mosis's schema breaks down, however, when one sees that far more parallels are drawn between Hezekiah and Solomon than between Hezekiah and David. Williamson (*IBC*, 119–25) has shown that Solomon is more clearly the paradigm for the Chronicler's Hezekiah than David, so that Williamson tends to view Hezekiah rather as a "second Solomon." A mediating position recognizes that the Chronicler's treatment of David and Solomon forms an indissoluble unity and sees themes drawn from both of these earlier reigns for the author's portrait of Hezekiah (Throntveit, 155–62; Ackroyd, 179–89).

(3) The Chronicler never tires of demonstrating the validity of his theology of immediate retribution (see the introductory essay to 2 Chr 10–26, "Reward and Punishment in Chronicles: The Theology of Immediate Retribution"). Hezekiah enjoys the blessing of God for his fidelity, blessing seen in loyalty and support of the populace, the reunification of the nation, building projects and prosperity, military victory and recognition among the nations. Hezekiah is presented almost as blameless as Solomon, with the exception of the enigmatic 32:24–26: Hezekiah was proud, but his repentance forestalled the wrath of Yahweh. See also *Comment* at 32:31.

Hezekiah Cleanses the Temple (29:1–36)

Bibliography

See the bibliography in the previous chapter, "The Chronicler's Hezekiah."

Translation

¹ *Hezekiah became king when he was twenty-five years old, and he ruled twenty-nine years in Jerusalem. His mother's name was Abijah,*ᵃ *daughter of Zechariah.* ² *He did what was right in the eyes of Yahweh just like all his father David had done.*

³ *In the first year*ᵃ *of his reign during the first month, he reopened the doors of the temple and repaired them.* ⁴ *He summoned the priests and Levites and assembled them in the eastern square.* ⁵ *He said to them:*

"Listen to me, O Levites: Sanctify yourselves now and sanctify the temple of Yahweh, the God of your fathers. Remove any defiled things from the sanctuary. ⁶ *Our fathers were unfaithful and did evil in the eyes of Yahweh our God. They forsook him; they turned their faces away from Yahweh's dwelling and turned their backs on him.* ⁷ *They even closed the doors of the portico and extinguished the lamps; they did not burn incense or offer burnt offerings in the sanctuary of the God of Israel.* ⁸ *The anger of Yahweh was aroused against Judah and Jerusalem; he made them an object of dread, horror, and derision, as you can see with your own eyes.* ⁹ *Indeed, our*ᵃ *fathers fell by the sword, while our sons, daughters, and wives were carried into captivity*ᵇ *because of this.*ᶜ ¹⁰ *Now I desire to make a covenant with Yahweh the God of Israel so that he will turn the wrath of his anger from upon us.* ¹¹ *Now, my sons,*ᵃ *do not be negligent, for Yahweh has chosen you to stand before him and to minister to him, to be his ministers and those who burn incense."*

¹² *Then these Levites set to work:*
from the Kohathites: Mahat son of Amasai and Joel son of Azariah;
from the Merarites: Kish son of Abdi and Azariah son of Mehallelel;
from the Gersonites: Joah son of Zimmah and Eden son of Joah
¹³ *from the descendants of Elizaphan: Shimri and Jeiel;*
from the descendants of Asaph: Zechariah and Mattaniah
¹⁴ *from the descendants of Heman: Jehiel and Shimei;*
from the descendants of Jeduthun: Shemaiah and Uzziel.

¹⁵ *They gathered their kinsmen and sanctified themselves; they went in to purify the temple of Yahweh as the king had commanded in accordance with the words of Yahweh.* ¹⁶ *The priests went inside the temple of Yahweh to purify it. They brought out into the courtyard of the temple of Yahweh all the unclean things they found in the temple of Yahweh; then the Levites received it and took it out to the Kidron Valley.* ¹⁷ *They began to sanctify the temple on the first*ᵃ *day of the first month. On the eighth day of the month they reached the portico of Yahweh; they sanctified the temple of Yahweh for eight days, and they finished on the sixteenth*ᵇ *day of the first month.* ¹⁸ *Then they went before King Hezekiah and said:*

"We have purified all the temple of Yahweh, the altar of burnt offerings and all its implements, the table for the consecrated bread and all its implements. ¹⁹We have prepared and sanctified all the implements that King Ahaz removed in his unfaithfulness during his reign; they are now before the altar of Yahweh."

²⁰Hezekiah arose and gathered the leaders of the city and went up to the temple of Yahweh. ²¹They brought seven bulls, seven rams, and seven male lambs,ᵃ along with seven male goats for a sin offering in behalf of the kingdom, the sanctuary, and Judah. He commanded the priests the descendants of Aaron to make the burnt offerings on the altar of Yahweh. ²²So they slaughtered the bulls, and the priests took the blood and sprinkled it on the altar; they slaughtered the rams and sprinkled the blood on the altar; they slaughtered the lambs and sprinkled the blood on the altar. ²³Then they brought the goats for the sin offering before the king and the assembly, and they laid their hands on them. ²⁴The priests slaughtered them and presented their blood on the altar as a sin offering to atone for all Israel, for the king had ordered that the burnt offering and sin offering be made for all Israel.

²⁵He stationed the Levites in the temple of Yahweh with cymbals, harps, and lyres, as had been commanded by David, Gad the seer of the king, and Nathan the prophet—this commandment was from Yahweh through his prophets. ²⁶The Levites took their positions with the instruments of David, and the priests with trumpets.

²⁷Hezekiah gave the order to make the burnt offering on the altar. At the time that the burnt offering began, the singing to Yahweh also began, accompanied by the trumpets and the instruments of David king of Israel. ²⁸All the congregation was worshiping; the singers were singing, and allᵃ the trumpeters were playing until the burnt offering was finished.

²⁹When the burnt offering was finished, the king and all who were with him bowed down and worshiped. ³⁰King Hezekiah and his officials ordered the Levites to praise Yahweh using the words of David and Asaph the seer. So they offered praises with joy, and bowed down and worshiped.

³¹Then King Hezekiah answered and said, "Now you have dedicated yourselves to Yahweh. Approach, and bring sacrifices and thank offerings to the temple of Yahweh." So the assembly brought sacrifices and thank offerings.ᵃ All who were willing brought burnt offerings.

³²The number of burnt offerings which the congregation brought was seventy bulls, a hundred rams, and two hundred male lambs; all these were burnt offerings to Yahweh. ³³The animals consecrated as sacrifices amounted to six hundred bulls and three thousandᵃ sheep and goats. ³⁴However, the priests were few in number and were not able to skin the burnt offerings, so their kinsmen the Levites assisted them until the work was done and until other priests had sanctified themselves, for the Levites had been more conscientious than the priests in sanctifying themselves. ³⁵There were also a great number of burnt offerings along with the fat of the fellowship offerings and with libations accompanying the burnt offerings. So the service of the temple of Yahweh was reinstituted.

³⁶Hezekiah and all the people rejoiced at what God had done for the people, for the work had been done speedily.

Notes

1.a. 2 Kgs 18:2, has a shorter form, "Abi."

3.a. G, καὶ ἐγένετο ὡς ἔστη ἐπὶ τῆς βασιλείας αὐτοῦ "it came about when he began his king-ship. . . ." G appears to have read either וְהָנָא or וַיְהִי for the MT הוא. The remainder is paraphrase, but also settles the ambiguity as to whether MT "first year, first month" is the first month of his reign or the first month of his first official full year, not counting the accession year.

9.a. G reads second person suffixes throughout the verse, "your fathers, your sons, your daughters, your wives." This is most naturally explained as an intra-G confusion of ἡμῶν and ὑμῶν.

9.b. G adds ἐν γῇ οὐκ αὐτῶν "in a land not their own." This appears to be an assimilation to the similar context mentioning sword, sons, and daughters in Jer 5:17, 19. See Allen, *GC* 2:62.

9.c. G translators took על זאת with the following verse. See Allen, *GC* 1:149.

11.a. G omits בני; see Allen, *GC* 2:133. OL *edificate*, "build," = בְּנוּ.

17.a,b. For MT "sixteenth," G^B reads "thirteenth." The change could be a scribal error based on the use of a system of abbreviations for numerals (Allen, *GC* 1:172, 2:85). Rudolph (294) regards it as a theologically motivated change, so that the purification of the temple was completed before the beginning of Passover. Whatever the origin of the second figure in G, the change from MT "first" to G^B* "third" is a mathematical correction to achieve the correct tally, rendered superfluous by the correction to "first" so that the total remained thirteen.

21.a. One need not with Rudolph (296) et al. suggest that לעלה dropped from the text at this point. It may assist the reader to insert the phrase "for burnt offerings" into the text of a translation (e.g., NEB) in order to anticipate at an earlier point the distinction made between the burnt offerings and sin offering (vv 22–23), but no versional evidence suggests the phrase was original, and the case for its accidental omission is poor.

28.a. הכל is missing in G, Syr, and Vg. Its omission in Par is reasonably common (Allen, *GC* 2:152–53), though it could be equally well understood as a gloss to MT or perhaps a dittogr from the preceding וכל or the following לכלות.

31.a. G adds εἰς οἶκον κυρίου, "to the house of the LORD," assimilating to the phrase in the earlier part of the verse.

33.a. G^B adds five hundred, for a total of thirty-five hundred small cattle. Allen (*GC* 2:102) explains this as an assimilation to 35:9.

Form/Structure/Setting

Hezekiah's reinstitution of legitimate temple worship early during his reign is described in four steps: (1) the instruction and ritual purification of the priests and Levites (29:3–15); (2) the purification of the temple and its precincts (29:16–19); (3) the rededication of the temple (29:20–30); (4) the participation of the populace (29:31–36). Estimates of the historicity of the events reported run the full gamut from regarding the entire chapter as a free composition of the Chronicler without historical foundation (Elmslie, 301) to accepting it as a reliable account (Myers, 169).

Though the account appears rather simple and straightforward, on closer reading various scholars have found it to be a highly complex composition of diverse sources that betray editorial activity and secondary expansions (Welch, *Work*, 103–7; Petersen, *Prophecy*, 79–83). Though the audience for Hezekiah's speech is initially stated as "priests and Levites" (29:4), Hezekiah addresses only "Levites" (29:5). In 29:12–15 it is only Levites who set out to follow Hezekiah's instructions. The remainder of the passage distinguishes the actions of the priests (29:20–24) and Levites (29:25–30). These references to the priests and their activities have commonly been viewed as the later insertions of a pro-priestly reviser who sought to attenuate somewhat the Chronicler's pro-Levitical stance.

Other commentators have argued in favor of the unity of the passage (Rudolph, 293–94; Williamson, 352–56). Though there is some confusion regarding the addressees, the speech of Hezekiah calls on his audience to "stand before him, minister to him, be his ministers, and burn incense" (29:11). Since the Chronicler is particularly concerned to restrict incense offering to the priests, the sons of Aaron (26:18), it must be assumed that the speech of Hezekiah was addressed to both priests and Levites even though only Levites are mentioned in 29:5. Hezekiah calls on his audience to rectify the evil done by Ahaz (29:7), including the reinstitution of rites and responsibilities restricted to the priests. The curious double occurrence of the verb "minister" (שרת) in 29:11 is also best explained as a reference to both priests and Levites: "to stand before and to minister" refers specifically to the duties of priests, whereas "to be his ministers" refers to the Levites. If Hezekiah's speech presumes the work of both priest and Levite, then in 29:5 the Chronicler is either (1) highlighting the Levites (Rudolph, 293), or (2) we should understand the term "Levites" as including both, i.e., though it is common for the writer to carefully distinguish these two offices, both could be designated as "Levites" on the principle that the broader includes the narrower. Though there are textual difficulties associated with these passages, cf. the author's designation of the priests as "Levitical priests" in the Hezekiah narrative (30:27) and elsewhere (1 Chr 9:2; 2 Chr 5:5; 23:18). The chapter does show some lethargy on the part of the priests and possibly some rivalry between the priests and Levites; these tensions may actually reflect the historical circumstances and need not be the end product of editorial history.

Hezekiah's speech (29:5–11) has been classified as a "Levitical sermon" (von Rad, *Hexateuch*, 275). It shows many of the features of this genre as von Rad described it: a historical retrospect (29:6–7), an allusion to a biblical text (29:8; Jer 29:18), and an exhortation (29:9–11).

Most of the paragraph boundaries in the text are marked by the use of an explicit subject (29:3, 12, 16, 31, 36), though not all explicit subjects in the passage appear to initiate a new paragraph (e.g., 29:26). The chapter is structured by various commands given in speeches and their fulfillment (e.g., 29:25–26, 29–30). One paragraph is begun with a ויהי-clause (29:32). In 29:28–29 there is an example of tail-head linkage between paragraphs: a phrase (the finishing of the burnt offering) at the end of one paragraph is repeated at the beginning of the next.

Comment

1–2 The Chronicler's account of the reign of Hezekiah (2 Chr 29–32) is almost completely independent of the parallel history (2 Kgs 18–20). He does draw his accession notice from the parallel text (2 Kgs 18:1–3), omitting the synchronism with the North.

The chronological notices surrounding the reigns of Jotham, Ahaz, and Hezekiah present one of the most difficult problems in the chronology of the kingdoms. Sorting out the issues involved would require a lengthy digression and is more the province of specialized studies (Catastini, Horn, Jenkins, McHugh, Payne, Stigers, Thiele); Hutter (52–55) and Konkel (9–43) provide a history of efforts to resolve these difficulties. Here we are following the system proposed by Thiele and thus dating Hezekiah's rule from 716/715 to 687/86 B.C., so that the twenty-nine-year reign includes the fifteen-year extension of his life (2 Kgs 20:6). If Hezekiah was twenty-five years old at the time of his accession (29:1) and his father was thirty-six at the time of his death (28:1), Hezekiah would have been born when Ahaz was about eleven years old; see *Comment* at 28:1.

The Chronicler has shaped his portrayal of Hezekiah as a second Solomon; see the introductory essay, "The Chronicler's Hezekiah." Here his likening Hezekiah to David is simply borrowed from the accession notice in 2 Kgs 18:3 (Williamson, 352).

3–4 The text is ambiguous as to whether the "first month, first year" was his first official year (postdating) or the first month after the death of his father (antedating); see Cogan, "Chronicler's Use of Chronology," 201–3. In either case the Chronicler is likening Hezekiah to Solomon in his concern with the temple from the time of his accession (2 Chr 1–2). The "eastern square" may be the same locale as the "square near the Water Gate" in Neh 8:1, 3, i.e., a location still outside the temple precincts; such squares were commonly found just inside city gates.

5–11 Hezekiah's father Ahaz had brought Judah to the same nadir that Jeroboam brought to Israel; see chap. 28, *Form/Structure/Setting.* Hezekiah's opening the doors of the temple, cleansing it, reestablishing worship, reinstituting incense rites and the care of the lampstands all reverse the actions of Ahaz (28:24–25) under whom Judah had lost the boast of its fidelity to Yahweh (13:10–11) that had characterized Solomon's rule (2:4; 4:7, 19–22).

Hezekiah's speech also recounts the military defeats suffered at the time of Ahaz when large segments of the population were deported (see *Comment* at 28:5–8, 17–18). The Chronicler borrows Jeremiah's description of the great exile of Judah (29:8; Jer 29:18) to describe the adumbration of that later event which occurred during the reign of Ahaz. Though similar language is found elsewhere, only Jer 29:18 has the complete form of the statement that Yahweh would make his people "an object of dread, horror, and derision" (von Rad, *Hexateuch,* 275; cf. Mic 6:16).

For the Chronicler's post-exilic audience the lesson could not be clearer: the path to restoration and blessing was the path of cultic fidelity.

The Chronicler also shapes Hezekiah's speech as a vehicle for pronouncements about retribution theology; see the introductory essay to 2 Chr 10–36, "Reward and Punishment in Chronicles: The Theology of Immediate Retribution." Being "unfaithful" (מעל) and "forsaking" (עזב) are two of the most characteristic terms in the Chronicler's speech materials; מעל in this context and others appears to refer more narrowly to cultic infidelity (cf. 29:19).

The Chronicler describes the temple cleansing as a covenant renewal (29:10). The statement recalls the language of Solomon's prayer at the dedication of the temple (6:14–16).

On the double use of "minister" (שרת), see above, *Form/Structure/Setting.*

12–15 The list of fourteen Levites is composed of (1) two representatives from each of the three Levitical families—Kohath, Merari, and Gershon; (2)

two representatives from the great Kohathite family of Elizaphan; and (3) two representatives from each division of the singers—Asaph, Heman, and Jeduthun. When compared with the list in 1 Chr 15:5–10, the Levitical singers have replaced Hebron and Uzziel, perhaps reflecting a growing influence on the part of the musical families (Petersen, *Prophecy*, 81). The family of Elizaphan had achieved sufficient importance as to be virtually a fourth Levitical clan, though in fact a subclan of Kohath (Num 3:30; 1 Chr 15:8).

The temple cleansing was carried out in accordance with the "words of Yahweh" (29:15). This statement may be part of the author's effort to parallel Hezekiah's reign with earlier events of Israel's history: just as the plans for the tabernacle, the temple (1 Chr 28:11–19), and Ezekiel's temple had come from the LORD, so instructions for its renewal have divine origin at the time of Hezekiah (see *Comment* at 29:25). Alternatively, the Chronicler may simply be indicating that Hezekiah's efforts were in conformity with the law, e.g., Deut 12:2–4.

16–17 Pagan cult objects were also burned in the Kidron at the time of Asa (15:16) and Josiah (30:14; 2 Kgs 23:4, 6, 12).

The purification of the temple required two weeks, one week in the outer courts and another in the building itself. The term *interior* (פנימה) may broadly refer to the interior of the temple (cf. 29:18) or more narrowly to the Most Holy Place (cf. 4:22; 1 Chr 28:11; 1 Kgs 6:27, 7:12, 50). It is not altogether clear in this case which is intended. The Levites were responsible for the inventory of the temple implements being taken in or out of the building (1 Chr 9:28), implying that they did not ordinarily enter the interior of the sanctuary; on the other hand, the Chronicler may be seeking to illustrate careful observance of the laws restricting access to the Most Holy Place to priests (5:4–11).

The cleansing continued until the "sixteenth" day of the first month, i.e., two days after Passover would ordinarily have begun (Num 9:1–11). This sets the stage for the delayed observance of Passover as reported in chap. 30.

18–19 P. Ackroyd ("The Temple Vessels—A Continuity Theme," in *Studies in the Religion of Ancient Israel*, ed. P. de Boer, VTSup 23 [Leiden: E. J. Brill, 1972] 166–81) notes the stress placed on the proper recovery and treatment of the temple implements, a theme important to the restoration community. These implements represented continuity with the glorious past and Solomon's temple (4:19–22; 1 Chr 28:14–17); whatever the fate of the building itself, the implements used in worship there survived (36:18; Ezra 1:7–11; Dan 5:2–3, 23; 2 Kgs 25:14–15).

20–24 A distinction is made between the burnt offerings (the seven bulls, rams, and lambs) and the sin offerings (the seven goats); see *Notes* at 29:21.a. The burnt offerings are most naturally understood as the same offerings mentioned again in 29:27 (contra Petersen, *Prophecy*, 82–83); the two paragraphs refer to the same offerings, but focus on the roles of different cultic personnel, the priests (29:24) and the Levitical musicians (29:27; Rudolph, 293).

The inclusion of the sin offerings finds its closest analog in the sin offerings mentioned in Ezekiel as part of the cleansing of the altar and sanctuary, the purification of priests, and preparation for celebration of Passover (Ezek 43:18–27; 45:1–3, 18–20; 44:27); this offering was made for the kingdom, the sanctuary, and the nation as a whole, i.e., for those involved in the apostasy under Ahaz (Williamson, 356).

Who actually slaughtered the burnt offerings? The "they" of v 22 appears to refer to the priests who are commanded to make the offerings (v 21; cf. v 34). However, the burnt offerings were ordinarily slaughtered by the offerer rather than the priest who was instead responsible for the blood rite (Lev 1:4–5). One need not suggest an earlier version of the account in which the laity performed the slaughter and which was modified at a later editorial stage to ascribe this task to the priests (Petersen, 82–83). If "they" is taken as an impersonal plural (Williamson, 356–57), tantamount to saying "the animals were slaughtered," this difficulty would disappear, for it would be the king and his officials who performed the slaughter. Alternatively, since the animals were not the offering of any particular individuals but were in behalf of the nation, it would be appropriate on such a unique occasion that the priests officiate in the slaughter as well. Either explanation suffices without suggesting some evolution of sacrificial practice eliminating lay slaughter by extending the role of the priests, though such an extension of priestly prerogatives remains plausible.

The offering was made for "all Israel" (29:24). The Chronicler may be using "Israel" as simply a synonym for Judah in this context (Rudolph, 294; cf. 29:21), or in light of Hezekiah's great interest in the Northern Kingdom, it may embrace a larger group than the priests initially thought (Williamson, *IBC*, 127).

25–26 This pericope prompts the question "Is David also among the prophets?" The Chronicler appears to regard him as such. The prophets were the recipients of the divine plans for the construction of Israel's sanctuaries: Moses received the plans for the tabernacle (Exod 25–30); Ezekiel saw the future temple (Ezek 40–48); and David received the plans for the temple "from the hands of the LORD upon me" (1 Chr 28:19). The Chronicler has gone out of his way to portray David as an occasional recipient of direct and unmediated revelation (1 Chr 22:8; 28:4–7, 19) in contrast to the account in Samuel where David receives revelation through prophets. See *Comment* at 29:15.

The Chronicler shows extensive interest in David's relationship to the cult and especially the Levites (1 Chr 23–27). He is no doubt in part seeking to establish the legitimacy of Levitical functions in his own day by reporting their origin at the time of David.

30 The Chronicler portrays the Levitical musicians as having a prophetic role (1 Chr 25:1–6; 2 Chr 20:14; 34:12–13 // 2 Kgs 23:2; 2 Chr 35:15; see Petersen, *Prophecy,* 55–87). This is probably best understood as evidence of the decline of the prophetic order in his own day, so that prophetic function or authority was associated with the Levitical musicians. The Chronicler is in effect legitimating an attitude to the Levitical musicians that was current in his time.

31–33 The idiom for "dedicated yourselves" (lit., "fill the hand") ordinarily refers to priestly investiture (13:9), but is used by the Chronicler also in a wider sense (1 Chr 29:5), and in this context clearly applies to the whole assembly and not just to the priests (cf. Williamson, 31).

One of the characteristic features of the Chronicler's work is his effecting parallels with earlier events in Israel's history. The spontaneity and extensiveness of the popular response to the restoration of the temple mirrors events at the time of David, Solomon, and Moses (Exod 36:6–7; 1 Chr 29:6–9; 2 Chr 7:7). The author was commending similar generosity to his readers in the post-exilic period.

34–36 It was ordinarily the duty of the offerer to slay and skin his offering (Lev 1:5–6), though by the period of Hezekiah, or at least on this occasion, the duty fell to the priests. See the discussion above at 29:20–24.

The author does not explain the lethargy or dawdling of the priests. Whatever the tension between the priests and Levites or between the priests and the king, the Chronicler clearly favors the Levites and provides a historical precedent for what may reflect the practice of his own day.

The people *rejoiced* at what Yahweh had done just as they had done at the dedication of Solomon's temple (7:10; cf. 30:25–26).

Explanation

The Chronicler is portraying Hezekiah as a second Solomon. After the fall of the Northern Kingdom, the spiritual successor of Israel is the united kingdom under Hezekiah. Though Judah had fallen to its nadir under Ahaz and had become just like the Northern Kingdom and had itself also endured an exile of large parts of its population, Hezekiah comes to bring restoration in the path of cultic fidelity. The lesson for the author's audience in the post-exilic period could not be missed: he summoned his readers to zeal for the LORD's house, to a national life of cultic fidelity, and to rejoicing over what God had done in their own day.

Christian readers of this chapter cannot but think of another cleansing of the Lord's temple, a time when zeal for the Lord's house would consume another son of David (John 2:17; Ps 69:9).

Hezekiah's Passover (30:1–27)

Bibliography

See the entries in the introductory chapter to 2 Chr 29–32, "The Chronicler's Hezekiah," particularly the items by Haag and Kraus. See in addition the following:

McConville, J. *Law and Theology.* 99–123. **Meier, W.** "'Fremdlinge, die aus Israel gekommen waren': eine Notiz in 2 Chronik 30:25f." *BN* 15 (1981) 40–43. **Segal, J.** *The Hebrew Passover.* London Oriental Series, 12. New York: Oxford UP, 1963. **Shaver, J.** *Torah.* 150–68. **Vaux, R. de.** *Ancient Israel.* New York: McGraw-Hill, 1965. 2:484–92.

Translation

[1] *Hezekiah sent messages to all Israel and Judah and also wrote letters to Ephraim and Manasseh to come to the temple of Yahweh in Jerusalem to celebrate Passover for Yahweh the God of Israel.*
[2] *The king, his officials, and all the assembly in Jerusalem decided to celebrate Passover in the second month;* [3] *they had not been able to celebrate it at that time* [a] *since a sufficient number of priests had not sanctified themselves, and the people had not assembled in Jerusalem.* [4] *The plan was right in the eyes of the king and the whole assembly.* [5] *They decided to send a proclamation through all Israel from Beersheba to Dan to come to celebrate Passover to Yahweh the God of Israel in Jerusalem, for they had not celebrated it in such large numbers* [a] *according to what was written.*
[6] *Heralds went out at the king's command through all Israel with letters from the king and his officials; they said,*
"Children of Israel, return to Yahweh, the God of Abraham, Isaac, and Israel, so that he will return to the remnant, those who are left to you from the hand of the kings [a] *of Assyria.* [7] *Do not be like your fathers and brothers who were unfaithful to Yahweh the God of their fathers, so that he made them an object of derision as you yourselves see.* [8] *Now do not be stiff-necked like your fathers. Reach out* [a] *to Yahweh and come to his sanctuary which he has sanctified forever, and serve Yahweh your God so that he will turn his fierce anger from you.* [9] *If you return to Yahweh, then your relatives and children will be shown mercy by their captors and returned to this land, for Yahweh is gracious and merciful, and he will not turn his* [a] *face from you if you repent."*
[10] *The heralds went from city to city in Ephraim and Manasseh as far as Zebulun; but the people mocked and ridiculed them.* [11] *However, some men from Asher, Manasseh, and Zebulun humbled themselves and came to Jerusalem.* [12] *Furthermore, in Judah the hand of God made them of one accord to fulfill the command of the king and his officials by the word of Yahweh.* [a]
[13] *A great number of people assembled in Jerusalem to celebrate the Feast of Unleavened Bread in the second month; it was a very great number of people.* [14] *They arose and removed the altars in Jerusalem; they removed all the incense altars and threw them into the Kidron Valley.* [15] *They slaughtered the Passover lamb on the fourteenth day of the second month. The priests and Levites were*

ashamed, so they sanctified themselves and brought burnt offerings to the temple of Yahweh. [16] *They stood in their customary places in accordance with the law of Moses the man of God. The priests sprinkled the blood they received from the Levites.* [17] *Since there were many in the assembly who had not sanctified themselves, the Levites slaughtered the Passover lambs for all who were ceremonially unclean and could not sanctify their lambs for Yahweh.* [18] *Although a great number of the people— most* [a] *of those who had come from Ephraim, Manasseh, Issachar, and Zebulun— had not consecrated themselves, they ate the Passover contrary to what was written; Hezekiah had prayed for them, "May Yahweh, who is good, forgive* [b] [19] *all who set their hearts on seeking God, Yahweh the God of their fathers, even if they are not ceremonially clean according to sanctuary rules." * [20] *Yahweh heard Hezekiah, and he healed the people.*

[21] *The children of Israel who were present in Jerusalem celebrated the Feast of Unleavened Bread with great joy for seven days; day after day the Levites and priests were singing praises to Yahweh with the mighty instruments of Yahweh.* [a]

[22] *Hezekiah encouraged the Levites who were showing great skill in serving Yahweh. They ate* [a] *the festival meal for seven days, sacrificing fellowship offerings and making confession to Yahweh the God of their fathers.*

[23] *The whole assembly agreed to celebrate another seven days, so they celebrated seven more days with joy.* [24] *Hezekiah king of Judah provided the assembly a thousand bulls and seven thousand sheep and goasts, and the officials provided them a thousand bulls and ten thousand sheep and goats. Great numbers of priests sanctified themselves.*

[25] *All the assembly of Judah—along with the priests, the Levites, all the assembly that had come from Israel, and the aliens who had come from Israel or lived in Judah—all rejoiced.* [26] *There was great joy in Jerusalem, for since the days of Solomon, son of David, king of Israel, there had not been anything like this in Jerusalem.* [27] *The Levitical priests* [a] *arose and blessed the people; God heard their voice, and their prayer reached heaven, his holy dwelling.*

Notes

3.a. "At that time" is an allusion to chap. 29; see *Comment*. It is not necessary to conjecture בְּעִתּוֹ "at its regular time"; cf. Rudolph, 300.

5.a. Tg paraphrases and expands, "because a large assembly had not celebrated Passover in Nisan at the time prescribed." For Tg that which was ככתב "as written" was not the national convocation ("large numbers") but the date.

6.a. MT; G, Syr, Vg correct to singular, probably a harmonization with accounts of the fall of the Northern Kingdom; cf. the pl form in Isa 37:11, 18.

8.a. For MT תנו יד "reach out a hand," Par has paraphrased, δότε δόξαν "give glory." Par occasionally paraphrases יד; see Allen, *GC* 1:52. Cf. in this v also ערפכם, G^B τὰς καρδίας ὑμῶν, "your hearts."

9.a. MT, "face"; versions read "his face." The versions appear to be a correction required for the target languages and in accord with the usual idiom.

12.a. Or possibly, "in matters pertaining to Yahweh." Cf. 19:11.

18.a. G omits רבת, "most." It may be a dittogr in the MT from v 17 or a gloss preserving an alternative reading; however, G could be omitting as superfluous. See Allen, *GC* 2:146.

18.b. The MT verse division here is curious. Ignore the *soph-pasuq* and read בעד with v 19. Cf. בעד after כפר in Exod 32:30, Lev 9:7, et al.

21.a. The often suggested emendation to בכל עז "with all [their] might" (cf. 1 Chr 13:8) is appealing, but would make the second occurrence of ליהוה superfluous. Cf. Rudolph, 302.

22.a. G συνετέλεσαν, "completed, finished." G appears to have read ויכלו for ויאכלו. MT could have assimilated to אכלו את הפסח, "ate the Passover," in v 18. Alternatively, G may have assimilated to the sense of the context since "completing the observance of a מועד" may provide a more appropriate verb for the direct object. See the discussion in Allen, *GC* 2:99.

27.a. A few Heb. MSS, G^A, OL, Vg, Syr, and Arab all read "priests and Levites." Cf. the similar textual difficulty at 5:5 and 23:18. It was the prerogative of the priests to bless the people (Num 6:22–26), a practice with which the MT would be in accord. Vg, in translating the conjunction *atque*, may be highlighting the conjunction, "priests as well as Levites" or "priests and even Levites." Cf. vv 15, 21, 25.

Form/Structure/Setting

The Chronicler's account of Hezekiah's Passover bristles with exegetical and historical questions; to treat these issues adequately would require separate monographs. For the sake of convenience we can summarize these issues under three categories: (1) the question of historicity, (2) Hezekiah's Passover praxis compared with other legal and narrative portions, and (3) the function of the particular narrative in the Chronicler's history.

(1) The historicity question. Since observing Passover at a central sanctuary is widely viewed as an innovation of the deuteronomic reform at the time of Josiah (Deut 16; 2 Kgs 23:21–23), Hezekiah's Passover is commonly regarded as an anachronism. The Chronicler is thought to have borrowed from the deuteronomic historian's account of Josiah and to have fashioned Hezekiah in Josiah's image. The claim of the deuteronomic historian that at the time of Josiah no such observance of Passover had been held by any king of Israel or Judah (2 Kgs 23:22; cf. 2 Chr 35:18) makes Hezekiah's celebration historically suspect. Since the parallel history is silent regarding an observance of Passover at the time of Hezekiah, this chapter is widely considered the imaginary product of the Chronicler's desire to portray Hezekiah as a reformer at least as great and perhaps surpassing Josiah (as examples among many taking essentially this approach, see Michaeli, 231; C-M, 470–71; Elmslie, 310; Coggins, 270; de Vaux, 487). The Chronicler is thought to have had 2 Kgs 23:21–23 in mind in his heightening the observance under Hezekiah in both duration (two weeks instead of one) and breadth of participation (involving inhabitants of the North as well instead of Judeans alone).

Other scholars regard the chapter as faithfully recalling to various degrees an actual historical observance of Passover reported in sources used by the Chronicler. The Chronicler is ordinarily described as rather punctilious in matters regarding the cult, and it would be quite surprising for him in his idealization of Hezekiah to create *de novo* details of the observance of Passover in which the praxis was not strictly orthodox. The Chronicler reports the delay of the national observance of the feast by one month, the participation in the meal by those who were ceremonially unclean, and the prolongation of the observance by an additional week—all details which depart from "orthodox" practice; such details are improbable creations for the author and almost certainly rest on sources at his disposal (Moriarty, *CBQ* 27 [1965] 404–6). One would not expect the Chronicler to create such an illogical, heterodox fantasy. If the Chronicler's account were a figment of his own imagination, he could have as readily reported a "proper" observance in the first month on the part of an enthusiastic and ceremonially prepared crowd. The irregularities become a strong argument for genuineness.

The argument from the deuteronomic history has also undergone some recent reassessment. First, scholars readily admit that Deuteronomy contains much material older than the Josianic reform; there is no necessary reason why the centralization of Passover at the central sanctuary could not have taken place well before the time of Josiah. This factor may require some modification of older traditional critical approaches to the history and development of Passover and the Feast of Unleavened Bread. Second, some scholars have suggested alternate explanations for the deuteronomic history's subdued treatment of Hezekiah's reform. There is no real question that the deuteronomic history is keenly interested in Josiah's reform. While we cannot be absolutely certain regarding the compositional history of Kings, it is probable that one earlier phase in its editorial development had as its primary purpose to celebrate and legitimate Josiah's reign (cf. 1 Kgs 13:2; 2 Kgs 23:24–25). If an earlier stage of the deuteronomic history was edited by a contemporary partisan of Josiah, one would expect him to downplay the reforming activities of earlier kings (e.g., Asa, Jehoshaphat, Hezekiah) in order to heighten the importance, effect, and uniqueness of Josiah's reform (Rosenbaum, *HTR* 72 [1979] 23–43; McKenzie, 170–72). It is far more probable that the deuteronomic historian has suppressed material in his sources about Hezekiah than that the Chronicler has read Josiah's Passover back into the reign of Hezekiah. For that matter, rather than seeing Hezekiah as a shadow of Josiah in Chronicles, it may well be more probable that Josiah in Kings is somewhat modeled after that author's sources for the reign of Hezekiah.

Though no doubt considerable debate will continue regarding the particulars of 2 Chr 30, there appears no substantial reason to doubt the essential historicity of the narrative; to the contrary, there are many good reasons to regard the account as resting on reliable traditions.

(2) *Passover praxis.* Biblical texts treating Passover and the Feast of Unleavened Bread show significant variation in numerous features: the relation of the two festivals, whether the observance is set in the confines of the family or as a pilgrimage festival to the central sanctuary, the number and kinds of specified sacrifices, specification of a date for the observance. Critical scholarship has ordinarily construed these differences in a chronological scheme showing progressive development and reflecting the traditional order for the development of the pentateuchal law codes; see the summaries of this history in de Vaux (484–93) and Shaver (150–73).

Though the subject is more complex than space allows, a short summary of the relevant legal texts as widely understood in critical scholarship may be helpful. Passover and the Feast of Unleavened Bread are thought originally to have been independent observances, the latter a Canaanite agricultural celebration and the former deriving from a nomadic, pastoral background. The earliest pentateuchal calendars mention Unleavened Bread, but not Passover (Exod 23:14–17; 34:18–23). Unleavened Bread is a pilgrimage feast, whereas in its earliest mentions Passover is a family feast (Exod 12:21–13, 27b [J]). In the deuteronomic code Passover is associated with Unleavened Bread, and Passover has also become a pilgrimage feast (Deut 16:1–17), though the people return to their homes the next day (Deut 16:7) and presumably continue the seven days of Unleavened Bread from their cities of residence until the assembly on the seventh day; the sacrificial animal is to be boiled. In Lev 23 (the "Holiness Code" [H]) both festivals are conjoined and additional details are provided regarding the offerings for each day of Unleavened Bread. In Exod 12:1–20 (the "Priestly Code" [P]), Passover and Unleavened Bread are decentralized and observed in the home; the sacrificial animal is to be roasted, and specifically not boiled in water (Exod 12:8–9). P further allows for a delay of one month in observing Passover due to extenuating circumstances (Num 9:1–14). Cf. also Num 28:16–25, Ezek 45:21–24, Ezra 6:19–22. There are a number of other variations in the minutiae surrounding these two festivals.

In his reappraisal of the relevant legal corpora J. McConville (*Law and Theology*, 99–123) argues that the relevant texts have been misunderstood in the widely accepted critical consensus. McConville relates the particularities of the observance as described in Deuteronomy to the larger concerns of that book as a whole. He argues that Passover and Unleavened Bread were joined observances in all strata of pentateuchal legislation and raises telling questions regarding the consensus that Deuteronomy is prior to the laws of P. McConville contends that the usual exegesis of the law codes covering Passover and Unleavened Bread is fraught with difficulties, and he questions whether the various codes can be arrayed so as to plot the historical development of the feasts as part of a history of Israel's cult.

The history of this debate is of particular interest in assessing the Chronicler's account of Passover during the reigns of Hezekiah (this chapter) and Josiah (2 Chr 35:1–19). Does the Chronicler's account of Hezekiah's Passover correctly reflect the practices of the late eighth century, or to what extent does it mirror practices of the author's own day? Does the passage confirm the critical consensus regarding the development of the festivals? Which antecedent legislation was available to the Chronicler or to Hezekiah (30:5, 18), and does it reveal anything about the extent of canon in either period? Many different answers have been offered to these questions. De Vaux (487) argued that the Chronicler was following the stipulations of the Priestly Code in his account of Hezekiah's Passover, whereas von Rad (*Geschichtsbild*, 52–53) contended that the Chronicler depended almost entirely on D for his account. Shaver (187) concluded that in his use of Torah the Chronicler appealed to more than pentateuchal texts alone, and that his use of the pentateuchal traditions drew from all the major pentateuchal codes. These issues will surface briefly in the *Comment* section below.

(3) The place of the narrative in the Chronicler's theology. See the introductory chapter, "The Chronicler's Hezekiah," pt. 2, "The Narrow Focus." The Chronicler has portrayed Hezekiah as a second Solomon. Several features of this chapter contribute to that development: (a) Hezekiah reunites the nation in the proper worship of Yahweh, in a sense restoring Solomonic conditions (30:1–12). (b) Just as Solomon's dedication of the temple was accompanied by a two-week celebration, so also Hezekiah's rededication extends to two weeks (30:23; 7:9). (c) Hezekiah also presides over a national assembly at the dedication and leads in an efficacious intercessory prayer in behalf of those attending (30:18–19). This prayer in many respects recalls Solomon's great dedicatory prayer and the LORD's response (6:14–42; 7:12–22). The

chapter as a whole is concerned to show the fulfillment of the LORD's promise to Solomon in his response to the dedicatory prayer. 2 Chr 7:14 is for the Chronicler virtually the "charter" for his account of Judean history subsequent to Solomon. The author seems to go out of his way to introduce the language of that text (Williamson, 368): "humble" (30:11),"pray" (30:18), "seek" (30:19, with the synonym דרשׁ instead of בקשׁ), "turn" (30:9), "hear" (30:20), and "heal" (30:20). As God had promised, the prayer uttered at the temple would be heard in heaven (7:14). See the introductory essay to 2 Chr 10–36, "Reward and Punishment in Chronicles: The Theology of Immediate Retribution." (d) The Chronicler has signaled his intent to parallel Hezekiah and Solomon by specifically likening the celebration during both reigns (30:26).

These motifs find their center in the Chronicler's own hopes for the restoration community, his picture of a reunified, reestablished nation united in cultic fidelity. The path to restoration and blessing after exile (30:6–9) was the path of repentance and service at the sanctuary of God.

The paragraphs in this narrative are primarily marked by the use of explicit subjects (30:1, 2, 6, 10, 21, 23, 25). Vv 6 and 10 begin with the same phraseology, a device commonly known as head-head linkage, a second paragraph repeating the initial words of an earlier one. Vv 5 and 13 provide a possible example of tail-head linkage: the emphasis on the large numbers ends one paragraph (v 5) and begins another (v 13), even though there is intervening material.

Comment

1 This verse is a summary statement introducing the entire narrative (Rudolph, 299). The oral proclamation was accompanied by letters (cf. Esth 1:22).

For the Chronicler the North appears already to have suffered exile at the hands of the Assyrians by the time of Hezekiah's accession (30:6, 9), so that in the second month of his first year he is able to effect a tacit reunification of the nation around the Jerusalem temple, a possibility blocked since the time of Jeroboam I (13:9–12; 1 Kgs 12:25–33). This produces a tension with other chronological notices synchronizing the beginning of Hezekiah's reign with that of Hoshea (2 Kgs 18:1). The chronological notices surrounding Hezekiah's reign provide one of the most difficult conundrums of OT chronology; see *Comment* at 29:1–2.

It is also worth noting that the Chronicler's attitude to the North was not one of exclusivism, but to the contrary, inclusivism. The Chronicler was not part of some anti-Samaritan polemic.

2–5 The law allowed for a delayed observance of Passover in the second month for those who had become unclean through contact with a corpse or for those who had been on a journey (Num 9:9–11). The actions of Hezekiah appear to depend on an interpretive extension of these provisions to cover those ritually unclean for any reason ("the priests had not sanctified themselves," 30:3) and those journeying from the Northern Kingdom or who had not made the pilgrimage to Jerusalem ("the people had not assembled themselves," 30:3; cf. 30:17–18); exceptional provisos for individuals have been generalized to apply to the entire nation. The celebration of Passover at the time of Hezekiah thus provides a good example of intrabiblical legal interpretation. The apostasy under Ahaz presumably had left the priesthood in disarray, perhaps almost nonfunctioning, but at least in a ceremonially unacceptable state.

Talmon ("Divergencies in Calendar Reckoning in Ephraim and Judah," *VT* 8 [1958] 48–74) suggested that this delay was also intended to put the Judean religious calendar temporarily in synch with the calendar of the Northern Kingdom that had been retarded by one month since the time of Jeroboam I (1 Kgs 12:32–33). The delay would have the attendant benefit of facilitating participation from the Northern regions.

The statement that Passover had not been celebrated "in such large numbers according to what was written" is difficult to assess. Obviously larger numbers were possible with the participation of pilgrims from the North, and the statement may intend simply to note record attendance. On the other hand the contrast may be with the private or familial observance also associated with Passover (Exod 12:1–28, 43–49); the passage may intend to say that this was the first observance en masse at the sanctuary, as envisaged by Deut 16:1–8. It was, of course, the first observance of Passover as a united people since the days of Solomon; see *Comment* at 30:26. The appeal to "what was written" suggests that the provisions of Deut 16 were in view.

6–9 The Chronicler commonly uses speech materials as primary vehicles for his own theological viewpoints. In Hezekiah's letter to the cities of the Northern Kingdom the themes and characteristic vocabulary ("return," "be unfaithful") of the Chronicler's theology of immediate retribution are prominent; see the introductory essay to 2 Chr 10–36, "Reward and Punishment in Chronicles: The Theology of Immediate Retribution." The Chronicler's interest in the motifs of exile, restoration, and remnant was of paramount importance to his own generation; see above, *Form/Structure/Setting*, (3). Turning to the LORD was the prior condition of restoration (30:9).

The Chronicler always refers to Jacob under the name Israel (30:6—with the exception of 1 Chr 16:13, 17 where the two terms are in parallel poetic lines). See Williamson, *IBC*, 62–63.

In referring to the "kings" (30:6—see *Notes*) of Assyria, the author probably intends more than the destruction in 722 B.C. at the hands of Shalmaneser V and Sargon II, but also all other Assyrian intrusions against the Northern Kingdom, at least from the time of Tiglath-pileser III (28:16–21; 1 Chr 5:26), and perhaps even as far back as Shalmaneser III.

10–12 The chapter variously lists the involvement of the Northern tribes. All from Beersheba to Dan were to be invited (30:5), though the heralds only went as far as Zebulun (30:10); Northerners came from Asher, Manasseh, and Zebulun (30:11), and from Ephraim, Manasseh, Issachar, and Zebulun (30:18). The use of "Beersheba to Dan" should be viewed as a useful hendiadys for the full extent of the kingdoms, even if the heralds' itinerary was less than the entire land; the omission of the Transjordan tribes (Reuben, Gad, and half of Manasseh) and Naphtali (cf. 34:6) may reflect the longer period of Assyrian domination in these regions and the deportation of their populations under Tiglath-pileser III (1 Chr 5:26; 2 Kgs 15:29).

The people acted with "one accord" (30:12); the Chronicler is fond of emphasizing the undivided loyalty of the people toward pious kings (cf. 1 Chr 12:39 [38]).

13–20 The nation is to "celebrate the Feast of Unleavened Bread" (30:12, 13); earlier they were to "celebrate the Passover" (30:1, 2, 5). As elsewhere in both the OT and NT, the two festivals were so closely associated that the entire celebration could be denominated by either designation. It is also possible that the shift in designations for the festival reflects a change in the Chronicler's source.

The cultic personnel had cleansed the temple precincts (29:15–17), now the assembled populace carries the reform throughout the city (30:14; cf. 29:16). The personal ritual sanctification of the cultic personnel that had begun among the urban clergy (29:4, 15, 34) either now extended to priests and Levites coming to the city from their scattered patrimonies or involved a further reconsecration for these particular festivals. This was not the first, nor would it be the last, time in history when popular religious enthusiasm outstripped that of professional clerics to their shame.

The Passover sacrifice was ordinarily slaughtered by the laity (Deut 16:5–6; Exod 12:3–6, 21); however, since so many in the congregation were ritually unclean, the Levites performed this duty for them (cf. Num 9:12–13).

It has often been pointed out that for all of his concern with the cult and its personnel, the Chronicler was not content with a religion of mere external punctiliousness regarding the details of the law, but showed a concern with the spirit of the law where it was in tension with the letter (30:18–19). Hezekiah's prayer recalls Solomon's dedicatory prayer and God's response; see above, *Form/Structure/Setting*, (3). Though no physical illness is suggested in the passage, the Chronicler goes out of his way to introduce the term *heal* (30:20), a direct allusion to 2 Chr 7:14. All that the Chronicler may intend regarding the "sanctuary rules" (30:19) is not clear, but failure to observe them could be a capital offense (Lev 15:31).

23–27 The seven additional days of celebration are reported as part of the Chronicler's effort to parallel Hezekiah and Solomon (7:8–10; see the introductory essay, "The Chronicler's Hezekiah"). Both occasions were marked by joyous celebration; the Chronicler specifically likens the joy to that at the time of Solomon (7:10). See *Comment* at 35:18.

The numbers of offerings are large, but eclipsed by those during the reign of Josiah (35:7–9) and Solomon (7:5).

The priests blessed the people, presumably with the words of the Aaronic benediction (Num 6:22–27).

Explanation

This chapter functions on a number of levels for the Chronicler as he seeks to address the needs of his contemporaries. (1) It raises once again the theme of exile and restoration. The path to a restored kingdom is the path of cultic fidelity. This message is pressed home through the observance of Passover, itself a commemoration of redemption and release from bondage to a foreign power. (2) The Chronicler never tires of portraying the validity of his theology of immediate retribution. Particularly in this chapter he seeks to show the efficacy and validity of Solomon's prayer and God's promise, an efficacy he understood as relevant for his own generation as well. (3) Hezekiah is presented as an embodiment of the ideal Davidic successor. He is another David/Solomon ruling over a united kingdom with the support of the populace. It is hard to escape the conclusion that the Chronicler held out this portrayal also in speaking of future possibilities and hopes for his own generation.

Christian readers of the passage are likely to recall other analogies. (1) They will remember another occasion when the religious fervor of the populace before another Passover transcended that of professional clerics when another son of David came to cleanse the temple (Matt 21:1–16; Mark 11:1–18; Luke 19:28–48). (2) They will think of another joyous festal meal in a purified city of God (Matt 26:29; Rev 19:6–18; 21:1–10, 22–27; 22:12–15).

Hezekiah's Provision for the Temple and Its Personnel (31:1–21)

Bibliography

See the entries in the introductory chapter to 2 Chr 29–32, "The Chronicler's Hezekiah."

Translation

¹ When all this was done, all the Israelites present in the cities of Judah went out, smashed the sacred pillars, cut down the Asherah poles, and destroyed the high places and altars throughout Judah, Benjamin, Ephraim, and Manasseh, until they destroyed all of them. Then all the Israelites returned each to his own town and possession. ² Hezekiah appointed the priests and Levites to their divisions—allotting to each his duty as priest or Levite—for making burnt offerings and fellowship offerings, to minister,[a] to give thanks and to praise in the gates of the camp[b] of Yahweh. ³ As his portion the king provided from his own possessions the burnt offerings for the morning and evening sacrifices and the burnt offerings for the sabbaths, new moons, and appointed feasts, as written in the law of Yahweh. ⁴ He commanded the people living in Jerusalem to give the portion due to the priests and Levites, so that they could devote themselves to the law[a] of Yahweh.

⁵ As soon as the order was issued, the Israelites gave generously from the firstfruits of grain, new wine, oil, and honey, and all the produce of the land; they brought a great quantity, a tithe of everything. ⁶ᵃ The Israelites and Judeans[a] living in the cities of Judah also brought a tithe of their herds and flocks and a tithe of their produce[b] dedicated[c] to Yahweh their God; they brought it and put it in many heaps. ⁷ They began to make the heaps in the third month and finished in the seventh. ⁸ Hezekiah and his officials came and saw the heaps, and they blessed Yahweh and his people Israel.

⁹ Hezekiah inquired of the priests and Levites regarding the heaps. ¹⁰ Azariah, the chief priest from the house of Zadok, answered him and said, "From the time that the people began to bring their contributions, there has been enough to eat and plenty to spare, for Yahweh has blessed his people, and this great quantity is left over."

¹¹ Hezekiah ordered them to prepare storerooms in the temple of Yahweh, and they did so. ¹² They faithfully brought the offerings and the tithes.[a] The leader in charge of them was Conaniah, the Levite, and Shimei his brother was second in command. ¹³ Jehiel, Azaziah,[a] Nahath, Asahel, Jerimoth, Jozabad, Eliel, Ismakiah, Mahath, and Benaiah[b] were officers under Conaniah and his brother Shimei, and at the appointment of King Hezekiah and Azariah, the overseer of the temple of God. ¹⁴ Kore son of Imnah, the Levite, keeper of the East Gate, was in charge of the voluntary offerings given to God; he was responsible for distributing the offerings given to Yahweh and the dedicated gifts. ¹⁵ He was faithfully assisted by Eden, Miniamin, Jeshua, Shemaiah, Amariah, and Shekaniah in the priests' towns, to

distribute to their relatives by their divisions, old and young alike. [16] *They distributed to all males three years old and up, irrespective* [a] *of their place in the genealogical records, to all who entered the temple of Yahweh to perform the daily duties of their service, by their courses and divisions.* [17] *They distributed to the priests registered by their paternal households and to the Levites from twenty years old and up by their courses and divisions;* [18] *they were registered with all their dependents—wives,* [a] *sons, and daughters—the entire community, for they were faithful in consecrating themselves.* [19] *As for the priests, the sons of Aaron, living in the fields of common lands around their cities—city by city—men were appointed by name to distribute portions to every male among the priests and registered in the genealogies of the Levites.*

[20] *Hezekiah did this throughout Judah; he did what was good, right, and true before Yahweh his God.* [21] *In everything he undertook in the service of God's temple and in obedience to the law and the commandment to seek his God, he did it with his whole heart, and he succeeded.*

Notes

2.a. G transposes לשרת to read "serve/minister in the gates," the duty of the Levitical gatekeepers (1 Chr 26:1)—the musical thanks and praise would not likely occur "in the gates." Many follow the G order as preferable and as reflecting the G *Vorlage.* The change does appear to be motivated, i.e., it simplifies or clarifies the passage by adjusting it to its context, and therefore is probably secondary, either introduced by a copyist or the G translator. The difficulty disappears if בשערי is understood as "within/inside the gates" or simply as somewhat awkward style—MT is most likely correct.

2.b. The Chronicler uses an unusual term to designate the temple: מחנות "camp, encampment." Cf. 1 Chr 9:18–19. The Chronicler shows much interest in holy war, and this semi-military term may recall the tabernacle traditions (Num 2:3, 9). G αὐλαῖς οἴκου "courts of the temple" reflects a paraphrase rather than dependence on a *Vorlage* with חצרות.

4.a. G instead of "law of Yahweh" reads "in the service of the house of the LORD." This is probably an adjustment to context of the part of G translator or an earlier scribe; the priests and Levites are to devote themselves to the service of the temple instead of seeking a living in some other way. See Allen, *GC* 2:99.

6.a-a. G omits the conj and takes "children of Israel and Judah" as the subj of the last verb ("brought") in the preceding verse, so that the subj of the first clause in v 6 is "those living in the cities of Judah."

6.b. Lit., "a tithe of dedicated things"; the word "produce" is inserted as required by the following clause, since animals would scarcely be arranged in heaps. There is no need to suggest an alternative text including תבאה (cf. v 5) since it is implicit in the context.

6.c. G ἐπιδέκατα αἰγῶν "a tithe of goats" is an intra-Greek corruption; αἰγῶν was read for ἁγίων "holy things." The opposite error is made at 35:7 and in Exod 35:26. See Allen, *GC* 2:28–29.

12.a. MT adds והקדשים "and the dedicated things," probably as a later harmonization with v 6. It is not found in G.

13.a. A few Heb. MSS, G^{B,L}, OL, Syr, "Uzziah"; a few other Heb. MSS and Vg, "Azariah."

13.b. G adds καὶ οἱ υἱοὶ αὐτοῦ, presumably a double reading of ובניו and ובניהו "and Benaiah."

16.a. G^B ἕκαστος "each" is an intra-Greek error for ἐκτὸς "beside, except" (G^{A,L}). See Rudolph, 306.

18.a. G omits "their wives." G translator may have taken טף in the sense of "children" instead of "dependents" and therefore have omitted "wives" since he understood "sons and daughters" as explanatory of the first term. Conversely, a scribe could have inserted "wives" into the MT by noting their omission from a group of dependents. The internal evidence appears to be a draw.

Form/Structure/Setting

The Chronicler shows some dependence on Kings in this chapter. 31:1 roughly parallels 2 Kgs 18:4, and 31:20–21 paraphrases 2 Kgs 18:5–7a. Apart from these approximations to Kings, the remainder of the chapter is once again unique to Chronicles.

Whatever the sources available to the Chronicler, the author's controlling interests in the cult and in portraying Hezekiah as a reflection of David and Solomon predominate. The royal supervision of cultic personnel, the generosity of king and populace, the lists of personnel, and divine blessing consequent upon obedience are all motifs characteristic of the Chronicler's earlier portrayal of David and Solomon. The recurrence of these themes need not impugn the historicity of the author's account, but does highlight the influence of the author's controlling selectivity. The Chronicler may have compressed reform activities that spanned a longer period so that they appear all to have been achieved in the first year of Hezekiah's reign: the temple was cleansed in the first month (chap. 29), Passover observed in the second (chap. 30), and provisions made for personnel and sacrifices from the third to the seventh month (31:7).

The paragraphs are introduced by the use of an explicit subject (particularly the name of the king, 31:2, 9, 11, 20) and temporal phrases with an infinitive construct (31:1, 5). Some are most easily seen as repartee units, e.g., question-answer (31:9–10), command-fulfillment (31:11–19).

Comment

1 Hezekiah's reform proceeded in concentric circles from the temple (29:3–36), through the city (30:13–14), and into the surrounding territory, including portions of the North (31:1). The same structure is followed by the deuteronomic historian for his account of Josiah's reform which radiates from the discovery of the law book in the temple (see *Form/Structure/Setting* in chap. 30 for some discussion of the relation of these two accounts), whereas the Chronicler highlights the chronological sequence of Josiah's reform.

The Chronicler alludes to the deuteronomic historian's judgment on Hezekiah (2 Kgs 18:4), though he omits any reference to the bronze serpent (see K. Joines, "The Bronze Serpent in the Israelite Cult," *JBL* 87 [1968] 245–56; H. Rowley, "Zadok and Nehushtan," *JBL* 68 [1939] 113–41; Yeivin, "The Sudden Appearance of the Bronze Serpent at the Time of Hezekiah," *BMik* 23 [1977] 10–11). For a recent survey of the evidence regarding the Asherah poles, see J. Day, "Asherah in the Hebrew Bible and Northwest Semitic Literature," *JBL* 105 (1986) 385–408.

2–4 The Chronicler continues to liken Hezekiah to Solomon by showing his oversight of cultic personnel (2 Chr 8:14; cf. 1 Chr 23–26). Just as David and Solomon provided from their own wealth for the temple (1 Chr 29:1–5; 2 Chr 9:10–11), so also Hezekiah provides from his property. The Chronicler is fond of showing that faithful and generous kings prompt similar generosity in the population (31:5–10; 24:8–14; 1 Chr 29:6–9).

The king was apparently responsible to provide the regular offerings as specified in 31:3 (cf. 2:4, 8:12–13; 1 Chr 16:37–40; Ezek 45:17, 22; 46:2);

at the very least the Chronicler describes the actions of Hezekiah in accord with the prescriptions of Ezekiel. In the Chronicler's own time the Persian kings showed similar largess (Ezra 6:9; 7:21–23). What was "written in the law" (31:3) was the list of offerings (Num 28–29) rather than the requirement that the king provide them.

Hezekiah restores the system of offerings used for the maintenance of the priests and Levites (31:4; Lev 6:14–7:36; Num 18:8–32; Deut 14:27–29; 18:1–8; 26:1–15) which had presumably been interrupted during the apostasy of Ahaz. These offerings were readily neglected by the people (Mal 3:8–12; Neh 13:10–13) and occasionally abused by the priests (1 Sam 2:12–16). Rather than describing these offerings as freeing the priests and Levites for devotion to the service of the temple (cf. G and text note 31:4.a), the Chronicler describes them as freeing the cultic personnel for devotion to the "law of Yahweh"; though both ways of describing the intended effect of the offerings may refer to temple duties, the Chronicler's phraseology could reflect the growing importance of the study of the law in the post-exilic period (Williamson, 374).

5–8 The firstfruits of grain, wine, and oil are specifically assigned to the priests (Num 18:12–13) and the tithe to the Levites (Num 18:21). Though "honey," actually a syruplike product from fruits, is excluded from burnt offerings, it was nevertheless suitable for the support of the priests and was brought as part of the firstfruits (Lev 2:11–12).

There is some ambiguity in the first phrase of 31:6 (Williamson, *IBC*, 129–30). In 31:5 "Israelites" appears to be a designation of the population of Jerusalem ("people living in Jerusalem," 31:4), though here it contrasts with Judeans and appears to refer to those coming from the North. Those at a distance from the city, i.e., those in the North and in the outlying cities of Judah, brought their offerings to the city in conformity with the provisions of Deut 12:17–18; 14:24–26. The Chronicler is concerned to portray "all Israel" acting in concert under Hezekiah; "Judeans" should not be eliminated as a gloss (Rudolph, 304; C-M, 479).

The amassing of the firstfruits and tithes continued from the third month (May/June, the time of the Feast of Pentecost and the grain harvest) through the seventh month (September/October, the time of the Feast of Tabernacles and fruit and vine harvests).

Hezekiah blesses the people (31:8), following the precedent of David and Solomon (1 Chr 16:2; 2 Chr 6:3).

9–10 The Chronicler modeled his account of the building of the temple after the building of the tabernacle; see the introductory essay to 2 Chr 1–10, "The Chronicler's Solomon." The superabundance of the people's contributions at the building of the tabernacle was repeated at the time of the temple (Exod 36:2–7; 1 Chr 29:6–9); the temple reform at the time of Hezekiah is similarly blessed with abundant giving. No doubt the Chronicler is intending a message for his own contemporaries in the post-exilic period. Cf. Neh 10:35–39.

This Azariah is not mentioned in the list of high priests in the genealogies (1 Chr 5:29–40 [6:3–15]). He is probably not the high priest who rebuked Uzziah (26:17) about forty years earlier; if the practice of papponymy (naming the son after the grandfather) also characterized this earlier period (cf. F. Cross, "A Reconstruction of the Judean Restoration," *JBL* 94 [1975] 4–18), he may have been the grandson of that priest.

11–19 The flow of thought and the precise significance of some of the details in this section are difficult. Hezekiah arranges for the storage and oversight of the offerings to be used to support the cultic personnel. Conaniah and Shimei are assisted by ten others responsible for the storerooms in the temple, while Kore and six others arranged distribution in the outlying priests' towns (1 Chr 6:54–60). This distinction between those living in Jerusalem and those in the outlying towns is reiterated in 31:16, 19; a distinction is also made in the basis for distribution between the priests (genealogical records) and the Levites (courses and divisions; 31:17).

Hezekiah is again likened to David in his provision for storerooms in the temple and in his assigning Levitical officials to care for them (31:11, 14; 1 Chr 9:26; 23:28; 26:22; 28:12).

The distribution included all males "three years old" and up, i.e., after weaning (31:16). Though no warrant can be found from the ancient versions, many have emended this figure to "thirty" years, the age at which duties were assigned in the temple (1 Chr 23:3). There is considerable variation in the age of Levites at their enrollments in various passages: twenty years (31:17), thirty years (1 Chr 23:3; Num 4:3), twenty-five years (Num 8:24); the considerations that prompted such variation are not clear.

20–21 The Chronicler is perhaps paraphrasing 2 Kgs 18:5–7a. He stops short of calling Hezekiah the best king ever (2 Kgs 18:5), a judgment which would conflict with his portrayal of David and Solomon. This summary assessment of Hezekiah serves as a literary marker: it ends the bulk of the material unique to the Chronicler's account of Hezekiah and marks a return to dependence on Kings (Williamson, 377). The record of obedience and fidelity in chaps. 29–31 prepares for the events of chap. 32. For the Chronicler's characteristic use of the term succeed, cf. 1 Chr 22:11, 13; 29:23; 2 Chr 7:11; 13:12; 14:6 [7]; 18:11, 14; 20:20; 24:20; 32:30; it is one of the terms serving as a frequent vehicle for his retribution theology.

Explanation

For most modern Western readers of the Bible this chapter reads somewhat awkwardly; it is one more example of the Chronicler's punctilious concern with matters cultic, an interest at great chronological and cultural distance from his readers today. But for the Chronicler and his own contemporaries, rather than a distant and curious pericope, this section would have been full of the utmost practical relevance for godly living. Its reports of generosity and its focus on the correct worship of God through giving and caring for his servants were practical exhortations of what it meant to seek God and to obey his commandments. For the Chronicler it was a lesson from history that needed to be heard in his own day, for it remained the pathway to success and blessing (31:21). Providing for the servants of God to free them for more important matters (31:4) is likewise a concern of the NT (Phil 2:25–30; 4:14–19; 2 Cor 8:10–9:15; Acts 6:1–4; 20:32–35).

Hezekiah's Victory and Illness   (32:1–33)

Bibliography

In addition to the items in the introductory essay to 2 Chr 29–32, "The Chronicler's Hezekiah," see also the following:

Ackroyd, P. "The Death of Hezekiah—A Pointer to the Future?" In *De la Torah au Messie: Mélanges H. Cazelles*, ed. M. Carrez, J. Dore, and P. Grelot. Paris, 1981. 219–26. **Rosner, F.** "The Illness of King Hezekiah and 'The Book of Remedies' Which He Hid," *Koroth* 9 (1985) 190–97.

Translation

¹*After these faithful acts,*[a] *Sennacherib king of Assyria came into Judah and encamped against its fortified cities, thinking to breach them for himself.* ²*When King Hezekiah saw that Sennacherib had come and intended to make war on Jerusalem,* ³*he consulted with his officials and his military staff about blocking the water from the springs outside the city, and they encouraged him.* ⁴*A large number of people were gathered, and they blocked all the springs and the stream that flowed through the land.*[a] *They reasoned, "Why should the kings*[b] *of Assyria come*[b] *and find*[b] *plenty of water?"* ⁵*He took courage*[a]*: he repaired all the broken sections of the wall and erected towers;*[b] *he built another wall outside that one and strengthened the supporting terraces of the City of David and provided a great number of weapons and shields.* ⁶*He appointed military officers over the people. He assembled them to himself in the square at the gate of the city*[a] *and spoke encouragingly to them. He said,*

⁷*"Take courage and be strong. Do not fear or be dismayed because of the king of Assyria and this great horde with him, for with us is one greater than with him.* ⁸*With him is the arm of flesh, but with us is Yahweh our God, to help us and to fight our battles."*
The people were encouraged by the words of Hezekiah king of Judah.

⁹ *After this, Sennacherib king of Assyria, while he was besieging Lachish with all his high command, sent his servants to Jerusalem to Hezekiah king of Judah and all Judah in Jerusalem with this message:* ¹⁰*Thus says Sennacherib*[a] *king of Assyria: "In what are you putting your trust that you stay in Jerusalem under siege?* ¹¹*Hasn't Hezekiah reduced you to forced labor, only to deliver you over to death by famine and thirst by his saying 'Yahweh our God will deliver us from the king of Assyria.'* ¹²*But isn't it Hezekiah who removed his high places and altars and commanded Judah and Jerusalem to worship and offer sacrifices*[a] *before only one altar?*[b] ¹³*Don't you know what my fathers and I have done to all the people of the lands? Were the gods of the nations of those lands able to deliver them from my hand?* ¹⁴ *Who among all the gods of the nations that my father exterminated was able to deliver his people from my hand? How will your god be able to deliver you*[a] *from my hand?* ¹⁵*Now do not let Hezekiah deceive you or mislead you like this. Do not believe him, for no god of any nation or kingdom has been able to deliver his*

people from my hand or the hand of my fathers. Nor will your gods deliver[a] *you from my hand."*

[16] *His servants spoke even more against Yahweh God and his servant Hezekiah.* [17] *He also wrote letters defying Yahweh the God of Israel, speaking against him, saying, "Just as the gods of the nations of the lands did not deliver their people from my hand, so also the god of Hezekiah will not deliver his people from my hand."* [18] *They*[a] *cried out in a loud voice in the language of Judah to the people of Jerusalem who were on the wall, in order to frighten and terrify them so they could capture the city.* [19] *They*[a] *spoke against the God of Jerusalem as if he were one of the gods of the peoples of the land, a product of the hands of men.*

[20] *King Hezekiah and Isaiah son of Amoz, the prophet, prayed about this and cried out to heaven.* [21] *An angel of Yahweh sent and annihilated*[a] *every warrior, commander, and officer in the camp of the king of Assyria. He returned to his land shamefaced, and when he entered the temple of his god,*[b] *some of his own progeny*[c] *cut him down there with a sword.* [22] *Yahweh saved Hezekiah and the inhabitants of Jerusalem from the hand of Sennacherib king of Assyria and from the hand of all others, and he gave them rest*[a] *on all sides.* [23] *Many came bringing offerings to Yahweh in Jerusalem and gifts to Hezekiah king of Judah, for he was exalted in the eyes of all nations from then on.*

[24] *In those days Hezekiah became mortally ill, so he prayed to Yahweh who answered*[a] *him and gave him a sign.* [25] *But Hezekiah did not respond according to the benefit shown him; rather his heart became proud, so wrath came upon him and upon Judah and Jerusalem.* [26] *But Hezekiah humbled himself from the pride of his heart—he and the inhabitants of Jerusalem—so the wrath of Yahweh did not come upon them in the days of Hezekiah.*

[27] *Hezekiah had exceedingly great riches and honor. He made treasuries for himself for silver, gold, precious stones, spices, shields,*[a] *and valuable things;* [28] *he made barns to store the harvest of grain, new wine, and oil and stalls for all kinds of cattle and pens for flocks.* [29] *He made towns*[a] *for himself, for he had a great number of flocks and herds since God had given him vast riches.* [30] *Hezekiah was the one who blocked the upper outlet of the waters of the Gihon and channeled them down to the west side of the City of David.*

Hezekiah succeeded in all that he did, [31] *and so when the envoys that the leaders of Babylon sent*[a] *to him to inquire about the sign observed in the land came, God left him, to test him, to know all that was in his heart.*

[32] *As for the rest of the deeds of Hezekiah and his acts of piety, they are written in the vision of Isaiah son of Amoz, the prophet, in the book of the kings of Judah and Israel.* [33] *Hezekiah rested with his fathers. They buried him in the upper area of the tombs of the sons of David; all Judah and the inhabitants of Jerusalem showed him honor in his death. Manasseh his son ruled in his place.*

Notes

1.a. The האלה refers to both preceding nouns, i.e., the construction is a hendiadys, "these deeds and faithfulness" for "these faithful deeds."

4.a. G τῆς πόλεως, = העיר "the city" instead of הארץ "the land." The G *Vorlage* may have assimilated to 2 Kgs 20:20 which says the water was brought into the city (Allen, *GC* 1:211) or even to 32:30 which also contains the word *city*. "The city" could also have been a correction for the more difficult "the land."

4.b. The two verbs will agree with the number of the noun. Where MT has the pl "kings," G, Syr, and Arab have the sg. Cf. the pl references in this chapter (32:13–15, 22) and 28:16. The pl also represents a more difficult reading.

5.a. G translator read the verb as ויתחזק and took it with the preceding v as referring to Sennacherib, "find plenty of water and take courage." A reviser later inserted the name of Hezekiah to make it clear that the clause belonged with v 5 as in MT, and thereby produced a double translation of the verb in G.

5.b. G omits ויעל על and reads πύργους "towers" as the second obj of the verb "build." This omission could reflect an awkward MT—the MT appears to require ויעל עליה, reading the article from המגדלות as the obj of the preceding prepn to give the sense "he erected towers upon it."

6.a. G defines the "city gate" more precisely as the valley (φάραγγος) gate, possibly assimilating to 26:9 which also speaks of the erection of towers (v 5).

10.a. The Chronicler substitutes Sennacherib's name for the epithet "the great king" in the parallel texts (2 Kgs 18:19; Isa 36:4). It is possible to see some theological motivation in this change, though it may be no more than paraphrase.

12.a. The Chronicler adds ועליו תקטירו, "offer sacrifices upon it." The verb קטר is ambiguous at this point and could refer to either burnt offerings or incense—both are characteristic concerns of the author.

12.b. Par θυσιαστηρίου τούτου "this altar" is an assimilation to Bas at 2 Kgs 18:22. This material is not found in G of Isa.

14.a. Instead of "you," 2 Kgs 18:35 // Isa 36:20 have "Jerusalem."

15.a. A few MSS and the ancient versions have a sg verb, in turn affecting the translation of אלהיכם, "nor will your God deliver you." The same verb is sg in v 17.

18.a. A few MSS, G* and Vg read a sg verb.

19.a. G and Vg read a sg verb.

21.a. The parallel texts use the verb נכה (2 Kgs 19:35; Isa 37:36) instead of כחד. The difference should not be attributed to *Tendenz* and may well have arisen from textual difficulties.

21.b. 2 Kgs 19:37 // Isa 37:38 include the name of his god, Nisroch.

21.c. The parallel texts also name the assassins as his sons Adrammelek and Sharezer. The Chronicler's choice of wording is worthy of note: instead of "his sons" (Isa 37:38), the Chronicler describes them as "those who came out of his loins"; cf. the reverse change at 2 Sam 7:12 // 1 Chr 17:11.

22.a. With G (κατέπαυσεν αὐτούς) and V (*praestitit eis quietem*), = וינח להם. MT וינהלם, "he guided/took care of them on every side." The difference is significant. The Chronicler uses the verb נוח, "rest," in a distinctive way; if G and Vg preserve the correct text, this is one other instance of Hezekiah's being likened to David and Solomon. See *Comment* at 14:1; and Braun, 198–99, 223–24.

24.a. In the parallel passages (2 Kgs 20:2–3 // Isa 38:2–3) the ויאמר introduces the content of Hezekiah's prayer, "Hezekiah prayed to Yahweh and said. . . ." In Chr however, the subject of the verb is Yahweh, "Hezekiah prayed to Yahweh and he [Yahweh] spoke to him." G translates the verb ἐπήκουσεν, "heard him"; this is not evidence for an alternate text (ויעתר, cf. 33:13), but rather the verb used by Par to designate answered prayer irrespective of the Heb. term. See Allen, *GC* 1:52. The change from the parallel texts may be simply an abridgment omitting Hezekiah's prayer, or it may reflect an effort to portray Hezekiah as the recipient of unmediated revelation, i.e., as a prophet like David and Solomon.

27.a. There is no need to emend מגנים "shields" to מגדנים "excellent things, gifts" (cf. 32:23, 21:3). Shields were kept in treasuries; this emendation would be at the expense of the author's effort to parallel Hezekiah with Solomon (9:16; 12:9).

29.a. The emendation from ערים "towns" to עדרים "herds" is appealing. However, it has no textual support. 1 Chr 27:25–31 and 2 Chr 26:9–10 imply the creation of settlements consisting of royal estates maintaining crown property.

31.a. The MT is intelligible as it is: the subj of the ptcp משלחים "sent" is שרי "leaders," i.e., "envoys whom the leaders of Babylon sent. . . ." However, the parallel text (2 Kgs 20:12) has a sg noun, שר "leader"; the pl in Chr may have arisen from a confusion of the *yod* and a *maqqef*. If the sg noun is read, the subj of the ptcp must be מליצי "envoys," and the ptcp must be repointed as a passive, e.g., מְשֻׁלָּחִים.

Form/Structure/Setting

The material devoted to Hezekiah's reform and his confrontation with Sennacherib, his illness, and meeting with envoys from Babylon in the three biblical accounts is in inverse proportion in Chronicles. Where the Assyrian campaign, the record of his illness and the visit of the envoys take up the largest part of the record in the other histories (2 Kgs 18:9–20:19; Isa 36:1–39:8), and the reform is only cursorily mentioned (2 Kgs 18:1–8), the Chronicler devotes the largest amount of his record to the reform (2 Chr 29–31) and treats the remainder in much smaller compass. The abundant biblical sources are supplemented by a variety of extrabiblical epigraphical materials ranging from multiple editions of Sennacherib's annals to Egyptian texts bearing especially on the chronological questions and assorted shorter inscriptions from the Levant.

The chronological and historical problems surrounding Hezekiah's confrontation with Sennacherib form one of the most difficult cruces in OT study, "a classic issue on which each new generation of biblical scholars seems constrained to test its mettle" (Childs, *Isaiah and the Assyrian Crisis*, 11). Though not without dissenting voices, a rough consensus has emerged among biblical scholars that the Kings account of Sennacherib's invasion is composed of three distinct sources: 2 Kgs 18:13–16 (A); 18:17–19:9a, 36–37 (B-1); 19:9b–35 (B-2), the latter two approximately parallel accounts. Whatever the provenance of these three accounts, D. Fewell (*JSOT* 34 [1986] 79–90) has described their rhetorical relationships and narrative function.

For the Chronicler there was no question of multiple invasions by Sennacherib or even of multiple appearances of his emissaries before Jerusalem. His narrative supports only one invasion and combines the two parallel accounts of Sennacherib's efforts at intimidation (2 Kgs 18:17–19:35) into a single narrative recast in accord with his own intentions. Accounts B-1 and B-2 were not read by him as successive events, but as varying versions of a single event which he has reintegrated.

The author is nevertheless clearly dependent on the parallel texts, presumably the book of Kings in particular. His omissions are instructive; though many should be attributed to an apparent desire to abridge the earlier accounts, some are related to his own *Tendenz*. Hezekiah in Chronicles is portrayed in the image of David and Solomon and consequently idealized in a similar way. He omits reference to 2 Kgs 18:14–16, not because it was not in his source, but because the spoliation of the temple and the defeat it implies would be out of accord with the faithful acts of Hezekiah. He omits most of 2 Kgs 18:17b–34 // Isa 36:2b–19: for the Chronicler, trust in foreign alliances was always wrong since it implied a distrust in Yahweh (see *Comment* at 16:7–10), and it would be out of accord with his portrayal of Hezekiah to suggest such dependence. He also omits most of 2 Kgs 18:36–19:34 // Isa 36:21–37:35: this omission downplays the role of Hezekiah's ministers, reduces the suggestion of fear on the part of the king and his government, and eliminates the mediatorial role played by Isaiah in receiving the oracle of deliverance; for the Chronicler Hezekiah is unafraid and is himself the recipient of direct revelation, again in the image of David and Solomon. The Chronicler closely relates the illness of Hezekiah and the visit of the envoys from Babylon, reinterpreting both, rather than treating them as discrete incidents (2 Kgs 20:3–19 // Isa 38:3–39:8).

The Chronicler's additions to the narrative are also instructive. 2 Chr 32:2–8 is unique to Chronicles and elaborates on the preparations for the siege and a speech given by Hezekiah. Such building programs in Chronicles are tokens of divine blessing for faithful kings; see the introductory essay to 2 Chr 10–36, "Reward and Punishment in Chronicles: The Theology of Immediate Retribution." 2 Chr 32:15–19 paraphrases and abridges material in the earlier account. 2 Chr 32:22–23, 27–30 directly model Hezekiah after Solomon in his achieving rest from enemies, fame among the nations, and wealth. 2 Chr 32:25–26 represent his understanding of Hezekiah's illness.

The speech in 32:7–8 has been identified as a Levitical sermon (von Rad, "Levitical Sermon," 274) drawing on Josh 10:25 and Jer 17:5. It could also be described as a holy war address (cf. Deut 20;2–4; 2 Chr 20:15–17), though here in the mouth of the king instead of a priest. The speech of the Assyrian emissary (32:10–15) shows the usual features of a messenger speech, but also the frequent use of rhetorical questions that characterizes lawsuit speeches.

At a number of points, particularly in his account of Hezekiah's illness and the Babylonian emissaries, the Chronicler's own record would be somewhat opaque without a knowledge of the earlier accounts, knowledge which the Chronicler is able to assume on the part of his reader.

The paragraphs in the narrative are marked by (1) temporal phrases (32:1, 9, 24), (2) the use of explicit subjects (32:2, 20, 22, 30b), and (3) a ‎וְיהי-clause.

Comment

1 The way the Chronicler introduces a narrative is often a key to his primary purpose in using it. Cf. 2 Chr 18:1: there the Chronicler modifies his *Vorlage* by mentioning Jehoshaphat's marriage alliance to the North; the following narrative of the battle for Ramoth-gilead becomes for him a chance to demonstrate again the evil of foreign alliances (19:1–3). Here the introductory phrase "after these faithful acts" is also diagnostic of the author's intent; it places the entire narrative that follows in the context of the author's theology of immediate retribution: a righteous king should enjoy victory in warfare and rest from his enemies, and this is the moral of the story (32:20–23).

The Chronicler does not mention the results of the Assyrian invasion reported in 2 Kgs 18:14–16; see *Form/Structure/Setting* above. He further mitigates Hezekiah's losses by reporting that Sennacherib "thought" (‎וַיֹּאמֶר) he would take the cities of Judah rather than saying he "conquered" them (‎וַֽיִּתְפְּשֵׂם, 2 Kgs 18:13 // Isa 36:1). Sennacherib's own annals claim the conquest of forty-six Judean cities.

2–5 Standard siege strategy calls for reducing a city through thirst by cutting off access to the water supply or by poisoning it; plentiful water only eases the task of the invading foe. Hezekiah's efforts at diverting and concealing the water sources in the area of Jerusalem anticipate the coming siege. Apart from the famous "Hezekiah's tunnel," the earlier Warren shaft, and an irrigation channel attributed to the Solomonic period (cf. Eccl 2:6; see H. Shanks, *The City of David* [Washington, DC: Biblical Archaeological Society, 1975]), comparatively little is known about the water supply of the City of David. Two springs are known to have been in the area, the famous Gihon (32:30) in the Kidron Valley east of the city and the spring at Enrogel, two miles south. See Y. Shiloh, "Jerusalem's Water Supply during Siege—The Rediscovery of Warren's Shaft," *BARev* 7/4 (1981) 24–39; and D. Cole, "How Water Tunnels Worked," *BARev* 6/2 (1980) 8–29.

The breaches in the wall may have come during the reign of Ahaz as part of his submission to Tiglath-pileser III. A breached wall left a city virtually defenseless; breaching a city was synonymous with conquering it (32:1). Hezekiah's decision to repair the breaches would be an overt signal of political rebellion against his Assyrian overlords. The population of Jerusalem grew considerably during the reign of Hezekiah, at least in part because of large numbers of immigrants coming to Jerusalem after the fall of the Northern Kingdom (M. Broshi, "The Expansion of Jerusalem in the Reigns of Hezekiah and Manasseh," *IEJ* 24 [1974] 21–26); the city expanded up to four times its former size. Archeological excavations in the Jewish Quarter of the Old City have uncovered portions of a wall that is attributed to Hezekiah.

Building projects such as these related to the water supply and the repair of the walls are not only prudent strategy; for the Chronicler they are tokens of divine blessing given to pious monarchs. It is striking that Isaiah took a different view (Isa 22:9–11) and warned about the danger of self-reliance and a tendency to forget Yahweh.

Strengthening the supporting terraces (the "Millo") likens Hezekiah once again to David and Solomon (1 Chr 11:8; 1 Kgs 11:27).

6–8 Just as Hezekiah had organized the priests (2 Chr 31), so also he provided a military structure; once again his actions mirror the earlier work of David (1 Chr 23–27).

Hezekiah's speech should be compared with other speeches before battle (20:15–17; 13:4–12); it is a classic summary of Israel's holy war ideology (Deut 7, 20). The speech itself is a concatenation of phrases and concepts found in other passages: Josh 10:25; Deut 31:6; 2 Kgs 6:16; Isa 7:14, 8:8–10; 31:3; Jer 17:5. The Chronicler does not mention the expectation of Egyptian help (2 Kgs 18:20–25); Hezekiah urges trust in Yahweh alone and thus avoids in the author's eyes the entangling foreign alliances that had brought judgment on Asa (2 Chr 16), Jehoshaphat (2 Chr 18:1–19:3), and Ahaz (2 Chr 28).

9–16 It is a form of psychological warfare: the commander of a powerful army sends messengers to intimidate surrounding cities into capitulation in the face of a threatened siege or disaster. Cf. the messages sent to Samaria by Ben-hadad (1 Kgs 20:2–12). When his messengers went to Jerusalem, Sennacherib "was besieging Lachish." It was literally a "monumental" campaign; Sennacherib commemorated the event with a mural over fifty feet long carved in stone in one of his palaces (D. Ussishkin, *The Conquest of Lachish by Sennacherib* [Tel Aviv: University Institute of Archeology, 1982]).

If Sennacherib's army was besieging Lachish, how is it that Jerusalem could be described as "under siege" (32:10)? The siege of Jerusalem had not yet begun, even though a great army accompanied Sennacherib's messengers (2 Kgs 18:17). The difficulty disappears (1) if the speech of the messenger is understood in a modal sense, e.g., "in what are you trusting that you are ready/willing to stay" (or, "going to stay/would stay") in Jerusalem under siege, or (2) if the siege was just beginning with the arrival of a large force. See Childs, *Isaiah and the Assyrian Crisis,* 107–9.

The messenger's speech is, of course, designed both to instill fear and to arouse discontent with Hezekiah. Hezekiah is charged with religious heresy, with abuse of power through forced labor, with deception, and with endangering the lives of his subjects. The "forced labor" (32:11) was presumably the conscripted assistance used for the water projects and repairing the walls and towers.

Ackroyd (193) sees in v 16 echoes of Ps 2:2: speaking against Yahweh and Hezekiah was speaking "against the Lord and his anointed." Hezekiah in Chronicles is idealized in the same way the author treated David and Solomon; he takes on messianic overtones that would be developed in the postbiblical literature of Judaism.

18 The term "Hebrew" is not used as a designation of the language of Israel in the OT. The "language of Judah" contrasts in this instance with Aramaic; the Chronicler appears to assume the reader's familiarity with the earlier accounts (2 Kgs 18:26–27; Isa 36:11–12). See E. Ullendorf, "The Knowledge of Languages in the Old Testament," *BJRL* 44 (1962) 455–65.

20–23 In 2 Kgs 19:1–4 // Isa 37:1–4 Hezekiah goes to the temple of the Lord and sends messengers requesting the prayers of Isaiah; the Chronicler interprets this as both men praying (cf. 2 Kgs 19:20). The author condenses much of the parallel account; instead of reporting Isaiah's oracle of deliverance and a second account of Sennacherib's emissaries, the royal prayers, and a second deliverance oracle (2 Kgs 19:5–34 // Isa 37:5–35), he moves immediately to God's answer to the prayer in the destruction of the Assyrian army. For the Chronicler it is another opportunity to demonstrate the validity of God's promise to hear Solomon's prayer at the dedication of the temple (6:28–31; 7:13–15).

The Chronicler omits the body count (2 Kgs 19:35 // Isa 37:36) reporting the death of 185,000 Assyrian soldiers. Herodotus (2:141) and Josephus (*Ant.,* 10.17–23) both preserve an independent tradition of some disaster causing Sennacherib to withdraw. The destroying angel recalls events after David's census (2 Sam 24 // 1 Chr 21) and the last plague (Exod 12).

The biblical histories all telescope the death of Sennacherib. The Assyrian king lives another twenty years until 681 B.C. Assyrian texts confirm Sennacherib's murder by a son (*ANET,* 288–89).

For the Chronicler's distinctive use of the "rest" motif, see *Notes* above on v 22.a. God gave Solomon rest from his enemies, and Hezekiah is allowed the same. Just as Solomon was exalted in the eyes of the nations (9:23–24), so is Hezekiah.

24–26 V 24 summarizes 2 Kgs 20:1–11 // Isa 38:1–22. In simply referring to the sign Hezekiah was given the Chronicler once again presumes his readers are familiar with the parallel accounts; the same information is assumed again in 32:31. Just as in 32:20–23, the author has abridged his material to bring into focus God's readiness to answer prayer as he had promised Solomon; Hezekiah prays and forthwith is healed, recalling the language of 2 Chr 7:14. See the introductory essay to 2 Chr 10–36, "Reward and Punishment in Chronicles: The Theology of Immediate Retribution." Illness in Chronicles ordinarily is the result of sin (16:7–12; 21:18–19; 26:19–21), though here the Chronicler does not provide any precipitating reason for Hezekiah's illness. Rather, his recovery and the sign he was given become the occasion for pride, from which Hezekiah must humble himself, recalling again the language of 2 Chr 7:14, and contrasting to Uzziah (26:16).

The incidents regarding the king's illness and the emissaries from Babylon in all three accounts are reported after the invasion of Sennacherib, though chronologically they were before (2 Kgs 20:6 // Isa 38:6). This has the advantage in Kings of recording a prophecy of the exile (2 Kgs 20:17) immediately before the judgment of exile announced during the reign of Manasseh (2 Kgs 21:10–15); in Isaiah it puts a prophecy of exile (39:5–7) immediately before the oracles of deliverance and restoration that begin in Isa 40.

It would make sense for Hezekiah and the Babylonians to coordinate their efforts to open a two-front war on Sennacherib shortly after his accession in 705 B.C. The "wrath" (32:25) that came on Hezekiah and Judah as a result of Hezekiah's pride would then be a reference to Sennacherib's invasion. Rather than the exile of the population occurring as threatened (2 Kgs 18:31–32 // Isa 36:16–17), this disaster did not come on Judah "in the days of Hezekiah" (32:26), but would fall instead on Manasseh (33:11) and ultimately on the entire kingdom (36:20; cf. 2 Kgs 20:17–19 // Isa 39:6–8). There would be "peace and security" (2 Kgs 20:19) during the lifetime of Hezekiah. This picture of events must also be compared with Sennacherib's claim to have deported 200,150 Judeans (*ANET*, 288); S. Stohlmann ("Judean Exile," in *Scripture in Context* [Winona Lake: Eisenbrauns, 1983]) argues that this figure represents the total number of Judean citizens counted as plunder by Sennacherib from his Judean campaign, while a much smaller number would actually have been deported.

Just as the Chronicler downplayed the mediatorial role of Isaiah during the Assyrian invasion (see *Form/Structure/Setting*), so here too he omits the involvement of Isaiah as described in the parallel texts, preferring to heighten the direct relationship of Hezekiah to God.

27–31 Hezekiah's wealth once again reflects the concern of the author to effect parallels with David and Solomon; see *Notes* above, 27.a. and 29.a. Riches and building programs are among the tokens of divine favor; Hezekiah's tunnel was a monumental undertaking, a task requiring the grace and favor of God; see 32:2–5.

חלצ, "succeed" (32:30), is another term characteristic of the Chronicler's theology of immediate retribution. In saying that Hezekiah succeeded in all that he did, the Chronicler is emphasizing only one part of the attitude taken to the Babylonian emissaries in the earlier two accounts (2 Kgs 20:17–19 // Isa 39:6–8). In the earlier accounts Hezekiah's display was a harbinger of a day when the Babylonians would carry away Judah's wealth and royal household, though Hezekiah would have peace and security during his reign. The Chronicler regards this testing as successful, focusing only on its positive outcome.

The Chronicler has also modified somewhat the reason for the visit of the Babylonians. In Kings and Isaiah they come with congratulations for his recovery from illness; the Chronicler presents instead an earlier visit of the magi inquiring about wonders in the heavens (cf. Matt 2:1–2), i.e., the widely known Babylonian interest in astrology prompted an inquiry regarding the declination of the sun (2 Kgs 20:10–11 // Isa 38:7–8). The more probable and pressing reason for the visit was cooperation between Merodach-baladan and Hezekiah in opening a two-front war on the Assyrians at the time of Sennacherib's accession, a strategy well attested in biblical history (16:1–3; 28:16–21; Isa 7). This cooperation with Babylon against Assyria may also explain why Manasseh was punished there by the Assyrians (33:11) and why Josiah sought to block the Egyptian advance (35:20–21). A. Shinan and Y. Zakowitch ("Midrash on Scripture and Midrash within Scripture," *Scripta Hieroslymitana* 31 [1986] 268–69) see Hezekiah as having failed the test: the Babylonians came prompted by the glory of God, while Hezekiah was interested only in his own grandeur and failed God's test.

32–33 "His acts of piety." See 6:42; 35:26; Neh 13:14; "Vision of Isaiah." See Isa 1:1. The inclusion of this source in a larger collection, "the book of the kings of Judah and Israel," indicates that this is not the canonical book of Isaiah.

The great "honor" shown Hezekiah at his death had to do with the observances attending his burial as well as the tomb site. The burial of a king was customarily accompanied by a great fire (16:14; Jer 34:5) in his honor, though such an honor could be withheld (21:19); the honor shown Hezekiah probably also included the quality and quantity of spices (16:14) that accompanied his interment. In addition to the intensification of customary royal burial observances, Hezekiah was assigned a particular place in the royal tombs. The precise meaning of the term מעלה is not certain. It has been taken as a topographical feature in the area of the royal tombs, "the upper part" (G ἐν ἀναβάσει), or as the upper tier of a two-level tomb or as an expression of quality, "better, finer." Ackroyd ("Death of Hezekiah," 222–25) sees the use of the term כבוד, "honor, glory," as contributing to the further development of later Jewish speculation about Hezekiah as a messianic figure. See F. Rosner (*Koroth* 9 [1985] 190–91) for a summary of later Jewish traditions regarding the king.

Explanation

Several planes of the Chronicler's central theological concerns intersect in this narrative. (1) It is an occasion for the Chronicler to reinforce his retribution theology. A king who has acted faithfully (32:1) will know the blessing of God through victory in war, building programs, wealth, fame among the gentiles, healing in times of illness, and the regard of his people at death. Readers of the NT will recall the statement of James, that "the prayer offered in faith will make the sick person well; the LORD will raise him up. If he has sinned, he will be forgiven" (James 5:15).

(2) The Chronicler had idealized David and Solomon by portraying them as all-but-sinless figures. For the Chronicler Hezekiah was the zenith of the

sons of David who followed. He draws many parallels between the reigns of those first rulers of a united kingdom and this ruler who was the first to rule alone after the Northern Kingdom had been carried away. See the introductory essay to 2 Chr 29–32, "The Chronicler's Hezekiah." In this regard the Chronicler can be thought of as the first of that long line of Jewish interpreters who would idealize Hezekiah and eventually treat him, along with David and Solomon, as messianic figures. In their faithfulness they embodied the hopes of Israel for the future, for the restoration of a united people enjoying peace, victory, and prosperity under the righteous rule of the sons of David.

(3) The Chronicler was much concerned with the themes of exile and restoration. Hezekiah is a model for avoiding exile or for enjoying restoration. He showed the path to recovery from the difficulties and foreign domination under Ahaz; his faithfulness avoided exile for Judah in his days (32:26). These were lessons for the post-exilic community.

The God of Israel will not brook hubris. Those who take their stand against him or his anointed are rebuked in his wrath (Ps 2). Taunts of an enemy delivered to those high on a city wall were answered by the power of a heaven-sent destroyer (32:21). Taunts delivered to one high on a cross were answered by resurrection from the dead, victory over that last and greatest enemy. The hubris of an Assyrian king was crushed by force; the hubris of mankind, by the foolishness of the cross. Let him who boasts, boast in the LORD (1 Cor 1:31).

Manasseh, 697/96–643/42, and Amon, 643/42–641/40 (33:1–25)

Bibliography

Broshi, M. "The Expansion of Jerusalem in the Reigns of Hezekiah and Manasseh." *IEJ* 24 (1974) 21–26. **Cogan, M.** *Imperialism and Religion.* 65–96. **Ehrlich, E.** "Der Aufenthalt des Königs Manasse in Babylon." *TZ* 21 (1965) 281–86. **Fuller, L.** *The Historical and Religious Significance of the Reign of Manasseh.* Leipzig: Brugulin, 1912. **Graham, P.** "Is There a Historical Basis for the Chronicler's Report of Manasseh's Captivity?" Paper read at the annual meeting of the Society of Biblical Literature, New Orleans, 1978. **Haran, M.** *Temples.* 276–84. **Malamat, A.** "The Historical Background of the Assassination of Amon, King of Judah." *IEJ* 3 (1953) 26–29. **McKay, J.** *Religion in Judah.* 20–27. **Nielsen, E.** "Political Conditions and Cultural Developments in Israel and Judah during the Reign of Manasseh." In *Proceedings of the Fourth World Congress of Jewish Studies, Jerusalem, 1965.* Jerusalem: World Union of Jewish Studies, 1967. 103–6. **Oded, B.** "The Reigns of Manasseh and Amon." In *Israelite and Judean History,* ed. J. Hayes and M. Miller. Philadelphia: Westminster Press, 1977. 452–58. **Spieckermann, H.** *Juda unter Assur.* **Stafford, J.** "The Reign of Manasseh in the Book of Chronicles." Thesis, Winnipeg Theological Seminary, 1986.

Translation

[1] *Manasseh was twelve years old when he became king, and he ruled fifty-five[a] years in Jerusalem.* [2] *He did what was evil in the eyes of Yahweh, just like the abominations of the nations that Yahweh drove out before the children of Israel.* [3] *He rebuilt the high places that his father Hezekiah had torn down.[a] He erected altars[b] to the Baals,[c] made Asherahs,[d] and bowed down and worshiped all the host of heaven.* [4] *He built altars in the temple of Yahweh of which Yahweh had said, "In Jerusalem my name shall dwell forever."* [5] *He built altars for all the host of heaven in the courts of the temple of Yahweh.*

[6] *He sacrificed his sons[a] in the fire in the Valley of Ben Hinnom[b] and practiced soothsaying, divination, and sorcery[c] and consulted mediums and spiritists. He did much evil in the eyes of Yahweh and provoked him.* [7] *He made a carved image[a] and put it in the temple of God, of which God had said to David and his son Solomon, "I will put my name forever[b] in this house and in Jerusalem, which I have chosen from all the tribes of Israel.* [8] *I will not again remove[a] the feet of Israel from the land I appointed[b] for your[c] fathers, if only they will do all that I command them, all the law, statutes, and precepts that came through Moses."*

[9] *But Manasseh misled Judah and the inhabitants of Jerusalem, so that they did evil more than the nations that Yahweh had destroyed before the children of Israel.*

[10] *Yahweh spoke to Manasseh and his people, but they did not heed.[a]* [11] *So Yahweh brought against them the leaders of the army of the king of Assyria, and they made Manasseh a prisoner, put a ring through his nose, bound him with fetters, and took him to Babylon.*

[12] *During his distress Manasseh entreated Yahweh his God and humbled himself greatly before the God of his fathers.* [13] *He prayed, and God accepted his prayer*

and heard his petition, and restored him to his kingdom in Jerusalem, and Manasseh knew that Yahweh was God.
¹⁴*After this he rebuilt the outer wall of the City of David from west of the Gihon Spring in the valley to the Fish Gate, enclosing the Ophel; he made it very high. He also installed military commanders in all the fortified cities of Judah.* ¹⁵*He removed the foreign gods and the carved image from the temple of Yahweh and all the altars he had built on the mountain of Yahweh's temple in Jerusalem, and he threw them out of the city.* ¹⁶*He restored*[a] *the altar of Yahweh and sacrificed fellowship and thank offerings upon it; he commanded Judah to worship Yahweh the God of Israel.* ¹⁷*However, the people continued sacrificing on the high places, though only to Yahweh their God.*

¹⁸*The rest of the acts of Manasseh—his prayer to God and the words that the seers spoke about him in the name of Yahweh the God of Israel—are in the* [a]*acts of the kings of Israel.*[a] ¹⁹*His prayer and the answer he received, all his sin and unfaithfulness, and the locations where he built high places and set up Asherah poles and idols before he humbled himself—these are written in the records of Hozai.*[a] ²⁰*Manasseh rested with his fathers, and they buried him in the palace grounds;*[a] *Amon his son ruled in his place.*

²¹ *Amon was twenty-two years old when he became king, and he ruled two years in Jerusalem.* ²²*He did what was evil in the eyes of Yahweh, just as Manasseh his father had done. Amon made sacrifices to all the idols his father had made and worshiped them.* ²³ *He did not humble himself before Yahweh as Manasseh his father had humbled himself; rather, Amon became even more guilty.* ²⁴*His servants conspired against him and killed him in his palace.* ²⁵*The people of the land struck down those who had conspired against King Amon; the people of the land then made Josiah his son king in his place.*

Notes

1.a. G^{A,V} lack "five," probably a case of haplography influenced by the preceding "fifty."

3.a. 2 Kgs 21:3, אבד, "destroyed."

3.b. G στήλας, "pillars," developed from misreading מצבות, so often associated with the Baals (2 Kgs 3:2; 10:26, 27). There could be some influence from 31:1: Manasseh restores those items Hezekiah removed.

3.c. 2 Kgs 21:3, sg. Chr has pl. where Kgs has sg also for *Asherahs* (33:3) and *sons* (33:6). These are commonly attributed to a desire on the Chronicler's part to enhance the apostasy of Manasseh. However, the Chronicler uses the pl "Baals" frequently in other contexts without direct parallels in Kgs (17:3; 24:7; 34:4)—it may be that the pl in this case should be attributed to his customary usage or the influence of other pls in the immediate context rather than the theological motive of enhancing Manasseh's impiety. See *Comment* at 17:3–4.

3.d. 2 Kgs 21:3, sg. The Chronicler uses the term "Asherah" ten times, only once in the sg, suggesting again a preference for the plural form rather than a theological motive. Chr also omits the phrase in 2 Kgs 21:3 likening Manasseh to Ahab.

6.a. 2 Kgs 21:6, sg,"his son." Chr MT may have depended on a *Vorlage* similar to that used by the Bas translator who also has a plural, τοὺς υἱοὺς αὐτοῦ. The difference between Kgs and Chr in this case should be regarded as a text critical question rather than as an example of the Chronicler's *Tendenz.* Cf. the same issue in 28:3.

6.b. Not in 2 Kgs 21:6.

6.c. Chr adds כשף, "practice sorcery," not in the parallel at 2 Kgs 21:6. This addition should be attributed to the influence of Deut 18:10.

7.a. 2 Kgs 21:7, פסל האשרה, "carved Asherah."

7.b. MT עילום is probably a scribal error for עולם.

8.a. 2 Kgs 21:8, לְהָנִיד, "cause to wander."

8.b. 2 Kgs 21:8, נָתַתִּי, "I gave." Par is influenced by Bas.

8.c. 2 Kgs 21:8, "their fathers." Par again is influenced by Bas.

10.a. All of 2 Chr 33:10-17 is contained in one twelfth-century cursive of Bas, obviously not a variant text of Kgs, but rather an intrusion into Kgs from Chr. See Lemke, *Synoptic Studies*, 220.

16.a. K, וַיִּכֶן (cf. G); Q, וַיִּבֶן, "he built" (cf. some MSS, Syr, Tg, Arab).

18.a.–a. Missing in G. The concluding notice for Manasseh's reign (33:18–19) is uncharacteristic for Chr and appears expanded and corrupt. The sources are introduced twice (הִנָּם, 18, 19) and there is some redundancy between them in the information each is reported to contain. The citation of the "acts of the kings of Israel" itself appears fragmentary; in light of the customary source citations in Chr, one would expect something like "behold they are written in the book of the kings of Israel and Judah." Since this citation is also missing in G, it is probable that Chr MT has undergone some secondary expansion or that a kind of dittography was introduced by a scribe anticipating the usual source citation. See Lemke, *Synoptic Studies*, 222–23; contrast Allen, *GC* 2:55.

19.a. MT appears to be the name of an otherwise unknown prophet Hozai. G reads ὁρώντων, = חֹזִים, "seers." Alternatively MT may have a haplography for the ו of the suffix, so that חֹזָיו, "his seers," would be correct.

20.a. 2 Kgs 21:18, בְּגַן בֵּיתוֹ, "in the garden of his palace." Chr MT omits "garden." The word בַּיִת includes not only the building proper but also the surrounding grounds, whether applied to the royal palace or the temple. Chr MT may have omitted בְּגַן through a homoioarchon due to the initial ב, or Par (ἐν παραδείσῳ) may be paraphrasing to give the sense, perhaps with influence from Bas.

Form/Structure/Setting

Though the Chronicler was heavily dependent on Kings for his account of Manasseh (33:1–10 // 2 Kgs 21:1–10), the two accounts contrast sharply in their overall assessment of his reign. In the deuteronomic history Manasseh is the nadir of the kings of Judah and is the leading cause of a now irreversible exile, whereas in Chronicles he becomes repentant and a religious reformer. Though agreeing regarding his apostasy, the two historians come to opposite moral judgments.

Opinions on the historicity of the Chronicler's version of Manasseh have varied widely. The account is clearly influenced by two of the Chronicler's major theological motifs: (1) the Chronicler makes extensive use of the motif of exile and restoration; in his narrative Manasseh becomes an allegory for Israel's own exile (see *Explanation* below); (2) Manasseh is occasion to demonstrate once again the validity of the author's theology of immediate retribution. With the stamp of the author's own concerns so clearly imprinted on the text, many have concluded that the entire incident was a flight of the Chronicler's fancy, at least extensive embellishment if not outright fabrication, perhaps to harmonize the king's long reign with the author's retribution theology. Others assess the historical data in the narrative as quite in keeping with the political circumstances of Judah under the Assyrians.

Manasseh's humiliation, deportation and imprisonment in Babylon provide the focal point of historical concerns in the chapter. The only extant direct references to Manasseh in Assyriological texts portray him as a loyal vassal: during the reign of Esarhaddon, Manasseh was required to contribute materials for construction in Nineveh (*ANET*, 291), and during the reign of Asshurbanipal he is named among the vassal kings who participated in a campaign against Egypt (*ANET*, 294). With this evidence indicating a submissiveness to Assyria on Manasseh's part, the question naturally follows regarding what historical circumstances would have prompted his humiliation and punishment by his overlords. Several scenarios are commonly suggested: (1) The revolt of Shamash-shum-ukin in Babylon (652–648 B.C.) against his brother Asshurbanipal fomented unrest in other parts of the Assyrian empire, and it is entirely within the range of probability that Manasseh was guilty of allying himself with the Babylonians, as his father Hezekiah had also done (32:31), or at least that he was suspected of complicity. This would place Manasseh's rebellion fairly late in his reign and would explain also why the Assyrian chose to punish Manasseh in Babylon instead of Nineveh or some other location. (2) Others associate Manasseh's humiliation with the rebellion of Abdimilkutte of Sidon and Sanduarri of Kundu and Sizu in 677 B.C. (*ANET*, 290–91). They were quickly defeated, and afterward, Esarhaddon required the twenty-two kings of Hatti to bring construction materials to Nineveh; Manasseh is mentioned in this list of kings. However, there is no indication that all of the kings named were involved in the rebellion, and the place of their submission is Nineveh instead of Babylon; the kings appear to be rendering expected tribute to their suzerain rather than suffering some punishment for rebellion. (3) Between 675–673 B.C., Baal of Tyre allied himself with Tirhakah of Egypt, and Assyria attacked (*ANET*, 292). Manasseh is not mentioned in this text; though he may have shown sympathy for the rebels, there is no hint of deportation and humiliation. One should not generalize from the scant Assyriological evidence for Manasseh's loyalty to conclude that this was the pattern of his entire fifty-five-year reign. If one could generalize from parallels throughout ancient Near Eastern history, vassal alliances were tenuous at best and controlled by expedience and opportunism. The greater probability is that Manasseh would rebel if opportunity was afforded and there was some expectation of possible success.

While the historical concerns are most plausibly answered in option (1) above, it is at least possible that the Chronicler is using the term "Babylon" more broadly as a generalized reference to Mesopotamia in his effort to parallel Manasseh's experience with that of Israel, so that any punitive deportation of Manasseh to either Assyria or Babylon could meet the historical question. There is no evidence which overtly contradicts the Chronicler's account, and it has a fair amount of intrinsic probability given the political circumstances. Manasseh's reign spanned over half a century, and there are numerous occasions and long periods of time into which any number of unrecorded events could fit, events of which we as yet have no direct evidence.

In Kings the greatest king following David and Solomon was Josiah; his rule and reforms embody the ideals of that history. It has always been something of an enigma that, because of the sins of Manasseh, the exile has become a foregone conclusion before the appearance of Josiah (2 Kgs 21:12–15). Though Josiah is the zenith of the kings of Judah, his reign becomes somewhat anticlimactic since the exile is already decreed. One way this tension has been explained is by appeal to a theory of double redaction for Kings (F. Cross, *Canaanite Myth and Hebrew Epic* [Cambridge, MA: Harvard UP, 1973]; R. Nelson, *The Double Redaction of the Deuteronomistic History*. JSOTSup 18.

[Sheffield: JSOT Press, 1981]). An early or original edition (DH[1]) of the deuteronomic history was composed by a partisan of Josiah to provide an ideological foundation celebrating the rule of that king; this pre-exilic composition was modified by an exilic editor (DH[2]) who recast the ideological focus of the book, in part explaining the reason for the exile. 2 Kgs 21:11–16 is ordinarily assigned to this exilic editor. Assuming that the theory of a double redaction is helpful in explaining the present form of Kings, one can only wonder how the initial composition (DH[1]) would have treated Manasseh. Prior to the presumed deletion of some material and insertion of 2 Kgs 21:11–16 by DH[2], DH[1] could well have contained some record of the humiliation of Manasseh by Assyria. Some have argued that the Chronicler had only DH[1] without the additions of DH[2] before him as a source; though this position does not appear probable (see *Form/Structure/Setting* in chap. 36), it is possible that the Chronicler's sources contained material similar to what may have been in DH[1] (see S. McKenzie, *Chronicler's Use*, 163; J. Rosenbaum, *HTR* 72 [1979] 23–43). However, since the passage is so replete with features of the Chronicler's theology and style, and since his portrayal of Manasseh conflicts with the attitude to him not only in Kings, but also in Jer 15:4 and 2 Chr 33:22, Williamson (*VT* 37 112–13) disputes that the Chronicler used information from a hypothetical DH[1]; he regards the author as having at the least rewritten the periocope with his own emphases (exile and restoration, retribution theology), if the entire section is not his own composition.

The Chronicler's treatment of Amon's reign is fairly brief (33:21–25), likening Amon to Manasseh with Kings (2 Kgs 21:19–26), but also contrasting him with his father. In both histories Amon is treated more or less as a sequel to Manasseh.

The paragraphs in the narrative are somewhat ambiguous, but could be analyzed as marked by the following devices: (1) temporal phrases (33:12, 14); (2) explicit subjects (33:9, 10); (3) a circumstantial clause (33:6). Note the three occurrences of the phrase reporting that Manasseh "did evil" early in the paragraphs beginning with 33:2, 6, 9; repetition of such phrases is common on paragraph boundaries.

Comment

1 Taken at first impression, if the extension of Hezekiah's life by fifteen years is dated from the 701 B.C. Assyrian invasion, Manasseh would have been born in 698 B.C. to attain age twelve by the death of Hezekiah. The fifty-five years would then date from 686–633 B.C.; these dates would be too late and would contradict other chronological notices for the length of Josiah's reign. To adjust the chronology downward, Thiele (*Mysterious Numbers*, rev. ed., 173–74) introduces a coregency with Hezekiah of about ten years, reducing his sole reign to forty-five years instead of fifty-five. Appeal to coregencies to handle difficult chronological problems is a powerful and plausible tool, but occasionally appears used in an almost ad hoc manner. See Hobbs, 304–5.

Manasseh ruled longer than any other king of Judah. Many find in this fact the key to the Chronicler's treatment of this king. In light of his theology of immediate retribution, Manasseh would have represented something of a problem: how is it that this king who represented the pinnacle of evil also enjoyed the divine blessing of long life? The Chronicler's account of Manasseh's punishment, repentance, and reform removes the narrative from being a problem and makes it instead a dramatic confirmation of the validity of retribution theology and the efficacy of repentance. Some object that since the Chronicler makes no particular point about Manasseh's long life, it was not a formative factor in his narrative (Mosis, *Untersuchungen*, 194). However, the Chronicler does show awareness of length of reign as an indicator of divine blessing in one context (1 Chr 29:28; 2 Chr 24:15–16; see *Comment* at 1:12); length of life is simply an extension of the health/illness motif of which the Chronicler does make repreated use.

The Chronicler omits the names of the mothers of Manasseh (2 Kgs 21:1), Amon (2 Kgs 21:19), and Josiah (2 Kgs 22:1) contrary to his regular practice of including this information for the earlier kings. McKay (*Religion in Judah*, 23–25) argues that these omissions in the case of Manasseh and Amon were because the women in question were of Edomite or Arabian origin and brought the worship of Arabian deities into Judah. This line of argument does not appear very convincing. The Chronicler does not name the mother of any king after Hezekiah; though the first such omission in the case of Manasseh could have been in some way theologically motivated and may have set the precedent for the remaining accounts, it is also possible that the author is simply modifying his format for reasons no longer apparent to us. The name of the queen mother and the death formulae "with his fathers" and "in the City of David" all disappear from Chr after the reign of Hezekiah; McKenzie (*Chronicler's Use*, 174–76) and Macy (*The Sources of the Books of Chronicles*, Diss. Harvard, 1975) find in this data evidence for a change in the Chronicler's sources.

2 This verse is verbatim 2 Kgs 21:2, but functions somewhat differently in the earlier narrative. In Kings Manasseh's reign accounts for the exile; the abominations for which Yahweh drove the Canaanites from the land would eventually be the same reasons for which Israel was driven out (Deut 18:12; 2 Kgs 17:8, 16–20). This relationship between the deeds and exile of the Canaanites and the deeds and exile of Israel is somewhat muted in Chronicles and becomes the personal experience of the king rather than the nation.

3–5 Biblical scholarship has traditionally regarded the cycles of reform and apostasy in Judah during the period of Assyrian domination as the reflex of political realities: in societies where politics and religion were inextricably intertwined, apostasy derived from the imposition of Assyrian worship, and reform was but the religious counterpart of political rebellion against Assyria. This picture has changed radically in the last couple of decades, particularly due to the monographs by McKay (*Religion in Judah*) and Cogan (*Imperialism and Religion*), though not without dissent (Spieckermann, *Juda unter Assur*). The religious phenomena alleged to be distinctly Assyrian worship, such as the "hosts of heaven," are now understood as indigenous Canaanite cults. With the progress of epigraphic discovery we are now able to appreciate that the Assyrians respected local cults and imposed Assyrian worship only when territories were annexed as provinces in the empire. The way is open to appreciating with the Scriptures once again the formative impact of religious conviction in the life of the kingdoms, rather than simply reducing the religious to a reflection of the political, though of course, some interpenetration of concerns must be expected.

The Chronicler omits comparing Manasseh with Ahab (33:3 // 2 Kgs 21:3). In Kings this comparison was appropriate: Manasseh represented the nadir of the South, as Ahab had been in the North. For the Chronicler, however, Ahaz represented the nadir of Judean kings, and he may have omitted the comparison as part of his effort to rehabilitate Manasseh. Ahab is only mentioned in Chronicles in connection with the apostasy following intermarriage in Judah with his dynasty (2 Chr 18:1–3, 19; 21:6, 13; 22:3–8).

6–8   The passage is clearly dependent on Deut 18:9–13; the precise significance of all the terms is not clear. By its inclusion in this and similar contexts, the rite of child sacrifice apparently was a divinatory practice; see *Comment* at 28:1–4.

The "carved image" (v 7) is specifically an image of Asherah in 2 Kgs 21:7. McKay (*Religion in Judah,* 22–23) regards פֶסֶל as a Phoenician term referring to a Phoenician goddess, and suggesting some political/marriage alliances with the Phoenicians.

10–11   The Chronicler omits 2 Kgs 21:10b–16. The omission is symptomatic of the approach taken to the problem of guilt and punishment in both histories. For Kings as it stands in its final redaction, guilt was in a sense cumulative, "since the day their fathers came out of Egypt until this day" (2 Kgs 21:16), and it is this cumulative weight of guilt which would issue in the exile; this is in keeping with the intent of Kings to account for the end of the Davidic dynasty and the destruction of Jerusalem. For the Chronicler, however, each generation knew weal or woe depending on its own conduct. The judgment announced against Masasseh would not come in his own day in Kings (2 Kgs 21:12–14), but several decades later, whereas in Chronicles Manasseh is judged immediately for his own wrongdoing. See the introductory essay to 2 Chr 10–36, "Reward and Punishment in Chronicles: The Theology of Immediate Retribution."

Manasseh is treated much as one would subdue an animal—the nose ring would serve to humiliate him completely before his captors. Assyrian iconography portrays similar treatment of captives (*ANEP,* no. 447). Cf. 2 Kgs 19:28; Ezek 19:4. The fetters anticipate Jehoiakim bound in bronze shackles and taken to Babylon (2 Chr 36:6). "Babylon" (33:11): see *Form/Structure/Setting.*

12–13   The verb "humble" is one of the frequent terms that serves as a vehicle for the Chronicler's theology of immediate retribution. By reporting Manasseh's humbling himself and praying the Chronicler is reiterating the centrality of Solomon's prayer at the temple dedication and God's response, particularly 2 Chr 7:14 which serves virtually as a charter for Israel's history as seen through the Chronicler's eyes.

Those areas where the Bible is tantalizingly silent often provide the impetus for the production of the apocryphal literature. The interest in Manasseh's prayer (cf. 33:18–19) has either spawned the composition of the apocryphal book by that name, or at least provided the warrant for assigning that poem to this occasion.

14–17 Building programs and large armies are the lot of the righteous king in Chronicles, and the author's inclusion of this material relates no doubt to showing divine blessing following upon repentance. It is possible that such fortification was undertaken prior to his revolt against Assyria, and that it has been dischronologized to this point as part of the Chronicler's presentation; however, it is equally probable that the fortification was undertaken after his return from Babylon as part of the Assyrian efforts to buttress their southern borders against Egypt. Manasseh may have been repairing damage done to the city walls when he was taken captive. Cf. 32:5.

Whatever the extent of Manasseh's religious reforms, the idols were either quickly back in place after his death or some were never removed at all (33:22). Josiah would still need to remove from the temple the altars that Manasseh had built (2 Kgs 23:12; cf. Jer 15:4). The Chronicler himself concedes that Manasseh's reform was not pervasive or enduring (33:17). Cf. the similar question of whether Asa and Jehoshaphat did or did not suppress the high places (see *Comment* at 14:1–4).

18–20 The death formula in Chronicles is elaborated beyond that in the parallel text (2 Kgs 21:17–18; see *Notes* above). The Chronicler does not include the information that Manasseh was buried in the "garden of Uzza" (2 Kgs 21:18); he makes the same omission in reference to Amon (2 Kgs 21:26). McKay (*Religion in Judah,* 24–25) associates the name Uzza with an Arabian astral deity whose cult may have been introduced into Jerusalem by Manasseh's wife; the Chronicler's omission in that case could be assigned to his effort to show Manasseh as a reform king to the end of his life (see *Comment* at 33:1), but there would be no reason for a similar omission in the case of Amon's unabashed idolatry. It may be that the "garden of Uzza" has been omitted simply because it was no longer an identifiable area in the topography of Jerusalem during the Chronicler's own day. In saying that Manasseh was buried in the palace grounds the Chronicler makes Manasseh the fifth king of whom he notes that he was not buried in the royal tombs.

21–25 The name and lineage of the mother of Amon is omitted (2 Kgs 21:19); see *Comment* at 33:1 above. If Amon was twenty-two when he became king and ruled for two years, Josiah was born when Amon was about sixteen years old (34:1).

The Chronicler's account of Amon follows rather closely that in 2 Kgs 21:19–26. The most notable difference is that for the writer of Kings, Amon was "just like" his father Manasseh (2 Kgs 21:20 // 33:22), whereas in Chronicles Amon is contrasted to Manasseh because of his failure to repent (33:23). The Chronicler explicates "walking in all the ways his father walked" (2 Kgs 21:21) as "offering sacrifices and worshiping all the idols his father Manasseh had made" (33:22; see *Comment* at 33:14–17 above).

The reasons for Amon's assassination are not apparent. Malamat (*IEJ* 3 [1953] 26–29) finds motivation in international politics; he suggests that Amon's murder was because of his pro-Assyrian policies and may have been instigated by Egypt when the decline of Assyrian power provided opportunity for rebellion. Nielsen ("Political Conditions") finds an ideological or religious explanation: parties loyal to Hezekiah's reform opposed the foreign influences in the ruling circles.

This question is complicated in part by the difficulty of identifying the "people of the land" (עם הארץ). Scholars have reached a variety of conclusions regarding the sociopolitical identity of the group designated by the phrase; some conclude they were (1) a privileged social class composed of free landowners; (2) a collective designation for free people, citizens; (3) a reference to the population of the provincial towns as distinguished from the population of Jerusalem; (4) a proletariat of the common folk; (5) a national council composed of elders. See the following: E. Auerbach, "'Am-ha'areṣ," *Proceedings of the First World Congress of Jewish Studies* (Jerusalem: World Union of Jewish Studies, 1952) 362–66; S. Daiches, "The Meaning of 'Am-haaretz' in the Old Testament," *JTS* 30 (1929) 245–49; T. Isida, "The People of the Land and the Political Crises in Judah," *Annal of the Japanese Biblical Institute* 1 (1975) 23–38; E. Nicholson, "The Meaning of the Expression ''Am ha'areṣ' in the Old Testament," *JSS* 10 (1965) 59–66; M. Sulzberger, *'Am-ha-aretz, The Ancient Hebrew Parliament* (Philadelphia: Julius Greenstone, 1909); S. Talmon, "The Judean 'am ha-areṣ in Historical Perspective," *Fourth World Congress of Jewish Studies* 1 (1967) 71–76; R. de Vaux, "Les sens de l'expression 'peuple du pays' dans l'Ancien Testament et le role politique du peuple en Israel," *RA* 58 (1964) 167–72. The Bible itself makes no comment regarding the ideology or composition of the "people of the land," and all such conclusions are reached only by inference or by necessity from some controlling paradigm.

The Chronicler omits the source and burial notice for Amon (2 Kgs 21:25–26). Though the author often uses burial notices as one more means of showing divine blessing or disfavor, the complete omission of that notice in this case is surprising. It may be related to avoiding mention of an Arab astral deity Uzza (see above on 33:20). However, it is possible that the burial notice was omitted as a result of a homoioteleuton—the two occurrences of the phrase "Josiah his son in his place" (2 Kgs 21:24b, 26b) may have resulted in the Chronicler's omitting the intervening material and picking up after the second occurrence of that phrase (Lemke, *Synoptic Studies*, 225).

Explanation

The deuteronomic historian and the Chronicler reached opposite moral judgments on the reign of Manasseh—one finding him the nadir of Judah, and the other, a reformer. Yet both judgments are "word of God." At a theological level this tension can be reconciled in the awareness that all that we do is touched both by sin and by the grace of God. The best deeds of human beings are never devoid of the taint of sinfulness; conversely, men at their most evil are never utterly bereft of the restraining grace of God. Either view—that focusing on evil or grace—provides a coherent picture. The biblical historians in this sense are not reductionistic, but taken together display life in its complexity. One overarching theme of the Bible is that God is pleased with repentance—even the repentance of an Ahab or a Manasseh, or others among the "chief of sinners" (1 Tim 1:15). The principle is reiterated time and again that "everyone who exalts himself will be humbled, and he who humbles himself will be exalted" (Luke 14:11; 18:14; Exod 10:3; 2 Kgs 22:19).

The book of Kings assigns much of the blame for the exile to Manasseh. In Chronicles by contrast, Manasseh is not blamed for the exile, but rather his personal experience becomes an allegory for the experience of Israel and a realization of prophetic hopes. Manasseh undergoes judgment for sin, exile, and restoration. He is the embodiment of the ransomed of the LORD who return with joy to Zion (Isa 51:11; 35:10). He was freed from the hands of those who had enslaved him (Ezek 34:27; Isa 61:1; 42:7; 49:9; 58:6; Jer 29:10; 30:8; Ps 107:10–16). He returned to the city to rebuild the ancient walls and to fortify towns (Isa 58:12; Ezek 36:33, 35; Amos 9:11, 14). Manasseh knew the Lord (33:13) as would others released from captivity (Ezek 36:26). Restoration to Jerusalem brought with it pure worship in a consecrated temple (Zech 14:6; Isa 27:13). Numerous other motifs from prophetic expectations about the restoration could also be cited as realized also in the life of Manasseh. The Chronicler has made Manasseh a paradigm for the experience that Judah itself would undergo; his repentance led to the joys of restoration, a message dear to the Chronicler and his audience. At an even later stage these perceptions of a restored community are further developed and applied by NT writers in their description of the work of Christ and the church.

Josiah, 641–609 B.C.: His Reform (34:1–33)

Bibliography

Alt, A. "Judas Gaue unter Josia." *PJ* 21 (1925) 100–116. **Bayer, E.** *Das dritte Buch Esdras und sein Verhältnis zu den Büchern Esra-Nehemia.* Freiburg: Herdersche Verlagshandlung, 1911. **Begg, C.** "The Death of Josiah in Chronicles: Another View." *VT* 37 (1987) 1–8. **Breslauer, S.** "Scripture and Authority: Two Views of the Josianic Reformation." *Perspectives in Religious Studies* 10 (1983) 135–43. **Budde, K.** "Das Deuteronium und die Reform König Josias." *ZAW* 44 (1926) 177–224. **Claburn, W.** "The Fiscal Basis of Josiah's Reform." *JBL* 92 (1973) 11–22. **Cogan, M.** "The Chronicler's Use of Chronology as Illuminated by Neo-Assyrian Royal Inscriptions." In *Empirical Models for Biblical Criticism*, ed. J. Tigay. Philadelphia: University of Pennsylvania Press, 1985. 197–210. ———. *Imperialism and Religion.* **Couroyer, B.** "Le litige entre Josias et Nechao." *RB* 55 (1948) 388–96. **Cross, F.,** and **D. Freedman.** "Josiah's Revolt against Assyria." *JNES* 12 (1953) 56–58. **Delcor, M.** "Reflexions sur la Pâque du temps de Josias d'après II Rois 23, 21–23." *Henoch* 4 (1982) 205–19. **de Vaux, R.** *Ancient Israel.* New York: McGraw-Hill, 1965. 2:484–92. **Díaz, J.** "Le muerto de Josias en la redación deuteronomic de libre de los Reges como anticipación de la teología de libro de Job." *Homenaje a Juan Pedro.* Madrid: Inst. B. A. Montano, 1975. 166–77. **Dietrich, W.** "Josia und das Gesetzbuch (2 Reg. 22)." *VT* 27 (1977) 13–35. **Eshkenazi, T.** "The Chronicler and the Composition of 1 Esdras." *CBQ* 48 (1986) 39 61. **Freed, A.** "The Code Spoken of in 2 Kings 22–23." *JBL* 40 (1921) 76–80. **Frost, S.** "The Death of Josiah: A Conspiracy of Silence." *JBL* 87 (1968) 369–82. **Granild, S.** "Einige Voraussetzungen des Gesetzbuches in 2 Kön. 22:8." *DTT* 19 (1956) 199–210. **Gressmann, H.** "Josia und das Deuteronium." *ZAW* 42 (1924) 313–37. **Horst, F.** "Die Kultusreform des Königs Josias." *ZDMG* 77 (1923) 220–38. **Jepsen, A.** "Die Reform des Josias." In *Festschrift für A. Baumgärtel.* Berlin: Töpelmann, 1959. 97–108. **Kitchen, K.** *TIPE* 407. **Kraus, H.** "Zur Geschichte des Passah-Massot-Festes im Alten Testament." *EvT* 18 (1958) 47–67. **Malamat, A.** "Josiah's Bid for Armageddon." *JANESCU* 5 (1973) 267–78. ———. "Megiddo, 609 B.C.: The Conflict Reexamined." *AcAnt* 22 (1974) 445–49. **Margalit, O.** "The Death of Josiah." *BMik* 12/30 (1966/67) 111–15. **McConville, J.** *Law and Theology in Deuteronomy.* Sheffield: JSOT Press, 1984. 99–123. **McKay, J.** *Religion in Judah under the Assyrians.* **McKenzie, S.** *The Chronicler's Use of the Deuteronomistic History.* **Milgrom, J.** "Did Josiah Subdue Megiddo?" *BMik* 16/44 (1970/71) 23–27. **Myers, J.** *I and II Esdras.* AB 42. Garden City: Doubleday, 1974. **Nicholson, E.** *Deuteronomy and Tradition.* Philadelphia: Fortress Press, 1967. **Ogden, G.** "The Northern Extent of Josiah's Reforms." *AusBR* 26 (1978) 26–34. **Petersen, D.** *Late Israelite Prophecy.* 85–87. **Pohlmann, K.-F.** *Studien zum dritten Esra. Ein Beitrag zur Frage nach dem ursprünglichen Schluss des chronistischen Geschichtswerkes.* FRLANT 104. Göttingen: Vandenhoeck & Ruprecht, 1970. **Priest, J.** "Huldah's Oracle." *VT* 30 (1980) 366–68. **Robinson, D.** *Josiah's Reform and the Book of the Law.* London: Tyndale Press, 1951. **Rose, M.** "Bemerkungen zum historischen Fundament des Josiasbildes in II Reg. 22ff." *ZAW* 89 (1977) 50–63. **Rost, L.** "Josias Passa." *Theologie in Geschichte und Kunst, FS K. Elliger*, ed. S. Hermann. Wittenburg: Luther Verlag, 1968. 169–75. **Rowton, M.** "Jeremiah and the Death of Josiah." *JNES* 10 (1951) 128–30. **Segal, J.** *The Hebrew Passover.* London Oriental Series 12. New York: Oxford UP, 1963. **Sekine, M.** "Beobachtungen zu der josianischen Reform." *VT* 22 (1972) 361–68. **Shaver, J.** *Torah.* 150–68. **Spieckermann, H.** *Juda unter Assur in der Sargonidenzeit.* **Tadmor, H.** "Philistia under Assyrian Rule." *BA* 29 (1966) 86–102. **Todd, E.** "The Reforms of Hezekiah and Josiah." *SJT* 9 (1956)

288–93. **Weinfeld, M.** *Deuteronomy and the Deuteronomic School.* Oxford: Clarendon Press, 1972. **Welch, A.** "The Death of Josiah." *ZAW* 43 (1925) 255–60. ———. *Work.* 122–48. **Williamson, H.** "The Death of Josiah and the Continuing Development of the Deuteronomic History." *VT* 32 (1982) 242–48. ———. *Israel in the Books of Chronicles.* ———. "Reliving the Death of Josiah: A Reply to C. T. Begg." *VT* 37 (1987) 9–15. ———. Review of S. L. McKenzie, *The Chronicler's Use of the Deuteronomic History. VT* 37 (1987) 107–14. **Wiseman, D.** *Chronicles of the Chaldean Kings.* London: British Museum, 1956.

Translation

[1] *Josiah was eight years old when he became king, and he ruled in Jerusalem thirty-one years.* [2] *He did what was right in the eyes of Yahweh; he walked in the*[a] *ways of David his father and did not deviate to the right or left.*

[3] *In the eighth year of his reign, while he was yet a young man, he began to seek the God of his father David.*

In his twelfth year he began to purge Judah and Jerusalem of high places, Asherah poles, images, and pillars. [4] *At his behest the altars for the Baals were demolished; he smashed the incense altars that were above them. He broke up the Asherah poles, images, and pillars, pulverized them, and scattered them over the graves of those who had sacrificed to them.* [5] *He burned the bones of the priests on their altars,*[a] *and he purged Judah and Jerusalem.* [6] *In the towns of Manasseh, Ephraim, Simeon, and as far as Naphtali, he removed*[a] *their temples,* [7] *he demolished the Asherah poles, crushed the images to powder,*[a] *and smashed all the incense altars through all the land of Israel. Then he returned to Jerusalem.*

[8] *In the eighteenth year of his reign, when he had purged the land and the temple, he sent Shaphan son of Azalaiah and Maaseiah, governor of the city, and Joah son of Joahaz, the recorder, to repair the temple of Yahweh his God.* [9] *They went to Hilkiah the high priest and gave him the money that had been brought to the temple and collected by the Levitical gatekeepers from Manasseh, Ephraim, and from all the remnant of Israel, and from Judah and Benjamin, and the inhabitants*[a] *of Jerusalem.* [10] *They turned it over to the workmen*[a] *who had charge of the temple of Yahweh; the workmen who worked in the temple of Yahweh paid it out for the repair and restoration of the temple.* [11] *They gave it to the tradesmen and builders*[a] *to buy dressed stone and wood for joists and beams for the buildings that the kings of Judah had allowed to fall into disrepair.*

[12] *The men did their work faithfully. Those who were in charge were Jahath and Obadiah, Levites from the Merari clan, Zechariah and Meshullam, from the Kohath clan. The Levites—all skilled musicians—*[13] *were in charge of the porters and supervised all the workers,*[a] *job by job. Some of the Levites also served as scribes, officials, and gatekeepers.*

[14] *When they were bringing out the money that had been brought to the temple of Yahweh, Hilkiah the priest found the book of the law of Yahweh given through Moses.* [15] *Then Hilkiah*[a] *said to Shaphan the scribe, "I have found the book of the law in the temple of Yahweh." Hilkiah gave the book to Shaphan.*[b]

[16] *Shaphan then took the book to the king and reported to the king as follows: "Your servants have been doing all that was assigned to them.* [17] *They poured out the silver that was found in the temple of Yahweh and entrusted it to the foremen*

*and workers." * [18]*Shaphan the scribe also informed the king, "Hilkiah the priest has given me a book," and he read from it* [a] *in the presence of the king.*

[19]*When the king heard the words of the law, he tore his garments.* [20]*The king gave this order to Hilkiah, Ahikam son of Shaphan, Abdon* [a] *son of Micah,* [b] *Shaphan the scribe, and Asaiah the king's minister:* [21]*"Go seek Yahweh in my behalf and in behalf of the remnant of Israel and Judah concerning the words of the book that was found. Great is the wrath of Yahweh that is poured out* [a] *on us because our fathers have not kept* [b] *the word of Yahweh and done all that is written in this book."* [c]

[22]*So Hilkiah and those the king appointed* [a] *went to Huldah the prophetess, the wife of Shallum son of Tokhath* [b] *son of Hasrah,* [c] *the keeper of the wardrobe;* [d] *she was living in Jerusalem in the second quarter. They spoke to her about this.* [23]*She said to them, "Thus says Yahweh the God of Israel: Say to the man who sent you to me,*

[24]*"Thus says Yahweh: behold I am about to do harm to this place and its inhabitants in accord with all the curses written* [a] *in this book which was read before the king of Judah.* [25]*Because they have forsaken me and have offered sacrifices to other gods and have provoked me with all the works of their hands, so my wrath is poured out* [a] *on this place and will not be quenched.*

[26]*"To the king of Judah who sent you to seek Yahweh, say this: Thus says Yahweh the God of Israel concerning the words you heard:* [27]*Inasmuch as your heart is tender and you have humbled yourself before God when you heard his words* [a] *against this place and its inhabitants,* [b] *and because you have humbled* [c] *yourself before me and torn your garments and wept before me, so I have heard, says Yahweh.* [28]*Behold I will gather you to your fathers, and you will be gathered to your grave in peace; your eyes will not see all the harm that I am about to bring against this place and its inhabitants."*

So they reported her answer to the king.

[29]*The king sent and gathered all the elders of Judah and Jerusalem.* [30]*The king went up to the temple of Yahweh with all the men of Judah, the inhabitants of Jerusalem, the priests and Levites,* [a] *and all the people from the least to the greatest. He read in their hearing all the words of the book of the covenant that was found in the temple of Yahweh.* [31]*The king stood in his usual place* [a] *and renewed the covenant before Yahweh, to follow Yahweh, to keep his commandments, traditons, and statutes with all his heart and soul, and to perform the obligations of the covenant written in this book.* [32]*He had all who were present in Jerusalem and Benjamin* [a] *pledge themselves to it. The inhabitants of Jerusalem acted in accord with the covenant of God, the God of their fathers.*

[33]*Josiah removed all the abominations from all the lands that belonged to the Israelites, and he required all were were found in Israel to serve Yahweh their God. For the duration of his life they did not turn from following Yahweh the God of their fathers.*

Notes

2.a. 2 Kgs 22:2 adds "all."

5.a. With Q, G[L], Tg, מזבחתם; K appears to be an erroneous and conflated pl, a scribal lapse.

6.a. The K "he inspected their temples" relies on a lexically improbable meaning for the verb בחר. The Q בְּחַרְבֹתֵיהֶם "with their swords" ill fits the context. Other common solutions include (1) reading בְּחָרְבֹּתֵיהֶם "in their ruins" (also ill fitting the context) or (2) emending to ברחבתיהם "in their squares/streets" (possibly reflected in Par τοῖς τόποις αὐτῶν "in their places"). Par could also be explained as the translator's paraphrase of a text already difficult; Par does not use τόπος as its equivalent for the other occurrences of רחב in Chronicles (29:4; 32:6). The presumption that Chr was originally following Kgs at this point favors MT בתים "temples" (2 Kgs 23:19). The reading adopted in the translation above is based on a conjectured alteration of one consonant to בער "remove"; this reading would parallel the הסיר of 2 Kgs 23:19. Cf. the Chronicler's interchange of the two verbs in 19:3 and 17:6 in reference to Jehoshaphat's destruction of pagan cults. See further Williamson, 399; and I. Seeligmann, "Indications of Editorial Alteration," *VT* 11 (1961) 202.

7.a. The verb form is somewhat anomalous. One expects either וְחָזַק or לְחָזֵק.

9.a. With K, G, Vg, and some Heb. MSS, וַיֵּשֶׁב; Q, וַיָּשֻׁבוּ "and they returned" suggests the Levites had toured these areas collecting the funds; cf. 24:5–6. Benjamin and the inhabitants of Jerusalem are also paired in v 32.

10.a. Reading pl עשׁי with following ptcp, G, Vg, and many MSS.

11.a. 2 Kgs 22:6 adds גדרים "masons."

13.a. See n. 10.a.

15.a. 2 Kgs 22:8 adds his title, "high priest."

15.b. 2 Kgs 22:8 adds "and he read it."

18.a. 2 Kgs 22:10, ויקראהו "he read it" (cf. 2 Kgs 22:8); Chr, ויקרא בו "he read from it"; see *Comment* below.

20.a. 2 Kgs 22:12, "Achbor," possibly the father of Elnathan, a courtier of Jehoiakim (Jer 26:22; 36:12).

20.b. 2 Kgs 22:12, "Michaiah."

21.a. 2 Kgs 22:13, נצתה "kindled"; see the same differences in 34:25 // 2 Kgs 22:17. Chr may be using the verb נתך under the influence of the earlier use in v 17.

21.b. 2 Kgs 22:13, Par (ἤκουσαν) = שׁמעו. Allen (*GC* 1:179, 212) argues that the Chronicler often uses שׁמר with עשׂה in reference to the commands of God and that the change was therefore deliberate on the Chronicler's part. Bas may have influenced Par at this point.

21.c. Instead of "in this book," 2 Kgs 22:13 has "about/against us."

22.a. MT has a grammatically acceptable ellipsis; a variety of verbs have been supplied in the versions as needed for the target languages—cf. BHS.

22.b. 2 Kgs 22:14, תקוה "Tikvah." See Allen, *GC* 1:212.

22.c. 2 Kgs 22:14, חרחס "Harhas"; cf. BHS; and Allen, *GC* 1:212.

22.d. G τὰς ἐντολάς, "the commandments" is most probably an intra-Greek confusion due to influence of context and similarity with στολάς "garments, equipment." Allen (*GC* 2:13–14) suggests assimilation in Par to 34:31.

24.a. Instead of "all the curses written in the book," 2 Kgs 22:16 has "all the words of the book."

25.a. See n. 21.a.

27.a. 2 Kgs 22:19, "what I said."

27.b. 2 Kgs 22:19 adds, "that they would be a reproach and curse."

27.c. Chr adds "humbled yourself"; it is not found in the parallel at 2 Kgs 22:19 and reflects the distinctive vocabulary of the Chronicler's theology of immediate retribution.

30.a. 2 Kgs 23:2, "priests and prophets" instead of "priests and Levites"; see *Comment* below.

31.a. 2 Kgs 23:3 העמוד and Par ἐπὶ τὸν στῦλον "alongside the column." Cf. 23:13. MT "stood in his place" is favored by similar contexts in Chronicles using עמד עמדם (30:16; 35:10; cf. Neh 8:7; 9:3; 13:11). Par could have assimilated to Bas.

32.a. The mention of Benjamin is unexpected. Some suggest (e.g., Rudolph, 326; Williamson, 403; C-M, 512) that the word "Benjamin" is a scribal error for "covenant" (ברית): either the MT has an awkward ellipsis or one should eliminate "Benjamin" and read "he had all who were present in Jerusalem pledge themselves to the covenant"; the term "covenant" is found in the parallel text (2 Kgs 23:3). However, the Chronicler appears to be explicating the "all the people" of 2 Kgs 23:3; he does pair the inhabitants of Jerusalem and Benjamin in 34:9. The term "covenant" in 2 Kgs 23:3 may be properly parallel to the same term in the last phrase of 34:32.

Form/Structure/Setting

The Chronicler's account of Josiah (2 Chr 34–35) parallels the earlier account in 2 Kgs 22:1–23:30. The accounts are approximately the same length and treat the same subjects. The Chronicler's narrative can be divided as follows (Elmslie, 330):

(1) Eradication of pagan cults in Jerusalem, Judah, and Israel (34:2–7).
(2) Temple repairs and discovery of the law book (34:8–28)
(3) Covenant renewal (34:29–33)
(4) Observance of Passover (35:1–19)
(5) Death of Josiah (35:20–27)

The narrative in Kings contains the same elements, but in varying detail and in a different order. For item (1) Kings goes to greater length and delays the account until after the discovery of the law book (2 Kgs 23:4–20). In Kings items (2) and (3) precede (1), and the reform of Josiah flows from the discovery of the law book. The observance of Passover under Josiah (4) is summarized only briefly in Kings (2 Kgs 23:21–23), whereas it is greatly expanded in Chronicles.

The Chronicler uses one of his most characteristic compositional techniques in his account of Josiah. He introduces chronological notes that provide the structure for his narrative; see Dillard (*JETS* 23 [1980] 215) for a list of chronological notices unique to Chronicles. The author reports that Josiah began to seek God in the eighth year of his reign (34:3) and that he began to purge the pagan cults in his twelfth year, at age twenty (34:3); the reform was then well underway before the discovery of the law book in the eighteenth year of his rule (34:8 // 2 Kgs 22:3; 35:19 // 2 Kgs 23:23).

These chronological notices have provoked a wide range of opinion: some accept them at face value, whereas other regard them as theological fabrications on the part of the Chronicler. There can be no serious doubt that the decline of Assyrian power in the latter half of the seventh century contributed to conditions favoring the reestablishment of a strong Judean state. Cross and Freedman ("Josiah's Revolt against Assyria," *JNES* 12 [1953] 56–58) tied the Chronicler's chronological notices to particular events in the decline of Assyria that would have encouraged rebellion on the part of Josiah and other vassals: his "seeking the God of his father David" in his eighth year would have followed the death of Asshurbanipal in 633 B.C.; his extending his reform into the former Assyrian provinces in the north in his twelfth year (628 B.C.) was synchronized with the death of the Assyrian king Asshur-etil-ilani; and the further reforms in his eighteenth year followed closely the failure of Assyrian control in Babylonia in 623 B.C. Cross and Freedman felt that their synchronisms between the Chronicler's dates for Josiah and the proposed chronology for the last kings of Assyria were mutually reinforcing. This argument now requires modification due to clarification of the date for the death of Asshurbanipal, an event now assigned to 627 B.C. (J. Oates, "Assyrian Chronology," *Iraq* 27 [1965] 135–59).

At the other end of the spectrum regarding the significance of these dates,

M. Cogan ("Chronicler's Use of Chronology," 203–5) regards the data as schematic scaffolding developed by the Chronicler to show that a godly king like Josiah would certainly have begun his reform efforts before his eighteenth year. Cogan (205) sees the Chronicler as concerned with "the earliness and self-motivation of the king's piety"; he draws an analogy with an inscription from the reign of Esarhaddon also depicting the youthful piety and reforms of that king.

The discovery of the law book during repair work implies that some reform was underway already, even though earlier phases of Josiah's reform are not mentioned in Kings. The *Tendenz* of the author of Kings in his account is also quite clear—he wishes to trace Josiah's reforms to the discovery of the book. The book is central, and the narrative proceeds in concentric circles from the discovery of the book (2 Kgs 23:2) through the temple (2 Kgs 23:4), through the city of Jerusalem (2 Kgs 23:5–7), through Judah (2 Kgs 23:8–9), and into territories in the North (2 Kgs 23:15–20). The deuteronomic historian's concern to portray Josiah's fidelity to the law through Moses makes the discovery of the book the inciting event of the reform; the form of the narrative in Kings owes much to that author's purpose.

With the *Tendenz* of Kings so clearly to the fore in that account, one should not too quickly attribute the Chronicler's chronological notices to fabrication arising from that author's theological motives. It is possible both to regard the chronological notices as reflecting some accurate sources at his disposal and to appreciate that it may well suit the Chronicler's interests to portray Josiah's piety as stemming from a much earlier point in his reign. The theological interests need not be at the expense of historicity.

The narrative is divided into paragraphs using the following devices: (1) a ויהי-clause with temporal phrase (34:19); (2) a temporal phrase (34:3a, 3b, 8, 14); and (3) an explicit subject (34:12, 16, 22, 29, 33). The paragraphs beginning at 34:3a and 3b are further marked by the repetition of the initial phrase using the verb החל "he began" with an infinitive.

Comment

1–2 Many features of the Chronicler's presentation of Josiah have analogs in his account of Joash (2 Chr 24); see *Explanation* below. Both became king at a very early age; both presided over a refurbishing of the temple using the offerings brought there. Though neither biblical history reports such, it is highly probable that Josiah ruled until the age of his majority (34:3b) under the tutelage of one or more regents, acting perhaps in behalf of the "people of the land." Regarding the "people of the land" and the age of Josiah's father at the time of his birth, see *Comment* at 33:21–25. Regarding the omission of his mother's name (2 Kgs 22:1), see *Comment* at 33:1.

Though a number of kings are said to have followed the precedent set by their father David, only of Josiah is it said that he did not "deviate to the right or left."

Josiah died confronting Necho in 609 B.C., so his thirty-one-year reign would have begun in 640 B.C.

3 According to the Chronicler David described Solomon as נער ורך

"young and inexperienced" at the time of his accession (1 Chr 22:5; 29:1; cf. 2 Chr 13:7); both terms are used also of Josiah (cf. 34:27).

Josiah began to seek God at age sixteen in the eighth year of his reign, a time when he would still probably be under the tutelage of regents. Though his personal piety may have begun to stir at that time, he did not initiate acts of reform until his twelfth year at age twenty; this would be the age of his majority (Num 1:3; 26:2; 1 Chr 27:23; 25:5) and presumably then also the first year of his sole reign no longer under the authority of a regent.

4–7 These verses summarize aspects of Josiah's reform treated at much greater length in 2 Kgs 23:4–20; the Chronicler has chronologically positioned them before the discovery of the law book in the temple (see *Form/Structure/Setting*). The passage is somewhat reminiscent also of reforms under Asa (15:8–15) and Hezekiah (chap. 29).

Most of the Chronicler's omissions from the more extensive parallel history appear to reflect aspects of his own *Tendenz*. Sacral prostitution apparently was not as big a problem for post-exilic Judah, and the Chronicler routinely omits references to it (2 Kgs 23:7); see *Comment* at 14:2–5; and P. Dion, "Did Cultic Prostitution Fall into Oblivion in the Postexilic Era?" *CBQ* 43 (1981) 41–48. One would also not expect the Chronicler to elaborate on Josiah's removing the altars of Ahaz and Manasseh (2 Kgs 23:11–12) when he had reported the intervening reforms of both Hezekiah and Manasseh. The Chronicler's portrayal of a faultless Solomon would require omission of 2 Kgs 23:13 as out of accord with that portrait; see the introductory essay to 2 Chr 1–9, "The Chronicler's Solomon." The Chronicler did not report the visit of the man of God from Judah to the altar at Bethel (1 Kgs 13:1–32) and would then also omit 2 Kgs 23:15–18.

Though not explicitly stated, the Chronicler implies that Josiah executed the priests of Baal (34:4–5; cf. 2 Kgs 23:20), following the precedent set by Jehu (2 Kgs 10) and Jehoiada (23:17 // 2 Kgs 11:18). Josiah suits the punishment to the crime: the priests who burned sacrifices to Baal have their own bones burned on the same altars; some are even disinterred for this purpose (2 Kgs 23:16). The Chronicler does not report that the ashes from the defiled temple implements in Judah were carried to Bethel (2 Kgs 23:4).

The Assyrian empire was in an advanced stage of disintegration by Josiah's twelfth year (628 b.c.). Nineveh itself was under siege by Cyaxares and the Medes in 625 b.c. The Babylonians were newly independent, and mountain tribes from the north were raiding former Assyrian territory. During the death throes of the Assyrian empire the territories of the Northern Kingdom became a "no man's land" (Soggin, 245). It is intrinsically probable in these circumstances that Josiah would seek to extend his control and influence into Israel (34:6), even as far as the Upper Galilee (Naphtali). Others, however, find the notion of Josiah's northern expansion improbable, the pious wishes of the Chronicler (Spieckermann, 112–14, 150–52; G. Ogden, "The Northern Extent of Josiah's Reforms," *AusBR* 26 [1978] 26–34). There is some archeological confirmation for the extension of Josiah's kingdom in the South in the excavations at Mesad Hashavyahu (Yabneh-yam), En-gedi, and Arad. The destruction of an Israelite temple at Arad should probably be attributed to the centralization efforts of Josiah. While considerable circumstantial evidence favors the reliability of the Chronicler's report that Josiah extended his border northward, it is also a theme dear to his own *Tendenz:* Josiah is shown as the king of a united kingdom almost reaching its Davidic/Solomonic proportions; "all Israel" acts in concert under this righteous ruler. The phrase "land of Israel" (34:7) occurs only four times in Chronicles, once each during the reigns of David (1 Chr 22:2), Solomon (2:16 [17]), Hezekiah (30:25), and Josiah.

The range of territory suggested runs from Simeon to Naphtali, an approximate equivalent for "Beersheba to Dan." The fact that Simeon occurs in a list with Northern tribes here and in 15:9 has been understood as indicating that the Chronicler thought it was in fact a Northern tribe. Whatever the correct explanation (see *Comment* at 15:9; and Williamson, *IBC,* 104), the suggestion that the Chronicler was ignorant of the geography and the territorial allocation for that tribe would be quite improbable.

Regarding the "incense altars" (34:4, 7), see *Comment* at 14:4.

8–11 In Chronicles the discovery of the law book in the temple was one incident in the course of a larger reform, whereas in Kings it was the precipitating incident and primary motivation for the entire reform. The Chronicler picks up with the narrative at 2 Kgs 22:3, but inserts the clause "when he had purged the land and the temple" as a reference back to 34:3–7.

Temple construction and repair were undertaken at royal initiative during the reigns of David, Solomon, Joash, and Hezekiah, and were the responsibility of Zerubbabel in the post-exilic period (Zech 4:8–10). Representatives of both the crown and cult were involved in administering temple funds, not only in Israel but also in Mesopotamian temples, and it is to be expected that royal representatives (34:8; 24:11) had some sway in the expenditure of temple resources. One can readily appreciate the potential for conflicting interests between palace and temple on the use of temple revenues, a tension already seen in similar circumstances during the reign of Joash; see *Form/Structure/ Setting* in chaps. 23 and 24 and the *Comment* at 24:4–7 regarding some of the underlying sociological tensions.

Only Shaphan is mentioned in the parallel text at 2 Kgs 22:3. He is mentioned again in 34:20 as the father of Ahikam and may also have been the father of Elasah (Jer 29:3), Gemariah (Jer 36:10–12), and Jaazaniah (Ezek 8:11) if these all refer to the same Shaphan.

Where 2 Kgs 22:4 says the funds were collected "from the people," the Chronicler is less ambiguous and reiterates his concern with "all Israel" by specifying the involvement of "Ephraim, Manasseh, and all the remnant of Israel" (34:9). The funds may have been collected at the temple gates (2 Kgs 22:4) or through an itineration (see *Notes* at 34:9.a); both methods were urged during the reign of Joash (24:5–6, 8–9).

On the surface of the text there appears some tension between vv 9 and 10 regarding who received the funds: in v 9 Hilkiah receives them, whereas in v 10 they are paid directly to the workmen. Rudolph's suggested emendation in v 9 from ויתנו "they gave" to ויתכו "they poured out/melted down the money" (cf. 34:17) would solve the problem. However, it is equally possible that there is simply an ellipsis here: Hilkiah and his subordinates (34:12–13) administered the funds and distributed them to the workmen.

The kings of Judah who "allowed the buildings to fall into disrepair" (34:11) would certainly have included Manasseh and Amon, and possibly Ahaz (2 Kgs 23:12).

12–13 A building contractor or construction engineer in our own day would not likely draw much comfort from the fact that musicians would be supervising a major construction or renovation project. A considerable interest in the Levites, and especially the Levitical musicians, is a hallmark of the Chronicler's history; the note that musicians would be in charge of the construction work shows just how concerned the Chronicler was to stress that the entire work was done under Levitical supervision. The use of music during a construction project is well attested from the ancient Near East (Rudolph, 323); it set the pace for the various tasks much as the ubiquitous radios on a contemporary construction site. While the Levitical musicians may have accompanied the work, the Chronicler does not specifically mention this task; he describes instead a supervisory role. The Levites were also in charge of other renovation projects (chaps. 24 and 29; cf. 1 Chr 26).

Though the clans of Kohath and Merari are mentioned, no names are given from the Gershonites.

14–18 For the Chronicler the discovery of the law book was one part of the reward for Josiah's faithfulness (Williamson, 401).

There has been a long and vigorous debate over the identity of the book found in the temple. The general consensus is that it was Deuteronomy or some earlier stage of that book during its growth and formation. Numerous features favor the identification with Deuteronomy. (1) The centralization of worship in the one place chosen by God, the temple in Jerusalem, is envisaged in Deut 12. (2) The destruction of the high places and all rival cultic installations is enjoined in Deut 12. (3) The book has an extended section of curses (34:24; Deut 27:9–26; 28:15–68), including the threat of exile. (4) The character of the Passover observance reflects the stipulations of Deut 16. (5) A prophet is consulted to know the will of God (34:22–28; Deut 18:9–22). (6) The books of Kings are history viewed through spectacles consisting of the book of Deuteronomy; pentateuchal laws distinctive of Deuteronomy are the measure by which the kings of Israel and Judah are evaluated. It would be natural that the fidelity of Josiah in Kings flow from the stipulations of that book. (7) Deuteronomy shows many features in common with extrabiblical treaties or covenants, a fact which also favors its identification as "the book of the covenant" (34:30 // 2 Kgs 23:2). While some have regarded Deuteronomy as a "pious fraud" written at the time of Josiah and attributed to Moses only in an effort to legitimate Josiah's extension of his power, increasingly scholars have come to recognize the comparative antiquity of much of the book and to allow that many of its provisions antedate the time of Josiah. One need not have solved all the questions surrounding pentateuchal criticism to recognize the compelling evidence that Deuteronomy or a document somewhat like it was the motivating force behind Josiah's reform as described in Kings. How it could have dropped from view or lost its influence can only be a matter of speculation; it is at least conceivable that during the threat of invasion under Hezekiah or during the apostasy under Amon and Manasseh it was concealed in the temple.

The Chronicler has modified his *Vorlage* at a couple of points: he omits the statement that Shaphan read the book (2 Kgs 22:8 // 34:15); when Shaphan appears before the king, the Chronicler reports that "he read from it" (ויקרא בו, 34:18) instead of "he read it" (ויקראהו, 2 Kgs 22:10). The changes have prompted many commentators (e.g., Elmslie, 333–34; Williamson, 402; Michaeli, 245) to suggest that the Chronicler thought the entire Pentateuch was in view and therefore modified the earlier history since he knew the entire Pentateuch would not be read through twice in one day, and that the king was likely to have heard only sections "read from it." However, Hebrew grammar may not support the distinctions imposed upon it in this case (Ackroyd, 202). The use of the verb קרא "read" with a direct object does not seem to be distinguished from its use with the prepositional phrase; for example, Baruch "read from" (ויקרא ב־), Jer 36:6, 8, 10, 13, et passim) the prophecies dictated by Jeremiah, but the context suggests he was in fact reading through them all.

The verb נתך in 34:17 (cf. 34:21, 25) is somewhat ambiguous. If translated "pour out" (with 34:21, 25), it would most probably refer to the act of emptying the offering chest or to the dispersal of the funds; if translated "melt down" it would refer to processing the offerings to a finer grade of metal in a smelter. See the *Comment* at 24:8–11 for both practices.

22–28 The office "keeper of the wardrobe" (34:22) probably designated the temple functionary responsible for production and maintenance of the priestly and Levitical vestments.

Hezekiah had extended the walls of Jerusalem and had enclosed a portion of the hill west of the Tyropoean Valley; this area may have represented the "second quarter" of the city (cf. Zeph 1:10; Neh 11:9, 17). Alternatively the *Mishneh* could have been the northern reaches of the city.

The Chronicler would have found the account of Huldah's oracle in 2 Kgs 22:14–20 quite congenial to his own theology of immediate retribution. Two of the terms characteristic of the Chronicler's theological vocabulary already occur in the parallel text: עזב "abandon, forsake" (34:25 // 2 Kgs 22:17) and כנע "humble oneself" (34:27 // 2 Kgs 22:19—a second use of this verb is inserted by the Chronicler in 34:27). See the introductory essay to 2 Chr 10–36, "Reward and Punishment in Chronicles: The Theology of Immediate Retribution."

The "curses" written in the book (34:24) presumably refer to Deut 27:9–26; 28:15–68; if the book consisted of the entire Pentateuch in the Chronicler's opinion, then passages such as Lev 26 would also have been in view.

Huldah's prophecy that Josiah would go to his grave in peace (34:28 // 2 Kgs 22:20) is problematic in light of events to follow (35:20–24; 2 Kgs 23:29–30) where the opposite seems to happen. Josiah did not live to see the destruction of Jerusalem (34:28), but his death at the hands of Neco scarcely seems like going to the grave in peace. Many have treated this as a literary critical problem: an old and reliable oracle prior to the events of 609 B.C. was later supplemented with a vaticinium ex eventu after 609 B.C.; cf. J. Priest, "Huldah's Oracle," *VT* 30 (1980) 366–68. However, it will not suffice to suggest that Huldah's original prophecy was unfulfilled or in error. This would have been anathema to the compilers of Kings who repeatedly use the fulfillment of prophetic pronouncements to confirm the efficacy of the prophetic word (Deut 18:14–22); it is hardly probable that such a lapse could escape editorial excision in Kings, much less also survive the Chronicler. A more natural understanding does not require literary critical effort. The compilers of Kings and Chronicles apparently understood the first half of Huldah's prophecy (going to his grave in peace) as defined by the second half (not seeing the destruction of Jerusalem). The analogy of Ahab may be helpful: his repentance forestalled the end of his dynasty (1 Kgs 21:27–28), but did not avert his own violent death (1 Kgs 22:34–35); cf. also Hezekiah (32:26).

The Chronicler has not reported that the exile is a foregone conclusion at this point in Judah's history (34:24–25, 28); that would have come as no surprise in the Kings account where Manasseh bears most of the responsibility for the coming judgment (2 Kgs 21:10–15). Huldah's oracle, which the Chronicler borrowed from Kings, presumes that the inevitability of the exile had already been announced.

29–32 Josiah leads the nation in a covenant renewal. The Chronicler has substituted "priests and Levites" (34:30) for the "priests and prophets" of his *Vorlage* (2 Kgs 23:2). The Chronicler often associates prophetic functions with the Levites (1 Chr 25:1–8; 2 Chr 20:14; 29:25, 30; 35:15; see D. Petersen, *Late Israelite Prophecy*, 85). The Levites may represent a continuation of cultic prophets, or in light of the demise of the prophetic succession in the post-exilic period, the Levitical preaching and teaching are understood as a continuation of that earlier prophetic function; see *Comment* at 29:30.

The conformity of the populace (34:32) was accomplished apparently without the measures taken during the reign of Asa (15:12–15).

33 This verse is a summary statement and forms somewhat of an inclusio with 34:6–7. As a summary it also suggests that the writer is departing from following Kings as his *Vorlage* and is turning to another source from which he will draw details regarding Josiah's observance of Passover (chap. 35).

Explanation

Many features of Josiah's reign have parallels with the reign of Joash (2 Chr 23–24). Both came to the throne while children. Both were involved in collection of funds at the temple and in subsequent renovations. Both are reported to have stood in the temple precincts in the king's place (34:31; 24:13); both led the nation in covenant renewal in the temple (34:29–32; 23:16–17). But here the parallels end. While Joash would remain faithful only so long as Jehoiada lived (24:2, 15–18), Josiah never turned from following the LORD to the right or left (34:2), and "for the duration of his life they did not turn from following Yahweh" (34:33). No foreign army would invade Judah in his day (34:24–25, 28; contrast 24:23–24).

For the Chronicler's audience the instruction regarding exile and restoration could not be missed. Josiah's faithfulness forestalled the disaster that would come on Jerusalem (34:28). Faithfulness was ever the path to enjoying the blessing of God.

Josiah's Passover; His Death   (35:1–36:1)

Bibliography

See entries for the preceding chapter (2 Chr 34:1–33).

Translation

¹ *Josiah celebrated Passover to Yahweh in Jerusalem;*[a] *they slaughtered the Passover lamb on the fourteenth day of the first month.* ² *He appointed the priests to their duties and encouraged them in the service of the temple of Yahweh.* ³ *He said to the Levites, who instructed*[a] *all Israel and were consecrated*[b] *to Yahweh:*

"Put[c] *the holy ark in the temple that Solomon son of David, king of Israel, built.*[d] *You are not to carry it on your shoulders. Now serve Yahweh your God and*[e] *his people Israel.* ⁴ *Prepare*[a] *yourselves by your fathers' houses and according to your divisions as written by David king of Israel and* [b]*his son* [c]*Solomon.* ⁵ *Stand in the Holy Place in family groups representing your fellow countrymen, the laity, a division of Levites for each clan.* ⁶ *Slaughter the Passover lamb; prepare the holy offerings*[a] *for your fellow countrymen in order to celebrate in accord with Yahweh's command through Moses."*

⁷ *Josiah provided the laity with thirty thousand small cattle—sheep and goats—* [a]*all for Passover offerings for all who were present,*[a] *along with three thousand bulls, all from the king's property.* ⁸ *His officials contributed willingly for the people, the priests, and the Levites. Hilkiah, Zechariah, and Jehiel, the chief officers of the temple of God, gave two thousand, six hundred small cattle and three hundred bulls as Passover offerings for the priests.* ⁹ *Conaniah,*[a] *along with Shemaiah and Nethanel, his brothers, and Hashabiah, Jeiel, and Jozabad, the leaders of the Levites,*[b] *provided five thousand small cattle and five hundred bulls as Passover offerings for the Levites.*

¹⁰ *The service was prepared; the priests took their positions, and the Levites stood in their divisions as the king had commanded.*[a] ¹¹[a]*They slaughtered the Passover offerings; the priests sprinkled the blood*[b] *they received while the Levites skinned the animals.* ¹² *They set aside*[a] *the burnt offerings to give them to the groups of clans among the laity to offer to Yahweh as written in the book of Moses. They did the same with the bulls.*[b] ¹³ *They roasted*[a] *the Passover offerings in the fire as prescribed; they cooked the holy offerings in pots, cauldrons, and pans*[b] *and served them quickly to all the laity.* ¹⁴ *After that they prepared the animals for themselves and the priests. Since the priests, the sons of Aaron, had been making the burnt offerings and fat offerings until nightfall, the Levites prepared for themselves and for the priests, the sons of Aaron.* ¹⁵ *The musicians, the descendants of Asaph, were standing in their places in accord with the command of David, Asaph, Heman,*[a] *and Jeduthun, the king's seer;*[b] *the gatekeepers were at each gate. There was no need for them to leave their posts since their relatives the Levites had made the preparations for them.*

¹⁶ *All the service of Yahweh was prepared that day for observing Passover and offering burnt offerings on the altar of Yahweh, as King Josiah had commanded.* ¹⁷ *The Israelites who were present observed Passover at that time and the Feast of*

Unleavened Bread for seven days. [18] *No Passover like it had been observed in Israel from the days of Samuel the prophet.*[a] *None of the kings of Israel*[b] *had ever observed such a Passover as Josiah did, with the priests and Levites and all Judah and Israel present with the inhabitants of Jerusalem.* [19] *This Passover was observed in the eighteenth year of Josiah's reign.*[a]

[20a] *After all this, when Josiah had set the temple in order,*[a] *Neco king of Egypt came up to do battle at Carchemish on the Euphrates, and Josiah went out to meet him.* [21] *He sent messengers to him, who said, "What is there between you and me, O King of Judah? I have not come against you*[a] *this day, but against the house with which I am at war.*[b] *God has told me to hurry. God is with me, so restrain yourself so he will not destroy you."* [22] *But Josiah would not turn away from him.*[a] *Instead he disguised himself*[b] *to do battle with him and would not listen to the words of Neco*[c] *from the mouth of God; he went to fight at the plain of Megiddo.*

[23] *Archers shot*[a] *Josiah, and he said to his servants, "Take me away—I've been gravely wounded!"* [24] *So his servants took him out of the chariot,*[a] *put him in a second chariot, and took him to Jerusalem. He died and was buried in the tombs of his fathers; all Judah and Jerusalem mourned Josiah.*

[25] *Jeremiah composed laments for Josiah, and all the singers—both men and women—commemorate Josiah in their laments to this day. These became a tradition in Israel and are written in the laments.*

[26] *As for the rest of Josiah's deeds, his acts of piety in accord with what was written in the law of Yahweh,* [27] *and the events of his reign from beginning to end, these are written in the book of the kings of Israel and Judah.*

[36:1] *The people of the land took Josiah's son Jehoahaz*[a] *and made him king in Jerusalem*[b] *in place of his father.*

Notes

1.a. 2 Kgs 23:21 has the additional phrase, "as written in this book of the covenant." The Chronicler provides this emphasis also in 35:6, 12, 26.

3.a. The K form appears to be a substantive, whereas the Q and a number of MSS treat as a ptcp; cf. Neh 8:7, 9. G τοῖς δυνατοῖς "those in charge" may derive from a misreading of the Heb. original as הַמּוּכָנִים (as in two Heb. MSS) or alternatively is an intra-Greek misreading of τοῖς συνετοῖς commonly used with its cognates in G as the equivalent for forms of בִּין (Allen, *GC* 2:32). 1 Esdr 1:3 ἱεροδούλοις "temple servants" is that translator's normal equivalent for נְתִינִים wherever it occurs in Ezra (1 Esdr 5:29, 35; 8:5, 22, 48), and suggests that his *Vorlage* contained that Heb. term or was misread.

3.b. G ἁγιασθῆναι αὐτοὺς and 1 Esdr 1:3 ἁγιάσαι αὐτοὺς both appear to have read הַקְדִּשְׁתֶּם "(ordered the Levites . . .) to sanctify themselves" (Allen, *GC* 2:78).

3.c–d. MT "put the ark" suggests that the ark had been removed from the Most Holy Place for some reason, perhaps in connection with the apostasy under Manasseh and Amon, or that its installation was ceremonially or symbolically reenacted so that the rededication of the refurbished temple under Josiah was likened to its initial dedication under Solomon; however, these are only inferences. There is no other evidence that the ark was removed or that its installation was reenacted; had the ark been removed, one would expect it to have been returned to its place earlier during the repairs. Since only the priests were to enter the Most Holy Place (cf. 5:7), one would not expect the Chronicler to enjoin the Levites to do so. Some translate the MT as "leave the ark in the temple" (e.g., Williamson, 405), a reference to 1 Chr 15:15–16; 16:4; 23:24–26. Rudolph (326; cf. Welch, *Work*, 70) reads נְתֹנַנּוּ and subordinates the clause to the following sentence: "since the holy ark was deposited in the temple . . ., there has been no need for you to carry it"; 1 Esdr 1:3 ἐν τῇ θέσει might be construed similarly, though more probably belongs with the preceding, "to sanctify themselves when putting the ark. . . ." G καὶ ἔθηκαν "and they put" may reflect ויתנו. The insertion in Par (3.d.), "and the king said," shows clearly that the translators of G did not construe the two clauses together.

3.e. 1 Esdr 1:4 adds θεραπεύετε "minister (to his people Israel)."

4.a. 1 Esdr 1:4, Syr, and Tg read a hiph impv with the Q, והכונו; G and Vg read a niph impv with K, והכונו‎ [והכונו].

4.b. The translators of 1 Esdr (1:4, μεγαλειότητα "splendor, magnificence") and Par (διὰ χειρός "through the hand of") took care to distinguish כתב and מכתב in the MT. 1 Esdr appears to have read its *Vorlage* as containing a form of כבד, though μεγαλειότης is not used as a translation equivalent for this term in G. T. Eshkenazi (*CBQ* 48 [1986] 45) sees this difference as a tendentious modification in 1 Esdras heightening the emphasis in that work on the dynasty of David. The preps before both terms appear to have been read as כ instead of ב in the versions.

4.c. G reads "King Solomon." The מלך may be a vertical dittogr from "King David" in the preceding line; it is not found in the parallel at 1 Esdr 1:4.

6.a. With 1 Esdr 1:6, καὶ τὰς θυσίας; 1 Esdras appears to have read והקדשים "holy things, offerings" as the object of the verb "prepare." G^BL omits והתקדשו. MT, "slaughter the Passover, sanctify yourselves . . .," is problematic: personal consecration would ordinarily precede the slaughter of the sacrifice. Translating "prepare the holy offerings for your fellow countrymen" accords with the actual actions of the Levites in fulfillment of the king's command (35:13–15).

7.a-a. This phrase is omitted in 1 Esdr 1:7.

9.a. G adds a name: χωνενίας καὶ βαναίας. The additional name probably arose as a correcting gloss preserving an original בניהו in place of the MT כונניהו. See Allen, *GC* 1:164.

9.b. For שרי הלוים "leaders of the Levites," 1 Esdr 1:9 uses χιλίαρχοι; G ἄρχοντες.

10.a. 1 Esdr 1:10 omits "king"; ἄζυμα "unleavened bread" suggests מצות was read instead of מצות "commandments." See E. Bayer, 22.

11.a-12.a. 1 Esdr omits 2 Chr 35:11 and the first three words of 35:12. The omission approximates a haplogr between the mention of the clerical and family groups (מחלקותם [35:10] and מפלגות [35:12]). See E. Bayer, 15; and J. Myers, AB 42, 27–28.

11.b. The versions insert the word "blood" (דם); it may have been an ellipsis in the MT or have been dropped due to homoiotel with מידם.

12.a. G καὶ ἡτοίμασαν "and they prepared" may have read ויכינו. See Allen, *GC* 2:152.

12.b. 1 Esdr 1:10, G, Syr, Tg, and a few Heb. MSS read בקר "morning" instead of בקר "bulls." The reading may have been prompted as a contrasting starting point to the עד לילה "until night" of v 14 (Allen, *GC* 2:69).

13.a. If בשל has only the meaning "boil," then the phrase בשל באש "boil in the fire" would be a curious and incongruous conflation of Exod 12:8–9 and Deut 16:7. However, בשל appears rather to be a more general term for food preparation, its precise significance depending on the context (cf. 2 Sam 13:8). In this case no tension would exist between Deut and Exod regarding the means of preparing the Passover animal. The Chronicler may be integrating terminology from both passages, but the semantic incongruity would not be there. The cooking would be in accord with custom (כמשפט), i.e., in fire and without water.

13.b. 1 Esdr 1:12 μετ' εὐωδίας "with a good savor" (either an alternate spelling or a transcriptional error for εὐοδίας "success") and G εὐοδώθη "it went well" both appear to have read a form of צלח "have success, prosper." The word in the MT may have been unfamiliar to the translators. See E. Bayer, 22.

15.a. 1 Esdr 1:15, "Zechariah" may be an assimilation to 1 Chr 15:18; 16:5. However, the presence of the name "Zechariah" could be interpreted as representing an earlier stage in the development of the Levitical singers (Gese's IIIA) prior to the hegemony of the Heman group (Gese's IIIB), so that MT's "Heman" would represent a later correction.

15.b. Two Heb. MSS, the versions, and 1 Esdr 1:15 read as pl, חוזי "seers"; cf. 1 Chr 25:1.

18.a. Cf. 2 Kgs 23:22, "since the days of the judges who judged Israel."

18.b. 2 Kgs 23:22, "kings of Israel and Judah." The Chronicler uses the term "Israel" here to refer to the entire nation as a unified entity.

19.a. Both 1 Esdr and G have additional material between vv 19 and 20.

1 Esdr 1:21–22 reads as follows: "The works of Josiah before the LORD were upright and he was full of piety in heart. Those things pertaining to him were written in former times, regarding how they sinned and were impious to the LORD with every nation and kingdom, and

how they grieved him and the words of the LORD were fulfilled against Israel." This section is regarded by many as reflecting the earlier text of Chronicles; it appears to be a paraphrase of 2 Kgs 23:24–27.

2 Kgs 23:24–27 is also found as an addition in G. However, the reference to Manasseh (2 Kgs 23:26) would be out of accord with the Chronicler's handling of that king, and suggests that this material was added from Kings at a later point and was not a part of the Chronicler's original text. The addition was already present in Par's Hebrew *Vorlage*: the transliteration καρασείμ (35:19a) is probably a misreading of קדשׁים // 2 Kgs 23:24 שׁקצים. This would suggest that 1 Esdr and Par were both using a *Vorlage* of Chronicles containing this secondary material; the absence of reference to Manasseh in the 1 Esdr addition suggests that this apocryphal work did not originally include an account of the reign of that king, and that therefore 1 Esdr is not a fragment of a larger composition including earlier portions of Chronicles. See Allen, *GC* 1:213–16; *HTR* 61 (1968) 483–91; R. Klein, *HTR* 60 (1967) 93–105; 61 (1968) 492–95; H. Williamson, *IBC*, 16–20.

20.a-a. Added by the Chronicler; not found in the parallel at 2 Kgs 23:29. A paraphrase of this phrase is found in 1 Esdr 1:23 ("And after all this activity on the part of Josiah, . . ."), but not in G.

21.a. MT takes אתה as the 2d person pronoun reinforcing the pronominal suffix of עליך; the verb is supplied though ellided. G ἥκω "I have come" read אָתָה; since this verb occurs in the remainder of the OT only in poetic sections, the MT has pointed correctly (Allen, *GC* 2:72).

21.b. The enigmatic בית מלחמתי has been taken many ways; see Rudolph, 330: (1) "the house with which I am at war" (cf. 1 Chr 18:10 // 2 Sam 8:10, "man of the war of Tou" = "man who waged war with Tou"; Keil, 505). (2) "garrison city, fortified base," possibly referring to Carchemish or Riblah or Megiddo (B. Alfrink, *Bib* 15 [1934] 173–84; A. Malamat, *JANESCU* 5 [1973] 276–77). (3) G omits the phrase. (4) 1 Esdr 1:25 appears to have read בית as פרת "my war is on the Euphrates."

22.a. 1 Esdr 1:26, ἐπὶ τὸ ἅρμα αὐτοῦ "to his chariot." 1 Esdr either read וישב as וירכב or was paraphrasing.

22.b. G ἐκραταιώθη "strengthened himself" may have read התחזק; 1 Esdr 1:26 ἐπιχειρεῖ "undertook" may have read חשׁב. A. Malamat (*JANESCU* 5 [1973] 278) disputes that התחפשׂ means "disguise" and suggests its occurrence in other contexts favors a meaning "cover the head, put on a helmet." Williamson (408–11) sees the influence of 1 Kgs 22:30 on a text of Kings used by the Chronicler as a source here; see *Comment* below. Josiah's death is described with similar details to Ahab's, a fact which favors the correctness of MT in this case.

22.c. 1 Esdr 1:26, "words of the prophet Jeremiah"; see *Comment* below.

23.a. 1 Esdr 1:27, κατέβησαν οἱ ἄρχοντες "the princes came down," read וירדו החרים instead of MT וירו הירים.

24.a. 1 Esdr 1:28, ἀπὸ τῆς παρατάξεως "from the ranks" misread מן המערכה.

36:1.a. Bas and Par add, "and they anointed him." Par is heavily influenced by Bas through chaps. 35–36; this addition should be attributed to that influence.

1.b. "In Jerusalem" is not found in G^B, 2 Kgs 23:30, or 1 Esdr 1:32.

Form/Structure/Setting

The study of 2 Chr 35–36 is both complicated and enhanced by the fact that the apocryphal work 1 Esdras (also known as 3 Esdras [Vg] or Esdras a [G]) begins with 2 Chr 35 and continues through Ezra-Nehemiah, omitting material relating to Nehemiah. A wide variety of opinions have been advanced regarding the relationships among these books, particularly as touching questions of authorship and priority. Three hypotheses dominate the discussion at this point:

(1) Fragmentary hypothesis. This position argues that 1 Esdras is a fragment of the original work of the Chronicler which embraced Chronicles-1 Esdras; on this view canonical Ezra-Nehemiah is a later edition of that material, sepa-

rated from Chronicles and with the addition of the Nehemiah traditions. This approach was most recently and extensively argued by K.-F. Pohlmann (*Studien zum dritten Esra*) and was also advocated in varying forms by J. Michaelis, A. Treuenfels, H. Howorth, J. Marquart, C. Torrey, and G. Hölscher (T. Eshkenazi, *CBQ* 48 [1986] 41). There are numerous analogs in this approach to the position of F. Cross (see "A Reconstruction of the Judean Restoration," *JBL* 94 [1975] 4–18) which is also argued in a number of dissertations done under his direction (see S. McKenzie, *Chronicler's Use*, 1–26). Various scholars taking essentially this approach differ on the extent of the original composition and the subsequent history and sequence of its redaction to yield the canonical books, but nevertheless, agree on the priority of 1 Esdras to the canonical text of Ezra-Nehemiah.

(2) Compilation hypothesis. This approach argues that 1 Esdras is a secondary composition presupposing essentially the canonical form of Chronicles and Ezra-Nehemiah. This approach was most recently and comprehensively argued by H. Williamson (*IBC*, 12–36; *VT* 37 [1987] 108); this position was also advocated in varying forms by L. Bertholdt, E. Bayer, B. Walde, and W. Rudolph (T. Eshkenazi, *CBQ* 48 [1986] 41). Williamson's arguments in turn were vigorously rejected by S. McKenzie (*Chronicler's Use*, 18–23), to whom Williamson replied in a review (*VT* 37 [1987] 107–14). Though Williamson does consider 1 Esdras to be fragmentary in its present form, particularly with reference to its abrupt beginning (*IBC*, 14–21, 35–36), he considers it to have begun after Manasseh as a derived composition.

(3) Distinct composition hypothesis. T. Eshkenazi (*CBQ* 48 [1986] 39–61) argues that 1 Esdras is a distinct composition by the person, circle, or school responsible for Chronicles. Eshkenazi assesses the differences between 1 Esdras and Ezra-Nehemiah as bringing the material of Ezra-Nehemiah into conformity with the ideology of Chronicles. Those characteristics which distinguish the outlook of Chronicles from that of Samuel-Kings are the same features that distinguish 1 Esdras from Ezra-Nehemiah. On her view then 1 Esdras was a compilation from Ezra-Nehemiah, a discrete book by the Chronicler and not a fragment of some larger unity. While concurring with the compilation hypothesis that 1 Esdras is secondary, she concurs with the fragmentary hypothesis in considering the Chronicler as also responsible for 1 Esdras.

Opinions remain divided on the entire range of questions posed by the existence of 1 Esdras; no consensus has been achieved. This commentary has been written throughout from the perspective that Ezra-Nehemiah and Chronicles are not a unity; the balance of the arguments appear to favor viewing 1 Esdras as a secondary composition presuming canonical Ezra-Nehemiah. In any event it remains an ancient text of 2 Chr 35–36 and is important to text critical questions in these chapters; though it is not a strictly literal translation, most of its divergences from the MT are readily explainable.

2 Chr 35 reports (1) the observance of Passover in the eighteenth year of Josiah's reign (35:1–19) and (2) the events surrounding Josiah's death (35:20–27).

The account of Josiah's Passover observance is a considerably expanded version of 2 Kgs 23:21–23. The differences largely concern additional attention to the role of the Levites and to the details of the ritual, both leitmotifs of

Chronicles. What sources were available to the Chronicler for these additional details can only be conjectured. Some regard the additional material as a free composition of the Chronicler reflecting his view of how Passover should be observed or reflecting the practices of his own day (J. Segal, *Hebrew Passover*, 14–19). There has also been considerable discussion of how to relate 2 Chr 35 in the sequence of law codes and narratives dealing with Passover; see the brief summary under *Form/Structure/Setting* in reference to 2 Chr 30.

The account of Josiah's death differs from the parallel account (2 Kgs 23:29–30) largely due to the additional information concerning (1) Neco's message and its designation as God's command, (2) Josiah's disguising himself for battle, (3) his being wounded by archers, (4) his transfer to a second chariot, and (5) his place of death and the subsequent mourning. In the earlier account it is not unambiguously clear that Josiah had set out to do battle with Neco, but only to "meet" (2 Kgs 23:29) him. The earlier, briefer account led many to conclude that a battle did not in fact take place, but that Neco had summoned Josiah and seized him and that the Israelite forces quit the field after Josiah's death (see for example M. Noth, *The History of Israel*, tr. S. Godman [New York: Harper's, 1958], 279; A. Welch, "Death of Josiah," *ZAW* 43 [1925] 255–60; T. Robinson, *A History of Israel* [Oxford: Clarendon Press, 1932], 1:424). However, since the publication of the Babylonian chronicles (D. Wiseman, *Chronicles of the Chaldean Kings* [London: British Museum, 1956]) and their confirmation of the general geopolitical and historical circumstances, few have questioned that a battle between Neco and Josiah did in fact take place.

There has also been considerable debate regarding the source of the Chronicler's additional information concerning Neco and Josiah. H. Williamson (408–11; *VT* 32 [1982] 242–48; *VT* 37 [1987] 9–15) has argued that the additional details regarding the confrontation with Neco were already found in the Chronicler's *Vorlage* of Kings and represent a further stage in the continuing literary development of the deuteronomic history beyond its canonical shape. Williamson cites four lines of evidence for this conclusion:

(1) The Chronicler invariably introduces his source citations at the same point where they occur in the deuteronomic history in every case except 2 Chr 35:26–27. This creates a strong presumption that he was following a text of Kings in which the source citation was located after the reference to Josiah's death instead of before (2 Kgs 23:28); see particularly his defense of this argument in *VT* 37 (1987) 10–12.

(2) Williamson considered it highly improbable that Neco would have in fact explained his movements theologically (2 Chr 35:21) or that the Chronicler would have introduced this gentile king as a divine messenger in place of his usual use of prophets or Levites as vehicles of the word of God. This creates the presumption that the Chronicler was composing under the restraint of prior tradition.

(3) The characteristic vocabulary associated with the Chronicler's theology of immediate retribution is also entirely lacking in the passage; terms such as "seek, humble, be unfaithful, forsake" do not occur.

(4) Williamson felt that the regular lamentations for Josiah would not

have continued into the Chronicler's day (35:25), and that therefore this note was found and appropriate in his source, a further edited version of Kings.

C. Begg ("The Death of Josiah in Chronicles: Another View," *VT* 37 [1987] 1–8) contested Williamson's conclusions; Williamson defended his position in a rejoinder ("Reliving the Death of Josiah: A Reply to C. T. Begg," *VT* 37 [1987] 9–15). Begg considered the overriding concern of the narrative to be reiterating the validity of retribution theology, the demonstration of the connection between affliction and sin: the death in defeat of a righteous king was explained as due to his own transgression of a message from God. Begg also considered the employment of the narrative as characteristic of the Chronicler: he reports other kings who began in piety, but rebelled later in their reigns, and makes frequent use of the warning speech addressed to a king regarding the conduct of war. After contesting each of Williamson's points, Begg concluded that the narrative of Josiah's death in Chronicles, whatever independent sources were available to him, bears all the marks of his own composition rather than providing warrant for some intermediate stage between Chronicles and Kings. The reader can consult these more detailed arguments in the respective articles. With reference to Williamson's arguments, even if the Chronicler's source citations are pedantically located in the same position as those in the deuteronomic history, one cannot thereby assume that the desire to do this represented some high priority compositional principle for the author; departure from this positioning could be viewed as "the exception that proves the rule"; such vagaries are often taken as marks of genuineness in information theory. Rather than finding it improbable that Neco would explain his own movements theologically, to the contrary we should consider it quite probable: it appears to have been common practice to allege the favor and beneficence of an opponent's deity, as was done by Sennacherib's emissaries (2 Kgs 18:25); the Assyrians routinely claimed that local deities, controlling the destinies of their adherents, acted in behalf of Assyria (M. Cogan, *Imperialism and Religion*, 11–21, 111). The surprising element in this account is not the theological rationalization on the part of the Egyptian Pharaoh, but rather that the Chronicler would view his protestations as genuinely a divine message to Josiah. The objection to the Chronicler's seeing Neco as a divine messenger merely pushes the problem back one step—it would seem improbable that any scribe in Israel's religious tradition would have treated him so, i.e., it is equally improbable that the Kings *Vorlage* had been modified. The absence of the Chronicler's characteristic vocabulary, which is particularly common in speech materials, is indeed striking. The sources used by the Chronicler in this pericope will continue to be debated. Use of a more developed version of Kings seems probable: the details would have come from a period closer to the events and would therefore also have a higher intrinsic probability for historical reliability.

The paragraphs in the chapter are marked by the following devices: (1) use of an explicit subject (35:1, 7, 23, 25; 36:1); (2) repetition of an initial phrase (העבדה ותכון "the service was prepared," 35:10, 16); and (3) a temporal phrase (35:20).

Comment

1–2 The Chronicler specifies the precise date of the observance, information not provided in the parallel text (2 Kgs 23:21–23) and included as a contrast to the delayed observance under Hezekiah (30:2–3; cf. Exod 12:6; Lev 23:5; Num 9:3).

Josiah's encouraging the priests may recall the contrast in other contexts between the willingness of the Levites and the reluctance of the priests (29:12–19; 30:3; Williamson, 404), though that contrast is not explicit in this context.

3–6 With reference to the teaching function of the Levites, see 17:7–8 and Neh 8:7–9.

With reference to the instructions regarding the ark, see *Notes* at v 3.c,d.

The Chronicler specifically parallels David and Solomon in three passages (35:4; 11:17; 7:10 [contrast 1 Kgs 8:66]), all passages putting Solomon in a favorable light. See the introductory essay to 2 Chr 1–9, "The Chronicler's Solomon." For their roles in assigning the courses and divisions of the priests and Levites, see 1 Chr 24:4, 19–20, 30–31; 28:19–21; 2 Chr 8:14.

Though the Passover animal was ordinarily slaughtered by the lay offerer (Deut 16:5–6; Exod 12:3–6, 21), the Chronicler understands that Josiah continued the practice of slaughter by the Levites as begun under Hezekiah (see *Comment* at 30:13–20). Under Hezekiah this practice was explained as exigency due to the ritual impurity of some participants; the practice has either become normalized by the time of Josiah (Rudolph, 325; C-M, 513; Myers, 212), or we are invited to infer a further exigency, perhaps the sheer number of participants (35:14, 18).

7–9 The Chronicler often reports the voluntary and joyful giving of king and people (24:8–14; 29:31–36; 31:3–21), presumably with hortatory intent for his readers. The giving of the king and his officials recalls the similar events during the reign of David (1 Chr 29:3–9).

The law prescribed small cattle—sheep and goats—for the Passover offerings (Exod 12:3–5; cf. Deut 16:2). The offering of bulls probably does not represent a modification of the stipulations in this regard; rather, the bulls constituted additional offerings as part of the concurrent Feast of Unleavened Bread (McConville, *Law and Theology*, 117).

The total number of small cattle enumerated was 37,600; of bulls, 3,800. These totals are nearly double the offerings at Passover under Hezekiah (30:24) but much less than the offerings at the dedication of the temple (2 Chr 7:5 // 1 Kgs 8:63). Population estimates for ancient societies are notoriously difficult; sober estimates would put the population of Iron Age Judah around 300,000 people (Y. Shiloh, "Population Estimates of Iron Age Palestine in the Light of a Sample Analysis of Urban Plans, Areas, and Population Density," *BASOR* 239 [1980] 25–35). For the celebration of Passover and Unleavened Bread involving a large percentage of the population of Judah and participants from the North, the figures are not unrealistic. The logistics for the resident population of Jerusalem must have been considerable.

The same names occur in 31:12–13 for Levites who were active during Hezekiah's reign; these individuals having those names during Josiah's reign

(35:9) were probably the grandsons of those mentioned earlier, a fact providing evidence for the practice of papponymy in monarchic Israel.

10–15 For a time the temple would have become a slaughterhouse, a stream of celebrants coming to receive animals for use in their observances. After the animals were slain and skinned, the Levites removed those portions used as burnt offerings and gave them to the family representatives who would present them to the priests for the burning. Details of this ritual are not prescribed in legislation pertaining to Passover; rather, the appeal to what was "written in the book of Moses" (35:12) probably pertains to provisions for fellowship offerings, the fat portions of which were burned on the altar (Lev 3:6–16); the burnt offerings and fat offerings (35:14) may refer to the same thing (Keil, 502; Williamson, 407).

The element of haste (Exod 12:11) may have been transferred in these observances to the quick service (35:13) by the Levites (Ackroyd, 204).

The Chronicler once again associates the Levites with prophetic authority (35:15; see 34:30; 29:25; 20:14; 1 Chr 25:1–8). See See D. Petersen, *Prophecy*, 86–87.

18–19 The deuteronomic historian had said there was no observance of Passover like this since "the days of the judges who led Israel, or throughout the days of the kings of Israel and Judah" (2 Kgs 23:22). The Chronicler's changes in this wording are striking: he speaks only of the "kings of Israel," using this term in reference to both kingdoms. Though the time period is the same, instead of referring to the period of the judges, the Chronicler prefers to speak of "the days of Samuel the prophet." All commentators recognize the emphasis the Chronicler placed on the role of the Levites in general and in particular their functions in Josiah's Passover; this shift of wording from the parallel account may reflect the Chronicler's desire to introduce a Levitical prophet into the narrative once again (1 Chr 6:25–28; cf. 1 Sam 1:1).

18 This verse should also be compared with 30:26. The Chronicler has incorporated both statements from his sources without feeling the need to harmonize them; the numbers of offerings and celebrants at Josiah's Passover exceeded that of Hezekiah.

19 This verse may form an inclusio with 34:8; it is drawn from the parallel text at 2 Kgs 23:23.

20–27 The narrative takes a chronological jump from the events of Josiah's eighteenth year (622 B.C.) to the year of his death (609 B.C.).

Israel's strategic location on the sole land bridge linking three continents has always been a major factor in her history. For all the biblical focus on Josiah, events in Judah paled in significance on the larger scale: the decay of the Assyrian empire induced the resurgence of two great powers that had long been held subject to Assyria (Egypt and Babylon); each sought to reestablish its ancient spheres of influence and territorial claims. These events were full of ominous portent for Judah.

Neco's messengers had sought free passage for the Eyptian army; Josiah's choosing instead to intercept and attack may have been the result of his own anti-Assyrian bias or of a coalition with Babylon or even of his own desire to maintain Judean independence from Egyptian incursion. The choice of Megiddo for the confrontation reflects the traditional strategic importance of the site at the mouth of the Nahal Iron, a pass through the Carmel range. Neco was en route to Carchemish as the ally of Assyria against Nabopolassar of Babylon, but inasmuch as Egyptian self-interest was the motivating force, it is quite accurately said that he was campaigning "against Assyria" (2 Kgs 23:29). The Babylonians had forced Ashur-uballit to move his capital from Harran to Carchemish half a year before the battle at Megiddo (D. Wiseman, *Chronicles*, 17–19; A. Malamat, *JANESCU* 5 [1973] 274).

For the Chronicler the death of Josiah presented a challenge to his theology of retribution; defeat in battle for him represented divine disfavor, whereas victory was a token of blessing. If Josiah was such a pious king, how is it that he suffered defeat and died in battle? The Chronicler demonstrates the validity of his retribution theology by modifying the Kings account to show that Josiah's death resulted from his disobedience to a divine oracle. Speech materials are commonly in Chronicles the vehicle of the author's theological viewpoints; just as other war oracles resulted in weal or woe for the king receiving them (2 Chr 11:1–4; 13:4–12; 18:16–22; 25:17–24; cf. 16:7–9), here the warning is given by a gentile king. The author informs the reader that retribution theology is the focus of his concern by introducing the narrative of Josiah's death with the additional phrase, "after all this, when Josiah had set the temple in order . . ."; the Chronicler commonly uses such introductory phrases to signal the focus of his interest (see *Comment* at 18:1).

Some of the additional details introduced by the Chronicler may reflect the influence of the accounts of the deaths of Ahab (1 Kgs 22:29–40) and Ahaziah (2 Kgs 9:27; cf. 2 Chr 22:8–9). All three kings died after fleeing the field of battle in their chariots. Ahab and Josiah both had gone into the battle disguised, both were wounded by archers, and both instructed subordinates to remove them from the battle.

The biblical histories appear to differ on the place of Josiah's death. Whereas 2 Kgs 23:30 states that Josiah's servants took him "dead from Megiddo," the Chronicler is at pains to show that "they brought him to Jerusalem and he died" (35:24). Williamson (409) regards this modification in Chronicles as the author's effort to ease the difficulty with Huldah's prophecy that Josiah would go to his grave in peace (see *Comment* at 34:28; cf. McConville, 264), though the Chronicler provides no hint of this intent in the immediate context. Gray (748) harmonizes 2 Kgs 23:30 with 2 Chr 35:24 by translating 2 Kgs 23:30, "his retainers drove him dying from Megiddo . . ."; cf. Rudolph, 333. Cf. the similar question regarding the place of death in the case of Ahaziah and Jehoiakim (see *Form/Structure/Setting* in chap. 22). The change to a second chariot was probably an effort to provide comfort or space for the recumbent king.

While it is clear that the Chronicler regards Neco's speech as a genuine word of God to Josiah (see above, *Form/Structure/Setting*), readers wonder how Josiah would have recognized this. This difficulty is probably the reason for the explanation offered in 1 Esdr 1:26 (see *Notes* at 22.c.): Neco's words were interpreted and validated by Jeremiah (cf. 36:12).

Jeremiah unquestionably held Josiah in high esteem (Jer 22:15–16); his instructions to "weep not for the dead king" (Jer 22:10) are testimony to the practice of uttering laments for Josiah. One can only speculate on the nature, extent, and fate of the collection of laments to which the Chronicler refers (35:25).

26–36:1 With reference to Josiah's "acts of piety," see 32:32 and 6:42.

The people of the land once again took a role in the royal succession; see *Comment* at 33:18–20. Josiah was the only king of Israel to be succeeded by three of his own sons and one grandson. Jehoahaz was also known as Shallum (1 Chr 3:15; Jer 22:11). The reasons for bypassing his older brothers are not directly addressed in the text; perhaps he was expected to continue Josiah's political policies (if not his religious fidelity [Jer 22:11–17]), and therefore, was in turn removed by Neco (36:3).

Explanation

Josiah's Passover was a pilgrimage feast: just as Israel had received its identity as a nation in the great assembly before Yahweh at Sinai, the law provided that during the pilgrimage feasts the nation would assemble before his sanctuary at least in part as a visible reminder of a corporate national existence. In this way the individual Israelite learned afresh what it meant to be Israel: that Yahweh had chosen them as his own and that he dwelled in their midst. Centuries later Jesus' parents annually made this same pilgrimage; they discovered that though he was still a child, Jesus knew more about the meaning of Passover than they (Luke 2:41–51; G. McConville, 260–61).

While the biblical historians regarded the reform under Josiah as approximating the zenith of religion in the kingdom of Judah, national or official reforms may not really change people or have lasting effect. Josiah's renewed covenant (34:30–31) was quickly abandoned by his successors; Josiah's contemporary Jeremiah would look for a day when a new covenant would be written on individual hearts, a new covenant that would effect a genuine change (Jer 33).

For the Chronicler, Josiah's fidelity did not cancel the inexorable validity of retribution theology: Josiah died in defeat when he transgressed the command of God. For the Christian reader, Josiah's failure drives us to look for yet another son of David who will rule the people of God in righteousness without lapse.

The Last Kings of Judah, 609–598 B.C.; Cyrus's Decree (36:2–23)

Bibliography

Bayer, E. *Das Dritte Buch Esdras und sein Verhältnis zu den Büchern Esra-Nehemia.* Freiburg: Herdersche Verlagshandlung, 1911. **Bickerman, E.** "The Edict of Cyrus in Ezra I." *JBL* 65 (1946) 249–75. **Cazelles, H.** "Le roi Yoyakim et le Serviteur du Seigneur." *Proceedings of the Fifth World Congress of Jewish Studies, Jerusalem, 1969.* Jerusalem, 1973. 1:121–26. **David, M.** "The Manumission of Slaves under Zedekiah." *OTS* 5 (1948) 63–79. **Freedy, K.,** and **D. Redford.** "The Dates in Ezekiel in Relation to Biblical, Babylonian and Egyptian Sources." *JAOS* 90 (1970) 462–85. **Ginsberg, H.** "Judah and the Transjordan States from 734–582 B.C." *Alexander Marx Jubilee Volume.* New York: Jewish Publication Society, 1950. 347–68. **Green, A.** "The Fate of Jehoiakim." *AUSS* 20 (1982) 103–9. **Larsson, G.** "When Did the Babylonian Captivity Begin?" *JTS* 18 (1967) 117–23. **Malamat, A.** "The Last Kings of Judah and the Fall of Jerusalem." *IEJ* 18 (1968) 137–56. ———. "The Twilight of Judah: In the Egyptian-Babylonian Maelstrom." *Congress Volume, Edinburgh, 1974.* VTSup 28. Leiden: Brill, 1975. 123–45. **McKenzie, S.** *Chronicler's Use.* 181–88. **Myers, J.** "Edom and Judah in the Sixth-Fifth Centuries B.C." In *Near Eastern Studies in Honor of William Foxwell Albright,* ed. H. Goedicke. Baltimore: Johns Hopkins Press, 1971. 377–92. ———. *I and II Esdras.* AB 42. Garden City, NY: Doubleday, 1974. **Stern, E.** "Israel at the Close of the Period of the Monarchy: An Archaeological Survey." *BA* 38 (1975) 26–54. **Tadmor, H.** "Chronology of the Last Kings of Judah." *JNES* 15 (1956) 226–30. **Vaux, R. de.** "The Decrees of Cyrus and Darius on the Rebuilding of the Temple." *The Bible and the Ancient Near East.* Translated by D. McHugh. London: Darton, Longman, and Todd, 1972. 63–96. **Williamson, H.** *IBC.* 7–11. ———. Review of S. L. McKenzie, *The Chronicler's Use of the Deuteronomistic History.* VT 37 (1987) 107–14. **Wiseman, D.** *Chronicles of the Chaldean Kings.* London: British Museum, 1956.

Translation

[2]*Jehoahaz was twenty-three years old when he became king, and he ruled three months in Jerusalem.* [3]*The king of Egypt[a] took him captive[b] in Jerusalem[c] and imposed on the land a payment of one hundred talents of silver and a talent of gold.* [4]*The king of Egypt[a] made Eliakim his brother[b] king over Judah and Jerusalem and changed his name[c] to Jehoiakim; Neco took his brother Jehoahaz and carried him away to Egypt.[d]*

[5]*Jehoiakim was twenty-five years old when he became king,[a] and he ruled eleven years in Jerusalem;[b] he did what was evil in the sight of Yahweh his God.[c]* [6a]*Nebuchadnezzar king of Babylon came up against him,[b] and bound him in bronze shackles to take him to Babylon.* [7]*Nebuchadnezzar took some of the implements from the temple of Yahweh to Babylon and put them in his palace in Babylon.[a]* [8]*As for the rest of the acts of Jehoiakim, the detestable deeds that he did and all that was charged against him, these are written in the book of the kings of Israel[a] and Judah.[b] Jehoiachin his son ruled in his place.*

[9]*Jehoiachin was eighteen[a] years old when he became king, and he ruled three months[b] in Jerusalem;[c] he did what was evil in the eyes of Yahweh.* [10]*At the turn*

of the year King Nebuchadnezzar sent [a] *and brought him to Babylon with the precious implements from the temple of Yahweh, and he made his kinsman* [b] *Zedekiah king in his place.*

[11] *Zedekiah was twenty-one years old when he became king, and he ruled eleven years in Jerusalem.* [12] *He did what was evil in the eyes of Yahweh his God;* [a] *he did not humble himself before the word of Yahweh from the mouth of Jeremiah the prophet.* [13] *He also rebelled against King Nebuchadnezzar who had imposed on him an oath in the name of God. He became stiff-necked and hardened his heart rather than turning to Yahweh the God of Israel.* [14] *All the leaders* [a] *of the priests and the people* [b] *became more and more unfaithful, following all the detestable practices of the nations; they defiled the temple of Yahweh which he had consecrated in Jerusalem.*

[15] *Yahweh the God of their fathers sent word to them through his messengers* [a] *time and again,* [b] *for he had pity on his people and his dwelling.* [16] *But they mocked the messengers of God, despised his words,* [a] *and scoffed at his prophets until the wrath of Yahweh rose against his people, until there could be no recovery.* [b] [17] *He brought against them the king of the Chaldeans who killed their young men with a sword in the sanctuary and had no pity on young man or young woman, the old or the infirm.* [a] *God delivered them all into his power.* [18] *All the implements of the temple of God, both large and small, and the treasures* [a] *of the temple of Yahweh and the treasures of the king and his officials* [b] —*he took it all to Babylon.* [19] *They burned the temple of God and tore down the wall of Jerusalem; they burned all the palaces with fire and destroyed anything of value* [a] *there.* [20] *He carried the remnant that had escaped the sword into exile in Babylon where they became slaves to him and his sons until the kingdom of Persia* [a] *came to power.* [21] *The land enjoyed its sabbath rests until the fulfillment of the word of Yahweh through Jeremiah; all the days of its desolation it rested until the fulfillment of the seventy years.*

[22] *In the first year of the reign of Cyrus king of Persia, to fulfill the word of Yahweh through Jeremiah, Yahweh aroused the spirit of Cyrus king of Persia to make a proclamation throughout his kingdom and to commit it to writing, as follows:*

[23] *"This is the word of Cyrus king of Persia:*

'Yahweh the God of heaven [a] *has given to me all kingdoms on earth; he has appointed me to build him a temple at Jerusalem in Judah. Whoever among you is from among his people, may Yahweh* [b] *his God be with him, and let him go up.'"*

Notes

3.a. G καὶ μετήγαγεν αὐτὸν ὁ βασιλεὺς εἰς Αἴγυπτον, "the king took him to Egypt." 36:1–8 in Par has assimilated to Bas or reflects a Heb. *Vorlage* for Par which had incorporated 2 Kgs 23:30–24:6. It is not clear whether the material unique to Chronicles was displaced by the material borrowed from Kings and only later reintroduced, or whether the Kings text was introduced to a text that retained the features of Chr MT. The text type of the supplements from Kings may reflect G[L]. See the discussion in Allen, *GC* 1:216 and *HTR* 61 (1968) 483–91; and R. Klein, *HTR* 60 (1967) 93–94; 61 (1968) 492–95. 1 Esdras reflects the MT of Chr.

3.b. Reading ויאסרהו with 2 Kgs 23:33 and G. MT, "removed, deposed." MT would be eased by the addition of a phrase, "deposed him *from being king* in Jerusalem"; if so, 1 Esdr 1:33 βασιλεύειν is the product of translational dynamics rather than an alternative text (cf. 2 Kgs 23:33).

3.c. G does not include "in Jerusalem."

4.a. Par follows Bas and 2 Kgs 23:34, "Pharaoh Neco"; 1 Esdr 1:35 reads with MT.

4.b. Par follows Bas and 2 Kgs 23:34, "son of Josiah"; 1 Esdr 1:35 reads with MT.

4.c. 1 Esdr 1:36. καὶ ἔδησεν Ἰωακὶμ τοὺς μεγιστᾶνας "And Jehoiakim bound the nobles," may depend on reading שׂרי את ויאסר. The translator of 1 Esdras has not referred to Jehoiakim by his earlier name Eliakim, and so would not report the change of name. See Bayer, 23.

4.d. Par has an addition drawn from Bas at 2 Kgs 23:34d–35 reporting Jehoahaz's death in Egypt and the program of taxation to pay Neco's demands.

5.a. 1 Esdras 1:37 adds "of Judah and Jerusalem."

5.b. 1 Esdr 1:37 omits the length of reign; G includes the length of reign and name of his mother.

5.c. Par follows Bas and adds the last clause of 2 Kgs 23:37, "according to all his fathers had done."

6.a. Par follows Bas and includes 2 Kgs 24:1a.

6.b. Par adds "into the land" at the end of the addition from 2 Kgs 24:1a.

7.a. Chr MT omits, though Par includes, 2 Kgs 24:1b–4 which reports Jehoiakim's three-year vassalage to Nebuchadnezzar and his rebellion.

8.a. 2 Kgs 24:5, Bas, Par and 1 Esdr 1:40 omit "Israel."

8.b. 1 Esdras 1:40 also omits "Judah." Par contains the additional note in Bas (2 Kgs 24:6) that "Jehoiakim slept with his fathers" and adds further with the Lucianic text of Bas, "he was buried in the garden of Uzza with his fathers" (cf. 2 Kgs 21:18, 26).

9.a,b. 2 Kgs 24:8 reports that Jehoiachin was eighteen years old at his accession and ruled for three months, in contrast to Chr MT which gives his age as eight and his reign as three months and ten days. The translation provided here understands the ten to have been a misplaced corrector's gloss that should have been read with the eight to give his age at accession as eighteen. See the discussion by A. Green, "The Fate of Jehoiakim," *AUSS* 20 (1982) 105.

9.c. The Chronicler omits the names of the queen mothers from his accession notices for all the kings of Judah after Hezekiah (see *Comment* at 33:1). Par is conflated with material from Bas through 36:8 (see *Notes* at 3.a); Par has followed Bas and included the mothers' names in 36:2, 5 but not in 36:9, 11.

10.a. Chronicles omits 2 Kgs 24:10b–16a and its details regarding the exile of Jehoiachin and ten thousand others; see Hobbs, 353.

10.b. Literally "his brother," though in fact he was an uncle (2 Kgs 24:17). The term אח of course has a wider semantic range, "relative"; Par's "brother of his father" is the translator's effort to harmonize. Cf. the similar phenomenon in 22:8.

12.a. 2 Kgs 24:19 and Jer 52:2 add, "according to all Jehoiakim had done."

14.a. G, "all the leaders of Judah and the priests"; 1 Esdr 1:47, "all the leaders of the people and the priests. . . ." G may have developed from misreading an abbreviation: שׂרי = שׂרי־י יהודה; see Allen, *GC* 2:84.

14.b. G, "people of the land."

15.a. 1 Esdr 1:48 reads singular, τοῦ ἀγγέλου αὐτοῦ = מלאכו "his messenger." Cf. the plural in v 49 // 36:16.

15.b. 1Esdr 1:48, μετακαλέσαι "to call them back"; the translator appears not to have understood the idiom השכם ושלוח.

16.a. 1 Esdr 1:49, καὶ ᾗ ἡμέρᾳ ἐλάλησεν κύριος "on the day in which the LORD spoke, they . . .," read וביום דברי for MT ביום דבריו. See Bayer, 23.

16.b. 1 Esdr 1:49, διὰ τὰ δυσσεβήματα προστάξαι "provoked by their apostasy." See Bayer, 23.

17.a. 1 Esdr 1:50 νεωτέρου may have read יונק for MT ישׁשׁ; cf. Syr. However, 1 Esdr appears to have leveled the text by making the second element in this second pair of nouns an antonym in keeping with the first pair ("young man or young woman"). Since such pairs of antonyms are commonly used in the OT to represent an entirety, it would be a form of contextual assimilation for a scribe to introduce an antonym here as well. G ἀπήγαγον "led away" may have read ישׁיב.

18.a. 1 Esdr 1:51 κιβωτούς "arks" appears to have read ארנות for MT אצרות. See Bayer, 23.

18.b. 1 Esdr 1:51, ἀναλαβόντες "took away" may have read ישׂאו for MT ושׂריו.

19.a. 1 Esdr 1:53, καὶ συνετέλεσαν πάντα "they completely demolished" read וכלו כל.

20.a. G, "Medes," but cf. v 22.

23.a. 1 Esd 2:2, "the LORD of Israel, the most high LORD."

23.b. Ezra 1:3 and Par read יהי "may (God) be" for MT יהוה; cf. 1 Esdr 2:3.

Form/Structure/Setting

The Chronicler treats the reigns of the last four kings of Judah rather quickly; much of the detail found in Kings (and its parallels in Jeremiah) is eliminated (2 Kgs 23:31b–32, 34d–35; 24:1b–4, 7, 10b–16a, 18b, 20; 25:1–30). The Chronicler either sharply abbreviates these accounts or has relied on sources other than the deuteronomic history. He not only provides much less detail, but also he drops the formulaic references to maternal lineage (see *Comment* at 33:1) and death notices for these kings. The Chronicler has arranged the accounts to portray two themes (cf. Williamson, 412): (1) the common fate of the last four kings, each ending in exile, and (2) the tribute paid by each, largely through spoliation of the temple. This has the effect of drawing a parallel between the fate of the Davidic dynasty and the temple: both destined for exile, but with hope of restoration.

The Chronicler's penchant for adopting patterns or typologies around which to shape his narratives is one of his most characteristic compositional techniques. These two themes are sufficient in large measure to account for the contours of the Chronicler's treatment of the last kings of Judah; they provide a rationale for the pattern of the material he has selected. However, since the Chronicler shows so much less dependence on Kings for this material than might ordinarily be expected, many have speculated that the Chronicler did not have Kings before him as a source for these reigns. S. McKenzie (*Chronicler's Use*) has sought to test some features of F. Cross's views regarding the redactional history of the deuteronomic history. Cross considers all material after 2 Kgs 23:25b along with material blaming Manasseh for Judah's fall (2 Kgs 21:10–16) and other passages to belong to DH[2]; McKenzie seeks to determine if the Chronicler had at his disposal only DH[1] without the additional material from DH[2] and if Chronicles, therefore, can be used as an objective criterion for isolating DH[2] material in Kings. McKenzie (206) concludes that Chronicles cannot be used reliably in this way, though it is of some use. The apparent absence of dependence on Kings for narratives of reigns after Josiah is the strongest argument in favor of the position that the Chronicler was dependent on DH[1] without DH[2]. However, if one takes into account the deliberate shaping of the chapter around the themes identified by Williamson, there is no reason to argue that the Chronicler did not have Kings with DH[2] available to him. The chapter in its present form is evidence of the particular interests of the author rather than evidence for the absence of DH[2] material in his sources. See also Williamson's review of McKenzie's work (*VT* 37 [1987] 107–14). The Chronicler does appear dependent on 2 Kgs 23:31–36 for his account of Jehoahaz (36:2–5); the two sections have in common the report of his deposition, the precise amount of tribute levied, the infrequent root עֲנשׁ, the name change for Eliakim, and the exile to Egypt. McKenzie (185) assigns these parallels to some independent oral or written source other than Kings, but only it seems in light of his controlling thesis that the Chronicler did not have DH[2] material at his disposal; in reality these parallels may prove just the opposite: that the Chronicler did have 2 Kgs 24–25 at his disposal, but used it only in the most cursory fashion due to other controlling interests of his own.

The repetition of the decree of Cyrus at the end of Chronicles (36:22–23) and at the beginning of Ezra (1:1–3) constitutes an important issue in the debate regarding the relationship of Chronicles and Ezra-Nehemiah; see the summary of this debate in H. Williamson, *IBC*, 7–10. The same data is put into the service of opposite arguments: on the one hand, the repetition is viewed as a deliberate overlap introduced to preserve the original connection when Chronicles was separated from Ezra; on the other hand, the repetition is viewed as a deliberate stitching together of two originally separate documents. Williamson (*IBC*, 9) regards the abrupt ending with ויעל "let him go up" as unnatural, an unsatisfactory ending for Chronicles which gives the appearance of having been extracted from Ezra 1:1. Since 36:21 could provide a satisfying ending to the work, Williamson regards the addition of Cyrus's decree at the end of Chronicles as a secondary expansion. T. Eshkenazi (*CBQ* 48 [1986] 56–57), who regards 1 Esdras also as a work of the Chronicler, points to the abrupt, midsentence ending of both 1 Esdras (9:55) and Chronicles as further evidence for their having a common author.

A wealth of both biblical and extrabiblical evidence is available for the study of the closing decades of the kingdom of Judah. Within the canon the historical records in Kings and Chronicles are supplemented particularly by Jeremiah and Ezekiel. Outside the canon abundant Egyptian and Babylonian epigraphic materials, as well as some discoveries in Israel, supplement the biblical accounts; pride of place in this regard must go to the Babylonian chronicles (see D. Wiseman, *Chronicles*). For efforts to integrate the details of these sources, see the chapter bibliography, particularly the entries by Malamat, Tadmor, Ginsberg, Myers, and Green. E. Stern (*BA* 38 [1975] 26–54) provides a summary of the material evidence.

The onsets of paragraphs in this chapter are marked by the recurring phrase שנה . . . בן (36:2, 5, 9, 11), a temporal phrase (36:22), and the use of an explicit subject (36:15).

Comment

2–3   In the latter half of 609 b.c. Judah underwent great political turmoil and experienced three successive changes of monarch. Josiah's death was followed by the three month rule of Jehoahaz who was in turn succeeded by Jehoiakim.

Jehoahaz, also known as Shallum, was not Josiah's firstborn; he had at least two older brothers (1 Chr 3:15). Nothing is known of the fate of Josiah's firstborn Johanan; he may have died before Josiah's own death. Jehoahaz came to the throne at age twenty-three and was succeeded three months later by Jehoiakim, who was twenty-five. The people of the land made Jehoahaz king, setting aside the right of primogeniture (21:3) probably in an effort to continue the anti-Egyptian or pro-Babylonian policies of Josiah. The same anti-Egyptian posture may explain Nebuchadnezzar's later choice of Zedekiah, Jehoahaz's younger brother by the same mother, Hamutal (2 Kgs 23:31; 24:18; see Malamat, "Last Kings," 140; "Twilight," 126).

Jehoahaz ruled for three months in 609 b.c.; Neco removed him while he was still in northern Syria (2 Kgs 23:33) and carried him to Egypt (Jer

22:11–12; cf. Ezek 19:1–4). The fine Neco imposed on Judah (a hundred talents of silver and one talent of gold) was much less than that levied by Sennacherib on Hezekiah (2 Kgs 18:14). The Chronicler does not specify the sources from which this sum was exacted: the people of the land who had enthroned Jehoahaz are those who carried the burden of making that payment (2 Kgs 23:35). Neco's hegemony over Judah ended the years of independence enjoyed under Josiah.

The Chronicler makes no overt moral judgment on Jehoahaz's reign, content to present the themes of exile and tribute that characterize his treatment of the last four kings of Judah. The deuteronomic historian does provide a brief, formulaic moral judgment (2 Kgs 23:32). Jeremiah provides more information regarding the actual character of his reign; it is an indictment for self-aggrandizement and injustice (Jer 22:11–17).

4–8 Jehoiakim reigned from Tishri, 609 B.C. until his death in the seventh year of Nebuchadnezzar, 598/97 B.C. For detailed discussion of the chronological issues in this period, see the bibliographic entries above by Freedy and Redford, Malamat, and Tadmor.

Three of the last four kings of Judah are known by more than one name: Shallum/Jehoahaz, Eliakim/Jehoiakim, Mattaniah/Zedekiah, the latter two receiving their throne names from the monarchs who installed them. The right to assign a name to an individual implied authority over him.

The Chronicler omits much of the detail contained in the earlier account of Jehoiakim's reign (2 Kgs 23:36–24:7). While Kings reports his death (2 Kgs 24:6), the Chronicler does not report the death of any of the last four kings of Judah. Instead of reporting Jehoiakim's death, the Chronicler chooses to report an incident from earlier in his reign in which Jehoiakim was either taken into temporary exile or at least prepared for it. This change is motivated by his structuring the account of these last four reigns around the twin themes of exile and tribute. No extant evidence corroborates an exile for Jehoiakim at some earlier point in his reign, and scholarly opinion is divided on whether such an exile took place or was only provided for or intended; the language of the Chronicler (36:6, "bound him to take him") makes allowance for the latter approach. It is conceivable that the binding of Jehoiakim was a symbolic demonstration of his status (McConville, 266); the threat alone may have made actual deportment unnecessary. If a literal deportation is intended, it should be associated with the deportation of Daniel and his friends along with articles from the temple (36:7; Dan 1:1–3; Jer 46:2) in Jehoiakim's third year (605 B.C.) after Nebuchadnezzar defeated Neco at Carchemish.

The temple vessels are an important theme in the biblical historical and prophetic writings; see *Comment* at 29:18–19. The temple vessels are not mentioned in connection with Jehoiakim in Kings; their inclusion in 36:7 reflects once again the Chronicler's interest in the themes of exile and tribute in his account of the last four kings of Judah.

Jehoiakim remained the submissive vassal of Nebuchadnezzar for three years (2 Kgs 24:1), but then rebelled. His death left his son Jehoiachin to bear the brunt of the Babylonian reaction.

Jeremiah is once again the source for much additional detail regarding Jehoiakim (Jer 22:18–23; 25:1–26:24; 36:1–32). Jehoiakim's death is mentioned in Kings (2 Kgs 24:6), but his burial is not, a fact consonant with Jeremiah's utterances about him (Jer 22:18–19). Jeremiah's prophecy suggests that Jehoiakim did not die a natural death but may have been assassinated at approximately the time the armies of Nebuchadnezzar set out to retaliate for his rebellion, though there is no direct confirmation for this.

9–10   The Chronicler does not include most of the details from the longer account of Jehoiachin's reign in 2 Kgs 24:8–17; 25:27–30; he reports only his exile and payment of tribute from the temple implements.

The submission of Jerusalem to Nebuchadnezzar is dated in the Babylonian Chronicle on the second day of Adar in Nebuchadnezzar's seventh year (16 March 597 B.C.). The Babylonian Chronicle provides striking confirmation of the biblical accounts: "In the seventh year [of Nebuchadnezzar], the month Kislev, the king of Akkad mustered his trooops, marched to the Hatti-land, and encamped against the city of Judah, and on the second day of the month of Adar he seized the city and captured the king. He appointed there a king of his own choice, received its heavy tribute and sent them to Babylon" (Wiseman, *Chronicles,* 73).

For the compiler of Kings the release of Jehoiachin from prison during the reign of Amel-Marduk (562–560 B.C.) demonstrated that the house of David was the continuing object of divine favor even during the captivity (2 Kgs 25:27–29). Cuneiform administrative documents known as the Weidner tablets (*ANET,* 308) record supplies delivered to Jehoiachin and his household during their captivity in the reign of Nebuchadnezzar. The Chronicler records the royal genealogy through Jehoiachin's line into generations after the exile (1 Chr 3:16–24).

11–14   The Chronicler's account of Zedekiah's rule (597–586 B.C.) is also shorter than that in the earlier history (2 Kgs 24:18–25:7; cf. Jer 52:1–11; 39:1–7) and shows once again concern with the exile of the king and the spoliation of the temple. In this particular account the characteristic vocabulary and themes of the Chronicler's theology of immediate retribution are also prominent. The following terms are frequent in passages reflecting the author's theology: "humble," כנע; "turn," שוב; "unfaithful," מעל. The fact that there could be no recovery (מרפא, 36:16) also recalls language of 2 Chr 7:14. See the introductory essay to 2 Chr 10–36, "Reward and Punishment in Chronicles: The Theology of Immediate Retribution."

Narratives and sermons in Jeremiah (Jer 27:1–28:17; 34:1–22; 37:1–38:28) once again provide more background on the reign of Zedekiah. Though the prophet repeatedly urged the king to submit to the Babylonians rather than look to Egypt (cf. Ezek 17:12–15) for help, Zedekiah took instead the advice of his "hawks" and rebelled. The oath Zedekiah had sworn to Nebuchadnezzar was probably similar to the vassal oaths known from Assyrian treaties which were sworn also in the name of the vassal's deities; Ezekiel too recalls this oath (Ezek 17:12–17), though it is not mentioned in Kings or Jeremiah.

15–21   The prophets and messengers spoken of in vv 15–16 probably refer to more than those who were active only in the last decades before the exile; the author appears to be speaking of the entire prophetic succession, though this is not unambiguously clear. The role of the prophets in Chronicles is primarily that of guardians of the theocracy; they are the bearers of the word of God to kings, who are in turn blessed or judged within a short time in terms of their response. Here, however, the Chronicler describes the guilt of Israel as cumulative: rather than each generation or king experiencing weal or woe in terms of its own actions, there is a cumulative weight of guilt which ultimately irretrievably provokes the wrath of God and brings the great exile.

There is some ambiguity as to the subject of v 17. It is possible to translate the two clauses after the initial clause in the verse that it was God (rather than the "king of the Chaldeans") who killed the young men and had no pity on the populace. Though it is a syntactic possibility, it seems improbable.

The temple vessels are an important theme in this last chapter of 2 Chronicles; see the *Comment* at 29:18–19.

The Chronicler's account of the destruction of the city is also considerably abbreviated from that found in 2 Kgs 25:8–26. Details regarding the actions of the Babylonian army, the name of its commander, the list of plunder, names of deportees, and the government under Gedaliah are all omitted. The Chronicler does not specify the number of captives; see the discussion of this question in Malamat, "Twilight," 133–34.

Jeremiah's "seventy years" have been variously dated, and the biblical text itself may show multiple understandings of the span of time intended in the reference. At least three possibilities offer themselves. (1) The exile ran from the first deportation (605/4 B.C.) until the decree of Cyrus (539 B.C.). The time period is not exactly seventy years, but close enough. This seems to be the understanding of Dan 9:25 where the end of the seventy years is associated with the decree to rebuild; Daniel himself would have been an exile for this period. The Chronicler (36:20–22) clearly associates the end of Jeremiah's seventy years with Cyrus's decree. (2) The exile ran from the destruction of the temple in 586 B.C. to the dedication of the second temple in 516 B.C. This may be the understanding of a passage like Zech 1:12–17: Zechariah, from his vantage in 520 B.C., still looks for an end to the seventy years; the end of that period is associated with the reconstruction of the city and God's return to the temple. (3) It is possible that the seventy-year figure is not intended to have a literal referent, but is symbolic for a less defined period of judgment. It is striking that both Daniel and Chronicles use the seventy-year figure as symbolic of larger time periods which also do not have clear referents (36:21; Dan 9:24–27).

The Chronicler has conjoined his citation of Jeremiah (25:11–12; 29:10) with a citation of Lev 26:34–35, 43. While the context in Lev 26 is stressing punishment for disobedience, including exile and fallow land, the Chronicler takes a slightly different view. From the vantage of the restoration, the seventy years of sabbatical rests prepared the land for the returnees; it allowed time for recuperation. In his citation of Lev 26:34–35 the Chronicler quite probably also has in view the promises of restoration and favor in Lev 26:40–45: they have paid for their sins, and God has not forgotten his covenant. One overarching concern of the Chronicler has been the question of the continuity of the restoration community with the past: "on the other side of exile and judgment, are we as a people still the particular object of God's favor?" In his tracing the history of the universe from Adam (1 Chr 1:1) to approximately his own day, the Chronicer is answering that question with a ringing affirmation. He is saying in effect, "God has loved us from the foundation of the world; we are a prepared people brought to a prepared land. It is a new day."

Since each of Jeremiah's seventy years represented an unobserved sabbatical year, it is also natural to ask whether the Chronicler had in mind some definite 490-year period during which the laws regarding the sabbatical year (Lev 25) had not been observed. Many suggestions have been offered: C-M (524) related the 490 years to the beginning of the period of the judges. Williamson reckons the period as beginning with the monarchy, a suggestion which is commended by the fact that this is the period covered by the Chronicler's narrative. Yet these and other suggestions are all problematic; it would seem best to take this number, like the number of years for the exile itself, as symbolic of an indefinite period.

22–23 There has been considerable debate regarding whether these verses are original with the Chronicler or a secondary addition; see the discussion above under *Form/Structure/Setting*.

The decree of Cyrus is found in a longer form in Ezra 1:2–4; 6:2–5. The authenticity of these documents has been ably argued by Bickerman ("The Edict of Cyrus in Ezra 1," *JBL* 65 [1946] 249–75) and de Vaux ("The Decrees of Cyrus and Darius on the Rebuilding of the Temple," in *The Bible and the Ancient Near East*, trans. D. McHugh [London: Darton, Longman, and Todd, 1972], 63–96).

The tabernacle, first and second temples were all built in part with funds provided from gentile nations; see *Comment* at 5:1. Cyrus's authorization for the rebuilding of the temple included not only the return of the implements taken from the first temple by the army of Nebuchadnezzar, but also funding from the Persian exchequer (Ezra 6:4–5; cf. Isa 44:28; 45:13).

Concluding the narrative with these two verses highlights the hopefulness already intimated in 36:20–21 and directs the reader to the continuation of the narrative in Ezra. The book ends with a new exodus at hand: not because God forced the hand of a reluctant Pharaoh, but because he moved the heart of a Persian king. The people of God will again go free and build a sanctuary.

Explanation

After his account of the reign of Josiah the Chronicler moves quickly through the reigns of the last four kings. Each king anticipates the fate of the nation through his own experience of exile; the temple too is successively plundered, anticipating its ultimate destruction. But this is not the end of the story: as nation and temple were inextricably bound in destruction, so they are also linked in restoration and renewal. A prepared and purged people return to a prepared land to build again the temple of God.

A great number of the motifs and themes found in this chapter are further developed in other passages in both Old and New Testaments; space allows only a quick intimation of a few directions in which these can be developed.

The true prophets far more often than not lived lives in tension with popular hopes and expectations; their messages contradicted the vox populi, so that they often became the object of the ire of king and populace. The history of the prophetic order is virtually summed up in the statement that their words were scoffed at, mocked, and despised (36:15–16). The utterances of these messengers in God's covenant lawsuit with Israel were finally vindicated in the destruction of the city and temple. Another lawsuit messenger was yet to come; he would once again warn the nation of coming wrath, that the axe was going to the root of the tree (Matt 3:7–12). After him would come God's own Son, the heir of all things (Matt 21:33–41; Hebr 1:1–2).

Zedekiah was the last king of Judah. Jeremiah uses his name to form the basis of a sermon (Jer 23:6; 33:16). When Nebuchadnezzar changed his name from Mattaniah to Zedekiah, the meaning of that new name was "Yahweh is righteous." To know Yahweh in his righteousness was to know him as judge. But Jeremiah anticipates another day when another son of David, a righteous Branch, would rule, and the name by which he would be called was "Yahweh is our righteousness." To know Yahweh this way was to know him in grace and mercy. Zedekiah was not that righteous king who would embody the Davidic ideal; he was judged, went into exile and death. With Jeremiah we look to another king, one who would be our righteousness. He too would endure exile (Matt 27:46; Mark 15:34), not for his own sins, but rather bearing the sins of others. He too would know restoration, and as the embodiment of the faithful remnant would become the nucleus of a new Israel; he would reign until all enemies be put under his feet.

In this new Israel Jew and Gentile together (Gal 3:7–9, 28–29; Eph 3:6) build, even constitute, a new dwelling for the Spirit of God (1 Cor 3:9–17; 1 Pet 2:5; Eph 2:19–22). This new Israel lives in anticipation of yet a further renewal—the renewal of the heavens and earth, when the dwelling of God will be with men (Rev 21:1–3).

Index of Authors Cited

Index of Principal Subjects

Index of Biblical Texts

A. Old Testament

B. Apocrypha

C. New Testament